DEMENTIA, AGING, AND INTELLECTUAL DISABILITIES: A HANDBOOK

DEMENTIA, AGING, AND INTELLECTUAL DISABILITIES: A HANDBOOK

edited by
Matthew P. Janicki
Arthur J. Dalton

USA	Publishing Office:	BRUNNER/MAZEL
		A member of the Taylor & Francis Group
		325 Chestnut Street, Suite 800
		Philadelphia, PA 19106
		Tel: (215) 625-8900
		Fax: (215) 625-2940
	Distribution Center:	BRUNNER/MAZEL
		A member of the Taylor & Francis Group
		47 Runway Road, Suite G
		Levittown, PA 19057-4700
		Tel: (215) 269-0400
		Fax: (215) 269-0363
UK		BRUNNER/MAZEL
		A member of the Taylor & Francis Group
		1 Gunpowder Square
		London EC4A 3DE
		Tel: 171 583 0490
		Fax: 171 583 0581

DEMENTIA, AGING, AND INTELLECTUAL DISABILITIES: A Handbook

1 2 3 4 5 6 7 8 9 0

Printed by Hamilton Printing Co., Castleton, NY, 1998.

A CIP catalog record for this book is available from the British Library.
∞ The paper in this publication meets the requirements of the ANSI Standard Z39.48-1984 (Permanence of Paper)

Library of Congress Cataloging-in-Publication Data

Dementia, aging, and intellectual disabilites: a handbook
   / edited by Matthew P. Janicki and Arthur J. Dalton.
        p. cm.
      Includes bibliographical references and index.
      ISBN 0-87630-915-5 (hbk. : alk. paper). --ISBN 0-87630-916-3
   (pbk. : alk. paper)
      1. Alzheimer's disease. 2. Mentally handicapped aged -- Mental
health. 3. Dementia. I. Janicki, Matthew P., 1943-
II. Dalton, A. J. (Arthur J.)
RC523.D455 1999
618.97'683--dc21   98-26774
                                                            CIP

ISBN: 0-87630-915-5   (case)
ISBN 0-87630-916-3   (paper)

Dedication

To my lifelong companion and wife, Bonnie, who provided exceptional moral support and encouragement while I did my part assembling this text. —*MPJ*

To Kalli who has made my contribution joyful from beginning to end. —*AJD*

Contents

PART 6.
EDUCATION AND POLICY CONSIDERATIONS

CONTRIBUTORS

Matthew P. Janicki, Ph.D.,

Is research associate professor of Human Development at the Institute of Disability and Human Development at the University of Illinois at Chicago and director for technical assistance at the Rehabilitation Research and Training Center on Aging with Mental Retardation (University of Illinois at Chicago). He was formerly director for aging and special populations for the New York State Office of Mental Retardation and Developmental Disabilities, as well as deputy director for the center for aging policy studies at the New York Institute for Basic Research in Developmental Disabilities. Dr. Janicki has more than 25 years of experience in the area of intellectual disabilities. Dr. Janicki founded the special interest group in aging (now the gerontology division) of the American Association on Mental Retardation and chairs the aging and intellectual disability special interest research group of the International Association for the Scientific Study of Intellectual Disability. Dr. Janicki was a Joseph P. Kennedy, Jr., Foundation Public Policy Fellow with the National Institute on Aging and with the United States Senate. A fellow of the American Psychological Association and the Gerontological Society of America, he is the editor and author of several books, publications and articles on aging and intellectual and developmental disabilities.

Arthur J. Dalton, Ph.D.,

Is co-deputy director for the center on aging policy studies at the New York State Institute for Basic Research in Developmental Disabilities. He has 25 years of research experience in the field of mental retardation and developmental disabilities and he served as associate professor in the department of physiology in the Faculty of Medicine at the University of Toronto, Canada. He was Director of the behavior research program and director of research development for Surrey Place Centre in Toronto. He has more than 10 years of voluntary experience in working directly with families and health-care and individuals affected with Alzheimer disease.

He was one the coauthors of a report on aging of persons with cerebral palsy and workgroup chair for a special training initiative on aging, Down syndrome, and Alzheimer disease co-sponsored by the New York State Developmental Disabilities Planning Council. He was one of the founders and president for three years of the Alzheimer Society of Canada, the world's first self-help, nonprofit national organization devoted to family support, public education and advocacy for individuals affected with Alzheimer disease. Dr. Dalton was a member of the board of directors of the National Down Syndrome Congress.

Elizabeth H. Aylward, Ph.D.,
Is an associate professor in the Department of Radiology at the University of Washington in the Department of Psychiatry and Behavioral Sciences at The Johns Hopkins University School of Medicine. She has conducted longitudinal research in neuroanatomical, clinical, neuroimaging, and neuropsychological correlates of aging in adults with Down syndrome.

Penni Benedetti,
Is a program coordinator for Community Access, Inc. of Elizabeth, New Jersey and was the assistant director for residential services at The Arc of Ocean County, Lakewood, New Jersey.

Diana B. Burt, Ph.D.,
Is clinical assistant professor of Psychiatry and Behavioral Sciences at the Center for Human Development Research, University of Texas—Houston Health Science Center. For 10 years, she has conducted a longitudinal study on aging, dementia, and depression in adults with intellectual disability. The focus of her publications in this area has been on differentiating "normal" aging from dementia, establishing standardized diagnostic criteria and procedures for identifying dementia, and emphasizing the need for differential diagnosis (i.e., primary dementia versus dementia secondary to depression).

Brian Chicoine, M.D.,
Is the medical director of the Adult Down Syndrome Center of Lutheran General Hospital in Park Ridge, Illinois. Dr. Chicoine is cofounder of the Adult Down Syndrome Center. This center has served and documented the health and psychosocial needs of over 500 adults with Down syndrome since is inception in 1992. Dr. Chicoine graduated from Loyola University Stritch School of Medicine and completed his Family Practice residency at Lutheran General Hospital. He has provided medical care for adults with developmental disabilities for more than 10 years. He has

made many national and local presentations and published several articles on this topic.

David Davis,

A graduate of Butler University, is a former member of the Indiana State Board of Tax Commissioners and was the first chairman of the Indiana School Reorganization Commission. He was employed for 26 years as the Executive Director of the Indiana Petroleum Council, a division of the American Petroleum Institute. He and wife, Gayle, were part of the group of parents who were the founders of the organization that has become the Noble Centers of Indianapolis (Indiana). They have served on boards of directors and communities of organizations interested in the welfare of persons with intellectual and developmental disabilities.

Heleen Evenhuis, M.D., Ph.D.,

Is a general practitioner who works with people with intellectual disabilities. She has worked since 1973 in the geriatrics section of Hooge Burch, a center for people with intellectual disability. She initiated the Dutch consensus group on diagnosis and treatment of sensory impairment in children and adults with intellectual disability and is now preparing an international consensus development on this topic. Her scientific work has been in the area of differential diagnosis of dementia, sensory impairment, and physical aspects of aging. Since 1995, a personal grant from the government of the Netherlands has enabled her to stimulate and conduct medical research in the field of intellectual disability.

Larry T. Force, Ph.D.,

Is an assistant professor of Psychology at Mt. St. Mary College and is the chairperson of the aging services committee for Letchworth District Developmental Services Office of the New York State Office of Mental Retardation and Developmental Disabilities. He has worked in the field of aging and disabilities for over 19 years and has authored and collaborated on articles, chapters, and technical reports that address topics of developmental models of aging, life-long disabilities, adult day services, and Alzheimer's disease.

Barbara Hammond,

Is the director of residential services for The Arc, Ocean County Chapter in Lakewood, New Jersey. She has 15 years experience working in the area of intellectual disabilities and oversees the operation of eight community-based housing programs serving 57 adults with intellectual disabilites.

Janice Herlihy, M.S.W., Lic. S.W.,

Is a clinical social worker with the Massachusetts Department of Mental Retardation at its Northampton area office. Ms. Herlihy, whose graduate specialization is in gerontology, has had more than 20 years of professional work experience in the fields of aging and mental retardation. A common theme in all of her work has been helping people return or stay at home in dignified, individualized, and supportive settings.

Anthony J. Holland, M.D.,

Is a university lecturer in the Section of Developmental Psychiatry, Department of Psychiatry, University of Cambridge and a consultant psychiatrist with Lifespan NHS Trust, Cambridge. He has a longstanding research interest in the relationship between Down syndrome and Alzheimer's disease and has published papers and jointly edited a book on this subject. He is a psychiatrist with the local specialist community health team for adults with learning disabilities (intellectual disabilities).

Liz Kendall, R.N., B.S.N.,

Caregiving and health education specialist, is a research associate and consultant to the Center on Aging Studies and the Institute for Human Development Interdisciplinary Training Center on Gerontology and Developmental Disabilities at the University of Missouri–Kansas City. She has worked with individuals with Alzheimer's disease, their families, and professional carers for more than 15 years and has conducted research and program evaluation on Alzheimer's disease and Down syndrome services and health and carer education projects for older adults. She serves on committees of the national Board of Directors of the Alzheimer's Association.

Diane Lavoie,

Is a service coordinator with the Massachusetts Department of Mental Retardation in the Westfield area office. Ms. Lavoie has worked in the field of developmental disabilities for over 20 years. She began working in an institutional setting, but the majority of her career has been spent in the community-based system. It has been and continues to be a very meaningful, enjoyable, and personally rewarding career for her.

Philip McCallion, Ph.D., A.C.S.W.,

Is an assistant professor in the School of Social Welfare at the University at Albany and a faculty research associate at the Ringel Institute of Gerontology. His research is focused on understanding the interaction of informal family care with formal services, evaluating the effectiveness of psychosocial interventions for carers, and exploring the experiences of multicultural families. Dr. McCallion is coeditor of the book, *Total Quality Management in the Social Services: Theory and Practice,* and is coauthor of the dementia care training package, *Maintaining Communication with Persons with Dementia.*

Dennis McGuire, Ph.D.,

Is coordinator of psychosocial services for the Adult Down Syndrome Project and is associated with the Institute on Disability and Human Development at the University of Illinois at Chicago. Dr. McGuire helped established the Adult Down Syndrome Center located at Lutheran General Hospital. Dr. McGuire received his master's degree from the University of Chicago and his doctorate from the University of Illinois at Chicago. His work includes over 20 years in mental health and developmental disabilities.

Chris Oliver, M.Phil, Ph.D.,

Is professor of Clinical Psychology at the University of Birmingham, England. He is engaged in research in the psychological, social, and biological concomitants of dementia in persons with Down syndrome as well as researching the determinants of self-injurious and other challenging behavior in persons with intellectual disability.

Marie O'Malley,

Is associated with Mount Saint Mary College. As a returning adult student, Ms. O'Malley has collaborated on research projects targeting caregiving strategies in the elderly and has presented her research at regional conferences. Her interest in the field of developmental disabilities began when her youngest child was diagnosed with a seizure disorder and developmental delay.

Marie E. Percy, Ph.D.,

Is associate professor of Physiology and Obstetrics & Gynecology at the University of Toronto, Canada, and Director of the Neurogenetics Laboratory at Surrey Place Center. After completing a Ph.D. in Biochemistry from the University of Toronto and postdoctoral training in immunology at the Agricultural Research Council (ARC), Institute of Animal Physiology (Babraham, UK), and in genetics at the Hospital for Sick Children (Toronto), she established a multidisciplinary research program in Risk Factors in Human Disease at the University of Toronto as a National Health Research Scholar (Health and Welfare Canada). Most recently, she has been studying genetic and peripheral biological markers in Alzheimer's disease in the general population and in Down syndrome and the significance of these markers in the etiology of Alzheimer's disease and in eliciting the disease.

V. P. Prasher, M.D.,
Is a senior clinical lecturer, Department of Psychiatry, University of Birmingham (UK) and a consultant psychiatrist for people with intellectual disability in Birmingham. He is a member of the Royal College of Psychiatrists, completed his master's of medical science degree in 1992 and doctorate of medicine in 1994. He has published numerous articles on differing aspects of health morbidity in adults with Down syndrome, particularly related to aging and dementia.

Christine Rinck, Ph.D.,
Is director of the University of Missouri–Kansas City Institute for Human Development Interdisciplinary Training Center on Gerontology and Developmental Disabilities. She has worked in the field of aging and developmental disabilities for over 12 years and has written many articles and reports in this area. Her areas of expertise have been in psychotropic medications and their effects on older persons, assistive devices, and community inclusion into generic senior services.

Stephen S. Rubin, Ph.D.,
Is a research fellow at the Institute on Disability and Human Development at University of Illinois at Chicago. Within the institute, he is involved in joint projects with the Rehabilitation Research and Training Center on Aging and Mental Retardation, Family Clinic, and Adult Down Syndrome Clinic. His work involves assisting practitioners in the development of research to best address intervention and treatment strategies and to investigate survey methodologies that better address individuals with limited cognitive abilities.

Kathryn Pekala Service, M.S., R.N.C/N.P., C.D.D.N.,
Has been a registered nurse since 1973. She is certified in developmental disabilities and has been working in the field of developmental disabilities for over 20 years, first as an R.N. and since 1979 as a nurse practitioner both in the institutional and community settings. Her master's degree is in nursing with a gerontological focus. Her current role is as a health care consultant, educator, and advocate to people with developmental disabilities, their families, staff, and to other health care providers in the general community.

Lilian U. Thorpe, M.D.,
Is an associate professor of psychiatry at the University of Saskatchewan, Saskatoon, Canada. Her main area of specialization is geriatric psychiatry, with a special interest in aging in intellectual disabilities. She is

involved in a longitudinal study of physical, psychiatric, and cognitive changes with aging in an intellectually disabled cohort, and is active in teaching in this area.

John A. Tsiouris, M.D.,

Is associate director of psychological/psychiatric services in the George A. Jervis Clinic, a tertiary clinic for individuals with developmental disabilities, at the New York State Institute for Basic Research in Developmental Disabilities. Dr. Tsiouris is also clinical assistant professor in the Department of Psychiatry at the State University of New York Health Sciences Center at Brooklyn. As a practicing clinician, he has evaluated and treated numerous adults with challenging behaviors, psychiatric disorders, or dementia.

Leslie Udell,

Is program coordinator with Winnserv, Inc., in Winnipeg, Manitoba, Canada. She received her education in Alberta, Canada, as a rehabilitation practitioner and has worked in the field for more than 14 years. She supervises several group homes for adults with intellectual disabilities. Over the past several years, she has worked with her agency to plan and implement residential supports for adults diagnosed with probable Alzheimer's disease.

John R. Wherrett, M.D.,

Is professor in the Division of Neurology, University of Toronto, Senior Physician at the Toronto Hospital and Consultant in Neurology to the Huronia Regional Centre. He has worked in the field of neurodegenerative diseases of both early and late onset, and his publications have concerned the clinical and biochemical aspects of these disorders.

T. Franklin Williams, M.D.,

Is professor of medicine emeritus at the School of Medicine and Dentistry, University of Rochester (New York). Dr. Williams is the former director of the National Institute on Aging in Bethesda, Maryland.

Henryk M. Wisniewski, M.D., Ph.D.,

Is director for the New York State Institute for Basic Research in Developmental Disabilities, Staten Island, New York. Dr. Wisniewski is an internationally recognized scientist and leader in the field of research and Alzheimer's disease. He has authored more than 650 articles with an emphasis on basic research in the neuropathology of Alzheimer's disease, particularly as it affects adults with Down syndrome.

Linda J. Wright, R.N., M.P.A.,

A specialist in geriatric nursing, is project director at the Center on Aging, University of Kansas Medical Center in Kansas City. She has more than 15 years of experience working with family carers and individuals with Alzheimer's disease and has conducted research on Alzheimer's disease including adult day care utilization, drug study participation, and sexual–intimate relationships. She is currently a member of the board of the national Alzheimer's Association.

FOREWORD

Living into older age is a relatively new phenomenon for more and more persons, including those with lifelong intellectual disabilities. With this change come the challenges to understand and respond effectively to aging-related conditions and, in particular, dementia, as these affect persons with intellectual disabilities and their carers. This book is a comprehensive response to these challenges.

Much of what is being learned about older persons without underlying intellectual disability is applicable to those with Down syndrome and other intellectual disabilities when further loss of cognitive function appears. As emphasized in several chapters in this book, it is especially important to look for and treat appropriately reversible causes of dementia, such as depression, medications, low thyroid function, and vitamin deficiencies, and not write off the changes as just a progression of the basic intellectual condition.

As is also carefully addressed in this book, it is essential to document any changes in intellectual function regularly over time and to obtain any evidence of progressive dementia that may fit the diagnostic criteria for Alzheimer's disease, as well as to assist in planning for further care needs.

The basic question of whether persons with Down syndrome, more than the general population, are predisposed to developing Alzheimer's disease, is carefully examined. A number of questions still to be answered are addressed, including the roles of other risk factors and the interpretation of the pathologic changes in the brain.

Also in this volume, attention is given to the roles of targeted supportive environments and of psychotropic medications and to the needs of carers who, usually aging themselves, now face these additional challenges. Frontiers for further research and development, and significant issues of policy, are addressed.

This book should be a valuable, practical guide, and a stimulus to further innovative steps for all those involved in the ongoing care and concern for older persons with intellectual disabilities.

T. Franklin Williams, M.D.
Professor of Medicine Emeritus
University of Rochester
School of Medicine and Dentistry
Rochester, New York

PREFACE

We assembled this handbook for a number of reasons. First, because we had a vision that this topic was already an area of increasing effort by people working in the field of intellectual disabilities and particularly among those persons interested in aging. Although much thought had already been given to how Down's syndrome and Alzheimer's disease were connected, no one text was available that examined the impact of Alzheimer's disease and other dementias on people with intellectual disabilities with and without Down's syndrome. We recognized from our collective experiences that the focus of this text would highlight those questions arising relative to the diagnosis and care management challenges for the broader population of adults with intellectual disabilities.

The 1994 International Colloquium on Alzheimer Disease and Mental Retardation, which we helped organize and coordinate, served as the first significant forum for the exchange of ideas in this broader area. It brought together researchers and professional clinicians who were familiar with each other's work but who had not had an opportunity to engage in an intensive exchange of knowledge and ideas. The outcome of this meeting was everything we had hoped for and resulted in the publication of the three seminal reports on care management, diagnostics, and epidemiology. It was also at the meeting that the need for this handbook was conceived as an effort that would combine the most recent research and clinical findings along with the best insights of this multidisciplinary and international group. The aim was to give the professional community as a whole the benefit from the latest thoughts and insights concerning Alzheimer's disease and associated conditions in people with intellectual disabilities.

Also, we recognized that there was a large body of informal knowledge based on extensive experience by clinicians and research workers that has not been brought together before. In particular, the development of diagnostic and management practices has grown by leaps and bounds in an international quest to provide better care and quality of life for aging adults with intellectual disabilities. A handbook appeared to be the best format to capture this knowledge. It permits its presentation in a practical fashion and leaves room for revisions and additions as knowledge and experience accumulates. Together, the editors have added the perspectives of research and care management. These perspectives made it possible to build the handbook on a base of clinical and programmatic knowledge supported by an appreciation of the research literature.

Third, in speaking with clinicians and families, we became aware that there were many more questions than answers confronting persons with a family member facing onset or progression of something as insidious and lethal as Alzheimer's disease. We felt compelled to ask contributors to deal with many sensitive topics and we sought out personal experiences by family members and careproviders. It is our view that the content of this volume will provide better recognition of the enormous value and importance of caregiving of individuals affected with dementia.

This handbook is intended to provide an up-to-date analysis and review of current knowledge that has direct or indirect relevance to diagnosis, assessment, treatment, management, and care practices related to dementia in persons with intellectual disabilities. Insofar as it is possible, given the present state of knowledge, the handbook is presented from an applied and practical perspective aimed at a general readership of clinical and care-provider professionals and agencies. The wide ranging array of topics in the handbook reflects the fact that dementia of the Alzheimer type is not well understood. Its causes, treatment, and prevention are unknown at this time. What is clear is that it appears to have multiple causes with enormous variability in the clinical expression including age of onset, duration, and number and severity of signs. These are accompanied by the progressive and widespread distribution of neuronal cell death and deleterious consequences in many other tissues and organs of the body. Thus, the handbook begins with a review of biological and clinical aspects of the disease, ending with descriptions of the best practices currently available to meet the needs for management of quality of life, declines in many functions and social skills, and the losses and grief associated with death in the terminal stages. We also wanted to raise policy issues, since these are rarely addressed and continue to change rapidly in response to growing needs for services everywhere.

Also, a note on terminology: We recognize that the use of the term "mental retardation" is prevalent in the United States, but we also recognize that the world disability community has moved toward universal adoption of the more descriptive "intellectual disabilities." Although the terms mental retardation, learning disability (as used in the United Kingdom), and developmental or mental handicap are synonymous (see Fernald, 1995), we felt that intellectual disability is more inclusive and a more effective and recognizable representation of the impairment under discussion in this text. It is also better suited as a descriptor when discussing further cognitive decline such as that associated with Alzheimer's disease and related dementias. Thus, the term intellectual disability is used in this text to represent cognitive impairments of a developmental etiology. In the glossary at the end of the text, we have provided additional definitions for most of the technical terms used in this text that are currently in use among professionals involved in the field of intellectual disabilities as well as dementia research and care management.

☐ Reference

Fernald, C. D. (1995). When in London . . . : Differences in disability language preferences along English-speaking countries. *Mental Retardation, 33,* 99–103.

ACKNOWLEDGMENTS

First, we want to acknowledge the invaluable contributions of the participants at the International Colloquium on Alzheimer Disease and Mental Retardation, the participants in the three working groups that emanated from the colloquium, and all of those persons who served as reviewers, offered comments, or otherwise provided input into the postcolloquium products. We are particularly grateful to our handbook contributors, who have helped to expand on the discussions of the colloquium without whose expertise and wisdom this handbook would not have been possible.

We also want to acknowledge the help of Wanda Janicki, who helped edit and review select chapters. We also want to acknowledge the funding provided by the National Institutes of Aging and Child Health and Human Development as well as the National Institute of Disability Rehabilitation and Research, without whose help we could have not held the Minneapolis colloquium and working group meetings. It was the foresight of these organizations that helped to bring together the international network of researchers, workers, and families who made this handbook possible.

Last, we want to recognize that much of this work would have not been possible without the lifelong contributions of a number of persons with intellectual disabilities who we came to know while they aged and were affected by dementia. Thus, we offer this text in memory of RM, Jan, David, Frank, Bill, and all of the others whose lives enriched, and whose struggles with Alzheimer's disease left a profound impression on us, their families, and carers.

1

INTRODUCTION

The three chapters in this section provide varying perspectives on the changes in behavior, personality, and physical and mental health that occur in individuals with Down syndrome affected by Alzheimer's disease. Each serves as a dramatic anchor linking the rest of the chapters in this volume. First, after briefly defining the terms aging, dementia, and Alzheimer's disease, the authors of the opening chapter review alternative current research hypotheses, which have implications for the potential treatment of Alzheimer's disease, namely, the role of beta amyloid, oxidative damage, and inflammatory mechanisms. The authors then introduce the notions of staging of the onset and progression of the disease, and the problem of diagnosis with a particular emphasis on medical and other conditions that may accompany Alzheimer's disease as an associated or comorbid condition. Since these notions appear and reappear throughout the volume in different guises, this chapter sets the tone for the analyses and commentaries that follow and emphasizes their central importance in meeting the challenges of dementia and aging in persons with intellectual disabilities. The bulk of the chapter is then devoted to a detailed presentation of RM, a woman with Down syndrome and dementia, that provides a vivid clinical picture of the broad array of complex issues that must be addressed on a case-by-case basis when offering services to meet the needs of affected individuals.

The authors of the second chapter were professionally involved on a daily basis with the care and management of Jan, a woman with Down syndrome, whose onset of dementia was first noted at the age of 47 and who quickly deteriorated over a period of two years, dying at the age of 49 of complications arising from respiratory disease. It is a gripping chronology of deterioration and suffering, which the authors observed in a woman whom they knew as a happy, sociable, nearly independent person prior to her illness. The narrative only indirectly reveals the intensity of the feelings of anxiety and affection which were felt by the care provider staff who was involved with Jan on a daily basis. One year before Jan's death, they were helpless to stop the disease and could only provide palliative care, a situation that is presently inescapable because of the absence of any known effective treatment for Alzheimer's disease. The heartbreaking story brings all of us closer to the human drama of Alzheimer's disease.

The third chapter is authored by a father who, along with his wife, spent a lifetime of love, devotion, and attention to their son, David, who had Down syndrome. Their story only begins to touch on some of the milestones that are particularly memorable to the family. Yet, it is possible to see, between the lines, a family's quiet resolution and determination to raise a child with Down syndrome from his infancy, childhood, and adolescence to his adulthood and older age. Their story will no doubt sound a familiar note for many, if not all, families of this generation who are raising an adult child with Down syndrome who was born 40 to 50 years ago. The problems and frustrations that parents faced and successfully solved in the early fifties to obtain and provide schooling for children and then find appropriate activities, jobs, and other occupations for them as adults, can be traced in the story of David. Similarly, the almost ubiquitous problems of finding good care from a medical community which was mostly ignorant of the unique problems of aging individuals with Down syndrome are evident when David reaches middle age. The struggles were renewed again when the parents had to deal with a medical community which was mostly ignorant of the connection between Alzheimer's disease and Down syndrome. The parents were left with very little support in coping with the declining functions of their son. They offer us much to contemplate with regard to how we can begin to provide aging-associated services to this generation of parents. Their story is emotionally compelling even though it is presented in an understated fashion.

Arthur J. Dalton
Matthew P. Janicki

Aging and Dementia

Aging, dementia, and Alzheimer's disease are defined carefully to ease the task of identifying their relationships to older individuals with intellectual disabilities. Known risk factors, current mechanisms underlying the development of Alzheimer's disease, and a three-stage model of the progression of dementia of the Alzheimer type are briefly described. The three-stage model is used as the framework for understanding the detailed clinical presentation and management practices utilized for RM, a woman with Down's syndrome who was systematically followed for a period of 20 years while she was alive with a confirmed postmortem neuropathological diagnosis of Alzheimer's disease. References to relevant chapters in this volume are also liberally interspersed throughout the account of RM. These citations provide the reader with current knowledge bearing on many aspects of the management and care of affected individuals with intellectual disabilities.

The authors would like to express their gratitude to the staff, residents, families, and friends of the Huronia Regional Centre, Orillia, Ontario, Canada, without whose cooperation for the past 25 years the reconstruction of RM's history would not have been possible. The authors also acknowledge the contribution of Catherine Bergeron, M.D., staff neuropathologist at the Canadian Brain Tissue Bank and the University of Toronto, Toronto, Ontario, Canada, who made the neuropathological diagnosis of Alzheimer's disease from examination of brain tissue specimens of RM. The authors are grateful for the contributions to portions of this chapter by Mary C. Sano and Paul S. Aisen.

Address correspondence to: Arthur J. Dalton, Ph.D., New York State Institute for Basic Research in Developmental Disabilities, 1050 Forest Hill Road, Staten Island, NY 10314.

Aging is a progressive, predictable process that involves the evolution and maturation of living organisms; it is evitable but varies greatly in terms of rate among individuals (Williams, 1995). From the perspective of the biological sciences, aging is defined as a cumulative, universal, progressive, internal, and deleterious set of processes that begin at the moment of conception and that are active until the death of the individual (Machemer, 1993). The processes of aging are unique for each species and they are genetically determined. It is essential to distinguish universal aging processes from age-associated diseases and disorders such as dementia and Alzheimer's disease, which appear in some, but not all individuals, in late life. Dementia represents an acquired loss of intellectual ability that occurs over a long period of time and affects many areas of cognitive functioning (Williams, 1995). Prior to the early 20th century the term dementia was used interchangeably with the word senility. Senility was then considered a normal consequence of aging, which included all the physical and mental infirmities that can affect the elderly (Hendrie & Hingtgen, 1990). Gradually, the growing realization became more widespread that the degenerative changes were due to disease processes rather than to normal aging. This changing view was finally accepted by the medical community by the mid-20th century. A detailed analysis of the term applied to individuals with intellectual disabilities is provided by Burt and Aylward (this volume) and some of the complexities of using the term in the context of psychiatric disorders is illustrated by Burt (this volume). A glossary at the end of the volume provides six other definitions of the term that are currently in use among professionals involved in the field of intellectual disabilities.

For the first half of this century, Alzheimer's disease was a term reserved to describe "senility" in the presenium, that is, the severe mental and personality deterioration that occurred at ages younger than 60 years. The term, like the word dementia, has also undergone a number of transformations since then. It is now applied to older adults of any age who show a pattern of progressive mental deterioration coupled with personality changes in a state of clear consciousness associated with a specific configuration of neuropathological changes in the brain (Reisberg, Ferris, & DeLeon, 1989; Berg, Karlinsky, & Holland, 1993). A glossary at the end of this text provides additional definitions which distinguish familial from sporadic forms of the disease. The cause(s), treatment, and prevention of this disease are presently not known. It affects about 10% of the general aging population over 65 years of age and represents a significant risk factor for all persons with Down's syndrome over the age of 40 years or so.

☐ Prevalence and Incidence of Alzheimer's Disease

The exact prevalence of Alzheimer's disease among adults with intellectual disability is unknown. For adults with Down's syndrome, recent research suggests that the neuropathological features of Alzheimer's disease may be much more common in this group than previously suspected (Wisniewski, Silverman, & Wegiel, 1994) and, consequently, dementia may also be more common. Zigman, Schupf, Haveman and Silverman (1995; 1977) in a comprehensive review of the epidemiological literature concluded that the age-specific prevalence rate of Alzheimer's dementia among adults with Down syndrome was consistently high, even though estimates of age-specific prevalence varied widely across studies. They attributed much of this variability to divergent sampling techniques and subject populations, varying assessment instruments, and nonstandardized diagnostic criteria. For those adults with intellectual disabilities other than Down's syndrome, the prevalence rates are not yet determined and studies show varying rates. For example, Cooper (1997) noted that dementia occurs at a much higher rate among older adults with intellectual disability than it does in the general population. In a population survey, Cooper found 22% of persons aged 65 and older with dementia. In contrast, others have noted rates equivalent to those of the general population. Haveman, Maaskant and Sturmans (1989) found dementia occurring in 10% of older adults with intellectual disability. Janicki and Dalton (1997; 1998) found dementia occurring in 6% of adults aged 60 and older and 12% of adults aged 80 and older.

☐ Neuropathology of Alzheimer's Disease

The loss of millions of brain cells is the most dramatic physical evidence of Alzheimer's disease. The processes whereby these nerve cells die in such numbers and the significance of the selective losses in particular regions (such as the nucleus basalis) and the death of specific types of nerve cells are not known. The search for infectious or transmissible agents, genetic or inherited abnormalities, and environmental toxins has yielded a large and important body of knowledge, but no specific cause(s) for Alzheimer's disease has been established. No infectious or viral agent has yet been identified and there have been no reported instances of one affected person transmitting the disease to any other. The neurofibrillary tangles and the senile plaques which are found in widespread regions of the brains of affected individuals have been the subject of intense research over many years (see recent reviews by Iqbal et al., 1993; Wisniewski & Wisniewski, 1992) and data from such studies hold promise for the development of potential biomarkers useful in diagnosis and rational approaches to drug therapies. Unfortunately, it is not clear whether the neurofibrillary tangles or the senile plaques or both are causes of Alzheimer's disease or whether they simply represent the debris or consequences of some as yet undetermined process or unidentified causative event.

Neurofibrillary tangles are bundles of filaments in the cytoplasm of the neuron that displace or encircle the neuron. Immunocytochemical studies suggest that when the neuron is still intact, a major surface antigen of the tangles is phosphorylated tau protein. They are stained strongly by silver (e.g., Bielchowsky methods). They are a characteristic feature of Alzheimer's disease, but tangles in relatively small numbers appear in the brain tissues of elderly individuals with no apparent dementia. *Senile plaques* are areas of incomplete degeneration in the brains of elderly individuals or person with Alzheimer's disease. These are focal collections of tortuous silver-staining processes. Microglial cells and reactive astrocytes can be seen around the periphery. Early plaques have only neuritic processes (remnants of axons and/or dendrites), but later in evolution they develop a central amyloid core around which a clear halo tends to form. These are often present in the brains of aging individuals without signs of dementia while alive.

The possibility of a genetic basis for Alzheimer's disease has received a significant boost since the discovery of a location on chromosome 21 for the genetic blueprint for an important protein associated with deposits of beta-amyloid in senile plaques and blood vessels of the brain (Robakis et al., 1987). While this gene may lead to the over-production of beta-amyloid, there is no proof that it causes Alzheimer's disease. Understanding of the molecular events which are involved in the production, breakdown, modification, and regulation of beta amyloid may yield important new treatment strategies.

☐ Risk Factors for Alzheimer's disease

Besides age, the presence of trisomy 21 is the only well-established risk factor for Alzheimer's disease. For more than 60 years since Struwe's first report (Struwe, 1929), all reports of postmortem examinations of brain tissue specimens from virtually all individuals with Down's syndrome who have died after the age of 40 years show the characteristic lesions of Alzheimer's disease. Other genetically based risk factors have been suggested. Variants of some genes located on chromosome 19, 14, and 1 and specific point mutations in two mitochondrial genes raise the possibility that they contribute to the pathology of Alzheimer's disease. Laboratory, clinical, and epidemiological studies have also identified a number of environmental risk factors that may predispose persons to the development of Alzheimer's disease, including head injury, depression, hypothyroidism, poor nutrition, and neurotoxic environmental agents.

A review of these possibilities and a critical examination of the literature are provided elsewhere (Percy, this volume). Two excellent reviews with extensive references to the literature dealing with the long-standing controversy about the role of the salts of "trace metals," such as aluminum and iron, in Alzheimer's disease have been recently published (Markesbery & Ehmann, 1994; McLachlan, 1995).

Amyloid Precursor Protein (APP).   Several observations firmly link Alzheimer's disease to the gene for APP. One of the most characteristic changes in the Alzheimer's disease brain is the accumulation of amyloid plaques. Amyloid β peptide (Aβ), a product of the metabolism of APP, is the major component of the plaques. Aβ is a 39–43 amino acid peptide resulting from cleavage of APP that forms the core of the amyloid plaques in the Alzheimer's disease hippocampus and neocortex. An inflammatory reaction, including activated microglia and astrocytes, with increased levels of inflammatory cytokines, acute phase proteins, complement proteins, and cyclooxygenase, accompanies the dystrophic neurites around mature plaques.

In certain families with autosomal dominant familial Alzheimer's disease, the disease is caused by mutations in the APP gene. Transgenic mice expressing such mutant APP genes develop neuritic plaques similar to those found in the Alzheimer's disease brain (Holzman, Li, Gage, Epstein, & Mobley, 1992; Games et al., 1995; Hsiao et al., 1996). The APP gene is located on chromosome 21; thus, there is an extra copy of the APP gene in persons with Down's syndrome. The relationship between the APP gene, Alzheimer's disease, and Down's syndrome has been discussed extensively (Beyreuther et al., 1992, Schellenberg, Kamino, Bryant, Moore, Bird, 1992). The mechanism by which Aβ production and/or plaque deposition results in neurodegeneration and dementia is far from clear. Two theories, which are by no means mutually exclusive, invoke free radical damage and destructive inflammation in the pathophysiology of Alzheimer's disease.

Oxidative Damage.   Free radicals are molecules with unpaired electrons, formed as by-products of metabolic processes (Halliwell & Gutteridge, 1989). They are highly reactive with macromolecules including lipids and thus can readily damage cell membranes. When the balance between free radical production and cellular antioxidant defenses is lost, cellular damage may ensue; such an imbalance has been invoked to explain age-related deterioration in many tissues. In vitro studies support a possible link between free radicals and Alzheimer's disease. Aβ protein generates free radicals in cell culture and in cell-free solution (Hensley et al., 1994), and the toxicity of Aβ in vitro can be limited by antioxidants (Bruce, Malfroy, & Baudry, 1996; Tomiyama et al., 1996). If free radicals play a significant role in neuronal loss in Alzheimer's disease, then antioxidants that accumulate in cell membranes within the brain would be expected to slow the neurodegeneration. The results of a recent trial of vitamin E and selegiline (Sano et al., 1997) provide encouraging support to this hypothesis. The topic has been recently reviewed in detail by Cohen and Werner (1994) and Beal (1995).

Oxidative stress may be particularly relevant to neurodegeneration in adults with Down's syndrome (Percy et al., 1990; Volicer & Crino, 1990). The gene for copper-zinc superoxide dismutase (SOD-1), is located on chromosome 21, and mean blood levels are elevated in individuals with Down's syndrome (De la Torre, Casado, Lopez-Fernandez, Carrascosa, Ramirez, & Saez, 1997). SOD-1 has an important role in protection against free-radical tissue damage. SOD converts superoxide radicals, which are released by stimulated inflammatory cells, into hydrogen peroxide, which in turn can be eliminated by catalase or glutathione peroxidase.

It is unclear whether an excess of SOD-1 has a protective or detrimental effect on free-radical-mediated damage, but it has been hypothesized that an excess of SOD-1 relative to catalase and glutathione peroxidase results in accumulation of damaging hydrogen peroxide in the brain, contributing to neurodegeneration (De Haan, Cristiano, Iannello, & Kola, 1997). Plasma vitamin E levels are lower in individuals with Down's syndrome and evidence of Alzheimer's disease when compared with non-dementing Down's syndrome controls (Jackson, Holland, Williams, & Dickerson, 1988).

Inflammatory Mechanisms.   Many different lines of evidence point to the importance of inflammatory mechanisms in Alzheimer's disease. Histopathologically, acute phase proteins, inflammatory cytokines, complement proteins, complement regulatory proteins, and activated microglial cells are all associated with neuritic plaques (Aisen & Davis, 1997). Laboratory studies support the theory that activation of inflammatory pathways contributes to neurodegeneration in Alzheimer's disease. The interleukin, Il-1, augments Aβ cytotoxicity in vitro (Fagarasan & Aisen, 1996). Alpha-1 antichymotrypsin may contribute to Aβ aggregation (Ma,

Yee, Brewer, Das, & Potter, 1994) and may influence APP processing. Complement proteins can bind Aβ, increasing aggregation, and may also contribute to Aβ cytotoxicity (Pasinetti, 1996). Activated microglial cells are associated with maturation of neuritic plaques and they may contribute to neurodegeneration (Giulian, Li, Leara, & Keenen, 1994; London, Biegel, & Pachter, 1996).

Epidemiological evidence also supports the hypothesis that inflammation contributes to neuronal loss in Alzheimer's disease. Alzheimer's disease and rheumatoid arthritis coexist less often than expected. This may suggest that the antiinflammatory drugs used to treat rheumatoid arthritis protect against the expression of Alzheimer's disease (McGeer, McGeer, & Sibley, 1990). Retrospective studies support this notion. The use of nonsteroidal antiinflammatory drugs (NSAIDs) seems to delay the expression of Alzheimer's disease (McGeer, Schulzer, & McGeer, 1996). The contribution of inflammatory/immune processes to Alzheimer's disease pathology in Down's syndrome may differ from sporadic Alzheimer's disease. Several genes may play a role in the inflammatory response including SOD-1, interferon receptor, and S-100 beta, which are all located on chromosome 21 (Sustrova & Sarikova, 1997).

Immunological alterations in adults with Down's syndrome have been reported (Cuadrado & Barrena, 1997). It has not been demonstrated, however, that these genetic differences appreciably alter the role of inflammation in the pathogenesis of Alzheimer's disease. As a result of the histopathological and in vitro laboratory studies and the epidemiological data, much effort is now being directed to controlled clinical trials of antiinflammatory drugs in Alzheimer's disease, sponsored by industry and by the National Institute on Aging.

☐ A Model for the Staging of Alzheimer's Disease

The onset and progression of dementia have been classified into a small number of stages to help deal with the numerous signs and symptoms that appear at different times during the course of the disease. Reisberg and his colleagues (1989) have demarcated seven stages. However, for older persons with Down's syndrome or other developmental disabilities who have very limited language and communication skills, it may be difficult to discriminate so many stages. Consequently, three-stage models may be more practical for them (Janicki, Heller, Seltzer, & Hogg, 1996). Several three-stage models have been used over the past 30 years which all share the same framework with differences only in the details (e.g.,

FIGURE 1.1: Process and diagnostic function of dementia

Early stage	*Behavior:* Onset features (short-term memory, language disruption, vocational dysfunction) *Dx:* Initial diagnosis *Care management:* Support compensations *Time frame:* 1–5 years (less in DS)
Mid stage	*Behavior:* Pronounced losses and decline (distinct losses in language, comprehension, disorientation, confusion, short-term memory losses, ADL losses, personality changes) *Dx:* Confirmatory diagnosis *Care management:* Close supervision, controls for wandering, day activities *Time frame:* 5–15 years (less in DS)
Late stage	*Behavior:* Significant decline and complete loss of function and basic skills, long- and short-term memory losses, loss of balance, and ambulation *Dx:* Upon autopsy *Care management:* Complete oversight and total care, infirmity, danger of infection and pneumonia, death *Time frame:* 3–5 years (less in DS)

Sim, 1965; Sourander & Sjögren, 1970; Crapper-McLachlan, Dalton, Galin, Schlotterer, & Daicar, 1984). Figure 1.1 illustrates the stages and the characterization of concerns related to each stage.

The early stage, characterized by onset features, dementia psychometric examinations usually reveal that memory performance is impaired prior to psychomotor performance and language performance is least involved. In this stage, IQ scores decline at variable rates but on average, a change of eight to ten points per year is frequently encountered (Crapper-McLachlan et al., 1984). The date of onset of the illness, as reported by family members, seems to be correlated best with the onset of change in the performance parts of IQ tests, such as the Wechsler Adult Intelligence Scale. For example, Crapper-McLachlan et al. noted that based on the date of onset reported by relatives judged to be reliable witnesses, a group of 10 patients examined at six-month intervals revealed that memory test scores (Wechsler Memory Scale, Form 1) begin to decline 12 to 18 months prior to the onset of other behavioral changes. With progression of the disease, changes in affect or emotional impulse control become apparent as well as motivation and general interest. At an early stage, slow waves appear in the electroencephalogram (EEG) and the proportion of the

EEG occupied by abnormal slow waves gradually increases as the disease progresses, until there is slow-wave domination of the EEG. When intellectual deterioration is moderately severe and the adult requires supervision, palmomental reflexes may appear. This abnormal reflex often appears about the time that the EEG abnormalities are obvious.

With further progression, dyspraxias and agnosias are apparent, and as the adult enters the middle stage of the illness, the superficial facial reflexes including the pout, snout, and glabellar reflexes may be elicited. Toward the end of the middle stage, there is altered muscle tone which first appears as mild gegenhalten (disturbed body counterbalancing abilities) and is often associated with bradykinesia. As the disease progresses there is frequently a general increase in muscle tone, particularly in the flexor groups and often most pronounced in the upper limbs. Myoclonic jerks or general seizures may occur during the latter stages of the disease. There may also be defective upward gaze with preservation of downward gaze. With loss of useful intellectual and motor function the sucking and grasp reflexes appear and the palmomental reflex disappears.

In the late or terminal stage of the illness, urinary incontinence and the loss of most motor functions necessitate total nursing care and predisposes to the terminal events of cachexia and bronchopneumonia. After a bout of pneumonia or other systemic illness, the plantar response may become extensor, and focal neurological signs such as hemianopia, hemiparesis, or unilateral tone changes may appear. However, focal neurological signs of this type are not characteristic of the disease, which may have a course as short as 18 months or as long as 27 years, but the average duration of illness is about 10 years. The pattern of functional changes described above includes specific functional changes occurring early, which are gradually followed by increasing severity and number of symptoms until global deterioration occurs late in the condition. The subtlety and insidious development of one or a few symptoms at the start in the absence of global deterioration are hallmarks of the dementia associated with the disease.

☐ Toward Diagnosis

The contributors to this volume explicitly or implicitly recognize the fundamental importance of an accurate and careful diagnosis. During the last two decades, substantial progress has been made in the development of the concepts of dementia which provide the underpinnings for diagnosis. There have been several useful attempts to define clinical syndromes of dementia and to correlate these syndromes with pathology. This has led to several theoretical schemes in which the course of dementia is described in stages. The most frequently employed scheme is to characterize dementia into mild, moderate, and severe signs, corresponding to the early, middle, and late or terminal stage. The scheme incorporates the progressive nature of the disease as well as the temporal features.

Other distinctions are of growing importance as diagnostic practices improve. These include classifications of dementia into "cortical" and "subcortical" varieties. These and related aspects of definition are explored in some detail by Wherrett (this volume). He also describes the precise role of the neurologist in the diagnosis and care of persons with intellectual disabilities who exhibit symptoms and signs of dementia. The neurologist must characterize, through precise diagnosis and functional assessment, the nature of the impairment that has a neurologic substrate and to institute measures to reverse, stabilize, or facilitate adaptations to the impairments. The standard diagnostic approach of the neurologist who seeks to identify the functional impairment and anatomical localization of lesions should be used for persons with intellectual disabilities just as it is for aging persons from the general population who are showing newly developing signs of abnormality.

Comorbid Conditions.   It is well known that persons with Down's syndrome affected with dementia have a higher prevalence of congenital heart defects, hypothyroidism, hearing impairments, and a history of hepatitis B infections (Van Schrojenstein Lantman-de Valk, Haveman, & Crebolder, 1996). Depression may also be a comorbid condition in aging persons with Down's syndrome (Burt, Loveland, & Lewis, 1992; Prasher, 1995e; Prasher & Hall, 1996; Burt, this volume). For persons with other etiologies such presentations are similar to others in the general population.

The relatively high prevalence of psychotic delusions and hallucinations associated with Alzheimer's disease in persons from the general population seems to be substantially lower in persons with Down's syndrome suffering from Alzheimer's disease. Delusions and hallucinations are almost never reported for persons with Down's syndrome who are suffering from dementia, according to a recent review of 86 cases described in 15 reports published between 1948 and 1992 (Prasher 1997). Another recent, carefully conducted evaluation of the mental health, physical health, and adaptive behavior of 12 adults who were 50 years of age and older, with intellectual disabilities (5 with Down's syndrome, 7 without Down's syndrome), each with a clinical diagnosis of dementia, reported 7 areas of significant mental symptoms (sleep difficulty, hypersomnia, irritability, inefficient thought, anhedonia, social withdrawal, and anergia) but failed to report any delusions or hallucinations (Moss & Patel, 1997).

Other psychiatric conditions are also receiving some attention (e.g., Prasher, 1995a; Prasher & Day, 1995; Thorpe, this volume). Deterioration in sensory functions (Evenhuis, van Zantan, Brocaar, & Roerdinkholder, 1992; Cronin-Golomb, 1995; Cronin-Golomb, Corkin, & Growdon, 1995; Prasher, 1994a, 1995b this volume; Van Schrojenstein Lantman-de Valk et al., 1997), the appearance of thyroid abnormalities (Murdoch, Ratcliffe, McLarty, Rodger, & Ratcliffe, 1977; Prasher & Krishnan, 1993; Prasher, 1994b, 1995c, 1995e), seizures (Johannsen, Christensen, Goldstein, Nielsen, & Mai, 1996; McVicker, Shanks, & McClelland, 1994; Prasher, 1995d; Prasher & Corbett, 1993), and other conditions (Prasher, 1994c) frequently occur at the same time as signs or symptoms of dementia. Rocco, Cronin-Golomb, and Lai (1997) have reported visual impairments of color discrimination (blue hues), stereoacuity, and contrast sensitivity in adults in a small, selected group of aging adults with Down's syndrome (mean = 45.5 years, plus or minus 9.3) but not in a comparable group of adults with intellectual disability without Down's syndrome. They considered the impairments to be Alzheimer-like, even though they appeared to be present before and to be independent of age-associated dementia. Finally, Collacott, Cooper, and Ismail (1994) have suggested that evidence of cerebrovascular disease may be overlooked and that multiinfarct dementia may be underreported among older individuals.

From an applied perspective, there are significant problems in assigning an accurate clinical diagnosis of dementia in persons with levels of intellectual disability in the severe to profound range. Moreover, there is no definition of dementia specific for individuals with intellectual disabilities, and the existing Diagnostic and Statistical Manual of Mental Disorders (DSM-IIIR) and International Classification of Diseases (ICD-10) standards for clinical diagnosis are silent for these individuals. The lack of a completely valid and reliable diagnosis and the absence of standardized neuropsychological and other tests able to reliably detect changes over time in the presence of the preexisting intellectual disabilities also create important obstacles. As Burt and Aylward (this volume) indicate, "misconceptions regarding the prevalence of dementia in adults with Down's syndrome and failure to follow nationally accepted standards for differential diagnosis have resulted in misdiagnoses of Alzheimer's disease." Further, when prevalent tests are applied to standards for assessing dementia in general, reliability across instruments appears uncertain (see Erkinjuntti et al., 1997)

Can it be assumed that the clinical presentation seen in patients with Alzheimer's disease is also similar for affected individuals with intellectual disabilities and, in particular, for those with Down's syndrome who are known to be at a high risk for developing the signs of dementia of the Alzheimer type in the sixth decade of life? An affirmative answer to this question provides the underpinnings for those chapters of this volume that focus largely or entirely on persons with Down's syndrome. Unfortunately, there are very few systematic studies of individuals with intellectual disabilities without Down's syndrome who have developed dementia with confirmed postmortem Alzheimer's disease. Nevertheless, until research provides the relevant data, it is practical to assume that the features of the disease in persons with intellectual disabilities without Down's syndrome will be similar in most respects to those observed in persons with Down's syndrome. The history of RM, a woman with Down's syndrome with a confirmed postmortem neuropathological diagnosis of Alzheimer's disease, provides a focus for many of the diagnostic, care, and management concerns addressed in this volume. Wherever possible, parts of RM's story are linked to specific chapters where the reader can obtain an in-depth treatment in a broader context beyond the single case.

The history of RM is also presented in some detail because the onset and progression of the signs and symptoms of dementia as well as the occurrence of a number of comorbid conditions illustrate the usefulness of the three-stage model discussed above. Also, RM was singled out along with others by a clinical research team for long-term follow-up study over a period of 20 years while she was alive. Finally, her sister gave permission and consent for the donation of brain tissue, which upon microscopic examination yielded a postmortem confirmation of the diagnosis of Alzheimer's disease. The story of RM is presented from a clinical perspective. The reader is invited to compare this perspective with a care-provider perspective, which is evident in the story of "Jan. S." by Hammond and Benedetti (this volume), and the personal perspective of Davis, a parent coping with dementia which affected his middle-aged son with Down's syndrome (this volume).

☐   Case History of RM

RM was born in 1928 following an uneventful, full-term birth without injury to a mother who was 36 years of age at the time. RM was the fifth child in a sibship of 6 children. She was admitted in 1934, when she was 6 years of age, to a large institution for persons with intellectual disabilities located in a rural community of Canada, 80 miles north of Toronto, Ontario. She lived there throughout life until her death in 1992 of respiratory failure and chronic obstructive pulmonary disease at the age of 64 years. Her IQ at the time of her admission in 1934 was estimated at 21 points with a mental age of 1.2 years. Psychometric examinations 40 years later, in 1973, as well as in 1975 and 1977 using the Leiter International Performance Scale yielded similar IQ scores of 19, 25, and 23 points, respectively (profound to severe mental retardation). No further IQ scores are available for the period between 1977 and 1992. Throughout her life, RM had limited speech, but she could use a few words combined with gestures even though she was hard to understand.

Medical Conditions.   RM had the usual childhood illnesses before the age of 10 years including mumps (age 4 years), measles (age 5 years), German measles (age 7 years), and chicken pox (age 8 years), as well as an early episode of pneumonia (age 8 years). She suffered an acute bout of bronchitis when she was 11 years old, started menorrhea when she was 16 years of age and menopause when she was 47 years old. A systolic heart murmur (V/VI) was noted when she was 23 years of age, and she became edentulous at age 42 years. Her heart was considered normal on admission to the institution, but at age 23 a soft systolic murmur was noted for the first time and several times thereafter. An examination when she was 61 years old failed to detect any sign of a heart abnormality or murmur. Electrocardiograms at ages 54, 55, and 59 years were all described as normal. The significance of many of the medical conditions that affected RM are discussed in more general terms for all aging persons with intellectual disabilities by Evenhuis who underscores their implications for diagnosis and care practices elsewhere in this volume.

Chromosomal studies conducted when RM was 45 and 62 years of age confirmed the presence of classical trisomy-21. RM had normal thyroid function test results at age 56 years. This is a noteworthy observation because of an increasing number of reports of an association between thyroid abnormalities and Alzheimer's disease. Also, a form of autoimmune thyroiditis associated with "subclinical hypothyroidism" has been identified in persons with Down's syndrome who show signs of dementia. For a detailed discussion of this topic the reader is referred to the chapter by Percy (this volume). No evidence of malignancies were recorded.

Neurological Aspects.   At 61 years of age, after an apparent seizure episode, a neurological examination was performed which revealed an alert, cooperative woman with a full range of eye movements including upward and downward gaze. The overall impression at the time was that a minor seizure may have accounted for the changes in her behavior noted by staff. Deep tendon reflexes were normal with a very weak early grasp reflex bilaterally and a weak right palmomental reflex without a left palmomental reflex. The snout reflexes were just beginning to appear. The sucking or rooting reflexes were absent. Her stance and gait were quite normal at the time, but she was unable to perform tandem gait. A second neurological examination performed 4 months later resulted in neurological findings that were essentially unchanged except for an occasional myoclonic jerk during the examination. The role of the neurologist in the assessment and management of dementia occurring in adults with intellectual disabilities is discussed in detail by Wherrett (this volume) who frames the question of Alzheimer's disease in the context of the more recently characterized forms of primary dementia such as Lewy body disease, and fronto-temporal and vascular dementias. The changes in cognition and a wide range of behaviors that are associated with this chronic neurodegenerative disease are treated elsewhere in this volume from the psychological perspective by Oliver (this volume) and Burt and Aylward (this volume).

Pharmacological Considerations.   A detailed review of her physician's prescriptions for medications for the period of 7 years up to the day before her death revealed that there were no apparent reasons for any psychopharmacological interventions. RM was never given any antipsychotic, antidepressant, or antianxiety agents, or stimulants or mood stabilizers, or antidyskinetics or antihistamines, suggesting that she suffered from no specifically diagnosed psychiatric condition for which such agents would be indicated. She was placed on dilantin for a minor seizure when she was 61 years of age. Two years later she was treated with heparin and coumadin and later with antibiotics and prednisone following a deteriorating respiratory condition. When she was 56 years of age she was given topical medications to treat mycotic toenails. The only other medications mentioned in her day-to-day medical records were vitamin C, lactulose, calamine, and kaopectate. The nature, variety, and prevalence of psychiatric conditions in aging persons with intellectual disabilities, are addressed in detail with several illustrative case studies by Thorpe elsewhere in this volume. The management implications of prescribing psychotropic medications for the treatment of a variety of conditions associated with aging in persons with intellectual disabilities, are extensively examined by Tsiouris in this volume.

Changes in Sensory Functions.   Sensory changes and deterioration are commonly observed among normal aging persons as well as among older persons with Down's syndrome. They may be misinterpreted as signs of dementia, particularly among aging persons with intellectual disabilities living at that time in institutions. Records indicate that formal audiological assessments of RM were conducted at least twice, when she was 47 and 53 years of age. The first evaluation was inconclusive because of occluded ear canals, a common condition found among institutional residents with intellectual disabilities. The second assessment revealed the presence of speech reception thresholds at 60 DB bilaterally, bone conduction responses to speech noted at 40 to 45 DB, with a moderate mixed hearing loss. Acoustic impedance measurements indicated occluded Eustachian tubes at the time of this assessment. At age 53, she was fitted with a hearing aid. Shortly thereafter, bilateral myringotomy with tubes was performed (retraction of both drums with negative middle ear pressure, chronic serous otitis). Frequent impacted wax in both external ear canals was regularly observed leading to severe to profound hearing loss at about this time.

Internal strabismus was noted when she was 40 years old, with the identification of congenital cataract with left corneal abnormality at age 46 years; left esotropia was noted at age 47 years with bilateral keratoconus. At age 55 years, RM was fitted with glasses. Ophthalmologic assessments were conducted several times. At age 56 years, she was diagnosed with congenital cataracts. At 60 years of age, an ophthalmologic examination concluded that she could see gross objects. At age 62 years, she was declared legally blind. Visual and auditory deterioration frequently increase with age, particularly among persons with Down's syndrome. These sensory changes make the diagnosis of dementia increasingly difficult. It is a sufficiently important issue to be addressed in detail by Evenhuis in this volume.

RM was reported to be hepatitis B positive for the first time at age 51 years and continued to have antibodies to hepatitis B. At 63 years of age, tests for malignancy were negative. A CT scan of the brain at age 59 years revealed the presence of cerebellar and cerebral atrophy with partially empty sella turtica, consistent with a diagnosis of Alzheimer's disease.

Cognitive Tests for Early Dementia. In 1972, at age 44, RM was enrolled in a long-term longitudinal study of 20 adults with Down's syndrome and 20 adults with intellectual disability but without Down's syndrome all residing at the same institution. Her cognitive functions were evaluated 7 times, on an annual basis between 1972 and 1983 using two matching-to-sample (MTS) tests of learning and two delayed-matching-to-sample (DMTS) recognition memory tests developed by Dalton and his colleagues (Dalton, Crapper, & Schlotterer, 1974; Dalton, 1992). The MTS tests not only provide an indicator of learning abilities but also an indication of visual function. Her performances on these tests provided the earliest sign of deterioration, which alerted care providers to the possibility of dementia. A standard or "Z" score of −2.00 was used as the "cut-off score" to define "suspicion of dementia." The standard scores were based on the performances on the same tests by a standardization sample of 109 persons with Down's syndrome who were healthy and unaffected by dementia or other serious condition. Details are provided elsewhere (Dalton, 1992). Her standard (Z) scores on the MTS (circles vs. squares) learning tests were -1.74, -0.08, -4.31, -4.31, -4.31, and her Z scores on the DMTS (circles vs. squares) memory test were -1.04, $+0.58$, -3.88, -3.88, and -3.88 at ages 44, 47, 49, 52, and 55 years, respectively. She exceeded the cut-of scores at the age of 49 years, raising the suspicion of dementia for the first time.

At the same time she was failing on the circles vs square test, she successfully met the learning criterion on the colored pictures MTS test until the last test in 1983. This finding suggests that loss of eyesight cannot explain her failure on the memory test because she was able to see well enough to learn the MTS tests. Mild deterioration on an easier test of memory (DMTS colored pictures) test was not evident until she reached the age of 55 years. In summary, subtle changes in cognitive functions which were indicative of "suspicion of dementia" were first noted when she was 49 years of age. Using these scores as the time of "onset," the total duration of dementia was estimated between 12 to 15 years prior to her death. The issues of cognitive evaluations are addressed in this volume by Oliver, Prasher, and Holland.

Activities of Daily Living. RM's daily living skills (ADLs) were repeatedly evaluated with the two-part Basic Life Skills (BLS) Scale behavior rating scale consisting of 259 items in Part 1, which assess motor skills, perceptual skills, self-care skills, communication skills, social skills, community living skills, academic skills, and 60 items in Part 2, measuring adaptability, sociability, cooperation, motivation, frustration tolerance, tolerance toward pressure, activity level, emotional maturity, absence of abnormal behavior and predictability of behavior (Cibiri & Jackson, 1976). The BLS scores are highly correlated with the AAMR's Adaptive Behavior Scale (ABS). The BLS scores were used because this scale was routinely employed with every institutional resident on an annual basis, it makes no assumptions about development, and it is more sensitive to the low end of the IQ scale than the ABS. RM's overall Index of Functional Independence (IFI), which is a mean score based on all BLS items, did not change significantly at any time for 12 years, when she was between the ages of 49 and 61 years, three years before she died. Her IFI scores for the 10 year annual evaluations ranged between 56 and 59 points all within 5 points of the mean (on the BLS scale of scores from 0 to 100) for a standardization sample of 114 adults with Down's syndrome and a sample of 691 individuals with intellectual disabilities without Down's syndrome, all from the same institution.

At the age of 62 years her scores fell precipitously, consistent with the appearance of the late stage of dementia. The evaluation of daily living skills and adaptive behaviors in aging persons with intellectual disabilities, more generally, has rightfully taken a prominent place in the assessment of individuals as the practice of using IQ scores alone has become less acceptable. A critical review and the current status of knowledge of these issues is provided by Prasher in this volume.

Month-by-Month Residential Life Summary.   Detailed daily and monthly reports on RM were available for the last 11 years of her life. In 1981, at the age of 53 years, notwithstanding the development of serious hearing losses, RM continued to participate in all of her daily activities, including shopping and going to church at Christmastime, and she continued working in the institution laundry. This level of activity continued throughout her 55th year, and it included participation in outings and cookouts as well as shopping and working in the laundry. Her severe hearing loss was still evident even with frequent consultations and removal of wax from her ears. When she was 55 years of age, at the time she was failing on the cognitive tests of learning and memory, she was still performing adequately in her everyday routines as well as in a visit to a fair in Toronto organized by staff. Assays of blood specimens revealed that her thyroid functions were normal with a weakly positive antithyroglobulin titer. Hypothyroid function is a common health problem among persons with Down's syndrome and may be implicated in the pathophysiology of Alzheimer disease (Percy, this volume).

When RM was 57 years of age she was placed on a diet of soft food to compensate for the gradual total loss of her teeth. Throughout, she had an active social life and her two sisters and brother frequently sent her gifts. They kept frequent contacts with her and the staff of the institution. In regular monthly reports until she was 58 years of age, RM continued to go to the hairdresser every week and to participate in all of her regular activities. At the age of 60 years, RM underwent 24-hour ambulatory EEG studies, which revealed only "moderate abnormality" consisting of generalized dysrhythmia without definite epileptic activity.

At the age of 61 years, the monthly reports indicate the onset of several bouts of incontinence and occasional incidents of crying, which may have been associated with gastro-intestinal problems. At this age, RM fell and injured herself without breaking any bones. During the same year, the monthly report noted an incident of "wandering." Also, in the same year, she continued to be incontinent and also appeared "confused." Chest pains were diagnosed as a "transient ischemic attack" when RM was 61 years of age. Her confusion continued to increase at this time as well as episodes of urinary incontinence. The monthly reports include instances of improper clothing (e.g., wearing pajamas at wrong times) and undressing at inappropriate places. By this time, she needed constant assistance with self-help skills such as dressing. Her eating skills deteriorated as well (e.g., pouring milk into a bowl of beans, trying to eat soup with a knife). Instances of refusal to cooperate were noted, as well as the emergence of a fear of stairs (which may have been related to her vision problems). She was placed on dilantin to control seizures, which started at about this time. During this year, at age 61, she became increasingly unsteady in her movements, and she could climb stairs only with assistance and with great difficulty. Her behavior became more problematic. She undressed and stuffed her clothing in the toilet, tended to wander off, and needed constant supervision. One year later, RM was provided with a wheelchair because of her mobility problems. She was now sleeping most of the day and could no longer walk. At the age of 62 years, deterioration continued with incidents of smearing feces on her bed, and she now required constant supervision and care.

RM's deteriorating condition was carefully monitored and managed. Social contacts with family members decreased beginning when she was 63 years of age, about 13 months prior to her death. Monthly reports at this time noted that she had occasional incidents of abrupt jerking movements and few behavior problems other than occasional incidents of stripping. Three such incidents when she was 63 years of age were classified as "seizures." She was no longer involved in any programs. Her appetite remained good until the last few weeks before her death although she had to be spoon fed with pureed food. One month before she died she weighed 105 pounds. Monthly reports thereafter until her death revealed that she had chronic obstructive pulmonary disease. She spent most of her waking time just sitting in her rocking chair and dozing on and off. She was continued on medications, including valproic acid to manage seizures which appeared for the first time when she was 63 years old. The increasing number and severity of the health problems experienced by RM reflect the progressively more deleterious consequences of Alzheimer's disease. At age 64, RM died of respiratory failure and chronic obstructive pulmonary disease. There was no evidence in any of the physician's prescription notes for the 11 years before her death that she was ever given major or minor tranquilizers, antidepressants, anxiolytics, or other mood and psychoactive medications, suggesting an absence of psychiatric signs.

Table 1.1 summarizes the main signs and symptoms in RM's adult life beginning at the age of 40 years (when individuals with Down's syndrome are considered to have the brain pathology of Alzheimer's disease). The numbers in the age column (years) indicates her age when each sign or symptom was first noted. The information was obtained from a recent detailed review of her entire institutional records as well as research data accumulated during the period from 1972 to 1987.

TABLE 1.1.   First appearance of sign or symptom

	Age (years)
internal strabismus	40
intact memory (DMTS) and learning (MTS) abilities[1]	44
corneal abnormality	46
left esotropia with keratoconus	47
first decline in memory (DMTS) and learning (MTS) abilities[1]	49
hepatitis B positive	51
moderate to profound hearing loss	53
visual impairments	55
continued decline in memory (DMTS) and learning (MTS) abilities[1]	55
cataracts	56
CT brain scan evidence of atrophy	59
EEG: dysrhythmia with superimposed sharp wave activity	59
24-hour ambulatory EEG: generalized dysrhythmia, no epilepsy	60
gross visual impairments	60
confusion	61
incontinence	61
wandering	61
refusal to cooperate	61
gait impairment	61
seizures	61
reflexes hyperactive for first time	61
requires constant supervision	61
intact ADL skills for past 12 years, evaluated annually	61
first decline in ADL skills	62
declared legally blind	62
myoclonic jerks	62
respiratory failure and death	64

[1]Slightly different procedures were used over a 12-year period; these are described in Dalton, Crapper, & Schlotterer, 1974; Dalton & Crapper, 1977; Dalton & Crapper McLachlan, 1984).

The problems and limitations of the general strategy of conducting longitudinal followups in assessment (illustrated here by the case of RM) and the value of employing experimental procedures for testing memory functions in persons with intellectual disabilities are discussed extensively by Oliver in this volume. He suggests that the longitudinal approach is highly recommended, but it has the disadvantage of being time consuming and requires more extensive resources because it involves repeated assessments at regular and sometimes frequent intervals.

The onset and progression of signs and symptoms shown in the table can be divided into those appearing during a "prodromal" period and those appearing during the formal stages. The first four signs of impairment (between the age of 40 and 47 years) can be considered prodromal because they have not been generally accepted as signs of the early stage Alzheimer's disease in persons with Down's syndrome. Also at this time, her visual learning and memory functions were found to be intact. Nevertheless, this claim for a prodromal period must be offered with reservations. Newly developed tests that were not available in the 1970s suggest that adults with Down's syndrome in their forties show Alzheimer-like visual deficits in the absence of any other signs of dementia and in the absence of significant peripheral ocular defects such as cataracts and refractive errors (Rocco et al., 1997). These visual deficits include impairments in color discrimination (blue hues, but not others), stereoacuity, and contrast sensitivity across the frequency range, all of which are mediated by visual primary and association cortex. No data on these visual functions were available for RM.

Formal stage-one signs and symptoms began at about the age of 49 years when RM showed the first evidence of cognitive deterioration (learning and memory losses) and extended to about the age of 55 years. The second or middle stage of the disease spanned the period when RM was about 56 years to 60 years, during which interval she developed cataracts and showed CT brain scan evidence of atrophy. The third or terminal stage of the disease covered the last 4 years of her life between the ages of about 61 to 64 years. It is also evident that the borders between the stages of disease are somewhat arbitrary especially since it is now generally accepted that there are wide individual differences in the number, age at appearance, and severity of the signs of dementia that occur in affected persons with Down's syndrome.

Neuropathological Diagnosis. RM's sister generously gave permission for postmortem removal and examination of some brain tissue specimens. The examination of the tissue and the neuropathological diagnosis of Alzheimer's disease was performed by a staff neuropathologist of the Toronto Hospital, Toronto. The brain weighed 1,010 grams after fixation and revealed a marked degree of diffuse cortical atrophy and enlargement of the sulci. Atrophy was marked in the temporal lobes with severe atrophy of both the amygdala and hippocampus.

Sections from 13 regions of the brain were examined microscopically revealing moderate neuronal loss in nucleus basalis with scattered neurofibrillary tangles. The section of the basal ganglia revealed a moderate neuronal loss in the nucleus basalis with scattered tangles. The globus pallidus showed mineralization of scattered vessels. There were abundant plaques and tangles in the cingulate region, with severe neuronal loss in the amygdala and adjacent entorhinal cortex. Middle temporal gyrus revealed abundant plaques and tangles. The inferior parietal cortex was less involved with moderate numbers of plaques and tangles. The hippocampus revealed marked cell loss and innumerable plaques and tangles. The substantia nigra was well-populated. A rare tangle was observed but no Lewy bodies. In the medulla, mild neuronal loss and gliosis were present in the inferior olive. The thalamus and cerebellum were unremarkable on routine stains. There was no mention in the report of vascular amyloidosis in the brain.

☐ Commentary

The story of RM illustrates the lethal and progressive nature of Alzheimer's disease in a person with Down's syndrome. It also provides a vivid picture of the broad array of complex issues that must be addressed when aging human beings with intellectual disabilities are affected by Alzheimer's disease. The occurrence of dementia among individuals with intellectual disabilities requires more recognition of its profound impact on the quality of life for the affected individuals, their families, friends, and care providers (Janicki & Dalton, in press). What is not apparent are the ways in which the staff modified their own behaviors to better cope with RM's frailties in the terminal stage, how they prepared her for dying, and how they dealt with their own feelings at the time. Some of these issues are addressed by Service, Lavoie, and Herlihy in this volume. The story of the progression of functional decline in David (Davis, this volume) and Jan (Hammond & Benedetti, this volume) provide additional insightful and detailed personal experiences. When combined with similar anecdotal stories of the progress in clinical symptoms published in the literature (Dalton & Crapper-McLachlan, 1986; Wisniewski, Dalton, McLachlan, Wens, & Wisniewski, 1985) a picture gradually emerges suggesting many similarities between persons with Down's syndrome and persons from the general population who are affected by the disease. The differences appear to be quantitative rather than qualitative. Neuropathologically, the lesions of Alzheimer's disease are typically much more numerous and distributed over wider areas of the brain in persons with Down's syndrome.

Clinically, the symptoms appeared about 20 years sooner and with a generally shorter duration than in the general population (Prasher & Krishnan, 1993a). For health care professionals and service agencies confronted with the wide array of signs and symptoms, the cases also underscore the need for appropriate education and training experiences for staff and the need for policies to permit agencies to effectively allocate their financial, personnel, and other resources. These issues are addressed by Janicki and Dalton (in press) and in this volume.

The central problem for the diagnosis of Alzheimer's disease is the absence of a litmus test. It is necessary to exclude all other possibilities in a complex, time-consuming process relying ultimately on clinical judgment. The clinical presentation in all cases can be confused with comorbid conditions reflecting pathological aging processes that are superimposed on the normal processes of aging. Many of these conditions may differ in frequency and severity from occurrence in similarly affected individuals from the general population and from those with intellectual disabilities of other etiologies. These differences will have an impact on diagnosis of dementia. Whether or not these conditions play an active role in the pathogenesis of dementia in this population or are merely associated conditions is not known. In persons with Down's syndrome, there are additional problematic areas for diagnosis. The clinical team must distinguish the manifestations of the primary intellectual disability, the chromosomal trisomy condition, normal and pathological aging processes, as well as the insidious and slowly progressive signs of possible dementia. Until systematic research provides an effective treatment to slow down and prevent the progression of Alzheimer's disease, interventions must be aimed at palliative care and the preservation of human dignity.

With regard to a comparison of care recommendations, the reader is invited to examine Appendix 2, provided in this volume, which offers a model set of guidelines based on day-to-day experience with affected persons with Down's syndrome who were allowed to "age in place" until their death in a small, suburban, residential community (Newroth & Newroth, 1981). Appendix 2 also graphically illustrates the usefulness of the three-stage model of Alzheimer's disease developed in this chapter and some of the clinical practice recommendations found in this volume in the chapters by McCallion; Force and O'Malley; and Holland; and Chicoine, McGuire, and Rubin.

☐ **References**

Aisen, P. S., & Davis, K. L. (1997). The search for disease-modifying treatment for Alzheimer's disease. *Neurology, 48*(Suppl. 6), S35–S41.

Beal, M. F. (1995). Aging, energy, and oxidative stress in neurodegenerative diseases. *Annals of Neurology, 38,* 357–366.

Berg, J. M., Karlinsky, H., & Holland, A. J. (1993). *Alzheimer disease, Down syndrome, and their relationship* (preface). Oxford: Oxford University Press.

Beyreuther, K., Dyrks, K., Hilbich, K., Manning, U., Konig, G., Multhaup, G., Pollwein, P., & Masters, C. L. (1992). Amyloid precursor protein (APP) and A4 amyloid in Alzheimer's disease and Down syndrome. In L. Nadel & C. J. Epstein (Eds.), *Down syndrome and Alzheimer disease* (pp. 159–182). New York: Wiley-Liss.

Bruce, A. J., Malfroy, B., & Baudry, M. (1996). β-Amyloid toxicity in organotypic hippocampal cultures: Protection by EUK-8, a synthetic catalytic free radical scavenger. *Proceedings of the National Academy of Sciences USA, 93*, 2312–2316.

Burt, D. B., Loveland, K. A., & Lewis, K. R. (1992). Depression and the onset of dementia in adults with mental retardation. *American Journal on Mental Retardation, 96*, 502–511.

Cibiri, S. M., & Jackson, L. J. (1976). *Training developmentally handicapped persons in basic life skills*. Toronto: Ontario Ministry of Community and Social Services.

Cohen, G., & Werner, P. (1994). Free radicals, oxidative stress and neurodegeneration. In D. B. Calne (Ed.), *Neurodegenerative diseases* (pp. 139–161). Philadelphia: W. B. Saunders.

Collacott, R. A., Cooper, S.-A., & Ismail, I. A. (1994). Multi-infarct dementia in Down's syndrome. *Journal of Intellectual Disability Research, 38*, 203–208.

Cooper, S-A. (1997). High prevalence of dementia among people with learning disabilities not attributable to Down's syndrome. *Psychological Medicine, 27*, 609–616.

Crapper-McLachlan, D. R., Dalton A. J., Galin, H., Schlotterer, G., & Daicar, E. (1984). Alzheimer's disease: Clinical course and cognitive disturbances. *Acta Neurologica Scandinavica, 69*(Suppl. 99), 83–90.

Cronin-Golomb, A. (1995). Vision in Alzheimer's disease. *Gerontologist, 35*, 370–376.

Cronin-Golomb, A., Corkin, S., & Growdon, J. H. (1995). Visual dysfunction predicts cognitive deficits in Alzheimer disease. *Optometry and Vision Science, 72*, 168–176.

Cuadrado, E., & Barrena, M. J. (1997). Immune dysfunction in Down's syndrome: Primary immune deficiency or early senescence of the immune system? *Clinical Immunology and Immunopathology, 78*, 209–214.

Dalton, A. J. (1992). Dementia in Down syndrome: Methods of evaluation. In L. Nadel & C. J. Epstein (Eds.), *Alzheimer disease and Down syndrome* (pp. 51–76). New York: Wiley-Liss.

Dalton, A. J., Crapper, D. R., & Schlotterer, G. R. (1974). Alzheimer's disease in Down's syndrome: Visual retention deficits. *Cortex, 10*, 366–377.

Dalton, A. J., & Crapper, D. R. (1977). Down's syndrome and aging of the brain. In P. Mittler (Ed.) *Research to practice in mental retardation: Biomedical aspects* III (pp. 391–400). Baltimore, University Park Press.

Dalton, A. J., & Crapper McLachlan, D. R. (1984). Incidence of memory deterioration in aging persons with Down's syndrome. In J. M. Berg (Ed.) *Perspectives and progress in mental retardation* (pp. 55–62). Baltimore: University Park Press.

Dalton, A. J. & Crapper-McLachlan, D. R. (1986). Clinical expression of Alzheimer's disease in Down's syndrome. *Psychiatric Clinics of North America: Psychiatric Perspectives on Mental Retardation, 9*, 659–670.

De Haan, J. B., Cristiano, F., Iannello, R. C., & Kola, I. (1997). Cu/Zn-superoxide dismutase and glutathione peroxidase during aging. *Biochemistry and Molecular Biology International, 35*, 1281–1297.

De la Torre, R., Casado A., Lopez-Fernandez, E., Carrascosa, D., Ramirez ,V., & Saez, J. (1997). Overexpression of copper-zinc superoxide dismutase in trisomy 21. *Experientia, 52*, 871–873.

Erkinjuntti, T., Ostbye, T., Steenbuis, R., & Hachinski, V. (1997). The effect of different diagnostic criteria on the prevalence of dementia. *New England Journal of Medicine, 337*, 1667–1674.

Evenhuis, H. M., van Zanten, G. A., Brocaar, M. P., & Roerdinkholder, W. H. M. (1992). Hearing loss in middle-age persons with Down syndrome. *American Journal on Mental Retardation, 97*, 47–56.

Fagarasan, M. O., & Aisen, P. S. (1996). Il-1 and anti-inflammatory drugs modulate Ab cytotoxicity in PC12 cells. *Brain Research, 723*, 231–234.

Games, D., Adams, D., Alessandrini, R., Barbour, R., Berthelette, P., Blackwell, C., Carr, T., Clemens, J., Donaldson, T., Gillespie, F., Guido, T., Hagopian, S., Johnson-Wood, K.,

Khan, K., Lee, M., Leibowitz, P., Lieberburg, I., Little, S., Masliah, E., McConlogue, L., Montoyo Zavala, M., Mucke, L., Paganini, L., & Penniman, E. (1995). Development of neuropathology similar to Alzheimer's disease in transgenic mice overexpressing the 717V-F β-amyloid precursor protein. *Nature, 373*, 523–527.

Giulian, D., Li, J., Leara, B., & Keenen, C. (1994). Phagocytic microglia release cytokines and cytotoxins that regulate the survival of astrocytes and neurons in culture. *Neurochemistry International, 25*, 227–233.

Halliwell, B., & Gutteridge J. M. C. (1989). *Free radical in biology and medicine.* Oxford: Clarendon Press.

Haveman, M., Maaskant, M. A., & Sturmans, F. (1989). Older Dutch residents of institutions, with and without Down syndrome: Comparison of mortality and morbidity trends and motor/social functioning. *Australia and New Zealand Journal of Developmental Disabilities, 15*, 241–255.

Hensley, K., Carney, J. M., Mattson, M. P., Aksenova, M., Harris, M., Wu, J. F., Floyd, R. A., & Butterfield, D. A. (1994). A model for β-amyloid aggregation and neurotoxicity based on free radical generation by the peptide: Relevance to Alzheimer disease. *Proceedings of the National Academy of Sciences USA, 91*, 3270–3274.

Holzman, D. M., Li, Y., Gage, F. H., Epstein, C. J., & Mobley, W. C. (1992). Neurodegeneration and gene dysregulation: Studies utilizing the mouse trisomy 16 model of Down syndrome. In L. Nadel & C. J. Epstein (Eds.), *Down syndrome and Alzheimer disease* (pp. 227–244). New York: Wiley-Liss.

Hsiao, K., Chapman, P., Nilsen, S., Eckman, C., Harigaya,Y., Younkin, S., Yang, F. S., & Cole, G. (1996). Correlative memory deficits, Aβ elevation, and amyloid plaques in transgenic mice. *Science, 274*, 99–102.

Iqbal, K., Alonso, A., Gong, C. X., Khatoon, S., Kudo, T., Singh, T., & Grundke-Iqbal, I. (1993). Molecular pathology of Alzheimer neurofibrillary degeneration. *Acta Neurobiologiae Experimentalis, 53*, 325–335.

Jackson, C. V. E., Holland, A. J., Williams, C. A., & Dickerson, J. W. T. (1988). Vitamin E and Alzheimer's disease in subjects with Down's syndrome. *Journal of Mental Deficiency Research, 32*, 479–484.

Janicki, M. P., & Dalton, A. J. (1997). Pending impact of dementia related care on intellectual disability providers. *Proceedings of the International Congress III on the Dually Diagnosed—Mental Health Aspects of Mental Retardation,* Montréal, P.Q., Canada, 188–190.

Janicki, M. P., & Dalton, A. J. (1998). *Prevalence of dementia and impact on intellectual disability services.* Manuscript submitted for publication.

Janicki, M. P., & Dalton, A. J. (in press). Current practice in the assessment and care of persons with intellectual disabilities. In N. Bouras (Ed.), *Psychiatric and behavioral disorders in mental retardation.* Cambridge: Cambridge University Press.

Janicki, M. P., Heller, T., Seltzer, G., & Hogg, J. (1996). Practice guidelines for the clinical assessment and care management of Alzheimer's disease and other dementias among adults with intellectual disability. *Journal of Intellectual Disability Research, 40*, 374–382.

Johannsen, R., Christensen, J. E. J., Goldstein, H., Nielsen, V. K., & Mai, J. (1996). Epilepsy in Down syndrome—Prevalence in three age groups. *Seizure, 5*, 121–125.

Hendrie, H. C., & Hingtgen, J. N. (1990). In H. C. Hendrie, L. G. Mendelsohn, & C. Readhead (Eds.), *Brain aging molecular biology, the aging process and neurodegenerative disease* (Preface, p. vii). Toronto: Hans Huber.

London, J. A., Biegel, D., & Pachter, J. S. (1996). Neurocytopathic effects of Beta-amyloid-stimulated monocytes: A potential mechanism for central nervous system damage in Alzheimer disease. *Proceedings of the National Academy of Sciences USA, 93*, 4147–4152.

Ma, J., Yee, A., Brewer, H. B., Jr., Das, S., & Potter, H. (1994). Amyloid-associated proteins a1-antichymotrypsin and apolipoprotein E promote assembly of Alzheimer b-protein into filaments. *Nature, 372*, 92–94.

Machemer, R.M., Jr. (1993). The biology of human aging. In R. H. Machemer, Jr., & J. C. Overeynder (Eds.), *Aging and developmental disabilities—An in-service curriculum* (pp. 7–23). Rochester: University of Rochester.

Markesbery, W. R., & Ehmann, W. D. (1994). Brain trace elements in Alzheimer disease. In R. D. Terry, R. Katzman, & K. L. Vick (Eds.), *Alzheimer disease* (pp. 353–367). New York: Raven Press.

McGer, P. L., McGeer, E. J., & Sibley, J. (1990). Anti-inflammatory drugs and Alzheimer disease. *Lancet, 335,* 1037.

McGeer, P. L., Schulzer, M., & McGeer, E. G. (1996). Arthritis and anti-inflammatory agents as possible protective factors for Alzheimer's disease: A review of 17 epidemiological studies. *Neurology, 47,* 425–432.

McLachlan, D. R. (1995). Aluminum and the risk for Alzheimer disease. *Environmetrics, 6,* 233–275.

McVicker, R. W., Shanks, O. E. P., & McClelland, R. J. (1994). Prevalence and associated features of epilepsy in adults with Down's syndrome. *British Journal of Psychiatry, 164,* 528–532.

Moss, S., & Patel, P. (1997). Dementia in older people with intellectual disability: Symptoms of physical and mental illness, and levels of adaptive behaviour. *Journal of Intellectual Disability Research, 41,* 60–69.

Murdoch, J. C., Ratcliffe, W. A., McLarty, D. G., Rodger, J. C., & Ratcliffe, J. G. (1977). Thyroid function in adults with Down's syndrome. *Journal of Clinical Endocrinology & Metabolism, 44,* 453–458.

Newroth, S., & Newroth, A. (1981). *Coping with Alzheimer disease: A growing concern.* Downsview, Ontario, Canada: National Institute on Mental Retardation (ISBN 0-919648-26-6).

Pasinetti, G. M. (1996). Inflammatory mechanisms in neurodegeneration and Alzheimer's disease: The role of the complement system. *Neurobiology of Aging, 17,* 707–716.

Percy, M. E., Dalton, A. J., Markovic, V. D., Crapper-McLachlan, D. R., Hummel, J. T., Rusk, A. C. M., & Andrews, D. F. (1990). Red cell superoxide dismutase, glutathione peroxidase and catalase in Down syndrome patients with and without manifestations of Alzheimer disease. *American Journal of Medical Genetics, 35,* 459–467.

Prasher, V. P. (1997). Psychotic features and effect of severity of learning disability on dementia in adults with Down syndrome: Review of literature. *British Journal of Developmental Disabilities 43,* 85–92.

Prasher, V. P. (1995a). Prevalence of psychiatric disorders in adults with Down syndrome. *European Journal of Psychiatry, 9,* 77–82.

Prasher, V. P. (1995b). Screening of hearing impairment and associated effects on adaptive behavior in adults with Down syndrome. *British Journal of Developmental Disabilities, 41,* 121–132.

Prasher, V. P. (1995c). Reliability of diagnosing clinical hypothyroidism in adults with Down syndrome. *Australia & New Zealand Journal of Developmental Disabilities, 20,* 223–233.

Prasher, V. P. (1995d). Epilepsy and associated effects on adaptive behavior in adults with Down syndrome. *Seizure, 4,* 53–56.

Prasher, V. P. (1995e). Age-specific prevalence, thyroid dysfunction and depressive symptomatology in adults with Down syndrome and dementia. *International Journal of Geriatric Psychiatry, 10,* 25–31.

Prasher, V. P. (1994a). Screening of ophthalmic pathology and its associated effects on adaptive behavior in adults with Down's syndrome. *European Journal of Psychiatry, 8,* 197–204.

Prasher, V. P. (1994b). Prevalence of thyroid dysfunction and autoimmunity in adults with Down syndrome. *Down's Syndrome: Research and Practice, 2*(2), 67–70.

Prasher, V. P. (1994c). Screening of medical problems in adults with Down syndrome. *Down's Syndrome: Research and Practice, 2*(2), 59–66.

Prasher, V. P., & Corbett, J. A. (1993). Onset of seizures as a poor indicator of longevity in people with Down syndrome and dementia. *International Journal of Geriatric Psychiatry, 8*, 923–927.

Prasher, V. P., & Day, S. (1995). Brief report: Obsessive-compulsive disorder in adults with Down syndrome. *Journal of Autism and Developmental Disorders, 25*, 453–457.

Prasher, V. P., & Hall, W. (1996). Short-term prognosis of depression in adults with Down's syndrome: Association with thyroid status and effects on adaptive behavior. *Journal of Intellectual Disability Research, 40*, 32–38.

Prasher, V. P., & Krishnan, V. H. R. (1993). Hypothyroidism presenting as dementia in a persons with Down syndrome: A case report. *Mental Handicap, 21*, 147–148.

Reisberg, B., Ferris, S. H., & DeLeon, M. J. (1989). The stage-specific temporal course of Alzheimer's disease: Functional and behavioral concomitants based upon cross-sectional and longitudinal observation. In K. Iqbal, H.M. Wisniewski, & B. Windblad, (Eds.), *Alzheimer's disease and related disorders* (pp. 23–41). New York: Liss.

Robakis, N. K., Wisniewski, H. M., Jenkins E. C., Devine-Gage, E. A., Houck, G. E., Yao, X. L., Ramakrishna, N., Wolfe, G., Silverman, W. P., & Brown, W. T. (1987). Chromosome 21q21 sublocalisation of gene encoding beta-amyloid peptide in cerebral vessels and neuritic (senile) plaques of people with Alzheimer disease and Down syndrome. *Lancet, 1*(8529), 384–385.

Rocco, F. J., Cronin-Golomb, A., & Lai, F. (1997). Alzheimer-like visual deficits in Down syndrome. *Alzheimer Disease and Associated Disorders, 11*, 88–98.

Sano, M., Ernesto, C., Thomas, R. G., Klauber, M. R., Schafer, K., Grundman, M., Woodbury, P., Growdon, J., Cotman, D. W., Pfeiffer, E., Schneider, L. S., & Thal, L. J. (1997). A controlled trial of selegiline, alpha-tocopherol, or both as treatment for Alzheimer's disease. *New England Journal of Medicine, 336*, 1216–1222.

Schellenberg, G. D., Kamino, K., Bryant, E. M., Moore, D., & Bird, T. D. (1992). Genetic heterogeneity, Down syndrome and Alzheimer disease. In L. Nadel & C. J. Epstein (Eds.), *Down syndrome and Alzheimer disease* (pp. 215–226). New York: Wiley-Liss.

Sim, M. (1965). Alzheimer's disease: A forgotten entity. *Geriatrics, 20*, 668–674.

Sourander, P., & Sjögren, H. (1970). The concept of Alzheimer's disease and its clinical implications. In G. E. W. Wolstenholme & M. O'Connor (Eds.), *Alzheimer's disease and related conditions* (pp. 11–36). London: Churchill.

Struwe, F. (1929). Histopathlogische untersuchungen uber entstehung und wesen der senilen plaques. *Zeitschrift fur Neurologie und Psychiatrie, 122*, 291–307.

Sustrova, M., & Sarikova, V. (1997). Down's syndrome—Effect of increased gene expression in chromosome 21 on the function of the immune and nervous system. *Bratislavske Lekarske Listy, 98*, 221–228.

Tomiyama, T., Shoji, A., Kataoka, K., Suwa, Y., Asano, S., Kaneko, H., & Endo, N. (1996). Inhibition of amyloid β protein aggregation and neurotoxicity by rifampicin—Its possible function as a hydroxyl radical scavenger. *Journal of Biological Chemistry, 271*, 6839–6844.

Van Schrojenstein Lantman-de Valk, H. M., Haveman, M. J., & Crebolder, H. F. J. H. (1996). Comorbidity in people with Down's syndrome: A criteria-based analysis. *Journal of Intellectual Disability Research, 40*, 385–399.

Van Schrojenstein Lantman-de Valk, H. M., van den Akker, M., Maaskant, M. A., Haveman, M. J., Urlings, H. F., Kessels, A. G., & Crebolder, H. F. (1997). Prevalence and incidence of health problems in people with intellectual disability. *Journal of Intellectual Disability Research, 41*, 42–51.

Volicer, L., & Crino, P. B. (1990). Involvement of free radicals in dementia of the Alzheimer type: A hypothesis. *Neurobiology of Aging, 11*, 567–571.

Williams, M. E. (1995). *Complete guide to aging and health.* New York: Harmony Books.

Wisniewski, H. M., Silverman, W., & Wegiel, J. (1994). Ageing, Alzheimer disease and mental retardation. *Journal of Intellectual Disability Research, 38,* 233–239.

Wisniewski, K. E., Dalton, A. J., McLachlan, D. R., Wen, G. Y., & Wisniewski, H. M. (1985). Alzheimer's disease in Down's syndrome: Clinicopathologic studies. *Neurology, 35,* 957–961.

Wisniewski, T. M., & Wisniewski, H. M. (1992). Alzheimer's disease and the cerebral amyloidoses. In I. Kostovic, S. Knezic, H. M. Wisniewski, & G. J. Spillich (Eds.), *Neurodevelopment, aging and cognition* (pp. 157–172). Boston: Birkhauser.

Zigman, W., Schupf, N., Haveman, M., & Silverman, W. (1995). *Epidemiology of Alzheimer disease in mental retardation: Results and recommendations from an international conference.* Washington, DC: American Association on Mental Retardation.

Zigman, W., Schupf, N., Haveman, M., & Silverman, W. (1997). Epidemiology of Alzheimer disease in mental retardation: Results and recommendations from an international conference. *Journal of Intellectual Disability Research, 41,* 76–80.

Barbara Hammond
Penni Benedetti

Perspectives of a Care Provider

This chapter provides a descriptive chronology of a middle-aged woman with Down syndrome who, once diagnosed with Alzheimer's disease, follows a classic course of decline and eventual debilitation and death. Staff of her residence chronicled the progression of her dementia and provide some insights into the care management practices used in providing for her care. The authors place the course of her disease in perspective and offer comments on the stresses and strains on agency resources. Suggestions are offered for agencies facing similar challenges in providing day-to-day care for adults with dementia.

This chronology of a woman in her forties with Down syndrome describes the progressive development of Alzheimer's dementia and illustrates the concurrent decline of both mental and physical capabilities. Once those concerned about her begin to notice the significant changes in her abilities and behavior, the interval between the time she is first assessed and when she dies is quite short. She was 49 years old when she died of complications related to dementia of the Alzheimer type. This is her story told through a series of diary entries taken by staff at the group home where she lived.

Address correspondence to: Barbara Hammond, The Arc of Ocean County, 815 Cedarbridge Avenue, Lakewood, NJ 08701.

☐ Jan S.'s Chronology of Decline

—Jan S.[2] first became involved with our agency in 1982 and decided to move into a small group home that we operated. Several years later, yearning for a place of her own, she moved to an apartment that we located for her. Jan was quite capable when we first knew her. She lived quite well at the group home and once she decided she wanted to live on her own, we did what we could to help her. Initially, she needed some assistance to manage her life in her new home but was fairly independent otherwise.

Jan had a very interesting personality and enjoyed a vigorous lifestyle. She enjoyed a range of activities, such as bowling, dancing, tennis, choir, shopping, and spending time with her family and gentleman friend. She did not have a permanent vocation but attended a local occupational center. During the time we knew her, she was happy and productive. In 1990, she moved into her own apartment.

A couple of years after she moved into her apartment, we began to notice some subtle changes in her behavior. Sometime in 1993, we asked that she see a specialist at our local clinic. She was interviewed and examined by a physician who specialized in the treatment of persons with intellectual disabilities. Her general functional abilities were showing gross deterioration. He examined her and recommended that further assessment be done to rule out causes such as hypothyroidism or depression. He also suspected that she may be showing signs of dementia related to Alzheimer's disease.

By March of 1994, Jan began to show a further decline of skills, and the first significant signs were becoming evident. For the first time, she was incontinent and began to wear several sets of underwear to cover this up. About this time, her participation in active sports and other activities began to diminish and she became more of a spectator. She began to be very emotional, often weeping at times when nothing seemed to provoke it. Her participation in the occupational center was more difficult, and her time was cut down to half a day from a full day.

Thus began the serious decline. Jan, a woman who enjoyed the fruits of an active and independent life, became less active and less independent. What follows is the monthly chronicle of her decline and the course of her illness.

May 1994

Jan alternates between marked periods of confusion and alertness. This month there is a bed wetting incident. Jan gets lost on the grounds of

[2]Jan is a pseudonym, as are the other names in this chapter.

the condo where she lives. On May 26, Jan is seen by a geriatric neurologist. He states Jan displays some "emotional–actional" qualities of early-stage dementia of the Alzheimer type. She is treated for anxiety and depression.

June 1994

Jan is distressed and is weeping daily. She is confused and in one incident forgot how to buckle her seat belt. There is an increase of incontinence. Jan needs increased assistance with dressing. She is putting on one knee-high stocking and one anklet. She takes her clean clothes out of the closet and puts them in her dirty clothes hamper.

July 1994

Jan has periods of lucidity and disorientation. She is found naked in her bedroom. At a barbecue at one of the group homes, she is found in the bathroom totally undressed sitting on the bathroom floor. Jan has a seizure with unconsciousness. Jan has become unable to do daily tasks such as her laundry. Jan is having much difficulty dressing. She is putting clothes on backward and having difficulty finding her clothes.

August 1994

In the beginning of August Jan still attends a sheltered workshop on a part-time basis. She transfers to Heritage Institute, a geriatric day care center on August 9. Jan is still interested in TV, her coloring books, doing crafts, and attending choir practice. Jan is eating all her meals and taking her medication with no difficulty. Jan starts wearing Depends.[2] She is frequently having accidents in her clothes, on the bathroom floor, and in her room. Toward the end of the month Jan is found with feces all over herself, smeared all over her room and on the rug. Her wet underpants are under her pillow and soiled Depends are hidden in her closet. Jan needs assistance with bathing and washing her hair. When she does bathe herself, she is very proud of herself and says, "I did it." Jan complains of her clothes being too tight. In actuality, they are loose on her. Crying and mood swings are beginning. Toward the end of the month crying becomes more frequent and confusion starts on a regular basis. At

[3]A brand of adult diaper product for incontinence.

the end of the month, Jan is found on the floor, gasping for air. We call 911 for the emergency team and an ambulance takes her to the emergency room. Jan is released a few hours later, appearing to be fine. Jan is starting to shuffle and lean forward when she walks.

September 1994

At the beginning of the month, Jan is still socializing somewhat. She is still attending choir, doing crafts, and group shopping. Jan's crying seems to be increasing. One incident involves her being hysterical, crying when staff tries to get her out of the van. Crying and screaming also has started when staff helps her with her bath. Jan is complaining frequently of her stomach hurting; no medical cause can be found. Jan appears to be disoriented and confused at times. When she dressed herself, she put her clothes on backward. She sometimes has trouble locating her eating utensils and plate. Once she appeared to have trouble finding her mouth when eating. Many trips up and down stairs crying. She began tripping and forgetting where she was going.

Found in a closet behind clothes hiding. Jan fell several times this month. Several times found sitting on her bedroom or bathroom floor naked, with wet clothes around her. Jan started removing her Depends. Jan started going to bed early toward the middle of the month. By the end of the month she started getting up at night. Jan saw a neurologist due to previously reported seizures. Increased Depakote.

October 1994

Jan's crying and screaming have increased. Constantly yelling "leave me alone." Eating well, but requiring hand-over-hand assistance when eating. Jan is having trouble getting in and out of the van. She is starting to need assistance with walking. Jan is having trouble with the stairs. Jan still makes an effort to do for herself but becomes easily upset when she can't. Jan fell out of bed. Jan is getting up more frequently during the night. A home health aide is hired by Jan's mother to help staff with Jan's personal care as it has become difficult and time consuming.

November 1994

Mood swings continue. Whining, crying, and screaming is a daily occurrence. There are times when she is alert and appears happy. Jan still enjoys seeing her boyfriend and going out with her parents. Jan appears to have had another seizure. Jan fell several times this month. She is having a lot of trouble with stairs, needing assistance of staff. Does not want a bath, screams, and is combative when staff bathes her. Up more frequently at night. More evidence of confusion; cannot find her plate or utensils when they are set before her on the table.

December 1994

At beginning of month, Jan appeared very tired and weak. She is having great difficulty walking. She appears to have forgotten how to move her feet. It now takes two staff to get her up or down the stairs. Two staff are needed to bathe her. She screams and kicks. Jan has been talking to imaginary people. She also scrunched up her sweater while wearing it and said it was a teddy bear. Jan talked about a group home that she had lived in several years ago as if she still lived there. She also called her mother, Sharon, the name of the group home manager. Staff members have begun to feed Jan. Jan became very ill; a mattress was moved downstairs, as staff members can no longer get her up and down stairs. Jan has started refusing to go to day program. Jan frequently is up during the night. There were two or three days when Jan needed little assistance and was cooperative and cheerful. During the end of the month, Jan had a seizure. By the 22nd, Jan needed a wheelchair. Constantly complaining that her stomach hurts.

January 1995

Jan has begun staying up most of the night. At times she lays in bed singing. She wakes quite often screaming. Jan complains daily that her stomach hurts. There is some difficulty swallowing her medication. Jan has to be fed by staff. There is much difficulty giving Jan a bath, taking two or three staff members to do it. At times Jan is unresponsive to staff. She is starting to sleep a lot during the day. Jan refuses a few times to go to day program. The wheelchair is being used a lot more. Jan is screaming to go home, but she is already at home. Jan picks at her clothes and the Depends while screaming and crying. Jan is restless and easily agitated.

February 1995

Jan's agitation, screaming, and crying happen daily. During one incident, she bites herself. Jan is sitting on the couch yelling that the bag she is holding is hers. She also accuses people of taking her things. Jan's having some problems swallowing pills. She spit her vitamin out so staff now checks to make sure she takes her medication. Jan is falling. She needs a lot of help getting on the van. At Jan's birthday party, she was screaming and crying a lot. Jan pulls her Depends off and gets feces all over herself. She is constantly pulling at her clothes. Jan has become very disruptive at Heritage. She is not participating and is agitating other people who are there. This month, Jan got a urinary infection and hemorrhoids. There is some difficulty getting Jan off the couch or out of bed, as she has become dead weight. Jan is still able to identify staff. Jan awakes at night crying and appearing to be frightened. A psychiatrist sees Jan the end of the month. He agreed with the working diagnosis of Alzheimer's dementia. Due to her increased agitation, he prescribes Ativan.

March 1995

Jan has four seizures this month. All four occur in the early morning . Crying and screaming has continued on a daily basis. She is waking up many times during the night. Jan is getting sores on her upper thighs and buttocks. Jan is having much difficulty swallowing food and medication.

April 1995

Jan continues to have trouble swallowing. There are times when she refuses to eat or drink. Many times Jan has to be held upright to eat. Jan has become rigid. Benztropine is prescribed for rigidity in her muscles. Anxiety, crying, yelling is a daily occurrence. Thioridazine is prescribed for anxiety, but changed at the end of month to Risperdal. Jan is coughing up a lot of mucus. She is hospitalized on the 3rd and 10th. Jan punches a home health aide in the eye. Jan is grinding her teeth. At times she is unresponsive. Jan is moved to a first floor apartment. She is no longer at Heritage and spends a lot of time propped up on the couch with pillows. Jan spends a lot of time sleeping during the day. Jan has impacted feces that have to be manually removed. There is a reddened area on Jan's ankle which is a possible breakdown in her skin. Jan is still able to recognize people. Screaming and agitation continues. Has been eating baby food and other soft foods. Often screams during eating. Staff have been putting her on her side with Depends due to open sores on her buttocks.

May 1995

Glycerin sticks being used to clean Jan's mouth. Head falling forward, Jan having difficulty holding it up. Jan is now being given bed baths.

Screaming and crying on a daily basis. There are a few times she appears to be alert and content. Physically, Jan appears to be getting worse. She has difficulty in swallowing. Jan is now getting a red rash in the crease of her thighs. Her feet are getting red and dry. She appears to be having body tremors. Overnight finds her bleeding from the mouth, but cannot find a cut in her mouth. Jan's feet have turned blue and are cold to the touch. Once elevated, color returned. There is also some swelling. Jan is congested with a lot of coughing. Bronchitis is diagnosed. Jan still responding to and recognizes her boyfriend.

June 1995

Jan appears to be nonresponsive and confused. She is easily agitated and is screaming frequently. Jan has become very congested with a lot of coughing. She has a gurgling noise coming from her throat. Jan's breathing is shallow. Mouth is once again bleeding. Jan is admitted to the hospital on June 20, due to bronchitis. She does not return to the supervised apartment. She is moved to a nursing home, as her doctor feels that she needs 24-hour nursing care. While Jan is in the nursing home, her condition continues to decline. She has difficulty swallowing food and contracts pneumonia three times. There is less recognition of familiar faces and voices over a period of a year. She can no longer speak. Her eyes will follow a voice or someone moving in the room; however, she does not appear to know anyone, responding only to her mother's voice.

July 1995

Jan is continued at the nursing home. She is steadily worse and is now under total nursing care.

August 1996

On August 14, 1996, Jan passes away. She is 49 years old.

☐ Challenges for Care Managerment

In the beginning Jan's physical and mental changes were gradual and almost imperceptible. Because Jan had always been forgetful and somewhat moody, the changes in her personality and mood were not readily detected. Yet, at some point, our staff began to notice that Jan did not initiate tasks and needed a great deal of assistance to accomplish simple, everyday tasks. Not fully being aware of what was happening to Jan, we believed that the changes were part of a normal "slowing down" due to aging. We continued to challenge Jan to help her maintain her skills. It was important for us to give Jan the encouragement to overcome her moods and what we thought were transitory changes in behavior. In retrospect, we were operating in a void of information and resources and we did a great deal of denying and hoping she would "be herself" again.

After we began to notice significant physical changes, we knew we needed to access medical assistance. We began the assessment process with a complete physical, neurological, and psychiatric evaluation. We were told that three conditions could be present: hypothyroidism, major depression, or dementia. Given the findings and ruling out other problems, the diagnosis of Alzheimer's dementia seemed to fit. The course of her disease clearly contained the following: onset of seizures, personality change, significant loss of skills, incontinence, altered gait, and eventually, the inability to walk.

At this point, we searched for information about this condition as it related to individuals with Down syndrome. We had no idea what to expect or how to plan for what was to come. Very early on, we had to provide Jan with a one-on-one staff person. Her gait now consisted of pitching and shuffling forward. She appeared to have lost depth perception and would step in every direction, trying to mount a curb. To board a van, she was virtually carried on and to exit she would sit and shimmy down the steps with the assistance of two staff members. As Jan's needs increased, a third staff person was often called upon to assist during the evening hours. This, however, became cost prohibitive. Jan needed assistance to walk, bathe, and eat. She appeared to be hallucinating, batting and screaming at invisible forces. She was combative, especially at bath time, and it took two staff members to get her into the tub, bathe her, and then get her out. She screamed and cried throughout and seemed terrified of the water.

Jan's mother stepped in with some help. She hired a home health aide to assist Jan in the evenings, from four to eight. These were the most difficult hours. Jan became very agitated in the early evening, what we later learned was common among adults with Alzheimer's disease. One of our greatest problems was moving Jan. She could be totally limp and dead weight or her body could become rigid. Our staff for the most part had no experience in the moving and personal care of patients, and as the level of nursing care increased, they were clearly becoming frustrated and stressed.

It was difficult to take Jan to a physician's office, as her screaming disturbed the other patients. Because of this, we often had to go to the emergency room of our local hospital to obtain medical care. These visits could take up to six hours. A number of medications were tried to help Jan with her hallucinations and anxiety but none were really effective. Nothing was found to help her with muscle rigidity. She was repositioned constantly throughout the day. When swallowing became difficult, we began crushing her medications and feeding her soft foods, but she continued to choke on these, too.

Even though she was experiencing serious decline, she had been able to continue attending a day program. This time spent away from her apartment provided our staff with some respite and time to do other things. However, there came a point when her crying and agitation were disturbing the other participants in the day program, and she was asked to leave. This left us with the challenge of providing 24-hour staffing for Jan. This was perhaps the most difficult time we experienced, as having to do this stretched our budget and stressed our staff even more. We no longer had the fiscal and human resources to continue to provide 24-hour care to Jan in her apartment.

About this time, Jan developed pneumonia and was hospitalized. Her physician advised us to have her admitted to a nursing facility. We found that by this time Jan needed the kind of care that we no longer could provide. Like other persons who develop dementia and lose the ability to care for themselves, Jan had finally gone beyond the resources that were available to provide for her in her home. Within our stretched resources, we provided the supports she needed up to almost the very end. However, it was difficult for the staff and everyone involved to admit we could no longer find ways to help Jan and keep her at home. It was a very emotional time for everyone involved.

☐ Commentary

The challenges that someone like Jan presented will not be unique. We now have several other adults who have dementia and we know that it will be an ongoing challenge. What are the lessons from our experience? With regard to being prepared for dealing with the onset of dementia in agency clientele, conduct assessments regularly to track loss of skills, most preferably in conjunction with any ongoing annual reviews, and develop a team of medical professionals who are familiar with Down syndrome and Alzheimer's disease (including a psychiatrist, primary care physician, and neurologist). Further, to help provide tailored services, access community care providers, such as home health aides, visiting homemakers, and volunteers, once a resident becomes wheel chair bound and his or her needs exceed the ability of staff to routinely handle. Also, provide training in lifting and personal care and rotate staff who are providing direct care, since primary carers can quickly become overwhelmed. It is important to also provide ongoing supports and encouragement to staff who are providing direct care and avoid nursing facilities for as long as possible, because such facilities often relate to individuals with intellectual disabilities with difficulty and confusion and perceive such individuals as having "unique" problems in behavior as opposed to symptoms of dementia. Last, in considering how to prepare for the future, only develop wheel-chair-accessible and otherwise barrier-free houses and apartments.

David R. Davis

A Parent's Experience

This chapter provides an account of the experiences of a family with a child with Down's syndrome who eventually succumbs to dementia of the Alzheimer type. It includes a discussion of the difficult early years of the child's life and the challenges the family faced as he aged. It also examines the family's problems in recognizing that their son was experiencing the onset of dementia and his gradual decline until his death at age 46.

David was our firstborn. The time was the late 1940s. My wife and I were young parents at the time; my wife was 24 years old when David was born. From the beginning David was different, but I'm not sure that we realized it at the time. As an infant, he had difficulty nursing and he couldn't hold his head up. What he did eat, he had difficulty keeping the food down. He had trouble with his bowels, and he had what we thought were bronchial infections.

We took him first to a general practitioner who recommended that we take him to a pediatrician. That doctor, after examining David, asked to meet with me alone. During our conversation, he told me David was a "mongoloid child" and would require special care. After the meeting, my wife and I decided that we would not take his word and requested another opinion. We went to another doctor who, at that time, was the most highly regarded and respected pediatrician in Indianapolis. He looked at

Address correspondence to: David R. Davis, 8722 Ray Circle, Indianapolis, IN 46256.

David for a minute or two and said "this is a mongoloid child." He went on to tell us that David would not live very long and he would be a burden to us for as long as he lived. He told us that David would probably die of pneumonia before the age of 7. He concluded, "If I were you, I would leave right now and drive straight to the state Institution for the Feeble Minded at Muscatatuck, admit him, and forget about him; have more children, and get on with your lives."

This was a considerable jolt to a young couple who had been married for less than a year. For us there was no decision to be made. We knew that we wanted to keep David with us. We had very strong support in our decision from my wife's mother and other family members. Our other family members were also very supportive, but none helped us like my mother-in-law did.

Over the next few months, David's progress was slow. He was sick nearly all the time. We had a difficult time coming up with a formula to feed him. He had an abdominal hernia. He had ear infections. His bowel movements were a problem. Yet, he was a cute baby and responded very well to love and affection. He finally became adjusted to a formula, and he knew the people who loved and cared for him. During this time, things were rough for us, but there were encouraging things that happened as we went along.

A little more than 18 months after David was born, our second child, a little girl arrived (subsequently a brother and another sister were born). She was a perfectly healthy baby and, except for having her days and nights mixed up, she progressed as a baby should. However, for my wife it was like having twins. She had two babies to be fed bottles, two babies in diapers, and two essentially helpless little souls who required their mother's undivided attention. The two of them learned to sit up at about the same time. The little girl learned to walk before David did. She learned to talk, but David did not.

David never did become verbally fluent in the usual sense of the term. Somehow, the words that David wanted to say just never quite got out. Those of us who were around him all the time could understand him, and he did a good job of using props and making his wants known. He could say "Mom," "Dad," and "Grandma" very plainly. He did a fair job with the names of his brother and sisters and the names of close friends, but he was never able to put it all together very well. We could tell he wanted to communicate, but he just could not get the words to come out together. We sensed this was very frustrating for him.

As David grew older he continued to have various physical problems. He had chronic ear problems that were eventually corrected by surgery. The ear problems stemmed from a hole in his ear that resulted from ear infections he had when he was a baby. David continued to have problems eating. Until he was 12 years old, he ate only baby foods and was mostly on a liquid diet. Finally, a neighbor he liked to visit coaxed him into eating fried chicken. From then on he always loved fried chicken and was always able to eat regular food.

Until the last couple of years of his life David was a sweet and lovable person. He loved to be with people and to participate in all activities. Had he been normal, he would have been quite an athlete. He played with other children his own age and those a little older; he could always hold his own with them in the tussles children have. He loved to play basketball and to bowl. He bowled for years and had several shelves full of trophies.

When it was time for David to go to school, there were no schools in Indianapolis for children like him. Although the Indiana constitution provides that an education shall be available to all children, in 1953 there were no classes except in the state institution. This was no option for us. Fortunately, in the year in which David would have started school, we were part of a group of parents who met and organized a parents' cooperative. We called ourselves The Parents and Friends of Retarded Children. Our first objective was to start a school for our children who were excluded from the public schools. This would be a school for retarded children. After months of fund raising, remodeling an old Catholic community center, and putting together a staff of mostly retired former teachers, we opened The Noble School at Indianapolis in September of 1953.

David was one of the early students at Noble. The facility grew at a rapid rate and moved from the community center into an abandoned private school. In 1972, the school moved into a specially designed building, which was built after a community-wide fund raising effort. Subsequently, a second facility was built and opened on another side of the city, and now Noble Centers operates out of 11 facilities around the metropolitan Indianapolis area.

As the Noble Centers evolved, a sheltered workshop was opened and the clients of Noble had an opportunity to go to work. David worked at this sheltered facility for a number of years until it became too much of a frustration for him to keep up with the demands of his job. This began when David was in his thirties. When this happened, we arranged for David to attend a combination day activity program and workshop at another facility operated by Noble. Had we known what was happening to David and what to look for, we would have realized that the difficulties David was having in the workshop program were probably the first signs of the onset of dementia.

☐ The Onset of Dementia

When we look back, we can see that David was slowing down. The changes in his skills experienced at the workshop were the first signs. The next thing we noticed was that David was having a hard time in other activities. For example, he was now having difficulty keeping up with the activities at the bowling alley. It took him forever to deliver the ball. Consequently, to be fair to the other participants we took David out of bowling. We wondered if we had done the right thing about removing him from the workshop and bowling because it just seemed like David was continuing to slow down. Now we know that all of this was a part of the precocious aging he was experiencing.

As David was growing older, so were we. My wife and I began to think of our own mortality and our own slowing down. We wanted to be sure David would be able to adapt if he had to live away from us. For several years his name had been on a list for admission to a group home. When he was age 40, David moved into the group home.

The adjustment for David was not easy, nor was it for us; but I think my wife and I were able to make the adjustment much faster than David. However, we believe that he was more comfortable in the group home than he was in our home and this was good. We were both pleased that we made the decision we did and that we were able to help David with the adjustment in his lifestyle. In David's second year in the group home, the staff began to notice that he would fall occasionally. That year, we were on vacation in Michigan; David and all our other children and grandchildren were with us. One morning we found David lying on the floor in his bedroom and we thought this was strange. He had apparently fallen, as he had a chipped tooth. We took him to a dentist that same day and had the tooth fixed temporarily. We returned to the cottage and David seemed well. Later, we took David back to his group home and we went back to our cottage.

However, only a few days had gone by when we got a call from the group home staff director telling us that David was in the hospital after suffering a series of severe seizures. We returned home and were advised that he had degenerative brain atrophy. He was placed on medication and had considerable difficulty in adjusting to the medicine. In fact, he suffered an overdose of the drug Dilantin and required further hospitalization. After a while, the dosages of the drugs were adjusted and he appeared to improve.

Soon after, David moved to a different group home operated by another agency. The staff at this home was much more dedicated and took very good care of him. From this point on, he needed a lot of care. He began to have myoclonic seizures and they were quite frequent. On some days he would have none and on other days the seizures would be very severe. Also, David continued to decline in his abilities and continually needed more help with his personal care. One of the problems he was now experiencing was that he did not appear to have a very good idea of where he was in relation to things around him. He would want to sit in a chair and then try to sit down before he was even at the chair. At dinner, sometimes he seemed to have difficulty locating his plate and getting the utensil to his mouth when he was eating.

We also noted a number of changes in David that had to do with his mood and emotional state. He was now occasionally combative. He had never been combative in his life; he had always been very agreeable and friendly. Common activities did not appeal to him any longer. For example, he didn't seem to enjoy television anymore. Yet this may have been due to a vision disorder as he would watch television if he was very close to it. He suffered from severe mood swings. One minute he would be happy and laughing and the next he would be depressed and maybe a little tearful. His neurologist tried to treat the mood changes with Prozac but without much success.

However, everything was not bad. David continued to enjoy music. He particularly liked country music and show tunes from *Music Man, South Pacific*, and *My Fair Lady*. We found he would be happy if he was taken for a drive or to the store. He liked to go to the grocery store or to go shopping at discount stores with his mother. And he continued to enjoy eating.

☐ Coping with David's Dementia

Throughout his life David had suffered a number of physical problems. He had ear problems from the time he was a baby until they were corrected by surgery. As a small child and until he was a teenager he had an abdominal hernia which later disappeared. After that he had an inguinal hernia, which was surgically corrected. In the last years of his life his digestive and elimination problems required the attention of pediatric gastroenterologists. He also had dental problems that required treatment under anesthesia by specialists. Through all of this, David generally maintained a good and cooperative attitude.

At this stage of our lives, we were having difficulty coping with David and his problems. We just didn't have the stamina anymore to give him the attention he required. We had him home for most weekends, but we were exhausted by the time we left to go back to his group home. He continued to slip. He was experiencing changes that neither he nor my wife and I understood. He was getting good medical care, but we had the feeling that the doctors didn't seem to know much more about what was going on than we did.

We understood that this problem of precocious aging and the onset of Alzheimer's disease is a fairly common problem in people with Down's syndrome. I don't believe that too much has been known about this because until recently generally people with Down's syndrome did not live to be old enough to have these problems. Because of advances in medical science people are living longer, and in recent years precocious aging has begun to receive greater attention.

Our life with David was a series of ups and downs. Mostly it was up. We met and worked with some of the most dedicated and wonderful people in the world. In spite of his problems, David was a joy to us and his brother and sisters. He loved his nieces and nephews and, like everyone who had ever been in contact with David, they loved him.

David was now in his forties. In the late fall of 1992, David's seizures were occurring more frequently, and between Thanksgiving and Christmas his seizures were so severe that he required hospitalization. During one of the seizure episodes, he aspirated some vomited food into his lungs and developed a severe case of pneumonia. He was in the intensive care unit of the hospital for about 10 days and then spent another week in the hospital to complete his recovery. He was discharged from the hospital and returned to his group home. The staff at the group home did a wonderful job of taking care of David, and we continued to bring him home for special occasions and on weekends. He enjoyed being at home. He was particularly happy to be with his nieces and nephews, especially the two youngest ones who were little more than infants. Yet for us it became quite a chore to get David home. His ability to control his legs and arms had deteriorated considerably. He just about had to be lifted into and out of the automobile. He needed help with nearly every aspect of his life.

Because of David's physical condition and the rate of his seizures, the staff at the group home was having more and more difficulty in caring for him. After a particularly severe episode of seizures, he was once again admitted to a hospital. The staff at the hospital advised us that David would require more care in the future than the group home could give him and that we should find a nursing facility for him.

After looking at several facilities, we arranged for David to be admitted to a nursing home that was just across the street from the hospital where he was being treated. This was a very nice place; however, we found that we wanted to spend more time with David than we had when he was in the group home. He was becoming more helpless all the time, and now he had to have help with eating. Yet he did seem to enjoy having us visit him. Unfortunately, this was a problem for us as the drive to the nursing home was about a 20 miles round trip through heavy traffic.

We realized that if we wanted to spend more time with David, he would have to be closer to us. My wife was very anxious to be with him at least once every day and sometimes more often. So we decided to move him to a nursing home less than a mile from our home. Here it was much easier to visit with him. Not only would my wife and I visit, but also his brother and sisters and their children would come to see him. Yet David's condition, both mentally and physically, continued to deteriorate. He was now unable to walk. It was difficult to feed him, and we were not sure he always recognized us.

One encouraging incident happened at Christmastime that year. His oldest sister and her teenage son brought him a small Christmas tree. They played Christmas music on his tape player and decorated the tree. David's eyes lit up momentarily and he said, "Merry Christmas" as best he could. That was the last thing any of us heard him say.

Along with his other problems, David developed some severe dental problems that required oral surgery. As a result of the surgery, he developed an infection that required hospitalization. The last 10 days of David's life were spent in a hospital suffering from a severe infection. We spent most of our time with him at the hospital, and his brother and sisters, and their children, visited him every day. I doubt that David knew that we were there. Late one afternoon about five minutes after his sisters had left the hospital, David stopped breathing. He had found peaceful rest.

Two days after he died, there was calling at a local funeral home. Many of our friends and neighbors came by to visit with us. There were old friends from the Noble School; there were staff and residents from the group homes and the nursing home; there was staff from Noble School; and there were personal friends of ours and of our children's. The next day, more than a hundred friends and associates joined us at David's funeral.

☐ Commentary

Since he died, many people have asked us a variety of questions about David. We have thought about his life and the effect it had on us and the lives of our family. I would like to share some of these here. There is one thing of which we are very certain: family support is "the name of the game." Early on the support and encouragement of my wife's mother was very important. The advice we were receiving from professionals was very discouraging. We could not accept the thought of institutionalizing our son. Life for us was difficult at first, but with the help of my mother-in-law we were able to get away from time to time and enjoy a reasonably active social life.

Later the support and understanding that our other children gave us was indispensable. They accepted David and he was a part of their lives. We always took family vacations, and David was with us wherever we went. As our children started to drive, they took over the job of transporting David to school and activities, such as dances and bowling. We think that David's life made us and our children much better human beings. Certainly, he formed us into a closer knit family than we might have been otherwise. Because the only public resources for the education or training of children or adults with a developmental disability were the state schools for the feeble minded (that is what they were called at that time), it was necessary to get something started locally if you were going to keep your child at home. Fortunately, for us, a group got together and decided to start a "school" for children with mental retardation. Out of this has came the Noble Centers organization in metropolitan Indianapolis. In working with those parents and the professionals that came to help us, we became acquainted with some of the most wonderful and dedicated people in the world. As we were more involved in local activities for the disabled, we became aware of state and national organizations that were working to improve the lives of our children and we became involved in those activities. We also have had the opportunity to serve on a number of university- or agency-linked committees and groups looking to improve the lives of parents and persons with developmental disabilities. All of these associations have been very rewarding, and we feel that we have had an opportunity to make a contribution to improving the lives of persons with disabilities.

One of the questions we are asked most often has to do with the nature of the dementia that David experienced. In looking back, the onset was very gradual and, initially, was not perceptible to us. David seemed to slow down, but we didn't notice it at first. It was only after an accumulation of events that we realized that he was slower. At first we thought it was just a phase he was going through or maybe a temperamental problem. Frequently, we would become irritated with him. This upset David and all of us. It was very frustrating for us as well as for David. We wish we had understood the nature of his problem earlier in its progression.

Near the end of David's first hospitalization, a neurologist with a terrible bedside manner told us that David had degenerative brain atrophy and that he should go from the hospital to a nursing home. Neither we nor the staff at the group home where David was living were willing to accept that advice. This was not the first time in David's life that a doctor had made a recommendation for a poor quality of life for him. Although he did end up in a nursing home, David did enjoy more than a year living in a group home in a pleasant environment.

In David's case, the realization that something was wrong was slow to sink in with us. Had it not been for the seizures, which David had never before had in his life, we might have gone on for some time without knowing that there was something very seriously wrong. When he was hospitalized for the second time, we were able to make contact with a neurologist who had some knowledge of the association of Alzheimer's disease and Down's syndrome. However, even with this doctor we found that we were the ones who provided him with material (that was new to him) that we had received from a local university.

After we became aware of David's real problem, we could see where there had been signs that we could have detected had we known what to look for. His problems at the workshop, the bowling difficulties, the long meal times, and the prolonged sessions of personal grooming—these were probably all signs of dementia in its earliest stage.

Later we began to notice the progression of the dementia. It was becoming more difficult for him to get in and out of an automobile. He was having trouble sitting in a chair and getting up. He had to be reminded to eat the food that was placed before him, and he began to need help with eating. He was losing interest in what was going on around him; television didn't seem to be important to him anymore. He began to have trouble walking. Although he had never been very verbal, he was losing his limited ability to communicate. All of these changes occurred gradually over a period of two to three years.

In his final months, David's ability to do things for himself just left him. He could not walk; he was bedfast. He would only eat if food was forced on him. He lost control of his bodily functions. At the end he was quite uncomfortable, and his death relieved him of his discomfort and the abysmal quality of his life.

We viewed David's demise with mixed emotions. He had always been such a gregarious, cheerful, loving person that it was hard to lose him. However, toward the end, he had been so miserable we knew that he was at peace at last. Also, it had always been a great cause of concern to us as to what would happen to David once we were gone. We had been speaking with a lawyer regarding setting up a guardianship for David. Several years ago we felt we had taken the first step toward setting up his life after we were gone when we placed him in a group home. One of our children had volunteered to be David's guardian, and we were confident with his sibling overseeing things he could live comfortably in a group home. Because of the dementia and his death, none of these plans was implemented. With his passing, David escaped the suffering he was experiencing. Now, we as his parents will be able to live out our lives knowing that David is in God's hands and at peace.

2

BIOMEDICAL CONSIDERATIONS

Understanding the biology and physiology of dementia is a precursor to a better understanding of assessment and care management. We have compiled the contributions in this section to help provide a foundation for this understanding. The section begins with a comprehensive review of the current status of knowledge about the pathogenesis of Alzheimer's disease and closely examines the impact on diagnosis, assessment, and treatment. In the opening chapter, Percy provides an up-to-date review and a detailed analysis of the current state of knowledge about the biological mechanisms (genetic, neurotoxins, free radical damage, immune system alterations) that have been implicated in Alzheimer's disease. She synthesizes many disparate observations into hypotheses that have direct or indirect relevance to diagnosis and treatments of Alzheimer's disease. She also reviews what is currently known about "risk factors" and "protective factors" for Alzheimer's disease and their impact on prevention. We placed this chapter first, because we felt it would provide carers and diagnosticians with a solid base of knowledge about the current limitations of treatments and the most promising directions where progress in diagnosis and treatment can be expected to go in the near future. Percy's chapter is followed by contributions of a neurologist and specialist physician, which are designed to provide an in-depth perspective of what the general practitioner as well as the specialist in neurology should know.

In the second chapter of this section, Wherrett underscores the complex diseases and afflictions of the brain, other than Alzheimer's disease, which can be expected to occur with largely unknown prevalence among persons with intellectual disabilities as they grow older. The identification and delineation of a wide variety of dementia and dementialike conditions and the difficult problems of assessment present diagnosticians and carers with what may appear to be a formidable task. Thus, we have included this chapter on the neurological basis of age-related or age-associated conditions because it underscores the role and contributions of the neurologist as a member of the treatment team. Wherrett spells out this contribution in persuasive detail, highlighting lifelong conditions and episodic behaviors continuing to adulthood, all from a functional perspective. It is evident that the neurologist must exercise particular care in obtaining a good history by paying attention to the need for investigative procedures and show constant vigilance of special predispositions in the differential diagnosis of cognitive, behavioral, and motor decline in aging persons with intellectual disabilities. Later, in part 4 (clinical considerations), we give more time to the examination of the psychiatric aspects.

In the last chapter of this section, Evenhuis reviews the unique problems for the physician who is asked to conduct an assessment, reach a diagnosis, and make appropriate recommendations. She focuses on what is known about sensory impairments and movement-related disorders with an emphasis on some recent research findings on the most common medical conditions encountered in this effort. Since other medical conditions, particularly those most likely to affect persons with Down's syndrome with Alzheimer's disease, have been extensively reviewed extensively in other texts (for example, see Berg et al., 1993; Pueschel & Solga, 1992), they are not repeated here.

☐ References

Berg, J. M., Karlinsky, H., & Holland, A. J. (Eds.) (1993). *Alzheimer disease, Down syndrome and their relationship.* New York: Oxford University Press.

Pueschel, S. M., & Solga, P. M. (1992). Musculoskeletal disorders. In S. M. Pueschel and J. K. Pueschel (Eds.), *Biomedical concerns in persons with Down syndrome* (pp. 147–157). Baltimore: Paul H. Brookes.

4

CHAPTER

Maire E. Percy

Risk Factors and Biological Consequences

Considerable research effort has been dedicated to identifying genetic and biological markers of Alzheimer's disease in the general population in the anticipation that such knowledge will further our understanding of the cause of the disease and the mechanisms involved in the disease process and will help with the differential and early diagnosis of Alzheimer's disease. Such information also is expected to permit the more rational development of treatments to prevent or to slow down the progress of Alzheimer's disease. This chapter reviews recent issues and applications of biomarkers and environmental risk factors for Alzheimer's disease in the general population and contrasts this knowledge with what is known about corresponding issues in persons with intellectual disability. The very difficult issue of diagnosing dementia of the Alzheimer type in persons with Down's syndrome is highlighted.

Address correspondence to: Maire E. Percy, Ph.D., Surrey Place Centre, 2 Surrey Place, Toronto, Ontario M5S 2C2 Canada. Email: maire.percy@utoronto.ca.

Acknowledgment: The author's research in risk factors in human disease has been supported by grants from the Queen Elizabeth Hospital Research Institute (Toronto, Canada), the Ontario Mental Health Foundation, the Alzheimer Society of Canada, Health Canada, the Alzheimer's Association (US), the University of Toronto Work Study and Life Sciences (Physiology) Programs, the Scottish Rite Charitable Foundation of Canada, and the Canadian Federal Government Summer Career Placements Program.

55

☐ Risk Factors for Alzheimer's Disease in the General Population

Alzheimer's disease is a devastating disorder which affects a high proportion of elderly people. It is steadily increasing among all industrialized populations. This is the result, at least in part, of demographic factors, since more people now are living to an older age. Other factors associated with industrialization or differing diets also may contribute to the problem, since there are reported geographical differences in the prevalence of Alzheimer's disease relative to another type of dementia called multi-infarct dementia (MID) (Jorm, 1991). In North America and in most European countries, Azheimer's disease is the fourth leading cause of death. In the United States, a minimum of 150,000 deaths per year result from this disease. The prevalence of Alzheimer's disease increases dramatically with age, from about 5% at age 65 to as much as 50% by age 85 (Evans et al., 1989). Further, projections are that the prevalence will increase by threefold by 2050 (Hebert, Scherr, Beckett, & Evans, 1996). Although these statistics are depressing, the geographic and age effects on the prevalence of Alzheimer's disease raise the optimistic possibility that it should be possible to delay the onset of Alzheimer's disease or even eliminate it from the normal human life span by controlling environmental risk factors, diet (including nutritional supplements), and/or by therapeutic interventions (Casdorph & Walker, 1995).

Progress in developing treatment for Alzheimer's disease has been hindered by the tediousness and expense of diagnosing this condition. Until recently, a diagnosis of possible or probable Alzheimer's disease has been made on the basis of excluding other causes for the clinical symptoms. A diagnosis of definite Alzheimer's disease has been made on the basis of finding clinical signs of Alzheimer's disease and characteristic brain features of Alzheimer's disease (the presence of "senile" plaques—SPs—and neurofibrillary tangles—NFTs—in an autopsy; see Table 4.1—McKhann, Drachman, Folstein, Katzman, Price, & Stadlan, 1984). Without brain analysis, the accuracy of diagnosing Alzheimer's disease can be as low as 60% or 70%. Over the past decade much effort has been spent attempting to develop positive tests for Alzheimer's disease that are based on the analysis of tissues other than brain (such as blood, cerebrospinal fluid, skin, or urine) to help physicians rule out or diagnose Alzheimer's disease (Percy, 1993). Such tests would provide a faster answer, which will often be good news when Alzheimer's disease can be ruled out; enable drug treatments to be measured objectively, which will help researchers and doctors to find drugs for Alzheimer's disease; and have the potential for substantial cost savings for governments, taxpayers, insurance companies,

TABLE 4.1.   NINCDS/ADRDA clinical criteria for Alzheimer's disease in the general population.

Possible Alzheimer's disease
Diagnosis of possible Alzheimer's disease can be made

- in the presence of atypical features
- in the presence of a systemic disease (not considered to be the cause of dementia)
- in the presence of a single progressive cognitive deficit

Probable Alzheimer's disease
Criteria include

- the presence of dementia
- deficits in at least two areas of cognition
- progressive deterioration
- no clouding of consciousness
- age between 40 and 90 years
- absence of systemic disorders

Diagnosis supported by

- progressive deterioration of individual cognitive function
- impaired activities of daily living
- family history of dementia
- normal lumbar puncture, abnormal electroencephalogram, and evidence of atrophy (or progression) on computerized tomographic scan

Features consistent with diagnosis

- plateaus in the course of the disease
- associated psychiatric symptoms
- neurological signs
- seizures
- normal computerized tomographic scan

Diagnosis of Alzheimer's disease unlikely if

- sudden onset
- focal neurological signs
- seizures or gait disturbance early in the disease

Definite Alzheimer's disease
Criteria include

- presence of clinical criteria for probable Alzheimer's disease
- histophatological evidence of disease

Adapted from McKhann et al. (1984).

and patients, since billions of dollars currently are being spent on potentially unnecessary, repetitive, and inconvenient procedures in hospitals and clinics throughout the world (Nymox Pharmaceutical Corporation, 1996).

A practical advantage of an early detection of dementia is that the sooner the family and carers learn about the probable diagnosis, the more time they have to plan for future living arrangements and establish a support network. Also, an early diagnosis of dementia would help with the differential diagnosis of other treatable conditions that may mimic dementia, such as depression, thyroid problems, medication side effects, and nutritional disorders.

Tests based on the analysis of tissues other than the brain, such as blood, cerebrospinal fluid (CSF), skin, or urine, are known as tests of *peripheral biological markers*. Tests that can identify persons at high risk of developing Alzheimer's disease in the future are called *predictive tests*. Tests that indicate disease already present are called *confirmatory* or *antemortem tests*. In order to have clinical applicability, an antemortem test for Alzheimer's disease must be relatively simple to perform, cost-effective, reproducible, have a high degree of sensitivity (i.e., be able to detect Alzheimer's disease in early stages) and specificity (i.e., reflect Alzheimer's disease as opposed to other neurodegenerative diseases such as MID or Parkinson's disease), and not be traumatic to the patient. The potential advantage of a CSF-based test is that since Alzheimer's disease is primarily a central nervous system (CNS) disorder, aberrant biological processes in the CNS might be directly reflected in the CSF, particularly as the CSF is largely sequestered from the peripheral circulation by the blood–brain barrier (the epithelial cells lining the brain capillaries). The main disadvantage of the drawing of CSF is that this is a traumatic procedure not routinely done outside of a hospital setting. Obviously, blood-, skin-, or urine-based tests are less invasive, better tolerated, and would not require hospitalization for the samples to be obtained. Brain imaging techniques and sensitive neurocognitive and neurofunctional demential test batteries are also being explored as diagnostic aids for Alzheimer's disease (Albert, 1996). Refer to Table 4.2 for a comparison of the advantages and disadvantages of current diagnostics for Alzheimer's disease and a test based on a peripheral biological marker.

Genetic Risk Factors for Alzheimer's Disease

In a minority of people, genetic factors are strongly predictive that they will get Alzheimer's disease at a young or relatively young age. In many other cases, nongenetic factors may determine whether symptoms of Alzheimer's disease appear earlier than later. The identification of genetic

TABLE 4.2. Comparison of current indirect diagnosis for Alzheimer's disease and a direct test based on measurements of a biological marker (Neuron thread protein) in cerebrospinal fluid.

	Current Diagnostics for Alzheimer's Disease	Characteristics of a Direct Test for Alzheimer's Disease Based on Measurement of Neuron Thread Protein in CSF
Test Methods	Electroencephalography, CT scans, positron emission tomography studies, neuropsychological testing batteries (BDS, IMC, SBT, CDR, HDS, WAIS, WMS, GDS, MMSE, GERRI, MOSES, NOSGER, CAMDEX, etc.), serum chemistries (glucose, electrolytes, hepatic, renal, thyroid and other metabolic and endocrine function tests, B12, folic acid, etc.), SPECT scans, hematological profiles, lumbar spinal fluid testing, HIV testing, magnetic resonance imaging, urinalysis, & 24-hour urine collection for heavy metals, chest X-ray, syphilis serology, toxicology screens, multiple examinations by multiple professionals (family physicians, gerontologists, neurologists, psychiatrists, psychologists, nursing caregivers, other health professionals), repeat testings, and repeat examinations.	Measurement of neuron thread protein in CSF
Efficiency/Speed	Months to years	48 hours
Discomfort to Patient and Family	Maximal	Minimal
Cost Effectiveness	NO	YES
False Positive Results	YES	Minimal
Diagnostic Approach Methodology	Exclusion	Direct measurement

The neuron thread test for Alzheimer's disease has been applied extensively to persons in the general population but not as yet to persons with underlying intellectual disability. Refer to text and to Table 4.4 (ADTCTM) for additional details. Table courtesy of Nymox Corporation, Rockville, Maryland, and Montreal, Canada.

risk factors for Alzheimer's disease (i.e., mutations in particular genes or particular variants of normal genes) not only can aid with disease diagnosis in those possibly affected but also can be used to predict which persons are at highest risk of developing it (a group upon which preventive treatment should be focused). About 90% of cases of Alzheimer's disease in the general population manifest after the age of 65 years; this form of Alzheimer's disease is called *late-onset Alzheimer's disease*. The other 10% of cases manifest before 65 and are called *early-onset Alzheimer's disease*. In about 10% of Alzheimer's disease cases there is a family history of Alzheimer's disease; this form of Alzheimer's disease is called *familial*. In about 90% of Alzheimer's disease cases, there is no obvious family history of the disease. This form of Alzheimer's disease is called *sporadic*.

A striking feature of all cases of Alzheimer's disease is the accumulation of a substance called *amyloid beta (or A beta) protein* in blood vessels and in and around cells of the brain. Because A beta protein is a breakdown product of a large protein encoded by a single gene on chromosome 21 called amyloid precursor protein (APP), it is suspected that there is a problem with APP metabolism in all persons who develop Alzheimer's disease. For persons in the general population who have early onset familial Alzheimer's disease, mutations in the APP gene account for only 2% to 3% of cases (five different APP mutations associated with early onset familial Alzheimer's disease so far have been identified) (Hyman & Tanzi, 1995; Karlinsky et al., 1992). Mutations in a gene on chromosome 14 called presenilin 1 or PS-1 account for about 50% of early onset familial Alzheimer's disease. To date, 17 apparently pathogenic mutations resulting in familial Alzheimer's disease have been described in PS-1 (Rogaev et al., 1995; Sherrington et al., 1995; The Alzheimer's Disease Collaborative Group, 1995). Persons with such mutations in the APP and PS-1 genes usually (but not always) develop Alzheimer's disease. Some other cases of Alzheimer's disease are associated with mutations in the presenilin 2 or PS-2 gene on chromosome 1, but these occur rarely and are not always expressed. Moreover symptoms associated with PS-2 mutations are highly variable and are expressed over a wide age range (from 45 to 88 years) (Sherrington et al., 1996).

Variants of a chromosome 19 protein called apolipoprotein E (ApoE) primarily affect the risk for late onset Alzheimer's disease with or without evidence of family history (Saunders et al., 1993; Roses, 1995). Because we inherit one set of chromosomes from our mother and another set from our father (each set consists of 22 chromosomes called autosomes plus the sex chromosomes), we have two copies of every autosomal gene (one maternal, the other paternal). Alternative forms of genes are called *alleles*. There are three alleles for ApoE in the general population—E2,

E3, and E4; E3 is common, and E2 and E4 are relatively less common. Most frequently, people have two E3 alleles. Genetic linkage and association studies have shown that the E4 allele is overrepresented and the E2 allele is underrepresented in persons with Alzheimer's disease. The E4 allele, which is present in about 30% of the general population, increases the risk for late onset Alzheimer's disease in a dose-dependent fashion, the increased relative risk ranging from 3 to 10–30 depending on whether one carries one or two copies of E4. However, the E4 gene or allele is not predictive or diagnostic: more than 90% of people with E4 do not have Alzheimer's disease, and 40% of Alzheimer's disease cases do not have E4. The E2 allele appears to be protective against Alzheimer's disease. In contrast to APP and PS-1 gene markers, the E4 allele is not specific for Alzheimer's disease, as it is also a risk factor for heart disease, MID, and Parkinson's disease. Studies of E4 metabolism in cells, however, are providing valuable new information about aberrant biological processes that underlie the development of Alzheimer's disease and other serious diseases (see below). It has been suggested that screening for Alzheimer's disease gene markers on a research basis should include ApoE genotyping. Overall, only about 50% of Alzheimer's disease cases are accounted for, at least in part, by known genetic risk factors. Therefore, there must be other yet unidentified Alzheimer's disease susceptibility or resistance genes and/or environmental risk factors for Alzheimer's disease. Recently, a lowered age at onset of early-onset Alzheimer's disease was found to be associated with the HLA-2A locus in the major histocompatibility complex on chromosome 6 (Payami et al., 1997). Frecker, Pryse-Phillips, and Strong (1994) previously had reported that the HLA DRB3 allele was associated with familial Alzheimer's disease. In 1988, mutations in the promoter region of the APoE gene (Lambert et al., 1998), and in the alpha-Z macroglobulin gene (Blacker et al., 1998) were identified as new genetic risk factors for Alzheimer's disease.

In the absence of proven treatment to prevent Alzheimer's disease or to slow down its development, not everyone benefits to the same extent from knowledge about one's genetic makeup. Moreover, facilities simply are not adequate to screen all Alzheimer's disease cases for the APP and PS-1 or PS-2 mutations that are known to be linked to Alzheimer's disease in families, generally. Having a peripheral biological marker predictive or diagnostic for Alzheimer's disease might solve this problem, in part. Guidelines are being developed for genetic screening in Alzheimer's disease as in other serious genetic diseases (Lennox, Karlinsky, Meschino, Buchanen, Percy, & Berg, 1994; Post et al., 1997).

Other Risk Factors for Alzheimer's Disease

In addition to increasing subject age and genetic predisposing risk factors for Alzheimer's disease, other factors that have been shown by epidemiological studies to predispose to Alzheimer's disease include head injury, the female sex, depression, hypothyroidism and electromagnetic radiation (Burns & Murphy, 1996; Sobel, Dunn, Davanipour, Qian, & Chui, 1996). Poor nutrition and toxic metals—lead, aluminum, mercury (including mercury-silver amalgam fillings in teeth), cadmium, iron excess or deficiency, copper, arsenic, beryllium, nickel, and titanium are suspected culprits that may play a role in the development of Alzheimer's disease and other dementias. Other brain poisoning chemicals that should be investigated are alcohol, some prescribed drugs such as antiepileptics, and industrial products employed at home or work such as solvents, herbicides, and pesticides (Casdorph & Walker, 1995).

Many publications have dealt with the relation between aluminum in public drinking water and Alzheimer's disease. A relation has been found in many, though not all, of the studies. In some cases lack of a relation may have been because of the limited range or relatively low concentration of aluminum and other characteristics of the drinking water such as the form of aluminum that is present. One recent study has suggested that about 25% of Alzheimer's disease cases in Ontario might be caused and/or exacerbated by high residual aluminum in municipal drinking water (McLachlan, Bergeron, Smith, Boomer, & Rifat, 1996). The water purification process itself may be a major problem. Although the use of alum (aluminum sulphate) has been condemned from the earliest days of food regulation and is universally acknowledged as a poison and a deleterious substance in all countries, it still is used in many municipalities to clarify water, and residual levels are not always kept below acceptable limits (100mg/L). Aluminum also has been added to the food chain and other consumer applications by mankind. For example, certain antacids, douches, buffered aspirin, and antidiarrheal drugs contain high levels of aluminum. Items such as hair spray, cheese products, baking powder, pizza, tea, nondairy creamer, infant soy-based formulas, deodorant, talcum powder, lipstick and other cosmetics, and toothpaste may contain high amounts of aluminum (Casdorph & Walker, 1995).

There is evidence that dust carrying aluminum or other toxic substances can get into the brain through the nose and olfactory system as well as through ingestion or by skin contact. The simple act of breathing thus may be hazardous. If the small hairs in the nose do not keep the airways free of debris, dust particles can find their way to the olfactory nerve. Animal studies have shown how material applied to skin inside the nose can travel directly to the brain from the olfactory nerve into the olfactory bulb and from there into other brain regions that typically are affected in Alzheimer's disease (e.g., the amygdala, entorhinal cortex, inferior parietal cortex, and frontal lobe). Aluminum and other fine metallic particulates, products of industrialization and metal processing, may cause metal poisoning in the workplace. Such particulates also may slip through elaborate air-pollution control devices at industrial sites. These toxic particulates can remain in the atmosphere for weeks and be transported for hundreds of miles by the wind. Poisoning from these minuscule dust constituents is inescapable, and people worldwide are potential victims (Casdorph & Walker, 1995).

Some studies have implicated infections in the development of Alzheimer's disease. Frecker, Pryse-Phillips, and Strong, (1994) found an association between adult exposure to tuberculosis and familial Alzheimer's disease. Itzhaki, Lin, Shang, Wilcock, Faragher, and Jamieson (1997) have evidence that the combination of an ApoE4 genotype and expression of herpes simplex type I virus (HSVI) in brain is significantly associated with the clinical expression of Alzheimer's disease (HSVI is the cause of the common "cold sore"). Another group reported the presence of spirochaetes in brain and CSF of 100% of a series of Alzheimer's disease cases but in none of the gender and age-matched "control" group (Miklossy, Kasas, Janzer, Ardizzone, & Van der Loos, 1994). (*Spirochaetes* are slender, spiral, active microorganisms classified as bacteria. Different kinds of spirochaetes cause diseases such as syphilis, relapsing fever, and Lyme disease.) Interestingly, spirochaetes from the Alzheimer's disease cases and spirochaetes used as a laboratory reference were found to contain protein that reacted with antibody to APP. It was suggested that spirochaetes might be one source of A beta protein in the brain.

Protective Factors Against Alzheimer's Disease

Negative risk factors for Alzheimer's disease (i.e., protective factors) may include education, smoking, nonsteroidal anti-inflammatory agents (such as Tylenol and aspirin), estrogen, (Burns & Murphy, 1996) and antioxidants (Sano et al., 1996). Smoking is thought to cause nonspecific arousal-related changes in the brain that affect the speed or motor performance and can persist over a long period of time. Evidence for the protective effects of the anti-inflammatory agents is supported by many epidemiological studies that highlight this area as a particularly promising one for development (McGeer & McGeer, 1995). Attention currently is focusing on possible protective effects of estrogen supplement, since one study has indicated that postmenopausal women who take estrogen supplements may have a substantially decreased risk of developing Alzheimer's disease (Paganini-Hill & Henderson, 1996). Unknown, however, is what molecular form of hormone might be most beneficial, if males could be similarly helped, and what the long-term consequences might be, since prolonged use of estrogen may increase the risk of breast cancer (Skolnick, 1997). Very recently, a combination of vitamin E and selegiline were found to slow down deterioration of cognitive function (Sano et al., 1996). Vitamin E and selegiline are antioxidants (Lethem & Orrell, 1997). Selegiline previously was found to be beneficial in the treatment of Parkinson's disease.

Supporting the involvement of toxic metals in Alzheimer's disease are findings from a clinical trial in which the administration of desferrioxamine (a metal chelating agent used in the treatment of thalassemia) was found to slow down the course of Alzheimer's disease two- to three-fold (Crapper-McLachlan et al., 1991) (sources of metal ions that catalyse free radical production in Alzheimer's disease might be damaged brain cells and blood vessels that liberate free iron. Iron is essential for life; but if it is not complexed to proteins, it is toxic.) Further support for the toxic metal hypothesis is provided by anecdotal reports that clinical symptoms of dementia can be halted or even reversed in some cases by chelation therapy (the intravenous administration of a chemical called magnesium EDTA along with important vitamins and nutrients), a procedure that has been used for more than two decades in the treatment of heart disease (Casdorph & Walker, 1995). Chelation therapy is a controversial process that is not accepted by all segments of the medical profession; if not administered properly, it can be dangerous. However, a retrospective analysis of treatment results from patients with various chronic degenerative and age-associated diseases suggest that chelation therapy might benefit persons with "geriatric symptomatology of vascular origin" (Olzewer & Carter, 1988). Prospective studies must be carried out to prove whether or not this procedure works. Desferrioxamine and EDTA are thought to prevent cell damage and to promote healing of damaged cell membranes by removing metallic elements that increase damaging oxygen-free radicals that act as chronic irritants.

Proper nutrition (a low-fat vegetarian-based diet that includes important vitamins and minerals and adequate levels of omega fatty acids) and a variety of memory-improving drugs anecdotally are reported to be beneficial for some persons with possible or probable Alzheimer's disease. Proper nutrition is important throughout all life stages, particularly in neonates and young children (Casdorph & Walker, 1995). Currently, drug companies are focusing on the development of new substances that protect brain cells from injury rather than on ones that rescue dying neurons. Efforts should be mounted to test potentially simple and inexpensive treatments that might be protective against Alzheimer's disease such as antioxidants, different forms of chelation, or nonsteroidal anti-inflammatory drugs in large double-blind clinical trials, and to curb industrial pollution which, unfortunately, continues to increase. The reader is referred to the book *Toxic Metal Syndrome* (Casdorph & Walker, 1995) for further discussion about the relation between toxic metal ions and neurodegenerative diseases, and the authors' experience with chelation therapy, regular exercise, proper nutrition, vitamin and mineral supplementation, use of memory-improving drugs, and avoidance of tobacco and other damaging habits.

It has been suggested that prospective clinical trials of Alzheimer's disease treatments should include the collection of useful "quality of life" data as well as a comparison of pre- and posttherapy diagnostic tests to provide objective evidence of effectiveness. Data derived from such work may be used to help patients and caregivers make decisions about treatment options, to aid economic analyses and resource allocations, and to influence health care policy (Fallowfield, 1996).

☐ Changes in Brain and Other Tissues in Alzheimer's Disease in the General Population

Brain Changes in Alzheimer's Disease

The brains of all persons afflicted with Alzheimer's disease are characterized by the presence of two distinct types of lesions: SPs and NFTs. SPs develop before the NFTs. Detailed examination of brain tissue using immunohistochemistry has revealed the structure of these lesions (McGeer & McGeer, 1995). In SPs (which develop near blood vessels in the brain), cells called reactive astrocytes form an outer shell around the lesion with fibrils extending into the lesion, while cells called microglia are clustered within this shell around the inner mass of the SP, which is called the core (Figure 4.1). Insoluble fibrils of amyloid beta protein (the breakdown product of APP) are found in the plaque cores as well as in blood vessels. Three main types of SPs have been identified: immature plaques, which contain a disorganized array of damaged neurites (processes of axons and dendrites of neurons); mature plaques; and "burned out" plaques in which all neurites have disappeared. The mature plaques resemble another type of lesion, which develops in certain conditions (called chronic granulomatous lesions), where degenerating material is at the core, cells called macrophages engulf the material around the core, and other cells called fibroblasts form an outer shell to "wall off" the lesions. Neurons that contain tangles eventually leave behind extracellular neurofibrillary tangles (sometimes called "ghost tangles").

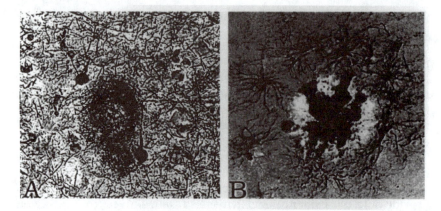

FIGURE 4.2 Schematic representation of chromosome 21, showing the localization of selected genes and the possible position of the "Down's syndrome critical region" in 21q22.2–22.3, which, when present in three copies, seems to be responsible for at least some of the major phenotypic features in Down's syndrome, such as the characteristic facies, lowered IQ, short stature, and heart defects. The two brackets illustrate the region of chromosome 21 triplicated in Down's syndrome patients with only a partial trisomy of 21. Genes shown are APP, amyloid precursor protein; SOD-1, superoxide dismutase-1 (Cu-Zn SOD); ETS2, the ets-2 oncogene; CBS, crystalline-B-synthase; and CRYA1, a crystallin lens protein. This same approach might reveal the position of the region of chromosome 21 that is responsible for the development of dementia of the Alzheimer type that develops in a substantial fraction of adults with Down's syndrome. (Adapted from Rahmani et al., 1989, and Korenberg et al., 1990; reproduced with permission from Thompson, McGinnes, & Willard, 1991.)

Tau protein (actually a family of proteins that forms the scaffolding for neurons) is the major component of NFT; when isolated from the Alzheimer's disease brain, tau has been found to contain many more phosphate groups than normal. Reactive microglia and reactive astrocytes are found near ghost tangles as well as around SPs, although their spatial organization around the tangles is not the same as that seen around the SPs. The signs and symptoms of Alzheimer's disease correlate better with levels of NFTs than SPs. There is no proven theory to explain how the diversity of genetic predisposing risk factors cause NFTs and SPs in Alzheimer's disease or the relationship (if any) between NFTs and SPs.

Controversy exists as to whether NFTs and SPs are "cause or effect" in Alzheimer's disease. It is speculated that a fundamental problem in Alzheimer's disease may be an impaired ability of neurons and other cells to protect themselves against various types of traumas including normal wear and tear. Perhaps NFTs and SPs develop as a response to injury of neurons and blood vessels and the deposition of amyloid beta protein is involved in this process. Markers on damaged neurons or blood vessels (or that are released by them) might muster the microglia and astrocytes into action to inactivate, engulf and/or "wall off" the injured cells (McGeer & McGeer, 1995).

Progress has been made in understanding the physiologic functions of the genes implicated in Alzheimer's disease development. Persons who have an ApoE4 allele tend to have a greater accumulation of amyloid beta protein in their brain and more NFT, whether or not they have clinical symptoms of dementia (Polvikoski et al., 1995). A protein called "low-density-lipoprotein-receptor-related protein," which is used by neurons to bind ApoE-lipid complexes, is also used to bind, internalize, and mediate the degradation of secreted APP. The PS-1 and PS-2 genes may directly or indirectly affect the transportation of APP to different compartments within neurons and ultimately determine whether or not it is converted into beta amyloid (Hyman & Tanzi, 1995). The final common pathway in Alzheimer's disease may be the aggregation of single molecules of beta amyloid (which are soluble) into the insoluble aggregated form which is found in mature SPs, a process which is promoted in the laboratory by certain metal ions such as copper, iron, or aluminum (Multhaup et al., 1996), and by APoE4 or another protein called alpha 1-antichymotrypsin (Ma, Brewer, & Potter, 1996).

There is evidence that neuron thread protein (NTP) are involved in neuronal repair and regeneration in the brain so that increased levels found in the Alzheimer's disease brain probably represent a normal defense against cellular damage brought about by neuronal degeneration (de la Monte & Wands, 1992; de la Monte, Volicer, Hauser, & Wands, 1992; de la Monte, YY, Hutchins, & Wands, 1996; de la Monte, Carlson, Brown, & Wands, 1996). These data are exciting because they provide optimism that treatments based on a rational understanding of the pathophysiologic mechanisms of risk factors may become realities, and that the effects of Alzheimer's disease treatments can be readily assessed.

There is evidence that chronic inflammation and immune processes occur in the Alzheimer's disease brain (McGeer & McGeer, 1995). The high load of beta amyloid and NFTs (which are highly insoluble and which may be responses to primary cellular injury) may be chronic irritants which accumulate over time and stimulate one type of immunity called the innate immune system in the brain of persons with Alzheimer's disease. In contrast to the adaptive immune system (which is well understood and involves the induction of specific antibodies and reactive T lymphocytes over a relatively long time period), the innate immune system (which is not well understood) responds immediately to cell injury or infection. Activation of the innate immune system involves production of the terminal components of complement (C5b-9) by microglia and astrocytes which assemble into a membrane attack complex (MAC) that inserts into cell membranes causing cell lysis and death of cells (McGeer & McGeer, 1995). Cells that engulf debris also produce bursts of oxygen free radicals in order to inactivate the material that is being digested. Healthy host cells are at significant risk of being damaged and disrupted by misdirected free radicals and MAC attack (a process called "bystander lysis") which increases the inflammatory response. This vicious cycle might be responsible for the dramatic increase in clinical symptoms of Alzheimer's disease which occur with increasing subject age in Alzheimer's disease. It is thought that once a certain threshold of destruction of brain tissue has been reached that clinical decline will be rapid. In theory, treatments that slow down or prevent cell injury and/or the inflammatory response both should be beneficial in Alzheimer's disease.

Recently, a member of the immunoglobulin superfamily of cell surface molecules called "RAGE" (receptor for advance glycation end-products) has been found to bind A beta protein expressed by both neurons and microglia. There is evidence that binding of A beta protein to RAGE on neurons stimulates the expression of factors that recruit microglia to sites of amyloid beta protein deposition (Stern, 1997).

Peripheral Biological Consequences in Alzheimer's Disease

Because brain tissue is bathed by CSF, there are changes in the composition of the CSF that reflect reactive and degenerative processes that are taking place in the brain. Hence, biological substances in the CSF that originate from brain tissue (or that are taken up from CSF by the brain) can reflect the degree of disease in the brain tissue itself. For example, levels of neuron thread protein (which is increased in the Alzheimer's disease brain probably in response to cellular damage) are up to 10 times higher in Alzheimer's disease CSF compared with normal controls (de la Monte & Wands, 1992; de la Monte, Volicer et al., 1992).

Tissue injury anywhere in the body (resulting from infection, inflammation, or other cause) may remain confined, or it may induce a peripheral acute phase response (APR) that involves the synthesis and release from the liver of a series of proteins called acute phase reactants. Output of certain other liver-derived proteins diminishes. The altered transcription of these genes is an adaptive response to the tissue injury which attempts to minimize damage and to help to restore the injured tissue to normal (Wilder, 1995). Activated phagocytic cells invade damaged tissues and release a number of factors into the blood serum including substances called cytokines (e.g., interleukins 1 and 6 [IL-1, IL-6] and tumor necrosis factor alpha [TNF alpha]) which induce the APR.

Because substances produced in a peripheral APR also have been found in the CSF of persons with Alzheimer's disease, it has been proposed that the brain itself might be mounting a localized APR in an attempt to minimize damage to brain tissue (Vandenabeele & Fiers, 1991; McGeer & McGeer, 1995). The region of the brain thought to control this process is the choroid plexus. Cytokine release by cells in the choroid plexus also might stimulate a peripheral APR, since elevated levels of a number of different acute phase proteins have been described in peripheral blood of affected individuals and in some cases in their first degree relatives (sisters/brothers and sons/daughters) who might have a very early stage of Alzheimer's disease (Percy, 1993). Because certain peripheral tissues of persons affected with Alzheimer's disease such as the skin, nasal epithelium, the adrenal gland, and blood cells have been shown to have abnormalities (see Percy, 1993), it cannot be excluded that a peripheral APR in these individuals might reflect damage in peripheral tissues as well as in the brain.

Many studies now have shown that the response to injury or stress in one part of the body may be manifested in more than just the part of the body being stressed. Wilder (1995) has described how communication about different types of stresses (including psychological stresses, virus infections, toxins, and physical injury) occurs throughout the body by means of interactions between the body's endocrine system, central nervous system, peripheral and autonomic systems, and the immune and inflammatory systems via signalling molecules, such as cytokines. Thus, acute phase responses in the brain and peripheral tissues of persons with AD may to some extent be coordinated.

Table 4.3 depicts how damage in the CNS in Alzheimer's disease might result in changes in peripheral biological markers. In Alzheimer's disease, the inflammatory reaction in the brain is postulated to be neverending because factors causing the injury (e.g., genetic mutations, infectious agents, environmental factors, and/or interactions between these) persist, and because of the bystander effects of reactive processes that compound the damage. A similar scenario is thought to occur in serious arthritic conditions (Aisen, 1997). Thus, in some respects Alzheimer's disease may be analogous to a serious form of arthritis.

Antemortem Tests for Alzheimer's Disease

Alzheimer's disease cannot be definitely diagnosed without a brain autopsy or biopsy. Furthermore, at present, a clinical diagnosis of probable Alzheimer's disease cannot be made until brain damage probably is irreparable. Hence there is a great need to develop tests that can diagnose

TABLE 4.3. Possible sequence of biological events taking place in the degenerating brain in Alzheimer's dementia.

RISK FACTORS
(genetic and/or environmental)
↓
PREMATURE DAMAGE OF NEURONS AND BLOOD VESSELS OF BRAIN
↓
INCREASED EXPRESSION OF AMYLOID BETA PROTEIN WHICH
BINDS TO "RAGE" RECEPTORS ON DAMAGED NEURONS
↓
ACTIVATION OF MICROGLIA (AND THE INNATE IMMUNE SYSTEM)
TO REPAIR AND/OR CLEAR THE DAMAGE
(attack of damaged cells, phagocytosis of damaged cells
and inactivation of material being engulfed by bursts of oxygen free radicals)
↓
BRAIN PATHOLOGY
(formation of senile plaques and neurofibrillary tangles
to "wall off" injured cells and to restrict the damage)
↓
DAMAGE OF HEALTHY BRAIN CELLS BY PROCESSES INTENDED
TO REMOVE DAMAGED CELLS
(through misdirected bursts of oxygen free radicals)
↓
INDUCTION OF A LOCAL ACUTE PHASE RESPONSE IN BRAIN
(cytokines released from primary sites of damage may induce an acute phase
response in the
choroid plexus of the brain in an attempt
to minimize brain damage in Alzheimer's disease)
↓
RELEASE OF BRAIN CONSTITUENTS INTO THE CEREBROSPINAL
FLUID AND PERIPHERAL CIRCULATION
↓
INDUCTION OF A PERIPHERAL ACUTE PHASE RESPONSE
(by the damaged brain and possibly also by damaged peripheral tissues)
↓
COORDINATION OF IMMUNE, ENDOCRINE, AND NEUROLOGICAL SYSTEMS
IN THE CENTRAL NERVOUS SYSTEM AND PERIPHERY

Refer to text for additional detail. This scheme represents the opinion of the author.
After McGeer and McGeer (1995), in part. See McGeer and McGeer, 1995.

Alzheimer's disease in the incipient stages or that can identify those at highest risk of developing Alzheimer's disease in the future.

Persons afflicted with Alzheimer's disease exhibit changes in personality, progressive declines in visual and verbal memory, impaired performance of routine tasks, time and space orientation, communication and language skills, abstract thinking, and ability to learn new material (Cohen & Freedman, 1991; Albert, 1996). According to some studies, people who develop Alzheimer's disease begin to lose visual memory sooner than expected in normal aging and long before other markers of dementia appear (see Rocco, Cronin-Golomb, & Lai, 1997). Olfactory deficits also have been described in persons with Alzheimer's disease (Serby, Larson, & Kalksteiln, 1991). In this chapter, the focus will be on advances that are being made in the development of peripheral *biological* tests for Alzheimer's disease.

CSF Tests

Many different substances have been examined in the CSF of persons with Alzheimer's disease, healthy normal individuals, and others with different types of neurodegenerative or neurological diseases (see Percy, 1993; Percy, Andrews, & Potter, in press). Although many of these may have potential as diagnostic aids, attention currently is focussing on three CSF tests: measurements of different molecular forms of tau, certain APP derivatives, and neuron thread protein.

Tau. The presence of elevated levels of tau (or phosphorylated tau) in CSF of Alzheimer's disease patients has been confirmed in quite a number of studies (Jensen, Basun, & Lannfelt, 1995; Andreasen et al., 1997; Vanmechelen, Blennow, Davidsson, Cras, & Van de Voorde, 1997). If a group of well-defined healthy normals is used as a comparative control, the specificity of detecting probable Alzheimer's disease is high (75% to 90%). However, the ability of this test to discriminate Alzheimer's disease from other types of dementia (e.g., vascular dementia, frontal lobe dementia, or Parkinson's disease) is more limited. It has been proposed that the use of CSF measures of tau in combination with measures of APP derivatives or other substances might be more specific for Alzheimer's disease (Motter et al., 1995; Percy, Andrews, & Potter, in press; Blennow and Vanmechelen, 1998). Since tau molecules in the CSF may be degraded at their ends, some groups are developing assays to detect regions of tau protein that do not become degraded (Mori et al., 1995).

APP Derivatives. A considerable number of studies suggest that CSF measures of A beta protein 1-40 on their own are not likely to be useful as a diagnostic aid for Alzheimer's disease. However, one type of A beta protein called A beta 1-42 (43) shows an overall decrease in the CSF of persons with Alzheimer's disease, although it is elevated in very early stages of Alzheimer's disease. The use of measures of different types of A beta in combination with measures of other substances in CSF is now being investigated as a diagnostic aid for Alzheimer's disease (Percy, Andrews, & Potter, in press).

Neuron Thread Protein.   Measures of CSF neuron thread protein (NTP) have been reported to distinguish 80% to 90% of autopsy-verified Alzheimer's disease cases from 95% of healthy normal individuals (Nymox Pharmaceutical Corporation, 1996). Increased NTP immunoreactivity has been noted in the brains of persons with Down's syndrome and it has been proposed that abnormal NTP expression and accumulation in the brain may be an early marker of Alzheimer's disease in this group (de la Monte, YY, Hutchins, & Wands, 1996). Values of NTP are elevated in some cases of other neurological conditions such as stroke, but these should pose no confusion to the competent clinician who makes the diagnosis. One group purports that it has developed an NTP test that can be applied to less than 0.5 ml of CSF and offers a testing service called AD7C(TM) with results delivered within 48 hours (Nymox Pharmaceutical Corporation, 1996). Tests for NTP might be a useful aid to the clinician investigating a patient with subtle or marginal symptoms, such as mental, emotional, cognitive, or behavioral, and might streamline the diagnostic work-up and follow-up management when used in conjunction with sound clinical judgment by a qualified medical doctor. Such a test would not replace the physician's diagnosis which is a responsible medical decision based on history, physical, and medical data. See Table 4.3.

Progress in Blood-Based Alzheimer's Disease Tests

Serum p97 Levels.   Many different blood tests are being investigated as antemortem tests for Alzheimer's disease. (See Percy, 1993; Percy & Potter, in press.) One blood-based test that appears very promising involves measuring levels of the iron-binding protein p97 in serum (Kennard, Feldman, Yamada, & Jefferies, 1996). Serum levels of p97 (recovered after refrigerating blood overnight) were reported to be greatly elevated in persons with Alzheimer's disease in comparison with gender- and age-matched healthy normal individuals, and to increase with increasing duration of Alzheimer's disease, implying that p97 might be an early biological marker for Alzheimer's disease. Characterization of serum

TABLE 4.4.   Comparison of three cerebrospinal-fluid-based tests as diagnostic aids for Alzheimer's disease.

Test	Sensitivity	Comments
Total tau/phospho-tau	75–90%	Distinguishes a high percentage of persons with Alzheimer's disease from healthy normal individuals; the test is not specific for Alzheimer's disease
Neuron thread protein AD7C(TM)	80–90%	5–7% of Alzheimer's disease cases and healthy normals are in the same range; the test may not be specific for Alzheimer's disease
A beta peptide	25%	80–90% of Alzheimer's disease cases and normals are in the same range; longer soluble derivatives of amyloid precursor protein may have a higher sensitivity.

Refer to text for addition detail. The three tests have been applied extensively to persons in the general population but not as yet to persons with underlying intellectual disability.

p97 levels in other neurodegenerative and neurological diseases is now under investigation. The reason for the elevation of p97 in the serum of Alzheimer's disease patients is not known.

Mitochondrial Mutations.   Persons with Alzheimer's disease have been found to have a higher percentage of mitochondria in their blood with specific types of mutations than healthy normal individuals. This observation may form the basis of a new diagnostic test for Alzheimer's disease (Davis et al., 1997). Because many healthy normal individuals also carry the same mutations as do persons with Alzheimer's disease (although smaller amounts), the significance of the finding is perplexing. Children inherit mitochondrial DNA only from their mothers. It has been suggested that children of mothers with a high proportion of mitochondrial mutations in their germ cells might be at increased risk of developing Alzheimer's disease.

Immune and Inflammatory Markers.   Singh (1997) has compiled evidence for altered immune function in Alzheimer's disease including circulating autoantibodies to A beta protein and enhanced suppressor T cell function and lower lymphocyte counts, enhanced proliferative activity, and increased production of interleukin 1 in persons with Alzheimer's disease. Trieb, Ransmayr, Sgonc, and Lassman (1996) have found that soluble A beta protein induces interleukin-2 receptors and proliferation of peripheral T cells in young and old healthy individuals but not in Alzheimer's disease cases. This important finding must be further investigated, as it would appear to have considerable clinical potential as a diagnostic aid for Alzheimer's disease. Heinonen et al. (1993) reported that cognitive function in persons with Alzheimer's disease correlated significantly with levels of circulating immune complexes in serum. McRae, Dahlstrom, & Ling (1997) found that a high proportion of Alzheimer's disease patients have antibodies in their CSF that react with brain microglia. It has been speculated that these may be secondary to faulty immune regulation in persons with Alzheimer's disease. Relations between autoimmune thyroid disease and familial Alzheimer's disease (Ewins, Rossor, Butler, Roques, Mullan, & McGregor, 1991; Genovesi et al., 1996) and diabetes mellitus and dementia (Ott et al., 1996) also have been described.

Other Peripheral Biological Indicators of Alzheimer's Disease

Possible Noninvasive Eye Pupil Test for Alzheimer's Disease.   Scinto et al. (1994) have described a potential noninvasive eye test for Alzheimer's disease. Marked hypersensitivity of the response of the pupil to the cholinergic antagonist drug called tropicamide was observed in a much higher percentage of persons with clinically diagnosed probable or suspected Alzheimer's disease compared with a series of elderly "control" individuals. Although some groups have confirmed this finding, others have not been able to. Like some CSF and blood tests, this eye pupil test may not be specific for Alzheimer's disease. However, because it is noninvasive and appears from longitudinal studies to be an early and sensitive indicator of Alzheimer's disease, effort should be devoted to identifying and controlling factors that currently are causing unexplained variability (reviewed by Percy, Andrews, & Potter, in press).

Increased Red Cell Copper, Zinc Superoxide Dismutase-1.   Increased production of free radicals resulting from altered oxygen metabolism has been postulated to cause damage to brain cells in Alzheimer's disease. In support of this finding is the observation that the activity of an enzyme called copper, zinc superoxide dismutase (SOD-1, which is

known to increase in cells that are exposed to oxidizing agents) is increased in red cells of persons with Alzheimer's disease (Serra, Famulari, Kohan, Marschoff, Dominguez, & de Lustig, 1994). Because there is a complex relationship between SOD-1 activity and age in Alzheimer's disease patients (this reaches a maximum at age 72 to 74 years), and because about one-third of first-degree relatives of persons with Alzheimer's disease have highly elevated red cell SOD-1, the use of red cell SOD-1 activity as an antemortem or predictive test for Alzheimer's disease will not be straightforward. Whether or not there is any relation between the ApoE4 genotype and SOD-1 activity has not been investigated.

Trisomy 21 Mosaicism in Tissues of Persons with Alzheimer's Disease. Some cells with an extra chromosome 21 have been detected in cultured lymphocytes or fibroblasts of persons with Alzheimer's disease. It has proposed that such mosaicism in brain tissue may be the cause of the neurodegeneration that is characteristic of Alzheimer's disease (Potter, 1991; Potter & Geller, 1996). Alternatively, this phenomenon may be an adaptive mechanism which is protective.

Platelet Abnormalities in Alzheimer's Disease. The external membrane of blood platelets has been found to be more compressible (i.e., more fluid) in persons with Alzheimer's disease than in healthy normal individuals. Measurements of platelet membrane fluidity have been found to be a significant predictor that Alzheimer's disease will develop in asymptomatic first-degree relatives of persons with Alzheimer's disease (Zubenko et al., 1996). Not clear is whether this platelet test is a better or worse predictor for Alzheimer's disease than having an ApoE4 genotype.

Dementia, Aging, and the Stress Response. There is evidence that metabolism of one type of steroid hormone called glucocorticoid is altered in Alzheimer's disease, depression, and in normal aging (Orell & O'Dwyer, 1995). As glucocorticoids play a fundamental role in regulating the body's response to many different types of stresses, whether stresses or the stress response is abnormal in Alzheimer's disease is currently under debate. In types of Alzheimer's disease that are causally associated with genetic mutations, the genetic mutations themselves may result in excessive internal stress to cells.

Future Directions. It is not likely that one peripheral biological marker will be found that identifies Alzheimer's disease with high sensitivity and specificity at a very early stage. Rather, a more practical approach might involve combining the results of genetic tests, neuropsychological tests, neurobehavioral tests, and measures of certain peripheral biological markers to yield a probability that a person will develop (or be affected by) Alzheimer's disease (Percy, Andrews, and Potter, in press). The author and her colleagues previously developed appropriate statistical approaches to combine genetic and biological information that improved the diagnosis of persons who were at risk of transmitting serious X-linked genetic diseases to their offspring (Percy, Andrews, Brasher, & Rusk, 1987).

☐ Applications to Intellectual Disabilities

Aylward, Burt, Thorpe, Lai, and Dalton (1997) have explained that the foremost impediment to progress in the understanding and treatment of dementia in adults with intellectual disability is the lack of standardized criteria and diagnostic procedures. The AAMR/IASSID working group (Aylward et al., 1997) proposed standardized criteria to use for diagnosis of dementia and procedures for determining whether or not criteria are met in individual cases. Nevertheless, important progress has been made in this field, particularly among persons with Down's syndrome (Brugge et al., 1994; Haveman, Maaskant, van Schrojenstein Lantman, Urlings, & Kessels, 1994; Janicki, Heller, Seltzer, & Hogg, 1995; Evenhuis, 1997). Down's syndrome usually is caused by the presence of an extra chromosome 21. Such persons have three copies of chromosome 21 instead of two (i.e., they have trisomy 21). In a small percentage of cases, Down's syndrome results from trisomy 21 mosaicism (these individuals carry two cell lines of which one is normal and the other is trisomy 21), or from duplication of only part of an extra chromosome 21 (partial trisomy 21), or from translocation trisomy 21.

Alzheimer-Type Dementia in Down's Syndrome

Reasons for studying risk factors and peripheral biological consequences of Alzheimer's disease in persons with intellectual disability are the same as in the general population. But it cannot be taken for granted that risk factors for persons with intellectual disability will be the same as for persons in the general population, especially when there is a genetic or chromosomal basis for the intellectual disability.

Dementia of the Alzheimer type is the most frequent cause of dementia among aging people with Down's syndrome. Research suggests that probably almost all people with Down's syndrome over the age of 35 develop the characteristic neuropathological changes of Alzheimer's disease, although the extent to which neuropathological changes result in cognitive decline and the eventual development of dementia is less certain (Mann, 1993; Holland & Oliver, 1995). Previous studies have reported that the clinical features of dementia in people with Down's syndrome increase with aging from 8% between 35 and 49 years of age, to approximately 75% in those over 60 years of age (Lott & Lai, 1982; Wisniewski, Wisniewski, & Wen, 1985; Lai & Williams, 1989; Dalton, 1992). Some recent studies (Devenny, Silverman, Hill, Jenkins, Sersen, & Wisniewski, 1996; Zigman, Schupf, Sersen, & Silverman, 1996), however, have found the prevalence of dementia in a population of adults with Down's syndrome to be less frequent than previously believed. Nevertheless, the high prevalence of clinical dementia in persons with Down's syndrome suggests that one or more genes on chromosome 21 are predisposing risk factors for Alzheimer's disease in this population. That a substantial fraction of persons with Down's syndrome do not develop clinical dementia suggests that there may be additional susceptibility and/or resistance factors for Alzheimer's disease in persons with Down's syndrome. It is speculated that the apparently protective effects of education against Alzheimer's disease may be more striking in persons with Down's syndrome and other forms of intellectual disability than in the population at large because of more profound interindividual differences in education and training. The achievements currently attained by some younger persons with an intellectual handicap could not have been envisioned even 15 years ago.

Importance of Cytogenetic Diagnosis of Down's Syndrome

Comparisons of DNA studies and clinical features of persons with Down's syndrome who have partial trisomy of the long arm of chromosome 21 (i.e., genotype–phenotype studies) are being used to molecularly map regions of the chromosome that are linked to characteristic features of Down's syndrome (Figure 4.3). Long-term follow-up of these individuals may also enable mapping of chromosome 21 region(s) that cause the Alzheimer's disease-linked brain changes and dementia. It would be particularly significant if certain individuals with partial trisomy 21 do not develop the brain features of Alzheimer's disease. If an Alzheimer's disease region on chromosome 21 that is distinct from the critical Down's syndrome region can be identified, then DNA analysis could be used to predict in rare cases whether a person with Down's syndrome due to partial trisomy 21 had a relatively low or high risk of developing Alzheimer's disease.

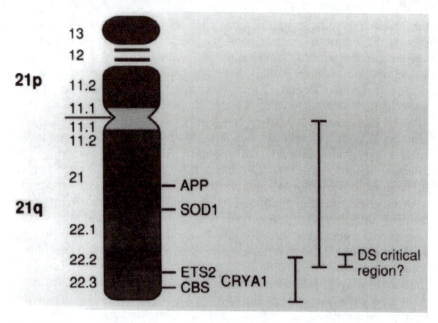

FIGURE 4.2.   Components of Alzheimer "senile" plaques. (A) Bielschowsky's silver stain demonstrating a mature senile plaque and two neurofibrillary tangles. The senile plaque shows a halo with trapped neurites characteristic of mature senile plaques. (B) Senile plaque triple stained to show the arrangement of glial cells. In the periphery, astrocytes immunostained for glial fibrillary acidic protein (GFAP) can be seen. In the center, the dark outlines of reactive microglial cells, immunostained for HLA-DR, are visualized. The light colored spherical mass is amyloid beta protein stained with thioflavin S. (Reproduced with permission from McGeer & McGeer, 1995.)

Genetic Risk Factors for Alzheimer's Disease in Down's Syndrome

A number of studies have explored the possibility that the ApoE4 allele is associated with "dementia" in Down's syndrome but findings have not been consistent (Martins et al., 1995; Helisalmi et al., 1996; Lambert, Perez-Tur, Dupire, Delacourte, Frigard, & Chartier-Harlin, 1996; Schupf et al., 1996; Alexander et al., 1997; Del Bo et al., 1997; Farrer et al., 1997). One problem may involve distinguishing "cognitive impairment" from "dementia." The ApoE2 allele may be associated with longevity and preservation of cognitive functioning in Down's syndrome (Lambert et al., 1996; Royston et al., 1996). There are no published studies investigating associations between APP, PS-1, or PS2 mutations and dementia in Down's syndrome. However, one linkage study found an association between the D21S121 locus and dementia in Down's syndrome but not between the APP locus or the ApoE4 allele and dementia (Farrer et al., 1997). Interestingly, Schupf, and Kapell, Lee, Ottman, and Mayeus (1994) found an increased risk of Alzheimer's disease in mothers of adults with Down's syndrome, a finding that might be related to the observation that the frequency of the ApoE4 allele is greater than expected in young mothers of children with Down's syndrome (Avramopoulos, Mikkelsen, Vassilopoulos, Grigiadouo, & Petersen, 1996).

Other Risk Factors for Alzheimer's Disease in Down's Syndrome

No epidemiological studies have been carried out to date to identify non genetic risk factors for dementia in persons with Down's syndrome or other forms of intellectual disability. However, increased levels of aluminum and iron have been detected in the Down's syndrome brain as in the Alzheimer's disease brain in the general population (Yoshida & Yoshimasu, 1996). The gastrointestinal absorption of aluminum is increased in Down's syndrome (Moore et al., 1997).

Possible Peripheral Biological Markers for Alzheimer's Disease in Persons with Down's Syndrome

Percy et al. (1990a, 1990b) have described some changes in peripheral biological markers in adults with Down's syndrome that are associated with increasing subject age and also with the presence of dementia in Down's syndrome. The copper, zinc superoxide dismutase (SOD-1) gene is located on chromosome 21. Because persons with Down's syndrome have an extra chromosome 21 in their cells, red cell SOD-1 in persons with Down's syndrome is 1.5 times that in normal individuals. With increasing age or the presence of dementia, the activity of red cell SOD-1 was found to decrease (Percy et al., 1990a). In contrast to persons with Alzheimer's disease in which lymphocytes tend to gain an extra chromosome 21 with increasing age (Potter, 1991), lymphocytes in persons with Down's syndrome have a tendency to lose a chromosome 21 (Percy, Dalton, et al., 1993). Not clear is that chromosome 21 loss precedes, coincides with, or follows the development of dementia (if at all). The possibility exists that changes in red cell SOD-1 and chromosome 21 loss are reactions to the Alzheimer process and have a protective physiological function rather than a destructive one.

There is evidence for altered immune and inflammatory responses in Down's syndrome as in Alzheimer's disease. For example, Mehta, Dalton,

Mehta, Percy, and Wisniewski (1993) have described elevations in serum interleukin-6 levels in older persons with Down's syndrome, but it is not clear whether these elevations reflect chronic hepatitis B (HBV) or other infections, autoimmune disease, or dementia. Biological studies also have provided new insights into possible biochemical aberrations underlying the development of dementia in Down's syndrome. Percy et al. (1990b) found that autoimmune thyroiditis (serum autoantibodies to thyroglobulin and/or thyroid microsomal antigens) associated with subclinical hypothyroidism was very common in adults with Down's syndrome, that this disorder increased with severity with increasing age, and was more severe in persons with Down's syndrome and clinical manifestations of Alzheimer's disease than in those of similar age who had no manifestations of Alzheimer's disease.

These findings have raised the possibility that autoimmune thyroiditis might cause dementia in some cases of Down's syndrome. New data continue to support these findings (Devenny et al., 1996). Nicholson et al. (1994), reported a significant association between autoimmune thyroiditis in Down's syndrome and the HLA 0301 allele. Data from an ongoing prospective longitudinal study indicate that 6 of 9 adults with Down's syndrome diagnosed with dementia have hypothyroid autoimmune thyroiditis (i.e., elevated levels of serum thyrotropin, antithyroglobulin, *and* antimicrosomal autoantibodies). In contrast, the frequency of this thyroid problem is only 20% in those with no clinical signs of dementia (Percy, Dalton, Mehta, Bauer, & Jeng, 1997). Importantly, chronic infection with HBV was found to be significantly associated with autoimmune thyroiditis in Down's syndrome but not in others with intellectual impairment (May & Kawanishi, 1996). Thus, chronic HBV infection may not only be a risk factor for autoimmune thyroiditis in Down's syndrome but for development of dementia in this population as well.

Continued longitudinal studies are essential to clarify these very important findings and to establish whether or not there is a significant link between chronic HBV infection, hypothyroid autoimmune thyroiditis, depression, and dementia in the Down's syndrome population. If this is the case, then immunization against HBV might prevent the development of these disorders in some cases. (Interestingly, published information suggests that there may be a link between a certain subtype of depression, thyroid dysfunction, and dementia in the population at large—Custro et al., 1994.) The lower than expected prevalence of dementia in Down's syndrome found in very recent studies might reflect an increasing tendency to immunize persons with Down's syndrome against HBV or to treat mild hypothyroid conditions that were not treated in the past. However, it has not been proven that treating subclinical hypothyroidism in Down's syndrome is beneficial. Oral zinc supplementation has been reported to restore certain serum parameters of thyroid function in children on a short-term basis, but the long-term consequences of zinc therapy are not known (Percy, 1993).

☐ **Commentary**

Genetic risk factors for Alzheimer's disease in the general population currently include mutations in the APP, PS-1, and PS-2 genes, and the APoE4 allele. These account for only about 50% of Alzheimer's disease cases, so there must be other yet unidentified Alzheimer's disease susceptibility genes or environmental risk factors. Mutations in mitochondrial DNA may contribute to the pathology of Alzheimer's disease. Toxic metal ions are other suspected culprits. Factors protective against Alzheimer's disease may include education and nonsteroidal anti-inflammatory agents. There is evidence that chronic inflammation and immune processes occur in the brain of people affected by Alzheimer's disease. Not clear is whether these processes cause Alzheimer's disease or are a consequence of neuronal injury. Efforts continue to develop a simple antemortem "Alzheimer test" based on measurements of biological parameters in tissues other than brain in living persons. Measurements of tau in combination with A beta derivatives, and neuron thread protein in the CSF, and of an iron-binding protein in the serum called p97, show promise as diagnostic aids for Alzheimer's disease. A potential noninvasive eye pupil test for Alzheimer's disease based on hypersensitivity of the eye pupil to tropicamide is being tested extensively.

In contrast to the general population, studies of biological markers of dementia in persons with intellectual disability are in their relative infancy. This is because of the difficulty in distinguishing features of dementia from those of the underlying intellectual disability. Intensive efforts are now underway to study the development of dementia in persons with Down's syndrome who are at peculiarly increased risk of developing an early onset form of Alzheimer-like disease that is not seen in other types of intellectual disability. Available data have raised the possibility that in Down's syndrome there may be a relation between chronic HBV infection, hypothyroid autoimmune thyroiditis, depression, and dementia. This possibility should be evaluated, since immunization against HBV might prevent development of these conditions in some cases. Such a study might provide new insights that could be applied to causes of dementia in the population at large.

With respect to the future direction of research, development of reliable methods to diagnose Alzheimer's disease in persons with intellectual disability will be dependent upon studies that correlate clinical findings and histopathological features of brain tissue. Thus, the creation of regional brain banks for Alzheimer's disease and other brain research in the developmental disability field must be promoted, and funding must be mobilized to ensure their continued operation. Further, longitudinal studies of the development of Alzheimer's disease-type dementia in persons with Down's syndrome and other forms of intellectual disability are extremely important. They can lead to the development of positive tests that can aid with the diagnosis of early stages of dementia and to the identification of genetic and environmental risk factors for dementia, and with help with the rational development of treatments for Alzheimer's disease in this population (which may not be the same as for persons in the general population). Finally, the formation of international networks without walls must be promoted and funding mobilized to support research and educational activities and clinical trials of the network.

☐   References

Aisen, P. S. (1997). Inflammation and Alzheimer's disease: mechanisms and therapeutic strategies. *Gerontology, 43,* 143–149.

Albert, M. S. (1996). Cognitive and neurobiologic markers of early Alzheimer disease. *Proceedings of the National Academy of Sciences USA, 93,* 13547–13551.

Alexander, G. E., Saunders, A. M., Szczepanik J., Strassburger, T. L., Pietrini, P., Dani, A., Furey, M. L., Mentis, M. J., Roses, A. D., Rapoport, S. I., & Schapiro, M. B. (1997). Relation of age and apolipoprotein E to cognitive function in Down syndrome adults. *Neuroreport, 8,* 1835–1840.

Alzheimer's Disease Collaborative Group (1995). The structure of the presenilin I (5182) gene and the identification of six novel mutations in early onset AD families. *Nature Genetics, 11,* 219–222.

Andreasen, N., Davidsson, P., Hesse, C., Lidstrom, A. M., van de Voorde, A., Vanmechelen, E., Winblad, B., & Blennow, K. (1997). A community-based follow-up study on cerebrospinal fluid tau protein in patients with dementia. In K. Iqbal, B. Winblad, T. Nishimura, M. Takeda, H. M. Wisniewski (Eds.), *Alzheimer's disease: Biology, diagnosis and therapeutics* (pp. 149–154). New York: Wiley.

Avramopoulos, D., Mikkelsen, M., Vassilopoulos, D., Grigoridou, M., & Petersen, M. B. (1996). Apolipoprotein E allele distribution in parents of Down's syndrome children. *Lancet, 347,* 862–865.

Aylward, E. H., Burt, D. B., Thorpe, L. U., Lai, F., & Dalton, A. (1997). Diagnosis of dementia in individuals with intellectual disability. *Journal of Intellectual Disabilities Research, 41,* 152–164.

Blacker, D., Wilcox, M. A., Laird, N. M., Rodes, L., Horvath, S. M., Go, R. C., Perry, R., Watson, B. Jr., Bassett, S. S., McInnis, M. G., Albert, M. S., Hyman, B. T., & Tanzi, R. E. (1998). Alpha-Z macroglobulin is genetically associated with Alzheimer disease. Nature Genetics, 19, 357–360.

Brugge, K. L., Nichols, S. L., Salmon, D. P., Hill, L. R., Delis, D. C., Aaron, L., & Trauner, D. A. (1994). Cognitive impairment in adults with Down's syndrome: Similarities to early cognitive changes in Alzheimer's disease. *Neurology, 44,* 232–238.

Burns, A., & Murphy, D. (1996). Commentary. Protection against Alzheimer's disease? *Lancet, 348,* 420–421.

Casdorph, H. R., & Walker, M. (1995). *Toxic metal syndrome: How metal poisonings can affect your brain.* Garden City Park, NY: Avery.

Cohen, S., & Freedman, M. (1991). Piecing together the signs of Alzheimer's disease. *The Canadian Journal of Diagnosis (March),* 81–92.

Crapper-McLachlan, D. R., Dalton, A. J., Kruck, T. P. A., Bell, M. Y., Smith, W. L., Kalow, W., & Andrews, D. F. (1991). Intramuscular desferrioxamine in patients with Alzheimer's disease. *Lancet, 337,* 1304–1308.

Custro, N., Scafidi, V., Lo Baido, R., Nastri, K., Abbate, G., Cuffaro, M. P., Gallo, S., Vienna, G., & Notarbartolo, A. (1994). Subclinical hypothyroidism resulting from autoimmune thyroiditis in female patients with endogenous depression. *Journal of Endocrinological Investigation, 17,* 641–646.

Davis, R. E., Miller, S., Herrnstaddt, C., Ghosh, S. S., Shinobu, L. A., Galasko, D., Thal, L. J., Beal, M. F., Howell, N., & Parker, W. D., Jr. (1997). Mutations in mitochondrial cytochrome c oxidase genes segregate with late-onset Alzheimer disease. *Proceedings of the National Academy of Sciences USA, 94,* 4526–4531.

de la Monte, S. M., & Wands, J. R. (1992). Neuronal thread protein over-expression in brains with Alzheimer's disease lesions. *Journal of the Neurological Sciences, 113,* 152–164.

de la Monte, S. M., Volicer, L., Hauser, S. L., & Wands, J. R. (1992). Increased levels of neuronal thread protein in cerebrospinal fluid of patients with Alzheimer's disease. *Annals of Neurology, 32,* 733–742.

de la Monte, S. M., Carlson, R. I., Brown, N. V., & Wands, J. R. (1996). Profiles of neuronal thread protein expression in Alzheimer's disease. *Journal of Neuropathology and Experimental Neurology, 55,* 1038–1050.

de la Monte, S. M., Xu, Y. Y., Hutchins, G. M., & Wands, J. R. (1996). Developmental patterns of neuronal thread protein gene expression in Down syndrome. *Journal of the Neurological Sciences, 135,* 118–125.

de la Monte, S. M., Ghanbari, K., Frey, W. H., Beheshti, I., Averback, P., Hauser, S. L., Ghanbari, H. A., & Wands, J. R. (1997). Characterization of the AO7C-NTP cDNA expression in Alzheimer's disease and measurement of a 41 kD protein in cerebrospinal fluid. *Journal of Clinical Investigation, 100,* 3093–3104.

Del Bo, R., Comi, G. P., Bresolin, N., Castelli, E., Conti, E., Degiuli, A., Ausenda, C. D., & Scarlato, G. (1997). The apolipoprotein E epsilon4 allele causes a faster decline of cognitive performances in Down's syndrome subjects. *Journal of the Neurological Sciences, 145,* 87–97.

Devenny, D. A., Silverman, W. P., Hill, A. L., Jenkins, E., Sersen, E. A., & Wisniewski, K. E. (1996). Normal ageing in adults with Down's syndrome: A longitudinal study. *Journal of Intellectual Disabilities Research, 40,* 208–221.

Evans, D. A., Funkenstein, H. H., Albert, M. S., Scherr, P. A., Cook, N. R., Chown, M. J., Hebert, L. E., Hennekens. C. H., & Taylor, J. O. (1989). Prevalence of Alzheimer's disease in a community population of older persons. *JAMA—Journal of the American Medical Association, 262,* 2551–2556.

Evenhuis, H. M. (1997). The natural history of dementia in aging people with intellectual disability. *Journal of Intellectual Disabilities Research, 41,* 92–96.

Ewins, D. L., Rossor, M. N., Butler, J., Roques, P. K., Mullan, M. J., & McGregor, A. M. (1991). Association between autoimmune thyroid disease and familial Alzheimer's disease. *Clinical Endocrinology, 35,* 93–96.

Fallowfield, L. (1996). Commentary. Quality of quality-of-life data. *Lancet, 348,* 421.

Farrer, M. J., Crayton, L., Davies, G. E., Oliver, C., Powell, J., Holland, A. J., & Kessling, A. M. (1997). Allelic variability in D21S11, but not in APP or APOE, is associated with cognitive decline in Down syndrome. *Neuroreport, 8,* 1645–1649.

Frecker, M. F., Pryse-Phillips, W. E., & Strong, H. R. (1994). Immunological associations in familial and non-familial Alzheimer patients and their families. *Canadian Journal of Neurological Sciences, 21,* 112–119.

Genovesi, G., Paolini, P., Marcellini, L.,Vernillo, E., Salvati, G., Polidori, G., Ricciardi, D., de Nuccio, I., & Re, M. (1996). Relationship between autoimmune thyroid disease and Alzheimer's disease. *Panminerva Medicine, 38,* 61–63.

Haveman, M. J., Maaskant, M. A., van Schrojenstein Lantman, H. M., Urlings, H. F., & Kessels, A. G. (1994). Mental health problems in elderly people with and without Down's syndrome. *Journal of Intellectual Disabilities Research, 38,* 341–355.

Hebert, L., Scherr, P., Beckett, L., & Evans, D. (1996). Projected incidence of Alzheimer's disease in the United States. *Neurobiology of Aging, 17* (Suppl.), S95.

Heinonen, O., Syrjanen, S., Soininen, H., Talasnieme, S., Kaski, M., Mantyjarvi, R., Syrjanen, K., & Riekkinen, P., Sr. (1993). Circulating immune complexes in sera from patients with Alzheimer's disease, multi-infarct dementia and Down's syndrome. *Neuroscience Letters, 149,* 67–70.

Helisalmi, S., Linnaranta, K., Lehtovirta, M., Mannermaa, A., Heinonen, O., Ryynanen, M., Riekkinen, P., Sr., & Soininen, H. (1996). Apolipoprotein E polymorphism in patients with different neurodegenerative disorders. *Neuroscience Letters, 205,* 61–64.

Holland, A. J., & Oliver, C. (1995). Down syndrome and the links with Alzheimer disease. *Journal of Neurology, Neurosurgery & Psychiatry, 59,* 111–114.

Hyman, B. T., & Tanzi, R. (1995). Editorial: Molecular epidemiology of Alzheimer's disease. *The New England Journal of Medicine, 333,* 1283–1284.

Itzhaki, R. F., Lin, W. R., Shang, D., Wilcock, G. K., Faragher, B., & Jamieson, G. A. (1997). Herpes simplex virus type 1 in brain and risk of Alzheimer's disease. *Lancet, 349,* 241–244.

Janicki, M. P., Heller, T., Seltzer, G., & Hogg, J. (1995). *Practice guidelines of the clinical assessment and care management of Alzheimer and other dementias among adults with mental retardation.* Washington: American Association on Mental Retardation.

Jensen, M., Basun, H., & Lannfelt, L. (1995). Increased cerebrospinal fluid tau in patients with Alzheimer's disease. *Neuroscience Letters, 186,* 189–191.

Jorm, A. F. (1991). Cross-national comparisons of the occurrence of Alzheimer's and vascular dementias. *European Archives of Psychiatry and Clinical Neuroscience, 240,* 218–222.

Karlinsky, H., Vaula, G., Haines, J. L., Ridgeley, J., Bergeron, C., Mortilla, M., Tupler, R. G., Percy, M. E., Robitaille, Y., Yip, T. C. K., Tanzi, R. E., Gusella, J. F., Becker, R., Berg, J. M., Crapper-McLachlan, D. R. C., & St. George Hyslop, P. H., Noldly, N. E., (1992). Molecular and prospective phenotypic characterization of a pedigree with familial Alzheimer disease and a missense mutation in codon 717 of the B-amyloid precursor protein (APP) gene. *Neurology, 42,* 1445–1453.

Kennard, M. L., Feldman, H., Yamada, T., & Jefferies, W. A. (1996). Serum levels of the iron-binding protein p97 are elevated in Alzheimer's disease. *Nature Medicine, 2,* 1230–1235.

Korenberg, J. R., Kawashima, H., Pulst, S. M., Ikeuchi, T., Ogasawara, N., Yamamoto, K., Schonberg, S. A., West, R., Allen, L., Magenis, E., Ikawa, K., Taniguchi, N., & Epstein, C. J. (1990). Molecular definition of a region of chromosome 21 that causes features of the Down syndrome phenotype. *American Journal of Human Genetics, 47,* 236–246.

Korenberg, J. R., Chen, X. N., Schipper, R., Sun, Z., Gonsksy, R., Gerwehr, S., Carpenter, N., Daumer, C., Dignan, P., & Disteche, C., Graham, J. M. Jr., Hugdins, L., McGilliuray, B., Miyazaki, K., Ogasawara, N., Park, J. P., Pagon, R., Pueschol, S., Sack, G., Say, B., Schuffenhauser, S., Soukup, S., & Yamanaka, T. (1994). Down syndrome phenotypes: The consequences of chromosomal imbalance. *Proceedings of the. National Academy of Sciences USA, 91,* 4997–5001.

Lai, F., & Williams, R. S. (1989). A prospective study of Alzheimer disease in Down syndrome. *Archives of Neurology, 46,* 849–853.

Lambert, J. C., Berr, C., Pasquier, F., Delacourte, A., Frigard, B., Cottel, D., Perez-Tur, J., Mouroux, V., Mohr, M., Cecyre, D., Galasko, D., Lendon, E., Poirier, J., Hardy, J., Mann, D., Amouyel, P., & Chartier-Harlin, M.C. (1998). Pronounced impact of Thl/E47cs mutation compared with—491 AT mutation on neural APDE gene expression and risk of developing Alzheimer's disease. *Human Molecular Genetics, 7,* 1511–1516.

Lambert, J. C., Perez-Tur, J., Dupire, M. J., Delacourte, A., Frigard, B., & Chartier-Harlin, M. C. (1996). Analysis of the APOE alleles impact in Down's syndrome. *Neuroscience Letters, 220,* 57–60.

Lethem, R., & Orrell, M. (1997), Antioxidants and dementia, *Lancet, 349,* 1189–1190.

Lott, I. T., & Lai, F. (1982). Dementia in Down syndrome: Observations from a neurology clinic. *Applied Research in Mental Retardation, 3,* 233–239.

Lennox, A., Karlinsky, H., Meschino, W., Buchanen, J. A., Percy, M. E., & Berg, J. M. (1994). Molecular genetic testing for Alzheimer's disease: Deliberations and preliminary recommendations. *Alzheimer's Disease and Related Disorders, 8,* 126–147.

Ma, J., Brewer, H. B., Jr., & Potter, H. (1996). Alzheimer A beta neurotoxicity: Promotion by antichymotrypsin, ApoE4; inhibition by A beta-related peptides. *Neurobiology of Aging, 17,* 773–780.

Mann, D. M. A. (1993). Association between Alzheimer disease and Down syndrome: Neuropathological observations. In J. M. Berg, B. Karlinsky, & A. J. Holland (Eds.). *Alzheimer disease, Down syndrome and their relationship* (pp. 71–92). Oxford: Oxford University Press.

Martins, R. N., Clarnette, R., Fisher, C., Broe, G. A., Brooks, W. S., Montgomery, P., & Gandy, S. E. (1995). ApoE genotypes in Australia: Roles in early and late onset Alzheimer's disease and Down's syndrome. *Neuroreport, 6,* 1513–1516.

May, P., & Kawanishi, H. (1996). Chronic hepatitis B infection and autoimmune thyroiditis in Down syndrome. *Journal of Clinical Gastroenterology, 23,* 181–184.

McGeer, P. L., & McGeer, E. G. (1995). Review article. The inflammatory response system of brain: Implications for therapy of Alzheimer and other neurodegenerative diseases. *Brain Research Reviews, 21,* 195–218.

McKhann, G., Drachman, D., Folstein, M., Katzman, R., Price, D., & Stadlan, E. M. (1984). Clinical diagnosis of Alzheimer's disease: Report of the NINCDS-ADRDA Work Group under the auspices of Department of Health and Human Services Task Force on Alzheimer's disease. *Neurology, 34,* 939–944.

McLachlan, D. R., Bergeron, C., Smith, J. E., Boomer, D., & Rifat, S. L. (1996). Risk for neuropathologically confirmed Alzheimer's disease and residual aluminum in municipal drinking water employing weighted residential histories. *Neurology, 46,* 401–405.

McRae, A., Dahlstrom, A., & Ling, E. A. (1997). Microglia in neurodegenerative disorders: Emphasis on Alzheimer's disease. *Gerontology, 43,* 95–108.

Mehta, P. D., Dalton, A. J., Mehta, S. P., Percy, M. E., & Wisniewski, H. M. (1993). Increased beta 2-microglobulin (B2M) and interleukin-6 (IL-6) in sera from older persons with Down syndrome. *Advances in the BioSciences, 87,* 95–96.

Miklossy, J., Kasas, S., Janzer, R. C., Ardizzoni, F., & Van der Loos, H. (1994). Further ultrastructural evidence that spirochaetes may play a role in the aetiology of Alzheimer's disease. *Neuroreport, 5,* 1201–1204.

Moore, P. B., Edwardson, J. A., Ferrier, I. N., Taylor, G. A., Lett, D., Tyrer, S. P., Day, J. P., King, S. J., & Lilley, J. S. (1997).Gastrointestinal absorption of aluminum is increased in Down's syndrome. *Biological Psychiatry, 41,* 488–492.

Mori, H., Hosoda, K., Matsubara, E., Nakamoto, T., Furiya, Y., Endoh, R., Usami, M., Shoji, M., Meruyama, S., & Nirai, S. (1995). Tau in cerebrospinal fluids: Establishment of the sandwich ELISA with antibody-specific to the repeat sequence in tau. *Neuroscience Letters, 186,* 181–183.

Motter, R., Vigo-Pelfrey, C., Kholodenko, D., Barbour, R., Johnson-Wood, K., Galasko, D., Chang, L., Miller, B., Clark, C., & Green, R., Olson, D., Southwick, P., Wolfert, R., Munroe, B., Lieberburg, I., Seubert, P., & Schenk, D. Reduction of beta-amyloid peptid42 in the cerebrospinal fluid of patients with Alzheimer's disease. *Annals of Neurology, 38,* 643–648.

Multhaup, G., Schlicksupp, A., Hesse, L., Beher, D., Ruppert, T., Masters, C. L., & Bayreuther, K. (1996). The amyloid precursor protein of Alzheimer's disease in the reduction of copper (II) to copper (I). *Science, 271,* 1406–1409.

Nicholson, L. B., Wong, F. S., Ewins, D. L., Butler, J., Holland, A., Demaine, A. G., & McGregor, A. M. (1994). Susceptibility to autoimmune thyroiditis in Down's syndrome is associated with the major histocompatibility class II DQA 0301 allele. *Clinical Endocrinology, 41,* 381–383.

Nymox Pharmaceutical Corporation: *European commercialization agreement for Nymox Alzheimer Diagnostic Test.* October 23, 1996.

Olzewer, E., & Carter, J. P. (1988). EDTA chelation therapy in chronic degenerative disease. *Medical Hypotheses, 27,* 41–49.

Orrell, M. W., & O'Dwyer, A. M. (1995). Dementia, ageing and the stress control system. *Lancet, 345,* 666–667.

Ott, A., Stolk, R. P., Hofman, A., van Harskamp, F., Grobbee, D. E., & Breteler, M. M. (1996). Association of diabetes mellitus and dementia: The Rotterdam Study. *Diabetologia, 39,* 1392–1397.

Paganini-Hill, A., & Henderson, V. W. (1996). Estrogen replacement therapy and risk of Alzheimer disease. *Archives of Internal Medicine, 156,* 2213–2217.

Payami, H., Schellenberg, G. D., Zareparsi, S., Kaye, J., Sexton, G. J., Head, M. A., Matsuyama, S. S., Jarvik, L. F., Miller, B., McManus, D. Q., Bird, T. D., Katzman, R., Heston, L., Norman, D., & Small, G. W. (1997). Evidence for association of HLA-A2 allele with onset age of Alzheimer's disease. *Neurology, 49,* 512–518.

Percy, M. E. (1993). Peripheral biological markers as confirmatory or predictive tests for Alzheimer disease in the general population and in Down syndrome. In J. M. Berg, H. Karlinsky, & A. J. Holland (Eds.), *Alzheimer disease and Down syndrome and their relationship* (pp. 199–223). Oxford: Oxford University Press.

Percy, M. E., Andrews, D. F., Brasher, P. M. A., & Rusk, A. C. M. (1987). Making the most of multiple measurements in estimating carrier probability in Duchenne muscular dystrophy: The incorporation of repeated measurements using logistic discrimination. *American Journal of Medical Genetics, 26,* 851–861.

Percy, M. E., Dalton, A. J., Markovic, V. D., McLachlan, D. R. C., Hummel, J. T., Rusk, A. C. M., & Andrews, D. F. (1990a). Red cell superoxide dismutase, glutathione peroxidase and catalase in Down syndrome patients with and without manifestations of Alzheimer disease. *American Journal of Medical Genetics, 35,* 459–467.

Percy, M. E., Dalton, A. J., Markovic, V. D., McLachlan, D. R., Hummel, J. T., Rusk, A. C., Gera, E., Walfish, P. G., & Andrews, D. F. (1990b). Autoimmune thyroiditis associated with mild "subclinical" hypothyroidism in adults with Down syndrome: A comparison of patients with and without manifestations of Alzheimer disease. *American Journal of Medical Genetics, 36,* 148–154.

Percy, M. E., Markovic, V. D., Dalton, A. J., McLachlan, D. R., Berg, J. M., Rusk, A. C., Somerville, M. J., Chodakowski, B., & Andrews, D. F. (1993). Age-associated chromosome 21 loss in Down syndrome: Possible relevance to mosaicism and Alzheimer's disease. *American Journal of Medical Genetics, 45,* 584–588.

Percy, M. E., Dalton, A. J., Mehta, P., Bauer, S., & Jeng, W. (1997, November). Thyroid involvement in Down syndrome revisited. Paper presented at the annual meeting of the Gerontological Society of America, Cincinnati, Ohio.

Percy, M. E., Andrews, D. F. & Potter, H. (in press). Diagnosis of Alzheimer disease from peripheral biological markers. Directions from the Alzheimer's pathogenic pathway. In C. F. M. Scinto & K. Dafner (Eds.), *Early Diagnosis and Treatment of Alzheimer's Disease*. Totawa, NJ: Humana Press.

Polvikoski, T., Sulkava, R., Haltia, M., Kainulainen, K., Vuorio, A., Verkkoniemi, A., Niinisto, L., Halonen, P., & Kontula, K. (1995). Apolipoprotein E, dementia, and cortical deposition of B-amyloid protein. *New England Journal of Medicine, 333*, 1242–1247.

Post, S. G., Whitehouse, P. J., Binstock, R. N., Bird, T. D., Eckert, S. K., Farrer, L. A., Fleck, L. M., Gaines, A. D., Juengst, E. T., Karlinsky, H., Miles, S., Murray, T. H., Quaid, K. A., Relkin, N. R., Roses, A. D., St. George-Hyslop, P. N., Sachs, G. A., Steinbock, G., Trushke, Z. F., & Zinn, A. B. (1997). The clinical introduction of genetic testing for Alzheimer disease. An ethical perspective. *Journal of the American Medical Association, 277*, 832–836.

Potter, H. (1991). Review and hypothesis: Alzheimer disease and Down syndrome—chromosome 21 non-disjunction may underlie both disorders. *American Journal of Human Genetics, 48*, 1192–1200.

Potter, H., & Geller, L. N. (1996). Alzheimer's disease, Down's syndrome, and chromosome segregation. *Lancet, 348*, 66.

Rahmani, Z., Blouin, J. L., Creau-Goldberg, N., Watkins, P. C., Mattei, J.-F., Poissonnier, M., Prieur, M., Chettouh, Z., Nicole, A., Aurias, A., Sinet, P.-M., & Delabar, J.-M. (1989). Critical role of the D21S55 region on chromosome 21 in the pathogenesis of Down syndrome. *Proceedings of the National Academy of Sciences USA, 86*, 5958–5962.

Rasmussen, D. E., & Sobsey, D. (1994). Age, adaptive behaviour, and Alzheimer disease in Down syndrome: Cross-sectional and longitudinal analyses. *American Journal of Mental Retardation 99*, 151–165.

Rocco, F. J., Cronin-Golomb, A., & Lai, F. (1997). Alzheimer-like visual deficits in Down syndrome. *Alzeimer's Disease & Associated Disorders, 11*, 88–98.

Rogaev, E. I., Sherrington, R., Rogaeva, E. A., Levesque, G., Ikeda, M., Liang, Y., Chi, H., Mar, L., Sorbi, Nacmirs, B., Placentini, S., Amaducci, L., Chunakou, I., Cohen, D., Iannfelt, L., Fraser, P. E., Rommers, J. M., & St. George Hyslop, P. H., Lin, C., Holman, K., & Tsuda, T. (1995). Familial Alzheimer's disease in kindreds with missense mutations in a novel gene on chromosome 1 related to the Alzheimer's disease type 3 gene. *Nature, 376* 775–778.

Roses, A. D. (1995). Apolipoprotein E genotyping in the differential diagnosis, not prediction, of Alzheimer's disease. *Annals of Neurology, 38*, 6–14.

Royston, M. C., Mann, D., Pickering-Brown, S., Owen, F., Perry, R., Ragbavan, R., Khin-Nu, C., Tyner, S., Day, K., Crook, R., Hardy, J., & Roberts, G. W. (1996). ApoE2 allele, Down's syndrome and Dementia. R., Crook, J., Hardy, & G. W., Roberts. (Eds.), *Annals of the New York Academy of Sciences, 777*, 255–259.

Sano, M., Ernesto, C., Klaubner, M. R., Schafer, K., Woodbury, P., Thomas, R., Grundman, M., Growdon, J., & Thal, L. J. (1996). Rationale and design of a multicenter study of selegiline and alpha-tocopherol in the treatment of Alzheimer disease using novel clinical outcomes. Alzheimer Disease Cooperative Study. *Alzheimer's Disease & Associated Disorders, 10*, 132–140.

Saunders, A. M., Strittmatter, W. J., Schmechel, D., George-Hyslop, P. H., Pericak-Vance, M. A., Joo, S. H., Rosi, B. L., Gusella, J. F., Crapper-MacLachlan, D. R., Alberts, M. J., Hulette, C., Crain, B., Goldgaber, D., & Roses, A. D. (1993). Association of apolipoprotein E allele E4 with the late-onset familial and sporadic Alzheimer Disease. *Neurology, 43*, 1467–1472.

Schupf, N., Kapell, D., Lee, J. H., Ottman, R., & Mayeux, R. (1994). Increased risk of Alzheimer's disease in mothers of adults with Down's syndrome. *Lancet, 344*, 353–356.

Schupf, N., Kapell, D., Lee, J. H., Zigman, W., Canto, B., Tycko, B., & Mayeux, R. (1996). Onset of dementia is associated with apolipoprotein E epsilon4 in Down's syndrome. *Annals of Neurology, 40,* 799–801.

Scinto, L. S. M., Daffner, K. R., Dressler, D., Ransil, B. I., Rentz, D., Weintraub, S., Mesulam, M., & Potter, H. (1994). A potential non-invasive biological test for Alzheimer disease. *Science, 266,* 1051–1054.

Serby, M., Larson, P., & Kalkstein, D. (1991). The nature and course of olfactory deficits in Alzheimer's disease. *American Journal of Psychiatry, 148,* 357–360.

Serra, J. A., Famulari, A. L., Kohan, S., Marschoff, E. R., Dominguez, R. O., & de Lustig, E. S. (1994). Copper-zinc superoxide dismutase in red blood cells in probable Alzheimer's patients and their first degree relatives. *Journal of the Neurological Sciences, 122,* 179–188.

Sherrington, R., Froelich, S., Sorbi, S., Campion, D., Chi, H., Rogaeva, E. A., Levesque, G., Rogaev, E. I., Lin, C., Liang, Y., Ikeda, M., Mar, L., Brice, A., Agid, Y., Percy, M. E., Clerget- Darpoux, F., Piacentini, S., Marcon, G., Nacmias, B., Amaducci, L., Frebourg, T., Lannfelt, L., Rommens, J. M., & St. George-Hyslop, P. H. (1996). Alzheimer's disease associated with mutations in presenilin 2 is rare and variably penetrant. *Human Molecular Genetics, 5,* 985–988.

Sherrington, R., Tsuda, T., Mar, L., Foncin, J.-F., Bruni, A. C., Montesi, M. P., Sorbi, S., Rainero, I., Piressi, L., Nee, L., Chumakov, I., Pollen, D., Brookes, A., Sanseau, P., Polinksy, R. J., Wasco, W., DaSilva, H. A. R., Haines, J. L., Pericak-Vance, M. A., Tanzi, R. E., Roses, A. D., Fraser, P. E., Rommens, J. M., & St. George Hyslop, P. H. (1995). Cloning of a gene bearing missense mutations in early onset familial Alzheimer's disease. *Nature, 375,* 754–760.

Singh, V. K. (1997). Neuroautoimmunity: Pathogenic implications for Alzheimer's disease. *Gerontology, 43,* 79–94.

Singh, V. K. (1996). Immune-activation model in Alzheimer disease. *Molecular and Chemical Neuropathology, 28,* 105–111.

Skolnick, A. A. (1997). Evaluating estrogen for Alzheimer disease poses ethical and logistical challenges. *Journal of the American Medical Association, 277,* 1831–1833.

Sobel, E., Dunn, M., Davanipour, Z., Qian Z., & Chui, H. C. (1996). Elevated risk of Alzheimer's disease among workers with likely electromagnetic field exposure. *Neurology, 47,* 1477–1481.

Stern, D. M. (1997, May). A cellular receptor for amyloid-beta peptide: From neurons to microglia with RAGE. Paper presented at the IBC's 6th Annual Conference on Alzheimer Disease: Exploiting Mechanisms for Drug Development and Diagnosis, San Francisco, California.

Thompson, M. W., McGinnes, R. R., & Willard, H. F. (1991). *Thompson & Thompson genetics in medicine* (5th ed.). Philadelphia: W. B. Saunders.

Trieb, K., Ransmayr, G., Sgonc, R., & Lassman, H. (1996). APP peptides stimulate lymphocyte proliferation in normals, but not in patients with Alzheimer disease. *Neurobiology of Aging 17,* 541–547.

Vandenabeele, P., & Fiers, P. (1991). Is amyloidosis during Alzheimer's disease due to an IL-1/IL-6 -mediated "acute phase response" in the brain? *Immunology Today, 12,* 217–219.

Vanmechelen, E., Blennow, K., Davidsson, P., Cras, P., & van de Voorde, A. (1997). Combination of Tau/Phospho-tau with other intracellular proteins as diagnostic markers for neurodegeneration. In K. B. Iqbal, T. Winblad, M. Nishimura, M. Takeda, & H. M. Wisniewski (Eds.), *Alzheimer's disease: Biology, diagnosis and therapeutics* (pp. 197–203). New York: Wiley.

Wilder, R. L. (1995). Neuroendocrine-immune system interactions and autoimmunity. *Annua. Review of Immunology, 13,* 307–338.

Wisniewski, K. E., Wisniewski, H. M., & Wen, G.-Y. (1985). Occurrence of neuropathological changes and dementia of Alzheimer disease in Down syndrome. *Annals of Neurology, 17,* 278–282.

Yoshida, H., & Yoshimasu, F. (1996). Alzheimer's disease and trace elements. *Nippon Rinsho, 54,* 111–116.

Zigman, W. B., Schupf, N., Sersen, E., & Silverman, W. (1996). Prevalence of dementia in adults with and without Down syndrome. *American Journal on Mental Retardation, 100,* 403–412.

Zubenko, G. S., Teply, I, Winwood, E., Huff, F. J., Moossy, J., Sunderland, T., & Martinez, A. J. (1996). Prospective study of increased platelet membrane fluidity as a risk factor for Alzheimer's disease: Results at 5 years. *American Journal of Psychiatry, 153,* 420–423.

John R. Wherrett

Neurologic Aspects

The role of the neurologist in the management of dementia occurring in adults with intellectual disability is discussed. Adults with intellectual disability are assumed to be generally at increased risk for secondary or symptomatic forms of dementia and some with particular diagnoses, such as Down's syndrome, are known to be at increased risk for primary dementias, such as Alzheimer's disease. Little is known about the risks for the more recently characterized forms of primary dementia such as dementia with Lewy bodies, frontotemporal dementias, and for vascular dementia. In the neurologic investigation of dementia occurring in intellectually disabled adults, special attention to aspects of the clinical assessment, to the need for investigative procedures, and to predisposition to the side effects of medication is necessary. In the differential diagnosis of dementia in intellectually handicapped individuals, delayed progression of the process that originally impaired development, as well as complications of this process such as epilepsy, hydrocephalus, hypothermia, and psychiatric disorder should be considered.

The role of the neurologist in the care of persons with intellectual disability who exhibit symptoms and signs of dementia is to characterize, through precise diagnosis and functional assessment, the impairment of the organic neurologic substrate and to institute measures to reverse,

Address correspondence to: John R. Wherrett, M.D., Edith Cavell Wing, 8th Floor, Room 024, Western Division of the Toronto Hospital, 399 Bathurst Street, Toronto, Ontario, Canada M5T 2S8. Email: j.wherrett@utoronto.ca stabilize, or facilitate adaptation to the impairment. The standard diagnostic approach of the neurologist that requires identification of functional impairment and anatomical localization of lesions should also be used in the assessment of newly developing symptoms and signs in aging persons with intellectual disability. Since intellectual disability in individuals is unique, assessment of newly occurring, late-onset neurologic impairment can be particularly challenging.

Depending on the context, the definition of dementia will vary. In neurology, the term may be used as a generic description of cognitive decline from any of a variety of causes (for example, head injury, stroke, anoxia) occurring at any stage of life beyond childhood. The term is applied more precisely in a diagnostic sense to persons in whom cognitive decline sufficient to impair personal, social, or occupational adaptation is the main presenting symptom, is persisting and progressive, and is associated with a chronic diffuse or multifocal brain disorder. Diagnostic criteria for specific dementing disorders have been established for research purposes by consensus groups of investigators. Examples are criteria for Alzheimer's disease (McKhann, Drachman, Folstein, Katzman, Price, & Stadlan, 1984), dementia with Lewy bodies (McKeith et al., 1995), frontotemporal dementia (Brun, Gustafson, Passant, Mann, Neary, & Snowden, 1994), and for vascular dementia (Roman et al., 1993). In addition to cognitive and behavioral features, these criteria may specify exclusions and other clinical and laboratory features. Since the pathological processes producing dementia may also involve brain structures that subserve functions other than cognition, such as motor function, symptoms and signs of involvement of these structures are often specified in the research criteria for the diagnosis of individual dementing disorders. Most research criteria elaborated for diagnosis of specific dementing disorders specify neuropathological criteria as well. Although these pathological criteria are commonly regarded as a *gold standard*, it should be appreciated that all of them, including those for Alzheimer's disease are to some extent controversial. Because of many recent advances in the pathology of neurodegenerative disorders, comprehensive studies of neurodegenerative changes in representative populations of persons with intellectual disability exhibiting dementia can only be anticipated and encouraged. From the neurologic perspective, these studies are essential to further understanding of causal mechanisms.

☐ Risk of Dementia

An important issue is whether intellectual disability of any cause predisposes to dementia. The diminished adaptability accompanying intellectual disability a priori would be expected to increase the risk of acquired brain injury from trauma, infection, toxins, and nutritional deficiency. Seizures that commonly accompany intellectual handicap induce changes in the brain (Lynch, Rutecki, & Sutula, 1996) that may increment cognitive impairment. Traumatic brain injury is a risk factor for Alzheimer's disease (Breteler, Claus, van Duijn, Launer, & Hoffman, 1992) and low levels of education may predispose (Katzman, 1993). It has been suggested that atherosclerotic vascular disease, a risk factor for vascular dementia, has a high incidence in adults with intellectual handicap other than Down's syndrome and a low incidence in Down's syndrome (Cole, Neal, Fraser, & Cowie, 1994). That single gene disorders causing intellectual disability may incorporate high risk of dementia is exemplified in Down's syndrome where virtually all adults with the syndrome will develop the neuropathological hallmarks of Alzheimer disease by age 40 (Dalton & Wisniewski, 1990) at least some of whom will have accompanying clinical findings of dementia (Brugge et al., 1994). A high proportion of adults with intellectual disability but without Down's syndrome manifest the neuropathological correlates of Alzheimer's disease, but evidence that this is accompanied by cognitive decline has not been clearly demonstrated (Wisniewski, Silverman, & Wiegel, 1994). It is theoretically plausible that single gene disorders other than Down's syndrome will confer either enhanced susceptibility for or protection from dementia.

Beyond the studies of Alzheimer's disease occurring in persons with Down's syndrome, there is little information about other forms of dementia occurring in Down's syndrome or indeed of dementias occurring in persons with other forms of intellectual disability. In the studies of the more recently identified syndromes of dementia, persons with intellectual disability have been excluded by definition, much less examined as a subgroup. Parkinsonism, as a clinical syndrome, has been found in a high proportion of individuals with Down's syndrome who have become demented. Isolated examples have been reported of persons with Down's syndrome found to have the pathological changes of dementia with Lewy bodies and of vascular dementia (Bodhireddy, Dickson, Mattiace, & Weidenheim, 1994; Collacott, Cooper, & Ismail, 1994). Thus, it can be assumed that virtually all forms of primary dementia and neurodegenerative disease will ultimately be found to occur in persons with intellectual disability should they survive long enough. From the standpoint of both those concerned with intellectual disabilities and those concerned with late-life dementia, the under- or overrepresentation of specific dementia syndromes is of great interest, at least by virtue of the light that these associations may shed on pathogenetic mechanisms.

TABLE 5.1. Primary dementias

---

1. The Alzheimer dementias (neuropathology of predominant and sufficient neuritic plaques and neurofibrillary tangles)
2. Dementia with Lewy bodies (neuropathology of widespread distribution of Lewy bodies in cortex as well as midbrain accompanied by Alzheimer pathology in about 50%)
3. Frontotemporal dementia
   (a) Frontal lobe degeneration type (neuropathology of frontal atrophy without distinctive histological features)
   (b) Pick type (neuropathology of severe asymmetrical frontotemporal atrophy, ballooned neurones, Pick bodies and severe sclerosis)
   (c) Motor neurone type (neuropathology of moderate frontotemporal atrophy, spinal motor neurone degeneration, and inclusions)
4. Progressive hippocampal sclerosis (neuropathology of severe neuronal loss in hippocampus with frontotemporal involvement)
5. Dementias with prominent subcortical features
   (a) Parkinson's disease
   (b) Huntington's disease
   (c) Progressive supranuclear palsy
   (d) Cortical basal ganglionic degeneration
6. Prion dementias

☐ Dementia Syndromes

In this section, current concepts of dementia occurring in individuals who do not have intellectual disability are summarized. The last two decades have seen useful attempts to define clinical syndromes of dementia and to correlate these syndromes with pathology (Table 5.1). Along with this has come a better appreciation of the behavioral manifestations of the various syndromes. A first attempt to classify dementing syndromes divided them into *cortical* and *subcortical* groups (Cummings & Benson, 1992). This remains a helpful concept, although there is considerable overlap between the two categories, both in the evolution of the clinical disorder and in the anatomical distribution of the pathology. "Cortical" dementias present with symptoms and signs of impairment of higher cortical functions including memory, language, integrated motor control, and integrated perception (amnesia, aphasia, apraxia, agnosia) but ultimately will progress to involve "subcortical" functions such as extrapyramidal motor control.

"Subcortical" dementias present as more subtle cognitive decline with slowing of the rate of cognitive processing and impaired retrieval of memory in the face of preserved storage, impaired executive function (activation and integration of other cognitive systems), and disordered mood.

Motor disturbances indicative of involvement of white matter or extrapy-ramidal structures may occur early in the course and may dominate the clinical picture initially. The "subcortical" group includes the dementias occurring in Huntington's and Parkinson's diseases, progressive supranu-clear palsy, communicating hydrocephalus (which some would not clas-sify as a primary dementia), and vascular dementias such as Binswanger's disease. These categories represent a rough division of dementing syn-dromes to guide further investigation.

Alzheimer's disease is the prototype of a cortical dementia and may present as impairment in an isolated cognitive domain other than mem-ory before multiple domains become affected. Also classified as a "corti-cal" dementia is Pick's disease, which has been a more complex clinicopathological construct (see below). Dementia commonly develops in Parkinson disease, a prototype of "subcortical" dementia (as does par-kinsonism in late Alzheimer's disease). In the past 12 years only, it has been discovered that a pathological hallmark of idiopathic Parkinson's disease, the Lewy body, which is a proteinaceous cellular inclusion re-stricted to the midbrain, occurs in the cerebral cortex in patients with both dementia and parkinsonism but without the pathological findings of Alzheimer's disease. This finding resulted from the use of newer immuno-histochemical staining techniques made possible by characterization of proteins in cellular inclusions and preparation of antibodies. Dementia with Lewy bodies is characterized by some unusual features in addition to the combination of dementia and parkinsonism (either may appear first) such as striking fluctuations in alertness and marked sensitivity to psychotropic medications. About half of the cases reported have had addi-tional pathology diagnostic of Alzheimer's disease. The frequency in which cortical Lewy bodies have been found suggests that dementia with Lewy bodies may be the most common form of dementia next to Alzhei-mer's disease. Incidence among persons with intellectual disability is un-known.

Recent attempts at clarifying Pick's disease and related syndromes sug-gest that a distinct group exists that has been recently designated as the "frontotemporal dementias." These forms are characterized by prominent behavioral features with frontal executive, but minimal memory impair-ment in the clinical presentation, by frontal atrophy and by combinations of cortical cell loss, ballooned neurones, proteinaceous cell inclusions called Pick bodies, and subcortical gliosis. There is a high familial inci-dence. Again, occurrences in adults with intellectual disability have not been reported.

A recently delineated dementia with clinical features similar to Alzhei-mer's disease but lacking Alzheimer pathology has sclerosis of the hippo-campus as the principal finding (Dickson et al., 1994). This has been found in elderly persons and may be associated with prominent vascular disease but not with stroke. The spectrum of dementias attributable to prion "infection" is widening with the addition of "thalamic" dementia or fatal familial insomnia (Prusiner, 1993) and possibly other inherited forms not involving mutations in the prion protein gene (Petersen et al., 1995). The occurrence of prion dementias in the various forms of intellectual disability needs elucidation.

The last form of dementia to be considered is vascular dementia. Vascular disease has long been considered a major cause of dementia, and there is no question that cognitive impairment is a common accompaniment of stroke. It is also clear that strategically located infarctions or hemorrhage can result in disabling cognitive impairment. It is much less obvious how often subtle strategically placed lesions or more diffuse lesions without infarction but resulting from vascular insufficiency are associated with syndromes of primary dementia in the absence of focal clinical phenomena suggestive of strokes. Nosology of vascular dementias may be further complicated by evidence that vascular function may be impaired in Alzheimer's disease (Thomas, Thomas, McLendon, Sutton, & Mullan, 1996). As noted earlier, both in theory and with some pathological support, adults with intellectual disability can be considered at increased risk for vascular disease and stroke. Again, this is an area in need of further investigation.

☐ Markers of Dementia

The investigation of primary dementias entails major effort in the definition of clinical–pathologic constructs. Further complicating attempts to precisely define specific dementias is the finding at postmortem that up to 40% of persons have multiple pathologies that could account for clinical dementia (Gearing, Mirra, Hedreen, Sumi, Hansen, & Heyman, 1995). A major advance in the characterization of the primary dementias has been the identification of mutant genes almost invariably accompanied by clinical and pathological Alzheimer's disease (Haass, 1996). These mutations provide biologic markers of high if not absolute specificity for forms of Alzheimer's disease. The genetic abnormality on chromosome 21 in Down's syndrome was the first marker to be detected. In addition to the absolute markers, polymorphism of another gene, the apo E gene, confers either susceptibility or resistance to Alzheimer's disease (Strittmatter & Roses, 1995). Thus, the clinical–pathological phenotype currently defined as Alzheimer's disease develops through the action of several different pathogenetic mechanisms. Identification of specific markers represents essential steps to the further clarification of clinical–pathological constructs of dementia.

☐ Diagnosis

A decline in behavior or cognition in adults with intellectual disability prompting suspicion of dementia will fall into one of three general categories: new neurologic disorders, including primary dementias; manifestations of delayed progression of the disorder that caused intellectual disability in the first place; and episodic manifestations of the primary disorder that continue to occur into adulthood.

There are special considerations in the assessment of new neurologic symptoms and signs in adults with intellectual disability. Much of the standard neurologic assessment depends on history obtained from the individuals affected. In dealing with cognitively impaired persons, we are much more dependent on history from family and care providers, and it is necessary to be persistent in obtaining this evidence. The more closely the collateral history giver is in contact with the patient, the more reliable the information. Use of video cameras is of great assistance in characterizing unusual behaviors, seizures, and intermittent movement disorders. Admission to an acute care unit for detailed monitoring is usually well tolerated and can be very informative. Because of the obstacles in obtaining a detailed history from persons with intellectual disability, a thorough physical examination assumes greater importance and, if necessary, sedation and/or anesthesia should be used to ensure the examination is complete. Advances in anesthesia have greatly reduced risk, and it may be employed in persons with intellectual disability with the reservation mentioned below. Few procedures used in neurologic investigation now pose risk, and they should be used where clinically indicated, taking into account the limited clinical information about patients with intellectual disability that may be available. The superimposition of one neurologic disorder on another represents a priori a complex medical circumstance, and application of care routines, developed for uncomplicated disorders, to adults with intellectual disability could be inappropriate.

☐ Dementia Disorders Arising "De Novo"

The primary dementias are discussed above. There are also secondary dementias, many of which can be controlled or reversed. The existence of a neurologic disorder causing intellectual disability does not preclude the occurrence of a second that will aggravate the disability. In the assessment of a decline in behavior, in communication, in activity of daily living skills, or in motor function, a very large number of disorders need to be considered that are potentially controllable or reversible. A list of considerations, by no means exhaustive, is given in Table 5.2. Investigations will need to be selected with the various listed categories in mind. A baseline of blood tests to look for evidence of infection, nutritional deficiency, endocrine disturbance, and systemic organ failure should be obtained. Careful consideration should be given to brain imaging studies in these individuals, under anesthesia if necessary, since clinical assessment often will be limited as a result of the intellectual disability. The same consideration should be given to lumbar puncture for sampling of spinal fluid when infection, inflammatory, or neoplastic disorder is suspected.

☐ Childhood Disorders Progressing into Adulthood

Pathogenetic mechanisms that impair brain development may continue to operate into adulthood with protracted, apparently or actually delayed, impairment of cognitive function. These individuals may have mild or more severe disorders presenting early in life that appear to be nonprogressive as development proceeds. However, decades later it may become apparent that progression of the underlying disorder is occurring with loss of cognitive and other skills. These disorders are either genetic or infective, and the protracted nature of the latter may reflect genetic predisposition. A large number of neurogenetic diseases can follow this course, many of which can be precisely diagnosed both from the characteristic clinical syndromes with neurologic and systemic features and from morphological and biochemical/molecular markers. These disorders are not easily classified. Included are protracted forms of lysosomal storage diseases (e.g., Salla, Gaucher type 1, ganglioside storage, Niemann-Pick C, ceroid-lipofuscinosis, and mucopolysaccharide storage diseases); leukodystrophies (e.g., metachromatic and globoid cell and other leukodystrophies); and mitochondrial disorders (e.g., the mitochondrial encephalomyopathy, lactic acidosis and stroke-like episodes, (MELAS) myoclonus epilepsy and ragged red fibres, and (MERRF) neuropathy, ataxia, and retinitis pigmentosa (NARP) syndromes; these syndromes are seen with mutations in the mitochondrial genome). For other neurogenetic-metabolic disorders such as phenylketonuria, homocystinuria, and Lesch–Nyhan and Coffin–Lowry syndromes there is little information about the natural history in adulthood to guide the clinician who encounters them first in later life.

There is one well-defined example of an infection contracted in utero that results in multiple developmental disabilities and that may persist or

---

TABLE 5.2.   Secondary causes of dementia

---

1. Physical trauma— chronic subdural hematoma, radiation encephalopathy
2. Infection
    (a) Bacterial— tuberculosis, Listeriosis, syphilis, Lyme disease, Whipples's disease
    (b) Fungal—cryptococcal meningitis, coccidiomycosis, histoplasmosis, etc.
    (c) Parasitic—toxoplasmosis, cysticercosis
    (d) Viral—progressive multifocal leukoencephalopathy, HIV
3. Other inflammatory disorders—Behcet's disease, thrombotic thrombocytopenic purpura, sarcoid
4. Nutritional, metabolic, toxic
    (a) Nutritional—deficiency of B12, folate, niacin, thiamine
    (b) Endocrine—dysfunction of thyroid, parathyroid, and adrenal glands
    (c) Systemic organ failure—chronic hepatic, renal or pulmonary failure, cerebral hypoxia
    (d) Prescribed drugs—psychotropic, anticholinergic, anticonvulsants, anti-Parkinson agents
    (e) Alcohol and illicit drugs
5. Neoplastic lesions—tumor, meningeal carcinomatosis, lymphoma
6. Vascular disorders (several inflammatory disorders are mainly vascular)
    (a) Recurrent embolization
    (b) Vasculitis—primary or associated with collagen vascular disease
    (c) Cerebrovascular atherosclerosis
    (d) Binswanger's disease, hypertensive encephalopathy
    (e) Amyloid angiopathy
    (f) Cerebral autosomal dominant arteriopathy with subcortical infarcts and leukoencephalopathy (CADASIL)
7. Multifactorial—communicating hydrocephalus

---

reactivate in adulthood. This is the congenital rubella syndrome which, in rare instances, will go on to a protracted encephalitis (progressive rubella panencephalitis) with dementia, seizures, and declining motor functions appearing 20 to 30 years later (Wolinsky, 1988).

☐   Episodic Disorders Continuing into Adulthood

The third category to be considered in the differential diagnosis of late cognitive decline in adults with intellectual disability includes those complications of the primary pathological process that present with episodic cognitive disturbances. Considered here are seizures and the therapy thereof, hydrocephalus, hypothermia, and depression.

Epilepsy is a very common manifestation of disorders, causing neurodevelopmental disorders, and the more severe the pathology, the more severe the seizures are likely to be. Uncontrolled convulsive attacks that are accompanied by asphyxia and metabolic acidosis pose a risk for incremental brain damage and deterioration of cognitive function.

Atypical clinical seizure patterns are to be anticipated in adults with neurodevelopmental disorder. Absence and partial complex seizures can be interpreted as episodes of confusion by care providers. The identification of these seizure patterns will often be hampered by the inability of affected individuals to describe the subjective experiences of their attacks. Indeed, by definition, it is only possible to make a diagnosis of partial complex epilepsy with a history of the subjective symptoms. However, subjective components of the seizure pattern may sometimes be inferred from behavior. Careful observation, sometimes with video or video-electroencephalography monitoring may be necessary.

Some adults with intellectual disability are skilled at mimicking seizures, and it may be very difficult to distinguish these "pseudoseizures" from true seizures. Video monitoring is essential to making this differentiation since the coincidence of both pseudo- and true seizures is very common, particularly in persons with intellectual disability. Repeated or prolonged convulsive seizures with rapid recovery unaccompanied by injury are likely to be pseudoseizures.

A common cause of cognitive and physical decline in persons with intellectual disability and epilepsy is toxicity from antiseizure drugs. These individuals are at particular risk for several reasons. In order to control intractable seizures, it is often necessary to escalate the dose of medication to the point where side effects appear. Agents for which efficacy is well established have specific side effects accompanied by confusion that are more likely to occur in individuals with intellectual disability. Carbamazepine can induce the syndrome of inappropriate secretion of antidiuretic hormone with hyponatremia, and valproic acid can induce hyperammonemia. Those most handicapped are most likely to have seizures that are difficult to treat and are most likely to have unusual responses to drugs, suggesting altered metabolism.

A commonly encountered issue in individuals with hydrocephalus, shunted or not, is whether cognitive or motor decline reflects increased intracranial tension. The more common presentation of an obstructed shunt is inattentiveness and deteriorating gait, often a festinating gait. If more detailed assessment is possible, the cognitive changes found are those of "subcortical" dementia. Late shunting of either obstructive or communicating hydrocephalus is usually followed by formation of subdural hematomas which pose a risk of enlargement and brainstem compression.

Another cause of recurring decline in function is hypothermia. A rare cause of severe spontaneous hypothermia is the Shapiro syndrome, which includes absence of the corpus callosum. The hypothermia is thought to result from an insensitive hypothalamic thermostat that fails to shut off sweating when the ambient temperature drops. A similar predisposition to hypothermia from defective hypothalamic regulation is probably more common among individuals who are severely impaired than the literature suggests and is a phenomenon that warrants further study (Chaney & Olmstead, 1994). Hypothyroidism and recurrent infection are to be ruled out as causes of hypothermia, the latter an unusual paradoxical response. Unrecognized recurring partial bowel obstruction from kinking of bowel, chronic constipation, or incomplete volvulus is a cause of lethargy that may be mistaken for persisting cognitive decline (Jancar & Speller, 1994).

A final and important consideration in the differential diagnosis of declining skills in communication, activities of daily living, and in motor function in persons with intellectual disability is psychiatric disorder ("dual diagnosis"). The psychomotor retardation in depression can be very difficult to distinguish from dementia (see Burt, this volume). Investigation and management of suspected dementia is optimally pursued as a collaboration of neurology, psychiatry, and geriatrics with essential contributions from neuropsychology and social services. These liaisons are often well established for persons with intellectual disability. Occasionally, after thorough investigation, a loss of skills cannot be attributed to any of the above causes and appears to reflect the effect of aging on a marginally maintained critical function.

☐ Commentary

Over the past 30 years, there has been major advance in understanding and management of dementia occurring in adults without prior neurologic disorder. Based on current understanding of dementing disorders, it is inherently plausible to suggest that adults with intellectual disability will be at increased risk for dementia. Among these persons, Down's syndrome serves as a prototype for dementia intervening in adulthood. However, there is little information about incidence and predisposition or resistance to various dementias in other forms of disability. Studies of aging and dementia in these other forms of intellectual disability are of great interest both for the guidance in management and for the understanding of the pathobiologic background to neurodevelopmental disorders and of the dementias of later life that they can provide. In the neurological investigation of dementia and intellectual disability, special considerations pertain. Particular care in obtaining collateral history, attention to need for investigative procedures, and awareness of special predispositions in the differential diagnosis of cognitive, behavioral, and motor decline are warranted.

☐ References

Bodhireddy, S., Dickson, D. W., Mattiace, L., & Weidenheim, K. M. (1994). A case of Down's syndrome with diffuse Lewy body disease and Alzheimer's disease. *Neurology, 44,* 159–161.

Breteler, M. M. B., Claus, J. J., van Duijn, C. M., Launer, L. J., & Hofman, A. (1992). Epidemiology of Alzheimer's disease. *Epidemiology Reviews, 14,* 59–82.

Brugge, K. L., Nichols, S. L., Salmon, D. P., Hill, L. R., Delis, D. C., Aaron, L., & Trauner, D. A. (1994). Cognitive impairment in adults with Down's syndrome. *Neurology, 44,* 232–238.

Brun, A., Gustafson, L., Passant, U., Mann, D. M. A., Neary, D., & Snowden, J. S. (1994). Clinical and neuropathological criteria for frontotemporal dementia. *Journal of Neurology, Neurosurgery and Psychiatry, 57,* 416–418.

Chaney, R. H., & Olmstead, C. E. (1994). Hypothalamic dysthermia in persons with brain damage. *Brain Injury, 8,* 475–481.

Cole, G., Neal, J. W., Fraser, W. I., & Cowie, V. A. (1994). Autopsy findings in patients with mental retardation. *Journal of Intellectual Disability Research, 38,* 9–26.

Collacott, R. A., Cooper, S. A., & Ismail I. A. (1994). Multi-infarct dementia in Down's syndrome. *Journal of Intellectual Disability Research, 38,* 203–208.

Cummings, J. L., & Benson, D. F. (1992). *Dementia: A clinical approach* (2nd ed.). Boston: Butterworth-Heinemann.

Dalton, A. J., & Wisniewski, H. M. (1990). Down's syndrome and the dementia of Alzheimer's disease. *International Reviews of Psychiatry, 2,* 43–52.

Dickson, D. W., Davies, P., Bevona, C., Van Hoeven, K. H., Factor, S. M., Grober, E., Aronson, M. K., & Crystal, H. A. (1994). Hippocampal sclerosis: A common pathological feature of dementia in very old (>80 years of age) humans. *Acta Neuropathologica* (Berlin), *88,* 212–221.

Gearing, M., Mirra, S. S., Hedreen, J. C., Sumi, S. M., Hansen, L. A., & Heyman, A. (1995). The Consortium to Establish a Registry for Alzheimer's Disease (CERAD). Part X. Neuropathology confirmation of the clinical diagnosis of Alzheimer's disease. *Neurology, 45,* 461–466.

Haass, C. (1996). Presenile because of presenilin: The presenilin genes and early onset Alzheimer's disease. *Current Opinion in Neurology, 9,* 254–259.

Jancar, J., & Speller, C. J. (1994). Fatal intestinal obstruction in the mentally handicapped. *Journal of Intellectual Disability Research, 38,* 413–422.

Katzman, R. (1993). Education and the prevalence of dementia and Alzheimer's disease. *Neurology, 43,* 13–20.

Lynch, M. W., Rutecki, P. A., & Sutula, T. P. (1996). The effects of seizures on the brain. *Current Opinion in Neurology. 9,* 97–102.

McKeith, I. G., Galasko, D., Kosaka, K., Perry, E. K., Dickson, D. W., Hanson, L. A., Salmon, D. P., Lowe, J., Mirra, S. S., Byrne, E. J., Quinn, N. P., Edwardson, J. A., Ince, P. G., Bergeron, C., Burns, A., Miller, B. L., Lovestone, S., Collerton, D., Jansen, E. N. H., de Vos, R. A. I., Wilcock, G. K., Jellinger, K. A., & Perry, R. H. (1995). Clinical and pathological diagnosis of dementia with Lewy bodies (DLB): Report on the CDLB Workshop, Newcastle upon Tyne, UK, October 1995.

McKhann, G., Drachman, D., Folstein, M., Katzman, R., Price, D., & Stadlan, E. M. (1984). Clinical diagnosis of Alzheimer's disease: Report of the NINCDS-ADRDA Work Group under the auspices of Department of Health and Human Services Task Force on Alzheimer's disease. *Neurology, 34,* 939–944.

Petersen, R. B., Tabaton, M., Chen, S. G., Monari, L., Richardson, S. L., Lynches, T., Manetto, V., Lanska, D. J., Markesbery, W. R., Currier, R. D., Autilio-Gambetti, L., Wilhelmsen, K. C., & Gambetti, P. (1995). Familial progressive subcortical gliosis: Presence of prions and linkage to chromosome 17. *Neurology, 45,* 1062–1067.

Prusiner, S. (1993). Genetic and infectious prion diseases. *Archives of Neurology, 50,* 1129–1153.

Roman, G. C., Tatemichi, T. K., Erkinjuntti, T., Cummings, J. L., Masdeu, J. C., Garcia, J. H., Amaducci, L., Orgogozo, J. -M., Brun, A., Hofman, A., Moody, D. M., O'Brien, M. D., Yamaguchi, T., Grafman, J., Drayer, B. P., Bennett, D. A., Fisher, M., Ogata, J., Kokmen, E., Bermejo, F., Wolf, P. A., Gorelick, P. B., Bick, K. L., Pajeau, A. K., Bell, M. A., DeCarli, C., Culebras, A., Korczyn, A. D., Bogousslavsky, J., & Hartmann, A. (1993). Vascular dementia: Diagnostic criteria for research studies. Report of the NINDS-AIREN International Workshop. *Neurology, 43,* 250–260.

Strittmatter, W. J., & Roses, A. D. (1995). Apolipoprotein E and Alzheimer disease. *Proceedings of the National Academy of Science USA, 92,* 4725–4727.

Thomas, T., Thomas, G., McLendon, C., Sutton, T., & Mullan, M. (1996). t3-Amyloid-mediated vasoactivity and vascular endothelial damage. *Nature, 380,* 168–171.

Wisniewski, H. M., Silverman, W., & Wegiel, J. (1994). Ageing, Alzheimer disease and mental retardation. *Journal of Intellectual Disability Research, 38,* 233–239.

Wolinsky, J. S. (1988). Rubella virus and its effects on the developing nervous system. In R. T. Johnson & G. Lyon (Eds.), *Viral Infections of the Developing Nervous System* (pp. 125–142). Lancaster, UK: MTP.

Associated Medical Aspects

Timely recognition and treatment of treatable physical conditions are important to prevent or delay functional deterioration in old age. However, the diagnosis of such conditions in people with intellectual disability is often hampered by the lack of self-report or atypical presentation of symptoms, the necessity to use modified diagnostic methods, and the physician's lack of knowledge and experience with these people. This chapter addresses the relevant conditions of old age and their frequencies in older people with intellectual disability, factors contributing to insufficient detection of these conditions, and recommendations for prevention and timely diagnosis, by means of health education for children and young adults with intellectual disabilities, guidelines and supports for general practitioners, screening programs, and advice on the design and illumination of homes. This service might be provided by specially trained general physicians and paramedics in regional expert teams and structured collaboration with specialist centers.

The presence of three copies of chromosome 21 in persons with Down's syndrome is universally regarded as a risk factor for the premature development of Alzheimer's disease. However, the dementia which is normally associated with Alzheimer's disease does not develop as frequently as expected. Older individuals with intellectual disabilities without Down's syndrome appear to develop Alzheimer's disease with no greater frequency than is found in the general population without intellectual disabilities (Evenhuis, 1997a). For these persons, dementia generally begins

Address correspondence to: Heleen M. Evenhuis, M.D., Ph.D., Hooge Burch, P.O. Box 2027, 2470 AA Zwammerdam, the Netherlands.

103

to occur around 65 and 75 years of age, whereas for those with Down's syndrome onset occurs between 50 to 60 years of age (e.g., Visser, Aldenkamp, van Huffelen, Kuilman, Overweg, & van Wijk, 1997). The differences in the risks, frequency, and clinical expression of dementia for persons with intellectual disabilities with and without Down's syndrome pose unique problems for the physician who is asked to conduct an assessment, reach a diagnosis, and make appropriate recommendations. This chapter will review some of these issues. It is beyond the scope of this chapter to examine all potentially relevant aspects. Thus, the reader is referred to a comprehensive text that has examined the relationship between Down's syndrome and Alzheimer's disease (Berg, Karlinsky, & Holland, 1993) and one that reports on the medical conditions that can affect individuals with Down's syndrome at any age (Pueschel & Solga, 1992).

The symptoms of dementia in persons with intellectual disabilities, with and without Down's syndrome, may be obscured for a considerable time by the simultaneous occurrence of physical, psychiatric, and other conditions. The behavioral consequences of depression, severe mobility impairments, sensory losses, and a number of chronic internal conditions may also pose distractions for the diagnostician. As a result, cognitive deterioration due to dementia may not be correctly recognized. On the contrary, the observed functional deterioration may actually be due to treatable conditions but wrongly interpreted as dementia. Furthermore, the effects of other conditions not only should raise concerns about accurate diagnosis but may also compromise accuracy in estimating the age of onset and the severity and extent of symptoms that may or may not be associated with dementia. The recognition and treatment of coexisting conditions are vitally important to prevent unnecessary aggravation of the deterioration process. In particular, depressive symptoms and episodes of delirium, which frequently accompany dementia in persons with intellectual disability (Moss & Patel, 1995; Evenhuis, 1997a), may be provoked by increased isolation due to insufficient management and treatment of mobility and sensory impairments. Depression may also have a direct impact on cognitive functions (e.g., Burt, this volume).

Thus, it is recommended that a careful diagnostic procedure that includes relevant psychiatric and physical conditions associated with aging be mandatory for all persons with intellectual disability over the age of about 40 years, who show signs of functional deterioration. This chapter will examine some of the important physical impairments and conditions of old age.

TABLE 6.1.   Risk factors for visual impairment

1. Congenital
   Down's syndrome
   Inborn errors of metabolism (mucopolysaccharidoses)
   A range of specific syndromes are associated with ophthalmological abnormalities (e.g. Bardet–Biedl syndrome)
2. Pregnancy and birth
   Intrauterine damage: rubella, cytomegalovirus, toxoplasmosis, fetal alcohol syndrome
   Pre- and dysmaturity (asphyxia, cerebral hemorrhagia, retinopathy)
3. Late-onset
   Meningitis
   Tumors
   Trauma
   Asphyxia (e.g. by near-drowning)
   Conditions related to Down's syndrome
   Old age

☐ Sensory Impairments

It is generally recognized that children and adults with intellectual disabilities suffer much more often than other people from visual and hearing impairments (Janicki & Dalton, 1998; McCulloch, Sludden, McKeown, & Kerr, 1996; Rijn, 1989; van Schrojenstein Lantman-de Valk, Haveman, Maaskant, Kessels, Urlings, & Sturmans, 1994; Warburg, 1994). Tables 6.1 and 6.2 provide a summary of risk factors that may be associated with such hearing impairment and visual impairments (Evenhuis, 1997c). Several prenatal and perinatal causes of cerebral damage may result in congenital eye or ear abnormalities or damage of cerebral sensory pathways as well, which will persist throughout life. Childhood meningitis is a notorious cause of hearing damage. Children with intellectual disabilities associated with craniofacial syndromes or hereditary metabolic diseases are also at risk for congenital or early childhood sensory impairment.

Conductive hearing loss in about 40% of children and young adults with Down's syndrome as a result of chronic or recurrent middle-ear infection is well known (Brooks, Wooley, & Kanjilal, 1972; Roizen, Wolters, Nicol, & Blondis, 1993). Eye abnormalities, such as strabismus, severe refractive errors, congenital cataracts, nystagmus, and keratoconus, often result in visual impairment in persons with Down's syndrome of all ages, from infancy to advanced age (Shapiro & France, 1985; Caputo, Wagner, Reynolds, Guo, & Goel, 1989; Prasher, 1994; Woodhouse et al., 1996). Congenital and early childhood sensory impairments also have high frequencies in the population of persons with intellectual disabilities other

---

TABLE 6.2. Risk factors for hearing impairment

---

1. Congenital
>   Hereditary sensorineural hearing impairment
>   Craniofacial syndromes
>   Inborn errors of metabolism (e.g. mucopolysaccharidoses, mucolipidoses, Refsum's disease)

2. Pregnancy and birth
>   Intrauterine infection: rubella, cytomegalovirus, syphilis, toxoplasmosis
>   Ototoxic drugs
>   Hyperbilirubinemia
>   Asphyxia (pre- and dysmaturity)

3. Late-onset
>   Meningitis (especially pneumococcal)
>   Ototoxic drug use
>   Conditions related to Down's syndrome
>   Old age

---

than those with Down's syndrome. Indeed, eye abnormalities are so frequently present and so infrequently recognized, even in countries with early detection programs for young children, that specialist ophthalmological evaluation of all young children with developmental delay has been recommended (Nagtzaam, 1997). Further, many adults with Down's syndrome suffer from increasing visual loss as a result of cataracts (Eissler & Longenecker, 1962; McCulloch et al., 1996) or secondary corneal changes in keratoconus (Walsh, 1981).

With regard to hearing, chronic and recurrent middle ear infections, resulting in conductive hearing loss, often continue during adulthood, whereas occlusion of the narrow external ear canals by impacted ear wax and scales is extremely frequent in this group. Moreover, from the age of about 30 years onward, progressive inner-ear hearing loss, probably as a result of premature presbyacusis, occurs in most adults with Down's syndrome and increasingly hampers their understanding of speech, thereby further impairing their communication skills (Buchanan, 1990; Evenhuis, Van Zanten, Brocaar, & Roerdinkholder, 1992).

The frequency of typical age-related sensory losses may be comparable with that in the general aging population for persons with intellectual disabilities without Down's syndrome who are aged 50 years and over (Evenhuis, 1995a; 1995b). Visual losses in this group result from increasing refractive errors, cataracts, glaucoma, and macular degeneration. However, because there is already a significant preexisting childhood impairment, the frequency and severity of visual impairments tend to be worse in the aging population with intellectual disabilities than in the population in general. In a study of 70 persons with intellectual disabilities, aged 60 years and over, it was found after correction with glasses that 18% had moderate (visual acuity ≤0.3) and 8% severe (≤0.1) visual impairment (Evenhuis, 1995a). By comparison, in one referent group (the U. S. general aging population) it was found that after optimal correction with glasses, the prevalence of *moderate* visual impairment was 0.6% in the group aged 60–69 years, and 9% in the group aged 80 years and older. The prevalence of *severe* visual impairments increases from 0.1% to 4% in these same age groups (Thielsch, Sommer, Witt, Katz, & Royall, 1990).

Other factors also contribute to impaired visual functions in aging persons with intellectual disabilities. Most have never been examined by an ophthalmologist, perhaps because referrals are not made or the individuals refuse to cooperate with the examination or are unable to do so. Still others may act so fearful that the specialist is unable to perform the assessments. As a result, optimal correction with glasses is not always feasible, especially for those with severe intellectual disabilities, dementia, or a physical illness. Many aging persons who need glasses cannot be readily persuaded to routinely wear them. Also, glaucoma may be overlooked for many years and only identified and treated in a stage of advanced visual field defects. For example, Evenhuis (Evenhuis, 1997a) reported that of the adults with intellectual disabilities and dementia in one Dutch group of 11 adults had visual functions of 0.3 units and lower.

Increasing age-related hearing losses have been reported in 35% of persons with intellectual disabilities aged 60–69 years and in 70% of those aged 70 years and older (Evenhuis, 1995b). This is comparable with frequencies reported for the general aging population living in Britain (Davis, 1991). However, hearing losses may be more severe in persons with intellectual disabilities as a result of lifelong, preexisting childhood hearing impairments and unrecognized middle ear pathology. In one longitudinal study of 11 persons with intellectual disabilities and dementia, eight had developed moderate (mean loss of 45 dB and greater) or severe (65 dB and greater) hearing losses prior to the onset of dementia (Evenhuis, 1997a). Occlusion of external ear canals by impacted ear wax in the population with intellectual disabilities is a common and frequently overlooked cause of hearing loss (Crandell & Roeser, 1993). During a recent screening of hearing function by means of oto-acoustic emissions in 155 adults with developmental ages lower than three years, removal of impacted ear wax was necessary in 55% of the individuals (Denkers & Evenhuis, 1996).

☐ Movement-Related Disorders

Mobility impairment is more frequent in aging persons with intellectual disabilities than in the aging population in general. About 30% of persons with intellectual disabilities have impaired walking capacities at 60 to 75 years of age and, after the age of 75 years, this impairment increases to around 60%. These findings have been confirmed in both institutionalized and group home residents (Day, 1987; Maaskant & Haveman, 1989; Kearny, Krishnan, & Londhe, 1993; Evenhuis, 1997b). In our longitudinal study of 11 aging persons with intellectual disabilities and dementia, four had severe mobility impairment prior to dementia and six developed it after the onset of dementia (Evenhuis, 1997a).

Many age-associated conditions such as osteoarthrosis, Parkinson's disease, stroke, hip fractures, backache, and painful foot problems also occur with varying frequency and severity among older persons with intellectual disabilities. As a result, many aging persons with intellectual disabilities need walking frames, wheel chairs, or support by others, with consequences for their social contacts, daily activities, and overall quality of life. The appearance of chronic secondary internal conditions is to be expected in older persons with intellectual disabilities and mobility impairment, including constipation, gastro-oesophageal reflux disease, deterioration of pulmonary function, coronary heart disease, and incontinence.

Dyspraxia is recognized as a frequent symptom of dementia of the Alzheimer type among aging persons from the general population. It consists of a partial loss of the ability to perform purposeful movements or skilled motor acts in the absence of paralysis, sensory loss, abnormal posture or tone, abnormal involuntary movements, incoordination, poor comprehension, or inattention (Lohr & Wisniewski, 1987). Recent reports have also appeared of reduced speech output and gait deterioration bradykinesia and difficulty in walking unaided (Prasher & Filer, 1995), in more than 80% of adults with Down's syndrome who have been clinically diagnosed with dementia of the Alzheimer type. The exact nature of the relationships between neurologic deterioration leading to mobility problems and unidentified visual impairment has not been systematically documented (Evenhuis, 1990).

☐ Internal Conditions

A variety of other medical conditions are generally present among older adults with intellectual disabilities. For example, among the participants in our study of 11 aging persons with intellectual disabilities and dementia, all suffered from chronic or recurrent, debilitating internal conditions, which mostly presented prior to the onset of dementia (Evenhuis, 1997a). Cardiovascular disease, chronic pulmonary disease, gastrointestinal conditions, and cancer seem to be as common among older people with intellectual disabilities as they are for the general population and these conditions also appear to be among the leading causes of death at this age (Evenhuis, 1997b; Janicki, Dalton, Henderson, & Davidson, 1996, in press).

Cardiovascular Disease.   It is generally recognized that about one-third of adults age 60 and older have cardiovascular disease both in the population with and among those without intellectual disabilities. Smoking, obesity, and physical inactivity are also recognized as risk factors in persons with intellectual disabilities, especially among those living in the community (Rimmer, Braddock, & Fujiura, 1994). The frequency of coronary heart disease in people with Down's syndrome has not been systematically studied or reported. Lower frequencies of such diseases may be expected due to the shorter life expectancy in this group and lower age-related blood pressure rates than in the general population. On the other hand, a relatively high frequency of cardiac valve pathology in this group might predispose to heart failure (Prasher, 1994).

Chronic Pulmonary Disease.   This frequent condition is associated mainly with smoking. However, the effects of "passive smoking" by non-smoking persons must also be kept in mind, because older persons with intellectual disabilities usually have been living in groups for several decades where smoking by others may have been common. Moreover, undetected recurrent aspiration as a result of gastro-oesophageal reflux or neurological swallowing problems may precipitate chronic pulmonary disease in people with mobility impairment, especially cerebral palsy (Turk, Overeynder, & Janicki, 1995). Persons with advanced dementia suffer increasingly from recurrent pneumonia, most probably as a result of aspiration which may be associated with dehydration and feeding problems in the late stage. Pneumonia is the most common immediate cause of death for persons with Alzheimer's dementia (Burns, 1992).

Gastro-Oesophageal Reflux Disease.   Improved assessment methods such as gastroscopy and intra-oesophageal pH measurement have led to the recent recognition that children and adults with intellectual disabilities are at a high risk of gastro-oesophageal reflux and secondary esophagitis. These conditions increase in frequency and severity with age (Roberts, Curtis, & Madara, 1986; Böhmer, Niezen-de Boer, Klinkenberg-Knol, Nadorp, & Meuwissen, 1996). This condition might be provoked by postural anomalies and impaired mobility and stimulated by psychotropic drug use. In our experience, reflux pain is a frequent but mostly unrecognized cause of sleeping, feeding, and behavioral problems in persons with all degrees of intellectual disabilities. Moreover, esophagitis is the underlying cause of many cases of previously unexplained chronic anemia.

Urinary Tract Infections and Incontinence.   The frequency of recurrent urinary tract infections (30%–40%) which often leads to incontinence, both in aging women and men with intellectual disabilities (Evenhuis, 1997b), is comparable with data reported on aging persons without intellectual disabilities but with chronic disabling conditions (Freedman, 1983). This may reflect increased disabilities in the older population with intellectual disabilities, compared with aging individuals from the population at large. It has to be stressed that the most frequent underlying causes (urethral stenosis, benign prostate enlargement, bladder stones, or neurological disregulation) are easily treatable, so diagnostic and therapeutic nihilism is not justified.

Chronic Constipation.   Constipation can be an underlying cause for many distressing conditions (for example, severe hemorrhoids, rectal prolapse, diverticula of the colon, acute intestinal obstruction, megacolon), which, all too frequently, necessitate surgical intervention particularly among frail, elderly persons. It affects about 50% of ambulatory and 85% of nonambulatory aging persons with intellectual disabilities (Evenhuis, 1997b). The frequent use of psychotropic and anti-epileptic drugs may play a role, as does a variety of mobility impairments.

Endocrine Disorders.   Diabetes mellitus has been reported for about 15% of individuals, and thyroid disease has been described for about 5% of older persons with intellectual disabilities. These frequencies are comparable with those reported for the general aging population. Hyperthyroidism often presents with cardiovascular and behavioral symptoms or weight loss, just like in older people without intellectual disabilities (Lazerus & Harden, 1964). However, in children and adults with Down's syndrome, thyroid disease is much more frequent than in the general population, increasing with age (Friedman, Kastner, Pond, & O'Brien, 1989). Hypothyroidism, in particular, appears to be frequently associated with functional deterioration both in young adults and in older persons with Down's syndrome and it has been implicated in those showing signs of dementia (Percy et al., 1990).

Cancer.   Cancer is a leading cause of death in aging people, and total frequencies are comparable in people with and without intellectual disabilities (Evenhuis, et al., 1996). Malignancies of the breast, lungs, large intestine, skin, and blood are the most common conditions. Women with intellectual disabilities may have a slightly elevated risk of breast cancer, probably because most of them do not bear children. Men with intellectual disabilities, as a group, have a decreased risk of pulmonary cancer, which may reflect the high percentage of nonsmokers among persons with severe and profound intellectual disabilities (Evenhuis, Oostindiër, Steffelaar, & Coebergh, 1996).

A three times elevated risk of esophageal cancer among adults with intellectual disabilities has been demonstrated in a Dutch study by Böhmer (1996). This increased cancer risk is probably the result of longstanding untreated gastro-oesophageal reflux disease in this group (Jancar, 1990; Bohmer, 1996) for reflux leads to Barrett's metaplasia in the oesophagus, a condition predisposing for carcinoma (Haggitt, Poon, & Doyle, 1994).

Although still rare among individuals with Down's syndrome, acute leukemia is frequently diagnosed in babies (Zipursky, Poon, & Doyle, 1992), and it is much more common in children and adults (Odell, 1988) compared with individuals in the general population. Further study is necessary to examine risks at older ages. It can manifest itself as tiredness, weight loss, and an overall general decline in functioning (Pary, 1992), which may be mistakenly identified as due to Alzheimer's disease. Adult cancers such as colon cancer seem to occur at the same rates as in the general population. Breast and cervical cancer in adults with Down's syndrome may occur less commonly than in the general population (Oster, Mikkalsen, & Nielsen, 1975).

☐ Diagnostic and Therapeutic Considerations

Failure to correctly identify impairments in sensory functions, as well as relevant internal conditions, is frequently attributed to highly variable language, communication, and self-reporting skills among adults with intellectual disabilities. The lack of self-reporting capabilities and spontaneous complaints are potentially particularly damaging to the establishment of adequate diagnosis and introducing adequate care management. To judge from the absence of such complaints, it appears that a wide array of conditions are tolerated, including marked visual impairments, hearing losses, chest pains, dyspnea, dyspepsia, arthritic pain, or micturition problems. Alertness is required by the physician because the symptoms can also be expressed atypically in the form of irritability, inactivity, loss of appetite or sleeping problems, or, in elderly persons, as functional deterioration. For the same reasons, symptoms are not easily recognized or identified by the family or other caregivers. These health problems, therefore, seldom receive the prompt medical attention that would be normally required (Wilson & Haire, 1990; Beange, McElduff, & Baker, 1995).

Finally, the work of physicians may be hampered also by the lack of comprehension and/or cooperation among persons with intellectual disabilities, which can be aggravated to a great extent by the onset of dementia. Therefore, the use of modified diagnostic methods is essential to achieve reliable results. Fortunately, new and useful resources are rapidly becoming more numerous and available. Recent advances have made the assessment of visual and hearing function much easier with persons with intellectual disabilities. Visual functions can now be measured more effectively using methods that were originally developed for infants and children. Among the best examples are the Stycar or LH vision tests or acuity card methods (Sheridan, 1981; Hyvärinen et al., 1992; Mackie & McCulloch, 1995; McCulloch, Sludden, McKeown, & Kerr, 1996), adapted methods for subjective audiometry including play audiometry, visual reinforcement audiometry, or behavioral response audiometry (Fulton & Lloyd, 1975), objective audiometry-like oto-acoustic emissions (Gorga, Stover, & Bergman, 1995; Denkers & Evenhuis, 1996), and auditory brainstem responses (van der Drift, Brocaar, & van Zanten, 1987; Maurizi, Ottaviani, & Paludetti, 1995). However, such methods are time consuming, require special equipment and experience, and are not always easily available.

Other diagnostic means are effective as well; for example, the forced oscillation method, developed for preschool children (Van de Woestijne, Desager, Duiverman, & Marchal, 1994) can be modified to measure pulmonary function among persons with moderate and severe intellectual disabilities. Diagnosis of gastro-oesophageal reflux by means of intra-oesophageal pH measurement is not always readily available, and this procedure is associated with some discomfort.

☐   Incomplete Diagnostic Efforts

In most countries, medical care is largely provided to persons with intellectual disabilities by physicians in the community. Most of them lack the necessary experience with this group. Only in a few countries, like the Netherlands, Belgium, the United Kingdom, and Finland, do physicians receive specialized training to work with this group. The lack of local physicians with specialized training means that reliance must be placed on scarce and regional resources. However, such regional resources or teams do not usually include physicians with knowledge of specific risk factors and atypical presentation of symptoms among older persons with intellectual disabilities. As a result, the quality of medical care for older people with intellectual disabilities is dependent on the individual preferences and experience of physicians and therefore the availability of appropriate services will be infrequent and/or inadequate (Strauss & Kastner, 1996). Further, aging persons with intellectual disabilities and functional decline in many countries are mainly referred for diagnostic evaluation to psychologists who do not have the training or expertise to diagnose or recognize the significance of undetected medical conditions. As a result, they may fail to make appropriate referrals for essential medical evaluations. This is an area that begs for remedy.

☐ Recommendations

People with intellectual disabilities and mild or moderate childhood mobility impairments do not always get regular specialist medical attention. Secondary effects on the motor system (arthrosis, postural problems) are therefore not anticipated or prevented. Moreover, their diagnosis may be delayed because many of these adults do not report pain or express their discomfort by behavioral problems. As a result, a rapid deterioration of ambulation skills may occur at any time during middle to old age, especially when visual loss is also insufficiently corrected. Homes are not in many cases designed for people who need physical accommodations, such as grips everywhere, room for their walking frames and wheel chairs, and illumination that is satisfactory. Yet these are all areas that can be managed.

Sensory impairments can be found and managed. According to a recently developed Dutch standard, screening of hearing function should be performed in all children with a developmental delay and every five years in adults aged 50 years and older. In children and adults with Down's syndrome, this evaluation should be performed routinely every three years throughout life (Evenhuis et al., 1996). The Oto-acoustic Emissions, a brief and objective screening method of hearing function, can be used for this purpose (Denkers & Evenhuis, 1996). In case of hearing impairment, carers should be instructed with guidelines for communication and creation of optimal hearing circumstances. Adequate fitting of hearing aids in persons with intellectual disabilities may require specialized technical experience of audiologists. Regularly they have to base their decisions on limited or incompletely reliable audiometric data, as well as knowledge of the hearing circumstances in group homes and activity centers, which are often unfavorable (noises of group life, activities, and background music). The choice of the type of hearing aid is also dependent on its intended use: improvement of verbal communication or, such as in people with profound intellectual disabilities, identification of environmental noises. It is even more important to note that acceptance of hearing aids by people with intellectual disabilities is to a large extent dependent on the assistance and support by parents, teachers, and carers.

The risk of coronary heart disease can be managed with the emphasis placed on prevention of risk factors like hypertension, smoking, obesity, and inactivity. Yet a timely diagnosis of coronary heart disease is often hampered because most people with even mild intellectual disabilities do not report chest pain. The situation is further complicated because cardiologists are not prepared to treat persons based on electrocardiographic changes alone. A screening in British group homes of persons with intellectual disabilities revealed previously undetected hypertension (Wilson & Haire, 1990). Further, it has be observed that obesity is often badly controlled (Rimmer, Braddock, & Fujiura, 1994; Prasher, 1995). Smoking has been identified as a frequent habit among men and women with mild and moderate intellectual disabilities (Burter, Wakham, McNeal, & Garvey, 1996; Rimmer, Braddock, & Fujiura, 1994) and this, too, can be managed with intervention programs. All of these observations underscore the need for preventive measures before symptoms become apparent.

☐ Commentary

Prevention and timely detection of deteriorating physical conditions associated with aging in the population with intellectual disabilities can provide important preventive and quality of life benefits. But the process must be started at an early age. Health education for children and young adults with intellectual disabilities should be stimulated, as well as instruction and training of caregivers. Guidelines and support for general practitioners, screening programs offered by regional expert teams (e.g., of sensory impairment, pulmonary function loss, and gastro-oesophageal reflux), and the ready availability of specialized advice should improve medical care. The benefits can only be achieved by the participation of many specially trained professionals including general physicians and paramedics in regional teams for intellectual disabilities and structured cooperation with qualified specialist centers.

The diagnosis of physical conditions that may cause functional deterioration and mimic dementia should not be delayed until deterioration becomes evident. At that point, cooperation may be more difficult to obtain, especially if symptoms of dementia are already present. Moreover, the beneficial effects of treatment, such as cataract surgery in persons with Down's syndrome, may be challenged at this stage. The adoption of recently recommended diagnostic criteria for the diagnosis of dementia among persons with intellectual disabilities (Aylward, Burt, Thorpe, Lai, & Dalton, 1997; Burt & Aylward, this volume) should lead to a systematic approach to diagnosis leading, ultimately, to the best and most cost-effective treatment and management decisions possible.

In persons with intellectual disabilities who show signs of functional deterioration, treatable causes should be actively searched for by expert medical examinations and treated adequately. In this way, functional deterioration may be halted in a number of cases. The progression of dementia, as well as depressive symptoms and delirium, may be slowed by treatment of reversible "comorbid" conditions.

☐ References

Aylward, E. H., Burt, D. B., Thorpe, L. U., Lai, F., & Dalton, A. J. (1997). Diagnosis of dementia in individuals with intellectual disability. *Journal of Intellectual Disability Research, 41,* 152–164.

Beange, H., McElduff, A., & Baker W. (1995). Medical disorders of adults with mental retardation: A population study. *American Journal on Mental Retardation, 99,* 595–604.

Berg, J. M., Karlinsky, H., & Holland, A. J. (Eds.). (1993). *Alzheimer disease, Down syndrome and their relationship.* Oxford: Oxford Medical Publications.

Böhmer, C. J. M., Niezen-de Boer, M. C., Klinkenberg-Knol, E. C., Nadorp, J. H. S. M., & Meuwissen, S. G. M. (1996). The prevalence of gastroesophageal reflux (GER) and refluxesophagitis in severely mentally handicapped. *Gastroenterology, 110,* A66.

Böhmer, C. J. M. (1996). *Gastroesophageal reflux disease in intellectually disabled individuals.* Unpublished master's thesis, Free University of Amsterdam, the Netherlands.

Brooks, D. N., Wooley H., & Kanjilal, G. C. (1972). Hearing loss and middle ear disorders in patients with Down's syndrome (mongolism). *Journal of Mental Deficiency Research, 16,* 21–29.

Buchanan, L. H. (1990). Early onset of presbyacusis in Down syndrome. *Scandinavian Audiology, 19,* 103–110.

Burns, A. (1992). Cause of death in dementia. *International Journal of Geriatric Psychiatry, 7,* 461–464.

Burtner, A. P., Wakham, M. D., McNeal, D. R., & Garvey, T. P. (1995). Tobacco and the institutionalized mentally retarded: Usage choices and ethical considerations. *Special Care in Dentistry, 15*(2), 56–60.

Caputo, A. R., Wagner, R. S., Reynolds, D. R., Guo, S. Q., & Goel, A. K. (1989). Down syndrome: Clinical review of ocular features. *Clinical Pediatrics (Phila), 28,* 355–358.

Crandell, C. C., & Roeser, R. J. (1993). Incidence of excessive/impacted cerumen in individuals with mental retardation: A longitudinal investigation. *American Journal on Mental Retardation, 97,* 568–574.

Davis, A. C. (1991). Epidemiological profile of hearing impairments: The scale and nature of the problem with special reference to the elderly. *Acta Otolaryngologica* (Stockh) *476* (Suppl.), 23–31.

Day, K. A. (1987). The elderly mentally handicapped in hospital: a clinical study. *Journal of Mental Deficiency Research, 31,* 131–146.

Denkers, I. A. M., & Evenhuis, H. M. (1996). *Otacoustic emissions as a screening method for hearing function in persons with severe intellectual disabilities.* Paper presented at the 10th World Congress of the International Association for the Scientific Study of Intellectual Disability, Helsinki, Finland.

Eissler, R., & Longenecker, L. P. (1962). The common eye findings in mongolism. *American Journal of Ophthalmology, 54,* 398–406.

Evenhuis, H. M. (1990). The natural history of dementia in Down's syndrome. *Archives of Neurology, 47,* 263–267.

Evenhuis, H. M. (1995a). Medical aspects of ageing in a population with intellectual disabilities: I. Visual impairment. *Journal of Intellectual Disability Research, 39,* 19–25.

Evenhuis, H. M. (1995b). Medical aspects of ageing in a population with intellectual disabilities: II. Hearing impairment. *Journal of Intellectual Disability Research, 39,* 27–33.

Evenhuis, H. M., on behalf of the consensus committee (1996). Dutch consensus on diagnosis and treatment of hearing loss in children and adults with intellectual disabilities. *Journal of Intellectual Disability Research, 40,* 451–456.

Evenhuis, H. M. (1997a). The natural history of dementia in ageing people with intellectual disabilities. *Journal of Intellectual Disability Research, 41,* 92–96.

Evenhuis, H.,M. (1997b). Medical aspects of ageing in a population with intellectual disabilities: III. Mobility, internal conditions and cancer. *Journal of Intellectual Disability Research, 41,* 8–18

Evenhuis, H. M., Mul, M., Lemaire, E. K. G., de Wijs, J. P. M. (1997c). Diagnosis of sensory impairment in people with intellectual disability in general practice. *Journal of Disability Research, 41,* 422–429.

Evenhuis, H. M., Oostindiër, M. J., Steffelaar, J. W., Coebergh, J. W. W. (1996). Incidentie van kanker bij mensen met een verstandelijke handicap (Cancer incidence in people with intellectual disabilities). *Nederlands Tijdschrift voor Geneeskunde, 42,* 2083–2087.

Evenhuis, H. M., van Zanten, G. A., Brocaar, M. P., & Roerdinkholder, W. H. M. (1992). Hearing loss in middle-age persons with Down syndrome. *American Journal on Mental Retardation, 97,* 47–56.

Freedman, L. R. (1983). Urinary-tract infections in the elderly. *New England Journal of Medicine, 309,* 1451–1452.

Friedman, D. L., Kastner, T., Pond, W. S., & O'Brien, R. D. (1989). Thyroid dysfunction in individuals with Down syndrome. *Archives of Internal Medicine, 149,* 1990–1993.

Fulton, R., & Lloyd, L. (1975). *Auditory assessment of the difficult-to-test.* Baltimore: Williams & Wilkins.

Gorga, M. P., Stover, L., & Bergman, B. M. (1995). The application of Otacoustic Emissions (OAEs) in the assessment of developmentally delayed patients. *Scandinavian Audiology, 24* (Suppl. 41), 8–17.

Haggitt, R. C. (1994). Barrett's esophagus, dysplasia, and adenocarcinoma. *Human Pathology, 25,* 982–993.

Hyvrinen, L., Colenbrander, A., & Mayer, L. (1992). *The LH Symbol Tests (Manual).* Long Island, NY: The Lighthouse Inc.

Jancar, J. (1990) Cancer and mental handicap: A further study (1976–85). *British Journal of Psychiatry, 156,* 531–533.

Janicki, M. P. & Dalton, A. J. (1998). Sensory impairments among older adults with intellectual disability. *Journal of Intellectual and Developmental Disabilities, 23,* 3–11.

Janicki, M. P., Dalton, A. J., Henderson, M., & Davidson, P. W. (in press). Mortality and morbidity among older adults with intellectual disabilities: Health services considerations. *Disability and Rehabilitation*.

Janicki, M. P., Dalton, A. J., Henderson, M., & Davidson, P. W. (1996). *Deaths among adults with mental retardation: Demographic and policy considerations.* Paper presented at the 10th World Congress of the International Association for the Scientific Study of Intellectual Disability, Helsinki, Finland.

Kearny, G. M., Krishnan, V. H. R., & Londhe, R. L. (1993). Characteristics of elderly people with a mental handicap living in a mental handicap hospital: A descriptive study. *The British Journal of Developmental Disabilities, 39,* 31–50.

Lai, F., & Williams, R. S. (1989). A prospective study of Alzheimer disease in Down syndrome. *Archives of Neurology, 46,* 849–853.

Lazerus, J. J., & Harden, R. M. (1964). Thyrotoxicosis in the elderly. *Gerontology Clinics, 11,* 371–375.

Lohr, J. B., & Wisniewski, A. A. (1987). *Movement disorders: A neuropsychiatric approach.* New York: Guilford Press.

Maaskant, M. A., & Haveman, M. J. (1989). Aging residents in sheltered homes for persons with mental handicap in the Netherlands. *Australia and New Zealand Journal of Developmental Disabilities, 15,* 219–230.

Mackie, R. T., & McCulloch, D. L. (1995). Assessment of visual acuity in multiply handicapped children. *British Journal of Ophthalmology, 79,* 290–296.

Maurizi, M., Ottaviani, F., & Paludetti, G. (1995). Objective methods of hearing assessment: An introduction. *Scandinavian Audiology, 24* (Suppl. 41), 5–7.

McCulloch, D. L., Sludden, P. A., McKeown, K., & Kerr, A. (1996). Vision care requirements among intellectually disabled adults: A residence-based pilot study. *Journal of Intellectual Disability Research, 40,* 140–150.

Moss, S., & Patel, P. (1995). Psychiatric symptoms associated with dementia in older people with learning disabilities. *British Journal of Psychiatry, 167,* 663–667.

Nagtzaam, L. M. D. (Ed). (1997). Richtlijnen voor diagnostiek en hehandeling van visuele stoornissen bij verstandelijk gehandicapten (Consensus on diagnosis and treatment of visual impairment in people with intellectual disability). Utrecht, the Netherlands: NVAZ.

Odell, J. D. (1988). Medical considerations. In C. Tingey (Ed.) *Down syndrome: A resource handbook* (pp. 33–45). Boston: College Hill.

Oster, J., Mikkalsen, M., & Nielsen, A. (1975). Mortality and life-table in Down's syndrome. *Acta Pediatrica Scandinavica, 64,* 322.

Pary, R. (1992). Differential diagnosis of functional decline in Down's syndrome. *Habilitative Mental Healthcare Newsletter, 11*(6), 37–41.

Percy, M. E., Dalton, A. J., Markovic, V. D., Crapper-McLachlan, D. R., Gera, E., Hummel, J. T., Rusk, A. C. M., Somerville, H. J., Andrews, D. F., & Walfish, P. E. (1990). Autoimmune thyroiditis associated with mild "subclinical" hypothyroidism in adults with Down syndrome: A comparison with and without manifestations of Alzheimer disease. *American Journal of Medical Genetics, 36,* 148–154.

Prasher, V. P. (1994). Screening of medical problems in adults with Down syndrome. *Down's Syndrome Research and Practice, 2,* 59–63.

Prasher, V. P. (1995). Overweight and obesity amongst Down's syndrome adults. *Journal of Intellectual Disability Research, 39,* 437–441.

Prasher, V. P., & Filer, A. (1995). Behavioural disturbance in people with Down's syndrome and dementia. *Journal of Intellectual Disability Research, 39,* 432–436.

Pueschel, S. M., & Solga, P. M. (Eds.). (1992). *Biomedical concerns in persons with Down Syndrome.* Baltimore: Paul H. Brookes.

Rimmer, J. H., Braddock, D., & Fujiura, G. (1994). Cardiovascular risk factor levels in adults with mental retardation. *American Journal on Mental Retardation, 98,* 510–518.

Roberts, I. M., Curtis, R. L., & Madara, J. L. (1986). Gastroesophageal reflux and Barrett's esophagus in developmentally disabled patients. *American Journal of Gastroenterology, 81,* 519–523.

Roizen, N. J., Wolters, C., Nicol, T., & Blondis, T. A. (1993). Hearing loss in children with Down syndrome. *Journal of Pediatrics, 123,* S9–12.

Shapiro, M. B., & France, T. D. (1985). The ocular features of Down's syndrome. *American Journal of Ophthalmology, 99,* 659–663.

Sheridan, M. D. (1981). *Manual for the Stycar Vision Tests.* Windsor, UK: NFER-Nelson.

Strauss, D., & Kastner, T. A. (1996). Comparative mortality of people with mental retardation in institutions and the community. *American Journal on Mental Retardation, 101,* 26–40.

Thielsch, J. M., Sommer, A., Witt, K., Katz, J., & Royall, R. M. (1990). Blindness and visual impairment in an American urban population. *Archives of Ophthalmology, 108,* 286–290.

Turk, M. A., Overeynder, J. C., & Janicki, M. P. (Eds.). (1995). Uncertain future—aging and cerebral palsy: Clinical concerns. Albany: New York State Developmental Disabilities Planning Council.

van der Drift, J. F. V., van der Brocaar, M. P., & van Zanten, G. A. (1987). The relation between the pure tone audiogram and the click auditory brainstem response threshold in cochlear hearing loss. *Audiology, 26,* 1–10.

van de Woestijne, K. P., Desager, K. N., Duiverman, E. J., & Marchal, F. (1994). Recommendations for measurement of respiratory input impedance by means of the forced oscillation method. *European Respiratory Review, 19,* 235–237.

van Rijn, P. M. (1989). Causes of early childhood deafness. Unpublished master's thesis, Nijmegen University, the Netherlands.

Van Schrojenstein Lantman-de Valk, H. M. J., Haveman, M. J., Maaskant, M. A., Kessels, A. G. H., Urlings, H. F. J., & Sturmans, F. (1994). The need for assessment of sensory functioning in ageing people with mental handicap. *Journal of Intellectual Disability Research, 38,* 289–298.

Visser, F. E., Aldenkamp, A. P., van Huffelen, A. C., Kuilman, M., Overweg, J., & van Wijk, J. (1997). Prospective study of the prevalence of Alzheimer-type dementia in institutionalized individuals with Down syndrome. *American Journal on Mental Retardation, 101,* 400–412.

Walsh, S. Z. (1981). Keratoconus and blindness in 469 institutionalized subjects with Down syndrome and other causes of mental retardation. *Journal of Mental Deficiency Research, 25,* 243–251.

Warburg, M. (1994). Visual impairment among people with developmental delay. *Journal of Intellectual Disability Research, 38,* 423–432.

Wilson, D. N. & Haire, A. (1990). Health care screening for people with mental handicap living in the community. *British Medical Journal, 301,* 1379–1381.

Woodhouse, J. M., Pakeman, V. H., Saunders, K. J., Parker, M., Fraser, W. I., Lobo, S., & Sastry, P. (1996). Visual acuity and accommodation in infants and young children with Down's syndrome. *Journal of Intellectual Disability Research, 40,* 49–55.

Zipursky, A., Poon, A., & Doyle, J. (1992). Leukemia in Down syndrome: A review. *Pediatric Hematological Oncology, 9,* 139–149.

3

ASSESSMENT CONSIDERATIONS

Taken together, the chapters in this section provide a comprehensive picture of the requirements for a valid and reliable assessment and diagnosis of dementia. At the same time, they provide in-depth analyses in several of the key areas of functioning that are inevitably affected by the onset and progression of dementia. We begin this section with a contribution by Oliver who presents a thorough and cautionary tale of the pitfalls and complexities of evaluating an adult with intellectual disabilities who is suspected of suffering from cognitive impairment. Is it dementia or is it some other condition or process? Oliver answers these and related questions by placing the spotlight on the contributions of neuropsychological testing to the evaluation and assessment of dementia in the presence of preexisting mental impairments, particularly those associated with intellectual disabilities. He recognizes, as do the other contributors to this section, that aging individuals with intellectual disabilities are difficult to evaluate because of their relatively low levels and wide heterogeneity in intellectual abilities, memory, and related functions. Many will show or develop varying degrees of visual and auditory impairments combined with a host of other age-associated conditions that will lower test scores leading to possible false diagnosis of dementia. Limited receptive and expressive language and reading skills greatly reduce the production of informed self-reports that would normally provide one of the most important and useful sources of data for diagnosis. Oliver defines the major problems and then examines the two major assessment strategies, retrospective and longitudinal, outlining the positive and negative features of both in the context of direct assessment and informant-based methods. Issues of reliability and validity as well as ethical considerations are underscored in this highly thought-provoking chapter.

The chapter by Burt and Aylward singles out the criteria for diagnosis of dementia for special attention. Without such criteria the effectiveness of care plans, management strategies, and interventions will be greatly reduced. They recognize that one of the most enduring and pressing problems is the absence of generally accepted criteria for the diagnosis of dementia and Alzheimer's disease among persons with intellectual disabilities. The existing criteria are silent where persons with intellectual disabilities are concerned. Burt and Aylward address these issues from the perspective of a series of resolutions and recommendations adopted after a series of meetings by an internationally recognized workgroup composed of clinicians and scientists who have been working in the field of intellectual disabilities. They describe and elaborate on the implications and application of the five criteria that have been proposed. These are a decline in memory, a decline in other cognitive abilities, an absence of clouding of consciousness, a decline in control of motivation, emotion and social behaviors, and a decline in memory and other cognitive functions of at least six months. The authors then examine the existing neuropsychological tests that may be appropriate for determining cognitive and other changes in function. These represent substantial contributions to the enhancement of the assessment and evaluation activities of clinical psychologists and other professionals engaged in practice with aging adults with intellectual disabilities.

In the last chapter, Prasher explores the literature from the perspective of assessing what has been said about adaptive behavior and reviews existing tests and ratings scales available for the assessment of adaptive behaviors from the perspective of their increasingly important role in differential diagnosis of dementia. He provides a detailed analysis of the relevant research literature that greatly facilitates the appreciation of the complex issues involved. The author also provides a research perspective on the limitations of retrospective approaches versus longitudinal evaluations. This contribution's focus on adaptive behavior reflects the particular importance of this dimension in the use of the recommended criteria for diagnosis of dementia and Alzheimer's disease in persons with intellectual disabilities.

7

CHAPTER   *Chris Oliver*

Perspectives on Assessment and Evaluation

The assessment of dementia in the presence of preexisting mental impairment presents significant problems for clinicians and researchers alike. The factors that contribute to the difficulties associated with assessment and the interpretation of results are reviewed. It is concluded that the level and variability of intellectual disability have both militated against the use of existing neuropsychological tests and promoted the use of informant-based interviews. However, more recently, neuropsychological tests have been developed that can be employed for individuals with severe mental retardation by using paradigms that ensure assessment integrity. This development is likely to enhance the reliability and validity of the assessment process. Alongside this trend, consideration needs to be given to the general strategy adopted for the assessment of dementia in the presence of intellectual disability. Whilst for the majority of individuals with intellectual disability retrospective assessment will probably prevail, for those who have Down's syndrome the high risk of an acquired dementia justifies a prospective strategy. It is proposed that serial assessments for persons who have Down's syndrome over the age of 35 should be conducted, with a decreasing interval between assessments over time.

Address correpondence to: Chris Oliver, Ph.D., School of Psychology, University of Birmingham, Edgbaston, Birmingham, United Kingdom, UK B15 2TT.

The assessment of dementia in adults with intellectual disabilities presents significant problems to both clinicians and researchers. Many of these problems arise from the variability in the degree of intellectual disabilities and the cognitive impairments associated with profound and severe intellectual disabilities (Oliver & Holland, 1986). These factors have immediate effects on the administration of assessments as well as indirect effects on the reliability and validity of the results of cognitive assessments. Severe and profound intellectual disabilities are usually associated with floor effects for most cognitive assessments. This problem is particularly relevant to the assessment of the early stages of dementia, when the cognitive signs may be subtle, for example, memory loss for recent events. Those individuals who have a greater degree of intellectual disabilities may have experienced lifelong difficulties in some or all cognitive domains that are compromised in dementia and, consequently, it may not be assumed that assessments necessarily indicate the recent development of a cognitive impairment.

At a more pragmatic level, a profound degree of intellectual disabilities means that trustworthy results of cognitive examinations are unlikely with persons who are nonverbal and unable to understand or to comply with language-laden test instructions. A more indirect effect of the degree of intellectual disabilities is that it may contribute to the masking of the early signs of dementia because of "diagnostic overshadowing." As persons with a greater degree of intellectual disabilities are likely to be in services in which a care culture is prominent, then cognitive and behavioral deficits acquired over time may simply be absorbed by the service in the same way that deficits of adaptive behavior associated with intellectual disabilities are managed. Consequently, any change in cognitive and behavioral status is masked.

The cumulative effect of these problems is an increased reliance on informant-based assessments. There are problems associated with any informant-based assessments that are usually manifest in indices of reliability and validity. However, for the assessment of an acquired dementia in the presence of preexisting cognitive impairments, these problems are exacerbated. Older adults with intellectual disabilities are more likely to be in residential services, as families are increasingly unable to offer support at home. This means that the informant will usually be a member of care staff. There are two consequences that then arise. First, the best informants (parents and family) on the past abilities of someone with intellectual disabilities may not be available. Second, there is generally a high rate of staff turnover in residential services for persons with intellectual disabilities. This means that staff may only have known the person with intellectual disabilities for a brief period of time. This is particularly problematic for the assessment of the early stage of dementia where changes are slow and subtle. These changes are frequently missed unless someone has known the individual well and for some time.

There are also problems that arise from staff expectations based on the prevailing "care culture" and the level of knowledge about Alzheimer's disease and Down's syndrome. It might lead to an underreporting of treatable conditions such as depression and an overreporting of dementia. For example, staff may expect functional changes to occur at specific ages for those with Down's syndrome to be the result of Alzheimer's disease. They may not consider or be fully alert to other possibilities such as the likelihood of changes associated with sensory losses or movement-related disorders (see Evenhuis, this volume), psychiatric (see Thorpe, this volume), or other neurological conditions (see Wherrett, this volume).

☐ Problems of Assessment

Differential diagnosis is one of the most significant problems when assessing dementia in someone with intellectual disabilities. The occurrence of changes in personally significant life events in persons who have Down's syndrome, which are likely to arise during their third and fourth decades of life, is a factor that has been greatly underrated. As there is a raised maternal age at birth for persons with Down's syndrome (Penrose, 1966), then it is more likely that parents will die during these decades. There are implications of this that relate both to bereavement and the likely change in living environment for persons with Down's syndrome. These issues may be associated with changes in behavior that are also seen in the early stages of dementia. The second problem is the effect of early institutionalization on an individual's abilities in later life. It is unclear how early institutionalization and the accompanying impoverished environments interact with cognitive ability and behavior in later life. However, it should be remembered that the early life experiences of persons with intellectual disabilities who were living in institutions may have been substantially different from those who were not institutionalized. For example, institutions until recently have been notorious for the presence of endemic hepatitis among all or nearly all of their residents (Van Schrojenstein Lantman-de Valk, Haveman, & Crebolder, 1996). Differences in exposure to other infectious agents, as well as significant differences in nutritional and health status, may also be associated with differences in risk for the development of dementia. Such possibilities are reflected in the inconsistencies evident in several recent reports of prevalence of dementia among institutionalized persons with Down's syndrome (Visser, Aldenkamp, van Huffelen, Kullman, Overweg, & van

Wijk, 1997) in comparisons with those living at home or in small group homes (Devenny, Silverman, Hill, Jenkins, Sersen, & Wisniewski, 1996).

A third general problem associated with assessing dementia in intellectual disabilities is that there is an implicit assumption in much of the research and clinical literature that the profile of decline evident in persons with intellectual disabilities is the same as that observed in persons who do not have intellectual disabilities. While there is good reason for believing that this is so, as much of the research demonstrates an acquisition of cognitive impairments which is similar (Oliver & Holland, 1986), there has perhaps not been as detailed an examination of this issue as is warranted. In the case of Down's syndrome, it is clear that before dementia occurs there are preexisting neurotransmitter and neurological differences between persons with Down's syndrome and persons who do not have Down's syndrome (Penrose, 1966; Blair & Leeming, 1984). How these differences interact with an acquired neurological change is unclear, but nevertheless the possibility that there is an interaction should challenge the assumption that the profile of acquired cognitive deterioration is the same in persons who have Down's syndrome and those with other causes of intellectual disabilities.

Perhaps the most substantial problem associated with assessing dementia in persons with intellectual disabilities is the possibility of a floor effect on a cognitive assessment which occurs with profound and severe intellectual disabilities. If an individual is unable to score at a level on a cognitive assessment that is above zero and above a level of test error, then it is not possible to use the assessment for follow-up to appraise decline. While the issue of a zero score is an obvious one, test error is equally critical. If change in scores is to be considered clinically significant, it must be greater than the size of the error, which is always a component of the test's reliability upon repeated use with the same person at different times. The problem of attributing low scores to cognitive decline, instead of the life-long intellectual disability, is more complex that it appears at first. Dramatic changes have been introduced over the past 20 to 30 years in educational and rehabilitation practices that have been provided to persons with intellectual disabilities. These practice changes could be reflected in equally dramatic changes for an individual whose cognitive functions were recorded 30 years ago and then are compared with those functions reported in place today. This "cohort effect," as it is called, will probably be evident both within cultures between times and between cultures. The variability in the degree of intellectual disabilities has been acknowledged in contemporary definitions of dementia in persons with intellectual disabilities (see Burt and Aylward, this volume). In addition, changes in the stability of normative data based on standardization samples over time may also represent another cohort effect.

The services that are available to persons with intellectual disabilities are generally based on a culture of caring for persons who have handicaps and disabilities. This promotes two problems for the assessment of dementia in persons with intellectual disabilities. First, the environments in which persons live on a day-to-day basis may be somewhat sheltered and consequently may not naturally present intellectual challenges. This may mean that the more subtle cognitive impairments, which are associated with the early stages of dementia, may not become apparent. In persons who do not have intellectual disabilities, the signs of dementia are usually initially evident because tasks need to be performed that require different cognitive processes. This situation is exacerbated when considering the various dimensions of cognitive function which include judgment, thinking, planning, organizing, and general processing of information (Aylward, Burt, Thorpe, Lai, & Dalton, 1995, 1997). If the environment does not present these intellectual challenges, then these signs may be masked. Second, even if cognitive decline is occurring over a period of time, the carers may adapt the environment to successfully meet the demands of diminishing functions of the individual in a gradual way, thereby masking the impact of any acquired cognitive deficits.

Medical and physical problems that are age associated in persons who do and persons who do not have intellectual disabilities may cause problems in the assessment of an acquired dementia (Dalton, Seltzer, Adlin, & Wisniewski, 1993; Evenhuis, this volume). These problems are particularly evident for persons with Down's syndrome because of the varied medical and physical conditions that are often associated with Down's syndrome, for example, cataracts (Van Schrojenstein Lantman-de Valk, Haveman, Maaskant, Kessels, Urlings, & Sturmans, 1994), hearing impairments (Buchanan, 1990; Evenhuis, this volume), and hypothyroidism (Lai, 1992; Prasher, 1995). These specific impairments lower test scores because of an inability to see test items correctly or to hear instructions, and not because of a dementia process. The same sensory impairments may lead to increased impairments in the skills of daily living that could incorrectly be interpreted as indicative of a dementia. This misdiagnosis is particularly likely to occur in the presence of undetected hypothyroidism (see Thase, 1982). Finally, sensory impairments themselves may directly contribute to some cognitive deterioration. The increases in sensory impairments which develop in later life among persons with Down's syndrome pose difficulties in the diagnosis of an acquired dementia such as Alzheimer's disease.

Assessment of the extent and rate of change in symptoms that takes place as dementia progresses in persons with intellectual disabilities is limited by the lack of normative data based on appropriate standardization samples. This problem is particularly acute for the evaluation of dementia in persons with Down's syndrome. There is clear evidence of age-associated physical changes such as alopecia and early menopause, signs that have been interpreted as indicative of accelerated aging. A slow change in cognitive abilities over time is normal (Selkoe, 1992). However, accelerated aging may be associated with cognitive change or with cognitive change and dementia. It may also be reflected in the appearance of a dementia alone without accelerated aging, or it could be that accelerated aging itself causes dementia. Resolution of these complex possibilities must await the results of systematic research.

Persons with greater degrees of intellectual disabilities may be unable to give sufficiently informed self-report about the cognitive and behavioral changes that they may be experiencing. This frequent situation leads to heavy reliance on the reports of others. The accuracy of such reports will be seriously affected by death of relatives, high staff turnover, unpredictable staff expectations, and the unavailability of the best informant.

To date, most of the research in the area of assessment has been derived from the study of the cognitive impairments that are seen in older adults with Down's syndrome. It is unclear whether the profile that has begun to emerge as a result of this research is equally applicable to persons with intellectual disabilities who do not have Down's syndrome. The assessment of dementia in persons with intellectual disabilities is confronted by problems arising between the interaction between preexisting and acquired neurological damage to the past and contemporary culture to which the person with intellectual disabilities is exposed. In order to offer services to persons who are developing dementia, it is important to be able to identify the early signs. It is precisely the subtlety of these signs that makes it most difficult to accurately identify dementia in persons with intellectual disabilities.

☐ Problem-Solving Strategies

There are two major strategies for addressing the problems of dementia assessment in persons with intellectual disabilities, namely, *retrospective* and *prospective strategies*. Both strategies require a prior determination of some of the properties of the assessment tests, particularly on their specificity and sensitivity. That is, how good are the tests in their applicability to persons with intellectual disability and their discernment and numerical quantification of dementia rather than other impairments? In addition, it is necessary to make a judgment about the suitability of the particular assessment method for each of the strategies. This preliminary judgment is most pertinent for persons with Down's syndrome where

TABLE 7.1.   A summary evaluation of the strategies that may be adopted for the assessment of dementia in persons with intellectual disabilities (ID).

		Reliability and Validity	Resources	Ethical Issues	Quality of Life Issues
Strategy	Prospective	High	High	Moderate	Moderate
	Retrospective	Low	Low	Substantial	Substantial
Method of Assessment	Informant Based	Low	Low	Moderate	–
	Direct	High	High	Moderate	–
Specificity of Assessment to ID and Dementia	Neither	Low	–	–	–
	Dementia Only	Low	–	–	–
	ID only	Low	–	–	–
	ID and dementia	High	–	–	–

the risk of acquiring dementia is extremely high and rises with age. An overview of some of the assessments on these dimensions is provided in Table 7.1.

The decision to adopt a retrospective assessment strategy involves review and analysis of data from past assessments that have employed generally accepted instruments used in clinical practice. This review is selectively aimed at those past assessments that have addressed cognitive abilities known to decline with dementia (such as memory, naming and related verbal skills, judgment, analytical abilities, and the like). The choice of data for analysis may also be theoretically driven. That is, data in the clinical records can be examined knowing that a particular acquired cognitive deficit is characteristic of the early expression of dementia. IQ scores might also be employed to assess global decline (see Hewitt, Carter, & Jancar, 1985; Nakamura, 1961; Fenner, Hewitt, & Torpy, 1987; Haxby, 1989) even though such scores are nonspecific to dementia and highly insensitive to subtle early changes in function. Similarly, a review of all available assessments, including vocational, educational, recreational, medical, and laboratory records, may lead to a convergence on dementia as a plausible account for the picture which is generated by these type of data.

The prospective strategy is increasingly being recommended as the approach of choice, particularly for persons with Down's syndrome (Aylward et al., 1995, 1997). Persons who are considered to be at high risk for acquiring dementia may be economically assessed at an age prior to the expected age of onset. Follow-up reassessment can be conducted using a wide array of tests, both standardized and experimental, to document any change, because each person's performance is compared with himself or herself on subsequent occasions. At this point, it is essential to determine whether or not the assessments that are employed will consist of direct observations of behavior including the test performances of the person or whether reliance will be place exclusively on "informant-based" instruments (i.e., questionnaires, behavior check lists). Direct assessments have the major advantage that experimental methods (e.g., Dalton, 1992) or nonstandardized modifications of existing tests (e.g., Wilson, Cockburn, & Baddeley, 1985) can be used effectively. A number of informant-based questionnaires have been developed specifically for measuring functions of persons with intellectual disabilities (e.g., Evenhuis, Kengen, & Eurlings, 1990; Gedye, 1995). Other, well-established methods that are nonspecific and insensitive, but that nevertheless are useful, include the AAMR Adaptive Behavior Scales (Nihira, Leland, & Lambert, 1993), which have been successfully employed to evaluate aging persons with Down's syndrome (Prasher, Krishnan, Clarke, & Corbett, 1994) and the Vineland Adaptive Behavior Scales (Sparrow, Balla, & Cicchetti, 1984). Finally, methods which have been developed for aging adults from the general population who are suspected of suffering from dementia, such as the Mini-Mental Status Examination (Folstein, Folstein, & McHugh, 1975) may also be helpful. A detailed discussion of various assessment methods for detecting dementia among persons with intellectual disabilities has recently been reported (Aylward et al., 1995, 1997).

☐   Critique of Strategies

An evaluation of the approach to assessment should consider a number of dimensions. The most important of these are test reliability and validity, ethical issues, the potential implications for the individual's quality of life, and resource issues. A summary evaluation of strategies on these dimensions is given in Table 7.2.

Prospective and Retrospective Strategies.   A retrospective approach to assessing dementia in persons with intellectual disabilities would commonly mean waiting for a referral to take place, which in turn is triggered by someone's observation that a suspicious change has taken place. Once the referral has been made, reports of current functioning are collected and evaluated. These are then compared with past assessments including retrospective interview material. The problems with this strategy is that the rate of change occurring between the assessments is unknown. A significant change could take place over 20 years or it may

TABLE 7.2.   An overview of the assessments that may be adopted for the assessment of dementia in persons with intellectual disabilities.

Specificity	Method of Assessment		
	Informant-Based Interview	Direct Testing	Informal
Neither		IQ assessments Rivermead Behavioural Memory Test (RBMT-C; Wilson et al.)	School reports, health records
Dementia only	Rarely employed	Severe impairment battery CANTAB (Sahakhian et al., 1988), MMSE (Folstein et al., 1975), CAMDEX (Roth et al., 1986)	
ID Only	AAMR Adaptive Behavior Scale Vineland Adaptive Behavior Scales		Hospital records, SEC reports, other assessments
ID and dementia	Dementia Questionnaire for Mentally Retarded Persons (Evenhuis et al., 1990), Dementia Scale for Down Syndrome (Gedye 1995), PAS-ADD (Moss, 1994)	Dalton/McMurray Visual Memory Test (Dalton & McMurray, 1995), Dyspraxis Scale for Adults with Down Syndrome (Dalton, 1996)	

occur in a brief six-month period. Neither situation may be recognized as a dementia, whereas a change over a year or so may provide more persuasive evidence for an acquired dementia. A second problem is that there may be few items that are included in assessments with known properties that have been used in the past that are specific to the early signs of dementia. Finally, the initial baseline may be low and when test error is taken into account, a "floor effect" at the initial assessment may be apparent. If past assessments using tests with known psychometric properties are employed that are not specific for the detection of cognitive impairments associated with dementia, then clearly the change that occurs may not be specific to dementia.

The question of the uncertain reliability of the information associated with use of this retrospective strategy is of paramount importance. Most of the time, such information should be used with caution and when no other more reliable data are available. There are important ethical questions associated with the retrospective strategy for the assessment of persons with Down's syndrome. Foremost among these is the consequence of deciding not to put the time and effort needed to conduct a proper prospective evaluation, knowing that these persons are at a high risk of developing dementia. Ethical concerns emerge in the decisions about what and how much information to provide or withhold from carers. Carers often struggle to provide support and services they deem appropriate in response to visible evidence of acquired cognitive deficits without possessing any satisfactory justification for their conduct. This all too common situation raises the likelihood of staff confusion and anxiety leading to unintentional ineffective planning for future service provision. It is against this background that the decision to use retrospective assessments should be made only with reluctance, particularly when it could affect persons with Down's syndrome over the age of 40 years or so who are at greatest risk for dementia.

The prospective assessment strategy is highly recommended, particularly for persons with Down's syndrome and others who are at high risk of developing dementia. However, this strategy is more time consuming and requires more extensive resources because it involves repeated assessments at regular and sometimes frequent intervals. Although such a strategy should be considered for all persons with Down's syndrome over the age of 30 years or so, it is not without problems of its own. There are similar ethical issues associated with the consequences of making "false positive" and "false negative" diagnoses. These types of error are difficult to estimate for any given test because there is no "gold standard" that could be used for comparative purposes. How the purpose of the assessments is described to persons with Down's syndrome and those who know and care for them can raise ethical concerns. Similarly, there can be the problem of giving or withholding information when functional decline is identified.

In addition to these ethical issues, there are also quality of life issues. If the early signs of dementia are identified, what are the implications for the individual's life and prospects for the future? It is likely that the individual will be compelled to move to another residential setting and that the individual's relationships with others will change dramatically for the worse. The diagnosis of dementia may overshadow other medical, social, and psychological needs of the individual. Notwithstanding these limitations, the prospective strategy promotes the use of actual performances on neuropsychological tests including direct behavioral observations. These data yield clear numerical scores that can be compared with those obtained by other individuals at risk. The psychometric properties of the tests can be calculated with a corresponding estimation of the nature and extent of measurement error. These assessments, ideally, are more likely to be sensitive and specific to cognitive changes even in the early stages of dementia.

Direct Assessments and Informant-Based Methods. Direct cognitive assessment as a strategy for assessing dementia in intellectual disabilities requires the performance of behaviors by the individual under special conditions arranged by the examiner. This can be intrusive, demanding, and sometimes threatening to self-esteem because most of these tests require performances of items of increasing difficulty, a procedure that is typically continued until the person fails two or three successive items. The newer psychological tests that are now coming into use require a higher degree of specialized training that may limit their wide availability. Floor effects exist for most of these direct neuropsychological tests that typically have been developed for persons with mild levels of intellectual disabilities. Administration of these tests usually requires more resources and scoring can be more complex. Finally, these tests, just like any other neuropsychological test, suffer from limited validity, reliability, sensitivity, and specificity. These issues are also important when using the well-known and standardized IQ tests. IQ and similar tests are neither specific nor sensitive to dementia, nor were they standardized on aging populations. Consequently, dementia may represent only one of several equally probable explanations for declines in IQ scores unless other possibilities are excluded by other methods. Individuals will rarely perform to the maximum score possible on these tests because of the impact of the life long intellectual disabilities. This means that there will be a much greater degree of variability in the scores between persons, even those without any cognitive declines, resulting in the presence of significant test error. This in turn leads to an inconsistent pattern of test scores across and within individual cognitive domains. It is quite possible to have significant decreases occurring in some domains and increases in performance in others.

A related approach is the use of batteries of neuropsychological tests to assess many cognitive domains, one or more of which will be affected if a dementia process is present. A comprehensive review of these studies and measures is beyond the scope of this chapter. However, detailed discussion and reviews have been published elsewhere (Oliver & Holland, 1986; Crayton & Oliver, 1993). There have also been an increasing number of reports of tests with a focus on specific functions such as short-term memory (Dalton, Crapper, & Schlotterer, 1974; Dalton, 1992; Wisniewski, Howe, Gwyn-Williams, & Wisniewski, 1978; Thase, Liss, Smeltzer, & Maloon, 1982, 1984; Haxby, 1989; Lai & Williams, 1989; Young & Cramer, 1991; Devenny, Hill, Patxot, Silverman, & Wisniewski,

1992), orientation (Owens, Dawson, & Losin, 1971; Wisniewski et al., 1978; Thase et al., 1982; Thase, Tigner, Smeltzer, & Liss, 1984; Haxby, 1989; Lai & Williams, 1989; Devenny et al., 1992), and dyspraxia (Dalton, 1992).

The assessment of orientation is particularly important in the diagnostic evaluation. However, it is nearly impossible to measure this function with neuropsychological tests in persons with intellectual disabilities, particularly those with severe to profound levels of intellectual disabilities. If orientation is assessed in an office or clinic away from where the person normally lives, confusion and disorientation may appear to be severe but merely reflect uncertainty in coping with an unfamiliar environment. The performance may also depend on the amount of information that has been given about where they have been taken to for the assessment. This is particularly problematic if early assessments take place in a clinic setting and, because of the effects of dementia, later assessments take place in the home environment. Some of these problems can be partly overcome by always conducting the assessment of orientation in the same environment during follow-up visits.

The assessment of short-term memory has similar problems. Most memory tests rely heavily on verbal instructions that require good comprehension as well as motivation to perform the test items. The ability of people with severe intellectual disabilities to understand verbal instructions which accompany memory tests may be compromised to the extent that short-term memory is not necessarily the cognitive domain that is being assessed. A similar problem arises with object memory. If individuals have idiosyncratic names for objects or they do not know the names of objects, then again errors may not necessarily be attributable to a short-term memory deficit. Naming and word finding may be similarly problematic, for example, as individuals may have never been able to accurately identify colors.

There are a number of other strategies in neuropsychological assessment that have been employed to overcome some of the problems described above. Assessments can employ a low floor, but these have a corresponding low ceiling (e.g., Dalton, 1992). This means that in sequential testing there is the capacity for appraising decreases in performance, but there is no room at the top of the test to identify improvements. Repeated examinations permit identification of idiosyncratic responses and the impact of preexisting intellectual disabilities can be estimated. Clearly this approach is particularly suitable for a prospective than a retrospective strategy.

The assessment of memory has perhaps been the most carefully adapted for people with intellectual disabilities. A number of studies have employed match to sample procedures to ensure that the individual is able to understand and perform the task before memory is assessed (Dalton, et al., 1974; Dalton, 1992; Thase et al., 1982, 1984). A greater variety of tests of this kind are increasingly required. They also provide a model for the development and construction of other tests that can lead to the development of a comprehensive battery, specific for individuals with intellectual disabilities.

While these problems are significant for neuropsychological test instruments, they are less evident when using behavior rating scales for the assessment of adaptive behavior. There are a number of rating scales for such a measurement whose psychometric properties are well established for appropriate populations of persons with intellectual disabilities. These informant-based assessments are popular because they usually do not require highly trained experts. They are quick to administer and usually cover a broad range of significant skills of daily life. They do not require either the presence or the participation of the individual. However, these instruments have a number of significant problems that need to be underscored. Informants selected from among staff of care-provider agencies frequently undergo "turnover." Different informants will have different skills and knowledge about the conditions being rated. They will also vary in the depth and duration of contact with the persons who are being rated. Often the informant is called upon to make subtle distinctions requiring psychiatric or medical training to separate out cognitive deficits specific to dementia from global deficits and specific deficits that are the result of lifelong intellectual disabilities. The extent to which the informant is able to perform these tasks cannot be estimated accurately. Consequently, the magnitude of errors introduced into the scores on these instruments cannot be calculated either, thereby raising doubts about reliability and validity. Fortunately, with careful planning, these instruments can yield scores that are "robust," that is, scores that are reliable. This is particularly so in the context of longitudinal prospective evaluations when the situation permits the same raters to conduct the follow-ups.

The issues of reliability and validity are particularly useful in planning for the use of informant-based assessments. It is important to establish interinterviewer (interexaminer) and interinterviewee reliability. These are seldom reported. Interviewee reliability is particularly important because of the frequent changes in the informant. The criterion used to assess validity requires even more careful examination. It may be questioned whether a diagnosis of dementia using, for example, Diagnostic and Statistical Manual of Mental Disorders (DSM-IV) criteria (American Psychiatric Association [APA], 1994) is valid for any persons with intellectual disabilities except under the most obvious circumstances. The validity is predicated on the assumption that the criteria for dementia used in

DSM-IV can be accurately assessed in the presence of intellectual disabilities. No systematic data supporting this assumption have been published to date. The validity of diagnosis must rest on postmortem evidence of the presence of the characteristic neuropathological brain lesions of Alzheimer's disease, until such time as a better criterion becomes available. The third problem with informant-based assessments is that it is quite possible that the changes in service delivery, which accompany age changes, are not taken into account. Consequently, if there is a decrease in an individual's opportunity to practice particular abilities, then any subtle cognitive deficits may be masked. This problem is more evident with informant-based assessments than with neuropsychological assessments.

A number of studies in the past have used informant-based assessments that are not specific to dementia in persons with intellectual disabilities. These measures are somewhat crude (insensitive and nonspecific) for detecting dementia. For example, the AAMR Adaptive Behavior Scale (Nihira, et al., 1993) is not only limited by the familiar reliability problems (both interexaminer and interviewee) but also by its nonspecificity and low sensitivity to dementia at least among individuals with Down's syndrome who are younger than 50 years of age (see Devenny et al., 1992, for a discussion of this point). However, these instruments are familiar and readily available and do not require intensive training, making them frequently the instrument of choice for those using the retrospective assessment strategy. Some neuropsychological tests and informant-based methods may be carefully adapted from other existing instruments for the assessment of dementia, such as the Mini-Mental Status Examination (Folstein, et al., 1975). A few can be used in their original form with little modification if they are employed with individuals with milder levels of intellectual disabilities. Because of the floor effects that constantly accompany the use of assessments standardized on persons who do not have intellectual disabilities, the adaptation of these instruments for use with persons with intellectual disabilities is warranted. However, floor effects are also a feature of these instruments, and appropriate adaptations have not yet been reported.

☐ Commentary

The last decade has produced a growing body of knowledge in the area of neuropsychological assessment of dementia among persons with intellectual disabilities. Most of the published work has been conducted with persons who have Down's syndrome. Consequently, the conclusions cannot be generalized to individuals with other forms of intellectual disabilities without the risk of substantial errors. A notable trend in the assessment procedures that have been employed in an increasing number of studies is a move toward developing assessments that are specific to people with intellectual disabilities and that employ strategies to overcome the problems of the variability of the degree of intellectual disabilities and the floor effects that are evident when assessing people with profound or severe intellectual disabilities. This trend is apparent in both direct neuropsychological assessments and informant-based assessments.

There is a rapidly growing need to develop an appropriate battery of neuropsychological tests with acceptable levels of validity and reliability. Mainstream research in the field of cognitive assessment of persons from the community at large with Alzheimer's disease is pertinent to this goal. Increased effort needs to be devoted to convert existing tests into ones that will produce valid and reliable assessments for people with intellectual disabilities. There is also a clear need to generate normative data and develop appropriate standardization samples for performances on those tests that already exist as well as new ones currently under development. These developments should occur in the context of the need to appraise an individual's performance on cognitive assessment against a level of performance predicted by other characteristics that are unaffected by dementia at the time that they are evaluated. This means generating normative data that contains an individual's past level of adaptive behavior at a time when dementia would be unlikely to be apparent. These data may make a significant contribution to one-time-only assessments.

The capability of accurately detecting the presence of cognitive impairment associated with dementia on the basis of a single assessment is unlikely for the foreseeable future. The problems of the variability of the degree of intellectual disabilities combined with those of test error make this assessment strategy prone to error. An approach that allows the appraisal of a single assessment against other information would be extremely beneficial. Meanwhile, a strategy of repeated test follow-ups on an annual or biannual basis appears to be the only viable course to contemplate seriously (see Burt and Aylward, this volume, for additional discussion of this point).

It is clear from reviewing the assessment instruments that are available that validity and reliability remain critical issues with regard to both direct and informant-based assessments. This is particularly true of the latter because of the nature of the assessment and the extent to which this increases the likelihood of test error.

For persons who have intellectual disabilities with etiologies other than Down's syndrome, it is likely that a retrospective strategy will continue to be used effectively. There is probably no good reason for adopting a prospective strategy unless appropriate resources are available. However, for persons with Down's syndrome a strong case can be made for routinely using a prospective assessment approach because these persons are at a uniquely high risk for developing Alzheimer's disease. Moreover, this risk increases dramatically with age (Visser et al., 1997). Routine periodic and comprehensive assessments should be conducted beginning at the time when risk is becoming significant, perhaps around the age of 35 years, with assessments being scheduled more frequently as the individual approaches the midforties to early fifties.

☐ References

American Psychiatric Association. (1994). *Diagnostic and statistical manual of mental disorders (DSM-IV)* (4th ed.). Washington, DC: Author.

Aylward, E. H., Burt, D. B., Thorpe, L. U., Lai, F., & Dalton, A. J. (1995). *Diagnosis of dementia in individuals with intellectual disability.* Washington, DC: American Association on Mental Retardation.

Aylward, E. H., Burt, D. B., Thorpe, L. U., Lai, F., & Dalton, A. J. (1997). Diagnosis of dementia in individuals with intellectual disability. *Journal of Intellectual Disability Research, 41,* 152–164.

Blair, J. A., & Leeming, R. J. (1984). Tetrahydrobiopterin metabolism, neurological disease and intellectual disabilities. In J. Dobbing with A. D. B. Clarke, J. A. Corbett, J. Hogg, & R. O. Robinson (Eds.), *Scientific studies in mental retardation.* London: Royal Society of Medicine and Macmillan Press.

Buchanan, L. H. (1990). Early onset of presbycusis in Down's syndrome. *Scandinavian Audiology, 19,* 103–110.

Crayton, L., & Oliver, C. (1993). Assessment of cognitive functioning in persons with Down syndrome who develop Alzheimer disease. In J. M. Berg, H. Karlinsky, & A. J. Holland (Eds.), *Alzheimer disease, Down syndrome and their relationship* (pp. 135–153). New York: Oxford University Press.

Dalton, A. J. (1992). Dementia in Down syndrome: Methods of evaluation. In L. Nadel & C. J. Epstein (Eds.), *Down syndrome and Alzheimer disease* (pp. 51–76). New York: Wiley-Liss.

Dalton, A. J. (1996). *Dyspraxia scale for adults with Down syndrome.* Staten Island, NY: Research Innovations. (5 Van Cortlandt Avenue, Staten Island, NY 10301).

Dalton, A. J., Crapper, D. R., & Schlotterer, G. R. (1974). Alzheimer's disease in Down's syndrome: Visual retention deficits. *Cortex, 10,* 366–377.

Dalton, A. J. & McMurray, K. (1995). *Dalton/Murray visual memory test.* Waterloo, Ontario: Bytecraft Ltd. (141 King Street West, Waterloo, Ontario, Canada).

Dalton, A. J., Seltzer, G. B., Adlin, M. S., & Wisniewski, H. M. (1993) Association between Alzheimer disease and Down syndrome: Clinical observations. In J. M. Berg, H. Karlinsky, & A. J. Holland (Eds.), *Alzheimer disease, Down syndrome and their relationship* (pp. 53–65). Oxford: Oxford University Press.

Devenny, D. A., Hill, A. L., Patxot, O., Silverman, W. P., & Wisniewski, K. E. (1992). Ageing in higher functioning adults with Down's syndrome: An interim report in a longitudinal study. *Journal of Intellectual Disability Research, 36,* 241–250.

Devenny, D. A., Silverman, W. P., Hill, A. L., Jenkins, E., Sersen, E. A., & Wisniewski, K. E. (1996). Normal aging in adults with Down's syndrome: A longitudinal study. *Journal of Intellectual Disability Research, 40,* 208–221.

Evenhuis, H. M., Kengen, M. M. F., & Eurlings, H. A. L. (1990). *Dementia Questionnaire for Mentally Retarded Persons.* Zwammerdam, the Netherlands: Hooge Burch Institute for Mentally Retarded People.

Fenner, M. E., Hewitt, K. E., & Torpy, D. M. (1987). Down's syndrome: Intellectual and behavioural functioning during adulthood. *Journal of Mental Deficiency Research, 31,* 241–249.

Folstein, M. F., Folstein, S. E., & McHugh, P. R. (1975). Mini-Mental State: A practical method for grading the cognitive state for the clinician. *Journal of Psychiatric Research, 12,* 189–198.

Gedye, A. (1995). *Dementia Scale for Down Syndrome (Manual).* Vancouver: Gedye Research and Consulting.

Haxby, J. V. (1989). Neuropsychological evaluation of adults with Down's syndrome: Patterns of selective impairment in non-demented old adults. *Journal of Mental Deficiency Research, 33,* 193–210.

Hewitt, K. E., Carter, G., & Jancar, J. (1985). Aging in Down's syndrome. *British Journal of Psychiatry, 147,* 58–62.

Lai, F. (1992). Clinicopathologic features of Alzheimer disease in Down's syndrome. In L. Nadel & C. J. Epstein (Eds.), *Down syndrome and Alzheimer disease* (pp. 15–34). New York: Wiley-Liss.

Lai, F., & Williams, R. S. (1989). A prospective study of Alzheimer disease in Down's syndrome. *Archives of Neurology, 46,* 849–853.

Moss, S. (1994). The psychiatric assessment schedule for adults with development disability (PAS-ADD). Manchester, UK: Hester Adrian Research Centre, University of Manchester.

Nakamura, H. (1961). Nature of institutionalized adult mongoloid intelligence. *American Journal of Mental Deficiency, 66,* 456–458.

Nihira, K., Leland, H., & Lambert, N. (1993). *AAMR Adaptive Behavior Scale—Residential and Community* (2nd ed.). Austin, TX: Pro-Ed.

Oliver, C., & Holland, A. J. (1986). Down's syndrome and Alzheimer's disease: A review. *Psychological Medicine, 16,* 307–322.

Owens, D., Dawson, J. C., & Losin, S. (1971). Alzheimer's disease in Down's Syndrome. *American Journal of Mental Deficiency, 75,* 606–612.

Penrose, L.S. (1966). *The biology of mental defect.* London: Sidgwick & Jackson.

Prasher, V. P. (1995). Age-specific prevalence, thyroid dysfunction and depressive symptomatology in adults with Down syndrome and dementia. *International Journal of Geriatric Psychiatry 10,* 25–31.

Prasher, V. P., Krishnan, V. H. R., Clarke, D. J., & Corbett, J. A. (1994). The assessment of dementia in people with Down syndrome: Changes in adaptive behaviour. *British Journal of Developmental Disabilities, 40,* 120–130.

Roth, M., Tym, E., Mountjoy, C. Q., Huppert, F. A., Hendrie, H., Verma, S., & Goddard, R. (1986). CAMDEX: A standardized instrument for the diagnosis of mental disorder in the elderly with special reference to the early detection of dementia. *British Journal of Psychiatry, 149,* 698–709.

Sahakian, B. J., Morris, R. G., Evenden, J. L., Heald, A., Levy, R., Philpot, M., & Robbins, J. W. (1988). A comparative study of visuospatial memory and learning in Alzheimer-type dementia. *Brain, 111,* 695–718.

Selkoe, D. J. (1992). Aging brain, aging mind. *Scientific American, 267*(Sept.), 96–103.

Sparrow, S. S., Balla, D. A., & Cicchetti, D. V. (1984) *Vineland Adaptive Behavior Scales.* Circle Pines, MN: American Guidance Service.

Thase, M. E. (1982). Reversible dementia in Down's syndrome. *Journal of Mental Deficiency Research, 26,* 111–113.

Thase, M. E., Liss, L., Smeltzer, D., & Maloon, J. (1982). Clinical evaluation of dementia in Down's syndrome: A preliminary report. *Journal of Mental Deficiency Research, 26,* 239–244.

Thase, M. E., Tigner, R., Smeltzer, D., & Liss, L. (1984). Age-related neuropsychological deficits in Down's Syndrome. *Biological Psychiatry, 4,* 571–585.

Van Schrojenstein Lantman-de Valk, H. M. J., Haveman, M. J., Maaskant, M. A., Kessels, A. G., Urlings, H. F., & Sturmans, F. (1994). The need for assessment of sensory functioning in ageing people with mental handicap. *Journal of Intellectual Disability Research, 38,* 289–298.

Van Schrojenstein Lantman-de Valk, H. M. J., Haveman, M. J., & Crebolder, H. F. J. M. (1996). Comorbidity in people with Down's syndrome: A criteria-based analysis. *Journal of Intellectual Disability Research, 40,* 385–399.

Visser, F. E., Aldenkamp, A. P., van Huffelen, A. C., Kullman, M., Overweg, J., & van Wijk, J. (1997). Prospective study of the prevalence of Alzheimer-type dementia in institutionalized individuals with Down syndrome. *American Journal on Mental Retardation 101,* 400–412.

Wilson, B., Cockburn, J., & Baddeley, A. D. (1985) *The Rivermead Behavioral Memory Test.* Reading, UK: Thames Valley Test Company.

Wisniewski, K. E., Howe, J., Gwyn-Williams, D., & Wisniewski, H. M. (1978). Precocious aging and dementia in patients with Down's syndrome. *Biological Psychiatry, 13,* 619–627.

Young, E. C., & Kramer, B. M. (1991). Characteristics of age related language decline in adults with Down's syndrome. *Mental Retardation, 29,* 75–79.

Diana B. Burt
Elizabeth H. Aylward

Assessment Methods for Diagnosis of Dementia

Standardized diagnostic criteria and procedures are proposed to further progress in the understanding and treatment of dementia in adults with intellectual disabilities. This chapter is a revised summary of previous reports prepared by participants of an international working group, which was conducted under the auspices of the International Association for the Scientific Study of Intellectual Disability and the American Association on Mental Retardation. Similarities in diagnostic issues between adults with intellectual disability and those in the general population are discussed, followed by a summary of issues unique to adults with intellectual disability. A brief overview of the application of International Classification of Diseases (ICD-10) diagnostic criteria to adults with intellectual disability is presented, including a description of procedures for determining whether criteria are met in individual cases. Finally, clinical and research recommendations are made.

Address correspondence to: Diana B. Burt, Ph.D., 6509 Gettysburg Drive, Madison, WI 53705.

This work was supported by grants from the National Institute of Child Health and Human Development (R01 HD30786, PI: Diana Burt) and the National Institute of Neurological Disorders and Stroke (R01 NS28115; PI: G. Pearlson).

141

Progress in the understanding and treatment of dementia in adults with intellectual disabilities has been hampered by the lack of standardized diagnostic criteria and procedures (Aylward, Burt, Thorpe, Lai, & Dalton, 1995, 1997). The lack of standardized criteria has led to significant differences among research groups regarding such basic findings as incidence and prevalence figures and age of onset (see Zigman, Schupf, Sersen, & Silverman, 1995). In both research and clinical settings, misconceptions regarding the prevalence of dementia of the Alzheimer's type in adults with Down syndrome and failure to follow nationally accepted standards for differential diagnosis (e.g., Clarfield & Foley, 1993; National Institutes of Health [NIH]) Consensus Development Conference, 1988) have resulted in misdiagnoses of Alzheimer's disease. For example, two adults with Down syndrome received misdiagnoses of Alzheimer's disease because a treatable cause of dementia (i.e., depression) had not been ruled out (Warren, Holroyd, & Folstein, 1989). When successfully treated for depression, the two adults returned to their premorbid levels of functioning.

To promote more rapid progress in research and to improve clinical practice, an international working group was convened to propose diagnostic criteria and procedures for assessing dementia in adults with intellectual disability (Janicki, 1994). The purpose of this chapter is to provide a summary of reports previously prepared by participants of the working group (Aylward et al., 1995, 1997). Similarities in diagnostic issues between adults with intellectual disability and those in the general population will be discussed, followed by a summary of issues unique to adults with intellectual disability. A brief overview of the diagnostic criteria will be presented, and clinical and research recommendations will be made.

☐ Diagnostic Issues Shared with the General Population

As in the general population, individuals with intellectual disability are living longer and thus are at increased risk for developing dementia (Dalton, Seltzer, Adlin, & Wisniewski, 1993; Eyman & Call, 1991; Janicki, Heller, Seltzer, & Hogg, 1996). Adults with intellectual disability, except those with Down syndrome, are believed to have the same risk for developing dementia due to various causes and at the same ages as adults in the general population (Barcikowska et al., 1989; Janicki & Dalton, 1993). That is, about 50% of dementia would be expected to be due to Alzheimer's disease, 25% would be due to multiple infarcts (strokes), and the remaining 25% would be due to other conditions (e.g., Parkinson's disease, Huntington's disease) (NIH, 1988). Compared with the general population, however, there is a possibility of increased risk for dementia due to adverse medication effects and/or psychiatric disorders (Harper, 1993).

In contrast, adults with Down syndrome are believed to be at increased risk at an earlier age for dementia of the Alzheimer type (as discussed in Dalton & Janicki, this volume). The exact prevalence of early occurring dementia of the Alzheimer type is unknown, however, because appropriate procedures regarding differential diagnosis were not usually followed in previous studies. Other types of dementia have been documented in adults with Down syndrome, including dementia due partially or completely to multi-infarcts (Dalton & Crapper-McLachlan, 1984; Hewitt, Carter, & Jancar, 1985; Evenhuis, 1990), Parkinson's disease (Lai & Williams, 1989), depression (Gedye, 1995; Warren et al., 1989), thyroid disease (Thase, 1982; Lai & Williams, 1989), and adverse effects of medication (Gedye, 1995). For all adults with intellectual disability, therefore, a thorough dementia work-up with appropriate exclusionary procedures is required first to diagnose dementia and second to determine possible causes. As in the general population, the diagnosis of dementia in an individual with intellectual disability in itself carries no connotation concerning a prognosis (American Psychiatric Association [APA], 1994). Cases of dementia that are identified by the criteria outlined here could be progressive or static, irreversible or reversible.

The classification of dementia is determined by the course of decline after initial onset (i.e., progressive or static), with reversibility being a function of the underlying pathology and timely application of effective treatment (APA, 1994). Progressive dementia is characterized by continued declines in functioning due to a degenerative disease like Alzheimer's disease, Pick's disease, Huntington's disease, and some forms of vascular disease (i.e., repeated ischemic attacks). Static dementia is characterized by a lack of further decline, such as dementia due to successfully treated vascular disease and head trauma (NIH Consensus Development Conference, 1988; see also Burt, this volume). At this time, many progressive and static dementias are irreversible (e.g., due to Alzheimer's disease and uncorrectable brain damage, respectively). That is, once declines in functioning occur significant improvements are not observed. In contrast, dementia due to conditions such as infections, endocrine disorders, toxic reactions to medicines, and depression are often completely reversible, such that premorbid levels of functioning return (NIH Consensus Development Conference, 1988; see also Thorpe, this volume, regarding reported cases of reversible dementia in adults with Down syndrome).

☐ Diagnostic Issues Specific to Adults with Intellectual Disability

When diagnosing dementia in adults with intellectual disability, several issues unique to this population must be considered (Dalton et al., 1993; Harper, 1993; Holland, Karlinsky, & Berg, 1993). The most important consideration is that the diagnosis requires a change in status from baseline functioning, not a change from a "normal" level. Thus, longitudinal assessment that documents baseline or "best" level of cognitive functioning in addition to changes in functioning is an absolute necessity before sufficient information can be obtained to make a diagnosis of dementia. Baseline functioning in individuals with intellectual disability is significantly more heterogeneous than in the general population, and individuals with various causes of intellectual disability have varying baseline profiles of strengths and weaknesses and varying sensory impairments (Gedye, 1995; Harper, 1993; Holland et al., 1993). In addition, they can have a wide range of behavior problems that are typical for them, and assessing the clinical significance of such behaviors requires a comparison with typical adulthood functioning (Harper, 1993).

The perception of cognitive decline will also depend, in most cases, upon the premorbid level of intellectual functioning and upon the demands required in the everyday life of the individual (Harper, 1993). Declines in individuals with mild intellectual disability could be very similar to those seen in the general population, whereas declines in individuals with more severe intellectual disability could be very different. In order to be clinically meaningful, any changes in performance obtained on cognitive tests must be accompanied by documentation of changes in everyday functioning, with changes being more apparent in settings that have heavier memory and cognitive demands. To be indicative of dementia, any changes over time must also be greater than those related to normal aging in adults with intellectual disability (APA, 1994; Dalton et al., 1993; Harper, 1993). Slight, gradual decreases (<1% per year) have been demonstrated in verbal, long-term memory for healthy adults with Down syndrome older than 50 (Devenny, Silverman, Hill, Jenkins, Sersen, & Wisniewski, 1996). Based on findings from the general population, gradual slowing of cognition and behavior would also be expected with aging (Harper, 1993; Salthouse, 1982).

☐ Diagnostic Criteria of the American Association of Mental Retardation/ International Association for the Scientific Study of Intellectual Disability (AAMR/IASSID)

Table 8.1 provides a summary of the World Health Organization's International Classification of Diseases (ICD-10) criteria for dementia. The AAMR/IASSID Working Group proposed using these criteria with individuals with intellectual disability. ICD-10 first outlines criteria for dementia and then lists additional criteria for the diagnosis of Alzheimer's disease (World Health Organization [WHO], 1992). In the following sections, issues unique to adults with intellectual disability are summarized, and procedures for determining whether criteria are met are briefly described.

Memory Decline in Individuals with Intellectual Disability. When assessing memory functioning in an individual with intellectual disability, it is critical to remember that premorbid memory functioning for adults with intellectual disability will be impaired relative to that in the general population (i.e., their baseline level of performance will be lower) (Hale & Borkowski, 1991; Kotz & Ellis, 1991; Nolan, Cottle, & Walker, 1985). In addition, there can be considerable baseline differences between verbal versus nonverbal memory skills. Thus, performance could depend upon whether words, pictures, or objects are used and upon whether a verbal or nonverbal response is required for recall or recognition (McDade & Adler, 1980; Varnhagen, Das, & Varnhagen, 1987). Assessment using only one modality, therefore, could misrepresent actual memory functioning. Finally, healthy adults with Down syndrome will often have reduced memory functioning compared with other adults with intellectual disability, despite comparable levels of intellectual functioning (Marcell & Weeks, 1988; Varnhagen et al., 1987).

Given all of these considerations, it is essential to record baseline or premorbid levels of memory functioning for all healthy adults with intellectual disability (see Aylward et al., 1997). Direct assessment of the individual is critical to supplement information supplied by carers, because carers are not often reliable in reporting memory or other cognitive functioning. In addition, carer reports or direct observations are usually required to document that any declines in memory are significant enough to affect daily functioning. Immediate and delayed memory span for digits, words, words in sentences, and/or objects could be assessed using appropriate memory scales from standardized tests such as the Wechsler

TABLE 8.1. ICD-10 criteria for dementia and Alzheimer's disease.

ICD-10 Criteria for Dementia
1. *Decline in memory.* Most evident in the learning of new information, although in more severe cases the recall of previously learned information may also be affected. The impairment applies to both verbal and nonverbal material.
2. *Decline in other cognitive abilities.* Characterized by deterioration in judgment and thinking, such as planning and organizing, and in the general processing of information. Deterioration from a previously higher level of performance should be established.
3. *Awareness of the environment.* Absence of clouding of consciousness for a period of time sufficiently long to allow the unequivocal demonstration of decline in memory and other cognitive functions.
4. *Decline in emotional control or motivation, or a change in social behavior.* Changes are manifested in at least one of the following: (1) emotional lability, (2) irritability, (3) apathy, or (4) coarsening of social behavior.
5. *Duration.* Decline of memory and other cognitive functions must be present for at least six months.

ICD-10 Criteria for Alzheimer's Disease
1. *All criteria for dementia are met.*
2. *Exclusionary Criteria.* No evidence from the history, physical examination, or special investigations for any other possible cause of dementia, a systemic disorder, or alcohol or drug abuse.
3. *Onset and progression.* For a diagnosis of Alzheimer's disease, there must be evidence of gradual onset and continuing cognitive decline.

Note. Both direct assessment of the individual with intellectual disability and collection of information from knowledgeable carers are required to determine that all criteria are met and to document that declines are significant enough to interfere with everyday functioning.

Adult Intelligence Scale-Revised, the Wechsler Intelligence Scale for Children and/or the Stanford–Binet (4th Edition), particularly if they were previously administered and performance was above floor levels (Dalton et al., 1993). In addition, memory tests such as the 4- to 6-year-old version of the Buschke Selective Reminding Test (Burt, Loveland, Chen, Chuang, Lewis, & Cherry, 1995; Devenny et al., 1996), the Dalton/McMurray Visual Memory Test (see Dalton, 1992, for a review), and/or appropriately modified mental status exams (e.g., Down Syndrome Mental Status Examination, Haxby, 1989; Test of Severe Impairment, Albert & Cohen, 1992) could be used. Carers should complete scales designed to assess everyday memory functioning in adults with mild to severe intellectual disability (e.g., Evenhuis, 1990) and moderate to profound intellectual disability (Gedye, 1995). For individuals with profound baseline impairments in functioning, or for nonverbal or nonresponsive individuals, changes in memory will usually have to be based on carer reports, unless tests specifically designed for this population are used (Dalton et al., 1993).

Decline in Other Cognitive Functions. Valid assessment of the onset of declines in other cognitive abilities depends upon an accurate indication of baseline functioning across a wide range of skill areas (Aylward et al., 1997; Harper, 1993; Holland et al., 1993; McKhann et al., 1984). In the absence of a baseline assessment, best level of functioning is sometimes documented in records. If previous standardized test performance was above floor levels (e.g., Leiter International Performance Scale, Wechlser Adult Intelligence Scale-Revised, Stanford–Binet), read-ministration of all or selected portions of the tests could be useful for detecting declines in reasoning, visual/perceptual/fine motor abilities, and expressive and receptive vocabulary (also see previous scores on the One Word Picture Vocabulary Test or the Peabody Picture Vocabulary Test-Revised).

Similarly, by readministering adaptive behavior scales or other living skills checklists to carers, the significance of cognitive losses in the daily lives of the individual can be documented (e.g., the Vineland Adaptive Behavior Scale—Sparrow, Balla, & Cicchetti, 1984; the Scales of Independent Behavior—Bruininks, Woodcock, Weatherman, & Hill, 1985; AAMR Adaptive Behavior Scale—Residential & Community Edition—Nihira, Leland, & Lambert, 1993; Disability Assessment Schedule—Holmes, Shah, & Wing, 1982). For example, losses in abstract reasoning skills can be documented in those who performed nonroutine tasks that required judgment, thinking, planning, and organization (e.g., selecting clothing that is appropriate for the weather, shopping, or complete meal preparation). In all individuals with intellectual disability, including those who performed only routine tasks (e.g., dressing, grooming and toileting, setting the table, social greetings), loss in motor abilities (apraxia) may be manifested as impaired ability to dress, self-feed, and brush teeth. Deterioration in language functioning (aphasia), as well as losses in ability to write, read, and calculate, can also be assessed using such scales.

Finally, for many individuals, declines in orientation to person, place, and time can be documented by repeated, standardized administration of mental status examinations designed for individuals with intellectual disability (e.g., Down Syndrome Mental Status Examination—Haxby, 1989; Mental Status Exam—Wisniewski & Hill, 1985; Test for Severe Impairment—Albert & Cohen, 1992). Dementia scales designed to allow the carer to estimate orientation skills are also useful (e.g., the Dementia Questionnaire for Mentally Retarded Persons—Evenhuis, Kengen, & Eurlings, 1990).

For the most severely impaired individuals, decline may be observed primarily as general slowing in all areas and greater impairments in attention. Increasing temporal or spatial disorientation, usually associated with later stages of dementia (such as the inability to distinguish between day and night or the inability to find the bedroom or kitchen), may be more salient than other cognitive deficits. For this reason, assessment of orientation to familiar environments is particularly important in these individuals. Visual and auditory impairment, which occur frequently in older individuals (and particularly often in those with Down syndrome), will affect the assessment of orientation and must be considered.

Documentation of dementia in individuals with intellectual disability requires that cognitive decline interferes with the previous level of social or occupational functioning (APA, 1994). It is recommended that a standardized instrument be administered on a longitudinal basis to document change (e.g., Scales of Independent Behavior, AAMR Adaptive Behavior Scale). When no baseline administration of these instruments has been performed, the clinician will have to rely on retrospective observations by the carer regarding changes in everyday functioning over time. Although such retrospective reports are valuable, clinicians must be aware of their potential lack of reliability.

Awareness of Environment (Delirium).   Diagnosis of delirium in individuals with intellectual disability should be made according to the same criteria used for the general population. (See Jarvik, Lavretsky, & Neshkes, 1992, for a thorough discussion of the diagnosis of delirium in elderly individuals.) Clinicians should be particularly aware, however, of the possibility of pharmacotoxic reactions that may cause delirium in individuals with intellectual disability (Tuinier & Verhoeven, 1994) and preexisting CNS abnormalities that may predispose these individuals to delirium (Lipowski, 1990).

Emotional Control, Motivation, or Social Behavior.   Individuals with intellectual disability and dementia present with a range of psychiatric and behavioral symptoms (e.g., sleep difficulty, hypersomnia, irritability, loss of interest; Moss & Patel, 1995; see also Thorpe, this volume). There is a high prevalence of behavioral abnormalities in some individuals with intellectual disability. These behaviors, which commonly occur, may be misperceived as being clinically significant, when a carefully taken history would indicate that such behaviors have always been typical for a given individual (Gedye, 1995; Harper, 1993; Holland et al., 1993). Conversely, abnormal behaviors may predate neurological changes of dementia and "overshadow" the true clinical syndrome (for further discussion, see Oliver, this volume). That is, all abnormal symptoms may be attributed to intellectual disability alone, rather than to a progressive dementing illness (Harper, 1993). This overshadowing is particularly problematic when professionals are not familiar with the behavior problems that commonly occur in individuals with intellectual disability or when longitudinal information on progression of behavioral abnormalities is unavailable.

Thus, behavioral/psychiatric functioning must be carefully evaluated for changes from earlier levels prior to the anticipated age of onset of dementia. As in the general population, behavioral/psychiatric symptoms may be misperceived and overly personalized by the carer, leading to subjectivity in the description of these symptoms. Thus, direct observation and/or evaluation of the individual with intellectual disability is an essential component of the behavioral/psychiatric assessment. Several instruments are available for the assessment of behavior problems including the maladaptive/problem behavior sections of the Vineland and Scales of Independent Behavior, the Aberrant Behavior Checklist (Aman, Singh, Stewart, & Field, 1985), the AAMR Adaptive Behavior Scale—Residential and Community Edition (Nihira et al., 1993), and the Disability Assessment Schedule (Holmes et al., 1982).

To determine whether behavior problems are severe and/or pervasive enough to indicate the presence of a psychiatric disorder several additional instruments are available. The Reiss Screen for Maladaptive Behavior (Reiss, 1987) is a carer-report instrument designed to screen for psychopathology in individuals with all levels of intellectual disability. Additional scales standardized on individuals with mild intellectual disability are the Emotional Problems Scales (Prout & Strohmer, 1991), and the Psychopathology Inventory for Mentally Retarded Adults (Matson, 1988), both of which have carer- and self-report versions. If psychiatric problems are indicated, it is recommended that the individual with intellectual disability be referred for complete evaluation and treatment by a psychiatrist or psychologist who has experience in working with individuals with intellectual disability, preferably in the differential diagnosis of dementia and other psychiatric disorders. It is particularly important that treatable psychiatric disorders, especially depression which is often difficult to differentiate from the early stages of dementia, be diagnosed and properly managed (Burt, Loveland, & Lewis, 1992; Dalton et al., 1993; Harper, 1993; Holland et al., 1993).

Duration.   For individuals with intellectual disability, there is a greater degree of variability of cognitive and behavioral functioning across time. Therefore, a diagnosis based on the recommended six-month duration for decline must be made with caution. It may be difficult to identify carers who have known the individual for a sufficient length of time to warrant a definite diagnosis.

☐ Criteria for Diagnosis of Alzheimer's Disease

Exclusionary Criteria.   Given the historical focus on the association between dementia of the Alzheimer type and Down syndrome, it is essential that all possible causes of dementia be considered and ruled out before a diagnosis of Alzheimer's disease is made. Examination and laboratory studies should meet nationally accepted standards for the evaluation of dementia in the general population (Clarfield & Foley, 1993; Consensus Conference, 1987; Jarvik et al., 1992; McKhann et al., 1984; Morris et al., 1989; NIH Consensus Development Conference, 1988). In addition, supplemental tests (such as electroencephalography (EEG) for detection of seizures and cervical spine X rays for individuals with Down syndrome to rule out atlanto-axial instability) should be performed to detect abnormalities that are more common in individuals with intellectual disability (Dalton et al., 1993). Other conditions that have been associated with dementia in this population should also be explored thoroughly (such as hypothyroidism; Lai & Williams, 1989; Thase, 1982), depression (see Burt, this volume; Burt et al., 1992; Gedye, 1995; Harper & Wadsworth, 1990; Warren et al., 1989); and adverse medication effects (Tsiouris, this volume).

It is also particularly important to screen for new-onset hearing and visual impairments, which individuals with intellectual disability may be unable to report. Although standard tests of vision and hearing can be used with individuals who are mildly or moderately cognitively impaired, special procedures will be necessary for more severely impaired individuals (see Evenhuis, van Zanten, Brocaar, & Roerdinkholder, 1992; Evenhuis, Mul, Lemaire, & de Wijs, 1997; Hyvarinen, Colenbrander, & Mayer, 1992; Mackie & McCullock, 1995). Additional diagnostic tests may be indicated, based on clinical presentation (e.g., Hachinski Ischemic Score—Hachinski, 1990) if multi-infarct dementia is suspected; CT or MRI to detect space-occupying lesions or normal pressure hydrocephalus; blood medication levels for patients on medications that may affect cognition, such as anticonvulsants, lithium, digoxin).

It is also very important to complete the standard neurological examination (see Adams & Victor, 1994) for localizing signs, paying particular attention to those that are frequently associated with dementia in individuals with intellectual disability (Wherrett, this volume; Dalton & Crapper-McLachlan, 1986; Evenhuis, 1990; Lai & Williams, 1989). Late-onset (i.e., not present during development) seizures (McVicker, Shanks, & McClelland, 1994), pathological reflexes, myoclonus, and gait disturbance are neurological abnormalities that are more likely to be indicative of dementia in adults with Down syndrome (Dalton & Crapper-McLachlan, 1986; Evenhuis, 1990; Lai & Williams, 1989). The clinician must also recognize that the prevalence of neurological abnormalities in nondemented individuals with intellectual disability is higher than in the general population (e.g., Wherrett, this volume; Habbak, Warren, Aylward, Jerram, & Pearlson, 1994), and thus may not necessarily be indicative of dementia. Again, a comparison with premorbid status is essential.

Progression and Onset.   Documentation of a progressive decline is required for a diagnosis of Alzheimer's disease. If adults with intellectual disability are initially assessed in the later stages of a degenerative disease, and if baseline assessments have not been conducted, progressive decline is often difficult to establish, except on the basis of carer reports. In preliminary, prospective studies average age of onset for clinical manifestations of Alzheimer's disease in individuals with Down syndrome is between 51 and 54 years of age (Lai, 1992), with no evidence for a bimodal distribution of age of onset. Although this is an average age of onset, evidence of decline may, of course, appear much earlier. Age of onset for individuals with intellectual disability due to causes other than Down syndrome tends to be after the age of 65 years (Janicki & Dalton, 1993), and there is currently no evidence regarding early- and late-onset of Alzheimer's disease for individuals in this subpopulation.

A diagnosis of definite Alzheimer's disease requires histopathological confirmation. It is currently not possible to distinguish the histopathologic abnormalities in those individuals with Down syndrome who demonstrate the clinical signs of dementia from those without the clinical signs (Rabe, Wisniewski, Schupf, & Wisniewski, 1990). Therefore, the working group did not advocate the confirmation of a diagnosis of Alzheimer's disease in individuals with Down syndrome through the use of histopathological analysis. Until research reveals descriptions of histopathological abnormalities specific to those individuals with Down syndrome who have clinical features of dementia, the working group recommended that the diagnosis of Alzheimer's disease in this group be based solely on clinical features. It is reasonable to assume, however, that currently accepted histopathological evidence of Alzheimer's disease is still valid for individuals with intellectual disability without Down syndrome.

☐ Clinical Recommendations

Dementia Work-Up. All procedures involved in the assessment of dementia in the general population (history, physical, and further investigations) should be followed as closely as possible (See Jarvik et al., 1992 for discussion of such an assessment), with necessary modifications to accommodate the individual with intellectual disability as previously outlined (also see Aylward et al., 1995; Holland et al., 1993).

Baseline Assessment. To establish a record of baseline functioning, the AAMR/IASSID Working Group (Aylward et al., 1997) recommended that all adults with intellectual disability be evaluated using standardized procedures to assess memory, other cognitive functions, and adaptive/maladaptive behavior at least once in early adulthood (by the age of 25 years). Without a baseline indication of functioning it is very difficult to determine whether current levels of memory and other cognitive, adaptive, and maladaptive functioning are related to level of intellectual disability, and thus are typical for an individual or whether they indicate declines related to dementia. Similarly, the validity of carer scales is maximized with a timely and preferably prospective account of functioning.

It is a challenge to perform an effective test administration to individuals with intellectual disability, especially with those who are becoming demented. As a result, many adjustments are necessary that may not be required for the general population. Cognitive testing should be performed by a psychologist who has prior test experience involving individuals with intellectual disability and who is thoroughly trained regarding the principles of psychological tests. Only under these circumstances can the appropriate adjustments be made. When possible, it is desirable to have subsequent tests administered by the same psychologist who performed the initial evaluation. The ideal carer interviewer should involve multiple informants, preferably family and nonfamily members who have observed the individual in a variety of settings. The cultural background of the individual and family being assessed needs to be taken into account, because what is typical or expected of an individual with intellectual disability may vary among cultures.

☐ Research Recommendations

The longitudinal use of a common set of standardized instruments, dementia scales, and mental status exams across research groups is recommended to determine their usefulness for assessing dementia in adults with intellectual disability (Aylward & Burt, 1998). Efforts are currently underway to assess a battery of tests, with a focus similar to that of the CERAD battery (Morris et al., 1989) which was developed for diagnosing Alzheimer's disease in the general population. This battery, which assesses general cognition, immediate and delayed memory, orientation, expressive and receptive language, fine motor speed, perceptual motor abilities, and adaptive behavior will be administered to a large multisite sample on an annual basis in an attempt to determine what declines are clinically significant and to establish a comparison standard for diagnoses based on dementia scales, mental status exams, and/or clinical judgment. Such collaboration, using multimethod, multisource (i.e., carer, self) techniques, will promote communication among various research sites and could eventually result in a centralized database for individuals with intellectual disability and dementia.

Using such a database, questions such as the following could be more efficiently examined: (a) What variations in course and areas of decline are observed? (b) Is the onset and course of dementia determined by the etiology of intellectual disability (e.g., Down syndrome versus other conditions), age, or premorbid level or pattern of functioning? (c) What psychiatric symptoms or disorders are associated with dementia? (d) How can dementia be differentiated from "normal" aging (i.e., what changes are clinically significant)? (e) How can the data be used to inform diagnostic decisions in individual cases, and (f) Do the data suggest useful techniques for improving the day-to-day lives of individuals with intellectual disability and dementia?

☐ **References**

Adams, R. D., & Victor, M. (1994). *Principles of neurology* (5th ed.). New York: McGraw-Hill.

Albert, M., & Cohen, C. (1992). The test for severe impairment: An instrument for the assessment of patients with severe cognitive dysfunction. *Journal of American Geriatrics Society, 40,* 449–453.

Aman, M. G., Singh, N. N., Stewart, A. W., & Field, C. J. (1985). The aberrant behavior checklist: A behavior rating scale for the assessment of treatment effects. *American Journal of Mental Deficiency, 89,* 485–491.

American Psychiatric Association. (1994). *Diagnostic and statistical manual of mental disorders* (4th ed.). Washington, DC: Author.

Aylward, E. H., Burt, D. B., Thorpe, L. U., Lai, F., & Dalton, A. J. (1997). Diagnosis of dementia in individuals with intellectual disability. *Journal of Intellectual Disabilities Research, 41,* 152–164.

Aylward, E. H., Burt, D. B., Thorpe, L. U., Lai, F., & Dalton, A. J., (1995). *Diagnosis of dementia in individuals with intellectual disability.* Washington, DC: American Association on Mental Retardation.

Barcikowska, M., Silverman, W., Zigman, W., Kozlowski, P. B., Kujawa, M., Rudelli, R., & Wisniewski, H. M. (1989). Alzheimer-type neuropathology and clinical symptoms of dementia in mentally retarded people with Down syndrome. *American Journal of Mental Retardation, 93,* 551–557.

Bruininks, R. H., Woodcock, R. W., Weatherman, R. F., & Hill, B. K. (1985). *Woodcock-Johnson Psycho-Educational Battery/Part Four: Scales of Independent Behavior.* Chicago, IL: Riverside.

Burt, D. B., & Aylward, E. H. (1998). *Test battery for the diagnosis of dementia in individuals with intellectual disabilities.* Washington, DC: American Association on Mental Retardation.

Burt, D. B., Loveland, K. A., Chen, Y. W., Chuang, A., Lewis, K. R., & Cherry, L. (1995). Aging in adults with Down syndrome: Report from a longitudinal study. *American Journal of Mental Retardation, 100,* 262–270.

Burt, D. B., Loveland, K. A., & Lewis, K. R. (1992). Depression and the onset of dementia in adults with mental retardation. *American Journal of Mental Retardation, 96,* 502–511.

Clarfield, A. M., & Foley, J. M. (1993). The American and Canadian consensus conferences on dementia: Is there a consensus? *Journal of American Geriatrics Society, 41,* 883–886.

Consensus Conference. Differential diagnosis of dementing diseases. (1987) *Journal of the American Medical Association, 258,* 3411–3416.

Dalton, A. J. (1992). Dementia in Down syndrome: Methods of evaluation. In L. Nadel & C. J. Epstein (Eds.), *Down syndrome and Alzheimer's disease* (pp. 51–76). London: Wiley-Liss.

Dalton, A. J. & Crapper McLachlan, D. R. (1984). Incidence of memory deterioration in aging persons with Down's syndrome. In J. M. Berg (Ed.), *Perspectives and progress in mental retardation* (pp. 55–62). Baltimore: University Park Press.

Dalton, A. J. & Crapper-McLachlan, D. R. (1986). Clinical expression of Alzheimer's disease in Down's syndrome. *Psychiatric Clinics of North America, 9,* 659–670.

Dalton, A. J., Seltzer, G. B., Adlin, M. S., & Wisniewski, H. M. (1993). Association between Alzheimer disease and Down syndrome: Clinical observations. In J. M. Berg, H. Karlinsky, & A. J. Holland (Eds.), *Alzheimer disease, Down syndrome, and their relationship* (pp. 54–69). New York: Oxford University Press.

Devenny, D. A., Silverman, W. P., Hill, A. L., Jenkins, E., Sersen, E. A., & Wisniewski, C. E. (1996). Normal aging in adults with Down syndrome: A longitudinal study. *Journal of Intellectual Disability Research, 40,* 208–221.

Evenhuis, H. M. (1990). The natural history of dementia in Down's syndrome. *Archives of Neurology, 47,* 263–267.

Evenhuis, H. M., Kengen, M. M. F., & Eurlings, H. A. L. (1990). *Dementia questionnaire for mentally retarded persons.* Zwamerdam, the Netherlands: Hooge Burch Institute for Mentally Retarded People.

Evenhuis, H. M., Mul, M., Lemaire, E. K. G., & de Wijs, J. P. M. (1997). Diagnosis of sensory impairment in people with intellectual disability in general practice. *Journal of Intellectual Disability Research, 41,* 422–429.

Evenhuis, H. M., vanZanten, G. A., Brocaar, M. P., & Roerdinkholder, W. H. M. (1992). Hearing loss in middle-aged persons with Down syndrome. *American Journal of Mental Retardation, 97,* 47–56.

Eyman, R. K., & Call, T. L. (1991). Life expectancy of persons with Down syndrome. *American Journal of Mental Retardation, 95,* 603–612.

Gedye, A. (1995). *Dementia scale for Down syndrome.* Manual. Vancouver: Gedye Research and Consulting.

Habbak, R., Warren, A. C., Aylward, E., Jerram, J., & Pearlson, G. (1994). Synkinesias are common in Down's syndrome. *Journal of Nervous and Mental Disorders, 192,* 667.

Hachinski, V. (1990). The assessment of multi-infarct dementia. In J. S. Chopra, K. Jagannathan, I. M. S. Sawhney, H. Lechner, & G. Szendey (Eds.), *Advances in neurology* (pp. 131–138). New York: Elsevier Science Publishers.

Hale, C. A., & Borkowski, J. G. (1991). Attention, memory and cognition. In J. L. Matson & J. S. Mulick (Eds.), *Handbook of mental retardation* (2nd ed., pp. 505–528). New York: Pergamon.

Harper, D. C., (1993). A primer on dementia in persons with mental retardation: Conclusions and current findings. In R. J. Fletcher & A. Dosen (Eds.), *Mental health aspects of mental retardation* (pp. 169–198). New York: Lexington Books.

Harper, D. C. & Wadsworth, J. S. (1990). Dementia and depression in elders with mental retardation: A pilot study. *Research in Developmental Disabilities, 11,* 177–198.

Haxby, J. V. (1989). Neuropsychological evaluation of adults with Down's syndrome: Patterns of selective impairment in non-demented old adults. *Journal of Mental Deficiency Research, 33,* 193–210.

Hewitt, K. E., Carter, G., & Jancar, J. (1985). Ageing in Down's syndrome. *British Journal of Psychiatry, 147,* 58–62.

Holland, A. J., Karlinsky, H., & Berg, J. M. (1993). Alzheimer disease in persons with Down syndrome: Diagnostic and management considerations. In J. M. Berg, H. Karlinsky, & A. J. Holland (Eds.), *Alzheimer disease, Down syndrome, and their relationship* (pp. 96–114). New York: Oxford University Press.

Holmes, N., Shah, A., & Wing, L. (1982). The Disability Assessment Schedule: A brief screening device for use with the mentally retarded. *Psychological Medicine, 12,* 879–890.

Hyvarinen, L., Colenbrander, A., & Mayer, L. (1992) *Manual. The LH symbol test.* New York: The Lighthouse Inc.

Janicki, M. P. (1994). *Alzheimer disease among persons with mental retardation: Report from an international colloquium.* Albany: New York State Office of Mental Retardation and Developmental Disabilities.

Janicki, M. P., & Dalton, A. J. (1993). Alzheimer disease in a select population of older adults with mental retardation. *Irish Journal of Psychology, 14,* 38–47.

Janicki, M. P., Heller, T., Seltzer, G. B., & Hogg, J. (1996). Practice guidelines for the clinical assessment and care management of Alzheimer's disease and other dementias among adults with intellectual disability. *Journal of Intellectual Disability Research, 40,* 374–382.

Jarvik, L. F., Lavretsky, E. P., & Neshkes, R. E. (1992). Dementia and delirium in old age. In J. C. Brocklehurst, R. C. Tallis, H. M. Fillit (Eds.), *Textbook of geriatric medicine and gerontology* (4th ed., pp. 326–348). Edinburgh: Churchill Livingstone.

Kotz, E. R., & Ellis, N. R. (1991). Memory for spatial location in retarded and nonretarded persons. *Journal of Mental Deficiency Research, 35,* 209–220.

Lai, F., & Williams, R. S. (1989). A prospective study of Alzheimer disease in Down syndrome. *Archives of Neurology, 46,* 849–853.

Lai, F. (1992). Clinicopathologic features of Alzheimer disease in Down syndrome. In L. Nadel, & C. Epstein (Eds.), *Down syndrome and Alzheimer disease* (pp. 15–34). New York: Wiley-Liss.

Lipowski, Z. J. (1990). *Delirium: Acute confusional states.* New York: Oxford University Press.

Mackie, R. T., & McCullock, D. L. (1995). Assessment of visual acuity in multiple handicapped children. *British Journal of Ophthalmology, 79,* 290–296.

Marcell, M. M., & Weeks, S. L. (1988). Short-term memory difficulties and Down's syndrome. *Journal of Mental Deficiency Research, 32,* 153–162.

Matson, J. (1988). *The Psychopathology Inventory for Mentally Retarded Adults.* Worthington, OH: International Diagnostic Systems, Inc.

McDade, H. L., & Adler, S. (1980). Down syndrome and short-term memory impairment: A storage or retrieval deficit? *American Journal on Mental Retardation, 84,* 561–567.

McKhann, G., Drachman, D., Folstein, M. F., Katzman, R., Price, D., & Stadlan, E. M. (1984). Clinical diagnosis of Alzheimer's disease: Report of the NINCDS-ADRDA

Work Group under the auspices of the Department of Health and Human Services Task Force on Alzheimer's disease. *Neurology, 34,* 939–944.

McVicker, R. W., Shanks, O. E. P., & McClelland, R. J. (1994). Prevalence and associated features of epilepsy in adults with Down's syndrome. *British Journal of Psychiatry, 164,* 528–532.

Morris, J. C., Heyman, A., Mohs, R. C., Hughes, J. P., van Belle, G., Fillenbaum, G., Mellits, E. D., & Clark, C. (1989). The consortium to establish a registry for Alzheimer's disease (CERAD). Part I. Clinical and neuropsychological assessment of Alzheimer's disease. *Neurology, 39,* 1159-1165.

Moss, S., & Patel, P. (1995). Psychiatric symptoms associated with dementia in older people with learning disability. *British Journal of Psychiatry, 167,* 663–667.

National Institutes of Health Consensus Development Conference Statement (Vol. 6, No. 11, July 6–8, 1987). (1988). Differential diagnosis of dementing diseases. *Alzheimer Disease and Associated Disorders, 2,* 4–15.

Nihira, K., Leland, H., & Lambert, N. (1993). *AAMR adaptive behavior scale—residential and community* (2nd ed.). Austin, TX: Pro-Ed.

Nolan, J. D., Cottle, D., & Walker, M. N. (1985). Conceptual organization and memory in nonretarded, mildly retarded, and moderately retarded adults. *Journal of Psychology, 199,* 261–264.

Prout, H. T., & Strohmer, D. C. (1991). *Emotional problems scale.* Odessa, FL: Psychological Assessment Resources, Inc.

Rabe, A., Wisniewski, K., Schupf, N., & Wisniewski, H. (1990). Relationship of Down's syndrome to Alzheimer's disease. In S. Deutsch, A. Weizman, & R. Weizman (Eds.), *Application of basic neuroscience to child psychiatry* (pp. 325–340). New York: Plenum.

Reiss, S. (1987). *Reiss screen for maladaptive behavior.* Worthington, OH.: International Diagnostic Systems, Inc.

Salthouse, T. A. (1982). *Adult cognition: An experimental psychology of human aging.* New York: Springer-Verlag.

Sparrow, S. S., Balla, D. A., & Cicchetti, D. V. (1984). *Vineland adaptive behavior scales.* Circle Pines, MN: American Guidance Service.

Thase, M. E. (1982). Reversible dementia in Down's syndrome. *Journal of Mental Deficiency Research, 26,* 111–113.

Tuinier, S., & Verhoeven, W. M. A. (1994). Pharmacological advances in mental retardation: A need for reconceptualization. *Current Opinion in Psychiatry, 7,* 380–386.

Varnhagen, C. K., Das, J. P., & Varnhagen, S. (1987). Auditory and visual memory span: Cognitive processing by TMR individuals with Down syndrome or other etiologies. *American Journal of Mental Deficiency, 91,* 398–405.

Warren, A. C., Holroyd, S., & Folstein, M. F. (1989). Major depression in Down's syndrome. *British Journal of Psychiatry, 155,* 202–205.

Wisniewski, K., & Hill, A. L. (1985). Clinical aspects of dementia in mental retardation and developmental disabilities. In M. Janicki & H. M. Wisniewski (Eds.), *Aging and developmental disabilities. Issues and approaches* (pp. 195–210.). Baltimore: Brookes.

World Health Organization. (1992). *ICD-10: International statistical classification of diseases and related health problems* (10th rev.). Geneva: Author.

Zigman, W. B., Schupf, N., Sersen, E., & Silverman, W. (1995). Prevalence of dementia in adults with and without Down syndrome. *American Journal on Mental Retardation, 100,* 403–412.

9

CHAPTER   *V. P. Prasher*

Adaptive Behavior

The assessment of adaptive behavior in people with intellectual disability is essential, particularly in relation to aging and dementia. During the last two decades, for older adults with intellectual disability, both cross-sectional and longitudinal studies have highlighted a significant association between decline in adaptive skills, aging, and dementia. Decline in adaptive skills is apparent after the age of 50 years with significantly greater loss for adults with Down's syndrome. Contributing factors include age, onset of dementia, underlying severity of intellectual disability, and presence of other forms of health morbidity. Future research issues are discussed.

Adaptive behavior has been and remains an area of considerable interest in the field of intellectual disability. Inadequacies of intelligence (IQ) testing (principally cultural bias, test bias, assumption of intelligence as a fixed value, inadequate assessment of all areas of intellectual functioning) led to a need to test "global functioning" of a person with an intellectual disability. This in the past was termed "social competence" (Doll, 1935)

Address correspondence to: V. P. Prasher, MBChB, MMEDSc, MCRPsych, M.D., Department of Psychiatry, University of Birmingham, Queen Elizabeth Psychiatric Hospital, Mindelshohn Way, Edgbaston, Birmingham, United Kingdom B15 2QZ. Email address: vprasher@compuserve.com

The author would like to thank Dr. Man Cheng Chung, Lecturer, University of Sheffield and M. S. Hague, Applied Statistician, University of Birmingham, for their help with statistical analysis.

157

but more recently termed "adaptive behavior" (Heber, 1961). Heber defined adaptive behavior as "the effectiveness with which the individual copes with the natural and social demands of his environment." Adaptive behavior has also been defined by the American Association on Mental Retardation as "the effectiveness or degree with which the individual meets the standards of personal independence and social responsibility expected of his age or cultural group" (Grossman, 1977). This allows people with intellectual disabilities to be viewed from a wider perspective rather than from a narrow viewpoint of impaired cognitive functioning. However, it must be borne in mind that testing of cognition and assessment of adaptive behavior are not substitutes for each other, rather they *complement* each other. This applies to all individuals with an intellectual disability but especially to the aging population where, for example, the diagnosis of dementia according to Diagnostic and Statistical Manual of Mental Disorders (DSM-IV) (American Psychiatric Association, [APA], 1994) or International Classification of Diseases (ICD-10) (World Health Organization [WHO], 1992) criteria include reference to both cognitive and social areas of functioning.

Tests of adaptive behavior assess an individual's current abilities (usually independent functioning, personal responsibility, and social responsibility) as they are manifested in a given situation. Several measures and patterns of behavior are assessed in different situations to give an overall assessment. Individual items are usually grouped together into domains such as language development, domestic activity, socialization. Commonly used measures of adaptive behavior are shown in Table 9.1.

☐ **Review of Cross-Sectional Studies**

Table 9.2 provides a synopsis of the outcomes of a number of cross-sectional studies. One of the first, conducted by Miniszek (1983), was an investigation of the systematic changes in adaptive behavior in elderly persons with an intellectual disability. Using the AAMR Adaptive Behavior Scale (ABS, Fogelman, 1975; Nihira, Foster, Shellhaas, & Leland, 1974), he was able to show that elderly people with Down's syndrome (N=15, age >50 years) scored lower than did younger persons with Down's syndrome (N=4, age <50 years) in every area of adaptive functioning except in domestic functioning. The elderly Down's syndrome group was divided into nine residents, judged to be severely regressing, and six who were still functioning relatively well. The regressed group scored much lower in all areas. An individual could, in comparison of their ABS profile with the above profiles, be reasonably diagnosed as

TABLE 9.1.   Instruments commonly used to assess adaptive behavior.

Scale	Authors	Main Use	Age Group	Administration/Completion
Vineland Social Maturity Scale	Doll (1935, revised 1965)	Assessment, planning, research	birth–30 years	informant-based interview
Cain–Levin Social Competency Scale	Cain, Levine, & Elzey (1963)	Assessment, planning	5–13 years	Informant based
Balthazar Scales of Adaptive Behavior (BSAB)	Balthazar (1973, 1976)	Assessment, planning research	5–57 years	Observer based
AAMD—Adaptive Behavior Scale	Nihira et al. (1974), Fogelman (1975)	Assessment, planning, research	3–69 years	Informant based
Progress Assessment Chart of Social & Personal Development	Gunzberg (1977)	Assessment, planning	6–16 years	Informant-based charts
System of Multicultural Pluralistic Assessment (SOMPA)	Mercer (1977)	Assessment	5–11 years	Informant based
Scale for Assessing Coping Skills (SACS)	Whelan & Speake (1979)	Assessment, planning	Adolescents–adults	Informant based
Disability Assessment Schedule (DAS)	Holmes, Shah, & Wing (1982)	Assessment, planning	Children–adults	Interview of informant
Hampshire Assessment for Living with Others (HALO)	Shackleton-Bailey & Pidcock (1983)	Assessment, planning	Children–adults	Observation, interview, informant
Vineland Adaptive Behavior Scales	Sparrow, Balla, & Cicchetti (1984)	Assessment, planning, research	Children–adults	Informant-based interview
ABAMR-Adaptive Behavior Scales	Nihira, Leland, & Lambert (1993)	Assessment, planning, research	3–69 years	Informant based

TABLE 9.2. Cross-sectional studies of adaptive behavior in adults with mental retardation.

Authors	Sample Size	Age Range (years)	Residence	Population Studied	Main Findings
Miniszek (1983)	19 DS+individuals 15 ID+individuals	34–70	institution	DS and ID	Older DS group scored lower in adaptive behavior than young DS group and matched non-DS ID group.
Janicki & MacEachron (1984)	7,823	53+	institution/ community	ID	Age-related differences found, particularly for cohort aged 73+I years. Greater decline for mild ID subjects.
Hauber, Rotegard, & Bruininks (1985)	403	40+	institution/ community	ID	Older adults (62+ years) less dependent in daily living skills than younger adults (40–62 years).
Hewitt, Carter, & Jancar (1985)	23	50–61	institution	DS	High rate of good self-care skills
Linter (1986)	63	20–85	institution	ID	Older group (60+ years) had greater self-care skills than younger groups (20–25, 40–45 years).
Janicki & Jacobson (1986)	10,532	45+	institution/ community	ID	Age-related differences in some domains of adaptive functioning at age 54 years; others apparent at 74 years.
Silverstein et al. (1986, 1988)	812 DS individuals 812 non-DS individuals	2–69	institution/ community	DS and ID controls	Age-related decline in some domains found for both groups. Significant decline in motor development for DS>60 years.

TABLE 9.2.   (continued)

Authors	Sample Size	Age Range (years)	Residence	Population Studied	Main Findings
Zigman et al. (1987, 1989)	2,144 DS individuals 4,172 non-DS ID individuals	20–69	institution/ community	DS and ID controls	For DS subjects adaptive competence declined with increasing age to greater extent than for ID controls. Marked differences present after age 50 years. Changes present irrespective of residence.
Janicki (1989)	883	45+	institution/ community	ID with cerebral palsy	Age-related decline in certain domains found. Group 75+ years had lowest independent individuals.
Haveman, Maaskant, & Sturmans (1989)	129 DS individuals 380 non-DS ID individuals	20–60+	institution/ community	DS and ID	Fall in some areas of basic personal skills for institutionalized DS adults 50+ years compared with ID group.
Barcikowska et al. (1989)	70	65+	institution	ID non-DS	Loss of adaptive behavior in 11%–32% of different adaptive behavior domains.
Collacott (1992)	308	18–60+	institution/ community	ID	Age-related decline present for 40 + years. Significant decline for subjects 60 + years. Change independent of residence.
Moss, Hogg, & Horne (1992)	122	50+	institution/ community	ID	No evidence of age-related decline. Relatively high functioning older adults.
Rasmussen & Sobsey (1994)	140 DS individuals 140 non-DS ID individuals		institution	DS and ID controls	No significant age-related differences for DS and ID control groups.
Prasher & Chung (1996)	201	16–72	institution/ community	DS	Age-related present irrespective of residence. Significant decline after 50 years. Age-associated decline present. Loss in skills greater for subjects with dementia.

*DS=Down's syndrome, †ID=intellectual disability.

having regression and dementia if other causes of regression were excluded (Prasher, Krishnan, Clarke, & Corbett, 1994).

Janicki and MacEachron (1984) analyzed information concerning demographic, functional, and service need characteristics of individuals with an intellectual disability derived form the Developmental Disabilities Information System (Janicki & Jacobson, 1982). The behavioral skills information from the Minnesota Developmental Programming System Behavior Scales (Joiner & Krantz, 1979) was used for this analysis. For the age groups 53–62, 63–72, and 73–99 years it was found that for increasing age there was a decline in mobility, toileting skills, eating, and dressing/grooming. Decline was most apparent for the elderly group. Individuals with severe intellectual disability had the greatest deficits in self-care skills but had the least decline in skills with increasing age. A greater percentage of individuals residing in the community was independent in mobility and daily living skills (although they also had a less severe intellectual disability and better health status). Similar findings were reported by Hauber, Rotegard, & Bruininks (1985) who found older adults (62+ years) were less dependent in activities of daily living than younger adults (40–62 years) and community residents performing more independently than institutionalized residents.

Subsequently, two relatively small institution-based studies were published reporting a high rate of good adaptive skills in elderly persons with Down's syndrome. Hewitt, Carter, & Jancar (1985) found using a nonstandardized interview that all persons were independent as regards to feeding; 70% were able to wash themselves independently although half of these required prompting; 74% were completely toilet trained; 22% were incontinent of urine; and one person had an in-dwelling catheter. All but two were independent in dressing skills. Linter (1986) again using a nonstructured assessment procedure found that elderly individuals with intellectual disability were quite able in terms of feeding, bathing, and dressing and all had good verbal skills.

In contrast with the above studies, several large studies were published that were based on the same data set as previously reported by Janicki and MacEachron (1984). Janicki and Jacobson (1986) investigated generational trends in sensory, physical, and behavioral abilities among 10,532 adults with an intellectual disability aged 45 years and older. For adults with mild to moderate intellectual disability, age-related differences in gross motor and independent living skills were present after the age of 54 years, but for domains toileting, dressing/grooming, eating, quantitative, language, reading/writing decline after the age of 74 years. A similar deficit at age 54 years in gross motor skills was found for adults with severe to profound intellectual disability. Maintenance or increase in skills for dressing/grooming, language, and independent living were seen to age 74 years, for eating and writing/reading to age 79, and for toileting and quantitative skills to age 84. Thereafter decline in skills was seen. This pattern of age-related differences was found for both institution and community residents. Generally, institutionalized adults exhibited greater differences and scored lower than their community counterparts. Zigman, Schupf, Lubin, and Silverman (1987) analyzed records of 2,144 individuals with Down's syndrome and of 4,172 controls with an intellectual disability other than Down's syndrome. Domains analyzed included gross-motor development, toileting, dressing, eating, independent living, language, reading, and writing. Scores of older adults with Down's syndrome (50 years and over) were worse than the scores for younger adults with Down's syndrome. For individuals with Down's syndrome at all levels of retardation, adaptive competence declined with increasing age to a greater extent than for controls with other intellectual disabilities. Particular areas affected were gross-motor functioning, toileting, dressing/grooming, eating, and independent living. Janicki (1989) examined aging in older adults with cerebral palsy and intellectual disability and found age-related differences in mobility, toileting, eating, and dressing/grooming skills. The lowest percentage of individuals independent for these activities of daily living was in the age group 75 years and over.

Silverstein, Herbs, Nasuta, and White (1986) and Silverstein, Herbs, Miller, Nasuta, Williams, and White (1988) found a less marked differential decline in adaptive behavior between adults with Down's syndrome and non-Down's syndrome controls. Effects of age on motor development, independent living skills, cognitive competence, social competence, social maladaption, and personal maladaption were assessed using the Client Development Evaluation Report (California State Department of Development Services, 1978). For the institutionalized population, factor analysis demonstrated that for motor development and independent living skills but not for cognitive or social competence, persons with Down's syndrome were functioning at a higher level than their counterparts. For some elderly adults with Down's syndrome (>60 years), there was a significant drop in motor development scores compared with younger adults (<60 years) and compared with age-equivalent adults without Down's syndrome. For the Down's syndrome and non-Down's syndrome groups living in the community, factor scores were higher than equivalent scores for institutionalized persons. For all factors, except cognitive competence, scores across age categories were higher for the Down's syndrome group than that for the non-Down's syndrome group. Nonsignificant decline in scores for motor development was seen for the Down's syndrome group aged 50+ years.

Haveman and colleagues (Haveman & Maaskant, 1989; Haveman, Maaskant, & Sturmans, 1989) investigated mortality and morbidity trends and motor/social functioning for 129 adults with Down's syndrome and for 380 adults with intellectual disabilities other than Down's syndrome living in institutions and group homes. Adaptive functioning was assessed using a scale for basic personal skills and a scale for linguistic skills (Kraijer & Kema, 1985). For institutionalized adults with Down's syndrome, 50 years and older, there was a substantial decline in basic personal and linguistic skills, but the non-Down's syndrome group continued to improve with increasing age.

Barcikowska et al. (1989), using results of neuropsychological diagnoses and retrospective study of clinical records, examined the relationship between neuropathological changes of Alzheimer's disease and clinical dementia in 70 adults without Down's syndrome, aged 65 years and older at the time of death. Activities of daily living skills were often affected with one-quarter of the sample showing significant decline in dressing/grooming, social and toileting skills, and motor ability. A smaller proportion of the sample had a significant decline in reading/writing, speech/language, and eating skills.

Collacott (1992), using the AAMR Adaptive Behavior Scale (ABS, Fogelman, 1975; Nihira et al., 1974), described results consistent with the emerging view of an age-related profile for adults with Down's syndrome. For persons in the age cohort 50 to 59 years, deterioration occurred in all domains with significant differences found for the domains of physical development, economic activity, numeracy and time sense, domestic activities, and vocational activities. After the age of 60 years, significant differences occurred in all Part I domains. For the total sample, decline with age followed an algebraic curve in which the overall ABS score was a function of the square of the individual's age. Persons resident in a hospital had poorer overall scores than those living in the community. However, using the same instrument, Moss, Hogg, and Horne (1992) demonstrated that age-related decline was not an inevitable consequence of aging. In 122 adults with an intellectual disability aged 50 years and over, factor analysis defined two dimensions, *personal competence* and *community competence*. Overall, the majority of individuals had a high level of toileting and dressing skills with no significant difference in scores for the groups 50 to 74 years and 75+ years of age.

Rasmussen and Sobsey (1994) reported results of the analysis of retrospective data of cross-sectional and longitudinal changes in adaptive behavior in institutionalized adults, with and without Down's syndrome. The Pyramid Scales, Criterion Referenced Measures of Adaptive Behavior in Severely Handicapped Individuals (Cone, 1984), were used. Findings for 140 adults with Down's syndrome were compared with 140 controls who did not have Down's syndrome. Each group was divided by age at initial assessment into under or over 40 years of age. No significant differences in adaptive skills were found for the two groups. The ages of the individuals were not given, but few were over the age of 50 years, implying that the study population was generally too young to experience age-related changes.

Prasher and Chung (1996) investigated the underlying causes of age-related differences in adaptive behavior in 201 adults with Down's syndrome using the ABS (Fogelman, 1975; Nihira et al., 1974). Significant age-related differences were seen for persons aged 50 years and over for all ABS domains except vocational activity. Aging, dementia, and severity of intellectual disability were found to be significant factors associated with decline in scores. Absence of a medical illness was a factor that predicted a higher level of adaptive behavior.

☐ Review of Longitudinal Studies

As shown in Table 9.3, Eyman and Widaman (1987) analyzed a database of a sample of 30,749 individuals with an intellectual disability over a four-year study period, for the presence of age-related differences in adaptive behavior using the Client Development Evaluation Report (Widaman, Gibbs, & Geary, 1987). Six factors were examined: motor, independent living, cognitive, social competence, social maladaption, and personal maladaption. Detailed data analysis was undertaken demonstrating a levelling-off or decline in skills with increasing age. Again severity of intellectual disability had a significant influence on the life-span trends, with the greater the level of intellectual disability, the lower the age-specific scores. Long-term follow-up studies (i.e., six to eight years) were recommended by the authors.

Other longitudinal studies have focused on adults with Down's syndrome. Schupf, Silverman, Sterling, and Zigman (1989) investigated changes in adaptive behavior ratings over the three years immediately preceding death in 99 adults with Down's syndrome and in 99 controls with intellectual disabilities other than Down's syndrome. The analytic procedures were similar to that used in other studies (Janicki & Jacobson, 1982). Greater decline in skills was seen for both older groups (>50 years) as compared with younger individuals. Regression was three to four times greater for older adults with Down's syndrome than for controls with other intellectual disabilities. Brown, Greer, Aylward, and Hunt (1990) also confirmed a significant decline in social/adaptive skills ratings with increasing age, with the least decline for those adults residing in an institutional setting.

TABLE 9.3.   Longitudinal studies of adaptive behavior in adults with mental retardation.

Authors	Sample	Age Range Years	Study Period (Years)	Residence	Population	Main Findings
Eyman & Widaman (1987)	30,749	4–90	4	institution/ community	ID	Decline in some areas of adaptive skills. 6–8 year longitudinal studies.
Schupf et al. (1989)	99 DS individuals 99 non-DS ID individuals	20–69	3	institution/ community	DS and ID controls	DS adults over 50 had significant greater regression than controls and younger DS subjects during last 3 years of life.
Brown et al. (1990)	130	1–59	—	institution/ community	DS	Age-related decline present. Least decline for individuals resident in institutional settings.
Rasmussen & Sobsey (1994)	56 DS individuals 64 ID individuals	—	4–4	institution	DS and ID	Decline in skills for subjects over 40 years of age. Particularly in self-help and communication skills. Adaptive skills more stable for ID group.
Burt et al. (1995)	34	22–56	3–4	community	DS	No age-related decline in nondemented middle-aged DS subjects. Level of ID significant factor in analysis.
Prasher et al. & Haque (1998)	128	16–72	3	institution/ community	DS	Decline in skills for middle-aged DS population over 3-year period of assessment. Only one significant factor for decline—dementia.

DS=Down syndrome; ID=intellectual disability.

Rasmussen and Sobsey (1994) reported longitudinal changes in adaptive behavior ratings in 56 institutionalized adults with Down's syndrome and 64 adults with other forms of intellectual disability over a three- to four-year period. Ratings from the Pyramid Scales: Criterion Referenced Measures of Adaptive Behavior in Severely Handicapped Individuals (Cone, 1984) were used. Findings were compared for groups below and above age 40 years. Significant decline in ratings of adaptive skills of washing/grooming, gross motor, receptive language, social interaction, dressing, domestic behavior, and toileting with age were found. Such findings were more apparent in Down's syndrome individuals over 40 years of age and also as compared with controls without Down's syndrome. Inconsistent results were reported by Burt, Loveland, Chen, Chuang, Lewis, and Cherry (1995) who made direct neuropsychological and behavioral examinations of 34 community-dwelling adults with Down's syndrome over a three-year period (age range 22 to 56 years; mean age of the sample not given). Individuals with dementia were not recruited into the study. Adaptive behavior skills were assessed using the Vineland Adaptive Behavior Scales, Interview Edition (Sparrow, Balla, & Cicchetti, 1984). The authors found no significant changes in performance over the study period and noted that neither age at entry nor gender had a significant effect on performance. However, IQ at entry had a significant effect on performance in all areas.

Prasher, Chung, and Haque (1988), using ratings from the Adaptive Behavior Scale (Fogelman, 1975; Nihira et al., 1974), examined the underlying factors for possible change in adaptive behavior in 128 adults with trisomy 21 over a three-year assessment period. Significant age-related decline in overall adaptive behavior scores was found for the domains independent functioning, numbers and time, self-direction, and responsibility. Presence of dementia was the only determining factor. No associations among sex, sensory loss, severity of intellectual disability, and place of residence were found. For those with no significant medical disorder adaptive scores were higher, but no significant decline was seen. These findings help clarify the apparent inconsistencies in the reports by Rasmussen and Sobsey (1994) and Burt et al. (1995) in that for a general middle-aged Down's syndrome population early decline in adaptive skills is seen, but this is mostly accountable by the onset of a dementing process. If dementia cases are excluded, no significant decline is found. The inconsistencies may also reflect the differences between informant-based rating scales and direct observations of functional changes and behavior.

☐ Findings from a Five-Year Longitudinal Assessment Study

Longitudinal data from the West Midlands Aging Study being conducted in the United Kingdom are of interest here. Prospectively collected data for 57 adults (32 male and 25 female) with cytogenetically proven trisomy 21, from their first five annual assessments, are reported. Nineteen adults were resident in institutions, 23 in community group homes, and 15 in their family home. Nine individuals had mild intellectual disability, 37 moderate, and 11 severe. Mean age for the total sample at entry was 43.0 years (SD 13.1, range 17 to 71 years). Individuals with other forms of Down's syndrome were excluded to control for cytogenetic variability significantly influencing outcome measures (e.g., adaptive behavior). Severity of intellectual disability was classified using ICD-10 criteria (WHO, 1992). Annual assessments for physical and psychological status were undertaken (for further details see Prasher & Chung, 1996; Prasher, Chung, & Haque, 1998). An evaluation for psychiatric disorders during the study period was made according to Diagnostic Criteria for Research (DCR-10; WHO, 1993). In this study individuals were included only in the "dementia group" when characteristic deterioration of Alzheimer's disease was evident for a minimum of three years. As previously done, adaptive behavior was assessed using the ABS; Fogelman, 1975; Nihira, Foster, Shellhaas, & Leyland, 1974), all domains of Part I (independent functioning) of the ABS were measured. The scale was completed by a person familiar with the person with intellectual disability and by a semi-interview assessment. Where possible, assessments were completed with the same carer over the study period. For persons living at home, the carer interviewed was a relative, but for other individuals it was a paid carer. The analysis of the ABS results was undertaken at the end of the study period to reduce bias.

Findings were analyzed for three groups: for all individuals *(total sample, N=57)*, individuals for whom no significant medical illness was present during the five-year period *(unaffected group, N=35)*, and for individuals with dementia only for whom the disorder was present for at least three years *(dementia group, N=12)*. The *unaffected group* consisted of individuals with no significant physical disorder, no hypothyroidism, and no evidence of dementia, depression, or other psychiatric disorder during the study period.

Mean overall Part I Total ABS Scores for the three groups are given in Figure 9.1. A decline in adaptive skills is seen for the total sample group and in particular for the dementia group but little decline for individuals who are otherwise well. Repeated measures ANOVA data analysis was

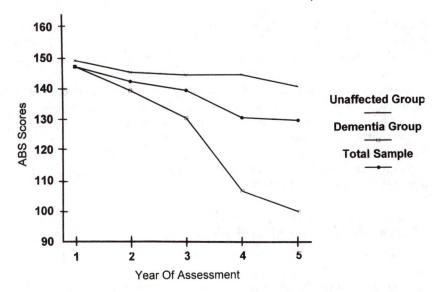

FIGURE 9.1.   Longitudinal mean overall part 1 total scores.

undertaken to compare decline between the ABS overall and 10 domain scores across the five years. For the *total sample*, the results showed that there was a significant decline in overall Part I score and for the following domains: independent functioning, physical development, language development, numbers and time, domestic activity, responsibility, and socialization. For the *unaffected group* the results showed no significant decline in overall Part I score over the five-year period and no significant decline for any of the domains. For the *dementia group* there was a significant decline in overall Part I scores and for the following domains: independent functioning, physical development, economic activity, language development, numbers and time, and domestic activity.

A factorial analysis indicated that for overall Part I scores there was a significant difference between the *dementia* and *unaffected groups*, but the change over time (i.e., interaction between time and *dementia* and *unaffected group*) was not significant. For the domain independent functioning there was a significant difference between demented and unaffected groups and there was a significant difference between the five years and the interaction term. For the domains physical activity and domestic activity there was a significant difference between the dementia and unaffected groups.

Linear regression analysis was performed on the change in overall ABS Part I total scores for the total sample (year 1–year 5). Independent variables used were presence of dementia, age at entry of study, intellectual disability, sex, and residence. Two factors, *presence of dementia* and *severity of intellectual disability*, were found to significantly predict decline in adaptive skills. Individuals with mild intellectual disability were more likely to show decline over time than individuals with severe intellectual disability.

These findings, over a longer study period than has been previously reported, confirm earlier studies that for a general population of middle-aged adults with Down's syndrome there is a decline in skills. Presence of dementia and underlying severity of intellectual disability are predictors of decline. Severity of dementia is associated with particular areas of loss of adaptive skills, and absence of significant illness implies absence of a significant decline in skills.

☐ Methodological and Assessment Issues

A series of methodological and assessment issues are discussed.

Cross-Sectional Versus Longitudinal Design. The majority of studies to date have been cross-sectional in nature (Table 9.2), but more recently longitudinal studies have been reported (Table 9.3). There remain a number of reasons why findings from cross-sectional studies should be accepted with caution: (1) age-cohort effect is likely to be significant (i.e., adaptive skills learned by a 20-year-old individual in the 1940s who is recruited into a study conducted in the 1990s aged 70+ will be significantly less than those learned by a 20-year-old adult raised today—an example of this would be independent travelling skills). (2) Older adults with an intellectual disability living today and assessed for adaptive behavior would have greater medical conditions as compared with a younger population. Compounding medical conditions themselves would impact on scores. (3) Older adults, due to poor education and social training, would have greater severity of intellectual disability as compared with younger individuals, and the underlying intellectual disability would result in older adults having lower scores. (4) "Healthy survivor effects" may diminish expected differences. For example, individuals who survive to age 80+ years may be individuals who have suffered few medical illnesses and therefore may not be representative of elderly people with intellectual disability as a whole. (5) Other methodological problems that may not be controlled for include fewer persons in older age groups, sex differences, and place of residence. (6) It is inappropriate in cross-sectional studies to talk in terms of a *decline* in skills with age when younger and older groups of different individuals are compared; it is more appropriate to state that older adults function at a lower level.

Differences reported from cross-sectional studies, therefore, may not be due to a *decline* in skills with age but artificial results secondary to underlying cultural/educational differences where studies cannot control for intraindividual and interindividual variability for the different age groups. Ideally prospective longitudinal studies are the choice in the assessment of age-related decline, but unfortunately due to the very nature of long-term data collection (fall in sample size over time, costs, etc.) such studies will prove to be difficult to undertake. At present no study has been published reporting detailed findings of adaptive behavior changes over more than a five-year period. Unless a concurrent illness is present, this is a relatively short period of time to detect significant decline.

Size of Sample Population.   Some studies have been of relatively small samples (e.g., $n<35$) (Miniszek, 1983; Hewitt, Carter, & Jancar, 1985; Burt et al., 1995), while others have been of considerably larger number of subjects (e.g., $n>5,000$) (Zigman et al., 1987; Janicki & Jacobson, 1986; Janicki & MacEachron, 1984), the latter being computer information system-based studies. The greater the sample population, the more likely it is that the study is representative of the total population of adults with intellectual disabilities. However, relatively smaller samples do allow more detailed assessments to be undertaken with more "hands on" data collection that can supplement findings from more epidemiological-based studies. For example, such studies are important when researching the impact of mental illness in people with an intellectual disability.

Age of Study Population.   The age of individuals studied has varied; for example, middle age and older (Table 9.2), to a more general age distribution (Table 9.2 and 9.3). Virtually all studies have included older adults with an intellectual disability, the very individuals for whom age-related decline should be evident. However, the advantage of including persons of a wide age range is to aid the determination of the age of onset of any decline and to help determine the severity and rate of loss over time. It is always pertinent to assess people with an intellectual disability when they are "well" and prior to the onset of any relevant medical disorder.

Place of Residence of the Sample.   Most studies to date have included individuals resident in institutional facilities, either as the only group studied or along with community-dwelling individuals (Table 9.2 and 9.3). Community care may have considerable variation, from a family home with highly involved relatives to large group homes not dissimilar to institutions. Studies of community-dwelling and institutional residents do allow the comparison of adaptive findings as determined by type of residence (Collacott, 1992; Prasher & Chung, 1996). However, for people with an intellectual disability, place of residence is not so categorical as often reported. Many older residents living at present in the community may have been long-term institutionalized residents. Individuals living in the community once they developed a number of medical conditions may have been transferred to institutions for further care. Certainly for future longitudinal studies it is highly probable that individuals will move from one form of residential situation to another. A study of aging in people with an intellectual disability who have had no contact with institutional care is awaited.

Individuals Studied. All studies have included individuals with an intellectual disability. These have been either as (1) Down's syndrome only (Hewitt, et al., 1985; Collacott, 1992; Prasher & Chung, 1996; Table 9.2); (2) identified Down's syndrome individuals and other forms of intellectual disability (Miniszek, 1983; Zigman et al., 1987; Silverstein et al., 1986, 1988; Schupf, Silverman, Sterling, & Zigman, 1989; Haveman & Maaskant, 1989; Haveman et al., 1989; Rasmussen & Sobsey, 1994); (3) general population of persons with intellectual disabilities (which would probably include individuals with Down's syndrome) (Linter, 1986; Hauber et al., 1985; Janicki & Jacobson, 1986; Janicki & MacEachron, 1984; Moss, Hogg, & Horne, 1992; Eyman & Widaman, 1987); and (4) intellectual disabled persons without Down's syndrome (Barcikowska et al., 1989) or intellectual disability and cerebral palsy (Janicki, 1989). Extrapolation of findings to the total population of adults with intellectual disabilities can only reliably be made if the sample population has the same makeup of individuals. Further, the majority of studies have focused on aging in adults with Down's syndrome. Findings to date have allowed either age-related differences in different age groups of adults with Down's syndrome to be determined or findings to also be compared with a general non-Down's syndrome population. Comparison between groups can help to determine whether aging is the same process irrespective of the underlying form of intellectual disability or whether this is an important factor. A failure of many of the studies is not to give the cause of intellectual disability in the persons studied. This means direct comparison of some studies is not possible and future replication is difficult.

Assessment of Physical and Psychiatric Morbidity. Adaptive behavior is very much determined by the health status of the individuals studied. Recently, several studies have been reported demonstrating the detrimental effect of physical disorders on adaptive behavior (Prasher, 1994, 1995; Roeden & Zitman, 1995) and of psychiatric disorders (Prasher & Hall, 1996; Zigman, Schupf, Sersen, & Silverman, 1995; Cooper & Collacott, 1993; Prasher et al., 1994) on adaptive behavior. The health status was reported in some studies assessing age-related adaptive behavior (Linter, 1986; Hewitt et al., 1985; Barcikowska et al., 1989; Janicki & Jacobson, 1986; Janicki & MacEachron, 1984; Haveman & Maaskant, 1989; Haveman et al., 1989; Prasher & Chung, 1996; Janicki, 1989; Hauber et al., 1985; Burt et al., 1995). The only studies directly investigating the possible interaction between age-related decline in adaptive behavior and presence of physical or psychiatric morbidity have been by Prasher and colleagues (1996, 1998, above). The demonstration of age-related decline is in itself important, but the factors causing the decline do need to be determined.

Underlying Severity of Intellectual Disability.   Most studies have commented on the status of the intellectual disability in their sample and many have directly investigated the impact of severity of intellectual disability on adaptive behavior (Janicki & MacEachron, 1984; Janicki & Jacobson, 1986; Zigman et al., 1987; Rasmussen & Sobsey, 1994; Prasher & Chung, 1996; Burt et al., 1995; Eyman & Widaman, 1987). From cross-sectional studies, conclusions regarding the effect of severity of intellectual disability on age-related differences are limited as level of adaptive behavior is very closely linked to level of intellectual disability. For any given age-specific group, the greater the severity of the underlying intellectual disability, the lower the adaptive behavior scores will be. It is only from longitudinal studies that the possible effect of intellectual disability on age-related decline can be fully assessed. For example, such questions may include the following: Do individuals of differing level of intellectual disability have different patterns of decline? Do individuals with severe/profound intellectual disability have the capacity for further decline in adaptive skills from an already low level (or is there a floor effect)?

Age-Associated Functional Decline (AAFD).   The concept of "normal aging" or AAFD (Prasher, 1996) remains an area for further research in people with an intellectual disability. Little information is available regarding decline in adaptive behavior associated with AAFD. Prasher in a series of reports (Prasher & Chung, 1996, Prasher et al., 1998; has investigated this area, demonstrating that for individuals with Down's syndrome who are otherwise well, some age-related decline is still apparent.

From the review of published reports a number of conclusions can be made: (1) A significant proportion of elderly people with intellectual disability (>50 years) remains relatively well and continues to maintain a high level of self-care skills. (2) For the elderly general intellectual disability population there is an age-related decline in adaptive skills. (3) Decline in adaptive skills begins at the age group 40–50 years following which there is a steady loss with increasing age. (4) For adults with Down's syndrome, decline in overall adaptive skills is greater as compared with age-specific controls who have an intellectual disability other than Down's syndrome. (5) The principal factor causing the differential decline is the increased incidence of clinical dementia in adults with Down's syndrome. (6) Age-related decline in adaptive behavior is a function of age, presence of dementia, and underlying severity of intellectual disability. (7). Age-related decline in adaptive behavior is not a function of sex and residence (although for the latter population skills are consistently lower). (8) The greater the severity of intellectual disability, the lower the level of adaptive skills, such that for individuals with mild/moderate intellectual disability there is a greater potential for age-related decline. (9) There is a differential decline in adaptive skills with age. (10) For persons with an intellectual disability, but without any significant medical disorder, age-related decline is seen and this probably reflects "age-associated functional decline."

☐ Future Research Issues

There remain several areas for future research with regard to investigating age-related decline in adaptive behavior in adults with an intellectual disability. These include:

(1) Further longitudinal studies for the general population of adults with intellectual disability are required. Follow-up studies of five years and over are awaited. Longitudinal studies to date have often assessed a sample population with a mean age in the fourth decade. Although such a middle-age population will present with some early age-related decline in adaptive skills, the aging process remains a condition associated with much older individuals and therefore a five- to 10-year longitudinal study of individuals age 50 years and older has yet to be reported.

(2) A wide variation of scales and instruments have been previously used. To ensure good reliability and validity an international consensus of the most appropriate measures is required (see Burt & Aylward, this volume).

(3) Future studies do need to describe the causes of the underlying intellectual disability in their subjects. This will aid with more direct comparison among studies, aid with the replication of findings, and

shed light on possible further differential age-related decline (as per the Down's syndrome population). For example, since in the future elderly people with fragile-X will be relatively common, this discrimination of etiology will be important to know to help understand how people with this disorder age. This also applies to other conditions, such as autism and Prader–Willi syndrome.

(4) The reasons why older adults with an intellectual disability lose significant adaptive skills with increasing age still need to be fully determined. The onset of a dementing process is probably the only established factor. The effects of other disorders, especially chronic physical conditions (e.g., loss of sensory function, immobility, undiagnosed thyroid dysfunction), still require further investigation. It is highly probable that decline in adaptive behavior will mirror decline in health status.

(5) "Normal aging" or " age-associated functional decline" (AAFD) has yet to gain the attention of researchers in the field of intellectual disability. Does such a concept exist? Is this really undetected/undiagnosed illness? The differentiation of AAFD from active disease processes remains an area for important future research.

(6) How well do changes in adaptive behavior reflect a dementing process, a disorder primarily of cognitive functioning? Which domains decline first? Is decline in adaptive behavior an early sign of dementia or is there a time lag between cognitive decline and decline in social skills? In people for whom cognitive assessments may not be possible (e.g., due to underlying intellectual disability, sensory impairment, poor cooperation with testing), can assessments of adaptive behavior (possible for all) be used as a more reliable measure of dementia?

(7) Correlation studies of decline in adaptive behavior, clinical changes of aging, and neuropathological findings are required.

(8) Is there a particular order of decline in the different adaptive domains? (For example, do older adults with an intellectual disability lose skills in language and mobility before domestic or vocational skills?)

(9) Management and possible treatment issues, although still a considerable distance away, may be the most important areas of future research. Are certain skills retrievable with behavioral therapy or drug therapy? How can the most up-to-date information be disseminated to care providers?

(10) Development of more appropriate services are needed for elderly people with an intellectual disability, where age-related declines in adaptive skills are taken into account.

☐ Commentary

The assessment of adaptive behavior in people with an intellectual disability is a fundamental part of the complete assessment of the individual.

No longer is IQ testing alone acceptable. Many different instruments are available to measure adaptive functioning, but probably the most widely used instrument is the ABS (Fogelman, 1975; Nihira, Shellhaas, & Leyland, 1974). Findings of cross-sectional and more recently longitudinal studies investigating age-related changes in adaptive behavior in adults with an intellectual disability suggest that there is a marked loss of skills with increasing age over 50 years. Onset of a dementing process and absence of medical disorders remain important factors. Longitudinal studies over a number of years, the role of adaptive behavior in the diagnosis of dementia, possible responses to treatment, and more appropriate service developments remain important areas for future research.

□ References

American Psychiatric Association, Committee on Nomenclature and Statistics. (1994). *Diagnostic and statistical manual of mental disorders* (4th ed.). Washington, DC: Author.

Balthazar, E. E. (1973). *Balthazar scales of adaptive behavior, part 1: scales of social adaptation.* Palo Alto, CA: Consulting Psychologists Press.

Balthazar, E. E. (1976). *Balthazar scales of adaptive behavior, part 2: scales of functional independence.* Palo Alto, CA: Consulting Psychologists Press.

Barcikowska, M., Silverman, W., Zigman, W., Kozlowski, P. B., Kujawa, M., Rudelli, R., & Wisniewski, H. M. (1989). Alzheimer-type neuropathology and clinical symptoms of dementia in mentally retarded people without Down syndrome. *American Journal on Mental Retardation, 93,* 551–557.

Brown, F. R., III., Greer, M. K., Aylward, E. H., & Hunt, H. H. (1990). Intellectual and adaptive functioning in individuals with Down syndrome in relation to age and environmental placement. *Pediatrics, 85,* 450–452.

Burt, D. B., Loveland, K. A., Chen, Y.-W., Chuang, A., Lewis, K. R., & Cherry, L. (1995). Aging in adults with Down syndrome: Report from a longitudinal study. *American Journal on Mental Retardation, 100,* 262–270.

Cain, L. F., Levine, S., & Elzey, F. F. (1963). *Manual for the Cain–Levine social competency scale.* Palo Alto, CA: Consulting Psychologists Press.

California State Department of Developmental Services. (1978). *Client Development Evaluation Report.* Sacramento, CA: Author.

Collacott, R. A. (1992). The effect of age and residential placement on adaptive behaviour of adults with Down's syndrome. *British Journal of Psychiatry 161,* 675–679.

Cone, J. (1984). *The Pyramid scales: criterion referenced measures of adaptive behavior in severely handicapped persons.* Austin, TX: Pro-Ed.

Cooper, S.-A., & Collacott, R. A. (1993). Prognosis of depression in Down's syndrome. *Journal of Nervous and Mental Diseases, 181,* 204–205.

Doll, E. A. (1935). The Vineland Social Maturity Scale. *Training School Bulletin. 32,* 1–7, 25–32, 48–55, 68–74.

Doll, E. A. (1965). *The Vineland Scale of Social Maturity: Condensed Manual of Directions.* Circle Pines, MN: American Guidance Service Inc.

Eyman, R. K., & Widaman, K. F. (1987). Life-span development of institutionalised and community-based mentally retarded persons, revisited. *American Journal of Mental Deficiency 91,* 559–569.

Fogelman, C. J. (Ed). (1975). *AAMD adaptive behaviour scale manual.* Washington DC: American Association on Mental Deficiency.

Grossman, H. J. (Ed). (1977). *Manual On terminology and classification in mental retardation* (1977 rev.). Washington, DC: American Association on Mental Deficiency.

Gunzberg, H. C. (1977). *Progress assessment chart of social and personal development.* Stratford-upon-Avon: SEFA Publications.

Hauber, F. A., Rotegard, L. L., & Bruininks, R. H. (1985). Characteristics of residential services for older/elderly mentally retarded persons. In M. P. Janicki & H. M. Wisniewski (Eds.), *Aging and developmental disabilities: Issues and approaches* (pp. 327–350). Baltimore: Brookes.

Haveman, M. J., & Maaskant, M. A. (1989a). Defining fragility of the elderly severely mentally handicapped according to mortality risk, morbidity, motor handicaps and social functioning. *Journal of Mental Deficiency Research, 33,* 389–397.

Haveman, M., Maaskant, M. A., & Sturmans, F. (1989b). Older Dutch residents of institutions, with and without Down syndrome: Comparisons of mortality and morbidity trends and motor/social functioning. *Australia and New Zealand Journal of Developmental Disabilities, 15,* 241–255.

Heber, R. (1961). A manual on terminology and classification in mental retardation (2nd ed.). *American Journal of Mental Deficiency* (Monograph Suppl.).

Hewitt, K. E., Carter, G., & Jancar, J. (1985). Ageing in Down's syndrome. *British Journal of Psychiatry, 147,* 58–62.

Holmes, N., Shah, A., & Wing, L. (1982). The Disability Assessment Schedule: A brief screening device for use with the mentally retarded. *Psychological Medicine, 12,* 879–890.

Janicki, M. P., & Jacobson, J. W. (1982). The character of developmental disabilities in New York State: Preliminary observations. *International Journal of Rehabilitation Research, 5,* 191–202.

Janicki, M. P., & Jacobson, J. W. (1986). Generational trends in sensory, physical, and behavioral abilities among older mentally retarded persons. *American Journal of Mental Deficiency 90,* 490–500.

Janicki, M. P., & MacEachron, A. E. (1984). Residential, health, and social service needs of elderly developmentally disabled persons. *Gerontologist, 24,* 128–137.

Joiner, L. M., & Krantz, G. C. (Eds.) (1979). *Assessment of behavioral competence of developmentally disabled individuals: The MDPS.* Minneapolis, MN: University of Minnesota Press.

Kraijer, D. W., & Kema, G. N. (1985). *Sociale Redzaamheidsschaal voor zwakzinnigen.* Lisse: Swets and Zeitlinger.

Linter, C. (1986). Aspects of ageing in mental handicap. *British Journal of Mental Subnormality, 31,* 114–118.

Mercer, J. R. (1977). *System of multicultural pluralistic assessment.* New York: Psychological Corp.

Miniszek, N. A. (1983). Developmental of Alzheimer's disease in Down's syndrome individuals. *American Journal of Mental Deficiency, 87,* 377–385.

Moss, S., Hogg, J., & Horne, M. (1992). Demographic characteristics of a population of people with moderate, severe and profound intellectual disability (mental handicap) over 50 years: Age structure, IQ and adaptive skills. *Journal of Intellectual Disability Research, 36,* 387–401.

Nihira, K., Foster, R. Shellhaas, M., & Leland, H. (1974). *AAMD adaptive behavior scale,* (1974 Rev.). Washington, DC: American Association on Mental Deficiency.

Nihira, K., Leland, H., & Lambert, N. (1993). *AAMR Adaptive Behavior Scales—Residential and Community.* Austin, TX: Pro-Ed.

Prasher, V. P. (1994). Screening of ophthalmic pathology and its associated effects on adaptive behaviour in adults with Down syndrome. *European Journal of Psychiatry, 8,* 197–204.

Prasher, V. P. (1995). Screening of hearing impairment and its associated effects on adaptive behaviour in adults with Down syndrome. *British Journal of Developmental Disabilities, 91,* 126–132.

Prasher, V. P. (1996). Age-associated functional decline in adults with Down syndrome. *European Journal of Psychiatry, 10,* 129–135.

Prasher, V. P., & Chung, M. C. (1996). Causes of age-related decline in adaptive behavior in adults with Down syndrome: Differential diagnoses of dementia. *American Journal on Mental Retardation, 101,* 175–183.

Prasher, V. P., Chung, M. C., & Haque, M. S. (1988). Longitudinal changes in adaptive behavior in adults with Down syndrome: Interim findings from a longitudinal study. *American Journal on Mental Retardation, 103,* 40–46.

Prasher, V. P., & Hall, W. (1996). Short-term prognosis of depression in adults with Down syndrome: Association with thyroid status and effects on adaptive behaviour. *Journal of Intellectual Disability Research, 40,* 32–38.

Prasher, V. P., Krishnan, V. H. R., Clarke, D. J., & Corbett, J. A. (1994). The assessment of dementia in people with Down syndrome: Changes in adaptive behaviour. *British Journal of Developmental Disabilities, 90,* 120–130.

Rasmussen, D. E., & Sobsey, D. (1994). Age, adaptive behavior, and Alzheimer disease in Down syndrome: Cross-sectional and longitudinal analyses. *American Journal on Mental Retardation, 99,* 151–165.

Roeden, J. M., & Zitman, F. G. (1995). Ageing in adults with Down's syndrome in institutionally based and community-based residences. *Journal of Intellectual Disability Research, 39,* 399–407.

Schupf, N., Silverman, W. P., Sterling, R. C., & Zigman, W. B. (1989). Down syndrome, terminal illness and risk for dementia of the Alzheimer type. *Brain Dysfunction, 2,* 181–188.

Shackleton-Bailey, M. J., & Pidcock, B. E. (1983). *Halo Report 1983: Hampshire Assessment for Living with Others—Research and Development Programme, 1981–1983.* Winchester, UK: Hampshire Social Services.

Silverstein, A. B., Herbs, D., Miller, T. J., Nasuta, R., Williams, D. L., & White, J. F. (1988). Effects of age on the adaptive behavior of institutionalized and noninstitutionalized individuals with Down syndrome. *American Journal on Mental Retardation, 92,* 455–460.

Silverstein, A. B., Herbs, D., Nasuta, R., & White, J. F. (1986). Effects of age on the adaptive behavior of institutionalized individuals with Down syndrome. *American Journal of Mental Deficiency, 90,* 659–662.

Sparrow, S. S., Balla, D. A., & Cicchetti, D. V. (1984). *Interview Edition. Expanded form manual. Vineland Adaptive Behavior Scales.* Circle Pines, MN.: American Guidance Service.

Whelan, E., & Speake, B. (1979). *Learning to cope.* London: Souvenir Press.

Widaman, K. F., Gibbs, K. W., & Geary, D. C. (1987). The structure of adaptive behavior: I. Replication across fourteen samples of non profoundly retarded persons. *American Journal of Mental Deficiency, 91,* 348–360.

World Health Organization. (1992). *The ICD-10 Classification of Mental and Behavioural Disorders. Clinical Descriptions and Diagnostic Guidelines.* Geneva: WHO.

World Health Organization. (1993). *The ICD-10 Classification of Mental and Behavioural Disorders. Diagnostic Criteria for Research.* Geneva: WHO.

Zigman, W. B., Schupf, N., Lubin, R. A., & Silverman, W. P. (1987). Premature regression in adults with Down syndrome. *American Journal of Mental Deficiency, 92,* 161–168.

Zigman, W. B., Schupf, N., Silverman, W. P., & Sterling, R. C. (1989). Changes in adaptive functioning of adults with developmental disabilities. *Australian and New Zealand Journal of Developmental Disabilities, 15,* 277–287.

Zigman, W. B., Schupf, N., Sersen, E., & Silverman, W. (1995). Prevalence of dementia in adults with and without Down syndrome. *American Journal on Mental Retardation, 100,* 403–412.

4

CLINICAL CONSIDERATIONS

In this section, we begin to enter the realm of treatment and coexistent conditions, some of which may present at first glance as dementia. We also proffer some information on the most prominent risk factors or prodromal symptoms associated with Alzheimer's disease in adults with intellectual disabilities. Thus, in the opening chapter, Holland offers us a brief, plain-language summary of what is currently known about the relationships between Down's syndrome and Alzheimer's disease viewed from the clinical perspective. He reviews the existing published research on the prevalence and incidence of dementia in this population and provides us with a detailed protocol for the assessment, differential diagnosis (Figure 10.1) and subsequent development of management strategies and regular reevaluation. In Figure 10.2, he greatly enhances the presentation by providing a flow chart of each of the steps and decision points in differential diagnosis. The reader is also provided with access to the work in the author's own laboratories at Cambridge University, which have provided experimental evidence of the usefulness of the modified Cambridge Examination for Mental Disorders of the Elderly (CAMDEX) and a concise neuropsychological test, the CAMCOG, to assist dementia diagnosis in persons with Down's syndrome.

In chapter 11, Burt discusses the notion that depression presents practitioners with a significant challenge when changes in cognitive function are observed as a prodromal syndrome for later development of Alzheimer's disease. Burt reviews the evidence available concerning reversible dementias that may contribute to misdiagnosis of Alzheimer's disease. A set of practical guidelines are then offered for the use of neuropsychological assessment methods. The author suggests the use of as many sources of information as possible, and the assessment of a wide range of behaviors viewed in as many situations as possible. She reflects on the limitations in sensitivity and specificity of the familiar dexamethasone suppression test in the diagnosis of depression. In this regard, she notes that similar criticisms can be leveled against psychopathology scales for detecting depression in adults with intellectual disabilities but which have not been designed for those with a possible comorbid dementia. She tells us also that aggressive treatment of correctly diagnosed depression with adequate follow-up is strongly recommended and that treatment of depression should be sustained because declines in function associated with this condition may endure for a number of years. Burt concludes this chapter by pointing out that there is a significant and growing need for improvements in the education of all health care professionals regarding psychiatric disorders in persons with intellectual disabilities and their rights to treatment.

Thorpe, in the following chapter, reviews the delineation and differentiation of the wide overlap between a variety of psychiatric disorders with depression and dementia in adults with intellectual disabilities. She points out that the emphasis should be on the accurate delineation of dementia from depression, bipolar disorders, anxiety and somatoform disorders, psychoses, and sleep disorders. The psychiatric perspective given to these issues is strongly supported by brief and precise examinations of seven cases supported by references to recent research literature. Thorpe, like several of the authors in this volume, underscores the imperative need to approach the demands of a clinical diagnostic work-up of aging adults with intellectual disabilities using a longitudinal, follow-up strategy.

The growing role and benefits of new psychopharmacologic agents in the management of many conditions associated with an aging population with intellectual disabilities are highlighted in detail by Tsiouris in the last chapter in this section. However, he underscores the need for extreme caution because the specific knowledge about the adverse effects of many of these medications on persons with intellectual disabilities is largely unknown. This situation is particularly acute concerning the sedative, anticholinergic, extrapyramidal, and hypotensive effects of drugs used with aging adults with intellectual disabilities. Nevertheless, these new agents give providers of services new options not previously available in the treatment and management of psychotic, depressive, bipolar, anxiety, and impulse control disorders as well as self-injurious behaviors, all of which are singled out for particular scrutiny by Tsiouris.

Anthony J. Holland

Down's Syndrome

Following the substantial improvement in the life expectancy of people with Down's syndrome, the prevalence of age-related health problems has become increasingly apparent. One particularly important association is the age-associated risk of Alzheimer-like neuropathological change and dementia of the Alzheimer type. The diagnosis of dementia in people with Down's syndrome is more difficult because of the likely preexisting intellectual impairment, and it relies on establishing evidence of a functional deterioration in memory and other cognitive abilities often in association with changes in personality. Other age-related problems, such as sensory impairments and thyroid dysfunction, or the possibility of depression, need to be considered, as any associated functional deterioration may well be reversible. The diagnosis of Alzheimer's disease is important in order to make sense of the changes that have been observed and to guide in the development of support for that individual.

Studies in the field of intellectual disability have in the past been criticized for what has often been seen as an overemphasis on the use of "diagnostic labels." However, more recent development in the behavioral sciences along with that of cytogenetics and molecular genetics has shown that

Address correspondence to: Anthony John Holland, B.SC., MBBS, MRCP, MRCPsych., MPhil, Dip Hum & Clin Genet. Section of Developmental Psychiatry, Cambridge University, Douglas House, 18b Trumpington Road, Cambridge, CB2 2AH, United Kingdom.

My thanks to Mrs. Robbie Patterson for her considerable administrative and secretarial support in the preparation of this chapter.

specific genetic or chromosomally determined disorders resulting in intellectual disability may also be associated with an increased propensity to specific types of cognitive deficits, problem behaviors, or particular physical or mental health problems (Flint, 1995). Knowing about the links between the cause of the disability, on the one hand, and the problem behavior or psychiatric disorder, on the other, can aid in diagnosis by making people aware of the potential for the development of such problems and, from a research prospective, help in the understanding of the possible underlying basis for the related problem. The association between Down's syndrome and the increased risk of developing in later life dementia due to Alzheimer's disease is an example of this (see Holland & Oliver, 1995 for review).

Although the cause of Down's syndrome was not known until 1959 when Lejeune, Gautier, and Turpin (1959) first described the characteristic trisomy 21, the fact that people with Down's syndrome may age prematurely and develop "senility" was reported over 100 years ago at a time when people with Down's syndrome rarely lived into adult life (Fraser & Mitchell, 1876). This long-standing observation has taken on a new significance as the life expectancy of people with Down's syndrome has improved so dramatically during this century. In this chapter the relationship between the presence of an extra copy of chromosome 21 from conception (trisomy 21) resulting in a child having Down's syndrome and the observed increased propensity to Alzheimer's disease in later life will be considered. From a service perspective this an important issue as Down's syndrome is the single most common cause of intellectual disability, and if the needs of this group of people are likely to change in later life, due to the onset of dementia, then services need to plan for this situation. From the individual's point of view, as well as that of their family and other carers, it is important to recognize when a problem such as dementia is developing so that an accurate diagnosis can be made and appropriate support strategies established.

☐ Aging in People with Down's Syndrome

Although the mean life expectancy of people with Down's syndrome still remains less than that of the general population, it has increased from less than 10 years in the early 1900s to nearly 50 years now, and 20% or more of the people with Down's syndrome may be over the age of 55 years at any one time (Penrose, 1949; Malone, 1988). This observation of a reduced life expectancy together with the age-associated changes that affect people with Down's syndrome has led to the proposal that people with Down's syndrome may age prematurely, and health-related problems which occur more frequently in the general population age 70 and over may occur in people with Down's syndrome as young as age 30 and over. There is some evidence for this in that people with Down's syndrome are at risk for hearing and visual impairments, thyroid disorder, and dementia of the Alzheimer type at a younger age than those without Down's syndrome. The importance of this is that in contrast to congenital problems associated with Down's syndrome (e.g., congenital heart disease), which are usually readily apparent at birth, problems associated with aging may develop insidiously and therefore can be missed easily.

Although clinical changes in later adult life and "early senility" were first described a long time ago, the recognition of an association with Alzheimer's disease depended on neuropathological studies that showed that people with Down's syndrome developed the plaques and neurofibrillary tangles characteristic of Alzheimer's disease as early as 30 years of age (e.g., Jervis, 1948; Malamud, 1964). More recently these studies have enabled a longitudinal picture of the brain changes associated with the ultimate development of the classical neuropathological features of Alzheimer's disease to be established (see Mann, 1993, for review). Early in childhood there appears to be increased diffuse deposition of the amyloid protein (characteristically found in Alzheimer's disease) followed later by the development of the classical plaques and neurofibrillary tangles (Mann & Esiri, 1989). It was this marked difference in terms of neuropathological change with increasing age between Down's syndrome and other causes of intellectual disability that subsequently led to a search on chromosome 21 for a possible "candidate gene" for Alzheimer's disease. The gene coding for the amyloid precursor protein (APP) was subsequently localized on chromosome 21 (Goldgaber, Lerman, MacBride, Saffioti, & Gajdusecek, 1987), and more recently increased amyloid levels in the blood as well as in the brains of people with Down's syndrome were reported (Rumble, Retallack, Hilbich, Simms, Multhaup, & Martins, 1989). Although excessive amyloid deposition and plaques and tangle formations in the brains of people with Down's syndrome are found at a young age, most studies report that the mean age for the onset of dementia is not until the early 50s. This marked difference in age between neuropathological and clinical change may reflect difficulties associated with detection of clinical change in people with a preexisting cognitive impairment. Therefore, the age at which dementia is first recognized is later than is in fact the case, or it may relate to the biological changes necessary for dementia to develop. For example, it may be that cerebral deposition of amyloid has to reach a critical level (Royston, Kodical,

Mann, Groom, Landon, & Roberts, 1994) or that some other neuropatho-logical event has to occur, such as changes in tau protein (Mukaetova-Ladinska, Harrington, Roth, & Wischik, 1994), before neuronal cell death occurs and markedly compromised cerebral function becomes apparent. Therefore, whether the amyloid gene and the excess production of amy-loid remain the key causative factor in the development of Alzheimer's disease in people with Down's syndrome remains open to question. In the general population, mutations in the APP gene have been shown to be associated with rare early-onset familial cases of Alzheimer's disease (Goate et al., 1991) indicating that a primary disorder of the amyloid can in these rare cases lead to the early onset of Alzheimer's disease.

   As with the general population, increasing age in people with Down's syndrome is the most significant risk factor for dementia in general as well as for Alzheimer's disease specifically; however, other factors in the general population have been shown to increase the age-specific risk. These include past head injury (Heyman, Wilkinson, Stafford, Helns, Sig-mon, & Weinberg, 1984) and/or depression and the presence of a thyroid disorder (Van Duijin & Hofman, 1992). In addition, a family history of Alzheimer's disease (Heston, Mastri, Anderson, & Anderson, 1981) or the presence of the ApoE 4 allele of the ApoE gene also increases the risk. The extent to which these factors influence the age-specific rates of Alz-heimer's disease in people with Down's syndrome has only been explored in a limited way. ApoE status does not appear to have a marked effect on cerebral amyloid deposition in young people with Down's syndrome but may have an adverse effect on life expectancy (Mann, 1993).

☐ Clinical Change in People with Down's Syndrome Associated with Increasing Age

Numerous neuropathological studies clearly established that marked changes in the brain occur with increasing age in people with Down's syndrome and that these were very similar to those found with Alzhei-mer's disease in the general population. It was therefore argued that a very significant proportion of people with Down's syndrome would de-velop dementia of the Alzheimer type in later life. Earlier cross-sectional clinical studies reported evidence of cognitive impairments in older rather than younger people with Down's syndrome (see Oliver & Holland, 1986, for review; Haxby, 1989; Thase, Tigner, Smeltzer, & Liss, 1984) but whether this was because the older group had declined cognitively due to the onset of dementia was uncertain. The diagnosis of dementia in people with a preexisting cognitive impairment was recognized as being more problematic in that it depends on the recognition of change in a number of domains of cognitive ability that may already be impaired due to preexisting intellectual disability but which may be deteriorating further due to dementia. Furthermore, the sensory impairments also associated with age together with thyroid disorder may mimic the onset of dementia.

There have been a number of longitudinal studies that have attempted to clearly establish the prevalence of dementia in people with Down's syndrome. These studies are problematic in their methodology, as in some cases they have used clinic or institutional samples and the criteria used for diagnosis have varied. Zigman et al. (1995, 1997) summarized these studies and reported rates of dementia of 8% in those between 35 and 49 years, increasing to between 50% and 75% in those over 60 years. (See Table 10.1.) In some studies rates of dementia were particularly high (Lai & Williams, 1989; Evenhuis, 1990; Holland, Hon, Stevens, & Huppert, 1996; Holland, Hon, Huppert, Stevens, & Watson, 1998). For example, Evenhuis (1990) in a prospective longitudinal study followed up 17 older people with Down's syndrome until their death and found that 15 of them developed dementia (mean age of onset was 51.3 years). In a population-based study undertaken in one health district in the United Kingdom, age-specific rates of dementia meeting International Classification of Diseases (ICD-10) and Diagnostic and Statistical Manual of Mental Disorders (DSM-IV) criteria of 0%, 3.4%, and 26% in the 30–39, 40–49, and 50–59 age groups, respectively, were observed (Holland et al., 1996). These closely follow the age-specific prevalence rates for presumed Alzheimer's disease found in the general population aged 70 years and older. Rates were higher if the criteria in the Cambridge Assessment for Mental Disorders in the Elderly (CAMDEX; Roth, Huppert, & Tym, 1988) were used (Holland et al., 1996). Personality changes, in the absence of diagnosed dementia, were reported in the younger group, and the authors proposed that the pattern of clinical change across different age groups may reflect the effect that previous abnormalities of brain development, primarily affecting the frontal lobe, might have on the "reserve capacity" of the frontal lobes in particular. Therefore, those functions served by the frontal lobes would be the first to be compromised with the development of increasing neuropathological change of the Alzheimer type. These prevalence studies are important, as they provide the figures that help to plan for services and give some idea about the clear age-specific risk for dementia.

Findings from brain imaging studies using different imaging techniques have provided support for these clinical findings. In essence studies of brain structure, function, and neuronal breakdown have indicated that

TABLE 10.1.   Studies assessing prevalence of dementia among adults with intellectual disabilities.

Study	N of Subjects	Age Range	Instruments	Prevalence	Comments
Ropper & Williams, 1980	20	30 and older	Medical record review	15%	Autopsy study
Thase, Liss, Smeltzer, & Maloon, 1982	40	25–64	Carer report Neuropsychological assessment Physical examination	15% 25–44, 45% 45–64	Cross-sectional study
Dalton & Crapper, McLachlan, 1984	59	19–58	Delayed-matching-to sample test of memory	24% in adults greater than 49 years of age	Longitudinal study
Hewitt, Carter, & Jancar, 1985	23	50+	IQ Scales Carer report Clinical assessment	39%	Cross-sectional study
Wisniewski, Wisniewski, & Wen, 1985	100	11–80	Medical record review	4% under age 30, 26% age 30+	Autopsy study
Haveman, Maaskant, & Sturmans, 1989	129	20+	Medical record review	0% 20–39, 9% 40–49, 20% 50–59, 75% 60+	Cross-sectional study
Lai & Williams, 1989	73	35+	Medical record review Carer report Clinical assessment	8% 35–49, 55% 50–59, 75% 60+	Longitudinal study
Schupf, Silverman, Sterling, & Zigman, 1989	99	20–69	MDPS [Minnesota Developmental Programming System]	4% 20–39, 26% 40–49, 51% 50–59, 59% 60–69	Retrospective cohort, followed until death

TABLE 10.1.   (continued)

Study	N of Subjects	Age Range	Instruments	Prevalence	Comments
Evenhuis, 1990	17	40+	IQ Scales Clinical assessment Medical record review	82.3%	Cohort study, followed until death
Francheschi, Comola, Piattoni, Gualandri, & Canal, 1990	50	20–52	Carer report Modified Blessed Carer report Global deterioration Scale	18% 0% 20–29, 33% 30–39, 55% 40–52	Cross-sectional study, mild mental retardation
Burt, Loveland, & Lewis 1992	61	20–60	IQ Scales Neuropsychological Adaptive behavior	8.2%	Cross-sectional study
Cole, Neal, Fraser, & Cowie, 1994	12	36–65	Clinical history Medical record review	83.3%	Autopsy study
Prasher, 1995	201	16–76	Medical record review Carer interview Clinical assessment Dementia assessment	0% 20–29, 2% 30–39, 9.4% 40–49, 36.1% 50–59, 54.5% 60–69	Prospective study, One time data
Zigman, Schupf, Sersen, & Silverman, 1996	2,376	21–70	MDPS	11% 21–40, 10% 41–50, 21% 51–60, 29% 61–70	Estimates change with varying cut points

Note: Adapted from Zigman et al., 1995.

cerebral atrophy, developing patterns of impaired brain function and neuronal loss, certainly in the fourth and fifth decade of life, occur in a significant proportion of people with Down's syndrome (Schapiro, Haxby, & Grady, 1992; Kesslak, Nagata, Lott, & Nalcioglu, 1994; Schapiro, Luxenberg, & Kayes, 1989; Murata et al., 1993).

☐ Differential Diagnosis of Decline in Older People with Down's Syndrome

Recognizing that decline is occurring and diagnosing the cause of that decline is critical; only then can appropriate treatment and management strategies be developed. There are two general problems that can lead to seriously erroneous outcomes. First, although the majority of people with Down's syndrome will have a significant intellectual impairment, there is a marked range of ability and therefore in later life if an individual is declining due to dementia this may not be recognized and observed disabilities are "labeled as due to the person's intellectual disability." Only if there is understanding about the person's past ability from the individual themselves, their family, or paid carers, who have known them for a long time, can the judgment be made about whether there has or has not been change. The diagnosis of dementia requires knowledge of the person over the previous months or years. Second, the opposite problem can occur in that as the link between Down's syndrome and Alzheimer's disease becomes more recognized, then it is assumed that apparent decline in a person with Down's syndrome is necessarily due to Alzheimer's disease. This is potentially a serious error, as the cause may be due to something that is treatable or at least partly remedial. It is well recognized that treatment of hypothyroidism, for example, can bring about a marked improvement in mental function (Thase, 1982). Similarly, people with Down's syndrome can also develop depression which may well mimic or coexist with dementia (Burt, Loveland, & Lewis, 1992; Burt, this volume). The main problems that can mimic dementia and have been reported to occur in people with Down's syndrome are shown in Figure 10.1. This is not a fully comprehensive list but rather the relatively common circumstances or conditions which should be considered.

The diagnosis of dementia in a person with Down's syndrome therefore requires evidence of a definite change in those areas of cognitive functioning that are known to deteriorate with Alzheimer's disease. These include the development of further impairments in the following areas: memory, language ability (aphasia), the ability to perform complex tasks (apraxia), orientation in time and place, everyday skills, and personality (see DSM-IV Criteria [American Psychiatric Association (APA), 1994]; WHO ICD-10 Criteria [World Health Organization (WHO), 1992]; Aylward, Burt,

FIGURE 10.1.   Differential diagnosis of apparent cognitive decline and loss of skills in a person with Down's syndrome.

- Dementia
- Depression
- Life events (e.g., bereavement)
- Physical illnesses
- Sensory impairments
- Thyroid disorder
- Combination of above

Thorpe, Lai, & Dalton, 1995, 1997; and Burt & Aylward, this volume). In the assessment of dementia in the general population a number of structured interviews as well as series of neuropsychological instruments are used in order to assess this. This includes such instruments as the CAMDEX (Roth et al., 1986), the CAMCOG (Huppert, Brayne, Gill, Paykel, & Beardsall, 1995), and the Mini-Mental State Examination (Folstein, Folstein, & McHugh, 1975). The CAMDEX informant interview and the CAMCOG and a memory battery (Rivermead Behavioural Memory Test; Wilson, Cockburn, & Baddeley, 1985) have been shown, with only minor modifications, to be useful in the assessment of people with Down's syndrome (Holland et al., 1996; Hon, Huppert, Holland, & Watson, 1998a, 1998b) and provide a valid and reliable measure of inquiring about change or measuring neuropsychological functioning over time. This process of assessment, differential diagnosis, and subsequent development of management strategies and regular reevaluation is summarized in Figure 10.2.

☐ Clinical Implications

It is generally accepted that, except for a few exceptions, people born with Down's syndrome develop over time the neuropathological features of Alzheimer's disease (Visser, Aldenkamp, van Huffelen, Kuilman, Overweg, & van Wijk, 1997). It is also clear that rates of dementia increase with increasing age. A more recent, as yet unpublished, study suggests that these age-specific prevalence rates closely mirror the age-specific rates of probable Alzheimer's disease found in the general population but occurring 40 years earlier and that some of the earliest changes may be due to compromised frontal lobe function. The diagnosis of dementia in this client group is more problematic because of the presence of preexisting intellectual impairments, and therefore disentangling what is due to the presence of intellectual disability, on the one hand, and what is

ASSESSMENT OF AGE-RELATED CHANGES IN PEOPLE WITH DOWN SYNDROME

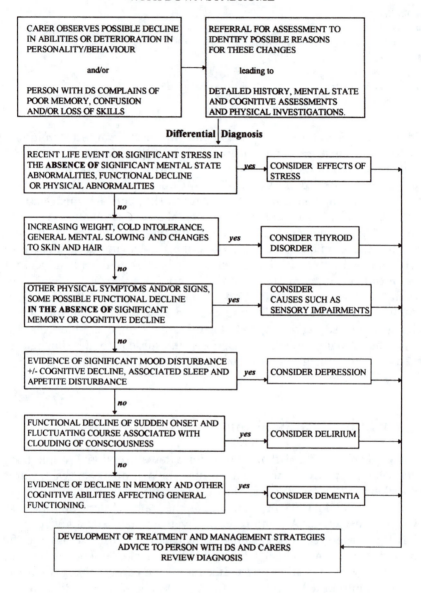

FIGURE 10.2. Assessment of age-related changes in people with Down's syndrome.

due to the onset of dementia, on the other, requires reliable longitudinal data both in the form of information on past and present functioning abilities and neuropsychological assessments.

In this context the role of those working in clinical services is to advise those with Down's syndrome, their families, and other carers about the diagnosis if a deterioration in functioning has been observed and, if the cause is established as being due to dementia, to help to develop longer-term support strategies that take into account the continuing deterioration in cognitive and functional abilities. Interventions include providing information about the likely course and consequences of a progressive disorder such as Alzheimer's disease, ensuring the maintenance of good physical health, recommending changes in the environment that may help to reduce the level of disability consequent on the deteriorating cognitive state of the person, and the development of consistent behavioral strategies to help manage any maladaptive behaviors that may occur (Holland, Karlinsky, & Berg, 1993).

☐ Commentary

Understanding observed changes in the behavior, mental state, and general well-being of people with intellectual disability requires a detailed and invariably multidisciplinary assessment. The purpose of such assessments is to identify those biological, psychological, and/or environmentally determined factors that might be contributing to this change so that the appropriate interventions can be undertaken to help the person concerned, their families, and other carers. People with Down's syndrome appear to have specific risks associated with increasing age, which includes that of developing Alzheimer's disease at a younger age than would be expected for those without Down's syndrome. The study of this association has been of great benefit to research in the general field of Alzheimer's disease, and it should be hoped that, with time, treatment options will be developed. However, at this point the recognition that a person with Down's syndrome has dementia is but the starting pointing in the development of an appropriate package of support that helps minimize the increasing disabilities that emerge as Alzheimer's disease progresses.

☐ References

American Psychiatric Association. (1994). *Diagnostic and statistical manual of mental disorders* (4th ed.). Washington, DC: Author.

Aylward, E. H., Burt, D. B., Thorpe, L. U., Lai, F., & Dalton, A. J. (1995). *Diagnosis of dementia in individuals with intellectual disability.* Washington, DC: American Association on Mental Retardation.

Aylward, E., Burt, D., Thorpe, L., Lai, F., & Dalton, A. J. (1997). Diagnosis of dementia in individuals with intellectual disability: Report of the task force for development of criteria for diagnosis of dementia in individuals with mental retardation. *Journal of Intellectual Disability Research, 41,* 152–164.

Burt, D. B., Loveland, K. A., & Lewis, K. R. (1992). Depression and the onset of dementia in adults with mental retardation. *American Journal on Mental Retardation, 96,* 502–511.

Cole, G., Neal, J. W., Fraser, W. I., & Cowie, V. A. (1994). Autopsy findings in patients with mental handicap. *Journal of Intellectual Disability Research, 38,* 9–26.

Dalton, A. J., & Crapper-McLachlan, D. R. (1984). Incidence of memory deterioration in aging persons with Down's syndrome. In J. M. Berg (Ed.), *Perspectives and progress in mental retardation: Biomedical aspects* (Vol. II, pp. 55–62). Baltimore: University Park Press.

Evenhuis, H. M. (1990). The natural history of dementia in Down's Syndrome. *Archives of Neurology, 47,* 263–267.

Flint, J. (1995). Behavioral phenotypes: A window onto the biology of behaviour. *Journal of Child Psychiatry and Psychology, 37,* 355–367.

Folstein, M. F., Folstein, S. E., & McHugh, P. R. (1975). Mini-Mental State. A practical method for grading the cognitive state of patients for the clinician. *Journal of Psychiatry Research, 12,* 189–198.

Francheschi, M., Comola, M. Piattoni, F., Gualandri, W., & Canal, N. (1990). Prevalence of dementia in adult patients with Trisomy 21. *American Journal of Medical Genetics Supplement, 7,* 306–308.

Fraser, J., & Mitchell, A. (1876). Kalmuc idiocy: Report of a case with autopsy with notes of 62 cases. *Journal of Mental Science, 22,* 161.

Goate, A., Chartier-Harlin, M. C., Mullan, M., Brown, J., Crawford, F., Fidani, L., Giuffra, L., Haynes, A., Irving, N., & James, L. (1991). Segregation of missense mutation in the amyloid precursor protein gene with familial Alzheimer's disease. *Nature, 349,* 704–746.

Goldgaber, D., Lerman, M. I., MacBride, O. W., Saffioti, U., & Gajdusecek, D. C. (1987). Characterization and chromosomal localization of a cDNA encoding brain amyloid of Alzheimer's disease. *Science, 235,* 877–880.

Haveman, M., Maaskant, M. A., & Sturmans, F. (1989). Older Dutch residents of institutions, with and without Down's syndrome: Comparison of mortality and morbidity trends and motor/social functioning. *Australia and New Zealand Journal of Developmental Disabilities, 15,* 241–255.

Haxby, J. V. (1989). Neuropsychological evaluation of adults with Down's Syndrome: Patterns of selective impairment in non-demented old adults. *Journal of Mental Deficiency Research, 33,* 193–210.

Heston, L. L., Mastri, A. R., Anderson, A. R., & Anderson, V. E. (1981). The genetics of Alzheimer's disease: Association with hematological malignancy and Down syndrome. *Archives of General Psychiatry, 34,* 976–981.

Hewitt, K. E., Carter, G., & Jancar, J. (1985). Ageing in Down's syndrome. *British Journal of Psychiatry, 147,* 58–62.

Heyman, A., Wilkinson, W. E., Stafford, J. A., Helns, M. J., Sigmon, A. H., & Weinberg, T. (1984). Alzheimer's disease: A study of epidemiological aspects. *Annals of Neurology, 15,* 335–341.

Holland, A. J., Hon, J., Stevens, F., & Huppert, F. A.(1996). *Population-based study of cognitive decline and dementia in older adults with Down's Syndrome.* Paper presented at the 10th

World Congress of the International Association for the Scientific Study of Intellectual Disabilities, Helsinki, Finland.

Holland, A. J., Karlinsky, H., & Berg, J. M. (1993). Alzheimer disease in persons with Down Syndrome: Diagnostic and management considerations. In J. M. Berg, H. Karlinsky, & A. J. Holland (Eds.), *Alzheimer disease, Down syndrome and their relationship* (pp. 95–114). Oxford: Oxford Medical Publications.

Holland, A. J., & Oliver, C. (1995). Down's syndrome and the links with Alzheimer's disease. *Journal of Neurology, Neurosurgery and Psychiatry, 59,* 111–114.

Holland, A. J., Hon, J., Huppert, F. A., Stevens, F., & Watson, P. (1998). Population-based study of the prevalence and presentation of dementia in adults with Down's syndrome. *British Journal of Psychiatry, 172,* 493–498.

Hon, J., Huppert, F. A., Holland, A. J., & Watson, P. (1998a). The value of the Rivermead Behavioural Memory Test (Children's Version) in an epidemiological study of older adults with Down syndrome. *British Journal of Clinical Psychology, 37,* 15–29.

Hon, J., Huppert, F. A., Holland, A. J., & Watson, P. (1998b). The value of the Cambridge Cognitive Examination (CAMCOG) in an epidemiological study of older adults with Down's Syndrome. Manuscript submitted for publication.

Huppert, F. A., Brayne, C., Gill, C., Paykel, E. S., & Beardsall, L. (1995). CAMCOG—A concise neuropsychological test to assist dementia diagnosis: Socio-demographic determinants in an elderly population sample. *British Journal of Clinical Psychology, 34,* 529–541.

Jervis, G. A. (1948). Early senile dementia mongoloid idiocy. *American Journal of Psychiatry, 105,* 102–106.

Kesslak, J. P., Nagata, S. F., Lott, I., & Nalcioglu, O. (1994). Magnetic resonance imaging analysis of age-related changes in the brains of individuals with Down's syndrome. *Neurology, 44,* 1039–1045.

Lai, F., & Williams, R. (1989). A prospective study of Alzheimer's disease in Down's Syndrome. *Archives of Neurology, 46,* 849–853.

Lejeune, J., Gautier, M., & Turpin, R. (1959). Étude de chromosomes somatiques de neuf enfants mongolien. *Comptes Rendus Hebdomadaires de Séances de l'Acádámie des Sciences, 248,* 1721–1722.

Malamud, N. (1964). Neuropathology. In H. A. Stevens & R. Heber (Eds.), *Mental retardation: A review of research* (pp. 429–452). Chicago: University of Chicago Press.

Malone, Q. (1988). Mortality and survival of the Down's Syndrome population in Western Australia. *Journal of Mental Deficiency Research, 32,* 59–65.

Mann, D. M. A. (1993). Association between Alzheimer disease and Down syndrome: Neuropathological observations. In J. M. Berg, H. Karlinsky, & A. J. Holland (Eds.), *Alzheimer disease, Down syndrome and their relationship* (pp. 71–92). Oxford: Oxford Medical Publication, Oxford University Press.

Mann, D. M. A., & Esiri, M. M. (1989). The pattern of acquisition of plaques and tangles in the brains of patients under 50 years of age with Down's syndrome. *Journal of the Neurological Sciences, 89,* 169–179

Mukaetova-Ladinska, E. M., Harrington, C. R., Roth, M., & Wischik, C. M. (1994). Distribution of Tau protein in Down's syndrome: Quantitative differences from Alzheimer's disease. *Developmental Brain Dysfunction, 7,* 311–329.

Murata, T., Koshino, Y., Omori, M., Murata, I., Nishio, M., Horie, T., Umezawa, Y., Isaki, K., Kimura, H., Itoh, S., Maeda, M., & Ishii, Y. (1993). In vivo proton magnetic resonance spectroscopy study on premature ageing in adult Down's syndrome. *Biological Psychiatry, 34,* 290–297.

Oliver, C., & Holland, A. J. (1986). Down's syndrome and Alzheimer's disease: A review. *Psychological Medicine, 16,* 307–322.

Penrose, L. S. (1949). The incidence of mongolism in the general population. *Journal of Mental Science, 95,* 685–688.

Prasher, V. P. (1995). Age-specific prevalence, thyroid dysfunction and depressive symptomatology in adults with Down syndrome and dementia. *International Journal of Geriatric Psychiatry, 10,* 25–31.

Ropper, A. H., & Williams, R. S. (1980). Relationship between plaques, tangles, and dementia in Down syndrome. *Neurology, 30,* 639–644.

Roth, M., Huppert, F. A., & Tym, E. (1988). *The Cambridge Examination for Mental Disorders of the Elderly.* Cambridge: Cambridge University Press.

Roth, M., Tym, E., Mountjoy, C. Q., Huppert, F. A., Hendrie, H., Verma, S., & Goddard, R. (1986). CAMDEX: A standardized instrument for the diagnosis of mental disorder in the elderly with special reference to the early detection of dementia. *British Journal of Psychiatry, 149,* 698–709.

Royston, M. C., Kodical, N. S., Mann, D. M. A., Groom, K., Landon, M., & Roberts, G. W. (1994). Quantitative analysis of β Amlyloid deposition in Down's syndrome using computerized image analysis. *Neurodegeneration, 3,* 43–51.

Rumble, B., Retallack, R., Hilbich, C., Simms, G., Multhaup, G., & Martins, R. (1989). Amyloid A4 protein and its precursors in Down's Syndrome and Alzheimer's disease. *New England Journal of Medicine, 320,* 1446–1452.

Schapiro, M. B., Haxby, J. V., & Grady, C. L. (1992). Nature of mental retardation and dementia in Down syndrome: Study with PET, CT and neuropsychology. *Neurobiology of Aging, 13,* 723–734.

Schapiro, M. B., Luxenberg, J. S., & Kayes, J. A. (1989). Serial quantitative CT analysis of brain morphometrics in adults with Down's syndrome with different ages. *Neurology, 39,* 1349–1353.

Schupf, N., Silverman, W. P., Sterling, R., & Zigman W. B. (1989). Down syndrome, terminal illness and risk for dementia of the Alzheimer type. *Brain Dysfunction, 2,* 181–188.

Thase, M. E. (1982). Reversible dementia in Down's syndrome. *Journal of Mental Deficiency Research, 26,* 111–113.

Thase, M. E., Liss, L., Smeltzer, D., & Maloon, J. (1982). Clinical evaluation of dementia in Down's syndrome: A preliminary report. *Journal of Mental Deficiency Research, 26,* 239–244.

Thase, M. E., Tigner, R., Smeltzer, D., & Liss, L. (1984). Age-related neuropsychological deficits in Down's syndrome. *Biological Psychiatry, 19,* 571–585.

Van Duijin, C. M., & Hofman, A. (1992). Risk factors for Alzheimer's disease: The EURODERM collaborative re-analysis of case-control studies. *Neuroepidemiology, 11* (Suppl. 1), 106–113.

Visser, F. E., Aldenkamp, A. P., van Huffelen, A. C., Kuilman, M., Overweg, J., & van Wijk, J. (1997). Prospective study of the prevalence of Alzheimer-type dementia in institutionalized individuals with Down's syndrome. *American Journal on Mental Retardation, 101,* 400–412.

Wilson, B., Cockburn, J., & Baddeley, A. D. (1985). *The Rivermead Behavioral Memory Test.* Reading, UK: Thames Valley Test Company.

Wisniewski, K. E., Wisniewski, H. M., & Wen, G. Y. (1985). Occurrence of Alzheimer's neuropathology and dementia in Down syndrome. *Annals of Neurology, 17,* 278–282.

World Health Organization. (1992). *ICD-10: International statistical classification of diseases and related health problems* (10th rev.). Geneva: WHO.

Zigman, W. B. Schupf, N., Haveman, M. J., Anderson, D., Babula, M., Collacott, R., Cooper, S.-A., Gerber, T., Lai, F., Prasher, V., Silverman, W., & Zigman, A. (1995). *Epidemiology of Alzheimer disease in mental retardation: Results and recommendations from an international conference.* Washington, DC: American Association on Mental Retardation.

Zigman, W. B., Schupf, N., Haveman, M.J., Anderson, D., Babula, M., Collacott, R., Cooper, S.-A., Gerber, T., Lai, F., Prasher, V., Silverman, W., & Zigman, A. (1997). Epidemiology of Alzheimer disease in mental retardation: Results and recommendations from an international conference. *Journal of Intellectual Disability Research, 41,* 76–80.

Zigman, W. B., Schupf, N., Sersen, E., & Silverman, W. (1996). Prevalence of dementia in adults with and without Down syndrome. *American Journal on Mental Retardation, 100,* 403–412.

Diana B. Burt

Dementia and Depression

The risk of misdiagnosing primary dementia and depression in adults with mental retardation is high, particularly for adults with Down's syndrome. Information and practice guidelines are provided that will reduce the risk of misdiagnosis in this population. Similarities and differences in risk factors for adults with mental retardation compared with adults in the general population are presented. Then relevant literature is briefly summarized, including the following: a description of 15 cases with a completely reversible dementia, prevalence figures for depression versus other psychiatric disorders, course of treatment for depression in adults with mental retardation, and psychiatric symptoms found in adults with mental retardation who appear to be demented. Finally, clinical, policy, and research recommendations are made.

When declines in memory and/or other cognitive functions occur within the context of depressive or other psychiatric symptoms, practitioners face a significant diagnostic challenge. Even in the general population, primary dementia and dementia secondary to depression are mistaken for each other at least 10%–20% of the time (desRosiers, 1992a, 1992b). The diagnostic challenge becomes even more daunting and the risk of misdiagnosis increases when the individual presenting with apparent dementia and psychiatric symptoms is an adult with intellectual disability

Address correspondence to: Diana B. Burt, Ph.D., 6509 Gettysburg Drive, Madison, WI 53705.

This work was supported by a grant from the National Institute of Child Health and Human Development (R01 HD30786, PI: Diana Burt).

(Burt, Loveland, & Lewis, 1992; Burt et al., 1996; Gedye, 1995; Warren, Holroyd, & Folstein, 1989). The purpose of this chapter is to provide information and practice guidelines that will reduce the risk of misdiagnosis in individuals with intellectual disability. In this population, the impact of a misdiagnosis of a progressive dementia like Alzheimer's disease can be profound. Problem behaviors that could be associated with dementia or depression are the leading reasons for institutionalization or reinstitutionalization of persons living in the community and also result in job loss or lowered job status (Bruininks, Hill, & Morreau, 1988). Conversely, misdiagnosing dementia as a psychiatric disorder or behavior problem could result in a referral only to a behavioral specialist (Des Noyers Hurley & Sovner, 1986), thus preventing an individual from receiving the appropriate dementia work-up to identify possible causes and treatment for reversible dementia, and appropriate planning for progressive or irreversible dementia (for definitions of types of dementia, see Wherrett, this volume).

Although many factors influencing diagnostic and follow-up decisions in adults with intellectual disability are similar to those identified in the general population, other issues specific to adults with intellectual disability increase the risk of misdiagnosis. After discussing similarities and differences in factors related to misdiagnosis, an update of relevant literature will be presented. Specifically, the following evidence will be summarized: (a) 15 documented cases of individuals with intellectual disability who had a completely reversible dementia; (b) the prevalence and treatment of depression in adults with intellectual disability; and (c) psychiatric symptoms found in adults with dementia who did not appear to have dementia secondary to depression. Finally, clinical assessment and follow-up recommendations will be presented, followed by recommendations for policy and research.

☐ Risk Factors for Misdiagnosis Shared with the General Population

The risk of misdiagnosing a treatable psychiatric disorder as a progressive, irreversible dementia appears to be greatest for adults with intellectual disability who are eventually diagnosed with depression (Burt et al., 1992; Gedye, 1995; Warren et al., 1989). No cases of reversible dementia secondary to other psychiatric disorders, except those apparently due to adverse effects of neuroleptic administration (Gedye, 1995), have been reported. Therefore, discussion will focus primarily on misdiagnosis related to depression, but dementia secondary to other psychiatric disorders cannot be ruled out without appropriate work-up. Three factors related to misdiagnosis between dementia secondary to depression and dementia of the Alzheimer type, which are applicable to the population of adults with intellectual disability, have been identified: (a) overlap of symptoms between depression and progressive dementia, (b) major depression identified as a prodromal syndrome for later development of dementia of the Alzheimer type, and (c) focal neurological signs in some adults with depression, suggesting an underlying organic process (desRosiers, 1992a).

Overlap of Symptoms.   As in the general population, there can be considerable overlap between symptoms of depression and dementia of the Alzheimer type in adults with intellectual disability, particularly those with Down's syndrome. For adults with Down's syndrome, two of the most commonly reported symptoms for Alzheimer-type dementia, apathy/inactivity and loss of self-help skills, are also typical of depression. Additional overlapping symptoms reported in at least two independent studies included depressed mood, urinary incontinence, irritability, slowing, becoming uncooperative, and losing housekeeping skills (Burt et al., 1992). Given the considerable symptom overlap in adults with intellectual disability, therefore, it is imperative for the clinician to consider whether any or all of the changes in functioning are related to depression or another treatable psychiatric disorder. If so, a psychiatric or psychological evaluation becomes most critical in the dementia work-up, and timely and appropriate referrals for further assessment and treatment are often required.

Major Depression as a Prodromal Syndrome for Later Progressive Dementia.   In the general population, major depression is diagnosed in 15% to 20% of patients who later develop Alzheimer's disease (desRosiers, 1992a). In adults with dementia secondary to depression, more than half of them eventually developed dementia of the Alzheimer type (Alexopoulos, 1991; Kral & Emery, 1989). In addition, when the first episode of depression occurs later in life, it is more likely to be associated with cognitive impairment, cerebral atrophy, deep white matter changes, recurrences, medical comorbidity, and mortality (National Institutes of Health Consensus Conference, 1992), suggesting that the depressive episode could signal an impending irreversible dementia (Alexopoulos, Abrams, Young, & Shamoian, 1988; Cummings, 1989; desRosiers, 1992b). Comparable longitudinal studies and studies involving examination of the brain have not been conducted to determine whether major depression or dementia secondary to depression are prodromal syndromes in some adults with intellectual disability. However, depression and depressive symptoms were observed in adults with Down's syndrome who later had clear neuropsychological evidence of a progressive dementia (Burt et al., 1996). Whether the depression was a prodromal syndrome or simply coincided with very early stages of the progressive dementia could not be determined, because of a lack of a thorough premorbid neuropsychological assessment indicating level of memory and cognitive functioning before the onset of depressive symptoms. In addition, previously depressed adults with intellectual disability were found to have impaired adaptive functioning relative to their nondepressed age-matched peers (Cooper & Collacott, 1993). Whether a significant percentage of them will develop dementia of the Alzheimer type will require further follow-up. Thus, an individual with a history of a previous depression, particularly depression associated with dementia, could be at increased risk for a later progressive dementia, suggesting that more frequent assessment of functioning could be warranted. Even if depression is associated with the early or later stages of a progressive dementia in an adult with intellectual disability, functioning and quality of life can be improved with treatment (Myers & Pueschel, 1995).

Focal Neurological Signs in Individuals with Depression. In the general population, some patients with depression have focal neurological signs, suggesting an underlying organic process (desRosiers, 1992a). Given that the prevalence of neurological abnormalities in adults with intellectual disability is higher than in the general population (Habbick, Warren, Aylward, Jerram, & Pearlson, 1994), it is important for the clinician not to assume that neurological abnormalities co-occurring with depression are indicative of an underlying progressive or static dementia without a comparison with premorbid status (Aylward, Burt, Thorpe, Lai, & Dalton, 1995, 1997). Neurological abnormalities most often associated with dementia in adults with Down's syndrome include onset of seizures (McVicker, Shanks, & McClelland, 1994), pathological reflexes, myoclonus, and gait disturbance (Lai & Williams, 1989; Dalton & Crapper-McLachlan, 1986; Evenhuis, 1990). To date, none of these symptoms has been associated with depression in adults with Down's syndrome or other forms of intellectual disability (Meins, 1993). If these symptoms have not always been typical of an individual, therefore, they would be considered to be more indicative of dementia than depression.

☐ Risk Factors for Misdiagnosis Specific to Adults with Intellectual Disability

Four factors that increase the general risk of misdiagnosis of psychiatric disorders in adults with intellectual disability (Sovner & DesNoyers Hurley, 1986) would increase the risk of misdiagnosis in individuals with apparent dementia even further (Moss & Patel, 1995).

Inability to Report Symptoms and History. Deficits in the ability to observe and describe one's behavior and inner states impair the individual's ability to provide an account of current symptoms and relevant history. Thus, although self-ratings of symptoms indicative of dementia and depression provide information that is not available from other sources, they require self-assessment and communication skills that are sometimes lacking in adults with mild and possibly moderate levels of intellectual disability and usually lacking in those with more severe retardation (Aman, 1991; Laman & Reiss, 1987; Moss & Patel, 1995). In addition, adults with intellectual disability appear to have difficulty reporting symptoms that would allow discrimination of particular types of psychopathology. Self-report interview formats, developed to minimize reading and speech demands (e.g., requiring yes–no responses to indicate presence of symptoms, pointing at bar graphs to indicate symptom severity), have led to high levels of inappropriate responses, response bias, and low to moderate levels of reliability (Laman & Reiss, 1987; Prout & Schaefer, 1985; Senatore, Matson, & Kazdin, 1985; Wyngaarden, 1981). In addition, symptoms indicative of depression or dementia are sometimes reported by the individual with intellectual disability but not a care provider or family member. Because agreement between self- and informant-ratings appears to be low for depression (Clark, Reed, & Sturmey, 1991), dementia (Moss & Patel, 1995), and other behaviors in adults with intellectual disability, it suggests that substantially different types of information may be obtained from the two sources (Wyngaarden, 1981).

Carer Report. The course of dementia (i.e., insidious versus abrupt onset, gradual versus steep decline) and presence or absence of precipitating negative life events (e.g., moves, losses) is often used to differentiate between various causes of dementia (e.g., senile dementia of the Alzheimer's type versus dementia secondary to depression) (desRosiers, 1992b). If an adult with intellectual disability is unable to report an accurate history, the clinician must rely on previous records or carer reports to give an indication of best level of functioning during adulthood and an indication of when and how symptoms relevant to the dementia were first manifest. Carer-report measures of dementia and depression have been developed, but the informant is still dependent on the individual with intellectual disability to communicate his or her own internal states or to display behaviors that indirectly indicate the presence of such states. Informant reports are subject to bias and distortion (Reiss, 1990) and are affected by the psychological needs of the informant, beliefs regarding behaviors typically associated with intellectual disability, carer tolerance levels, and the setting in which behaviors are observed (e.g., individual versus group home) (Borthwick-Duffy, 1990).

Vegetative symptoms of depression such as weight loss or sleep changes should be easier for an informant to observe and report reliably. However, many adults with intellectual disability receive psychotropic medications that affect appetite, weight, sleep patterns, and diurnal mood variation (Sovner & Des Noyers Hurley, 1983). Thus, reports of vegetative symptoms are often not useful in detecting depression (Wright, 1982), and like other measures, reports of vegetative symptoms have not been shown to be reliable in adults with intellectual disability (Carlson, 1979). Finally, abnormal vegetative symptoms are not pathonogmonic to depression but also occur in dementia (Cummings, 1989). Because of possible disparities between informant and self-report of symptoms, it is essential that a dementia work-up and follow-up assessment involve as many sources of information as possible and assess behaviors across as many situations as possible (Aylward et al., 1995; Gedye, 1995). If disparities arise, which are probably more likely in the early stages of dementia, clinicians will be required to use their own judgment to formulate an appropriate and perhaps tentative diagnosis (Sunderland, Hill, Lawlor, & Molchan, 1988).

Biochemical Markers.   The use of biochemical markers for depression, such as the dexamethasone suppression test (DST) has also been explored in persons with intellectual disability to aid in accurate diagnosis. It was found, however, to have low sensitivity and specificity (Pirodsky, Gibbs, Hesse, Hsieh, Krause, & Rodriguez, 1985; Wolkowitz, 1990). In addition, the DST has low specificity particularly in terms of distinguishing among cognitively intact persons with depression, those with dementia secondary to depression, and those with depression and a primary degenerative dementia (Alexopoulos, Young, Haycox, Shamoian, & Blass, 1985).

Symptom Presentation and Assessment.   A second factor that would increase the risk of misdiagnosis is that limited intellectual and social skills affect the way that symptoms of dementia or depression are manifest (Aylward et al., 1995; Charlot, Doucette, & Mezzacappa, 1993; Glick & Zigler, 1995; Reiss & Rojahn, 1993; Sovner & DesNoyers Hurley, 1986). In addition, persons with intellectual disability often have maladaptive behaviors (e.g., self-injury) in the absence of a psychiatric disorder, and it is essential to know what is typical for a given individual so that one can determine whether a reported behavior is clinically significant or not (Aylward et al., 1995; Gedye, 1995). Finally, "cognitive disintegration" could be more likely to occur as a response to stress (Sovner & DesNoyers Hurley, 1986), resulting in changes in both cognitive and emotional functioning, that may not be indicative of an underlying progressive dementia.

Psychopathology scales, developed for adults with intellectual disability, aid in determining what is "normative" for adults with intellectual disability (e.g., Reiss Screen, Reiss, 1988; Emotional Problems Scales, Prout & Strohmer, 1991; Psychopathology Inventory for Mentally Retarded Adults (PIMRA; Matson, 1988); Diagnostic Assessment for the Severely Handicapped (DASH; Matson, 1994), and usually have informant and self-report forms. Thus, they would be useful for indicating what symptoms are outside the typical range and for comparing self-report and informant ratings. However, their specificity is often low, and they were not designed to be used with individuals with a possible comorbid dementia. Regarding depression, there are no widely accepted criteria or scales for use in the diagnosis of depression in adults with intellectual disability (Aman, 1991; Dibble, 1986; Matson, Kazdin, & Senatore, 1984). Existing measures have unknown sensitivity and low specificity, and most are based on an untested assumption of syndrome equivalence for depression between adults with intellectual disability and those in the general population (Matson et al., 1984; Senatore, Matson, & Kazdin, 1985).

A depression scale with self-report and informant versions has been developed by the author, specifically to assess depression in adults with intellectual disability. The informant version was originally developed for use in adults with dementia in the general population (Sunderland et al., 1988). The self-report measure, which is considered appropriate for adults with mild levels of intellectual impairment, uses an either–or question format, which appears to be associated with relatively high reliability in adults with intellectual disability (Wyngaarden, 1981). The scale is in the development stages, but the symptoms being assessed by it are listed in Table 11.1, which provides an indication of how observable symptoms of depression are manifest in adults with intellectual disability.

Clinician Bias.   Other factors unique to adults with intellectual disability that increase the risk of misdiagnosis of dementia (particularly in adults with Down's syndrome) are related to clinician preconceptions regarding cause of behavioral change and clinician bias regarding the value of follow-up diagnostic tests once a dementing process is suspected. Misdiagnosis is often related to a bias toward a diagnosis of a progressive, irreversible dementia and away from a diagnosis of a treatable psychiatric condition, such as depression.

For years, it was believed that all adults with Down's syndrome over the age of 35 got dementia of the Alzheimer type (see Chapter 1). Thus, the diagnosis of dementia of the Alzheimer type is typically made at a much earlier age for adults with Down's syndrome and at a time in their lives when they appear to be at risk for depression and dementia that is likely to be due to treatable causes (Gedye, 1995; Warren et al., 1989).

TABLE 11.1.   Observable symptoms of depression in adults with mental retardation.

Core Symptoms Suggesting Depression:
1. Looks sad, downcast, preoccupied, or tearful
2. No longer initiates or participates in activities that previously enjoyed[a]
3. Gets irritable or upset easily, more than expected for a given situation
4. Looks restless or agitated

Additional Symptoms:
1. Looks sleepy or drowsy during the day[b]
2. Has trouble falling asleep, staying asleep, or waking too early[c]
3. Has had a decrease or increase in amount eats[d]
4. Complains about feeling bad or needing to go to the doctor
5. Looks anxious or concerned about something (does not duplicate other symptoms such as irritability)
6. Has low energy level
7. Has reduced physical and facial expressiveness to external stimuli (reduced smiling, looks bland)
8. No longer enjoys previously enjoyed activities (consistency between informant report and observations may be poor—get an overall picture)
9. Frequently asks for assistance, regardless of need for help
10. Speech has changed in terms of tone, rate, spontaneity, loudness
11. Has noticeable differences in mood throughout the day
12. Repeatedly does something to hurt him/herself (biting, hitting, head banging, scratching)
13. Sits and stares or sits stiffly
14. Looks slowed down
15. Is physically or verbally aggressive
16. Loss of daily living skills
17. Looks fearful

Note. Observable symptoms of depression were those reported in the literature for all adults with mental retardation and are based on a revised version of the Mood Assessment Scale for Demented Adults (Sunderland et al., 1988). Additional symptoms, such as suicidal ideation, hopelessness, guilt, low self-esteem have been reported in higher functioning adults. At least one "core symptom" and a total of five symptoms must be present nearly all day, every day for two weeks to satisfy modified DSM-IV criteria for depression (Sovner, 1986). In addition, to clearly be considered as clinically significant, symptoms *must* indicate a change from typical functioning for an individual.
[a]This item focuses on initiative and motivation. If failure to engage in previously enjoyed activities is related to restriction of activities for safety reasons in an individual with dementia (e.g., they are no longer allowed to ride their bike because of lack of judgment and wandering), this item would not be considered "present" for purposes of diagnosing depression.
[b]Medication effects must be considered.
[c]Carers must often go in to check for sleep symptoms, because self-reports may not always be accurate.
[d]Differentiation must be made between eating stemming from memory loss or confusion and physical hunger. Interviews with the individual, review of documented weight changes, and notation of eating habits are helpful. Also consider medication effects.

Anecdotal reports suggest that laboratory tests and diagnostic follow-ups are still being denied to individuals with Down's syndrome in their thirties based on this erroneous belief and assignment of an immediate, unsubstantiated diagnosis of Alzheimer's disease. Similarly, it was previously believed that adults with intellectual disability fail to develop to a level that would permit them to become depressed (Nezu, Nezu, & Gill-Weiss, 1992), and thus a bias against diagnosing a primary or comorbid depression would be greater in clinicians who are unaware of the prevalence or symptoms of depression in this population.

☐ Literature Findings

Given the high risk of misdiagnosis in adults with intellectual disability, it is imperative that clinicians are aware of reported cases of dementia that were completely or partially reversible, how common depression is in adults with intellectual disability, whether depression is associated with changes in functioning in nondemented adults with intellectual disability, how treatment for depression is sometimes lengthy and complicated, and what psychiatric symptoms are common in adults with dementia.

Reversible Dementia. Fifteen adults with Down's syndrome with completely reversible dementia have been described (Gedye, 1995; Warren et al., 1989). All of the cases had an onset of dementia before age 40, suggesting that the risk of misdiagnosing a reversible type of dementia as a progressive dementia is greater for younger adults with Down's syndrome (Gedye, 1995). Of the fifteen adults, 10 had dementia secondary to depression, as indicated by a complete return to premorbid functioning after depressive symptoms remitted (Cummings, 1989; Rabins, Merchant, & Nestadt, 1984). Five depressed adults, two of whom had a primary diagnosis of Alzheimer's disease, responded to electroconvulsive therapy (ECT) treatment for depression and had a complete remission of both affective and other symptoms (Warren et al. 1989). For the other five depressed adults, remission occurred in 4 to 6 years and was related to environmental adjustments, improved physical health, or improved vision (Gedye, 1995). Two other adults had neuroleptic-induced dementia that resolved completely after medication was withdrawn (Thioridazine, and Loxapine, respectively) (Gedye, 1995). Two additional adults had reversible dementia related to difficult-to-control seizures, which eventually were controlled, and one adult had hypothyroidism-induced dementia (Gedye, 1995). At least two other adults with apparent dementia showed partial, but not complete, recovery of function when psychiatric

TABLE 11.2. Prevalence of psychiatric disorders in adults with mental retardation.

Disorder	Prevalence (%)
Anxiety	1–25
Depression	5–67
Manic-Depression	Rare (7 cases with Down's syndrome reported)
Personality Disorder	15–35
Schizophrenia	21–24

Note. References include Anxiety, Personality Disorder, and Schizophrenia: Nezu, Nezu, & Gill-Weiss, 1992; Depression: Burt, Loveland, & Lewis, 1992; Campbell & Malone, 1991; Meins, 1993; Nezu, Nezu, & Gill-Weiss, 1992; Singh, Sood, Soneklar, & Ellis, 1991; Szymanski, 1988; Manic-Depression: Cooper & Collacott, 1993.

symptoms were treated in one case and when Halcion was withdrawn in a second (Burt et al., 1996). No cases of reversible dementia have been reported for adults with intellectual disability due to other causes. Thus, at this time it appears that adults with Down's syndrome are at greater risk for a reversible dementia secondary to depression compared with their peers with intellectual disability due to other causes.

Depression: Prevalence, Effects on Functioning, and Treatment.

As indicated in Table 11.2, prevalence figures for depression in adults with intellectual disability have a large range, probably related to inconsistently applied diagnostic criteria, assumptions of syndrome equivalence with the general population, and the source of the population sampled (i.e., clinical versus general) (Nezu, Nezu, & Gill-Weiss, 1992). The prevalence figures for other psychiatric disorders in adults with intellectual disability are presented for purposes of comparison, indicating that depression is at least as prevalent as other disorders. Regarding associations with declines in functioning, as mentioned previously, depression is associated with changes severe enough to be indicative of dementia in some adults with Down's syndrome. In addition, in nondemented adults with intellectual disability, primarily those with Down's syndrome, depression is associated with declines in intellectual, memory, language, and adaptive functioning (Benson, Reiss, Smith, & Laman, 1985; Burt et al., 1992; Kazdin, Matson, & Senatore, 1983; Laman & Reiss, 1987; Szymanski & Biederman,

1984; Warren et al., 1989). Whether the extent of the declines is associated with severity of depression or an impending dementia is not known at this time.

Even when depression is accurately diagnosed, it is necessary to successfully treat the depression and provide adequate follow-up to determine to what extent any cognitive declines and behavioral changes are related to the underlying depression and to what extent they could be related to a primary dementia (Cummings, 1989; Rabins et al., 1984). Research on the medical treatment of depression in adults with intellectual disability is mostly at the case study level and suggests that treatment often involves a long and varied course (Myers & Pueschel, 1995; Pary, 1991; Sovner, Fox, Lowry, & Lowry, 1993). For example, the duration of depression in treated adults has varied from three months to six years (Gedye, 1995; Myers & Pueschel, 1995). Warren et al. (1989) successfully used electroconvulsive therapy treatment in five adults with Down's syndrome who had dementia secondary to depression after they failed to respond to or developed adverse effects to antidepressants. Social skills training has been found to be effective for adults with milder forms of intellectual disability (Matson, 1986) and other nondrug therapies (e.g., grief therapy, Harper & Wadsworth, 1993) or therapies with minimal cholinergic effects would be preferred to prevent the possibility that adverse drug effects were contributing to further declines in functioning and additional diagnostic difficulties. In short, the treatment of depression can often involve a series of attempts involving various types of social skills training, psychotherapy, or medication. Individuals and/or their carers who are resistant to assessment and/or treatment make follow-up increasingly difficult (Myers & Pueschel, 1995).

The fact that depressive symptoms do not remit after one or two trials of various antidepressants does not necessarily imply that dementia is not secondary to depression, and continued efforts at treatment are necessary. In our longitudinal study, we have been unable to rule out depression as a possible cause for declines in functioning for periods as long as five years, at which time depressive symptoms remitted and further declines in cognitive functioning occurred. In other cases, when depression remitted, individuals improved in some or all areas of functioning (Burt et al., 1996).

Psychiatric Symptoms in Adults with Dementia.   The following psychiatric symptoms were reported to be likely in adults with dementia: loss of interest, sleep difficulty, irritability, and slowness and poverty of speech. In contrast, depressed mood and delayed sleep were reported to be less likely (Moss & Patel, 1995). Whether the stage of dementia (if progressive) or the underlying intellectual disability affected the manifestation of what appear to be depressive symptoms in adults with intellectual disability is unknown. In our own longitudinal study, depressive symptoms and symptoms meeting criteria for clinical depression have been present at early and later stages of progressive, irreversible dementia in adults with Down's syndrome. In addition, the following symptoms which were not typical for the individual were also noted during the course of the disease: behavioral outbursts, oppositional and aggressive behavior, self-injurious behavior, confabulation, auditory hallucinations, exposing self in public, delusions, and stealing (Burt et al., 1996). The occurrence of psychiatric symptoms in adults with dementia increases the risk of misdiagnosing a possible progressive dementia as a psychiatric disorder, making it imperative that the clinician follows recommended diagnostic, treatment, and follow-up recommendations as outlined below.

☐ Implications for Work/Research in Dementia and Intellectual Disabilities

Clinical Recommendations.   Given that misdiagnosis is probably more likely in adults with intellectual disability, particularly those with Down's syndrome who are believed to be at risk for Alzheimer's disease, several diagnostic and treatment issues must be addressed for each case that presents with possible dementia. First, are there documented changes in functioning indicative of dementia? Second, are the changes in functioning related to a treatable psychiatric disorder? Third, is the apparent dementia reversible, partially reversible, static, or progressive? Finally, what is the proper diagnostic work-up and follow-up? Guidelines for answering the first question have been discussed in Burt and Aylward, this volume. Once a suspected dementia has been established, a complete physical and laboratory analysis should be conducted, in addition to a psychological/psychiatric evaluation, to detect the presence of any comorbid psychiatric disorder, especially depression. The clinical interview should include questions regarding degree of social support and stressful life events that could have precipitated or continue to precipitate depression (Meins, 1993; Sung et al., 1997). Once a comorbid psychiatric disorder is suspected or identified, the steps for longitudinal follow-up outlined in Table 11.3 should be followed to confirm diagnosis and course of dementia. Given the challenges of diagnosing psychiatric disorders in adults with intellectual disability, and that information should ideally be integrated across sources (e.g., self, informants from various settings) and

TABLE 11.3.   Clinical follow-up for an individual with apparent dementia and suspected comorbid depression.

Depression Status	Memory/Cognitive/Behavioral Status	Appropriate Diagnoses	Follow-Up Action Required
Initial Presentation: Present	Documented decline from baseline	Dementia Major Depression	Dementia Work-up Psychiatric Evaluation/Treatment
Possible Later Presentation: Present identified periodic	Partial or complete return to baseline	Dementia secondary to possibly identified condition (e.g., thyroid disease, medication)	Continued treatment for condition and depression, screens for dementia
	Further declines, without increase in severity of depressive symptoms	Progressive dementia Major Depression	Continue treatment for depression, evaluate for adverse effects of treatment and other causes of dementia

TABLE 11.3. (continued)

Depression Status	Memory/Cognitive/Behavioral Status	Appropriate Diagnoses	Follow-Up Action Required
Possible Later Presentation:			
Absent	Complete return to baseline	Reversible dementia secondary to depression	Periodic screens for future dementia/depression, ensure documentation in permanent record
	Partial return to baseline	Dementia if meet criteria	Monitor for further declines or improvements and possible causes
	No change	Static dementia	Monitor for further declines or improvements and possible causes
	Further decline	Progressive dementia	Alzheimer's work-up, continued follow-up for treatable conditions

Note: In our experience, an extensive neuropsychological assessment of memory and other cognitive functions to document further declines becomes less informative when an individual has progressed from a higher level of functioning (i.e., IQ >40, Mental age (MA) > about 5 years) to a level in which their IQ is <20, or MA is < about 2 years. Of course, if reason for improvement is present, reassessment is necessary. Similarly, progression of memory and cognitive decline is difficult to document in individuals whose premorbid mental age is less than 2 years and who have few verbal skills. At least one memory test has been developed, however, to document changes in such individuals (Dalton & Crapper-McLachlan, 1986).

disciplines (e.g., psychiatry, neurology, psychology, social work), it is recommended that a multidisciplinary, criteria-based team approach be used to implement the recommended steps (see Verhey et al., 1993; Sung et al.). The "multiconditional nature of dementia" (Verhey et al. 1993) and the expected lack of consistency in information from various sources using various methods makes it crucial that members from all relevant disciplines meet to combine data and generate appropriate diagnoses and treatment plans.

In choosing diagnostic team members, it should be noted that the risk of misdiagnosis between depression and dementia is greater for professionals who have not been specifically educated or trained to make psychiatric diagnoses in older adults with intellectual disability. There is a great unmet need for graduate level and physician training regarding psychiatric disorders in persons with intellectual disability, particularly disorders associated with aging (Nezu et al., 1992). There is also a need to educate all health care professionals regarding the rights of persons with intellectual disability and regarding the productive lives led by adults with intellectual disability to prevent a bias not to follow up on diagnostic tests, which would increase the risk of misdiagnosis.

Policy Recommendations.   When establishing funding and/or residential policy for adults with intellectual disability, the issues raised here stress the need to base funding and living decisions on the current and projected needs of an individual, not on a diagnosis or "label." As stated previously, reversible dementia occurs in adults with intellectual disability, and it can take years from initial behavioral signs to establish a definite and accurate diagnosis. Individuals should be allowed to "age in place" (stay in their current residence) as long as possible, and support or living decisions should not be made on the basis of fears of future declines in functioning and high service needs. In addition, support for medical care needs to be based on current needs and not on whether an illness is currently deemed to be treatable or not. Even individuals with progressive dementia, consistent with that caused by Alzheimer's disease, can benefit from treatment of comorbid psychiatric symptoms. Finally, support needs to be provided for a baseline evaluation of memory, cognitive, and behavioral functioning in early adulthood and periodic evaluation of adults with Down's syndrome starting in their mid-30s and adults with other causes of intellectual disability in their mid-40s.

Research Recommendation.   Longitudinal, prospective studies involving individuals with and without Down's syndrome with clearly described cases of dementia (i.e., progressive or not, reversible or not) are needed to aid in diagnosis, treatment, and planning. Such research should be multisite to include as many cases with dementia as possible and must involve a cognitive and behavioral assessment of the individual, psychiatric assessment involving the individual and carer as much as possible, and a complete assessment of physical condition, including medications. Questions of interest that could be addressed by such research include: (a) Is depression prodromal to progressive dementia? (b) What is the appropriate assessment and treatment of depression in adults with dementia? (c) To what extent does depression with varying levels of symptom severity affect functioning, and is the association mediated by age or cause of intellectual disability? (d) What psychiatric symptoms or comorbid conditions are associated with varying types of dementia?

☐ References

Alexopoulos, G. S. (1991). Heterogeneity and comorbidity in dementia-depression syndromes. *International Journal of Geriatric Psychiatry, 6,* 125–127.

Alexopoulos, G. S., Abrams, R. C., Young, R. C., & Shamoian, C. A. (1988). Cornell scale for depression in dementia. *Biological Psychiatry, 23,* 271–284.

Alexopoulos, G. S., Young, R. C., Haycox, J. A., Shamoian, C. A., & Blass, J. P. (1985). Dexamethasone suppression test in depression with reversible dementia. *Psychiatry Research, 16,* 277–285.

Aman, M. G. (1991). *Assessing psychopathology and behavior problems in persons with mental retardation. A review of available instruments.* Washington, DC: Department of Health and Human Services.

Aylward, E. H., Burt, D. B., Thorpe, L. U., Lai, F., & Dalton, A. J. (1995). *Diagnosis of dementia in individuals with intellectual disability.* Washington, DC: American Association on Mental Retardation.

Aylward, E. H., Burt, D. B., Thorpe, L. U., Lai, F., & Dalton, A. J. (1997). Diagnosis of dementia in individuals with intellectual disability. *Journal of Intellectual Disability Research, 41,* 152–164.

Benson, B. A., Reiss, S., Smith, D. C., & Laman, D. S. (1985). Psychosocial correlates of depression in mentally retarded adults: II. Poor social skills. *American Journal of Mental Deficiency, 89,* 657–659.

Borthwick-Duffy, S. (1990). Application of traditional measurement scales to dually diagnosed populations. In E. Dibble & D. B. Gray (Eds.), *Assessment of behavior problems in persons with mental retardation in the community* (pp. 147–157, DHHS Publication ADM 90-1642). Rockville, MD: U.S. Department of Health and Human Services.

Bruininks, R. H., Hill, B. K., & Morreau, L. E. (1988). Prevalence and implications of maladaptive behaviors and dual diagnosis in residential and other service programs. In J. A. Stark, F. J. Menolascino, M. H. Albarelli, & V. C. Gray (Eds.), *Mental Retardation and Mental Health* (pp. 3–29). New York: Springer-Verlag.

Burt, D., Chen, Y. R., Loveland, K., Lewis, K., Lesser, J., Cherry, L., Breen, N., Cummings, E., & Primeaux, S. (1996, May). *Dementia in adults with Down syndrome: A report from a longitudinal study.* Paper presented at the meeting of the American Association on Mental Retardation, San Antonio, TX.

Burt, D. B., Loveland, K. A., & Lewis, K. R. (1992). Depression and the onset of dementia in adults with mental retardation. *American Journal on Mental Retardation, 96,* 502–511.

Campbell, M., & Malone, R. P. (1991). Mental retardation and psychiatric disorders. *Hospital and Community Psychiatry, 42,* 374–377.

Carlson, G. (1979). Affective psychoses in mental retardates. *Psychiatric Clinics of North America, 2,* 499–510.

Charlot, L. R., Doucette, A. C., & Mezzacappa, E. (1993). Affective symptoms of institutionalized adults with mental retardation. *American Journal on Mental Retardation, 98,* 408–416.

Clark, A. K., Reed, J., & Sturmey, P. (1991). Staff perceptions of sadness among people with mental handicaps. *Journal of Mental Deficiency, 35,* 147–153.

Cooper, S. A., & Collacott, R. A. (1993). Mania and Down's syndrome. *British Journal of Psychiatry, 162,* 739–743.

Cummings, J. L. (1989). Dementia and depression: An evolving enigma. *Journal of Neuropsychiatry, 1,* 236–242.

Dalton, A. J., & Crapper-McLachlan, D. R. (1986). Clinical expression of Alzheimer's disease in Down syndrome. *Psychiatric Clinics of North America, 9,* 659–670.

Des Noyers Hurley, A., & Sovner, R. (1986). Dementia, mental retardation, and Down's syndrome. *Psychiatric Aspects of Mental Retardation Reviews, 5(8),* 39–44.

desRosiers, G. (1992a). Primary or depressive dementia: Psychometric assessment. *Clinical Psychology Review, 12,* 307–343.

desRosiers, G. (1992b). Primary or depressive dementia: Clinical features. *International Journal of Geriatric Psychiatry, 7,* 629–638.

Dibble, E. D. (1986). Summary: Challenges for research. *Psychopharmacology Bulletin, 22,* 1086–1087.

Evenhuis, H. M. (1990). The natural history of dementia in Down's syndrome. *Archives of Neurology, 47,* 263–267.

Gedye, A. (1995). *Dementia scale for Down syndrome* (Manual). Vancouver: Gedye Research and Consulting.

Glick, M., & Zigler, E. (1995). Developmental differences in the symptomatology of psychiatric inpatients with and without mild mental retardation. *American Journal on Mental Retardation, 99,* 407–417.

Habbick, R., Warren, A. C., Aylward, E., Jerram, J., & Pearlson, G. (1994). Synkinesias are common in Down's syndrome. *Journal of Nervous and Mental Diseases, 192,* 667.

Harper, D. C., & Wadsworth, J. S. (1993). Grief in adults with mental retardation: Preliminary findings. *Research in Developmental Disabilities, 14,* 313–330.

Kazdin, A. E., Matson, J. L., & Senatore, V. (1983). Assessment of depression in mentally retarded adults. *American Journal of Psychiatry, 140,* 1040–1043.

Kral, V., & Emery, O. (1989). Long-term follow-up of depressive pseudodementia of the aged. *Canadian Journal of Psychiatry, 34,* 445–446.

Lai, F., & Williams, R. S. (1989). A prospective study of Alzheimer disease in Down syndrome. *Archives of Neurology, 46,* 849–853.

Laman, D. S., & Reiss, S. (1987). Social skill deficiencies associated with depressed mood of mentally retarded adults. *American Journal of Mental Deficiency, 92,* 224–229.

Matson, J. L. (1986). Treatment outcome research for depression in mentally retarded children and youth: Methodological issues. *Psychopharmacology Bulletin, 22,* 1081–1085.

Matson, J. L. (1988). *The PIMRA manual.* Orland Park, IL: International Diagnostic Systems.

Matson, J. L. (1994). *The diagnostic assessment for severely handicapped II.* Baton Rouge, LA: Scientific Publishers Inc.

Matson, J. L., Kazdin, A. E., & Senatore, V. (1984). Diagnosis and drug use in mentally retarded, emotionally disturbed adults. *Applied Research in Mental Retardation, 5,* 513–519.

McVicker, R. W., Shanks, O. E. P., & McClelland, R. J. (1994). Prevalence and associated features of epilepsy in adults with Down's syndrome. *British Journal of Psychiatry, 164*, 528–532.

Meins, W. (1993). Prevalence and risk factors for depressive disorders in adults with intellectual disability. *Australia and New Zealand Journal of Developmental Disabilities, 18*, 147–156.

Moss, S., & Patel, P. (1995). Psychiatric symptoms associated with dementia in older people with learning disability. *British Journal of Psychiatry, 167*, 663–667.

Myers, B. A., & Pueschel, S. M. (1995). Major depression in a small group of adults with Down syndrome. *Research in Developmental Disabilities, 16*, 285–299.

National Institutes of Health Consensus Development Conference Statement (Vol. 9, No. 3, November 4–6, 1991). (1992). Diagnosis and treatment of depression in late life. *Journal of the American Medical Association, 268*, 1018–1024.

Nezu, C. M., Nezu, A. M., & Gill-Weiss, M. J. (1992). *Psychopathology in persons with mental retardation: Clinical guidelines for assessment and treatment*. Champaign, IL: Research Press Company.

Pary, R. J. (1991). Towards defining adequate lithium trials for individuals with mental retardation and mental illness. *American Journal on Mental Retardation, 95*, 681–691.

Pirodsky, D. M., Gibbs, J. W., Hesse, R. A., Hsieh, M. C., Krause, R. B., & Rodriguez, W. H. (1985). Use of dexamethasone suppression test to detect depressive disorder in mentally retarded individuals. *American Journal of Mental Deficiency, 90*, 245–252.

Prout, H. T., & Schaefer, B. M. (1985). Self-reports of depression by community-based mildly mentally retarded adults. *American Journal of Mental Deficiency, 90*, 220–222.

Prout, H. T., & Strohmer, D. C. (1991). *Emotional problems scales*. Odessa, FL: Psychological Assessment Resources.

Rabins, P. V., Merchant, A., & Nestadt, G. (1984). Criteria for diagnosing reversible dementia caused by depression: Validation by two year follow-up. *British Journal of Psychiatry, 144*, 488–492.

Reiss, S. (1988). *The Reiss screen test manual*. Orland Park, IL: International Diagnostic Systems.

Reiss, S. (1990). The development of a screening measure for psychopathology in people with mental retardation. In E. Dibble & D. B. Gray (Eds.), *Assessment of behavior problems in persons with mental retardation in the community* (pp. 107–118, DHHS Publication ADM 90-1642). Rockville, MD: U.S. Department of Health and Human Services.

Reiss, S., & Rojahn, J. (1993). Joint occurrence of depression and aggression in children and adults with mental retardation. *Journal of Intellectual Disability Research, 37*, 287–294.

Senatore, V., Matson, J. L., & Kazdin, A. E. (1985). An inventory to assess psychopathology of mentally retarded adults. *American Journal of Mental Deficiency, 89*, 459–466.

Singh, N. N., Sood, A., Soneklar, N., & Ellis, C. R. (1991). Assessment and diagnosis of mental illness in persons with mental retardation. *Behavior Modification, 15*, 419–443.

Sovner, R. (1986). Limiting factors in the use of DSM-III criteria with mentally ill/mentally retarded persons. *Psychopharmacology Bulletin, 22*, 1055–1059.

Sovner, R., & DesNoyers Hurley, A. (1983). Do the mentally retarded suffer from affective illness? *Archives of General Psychiatry, 40*, 61–67.

Sovner, R., & DesNoyers Hurley, A. (1986). Four factors affecting the diagnosis of psychiatric disorders in mentally retarded persons. *Psychiatric Aspects of Mental Retardation Reviews, 5*(9), 45–49.

Sovner, R., Fox, C. J., Lowry, M. J., & Lowry, M. A. (1993). Fluoxetine treatment of depression and associated self-injury in two adults with mental retardation. *Journal of Intellectual Disability Research, 37*, 301–311.

Sunderland, T., Hill, J. L., Lawlor, B. A., & Molchan, S. E. (1988). NIMH dementia mood assessment scale (DMAS). *Psychopharmacology Bulletin, 24,* 747–749.

Sung, H., Hawkins, B. A., Eklund, S. J., Kim, K. A., Foose, A., May, M. E., & Rogers, N. B. (1997). Depression and dementia in aging adults with Down syndrome: A case study approach. *Mental Retardation, 35,* 27–38.

Szymanski, L. S. (1988). Integrative approach to diagnosis of mental disorders in retarded persons. In J. A. Stark, F. J. Menolascino, M. H. Albarelli, & V. C. Gray (Eds.), *Mental Retardation and Mental Health* (pp. 124–139). New York: Springer-Verlag.

Szymanski, L. S., & Biederman, J. (1984). Depression and anorexia nervosa of persons with Down syndrome. *American Journal of Mental Deficiency, 89,* 246–251.

Verhey, F., Jolles, J., Ponds, R., Rozendaal, N., Plugge, L. A., de Vet, R., Vreeling, F. W., & van der Lugt, P. (1993). Diagnosing dementia: A comparison between a monodisciplinary and a multidisciplinary approach. *Journal of Neuropsychiatry, 5,* 78–85.

Warren, A. C., Holroyd, S., & Folstein, M. F. (1989). Major depression in Down's syndrome. *British Journal of Psychiatry, 155,* 202–205.

Wolkowitz, O. M. (1990). Use of the dexamethasone suppression test with mentally retarded persons: Review and recommendations. *American Journal of Mental Retardation, 94,* 509–514.

Wright, E. C. (1982). The presentation of mental illness in mentally retarded adults. *British Journal of Psychiatry, 141,* 496–502.

Wyngaarden, M. (1981). Interviewing mentally retarded persons: Issues and strategies. In R. H. Bruininks, C. E. Meyers, B. B. Sigford, & K. C. Lakin (Eds.), *Deinstitutionalization and community adjustment of mentally retarded people* (pp. 107-129). Washington, DC: American Association on Mental Deficiency.

Lilian U. Thorpe

Psychiatric Disorders

The diagnosis and recognition of psychiatric disorders in old age among people with intellectual disabilities are complicated by comorbid illnesses and preexisting impairments as well as baseline cognitive and functional abilities. With the inclusion of the dementias, psychiatric disorders increase in old age. Depression and dementia have some overlapping clinical symptoms and need to be differentiated for treatment purposes. Bipolar illness is often misdiagnosed as either a behavioral problem or a schizophrenic illness. Psychotic illnesses are frequently overdiagnosed in people with intellectual disabilities. Anxiety disorders are very poorly studied in this group, although they continue to have a major impact on the quality of life of aging people with intellectual disabilities. General assessment difficulties are discussed and some suggestions made for further research in the area.

Biological, psychological, and social changes associated with aging interact with preexisting intellectual disabilities to make the recognition and treatment of psychiatric illness even more challenging than in the younger intellectually challenged population, or indeed in the general elderly population. As discussed in other chapters, the life span of people

Address correspondence to: Lilian U. Thorpe, M.D., FRCP(C), Clinical Gerontology, 701 Queen Street, Saskatoon, Saskatchewan, S7K 0M7 Canada. E-mail: thorpe@duke.usask.ca.

with intellectual disabilities is increasing, necessitating improvements in the clinical understanding of aging-related issues in this group. The accurate diagnosis and treatment of psychiatric disorders in this vulnerable group are critical for maintaining optimal levels of independent psychosocial functioning and facilitating good quality of life. This chapter reviews the major psychiatric disorders of old age with an emphasis on people with intellectual disabilities. Clinical case material illustrating various disorders and relevant assessment and treatment issues will be presented. Recommendations are made for further research in this challenging area.

Most researchers investigating the rate of psychiatric and medical disorders in older people with intellectual disability have found rates similar to the general elderly population, with a few significant differences (Day & Jancar, 1994). Behavioral disorders are more common, as is dementia of the Alzheimer type (specifically in those with Down's syndrome). There is also a high prevalence of reactive depressive and anxiety symptoms (Day, 1985; James, 1986), usually related to physical health problems or bereavement.

☐ Dementing Disorders

Dementia is the most notable psychiatric disorder linked to aging. In nonintellectually disabled populations over the age of 65, about 5% suffer from severe dementia, and 15% suffer from mild dementia. Over the age of 80 this rises to about 20% of people suffering with severe dementia (Kaplan, Sadock, & Grebb, 1991). The prevalence of dementia in populations with developmental disabilities depends on the cause of the disability. It is well known now that persons with Down's syndrome have a markedly increased likelihood of developing dementia (Karlinsky, Hardy, & Rossor, 1993). Other than among those with Down's syndrome (or possibly some of the other chromosomal disorders), however, the age-specific prevalence of dementia is likely similar to that of the general population.

Although baseline functional abilities are generally lower in those with intellectual disabilities, similar patterns of decline related to dementia are seen in all areas of functioning. Behavioral changes such as sleep difficulty, irritability, inefficient thought, loss of interest, and anhedonia have been particularly related to the development of dementia in persons with intellectual disability (Moss & Patel, 1995) and are similarly likely to cause caregivers stress as in the general population. Early signs of cognitive dysfunction, such as loss of conceptualization and abstraction, may not be apparent, especially in adults with more severe intellectual disabilities. The assessment of the severity of dementia in adults with intellectual disabilities is also much more difficult than in the general population (Janicki, Heller, Seltzer, & Hogg, 1995, 1996). In general, the usual assessment instruments are difficult to use, especially in people with very low intellectual functioning, as the score may already be so low that no changes are observed with a further dementing process.

Case One—MH

MH is a 55-year-old man with Down's syndrome. Two years prior to the initial psychogeriatric assessment he started wandering out of his group home at night, causing distress to carers, especially during cold weather. He developed difficulty finding his own room and lost the ability to fully dress himself. He was noted to have increasingly frequent episodes of urinary incontinence, without evidence of bladder infections. These losses came upon him gradually, with no major sudden drops in functioning. Two months prior to the initial assessment, MH developed his first seizure. On clinical assessment he had no disorders contributing to reduced intellectual functioning (such as thyroid disease or depression), but investigation of his functional abilities showed significant reductions compared with five years ago. He was given a diagnosis of Alzheimer's disease and eventually was transferred to the dementia unit of a local nursing home.

Dementia of the Alzheimer's type appears to be the most common among persons with lifelong disabilities, as it is in the general population. Adults with Down's syndrome are particularly likely to be affected by Alzheimer's disease (Wisniewski, Hill, & Wisniewski, 1992). In some community surveys however, particularly among African Americans and Japanese, the prevalence of vascular dementia has been found to be higher than that of Alzheimer's disease (Yoshitake et al., 1995). Vascular dementias include not only the dementias resulting from repeated large strokes but also dementias resulting from gradual and progressive small vessel disease (Emery, Gillie, & Ramdev, 1994). This may occur gradually and may be clinically indistinguishable from dementia of the Alzheimer's type. Consequently, although the older clinical lore suggested that vascular dementia typically has an abrupt onset and a stepwise progression in intellectual deficits, this may not always be the case. Fuller brain imaging studies, such as SPECT (single photon emission computerized tomography) scanning may be more helpful in making the differentiation between those two types of dementia (Read, Miller, Mena, Kim, Itabashi, & Darby, 1995).

Risk factors for vascular dementia include hypertension, diabetes, smoking, obesity, and arrhythmias. The significance of making a diagnosis of vascular versus Alzheimer-type dementia is that it enables the clinician to maximize the reduction of known risk factors such as hypertension as well as allows for better understanding of future clinical progression. The psychiatric presentation of vascular dementia may also be somewhat different. People with vascular dementia are more likely to have emotionality and other mood symptoms. Those with left-sided strokes are particularly likely to develop depression, which can often be successfully treated with antidepressant medications (Starkstein & Robinson, 1994). Stroke-related mania is less common, but it tends to appear more commonly in right-sided brain lesions.

Case Two—GR

GR is a man with Down's syndrome. At initial assessment he was 48 years old and had just been admitted to the dementia unit of a local nursing home. Eight months before that he had been living in a small private care home (sharing with four other people with intellectual disabilities) and attending a local sheltered workshop. Other than having had high blood pressure for the last few years, he had been well physically and had been able to perform most of his own self-care. He was able to converse with staff, make his needs known, and was very attached to his carer, with whom he had a longstanding supportive relationship. There was a family history of heart disease and stroke but no other psychiatric history. Eight months prior to nursing home admission, he suddenly developed increased confusion and lost his ability to speak more than occasional words. He developed incontinence and had weakness on the right side of his body. Since that time he developed more episodes of acute worsening of his intellectual and physical functioning, leading eventually to a complete inability to walk, feed himself, or talk. He still appeared to recognize his previous carer but was unable to speak with her. Further investigations determined the presence of multiple small strokes.

Interventions for those suffering from dementing illnesses and intellectual disabilities generally involve treating the behavioral and psychiatric symptoms of the dementing illness, as currently there are no known significantly successful treatments for the dementia itself (for a fuller description of research in drugs to treat dementia see Stern & Davis, 1996). Acetylcholine enhancing medications such as tacrine have indeed been used with some very small success in decreasing the symptoms of dementia, but a high prevalence of side effects has limited their use. Many other medications are currently in various stages of testing and some of these may eventually prove to significantly improve the core disabilities of dementia without having major side effects.

After the assessment of dementia and the identification of specific psychiatric and behavioral problems causing distress to the affected person and significant others, various biological, psychological, and social interventions can be offered. After the maximization of medical treatment of coexisting disorders, the most important intervention for those with dementia is to adapt the environment to the person's changing intellectual and functional needs (Calkins & Chafetz, 1996). Those with typical dementia-related behaviors such as wandering need to have safe environments enabling free movement, as this helps minimize the use of physical and chemical restraints. Wandering is a normal part of the dementing process and is often positive in its function in maintaining physical mobility. Physical and chemical restraints in the general population are associated with general physical decline and increased morbidity (Strumpf & Evans, 1991). Paradoxically, aggression rates may even increase rather than decrease among those who are subjected to various forms of restraint.

General information must be provided to carers so that realistic expectations of the person's abilities can be fostered. Difficult behaviors, such as aggression, paranoia, or the loss of bowel and bladder function are better tolerated by carers if the underlying dementing process is understood. Aggression is a frequent problem, as people with dementing illnesses have a reduced ability to understand the environment around them and can react to perceived threatening situations with a great deal of anxiety and aggression. Some clinicians believe that severe aggressive behavior in those with dementia may be occasionally related to early physical and sexual abuse that later leads to the misperception of personal care as a renewed assault (Tharinger, & Horton, 1990). This factor is particularly important to consider in older demented and intellectually disabled people in view of the vulnerability of disabled people to physical and sexual abuse (Sobsey, Wells, Lucardie, & Mansell, 1995) and their preexisting reduced abilities to accurately interpret the actions of others. Personally invasive care, then, must be sensitively approached, and attempts must be made to understand the origins of particularly emotional reactions to certain aspects of care.

Medications most commonly used to treat the difficult behaviors of dementia are neuroleptics (i.e., haloperidol or chlorpromazine). These can be most successfully used to treat psychotic symptoms like paranoia, which may be contributing toward aggression. They are also often used with some success to decrease aggressive agitated behavior, even in the absence of psychosis (Schneider & Sobin, 1994). To decrease further impairment of new learning as well as minimize stiffness, drowsiness, and later involuntary movements (tardive dyskinesia), the lowest possible doses of neuroleptics should be used. For example, haloperidol, 0.25 mg twice daily, should be an initial starting dose, and dose increases should ideally occur as slowly as weekly. Regular attempts to decrease the dosage should be made. Recently a new narcoleptic, risperidone, has become available. When used in low dosage, compared to haloperidol, it causes less stiffness, drooling, and tardive dyskinesia. When compared to chlorpromazine, it causes less sedation, blood pressure drop, and dry mouth. Risperidone is currently of great interest to geriatric psychiatrists for these reasons (Owens, 1994; Raheja, Bharwani, & Penetrant, 1995) and is the subject of a large ongoing international study involving adults with intellectual disabilities.

Depressive and anxiety symptoms are common in the early stages of dementia and generally do not respond as well to antidepressants as major depressive illness itself. They may require a great deal of reassurance and reevaluation of demands made on the person. Occasionally anxiolytics may be of help, but their use should be minimized to decrease the further impairment of intellectual functioning and to minimize the risk of falls.

☐ Depressive Illness

About 15% of all general elderly community dwelling adults have depressive symptoms, and there is a slight increase in those over 75. Major depressive illness itself, however, may decrease with age (Blazer, 1990) in the general population, although special populations such as those in institutions and in general medical hospital wards have higher rates. Day and Jancar (1994) reviewed mental and physical health among older adults with intellectual disability and concluded that psychiatric disorders are more common due to a higher frequency of behavioral disorders, but that the major psychiatric disorders do not increase with age. However, a particularly high prevalence of depression and anxiety reactive to physical illness or other events was noted.

Symptoms of depressive illness include physical ones such as reduced energy, concentration, sleep, appetite, and weight. It may also, however, include psychological ones such as deterioration of intellectual functioning, sadness, low self-esteem, worthlessness, occasional paranoid thoughts, and, less commonly, suicidal thoughts. Depressive symptoms related to a grieving process are common, particularly in middle-aged persons whose parents were primary carers, and who die, leaving a significantly diminished support network to the disabled person. Grieving reactions are fairly similar to the nondisabled population (Harper & Wadsworth, 1993). Completed suicides among people with intellectual disabilities are very rarely reported and are probably less common than in the general population, although suicidal gestures and related behaviors are frequently documented in clinical populations (Walters & Barrett, 1995; Reiss, 1994). Unfortunately, depression is more difficult to diagnose in those with low intellectual functioning, especially those adults who are nonverbal and thus unable to provide classical "depressive" descriptions of their thoughts and feelings (Matson, 1982). Consequently, in my clinical experience, depression is frequently missed in persons with intellectual disabilities, with the result that the major and minor tranquilizers are used in place of appropriate antidepressant treatment. The impact of an untreated depressive illness on an already vulnerable and fragile individual with intellectual disabilities can be catastrophic and may result in premature institutionalization and even death.

Case Three—LD

LD is a 60-year-old woman who was referred for increasing irritability, decreased food intake, weight loss, intermittent nighttime wakening, and disinterest in her usual interests over the last few months. She screamed at staff that tried to get her to eat and even occasionally hit other residents and staff when they tried to interact with her. She had only mild intellectual disabilities, so she was able to speak clearly. At the assessment interview she became very agitated and claimed that staff and other residents were all responsible for her problems and that nobody liked her. There was a family history of psychiatric illness of unknown type (LD was adopted). LD had been physically healthy, and repeated physical and laboratory examinations showed no medical illness. The diagnosis of depressive illness was made, and an antidepressant (nortriptyline) started. During the second week she started sleeping and eating better, and by the fourth week she became less irritable and more interested in her activities. By three months later she was functioning almost at her usual level.

☐ Bipolar Illness

Bipolar disorder (also known as manic–depressive illness) consisting of episodes of manic behavior (increased psychomotor activity, decreased sleep, increased irritability, and possibly euphoria) tends to begin in early to midadulthood in the general population. Some people appear to develop bipolar disorder in old age (Shulman & Post, 1980), and this may be due to organic causes such as vascular brain damage. Late onset bipolar disorder is not common in the general population and is likely also uncommon among adults with intellectual disability. However, cyclical changes in mood and behavior, when they do occur, are easily misdiagnosed as maladaptive behavior in those with severe disabilities. It is also quite common in my clinical practice to see patients with bipolar disorder diagnosed for years as having schizophrenia. Although a number of researchers skilled in intellectual disabilities have found a high rate of diagnosis of schizophrenia in people with intellectual disabilities who have been referred to psychiatrists (Bouras & Drummond, 1992), there is less evidence from the literature that schizophrenia is actually more common in this group overall, if nonreferred patients are included. Most likely, as with young children and minority culture groups who also tend to be misdiagnosed with schizophrenia (Weller & Weller, 1995; Jones & Gray, 1986), intellectually disabled adults have symptoms less easily interpreted by physicians, leading to difficulties with diagnosis. As in the general population, it is important to differentiate between bipolar disorder and schizophrenia so that mood stabilizers can be used to decrease both manic and depressive episodes. Older people are more vulnerable to the side effects of antipsychotic medications, so these should be used in the lowest possible doses and only if they are truly necessary.

Case Four—HG

HG is a 70-year-old, Native American woman with mild intellectual disability who had been living in a small group home for three years prior to initial assessment. She was institutionalized at the age of 18 when she had bizarre behavior consisting of not sleeping at night and wandering about in the bush near her reservation. She had been on neuroleptic medications in large doses for many years. An initial psychogeriatric referral, which was for difficult behavioral problems, found her to have significant tardive dyskinesia secondary to many years of neuroleptic use. She was also in a florid manic episode with pressure of speech, flight of ideas, and extreme motor hyperactivity. She responded very well to mood stabilizers and eventual discontinuation of all neuroleptic medications. Over the next three years her tardive dyskinesia significantly decreased. Her functional abilities also improved significantly in the workshop and in her group home.

☐ Anxiety Disorders

Analyzing the general population Epidemiologic Catchment Area (ECA) studies, Blazer, George, and Hughes (1991) found that the prevalence of major anxiety disorders decreased somewhat from middle age onward but was still 19.7% for a six-month prevalence period. The most common disorders were found to be phobias. Most anxiety disorders begin in early adulthood, but occasionally these can appear after age 60 in the general population. In the intellectually disabled population as a whole, there is a diversity of reported prevalence: some authors find that the rate is at least as common as in the nondisabled population (Allen, 1989), and others note decreases in the rates (Jacobson, 1990). In my clinical experience, anxiety disorders are as common in elderly people with mild to moderate intellectual disabilities as in general geriatric patients.

Certain groups of disabled people may have particularly high rates of anxiety symptoms such as obsessions and compulsions (Bodfish, Crawford, Powell, Parker, Golden, & Lewis, 1995). Anxiety states and symptoms appear to be particularly common in aging people with disabilities (Day, 1985; James, 1986). Both medications and behavioral/cognitive therapies are effective in anxiety disorders of elderly people and appear to be similarly effective in people with a mild intellectual disability, although formal studies in this area are sparse. Older people in general are more sensitive to side effects of benzodiazepine medications such as falls and further intellectual impairment. This is likely similar among those with intellectual disabilities. A tendency to use medications rather than cognitive behavioral techniques is tempting, especially in times of financial restraint and reduced availability of staff to do individual work. Various psychotherapeutic approaches have been used with people with intellectual disabilities (Des Noyers Hurley, 1989) and should continue to be included in the treatment planning.

Case Five—JK

JK is a 60-year-old man whose mother recently died. She was his main support. Following her death he developed increasingly troublesome obsessions and compulsions. He spent almost all his waking hours opening and closing doors and touched coresidents and staff on the head repeatedly. His compulsive symptoms gradually started decreasing after eight months on fluvoxamine, an antidepressant that is known to have antiobsessional properties in the general population.

☐ Somatoform Disorders

Somatoform disorders are disorders in which people have extensive physical symptoms that resemble medical illnesses but for which no objective causes are found. In the general population, hypochondriasis peaks in the 40- to 50-year-old age group. With age there is a higher prevalence of preexisting physical illness and, therefore, the somatoform disorders are more difficult to differentiate from true physical illness. Among seniors with intellectual disabilities there is also a high rate of physical disabilities but reduced "psychological mindedness" or the ability to analyze the role of psychological factors in the development of other symptoms. Quite frequently such people present with repeated physical complaints in numerous body systems rather than symptoms of psychological distress such as anxiety or depression.

Case Six—NW

NW is a 74-year-old intellectually disabled man who was initially referred for abdominal pain of unknown causes. He had numerous physical, laboratory, and radiological examinations to investigate this, all uneventful. In interviews, NW would discuss nothing except his pain. Relaxation techniques were attempted over a number of months, and trials of anxiolytic medications, antidepressants, and mood stabilizers had little effect on his anxious preoccupation with his health. After a few months though, the focus of his preoccupation moved from abdomen, to back, to the head, and then to the belief that he was going blind. Eventually, the focus of treatment became how staff could deal with him more effectively. Regular meetings were held to allow them to ventilate their frustration, and how to approach NW more consistently and calmly. Family members noted that NW's father had also always been worried about his health and had that he been a high-strung, anxious individual.

☐ Psychoses

Schizophrenia occurs in about 1% of the general population and is clinically similar in persons with intellectual disabilities, especially those with mild impairment. It usually starts in late adolescence or in the early 20s in men, somewhat later in women, and possibly earlier in those with intellectual disabilities (Meadows & Turner, 1991) and continues into old age. Late, chronic ("burned-out") schizophrenia can present a picture clinically similar to dementia. The main treatment is with the classical antipsychotic drugs, which are most useful for reducing active symptoms such as hallucinations and delusions but which are less successful in reducing negative symptoms such as apathy and withdrawal. Atypical agents like clozapine and risperidone are more effective at reducing these "negative" symptoms. People with disabilities (especially older ones) may be more likely to develop tardive dyskinesia (Gualtieri & Schroeder, 1986), so medications such as clozapine and risperidone, which are also less likely to cause extrapyramidal side effects or tardive dyskinesia, might be good choices. Unfortunately, clozapine has extensive other side effects requiring frequent blood monitoring, so is not generally indicated.

Case Seven—VR

VR is a 68-year-old man living in an institution. His records indicate that he had mild intellectual disability as a child but that he was fairly functional until his teenage years. At that point he became increasingly unusual, talking to himself, believing people were watching him, and that coresidents wanted to hurt him. He was institutionalized and required large doses of neuroleptics to control his paranoia. By the time he reached 60, he had developed extensive involuntary movements (writhing movements of his tongue, mouth, and jaw). By 68 he had also become apathetic, showing minimal interest in his surroundings. He had a lot of difficulty with constipation and dry mouth from his medications, but attempts to decrease his neuroleptics resulted in his increased suspiciousness. He was switched to risperidone, which gave him minimal sedation, and less constipation. Staff felt that he was less apathetic.

☐ Substance and Alcohol Abuse

Abuse of alcohol and illicit substances is not as common among people with intellectual disabilities, as in the general elderly population, where the abuse of prescribed medications such as anxiolytics is more significant. Many studies find a high overall rate of psychoactive drug use in intellectually disabled people (Kiernan, Reeves, & Alborz, 1995; Aman, Sarphare, & Burrow, 1995), and some authors (Pary, 1993) have specifically explored their use in elderly disabled people, finding an increase with age. In an unpublished study of a Saskatchewan, Canada, population of community-dwelling persons with intellectual disabilities, Thorpe (1996) also noticed a trend toward the increased use of anxiolytics and sedatives in the older cohorts. Factors associated with successful or unsuccessful withdrawal of antipsychotic drugs have been explored recently by Branford (1996).

☐ Sleep Disorders

Sleep disorders are very common in the general aging population. Older people tend to have more light stage sleep and more frequent wakenings during the night. They are also more likely to have sleep apnea (a pattern of intermittent failure to breathe due to an obstructed airway, followed by transient wakenings) and other medical disorders such as congestive heart failure that may affect sleep. Because of their typical constricted upper airway and decreased tone, adults with Down's syndrome are particularly likely to have sleep apnea (Marcus, Keens, Bautista, VonPechman, & Ward, 1991; Silverman, 1988; Stebbens, Dennis, Samuels, Croft, & Southall, 1991) resulting in nighttime sleep problems with daytime drowsiness and poor cognitive performance. Sedative medications can worsen clinical symptoms (and even cause death), as they may prevent a person with an obstructed airway from partially wakening enough to increase their airway tone and thus successfully take a deep breath. Typical nighttime observations are of a person who snores very loudly, then stops completely for a short while, followed by a much louder snorting intake of air.

☐ General Assessment Issues in Elderly Persons with Intellectual Disabilities

The greatest complicating factor in the general assessment of elderly people with intellectual disabilities is the disability itself and the related communication difficulties (Haveman, Maaskant, Van Schrojenstein Lantman, Urlings, & Kessels, 1994). However, in addition to communication, there are many other factors such as baseline behavioral abnormalities and abnormal psychosocial life experiences that offer complications (Menolascino & Fletcher, 1989). Different cultural groups vary in how they perceive and treat elders with disabilities (Moss, 1992), so assessment and treatment may vary depending on the country or, indeed, the cultural group within a particular country.

The time required for a full assessment is increased due to communication difficulties, the need to obtain information from a large number of sources, and a greater level of overall complexity. This can be a significant problem, depending on the funding arrangements of the clinician. Staff dynamics and even interpersonal interactions with other residents can have a major impact on psychiatric symptoms and behavioral difficulties and must be explored. Complicating preexisting medical problems (such as seizure disorders) superimposed on those already seen in the general aging population are common among people with intellectual disabilities, although possibly less common in the oldest group due to the healthy survivor effect (Hogg, Moss, & Cooke, 1988).

Medication use for cardiovascular, gastrointestinal, or respiratory conditions becomes more common with age, and this can cause mood and behavioral changes that are often difficult to separate from the major psychiatric disorders. Interestingly, Day (1987) and others have found that there seems to be a lower rate of regular medical drug therapy in older adults with intellectual disability than in those without such disability. Finally, there are not many clinicians who have expertise in both aging and intellectual disabilities, making the accurate assessment of elderly persons with intellectual disabilities even more difficult.

Formal psychiatric rating instruments, such as the psychiatric assessment schedule for adults with a developmental disability (PAS-ADD 10: Moss, 1994), may simplify this assessment process, especially for clinicians without extensive "dual" aging and disability experience. There are a variety of other rating scales for behavioral and psychiatric disorders in intellectual disability (see the summary of these in Reiss, 1994), but most of these are shorter screens rather than assessment schedules.

☐ Commentary

Although information about psychiatric disorders among elderly people with intellectual disabilities is increasing, there is still a need to develop more longitudinal information. Cohorts of currently old people have had very different lives from those who will be old in 20 years. It is important to develop ongoing studies to assess the individual impact of aging in terms of functional ability, psychiatric status, as well as vocational and recreational needs. Key issues such as whether demented people with intellectual disabilities should access generic aging services or should have specific services geared to their intellectual functioning will need to be addressed. Projections of the numbers of people with lifelong disabilities who will develop dementia will need to be available to each locality to enable resource adaptation and planning for the future. Last, research findings must be incorporated into the treatment planning of clinicians and agencies, involving increased educational intervention in medical schools, nursing homes, and community resources for those with intellectual disabilities.

☐ References

Allen, E. A. (1989). Behavioural treatment of anxiety and related disorders in adults with mental handicaps: A review. *Mental Handicap Research, 2,* 47–60.

Aman, M. G., Sarphare, G., & Burrow, W. H. (1995). Psychotropic medications in group homes: prevalence and relation to demographic/psychiatric variables. *American Journal on Mental Retardation, 99,* 500–509.

Blazer, D. (1990). Epidemiology of late-life depression and dementia: A comparative study. In A. Tasman, S. M. Goldfinger, & C. A. Kaufmann (Eds.), *Review of Psychiatry* (Vol. 9, pp. 210–219). Washington, DC: American Psychiatric Press.

Blazer, D., George, L. K., & Hughes, D. (1991). The epidemiology of anxiety disorders: An age comparison. In C. Salzman & B. D. Lebowitz (Eds.), *Anxiety disorders in the elderly: Treatment and research* (pp. 17–30). New York: Springer.

Bodfish, J. W., Crawford, T. W., Powell, S. B., Parker, D. E., Golden, R. N., & Lewis, M. H. (1995). Compulsions in adults with mental retardation: Prevalence, phenomenology, and comorbidity with stereotypy and self-injury. *American Journal on Mental Retardation, 100,* 183–192.

Bouras, N., & Drummond, C. (1992). Behavior and psychiatric disorders of people with mental handicaps living in the community. *Journal of Intellectual Disability Research, 36,* 349–357.

Branford, D. (1996). Factors associated with the successful or unsuccessful withdrawal of antipsychotic drug therapy prescribed for people with learning disabilities. *Journal of Intellectual Disability Research, 40,* 322–329.

Calkins, M. P., & Chafetz, P. K. (1996). Structuring environments for patients with dementia. In M. F. Weiner (Ed.), *The dementias: Diagnosis, management and research* (2nd ed., pp. 297–311). Washington, DC: American Psychiatric Press.

Day, K. (1985). Psychiatric disorder in the middle-aged and elderly mentally handicapped. *British Journal of Psychiatry, 147,* 660–667.

Day, K. A. (1987). The elderly mentally handicapped in hospital: A clinical study. *Journal of Mental Deficiency Research, 31,* 131–146.

Day, K., & Jancar, J. (1994). Mental and physical health and ageing in mental handicap: A review. *Journal of Intellectual Disability Research, 38,* 241–256.

Des Noyers Hurley, A. (1989). Behavior therapy for psychiatric disorders in mentally retarded individuals. In R. Fletcher & F. Menolascino (Eds.), *Mental retardation and mental illness: Assessment , treatment, and services for the dually diagnosed* (pp. 127–140). Lexington, MA: Lexington Books.

Emery, V. O. B., Gillie, E., & Ramdev, P. T. (1994). Vascular dementia redefined. In V. O. B. Emery & T. E. Oxman (Eds.), *Dementia: Presentations, differential diagnosis, and nosology* (pp. 162–194). Baltimore: Johns Hopkins University Press.

Gualtieri, C. T., & Schroeder, S. R. (1986). Tardive dyskinesia in young mentally retarded individuals. *Archives of General Psychiatry, 43,* 335–340.

Harper, D. C., & Wadsworth, J. S. (1993). Grief in adults with mental retardation: Preliminary findings. *Research in Developmental Disabilities, 14,* 313–330.

Haveman, M. J., Maaskant, M. A., Van Schrojenstein Lantman, H. M., Urlings, H. F. J., & Kessels, A. G. H. (1994). Mental health problems in elderly people with and without Down's syndrome. *Journal of Intellectual Disability Research, 38,* 341–355.

Hogg, J., Moss, S., & Cooke, D. (1988). *Ageing and mental handicap.* London: Chapman and Hall.

Jacobson, J. W. (1990). Do some mental disorders occur less frequently among persons with mental retardation? *American Journal on Mental Retardation, 94,* 596–602.

James, D. H. (1986). Psychiatric and behavioural disorders amongst older severely mentally handicapped inpatients. *Journal of Mental Deficiency Research, 30,* 341–345

Janicki, M. P., Heller, T., Seltzer, G. B., & Hogg, J. (1995). *Practice guidelines for the clinical assessment and care management of Alzheimer and other dementias among adults with mental retardation.* Washington, DC: American Association on Mental Retardation.

Janicki, M. P., Heller, T., Seltzer, G. B., & Hogg, J. (1996). Practice guidelines for the clinical assessment and care management of Alzheimer's disease among adults with intellectual disability. *Journal of Intellectual Disability Research, 40,* 374–382.

Jones, B. E., & Gray, B. A. (1986). Problems in diagnosing schizophrenia and affective disorders among Blacks. *Hospital & Community Psychiatry, 37,* 61–65.

Kaplan, H. I., Sadock, B. J., & Grebb, J. A. (1991). Geriatric psychiatry. In H. I. Kaplan and B. J. Sadock (Eds.), *Synopsis of psychiatry: Behavioral sciences, clinical and psychiatry* (6th ed., pp. 807–819). Baltimore: Williams and Wilkins.

Karlinsky, H., Hardy, J. A., & Rossor, M. N. (1993). Alzheimer disease. In J. M. Berg, H. Karlinsky and A. J. Holland (Eds.), *Alzheimer disease, Down syndrome, and their relationship* (pp. 3–18). New York: Oxford University Press.

Kiernan, C., Reeves, D., & Alborz, A. (1995). The use of antipsychotic drugs with adults with learning disabilities and challenging behavior. *Journal of Intellectual Disability Research, 9,* 263–274.

Matson, J. (1982). The treatment of behavioural characteristics of depression in the mentally retarded. *Behavior Therapy, 13,* 209–218.

Meadows, G., & Turner, T. (1991). Assessing schizophrenia in adults with mental retardation: A comparative study. *British Journal of Psychiatry, 158,* 103–105

Menolascino, F., & Fletcher, R. (1989). *Mental retardation and mental illness. Assessment, treatment, and service for the dually diagnosed.* Lexington, MA: Lexington Books.

Moss, S. (Ed.). (1992). *Aging and developmental disabilities: Perspectives from nine countries.* Durham: University of New Hampshire, Institute on Disabilities.

Moss, S. (1994). *The psychiatric assessment schedule for adults with development disability.* Manchester, UK: Hester Adrian Research Centre, University of Manchester.

Moss, S., & Patel, P. (1995). Psychiatric symptoms associated with dementia in older people with learning disability. *British Journal of Psychiatry, 167,* 663–667.

Owens, D. G. (1994). Extrapyramidal side effects and the tolerability of risperidone: A review. *Journal of Clinical Psychiatry, 55*(Suppl.), 29–35.

Pary, R. (1993). Psychoactive drugs used with adults and elderly adults who have mental retardation. *American Journal on Mental Retardation, 98,* 121–127.

Raheja, R. K., Bharwani, I., & Penetrant, A. E. (1995). Efficacy of risperidone for behavioural disorders in the elderly: A clinical observation. *Journal of Geriatric Psychiatry Neurology, 8,* 159–161.

Read, S. L., Miller, B. L., Mena, I., Kim, R., Itabashi, H., & Darby, A. (1995). SPECT in dementia: Clinical and pathological correlation. *Journal of the American Geriatric Association, 43,* 1243–1247.

Reiss, S. (1994). *Handbook of challenging behavior: Mental health aspects of mental retardation.* Worthington, OH: IDS.

Schneider, L. S., & Sobin, P. (1994). Treatments for psychiatric symptoms and behavioural disturbances in dementia. In A.S. Burns & R. Levy (Eds.), *Dementia* (pp. 519–540). London: Chapman and Hall.

Shulman, K. I., & Post, F. (1980). Bipolar affective disorder in old age. *British Journal of Psychiatry, 136,* 26–32.

Silverman, M. (1988). Airway obstruction and sleep disruption in Down Syndrome. *British Medical Journal (Clinical Research), 296,* 1618–1619.

Sobsey, D., Wells, D., Lucardie, R., & Mansell, S. (1995) *Violence and disability: An annotated bibliography.* Baltimore: Paul H. Brookes.

Starkstein, S. E., & Robinson, R. G. (1994). Neuropsychiatric aspects of stroke. In C. E. Coffey & J. L. Cummings (Eds.), *Textbook of geriatric neuropsychiatry* (pp. 457–477). Washington, DC: American Psychiatric Press.

Stebbens, V. A., Dennis, J., Samuels, M. P., Croft, C. B., & Southall, D. P. (1991). Sleep related upper airway obstruction in a cohort with Down's syndrome. *Archives of Disabled Children, 66,* 1333–1338.

Stern, R. G., & Davis, K. L. (1996). Research in treating cognitive impairment in Alzheimer's Disease. In M. F. Weiner (Ed.), *The dementias: Diagnosis, management and research* (2nd ed., pp. 331–353). Washington, DC: American Psychiatric Press.

Strumpf, N. E., & Evans, L. K. (1991). The ethical problems of prolonged physical restraint. *Journal of Gerontological Nursing, 17,* 27–30.

Thorpe, L. U. (1996). *Drug use in a Saskatoon, Canada population of adults with intellectual disabilities.* Unpublished manuscript. Saskatoon: University of Saskatchewan.

Walters, A. S., & Barrett, R. P. (1995). Suicidal behavior in children and adolescents with mental retardation. *Research in Developmental Disabilities, 16,* 85–96.

Weller, E. B., & Weller, R. A. (1995). Bipolar disorder in children: Misdiagnosis, underdiagnosis, and future directions. *Journal of the American Academy of Child & Adolescent Psychiatry, 34,* 709–714.

Wisniewski, K. E., Hill, L., & Wisniewski, H. M. (1992). Aging and Alzheimer's disease in people with Down syndrome. In I. T. Lott & E. E. McCoy (Eds.), *Down syndrome: Advances in medical care* (pp. 167–183). New York: Wiley-Liss.

Yoshitake, T., Kiyohara, Y., Kato, I., Ohmura, T., Iwamoto, H., Nakayama, K., Ohmori, S., Nomiyama, K., Kawano, H., & Ueda, K. (1995). Incidence and risk factors of vascular dementia and Alzheimer's Disease in a defined elderly Japanese population: The Hisayama Study. *Neurology, 45,* 1161–1168.

John A. Tsiouris

Psychotropic Medications

This chapter offers a review of geriatric pharmacology for older adults with intellectual disabilities. It briefly describes the different classes of psychotropics and the major psychiatric and behavioral disorders (including dementia) for which the psychotropics have been used in older people with intellectual disabilities. Issues of baseline behavioral data, the need for establishing a psychiatric diagnosis, pharmacodynamics, pharmacokinetics, and side effects are discussed. The chapter provides the presenting behaviors, general guidelines of geriatric psychopharmacology, and a commentary on depression and dementia as well as reasons for psychopharmacological interventions.

The psychopharmacology of challenging behaviors has developed in response to behaviors exhibited by persons with intellectual disability that interfere with functioning and that have not been managed with behavior modification or other nonpharmacological interventions. When it was recognized that persons with intellectual disability exhibit the same psychiatric disorders as persons without it and needed special ways of management, the term "dual diagnosis" was applied with beneficial effects on the mental health of these persons.

Address correspondence to: John A. Tsiouris, M.D., Associate Director, Psychological/Psychiatric Services, George A. Jervis Clinic, New York State Institute for Basic Research in Developmental Disabilities, 1050 Forest Hill Road, Staten Island, NY 10314.

Preparation of this article was supported in by the New York State Office of Mental Retardation and Developmental Disabilities. Grateful appreciation is also extended to Valerie Mazza for her assistance in preparing this chapter for publication.

Currently, the necessity of geriatric psychopharmacology for older adults with intellectual disability is developing for several reasons:

- In adults over 50 years of age with Down's syndrome, a high prevalence of Alzheimer's disease has been found (Dalton & Crapper-McLachlan, 1986; Evenhuis, 1990; Burt, Loveland, & Lewis, 1992; Collacott, Cooper, & McGrother, 1992; Wisniewski & Silverman, 1996). However, one recent 6-year follow-up study of 40- to 60-year-old adults with Down's syndrome found a low prevalence of Alzheimer's disease (Devenny, Silverman, Hill, Jenkins, Sersen, & Wisniewski, 1996).
- Other studies have shown that adults with intellectual disability and without Down's syndrome may be at higher risk for Alzheimer's-type neuropathology than are adults without intellectual disability (Popovitch, Wisniewski, & Barcikowska, 1990; Zigman, Silverman, & Wisniewski, 1996). Both a high and low incidence of Alzheimer's disease in non-Down's syndrome adults with intellectual disability have been reported (Cooper, 1996; Devenny et al., 1996).
- Depression is common in adults with Down's syndrome, while other psychiatric disorders are common in adults with intellectual disability without Down's syndrome (Collacott et al., 1992). Depression and Alzheimer's disease in Down's syndrome have many common symptoms and similar presentations (McGuire & Chicoine, 1996), and persons with Down's syndrome and Alzheimer's disease have associated psychiatric disorders, especially depression (Burt et al., 1992).
- In persons without intellectual disability, hippocampal atrophy as a marker for early detection of Alzheimer's disease has been suggested (deLeon et al., 1993). Hippocampal atrophy has been reported in persons with recurrent depression. The cause of atrophy is postulated to be due to hypercortisolism secondary to depression, which acts as a stressor (Sheline, Wang, Mokhtar, & Csernansky, 1996).
- Loss of family members, loss of support systems, relocations, demands for more independent functioning, and medical problems are experienced as stressors by elderly persons with intellectual disability, and may precipitate a relapse of old or trigger new psychiatric disorders or challenging behaviors, or both.
- Medications that were previously well tolerated may produce acute side effects in elderly persons. This may be due to changes in absorption, distribution, metabolism, and excretion rates in the elderly system with diminished physiological reserves (Salzman, Satlin, & Burrows, 1995).
- The long-term side effects of psychotropic medications for preexisting psychiatric disorders or challenging behaviors or both may emerge after elderly persons with intellectual disability have taken psychotropic drugs for many years.

===

TABLE 13.1. Presenting behaviors

===

A. *Challenging behaviors*

Noncompliance	Hypermotility (inability to sit still)
Screaming	Hypomotility (slowness in moving and
Feces smearing	performing or lying down constantly)
Aggression (threats, assaults)	Stripping
Aggression (self-injurious behavior)	Incontinence

B. *Psychiatric signs (observable)*

Sleep disturbances	Excessive energy level
Eating disturbances	Diminished energy level
Weight loss or gain	Affective disturbances
Mood changes	Inability to learn new skills
Disorganized, bizarre behavior	Inability to speak and express thoughts
Catatonic behavior	as before (aphasia)
Mutism	Inability to understand (agnosia)
Diminished interest	Inability to follow orders and execute them
	(apraxia)

C. *Psychiatric symptoms (subjective, verbalized, or observed)*

Hallucinations	Thought disorders, speech and language
Paranoid ideations	disturbances
Delusions	Memory, orientation, and judgment
Homicidal ideations	disturbances
Suicidal ideations	

☐ **Reasons for Psychopharmacological Intervention**

Physicians of different specialties, but especially psychiatrists, are asked to evaluate older persons with intellectual disability and prescribe psychotropics for a number of reasons (as seen in Table 13.1).

☐ **General Guidelines**

In view of the various reasons for drug intervention, there are a number of reasons why there is a need for general guidelines for psychopharmacology in older persons with intellectual disability (Reiss & Aman, 1997; Tsiouris & Adelman, 1997). First, psychotropic medications should not be used by persons with intellectual disabilities unless there is also a specifically diagnosed psychiatric condition for which such agents are indicated. These conditions might include, but are not limited to, acute psychosis; schizophrenia; psychotic disorders not otherwise specified

(NOS); schizoaffective, delusional, mood, anxiety disorders; impulse control and tic disorders; attention deficit hyperactivity disorder (ADHD); conduct disorders; stereotypic movement disorder; and severe destructive behavior to self or others. A psychotropic agent should never be used as a substitute for a carefully planned systematic intervention. It must be kept in mind that response to drug therapy may be paradoxical or cause side effects in a person with intellectual disability. The neurological and metabolic status of an individual must be carefully considered before drug intervention is undertaken.

Second, a psychiatric evaluation must be performed before psychotropics are prescribed, except in emergency situations. Psychotropics are prescribed, but at times inappropriately, for aggressive, destructive, self-injurious, and sexually inappropriate behaviors, and for temper tantrums and stereotypies, when the signs and symptoms of a psychiatric disorder are under control or in the absence of a concomitant psychiatric disorder. A definite or working/tentative psychiatric diagnosis has to be documented, and the psychotropic agents must be prescribed under the accepted practice of psychopharmacology corresponding to the diagnosis.

The physician diagnosing an older person with intellectual disability must take a good history and baseline data information from carers. Time must be allowed for close observation and follow-up visits by the physician for an accurate diagnosis and prescription of psychotropic drugs. At times, the patient's response to the medication may confirm the diagnosis. The examining physician must determine if the signs and symptoms of psychiatric disorders are new or old, with or without acute exacerbation; a justifiable response to environmental stimuli; due to medication side effects, a medical illness, or sensory deficits; responsive to behavior modification; part of a previous psychiatric disorder; age related, such as depression, delusional disorders, reactive psychosis, personality changes due to medical or neurological disorders; or a psychiatric disorder associated with Alzheimer's disease.

According to the concept of diminished physiological reserve, age-related changes in central nervous system (CNS) function may not become clinically evident until the individual is confronted with a stressful event. Following the event, the vulnerable system may reveal symptoms of medical or psychiatric disorders. The physiological and biochemical effects produced by a given drug are referred to as *pharmacodynamics*. Elderly persons are more sensitive than younger patients to the sedative effects (drowsiness), anticholinergic effects (dry mouth, urinary retention, constipation), extrapyramidal effects or parkinsonism (shakiness or trembling, stiffness of arms or legs, masklike face), and hypotensive effects (dizziness or fainting) of psychotropic drugs. Persons with Alzheimer's disease and acetylcholine deficiency are more sensitive to the anticholinergic effects of psychotropic drugs. The action of drugs in the body over a period of time is known as *pharmacokinetics*. Absorption, distribution, binding in tissues, biotransformation, and excretion (clearance) are the parameters that determine the bioavailability of a drug after administration.

Pharmacodynamic and pharmacokinetic changes have to be considered when any medication is initiated or added or both to the drug regimen of an older person. Disturbances in absorption decrease the bioavailability of a drug. Decreased lean body mass and increased body fat are age related and contribute to changes in body distribution of a drug according to its water or fat solubility. The age-related decrement in phase I oxidative biotransformation delays hepatic metabolism and prolongs the half-lives of many psychotropic drugs. Chronic inflammatory conditions or malnutrition may reduce the synthesis of plasma-binding proteins, resulting in a higher free-drug concentration. A reduced glomerular filtration rate in many older people impairs renal clearance of drugs. Chronic liver disease or congestion can further delay clearance of a drug, contributing to a higher concentration (Salzman et al., 1995).

☐ Fundamentals of Geriatric Psychopharmacology

The following should be considered when prescribing psychotherapeutic medications in older persons with intellectual disabilities: (a) start low and go slow (a geriatric maxim); (b) treat the underlying psychiatric disorder; (c) treat the challenging behaviors with the psychotropics that have been found to be effective in younger persons, if a psychiatric diagnosis cannot be made; (d) choose the psychotropic with the most benign side-effects profile; (e) evaluate the risk/benefit ratio of the prescribed medication and monitor its therapeutic effectiveness and adverse effects; and (f) consider pharmacodynamic and pharmacokinetic changes when any medication is initiated or added or both to the drug regimen of an older person.

☐ Classes of Psychotropics

There are several psychiatric disorders and many classes of psychotropic drugs. Studies have established the effectiveness of a particular class of psychotropics or a specific psychotropic for one or more psychiatric disorders (Raskind, 1995). *Comorbidity* is the term used when more than one psychiatric disorder is diagnosed in a person. A combination of different classes of psychotropics is often used to treat a person with one or more psychiatric disorders and is referred to as *copharmacy*. *Polypharmacy* means the use of more than one agent of the same category of use (i.e., two neuroleptics, two antidepressants, or two antianxiety agents) and is a practice that should be avoided.

Antipsychotics. Also called neuroleptics or major tranquilizers, antipsychotics are used mainly for the management of the manifestations of psychotic disorders. They are dopamine receptor antagonists. As noted in Table 13.2, this group of medications includes haloperidol, molindone, thiothixene, pimozide, loxapine, and the phenothiazines such as thioridazine, mesoridazine, chlorpromazine, perphenazine, fluphenazine, and others (United States Pharmacopeial Convention [USPC], 1996). Cognitive impairment, Parkinsonism, dystonia, tardive dyskinesia, and akathisia are often seen in elderly patients taking antipsychotic medications (Karson, Bracha, & Powell, 1990). Tardive dyskinesia is a movement disorder characterized by uncontrolled movements of the mouth, tongue, and cheeks, as well as the arms and legs. It has been found that elderly patients respond well to the atypical antipsychotics, risperidone and clozapine, which rarely caused the aforementioned side effects (Karson et al., 1990). Sedation, weight gain, and excessive salivation are the most serious side effects to be considered when the new atypical antipsychotic drugs are prescribed for elderly patients (Casey, 1996). Clozapine at low doses given to over 100 patients for treatment of psychosis in Parkinson's disease did not produce akathisia (Friedman, 1993). The greater effectiveness of the new atypical neuroleptic drugs and the decreased frequency of side effects like dystonias and dyskinesia may be due to a blockade of dopamine and serotonin receptors in the brain (Richelson, 1996).

Antidepressants. These are indicated for the relief of symptoms of major depressive episodes and dysthymia. All have major effects on brain neurotransmitters, mainly norepinephrine and serotonin, although their precise mechanism of action has not been established. Antidepressants may be grouped according to their chemical structures (tricyclics) or their mechanisms of action (monoamine oxidase inhibitors (MAOIs), and the selective serotonin reuptake inhibitors (SSRIs). Tricyclic antidepressants include amitriptyline, clomipramine, desipramine, doxepin, imipramine, nortriptyline, protriptyline, and trimipramine. MAOIs include isocarboxazid, phenelzine, and tranylcypromine. Fluoxetine, sertraline, and paroxetine are SSRI antidepressants. Bupropion, trazodone, fluvoxamine, venlafaxine, nefazodone, and maprotiline are other examples of antidepressants with varied chemical structures and unclear mechanisms of action (USPC, 1996).

TABLE 13.2.   Common medications for psychiatric disorders.

Antipsychotics
(typical)
   Chlorpromazine *(Thorazine)*
   Fluphenazine *(Prolixin)*
   Haloperidol *(Haldol)*
   Loxapine *(Loxitane)*
   Mesoridazine *(Serentil)*
   Perphenazine *(Trilafon)*
   Thioridazine *(Mellaril)*
   Thiothixene *(Navane)*
   Trifuoperazine *(Stelazine)*
(Atypical)
   Clozapine *(Clozaril)*
   Olanzapine *(Zyprexa)*
   Quetiapine *(Seroquel)*
   Risperidone *(Risperdal)*

Antianxiety Agents
(Benzodiazepines)
   Alprazolam *(Xanax)*
   Chlordiazepoxide *(Librium)*
   Clorazepate *(Tranxene)*
   Clonazepam *(Klonopin)*
   Diazepam *(Valium)*
   Lorazepam *(Ativan)*
   Oxazepam *(Serax)*
(Nonbenzodiazepines)
   Buspirone *(Buspar)*

Mood Stabilizers
   Carbamazepine *(Tegretol)*
   Lithium Carbonate *(Lithobid, Eskalith)*
   Valproic Acid *(Depakote, Depakene)*

Stimulants
   Dextroamphetamine *(Dexedrine)*
   Dextroamphetamine
   and amphetamine salts *(Adderall)*
   Methylphenidate *(Ritalin)*
   Pemoline *(Cylert)*

Antihistamines as Antianxiety/Sedative-
   hypnotic agents
Sedative-hypnotic
   Diphenhydramine *(Benadryl)*
   Hydroxyzine *(Atarax)*

Antidepressants
(Tricyclics)
   Amitriptyline *(Elavil)*
   Amoxapine *(Asendin)*
   Clomipramine *(Anafranil)*
   Desipramine *(Norpramin)*
   Doxepin *(Sinequan)*
   Imipramine *(Tofranil)*
   Nortriptyline *(Pamelor)*
   Protriptyline *(Vivactil)*
   Trimipramine *(Surmontil)*
(MAO Inhibitors)
   Phenelzine *(Nardil)*
   Tranylcypromine *(Parnate)*
(Selective SRIs)
   Fluoxetine (Prozac)
   Paroxetine *(Paxil)*
   Sertraline *(Zoloft)*
(Other SRIs)
   Fluvoxamine *(Luvox)*
   Nefazodone *(Serzone)*

(Others)
   Bupropion *(Wellbutrin)*
   Maprotiline *(Ludiomil)*
   Mirtazapine *(Remeron)*
   Trazodone *(Desyrel)*
Venlafaxine (Effexor)
Antidyskinetics
   Amantadine *(Symmetrel)*
   Benztropine *(Cogentin)*
   Biperiden *(Akineton)*

   Trihexyphenidyl *(Artane)*

Beta Blockers/Antianxiety Adjuncts
   Nadolol *(Corgard)*
   Pindolol *(Visken)*
   Propranolol *(Inderal)*

Opiod Antagonists
   Naltrexone *(ReVia, Trexan)*

Dementia Medications
   Tacrine *(Cognex)*
   Donepezil *(Aricept)*

Antianxiety Agents. These drugs are indicated mainly for the management of anxiety disorders or for the short-term relief of the symptoms of anxiety. The major group of antianxiety agents, the benzodiazepines, also have a sedative/hypnotic action. They are also used for short-term treatment of seizures or convulsions. Diazepam, chlordiazepoxide, lorazepam, clonazepam, alprazolam, clorazepate, and oxazepam are some examples of benzodiazepines. Another antianxiety agent is meprobamate. Buspirone is a new nonbenzodiazepine, antianxiety agent. It does not have significant sedative properties or produce psychological/physical dependence associated with the use of the aforementioned antianxiety agents.

Barbiturates. These drugs, especially phenobarbital, are indicated mainly for long-term anticonvulsant therapy in the treatment of certain types of epileptic seizures and for emergency treatment of certain acute convulsive episodes. Barbiturates, such as amobarbital, apobarbital, butabarbital, pentobarbital, phenobarbital, and secobarbital, have been used for the short-term treatment of insomnia and for routine daytime sedation to relieve anxiety, tension, and apprehension. However, barbiturates generally have been replaced by benzodiazepines for both daytime sedation and short-term insomnia treatment (USPC, 1996).

Chloral Hydrate. Although chloral hydrate has been used for the treatment of insomnia, it is effective only as a hypnotic to induce sleep. It generally has been replaced by agents with better pharmacodynamic and pharmacokinetic profiles. The use of chloral hydrate as a routine sedative has also generally been replaced by safer and more effective agents (USPC, 1996).

Stimulants. Amphetamine, dextroamphetamine, methamphetamine, methylphenidate, and pemoline are CNS stimulants used in the treatment of ADHD. The amphetamines and methylphenidate are also indicated for the management of symptoms of narcolepsy. In the treatment of ADHD, the stimulant medications decrease motor restlessness and increase the ability to pay attention. These actions are mediated through dopaminergic mechanisms, although the precise mechanism of action has not been established.

Mood Stabilizers. Lithium is the primary agent used in the treatment of bipolar disorder and for maintenance therapy to help diminish the intensity and frequency of manic episodes in patients with a history of mania. Carbamazepine, an anticonvulsant indicated mainly for the treatment of epilepsy, is also used alone or in combination with lithium or antidepressants and antipsychotics or both to treat some manic–depressive patients. The anticonvulsants, valproic acid and divalproex, have been approved for the prevention and treatment of manic–depressive illness. These agents have varied mechanisms of action, side effects, and interactions with other medications.

Antidyskinetics. Benztropine, trihexyphenidyl, ethopropazine, procyclidine, and biperiden are antidyskinetics with anticholinergic action and are used to treat the movement disorders of Parkinsonism and some extrapyramidal disorders induced by antipsychotic drugs, such as the phenothiazines. Amantadine, an antiviral medication, is also an antidyskinetic agent indicated for the treatment of drug-induced extrapyramidal reactions or Parkinsonism (USPC, 1996).

Antihistamines. Diphenhydramine is an antihistamine used as a sedative/hypnotic to treat insomnia and as an antidyskinetic agent for the symptomatic treatment of Parkinsonism and drug-induced extrapyramidal reactions in some elderly patients. Hydroxyzine is used as an antianxiety agent for the short-term relief of psychosis-related tension and for its sedative/hypnotic effects (USPC, 1996).

Other Medications Used as Psychotropics. Beta-adrenergic blocking agents, such as propranolol, nadolol, and pindolol, have been used as therapy adjuncts to control the physical manifestations of anxiety, such as tachycardia and tremor, hypertension and certain arrhythmias (USPC, 1996). They are useful for reducing anxiety and improving performance in specific stressful situations and for rage attacks, neuroleptic-induced akathisia (inability to sit still), aggressive, destructive, and self-injurious behavior.

Opioid antagonists are another group of medications used with adults with intellectual disability. One such agent, naltrexone, is indicated as an adjunct to other nondrug measures in the maintenance of an opioid-free state in detoxified, formerly opioid-dependent individuals. Naltrexone binds to opioid receptors in the CNS and competitively inhibits the action of opioid drugs. Studies support its use in the treatment of self-injurious behavior in some people with developmental disabilities (Sandman et al., 1993; Thompson, Hackenberg, Cerutti, Baker, & Axtell, 1994; USPC, 1996).

☐ Psychiatric Disorders and Psychotropics

Clinical experiences suggest that signs and symptoms of psychiatric disorders in older adults with intellectual disability are similar to those presented by adults without intellectual disability, and their response to psychotropics is the same.

Antipsychotic/Neuroleptics for Psychotic Disorders and Other Indications.

Schizophrenia is a psychotic disorder characterized by delusions, hallucinations, disorganized (incoherent) speech, and grossly disorganized or catatonic behavior; these are referred to as positive symptoms. Affective flattening, alogia, or avolition are referred to as negative symptoms (Diagnostic and Statistical Manual of Mental Disorders [DSM IV]; American Psychiatric Association [APA], 1994). Hostility, impulsivity, agitation, insomnia, withdrawal, poor self-care, and poor eating habits are behaviors associated with psychoses. Other psychotic disorders include schizophreniform disorder, brief psychotic episode, schizoaffective disorder, delusional disorder, psychotic disorder due to medical condition, substance-induced psychotic disorder, manic episode with psychotic features, and major depressive episode with psychotic features.

In terms of treatment, studies have supported the clinical efficacy of the neuroleptics in the treatment and control of the signs and symptoms of psychosis, especially those of schizophrenia (Poling, Gadow, & Cleary, 1991). These studies have been conducted in adults without intellectual disability. Neuroleptics have been commonly used to treat severe disruptive behaviors and psychosis in elderly adults without intellectual disability and with or without Alzheimer's disease (Wragg & Jeste, 1988). In children and adults with intellectual disability, the neuroleptics have been prescribed mainly to control psychosis; aggressive, destructive self-injurious behavior; severe agitation; and stereotypies (Baumeister, Todd, & Sevin, 1993). Older adults with intellectual disability and coexisting diagnoses of schizophrenia have been maintained on neuroleptics, at times on subtherapeutic doses. In a study of nonverbal older adults with severe or profound intellectual disability in whom the diagnosis of schizophrenia or other psychotic disorder was difficult to make, attempts to taper and discontinue neuroleptics were partially successful. Behavior problems, agitation, and psychotic symptoms reemerged and severe dyskinesia became evident (Gualtieri & Schroeder, 1986).

In older men with intellectual disability, exacerbations of previously diagnosed psychotic disorders can be managed well by increasing the dose or changing to another neuroleptic. If neuroleptics alone cannot treat the presenting problems, the previous diagnosis must be questioned and mood stabilizers, antidepressants, or beta blockers added, depending on the signs and symptoms. In new cases with presentation of *clear signs and symptoms of psychosis* with or without Alzheimer's disease, neuroleptic medications are indicated. In choosing the neuroleptic, the physician must be guided by the side-effect profile of each drug, concomitant chronic illness and medication, as well as the history of the patient and family, if possible, taking into account prior drug responses and experiences of adverse effects. Neuroleptics have anticholinergic effects causing constipation, dry mouth, decreased sweating, orthostatic hypotension, and drowsiness. At times, their sedative effects can be carried on through the next day if they have been used for agitation during the night.

Akathisia, blurred vision, dystonic and parkinsonian extrapyramidal effects, fainting, and tardive dyskinesia are frequent adverse effects of neuroleptics that require medical attention and are more likely to occur in the elderly than in younger adults (Lieberman, Kane, & Woerner, 1984; Karson et al., 1990; USPC, 1996), especially in older adults with cortical atrophy (Sweet, Benoit, & Mulsant, 1992). The neuroleptic risperidone causes fewer dystonic reactions in smaller doses, but it does produce unusual tiredness or weakness, drowsiness, dry mouth, headache, sore throat, rhinitis, and weight gain (USPC, 1996).

Clozapine is an atypical antipsychotic agent that does not produce extrapyramidal symptoms, dystonic effects, akathisia, or tardive dyskinesia except in rare cases, but more frequently it causes dizziness, drowsiness, headache, constipation, and profuse watering of the mouth. The need to monitor a patient's white blood cell count for signs of agranulocytosis (low white cell count) prior to initiating therapy, each week during clozapine therapy, and for 4 weeks after discontinuation of therapy, has prevented the use of clozapine in older adults with intellectual disability except in exceptional refractory cases. Olanzapine has recently been approved, and in the United States new neuroleptics with better side-effects profiles are currently in the pipeline for Food and Drug Administration (FDA) approval.

Since clinical experience has shown that older adults with intellectual disability and Down's syndrome are so vulnerable to the side effects of neuroleptics, their use should be avoided in this population, if possible. Neuroleptics have been used with beneficial effects for the following non psychotic disorders: Tourette's disorder (haloperidol, pimozide, risperidone); autistic disorder (haloperidol, risperidone, mesoridazine); anxiety not responsive to antianxiety drugs; agitation, hyperactivity, and conduct problems; and intractable hiccups.

☐ Antidepressants for Depressive Disorders

Major depression is one of the most common disorders diagnosed in older persons with an intellectual disability and, especially, among adults with

Down's syndrome. At times, the presentation of symptoms is similar to dementia (pseudodementia or reversible dementia). The diagnosis of major depression can be made easily in verbal and nonverbal adults with intellectual disabilities. According to the DSM-IV (APA, 1994), five out of nine criteria are required and six criteria are observable signs (depressed mood, loss of interest or pleasure, sleep disturbances, appetite disturbances and weight loss, psychomotor retardation or agitation, and fatigue or loss of energy). The other three criteria are subjective and many times are verbalized by adults with intellectual disability when properly questioned (Walters, 1990). These three criteria are feelings of worthlessness, diminished ability to think, and recurrent thoughts of death.

Medical conditions causing depression must be excluded or treated appropriately. Medications producing depression must be tapered or discontinued, if possible, in a person diagnosed with depression before treatment with antidepressants. The use of the tricyclic antidepressants (amitriptyline, imipramine, doxepin, and others) in therapeutic doses for the treatment of depression in older adults with intellectual disability is limited by their adverse effects (dizziness, drowsiness, dryness of mouth, constipation, difficult urination), although cases of successful treatment have been reported (Storm, 1990). Monoamine oxidase inhibitors are not used to treat older persons with intellectual disability because of the strict diet restrictions required to prevent hypertensive crisis. The introduction of the SSRIs with their more benign side-effects profile has vastly improved the ability of the physician to treat depressive disorders in older persons with intellectual disability, with or without Down's syndrome or depression associated with Alzheimer's disease.

Early diagnosis and aggressive treatment of the depressive disorder may relieve symptoms of depression and improve function (Cooper & Collacott, 1993), decreasing the number of nonresponders and the need of electroconvulsive therapy (Lazarus, Jaffe, & Dubin, 1990; Warren, Holroyd, & Folstein, 1989). Treatment with fluoxetine, sertraline, paroxetine, and, in some cases, with desipramine and trazodone, starting with small doses and gradually increasing the dose, has differentiated pseudodementia from dementia. Symptoms of depression associated with dementia in adults with Down's syndrome were relieved. Side effects were not noted (Tsiouris & Patti, 1997; McGuire & Chicoine, 1996). The most commonly reported side effects of SSRIs are headache, drowsiness, dizziness, insomnia, increased sweating, agitation and restlessness, and delayed sexual performance or decreased sexual desire (USPC, 1996). Some patients cannot tolerate SSRIs for unknown reasons. However, bupropion and the tricyclic antidepressants, nortriptyline and desipramine, may be used in such persons, or, if these are not tolerated, the antidepressants, venlafaxine and nefazodone, and the antiobsessional agent, fluvoxamine, may be used to treat their depression. Fluvoxamine has been found superior to placebo in reducing repetitive thoughts and maladaptive behaviors and improving some aspects of relatedness, especially language in a double-blind, placebo-controlled study of 30 adults aged 18 to 53 years with autistic disorder (McDougle, Naylor, Cohen, Volkmar, Heninger, & Price, 1996). Concurrent use of nefazodone and fluvoxamine with the antihistamines, astemizole and terfenadine, is contraindicated. To prevent adverse drug interactions, caution must be observed with any patient, especially older persons, taking antidepressants and other medication.

All the antidepressants can lower the seizure threshold and may produce nervousness or restlessness, excitation, hypomania, and aggressive behavior. Concurrent use of the antidepressant with divalproex, lithium, or carbamazepine may stabilize the mental status of the person without discontinuing the antidepressant. Other labeled or unlabeled indications for the antidepressants in young and older persons with or without intellectual disability are dysthymic disorder, obsessive compulsive disorder, post-traumatic stress disorder, panic disorder, social phobia, enuresis, low-level (defensive) aggression, and self-injurious behavior.

Mood Stabilizers for Bipolar Disorders.   Bipolar disorders are chronic mood disorders. Most of the older persons with intellectual disability and bipolar disorder have been correctly diagnosed and are being treated with mood stabilizers. However, attention must be paid to many cases of elderly persons with intellectual disability whose bipolar disorder had been misdiagnosed as schizophrenia in their younger years and who were then treated inappropriately for many years with antipsychotic drugs. In this category are persons with bipolar disorder, type I, having recurring hypomanic or manic episodes with psychotic features and very few depressive episodes in between; and persons with bipolar disorder, type II, having recurrent episodes of severe depression with psychotic features and brief hypomanic episodes in between.

A manic episode is characterized as a distinct period of abnormally elevated, expansive, or irritable mood lasting for seven or more days with three or more of the following factors: grandiosity, decreased need for sleep, overtalkativeness, flight of ideas, distractibility, increased goal-directed activity, and excessive involvement in pleasurable activities. When the episode is not severe enough to cause marked impairment in social or occupational functioning and lasts at least four days or more, it is characterized as a hypomanic episode. Rapid cycling is defined as four or more episodes of any combination of depression or mania during a 12-month period. In elderly persons with intellectual disability, the episodes are not well delineated, and often the following behaviors are observed: irritability, excitability, impulsivity, overactivity, low frustration tolerance, undressing, running away, increased verbalization, decreased need for sleep, and aggressivity in an attempt to dominate others.

Among treatment approaches, lithium has been found effective in bipolar disorders. Vomiting, diarrhea, tremor, and ataxia are a few of the side effects which can be minimized with dosage adjustment. Divalproex sodium is an anticonvulsant which also has been found to be very effective for bipolar disorder. Carbamazepine is another anticonvulsive used for bipolar disorders. Divalproex or carbamazepine should be used instead of lithium if there is a history of seizures or EEG abnormalities. Complete blood counts and liver function tests must be monitored when divalproex and carbamazepine are used and thyroid function and kidney clearance monitored when lithium is used. Serum drug concentrations have to be monitored frequently for all three drugs, especially lithium. Verapamil (Dubovsky, Franks, & Allen, 1986), nimodipine (Brunet, Cerlick, & Robert, 1990), thyroxine (Bauer & Whybrow, 1990), clonazepam, and lorazepam have been added to the mood stabilizers and tried in difficult cases of chronic hypomanic states and in rapid cycling conditions. In a few cases, the addition of an antipsychotic such as risperidone, haloperidol, or clozapine in small doses during or after the acute manic phase may be justified (Janicak, Davis, Ayd, & Preskorn, 1995).

☐ Antianxiety Drugs for Anxiety Disorders

Anxiety disorders include generalized anxiety disorder, panic disorder with or without agoraphobia, agoraphobia without history of panic disorder, specific phobia, social phobia, obsessive compulsive disorder, posttraumatic stress disorder, acute stress disorder, and anxiety disorder due to medical illness or induced by a substance. Older adults with intellectual disability may be receiving treatment for a preexisting anxiety disorder such as generalized anxiety disorder, obsessive compulsive disorder, agoraphobia or social phobia, or may present with new symptoms that may suggest post-traumatic stress disorder, panic disorder, acute stress disorder, or anxiety disorder due to medical illness or other medication. Anxiety disorders can precipitate depression and may also be induced or exacerbated by depression, separations, losses, relocation, and traumatic experiences (such as medical illness and hospitalization).

Antianxiety agents (anxiolytics) alone or in combination with an antidepressant have been used in the treatment of anxiety disorders in younger and older persons without intellectual disability. Anxiolytics reduce anxiety, produce sedation, and induce sleep. There are no studies on the use of anxiolytics for anxiety disorders in younger or older adults with intellectual disability (Chandler, Gualtieri, & Fahs, 1988). Anxiolytics have been used for control of disruptive behavior (Intagliata & Rinck, 1985) with no clear effects (Lipman, DiMascio, Reatig, & Kirson, 1978). Clinical experience suggests anxiolytics be used in similar ways and with the same precautions as in elderly adults without intellectual disability (Salzman, 1990).

Environmental changes for situation anxiety have to be considered. Medication (stimulants, antidepressants, neuroleptics with secondary akathisia) or other stimulants (caffeine) produce or exacerbate anxiety. They have to be tapered or discontinued, if possible, before initiating treatment with anxiolytics.

Benzodiazepines.   Anxiolytics should not be used for disruptive behaviors unless an anxiety disorder is the underlying cause for these behaviors, since sedation, ataxia with falling episodes, psychomotor slowing, and cognitive impairment occur with their administration (Salzman, 1990). In children and adults with intellectual disability, benzodiazepines, especially the short-acting lorazepam and alprazolam, have been observed, in some cases, to increase aggressivity and level of arousal (paradoxical reaction or disinhibition) (Barron & Sandman, 1985). Close observation is needed initially after administration of benzodiazepines.

After prolonged administration, benzodiazepines or barbiturates or both should be discontinued gradually to lessen the possibility of rebound (the reemergence of anxiety) or withdrawal symptoms. Alprazolam, clonazepam, diazepam, and lorazepam may be used for panic attacks, acute stress disorder, and post-traumatic stress disorder alone or with one of the antidepressants nortriptyline, desipramine, fluoxetine, sertraline, paroxetine, and others. Clonazepam is used alone for night terrors and myoclonus and for obsessive compulsive disorder in conjunction with clomipramine or an SSRI.   Clonazepam, lorazepam, and diazepam may be combined with an antipsychotic medication for rapid control of excited psychotic or manic states (McClellan & Werry, 1992). Lorazepam and alprazolam are used before medical appointments or procedures.

Nonbenzodiazepines.   Buspirone is an antianxiety agent that may alleviate anxiety, agitation, aggression, and self-injurious behaviors, as observed in a few cases of young adults with intellectual disability (Mandoki, 1994). It reduced agitation associated with dementia in adults without intellectual disability (Sakauye, Camp, & Ford, 1993). If the anxiety is acute, buspirone should not be used since one to two weeks of therapy may be required before the antianxiety effect is noticeable, as compared with the immediate effect of benzodiazepines. Buspirone causes less sedation in lower doses than other anxiolytics, but it has not been shown to be effective for long-term management of anxiety (more than three to four weeks) (USPC, 1996).

Hypnotics. For insomnia that is not a symptom of depression or psychosis, and especially for acute insomnia, the benzodiazepines estazolam, flurazepam, nitrazepam, quazepam, temazepam, and triazolam, and the nonbenzodiazepine, zolpidem, may be used for short-term treatment. Failure to remit or worsening of the insomnia after 7 to 10 days or the emergence of new unusual behaviors may signify an unrecognized psychiatric or physical disorder (USPC, 1996)

Beta-Adrenergic Blocking Agents for Impulse Control Disorders and Related Problems.
Intermittent explosive disorder, kleptomania, pyromania, pathological gambling, and trichotillomania are examples of impulse control disorders. Some older adults with intellectual disability may have an ongoing impulse control disorder or it may develop as the patient ages. Temper tantrums, during which aggressive, self-injurious and disruptive behaviors are exhibited, may occur at low intensity and frequency but become exacerbated as the patient ages. An underlying medical/neurological condition may cause an older adult with intellectual disability to become noncompliant and exhibit rage attacks secondary to personality changes. Pyromania and kleptomania are rare in older adults with intellectual disability. Trichotillomania (abnormal desire to pull out one's hair) occurs frequently. Clinical experience has shown that impulse control disorders in elderly persons with intellectual disability, in the absence of exacerbation by another underlying psychiatric or neurological disorder, have responded poorly to trials with various psychotropics.

Intermittent explosive disorder (rage attacks), severe tantrums, and aggressive/disinhibited behavior with intermittent self-injurious behavior in young adults with intellectual disability responded favorably to the beta blockers propranolol, pindolol, and nadolol in different doses (Ratey, 1986; Ratey & Lindem, 1991; Greendyke, 1986). There are no studies of beta blockers in older adults with intellectual disability and explosive disorders or disinhibited behaviors. Low doses of propranolol have been used in elderly adults with dementia without intellectual disability with modest results (Risse & Barnes, 1986; Weiler, Mungas & Bernick, 1988). In clear cases of rage attacks, severe tantrums, and disinhibited behavior in older adults with intellectual disability with or without dementia, small doses of a beta blocker, preferably a trial with pindolol for its low effect on blood pressure, is suggested.

Beta blockers are indicated also for the treatment of neuroleptic-induced akathisia; tremors, including essential, familial, senile, and lithium-induced; and the somatic symptoms (tremor, sweating, palpitation) of performance anxiety. Less frequent beta-blocker side effects that may need medical attention include: dizziness; swelling of ankles, feet, and/or lower legs; shortness of breath; and possible mental depression (USPC, 1996). Since contraindications indicate cardiac conduction abnormalities, the risk/benefit must be considered with existing medical conditions such as allergy, asthma or emphysema, congestive heart failure, diabetes, hyperthyroidism, and mental depression.

Opioid Antagonists for Self-Injurious Behavior. Although there are no studies of the use of opioid antagonists for self-injurious behaviors in older adults with intellectual disability, naltrexone may be tried if an older adult with intellectual disability exhibits severe self-injurious behaviors, and an underlying psychiatric disorder responsive to other psychotropics has been excluded as a cause of self-injurious behaviors. Clinical studies of its use for self-injurious behaviors in younger adults have found that naltrexone is a relatively safe drug with minor side effects; 35 to 40% of individuals with self-injurious behaviors tried on naltrexone responded positively to varied doses (Sandman et al., 1993; Thompson et al., 1994). Generally, the use of naltrexone is contraindicated for self-injurious behaviors if there is dependence on opioid drugs, liver failure, or acute hepatitis.

Dementia of the Alzheimer Type or Alzheimer's Disease. Many medications have been tried with limited beneficial effects in older persons with only Alzheimer's disease and without intellectual disability in an attempt to prevent, delay, or reverse the process of Alzheimer's disease. The diagnosis of Alzheimer's disease in persons with or without intellectual disability and with or without Down's syndrome is a difficult one to make in the early stages, but it can be made through exclusion of other disorders and close follow-up. Drugs that have been used or tried in persons without intellectual disability include cholinesterase inhibitors, cholinergic agonists, monoamine oxidase inhibitors, glutamatergic agents, anti-inflammatory agents, antioxidants, antifibrillization-of-the-amyloidogenic protein agents, GABAergic agents, noradrenergic agents, somatostatin, adrenocorticotropic hormone agonists, thyrotropin-releasing analogues, opiate receptor antagonists, calcium channel blockers, and hydergine (Raskind, 1995; Salzman et al., 1995).

Only two drugs, tacrine and donepezil, have been approved for treatment of Alzheimer's disease in the United States. Both drugs improve cognitive performance in the early stages of Alzheimer's disease. There is no evidence that either drug alters the course of the underlying dementing process. These medications or others have not been tested, as yet, in persons with intellectual disabilities. Trazodone was reported as effective in certain cases of Alzheimer's disease in patients without intellectual disability with insomnia, banging, and screaming (Greenwald, Marin, & Silverman, 1986). In a study of 10 persons without intellectual disability but with depression and advanced Alzheimer's disease, sertraline was used for treatment of depression. In eight of them, improvement of affect was observed. Six of these persons were also refusing food and sertraline diminished food refusal in five of them (Volicer, Rheaume, & Cyr, 1994). A meta-analysis of studies evaluating antipsychotic drugs in persons without intellectual disability suffering from dementia and exhibiting behavior problems (Schneider, Pollock, & Lyness, 1990) concluded that antipsychotic drugs are significantly more effective than placebo in this population. Tapering and discontinuing the antipsychotics after four months, when improvement was noted in behavior problems, was not followed by the reemergence of problems in eight out of nine older patients with dementia and agitation without intellectual disability (Risse, Cubberly, & Lampe, 1987). The mood stabilizers carbamazepine (Marin & Greenwald, 1989), divalproex (Mellow, Solano-Lopez, & Davis, 1993), and lithium (Holton & George, 1985) have been found effective in reducing hostility, agitation, and noncompliance in persons with dementia without intellectual disability.

It is important, especially in adults with Down's syndrome who exhibit a decline in cognitive and activities of daily living skills, to rule out any other reversible cause of decline or other type of dementia before making the diagnosis of Alzheimer's disease. This requires medical, neurological, and psychiatric evaluations with close follow-up visits. Older persons with Alzheimer's disease and intellectual disability often have other symptoms, such as memory and orientation problems, aphasia, agnosia, apraxia, and disturbances in planning and organizing, which are the characteristics of dementia. Depressive disorders are commonly associated with Alzheimer's disease, especially in persons with Down's syndrome. One study showed that trazodone and the SSRI antidepressants, fluoxetine, paroxetine, and sertraline, were found to relieve the symptoms of depression in six cases with Down's syndrome, Alzheimer's disease, and associated depression (Tsiouris & Patti, 1997). Noncompliance, eating and sleeping disturbances, and low energy level (slowness) were the target behaviors for which the antidepressant drugs had their most noted effects. Explosiveness, aggressivity, destructiveness, affective instability, and disorganized behavior not associated with depression, responded better to the anticonvulsant drugs divalproex and carbamazepine.

The intensity of paranoid thoughts and behaviors and the persecutory and erotomanic delusions, observed in a few of the cases studied, subsided when the mood disorder was treated with the SSRIs or divalproex. Antipsychotic drugs are not well tolerated and must be avoided (if possible) in older persons with intellectual disability, Alzheimer's disease, and especially in adults with Down's syndrome.

Small doses of risperidone, mesoridazine, thioridazine, loxapine, olanzapine, or haloperidol can be used only if, in addition to the diagnosis of Alzheimer's disease, clear and persistent signs and symptoms of a psychotic disorder (hallucinations, delusions, regression, bizarre behavior, and random aggressive and destructive behavior) are observed. Buspirone may be tried if anxiety and agitation are predominant behaviors. Sleep disturbance is a common behavior problem in persons with Alzheimer's disease and usually is a symptom of an associated psychiatric disorder which responds to corresponding psychotropics. A mild hypnotic or small doses of thioridazine or both can be tried if insomnia is an independent behavior. Melatonin is another substance that may be tried for regulation of sleep pattern disturbances (Jan, Espezel, & Appleton, 1994).

☐ Commentary

Advances in medicine and optimal care offered to persons with intellectual disabilities has helped to improve their quality of life and increase their longevity. Older persons with intellectual disability present new medical, psychiatric, and behavioral problems; thus providers need educational materials to address these issues. Further studies should be conducted regarding the aforementioned issues. Until then, especially from a psychiatric and psychopharmacological point of view, providers have to rely on the limited studies of geriatric psychiatry and psychopharmacology in the general aging population. The advancing everyday knowledge regarding the function of the brain, and an increasing number of new psychotropics with better side effects profile, has given providers new options. These advances coupled with patience, care, and sound medical practice by the providers can further improve the quality of life in aging persons with intellectual disabilities.

☐ References

American Psychiatric Association. (1994). *Diagnostic and statistical manual of mental disorders* (4th ed.). Washington, DC: American Psychiatric Association.

Barron, J., & Sandman, C. A. (1985). Paradoxical excitement to sedative-hypnotic drugs in mentally retarded clients. *American Journal of Mental Deficiency, 90,* 124–129.

Bauer, M. S., & Whybrow, P. C. (1990). Rapid cycling bipolar affective disorder, II: Treatment of refractory rapid cycling with high-dose levothyroxine: A preliminary study. *Archives of General Psychiatry, 47,* 435–440.

Baumeister, A. A., Todd, M. E., & Sevin, J. A. (1993). Efficacy and specificity of pharmaco-logical therapies for behavioral disorders in persons with mental retardation. *Clinical Neuropharmacology, 16,* 271–294.

Brunet, G., Cerlick, B., & Robert, P. (1990). Open trial of a calcium antagonist, nimodipine, in acute mania. *Clinical Neuropharmacology, 13,* 22.

Burt, D. B., Loveland, K. A., & Lewis, K. R. (1992). Depression and the onset of dementia in adults with mental retardation. *American Journal on Mental Retardation, 96,* 502–511.

Casey, D. E. (1996). Side effect profiles of new antipsychotic agents. *Journal of Clinical Psychiatry, 57*(Suppl. 11), 40–45.

Chandler, M., Gualtieri, C. T., & Fahs, J. J. (1988). Other psychotropic drugs. In M. G. Aman, & N. N. Singh (Eds.), *Psychopharmacology of the developmental disabilities* (pp. 119–145). New York: Springer-Verlag.

Collacott, R. A., Cooper, S.-A., & McGrother, C. (1992). Differential rates of psychiatric disorders in adults with Down's syndrome compared with other mentally handi-capped adults. *British Journal of Psychiatry, 161,* 671–674.

Cooper, S.-A. (1996, July). *The psychiatry of elderly people with learning disabilities.* Paper presented at the Tenth World Congress of the International Association for the Scien-tific Study of Intellectual Disabilities, Helsinki, Finland.

Cooper, S.-A., & Collacott, R. A. (1993). Prognosis of depression in Down's syndrome. *Journal of Nervous & Mental Disease, 181,* 204–205.

Dalton, A. J., & Crapper-McLachlan, D. R. (1986). Clinical expression of Alzheimer's disease in Down's syndrome. *Psychiatric Clinics of North America, 9,* 659–670.

deLeon, M. J., Golomb, J., George, A. E., Convit, A., Tarshish, C. Y., McRae, T., DeSante, S., Smith, G., Ferris, S. H., Moz, K., & Rusinek, H. (1993). The radiologic prediction of Alzheimer disease: The atrophic hippocampal formation. *American Journal Neuro-radiology, 14,* 897–905.

Devenny, D. A., Silverman, W. P., Hill, A. L., Jenkins, E., Sersen, E. A., & Wisniewski, K. (1996). Normal aging in adults with Down's syndrome: A longitudinal study. *Journal of Intellectual Disability Research, 40,* 208–221.

Dubovsky, S. I., Franks, R. D., & Allen, S. (1986). Calcium antagonists in mania: A double blind study of verapamil. *Psychiatry Research, 18,* 309–320.

Evenhuis, H. M. (1990). The natural history of dementia in Down's syndrome. *Archives of Neurology, 47,* 263–267.

Friedman, J. H. (1993). Akathisia with clozapine. *Biological Psychiatry, 33,* 852–853.

Greendyke, R. M. (1986). Propranolol treatment of assaultive patients with organic brain disease. *Journal of Nervous and Mental Diseases, 174,* 290–294.

Greenwald, B. S., Marin, D. B., & Silverman, S. M. (1986). Serotoninergic treatment of screaming and banging in dementia [Letter]. *Lancet, 2,* 1464–1465.

Gualtieri, C. T. & Schroeder, S. R. (1986). Tardive dyskinesia in young mentally retarded individuals. *Archives of General Psychiatry, 43,* 335–340.

Holton, A., & George, K. (1985). The use of lithium in severely demented patients with behavioral disturbance. *British Journal of Psychiatry, 146,* 99–100.

Intagliata, J., & Rinck, C. (1985). Psychoactive drug use in public and community facilities for mentally retarded persons. *Psychopharmacology Bulletin, 21,* 268–278.

Jan, J. E., Espezel, H., & Appleton, R. E. (1994). The treatment of sleep disorders with melatonin. *Developmental Medicine and Child Neurology, 36,* 97–107.

Janicak, P. G., Davis, J. M., Ayd, F., & Preskorn, S. H. (1995). Advances in the pharmaco-therapy of bipolar disorder. In P. G. Janicak, J. M. Davis, F. J. Ayd, Jr., & S. H. Preskorn (Eds.), *Update— Principles and Practice of Psychopharmacotherapy* [1(3), 20pp.]. Baltimore: Williams and Wilkins.

Karson, C. G., Bracha, H. S., & Powell, A. (1990). Dyskinetic movements, cognitive impair-ment, and negative symptoms in elderly neuropsychiatric patients. *American Journal of Psychiatry, 147,* 1646–1649.

Lazarus, A., Jaffe, R. L., & Dubin, W. R. (1990). Electroconvulsive therapy and major depression in Down's syndrome. *Journal of Clinical Psychiatry, 51,* 422–425.

Lieberman, J., Kane, J. M., & Woerner, M. (1984). Prevalence of tardive dyskinesia in elderly samples. *Psychopharmacology Bulletin, 20,* 22–26.

Lipman, R. S., DiMascio, A., Reatig, N., & Kirson, T. (1978). Psychotropic drugs and mentally retarded children. In M. A. Lipton, A. DiMascio, & K. F. Killam (Eds.), *Psychopharmacology: A generation of progress* (pp. 1437–1449). New York: Raven Press.

Mandoki, M. (1994). Buspirone treatment of traumatic brain injury in a child who is highly sensitive to adverse effects of psychotropic medications. *Journal of Child and Adolescent Psychopharmacology, 4,* 129–139.

Marin, D. B., & Greenwald, B. S. (1989). Carbamazepine for aggressive agitation in demented patients. *American Journal of Psychiatry, 146,* 805.

McClellan, J. M., & Werry, J. S. (1992). Schizophrenia. *Psychiatric Clinics of North America, 15,* 131–148.

McDougle, C. J., Naylor, S. T., Cohen, D. J., Volkmar, F. R., Heninger, G. R., & Price, L. H. (1996). A double-blind, placebo-controlled study of fluvoxamine in adults with autistic disorder. *Archives of General Psychiatry, 53,* 1001–1008.

McGuire, D., & Chicoine, B. A. (1996). Depressive disorders in adults with Down syndrome. *The Habilitative Mental Healthcare Newsletter, 15,* 1–7.

Mellow, A. M., Solano-Lopez, C., & Davis, S. (1993). Sodium valproate in the treatment of behavioral disturbance in dementia. *Journal of Geriatric Psychiatry and Neurology, 6,* 28–32.

Poling, A., Gadow, K. D., & Cleary, J. (1991). *Drug therapy for behavior disorders: An introduction.* New York: Pergamon Press.

Popovitch, E. R., Wisniewski, H. M., & Barcikowska, M. (1990). Alzheimer neuropathology in non-Down's mentally retarded adults. *Acta Neuropathology, 80,* 362–367.

Raskind, M. A. (1995). Treatment of Alzheimer's disease and other dementias. In A. F. Schatzberg & C. B. Nemeroff (Eds.), *Textbook of psychopharmacology* (pp. 657–665). Washington, DC: American Psychiatric Press.

Ratey, J. J. (1986). Beta-blockers in the severely and profoundly mentally retarded. *Journal of Clinical Psychopharmacology, 6,* 3–7.

Ratey, J. J., & Lindem, K. J. (1991). Beta blockers as primary treatment for aggression and self injury in the developmentally disabled. In J. J. Ratey (Ed.), *Mental retardation: Developing pharmacotherapies* (pp. 51–81). Washington, DC: American Psychiatric Press.

Reiss, S., & Aman, M. G. (1997). The international consensus process on psychopharmacology and intellectual disability. *Journal of Intellectual Disability Research, 41,* 448–455.

Richelson, E. (1996). Preclinical pharmacology of neuroleptics: Focus on new generation compounds. *Journal of Clinical Psychiatry, 57* (Suppl.), 4–11.

Risse, S. C., & Barnes, R. (1986). Pharmacologic treatment of agitation associated with dementia. *Journal of the American Geriatrics Society, 34,* 368–376.

Risse, S. C., Cubberley, L., & Lampe, T. H. (1987). Acute effects of neuroleptic withdrawal in elderly dementia patients. *Journal of Geriatric Drug Therapy, 2,* 65–77.

Sakauye, K. M., Camp, C. J., & Ford, P. A. (1993). Effects of Buspirone on agitation associated with dementia. *American Journal of Geriatric Psychiatry, 1,* 82–84.

Salzman, C. (1990). Practical considerations of the pharmacologic treatment of depression and anxiety in the elderly. *Journal of Clinical Psychiatry, 51*(Suppl.), 40–43.

Salzman, C., Satlin, A., & Burrows, A. B. (1995). Geriatric psychopharmacology. In A. F. Schatzberg & C. B. Nemeroff (Eds.), *Textbook of psychopharmacology* (pp. 803–821). Washington, DC: American Psychiatric Press.

Sandman, C. A., Hetrick, W. P., Taylor, D. V., Barron, J. L., Touchette, P., Lott, I., Crinella, F., & Martinazzi, V. (1993). Naltrexone reduces self-injury and improves learning. *Experimental and Clinical Psychopharmacology, 1,* 242–258.

Schneider, L. S., Pollock, V. E., & Lyness, S. A. (1990). A metaanalysis of controlled trials of neuroleptic treatment in dementia. *Journal of American Geriatrics Society, 38*, 553–563.

Sheline, Y. I., Wang, P. W., Mokhtar, H. G., & Csernansky, J. G. (1996). Hippocampal atrophy in recurrent major depression. *Proceedings of the National Academy Science, 93*, 3908–3913.

Storm, W. (1990). Differential diagnosis and treatment of depressive features in Down's syndrome: A case illustration. *Research in Developmental Disabilities, 11*, 131–137.

Sweet, R. A., Benoit, H., & Mulsant, M.D. (1992). Dyskinesia and neuroleptic exposure in elderly psychiatric inpatients. *Journal of Geriatric Psychiatry and Neurology, 5*, 156–161.

Thompson, T., Hackenberg, T., Cerutti, D., Baker, D., & Axtell, S. (1994). Opioid antagonist effects on self-injury in adults with mental retardation: Response form and location as determinants of medication effects. *American Journal on Mental Retardation, 99*, 85–102.

Tsiouris, J. A., & Adelman, S. A. (1997). *Guidelines/information on psychotropic and antiepileptic drugs for individuals with developmental disabilities.* Staten Island, NY: New York State Institute for Basic Research in Developmental Disabilities.

Tsiouris, J. A., & Patti, P. J. (1997). Drug treatment of depression associated with dementia or presented as "pseudodementia" in older adults with Down syndrome. *Journal of Applied Research in Intellectual Disabilities, 10*, 312–322.

United States Pharmacopeial Convention (USPC). (1996). *Drug information for the health care professional* (Vol. I, 16th ed.). Rockville, MD: United States Pharmacopeial Convention.

Volicer, L., Rheaume, V., & Cyr, D. (1994). Treatment of depression in advanced Alzheimer's disease using sertraline. *Journal of Geriatric Psychiatry and Neurology, 7*, 227–229.

Walters, R. M. (1990). Suicidal behaviour in severely mentally handicapped patients. *British Journal of Psychiatry, 157*, 444–446.

Warren, A. C., Holroyd, S., & Folstein, M. F. (1989). Major depression in Down's syndrome. *British Journal of Psychiatry, 155*, 202–205.

Weiler, P. G., Mungas, D., & Bernick, C. (1988). Propranolol for the control of disruptive behavior in senile dementia. *Journal of Geriatric Psychiatry and Neurology, 1*, 226–230.

Wisniewski, H. M., & Silverman, W. (1996). Alzheimer disease neuropathology and dementia in Down's syndrome. In J. A. Rondal, L. Nadel, J. Perrera (Eds.), *Down syndrome: Psychological, psychobiological and socioeducational perspective* (pp. 43–50). London: Cholin Whurr.

Wragg, R. E., & Jeste, D. V. (1988). Neuroleptics and alternative treatments. Management of behavioral symptoms and psychosis in Alzheimer's disease and related conditions. *Psychiatric Clinics of North America, 11*, 195–213.

Zigman, W., Silverman, W., & Wisniewski, H. M. (1996). Aging and Alzheimer's disease in Down syndrome: Clinical and pathological changes. *Mental Retardation and Developmental Disabilities Research Reviews, 2*, 1–7.

5

PROGRAM CONSIDERATIONS

Until recently, little guidance was available on programs and supports for aging-related and aging-associated problems among adults with intellectual disabilities. The focus of this section is to address this dearth of guidance. As older people are affected by age and by the special challenges inherent in growing older with a lifelong disability, both carers and agencies are confronted with how to design interventions and services to address their specific needs. The occurrence of Alzheimer's disease in persons with intellectual disabilities poses a special challenge to prevalent models of programming that are almost entirely based on skill and independence acquisition. With the onset of dementia and other age-associated conditions that manifest decline, such issues as communication, assessment services, day and residential supports, and responding to dying and death, are all especially germane. The chapters in this section offer overviews, as well as prescriptive help, for these programmatic issues.

In the opening chapter on communication, McCallion begins by exploring some of the limitations imposed on communication by decline and proposes some ways that older adults can be helped in coping with diminished capacities, memories, and verbal skills. He reviews a three-stage profile of changes in communication skills that occurs as dementia progresses to affect phonology, syntax, semantics, and pragmatics. The author then offers a lucid and comprehensive account of a five-part program for persons with dementia and intellectual disabilities designed specifically to meet their needs. The five parts include careful evaluation of strengths and weaknesses in the individual's functioning, which is used as the information base for making meaningful changes in the environment, training of staff to use prompts and cues, memory aids (e.g., strategic labeling, personal memory albums, memory charts, memory audiotapes), and taking care of the carer (e.g., information, supports, taking "breaks"). The author notes that these programmatic innovations will maintain and possibly enhance the quality of life of affected individuals with intellectual disabilities. In this chapter, McCallion also examines how families and other carers communicate and proposes remedial aids that can be useful for overcoming communication difficulties. Since families rely on communication for personal interactions and histories, he explores how families can be helped to cope with the communication losses associated with dementia and how they can build bridges over those losses as family members age.

Having a community resource that provides for assessment and clinical consultation for problems associated with aging can be an immensely valuable asset. In the next chapter, Chicoine, McGuire, and Rubin describe the history and establishment of a multidisciplinary assessment clinic as a programmatic response that grew out of the concerns of families and parents of aging individuals with Down's syndrome. The authors describe the rationale for incorporating a routine which assures that every adult is seen by a family practice physician, a social worker, an audiologist, and a nutritionist. Several assessments and the regular use of extensive questionnaires with a focus on health problems and psychosocial concerns are used and are combined with structured interviews with a family member or care provider and the adult. Personal well-being and an emphasis on health and wellness provide the anchor around which all contacts and services are provided. Analyses and reviews of the cases seen in the clinic over a number of years introduce the reader to the many reversible conditions that produce losses of function other than dementia of the Alzheimer type in this susceptible population. From their experience, the authors signal the importance of a complete and thorough assessment as a prerequisite for quality services.

In the next two chapters, Force and O'Malley and Udell examine aspects of specific service provision as they apply to situations involving dementia and other functional decline. Families and other carers often ask for adult day services in the community as an alternative to institutionalization of their aging relative with intellectual disabilities, according to Force and O'Malley. Three models of adult day care are reviewed briefly, namely, the health/medical model, the social model, and the specialty model. The approach presented is from the service agency perspective. Specific agency issues, such as mission statements, target service population, enrollment criteria, and assessment practices, standards for buildings and living areas, and documentation, are driven by a common prevention philosophy that involves preservation of remaining functions. The authors outline the broad array of activities currently occurring in adult day programs, including nutrition, community outings, on-site entertainment activities (amateur choir groups, crafts, cooking classes, music therapy, foster grandparents, senior companions), use of pets, modified dancing, aerobics, reminiscence sessions, to name only a few. These descriptions are then followed by their application to adults with intellectual disabilities and those affected by dementia of the Alzheimer type. Some of the problems of implementing day programs are illustrated by cases studies. The authors speculate that in the future more adult day services will become available in response to growing needs and that these services will converge for persons with Alzheimer's dementia whether or not there is an associated intellectual disability in the affected individuals.

Udell discusses residential supports for persons with intellectual disabilities affected by dementia from an organizational perspective, which is particularly relevant for agencies that operate small group home settings. Her presentation is based on the experience of a residential agency which provides services to adults with intellectual disabilities. The impact of current knowledge about risk factors, prevalence, and clinical presentation and progression of dementia, on the planning activities of the agency directors, is described. These include a perceptive discussion of issues, including the level of organizational commitment, requirements for modifications to provide accessible housing, assistive devices, staffing levels, and the financial implications for the organization. The author then shifts to staff training and the personal preparation of staff, which the organization recognizes as an essential requirement of effective and proactive intervention with persons who will show progressive decline until they become bedridden and physically as well as mentally incapacitated. The philosophical base is the provision of care that is best for the residents and what the residents would choose if they had the capacity to communicate their wishes. With the physical deterioration of affected individuals, the care shifts to a more medical orientation, with particular attention to appropriate medications, support, and patience in dealing with emotional and behavioral changes, providing palliative care, daytime supports, and activities. She also raises the difficult program issue of whether to proceed with providing care within an "aging in place" context or to begin to develop specialty homes for dementia care. Wisely, she leaves such thorny programmatic issues unresolved, but she permits the reader to use the information gleaned from her experiences to form his or her own opinions. Udell concludes by presenting four major recommendations that emerged from analysis of the experience of her agency in supporting people with Alzheimer's disease.

Last, Service, Lavoie, and Herlihy explore what may be the most difficult issue to address in any care system—the effects of death and bereavement on staff, carers, and friends. The authors address the sensitive issues of end-stage care and support of individuals with intellectual disabilities as they decline into the late or terminal stages of Alzheimer's disease. They note that this is a new activity for care providers. The knowledge base on the topic of losses, death, and grieving in the research literature is very limited. In this chapter, the authors utilize a "composite case" as a model to examine the sequence of responses that reflect a recognizable and somewhat predictable five-stage process (denial, anger/guilt, bargaining, depression, and acceptance). A detailed descriptive analysis is offered of the efforts at helping staff and families to cope with the dying or death of an affected person. We see in this chapter a thoughtful review of some of the issues related to dying within a living situation and its effects upon housemates and staff. We also see the dilemmas faced by agencies and staff that result from contending with religious and affiliative differences, family wishes and traditions, and ingrained agency practices. This chapter, in the end, helps us better understand how unprepared we often are for life's last challenge.

14
CHAPTER

Philip McCallion

Maintaining Communication

Longitudinal and cross-sectional studies suggest that persons with intellectual disabilities are at least as likely to experience symptoms of dementia as the general population. Useful models and training programs for families and carers for the general population with Alzheimer's dementia are already available. The progression of dementia among persons with intellectual disabilities appears to be similar to that in the general population. Therefore, existing service models and programs may be adapted for the population with intellectual disabilities. A five-part program, maintaining communication and independence (MCI), is proposed which adapts an existing program for persons with dementia to better meet the needs of persons with intellectual disabilities. The five parts to MCI include the following: (1) strengths identification and deficit assessment, (2) environmental modification, (3) good communication, (4) memory aids, and (5) taking care of the carer.

Understanding the experience of Alzheimer's dementia among persons with intellectual disabilities is complicated by the extent of deficits associated with concomitant disabilities, difficulties in diagnosing dementia,

Address correspondence to: Philip McCallion, Ph.D., ACSW, School of Social Welfare, Center on Intellectual Disabilities, University at Albany, 135 Western Avenue, Albany, NY 12222.

Development of this chapter was supported through grants from the New York State Department of Health Dementia Research Grants Program and from the U.S. Administration on Aging.

and other confounding features such as depression among persons with limited communication ability and poor existing medical and functional histories (Burt, Loveland, & Lewis, 1992, Janicki, Heller, Seltzer, & Hogg, 1995). Nevertheless, it is likely that the progression of the disease is similar to that in the general population, beginning with forgetfulness, personality changes, and lost skills, and moving progressively through early, moderate, and severe stages. Indeed, it has been suggested that the manifestation of later-stage Alzheimer's dementia among persons with Down's syndrome is no different from that described among the general population (Dalton & Wisniewski, 1990).

The increased longevity of persons with intellectual disabilities not only increases the occurrence of Alzheimer's dementia among this population, but it has also posed a challenge to prevalent models of programming. As Seltzer and Krauss (1987) pointed out, consideration of programs for persons with intellectual disabilities who are aging is a relatively new phenomenon. The primary service models were built at a time when the majority of persons with intellectual disabilities were not expected to live beyond middle age, and those models were focused on skill and independence acquisition. The models are not appropriate for aging persons with intellectual disabilities in general, and persons with Alzheimer's dementia in particular, where the focus needs to be on skill maintenance.

A particular concern is the emphasis on moving individuals with intellectual disabilities to the most independent levels possible. No provision has been made for the reintroduction of supports when they are required at a later time. The following is a typical situation:

> We knew that something was wrong with my son Mark the weekend of his 40th birthday. Just as he had for the last eight years he took the bus from his group home to our house. I was so proud of him the first time he came home independently on his own. It's a three-hour ride. I waited at our bus station like I always did. The bus arrived and he wasn't on it. We called the group home and they told us he got on the bus. Mark's father doesn't drive anymore, so we got our neighbor to drive to the next town where we found him. He got off at the wrong bus station, and he didn't know why. The group home doesn't have a staff member to travel with him, and it's too long a ride for me to go down and get him on the bus all in one day. Does this mean he won't come home anymore?

This vignette also illustrates that the declines experienced by a person with an intellectual disability and dementia also have an emotional as well as a practical impact on families and other carers. Carers and other family members have indicated that they need training and service models that assist them to maintain existing independence and living situations and to respond appropriately to the growing deficits associated with

Alzheimer's dementia among persons with intellectual disabilities (Anto-nangeli, 1995; Janicki & Dalton, 1993; Janicki & Dalton, this volume). Interventions are also needed that strengthen carers' own ability to cope with dementia-related declines.

Useful models and training programs for families and carers in the general population with Alzheimer's dementia are available, and adaptations of these can be made for the population with intellectual disabilities. One such adaptation, the five-part program, MCI, is explored in this chapter. MCI is adapted from the maintaining communication with persons with dementia program (Toseland & McCallion, 1998). The five parts to MCI include the following: (1) strengths identification and deficit assessment, (2) environmental modification, (3) good communication, (4) memory aids, and (5) taking care of the carer.

☐ Strengths Identification and Deficit Assessment

Much has been written about the difficulties in assessing the presence of dementia associated with Alzheimer's disease among persons with intellectual disabilities. Numerous workers (e.g., Aylward, Burt, Thorpe, Lai, & Dalton, 1995; Burt & Aylward, this volume) have reached the conclusion that many existing instruments used with the general population are not sensitive enough to identify additional changes beyond the cognitive deficits each person with an intellectual disability may already be experiencing. In addition, they are particularly concerned that there is not sufficient consideration of the effects of age-related changes or of other conditions such as depression. They underscore the need for gathering and monitoring information on behavior to confirm changes and the collection and consideration of detailed medical, neurological, and functional evaluations. Details on the issues involved in a diagnosis of Alzheimer's dementia are provided elsewhere. However, it is important to point out that the diagnostic process must rely ultimately on the confirmation of progressive deficits in functioning and cognition, over and above those associated with preexisting intellectual disabilities. For the purposes of this chapter, a diagnosis of probable Alzheimer's dementia is assumed. This assumption allows us to consider how the information gathered in the diagnosis process can be used to advance effective programming. For programming purposes, we need to shift attention away from impairments to a focus on what strengths remain. Such a shift provides the basis for interventions. Simultaneously, diagnostic teams must be encouraged to give detailed consideration to the status of concurrent age-related changes in communication and memory.

For all aging persons there are likely to be growing deficits in the sensory functions of vision, hearing, taste, smell, and touch. Biological changes both reduce sensitivity and increase the impact of interferences such as background noise, distracting odors, and poor lighting. Existing deficits for persons with intellectual disabilities are also likely to increase with age. There is a danger of assuming that because senses are deteriorating, nothing can be done. Yet easily achieved environmental changes may compensate for these changes. When senses are not stimulated, deterioration may accelerate, and people may withdraw from social contacts (Bourgeois, 1991). Periodic assessment of hearing and vision is clearly necessary, as is the use of hearing aids and glasses to compensate for treatable impairments.

With the onset of dementia, there is concern as to what effect dementia has on communication abilities. The profile of communication skills in dementia differs from the profiles of developmental aging and focal organic disorders (Frank, 1994; Santo Pietro, 1994). Adults generally show some episodic memory losses and slower reaction times as aging progresses. However, language disorders (such as aphasia and right hemisphere disorders) will affect specific language functions without affecting intellect and memory. Yet dementia affected communication generally progresses through three stages. In the first stage, deficits are primarily in the content area of lexical access and subtle conversational skills. In the second stage, there is increased difficulty in content areas, including concept formation, lexical access diminished graphic abilities reliance on syntactic abilities, and reduced memory function. The third stage of dementia may involve all of the above in a more severe manner, along with severe memory and intellectual deficits. Further, Alzheimer's dementia progressively alters four major components to communication skills: phonology, syntax, semantics, and pragmatics. *Phonology* involves the process of forming and producing words, *syntax* the processes of sentence comprehension and formulation, and *semantics* the knowledge of meanings of words. *Pragmatics* is the learned rule of managing communication such as maintenance of cohesion and coherence, taking turns, managing topics during a conversation, and ways to reengage another person when the conversation breaks down (Ripich, 1994).

Pragmatics of communication often breaks down earliest in the course of Alzheimer's dementia. For persons with intellectual disabilities, pragmatics may have never been well developed, meaning that breakdowns are likely to be dramatic, creating frustrating situations for families, other carers, and the person with an intellectual disability. Those frustrations encourage withdrawal from conversation, even when communication is still possible. It is important, therefore, to identify remaining communication assets for preservation in order to maintain communication and independence for the person with an intellectual disability (Fujiki & Brinton, 1993).

Meaningful communication also requires the processing of words, sounds, and symbols to produce and comprehend concepts. There are three levels of memory: sensory, primary, and secondary. *Sensory memory* is what we hear and see, while *primary memory* is where we interpret, code, and maintain what we see and hear based on coding schemes maintained in secondary memory. *Secondary or longer-term memory* also has three subcomponents. *Episodic memory* contains the conscious recollection of specific events in particular places and times; for example, "I was born on Independence Day, 1921, in Albany." *Semantic memory* contains vocabulary and general knowledge independent of time and context; for example, "a lot of people barbecue on Independence Day." *Procedural memory* is about knowing when to do something, what to do, and how to do it; for example, "You need to get the coals nice and gray before you put meat on the barbecue." More and more memories and encoding and interpreting processes are lost with the progression of Alzheimer's dementia. Long-held procedural memories, however, are usually retained the longest (Tomoeda & Bayles, 1990). An appreciation of these aspects of memory function is critical to the design of effective programming and communication interventions.

☐ Environmental Modification

Consideration of environmental modification must address both age-related changes and the specific functional losses associated with Alzheimer's dementia. Attention should be paid to increasing the brightness of lighting without adding to glare, using larger size lettering and a greater range of colors for signs, and enhancing the taste and aroma of food. Background noises and other distractions should be reduced to further compensate for normal age-related changes. Sitting someone close to the kitchen at meal times makes her/his care easier for staff, but doors opening and closing, people moving in and out, and the clatter of utensils may be very distracting. These distractions reduce conversations at meal times, whether or not the person is affected by Alzheimer's dementia. However, what may represent distractions in one situation become important sensory cues in another. For example, *redundant cueing*, the designed invoking of a number of senses to convey the same information, may be vital to maintaining understanding and communication when sensitivity of one of the senses is diminished (Christenson, 1990). The prompts of seeing signs for the dining room and plates and silverware on the table, hearing sounds from the kitchen, and smelling the aromas of newly cooked food, may increase the likelihood that an individual will continue to independently go to the dining area at appropriate times. Encouraging families and other carers to use redundant cuing techniques will increase the frequency of effective communications.

Other deficits associated with Alzheimer's dementia also require specific environmental modifications. Families and other carers need to consider the following 10 areas (Christenson, 1990):

Comfort.   Comfort is a subjective quality. Too often, we ask people to conform to average or majority expectations. There is not, for example, one wheelchair that is suitable for everyone. As infirmity increases, it is likely that persons will spend increasing amounts of time in a particular chair or in a particular area. Consideration must be given to the extent to which arrangements and furnishings cater to their comfort. Discomfort will amplify deficits in function.

Legibility.   Written word signs have limited value as a cue or landmark for persons with Alzheimer's dementia attempting to continue to negotiate around their living environment independently. The placement of furniture and the room layout of most buildings often give confusing messages to most persons with Alzheimer's dementia. Clutter should be reduced, purposeful cues increased, and consideration given to screening spaces that are not part of the world of the person with Alzheimer's dementia, such as a janitor's closet.

Autonomy.   Autonomy is about privacy, about having a place to be alone, and being able to choose when to be alone and when to participate in group activities. Active encouragement and attention to needs for privacy will reduce conflicts with others living in the same setting.

Accessibility.   Accessibility means ability to move about and to carry out activities independently or with minimal help. Strategies to enhance accessibility include providing wheelchair-wide corridors, shelves and cupboards at usable heights, signs, grab bars in bathrooms, curb cuts, and eliminating stairs and trip hazards. It may also mean adding chairs to hallways in larger congregate settings, because being able to rest periodically may be the difference between walking somewhere independently and being taken there. Again the focus should be on tailoring accessibility for the individual, not for most people.

Adaptability.   Alzheimer's dementia is progressive. The living environment must be modifiable as needs and level of functioning change. The pursuit of homes "just like others in the community" may mean for out-of-home providers that they have chosen homes that will require major renovation to remain suitable as individuals age and experience Alzheimer's dementia. This is also a concern for families. Anecdotal accounts of families locking persons experiencing Alzheimer's dementia in their rooms occur because the homes they are living in are not easily adaptable as care needs change. Consideration should be given to adaptability concerns in the selection and design of new alternative living settings and in the planning of renovations to existing settings and family homes.

Meaning.   How long an individual has lived in a particular place influences how meaningful the home is and how traumatic sudden changes may be. The feelings of reassurance and security provided by familiar objects, furniture, and people should not be underestimated.

Security.   The more privacy and meaning are valued, the safer the person with Alzheimer's dementia will feel. In addition, a focus on safety is likely to enhance independence by eliminating slippery surfaces and trip hazards, ensuring that adaptive aids are truly adaptive for the individual and that there are established approaches for responding to emergencies.

Socialization.   A range of opportunities to socialize are important to people at all stages of Alzheimer's dementia. For families caring at home, the use of day programs and respite is sometimes rejected, because parents see it as a selfish choice to meet their own needs. Yet the opportunity to occasionally see other people and to participate in group activities is often valued by the person with an intellectual disability, even in the later stages of Alzheimer's dementia. Indeed, there may be an increased need for physical contact with others to offset loneliness and fears associated with progressive dementia. In their own homes, families should be assisted in identifying ways to increase opportunities for interaction. They should also be encouraged to incorporate walks, shorts trips, and participation in previously enjoyed social activities into the daily routine for the person with an intellectual disability.

Congregate settings offer more opportunities for formal group activities. However, in these settings there may be less opportunities for time alone or for informal group participation. When individuals being cared for are seen to congregate around staff offices and in day rooms, the likely response is to criticize the programming being offered. It may also be indicative that there are no other locations where individuals can be alone or may choose to informally socialize in smaller numbers. Congregate settings must be designed or renovated to provide such opportunities.

Aesthetics.   It seems self-evident that living in a pleasant environment is more likely to help a person with an intellectual disability maintain skills and functions. The question is who defines the pleasant environment: the home owner or operator, the designer of the home, the family, or the person with an intellectual disability? Understanding and reflecting what is or has been valued by the person with an intellectual disability is critical to this definition. It "anchors" the person in his or her environment and often has a calming effect.

Sensory Stimulation.   Throughout our lives, some of us have been sensation seekers. Others have always preferred more subdued environments. The same is true for persons with intellectual disabilities. Regardless, both age-related changes and the progression of Alzheimer's dementia reduce the efficiency, intensity, and range of our senses. Environmental changes that create positive stimulation that compensates for recent deterioration are recommended.

A variety of materials are now widely available on how to make specific modifications that address these 10 areas (see, for example, Calkins, 1988; Christenson, 1990; and Cohen & Weisman, 1991).

☐ Good Communication

With the progression of the effects of Alzheimer's dementia there is a steady deterioration in memory and the ability to communicate. As one carer noted,

> A lot of people never found it easy to communicate with Mary. Her words could be hard to understand and she didn't use regular signs for things. I didn't have a problem and neither did my other children. Over the years we built up our own language and ways of making ourselves understood. That has all changed. She forgets what you just said to her and gets frustrated more easily. Lately she just seems more and more withdrawn.

Therapeutic interventions in communication generally involve maintaining an affected adult's communication abilities, as well as providing educational information for carers for more effective communication strategies (Frank, 1994). Changes in communication and memory do occur and create frustration for both the person with an intellectual disability and for family and other carers. Often the person withdraws and the family or other caregiver gives up trying to communicate. Giving up even seems justified, because family members and other carers are concerned with not frustrating the person unnecessarily.

However, although deficits in communication skills and in memory are evident, it is important to recognize that many long-term memories and learned communication behaviors will remain well into the later stages of Alzheimer's dementia. Simplification of conversations and greater use of prompts, cues, and structure will help maintain previous communication abilities and reduce frustrations (Fujiki & Brinton, 1993; Hart & Wells, 1997). It is particularly important to be aware that choice of words or complexity of language can affect agitation among persons in later stages of dementia. The language used by staff or carers should always match the comprehension level of the person affected by dementia, and by judicious use of language, the language should prevent agitation and aggressive behavior (Hart & Wells, 1997). Also, the individual with an intellectual disability understands more than he or she is able to convey and receives and sends nonverbal messages even in the severe stages of Alzheimer's dementia. As shown in Figure 14.1, there are a number of things that family members and other carers can do to maintain communication (McCallion & Toseland, 1996). Above all, families and carers must continue to make the effort to maintain communication and reduce the communication frustration experienced by the person with an intellectual disability. For many individuals with intellectual disabilities and Alzheimer's dementia, memory aids may be important parts of maintaining this effort.

☐ Memory Aids

Memory aids provide visual or auditory prompts that help to maintain communication during the progression of Alzheimer's dementia. There are four main types: strategic labeling, personal memory albums, memory charts, and memory audiotapes.

Strategic labeling is recommended particularly in the early stages of Alzheimer's dementia. Names in bold letters on important objects and places are often key to helping the person experiencing Alzheimer's dementia to maintain her/his orientation to her/his daily life by reinforcing verbal cues. For example, telling someone that she/he should brush her/his teeth requires the completion of a number of steps. She/he needs to go into the bathroom, get her/his toothbrush, and put toothpaste on it before she/he can brush her/his teeth. Each of those steps can be reinforced and previously learned sequences maintained when the steps are repeated, a corresponding written list is clearly visible, and each item needed is

FIGURE 14.1. Suggestions for effective communication.

1. Speak only when you are visible to the person.
2. Use overemphasis, gestures, facial expressions, and pointing to familiar objects to support the message expressed in words.
3. Give the person time to listen, think, and respond. What seems like a long and unproductive silence to you may instead be time needed by the person to concentrate, comprehend, and formulate a response.
4. If the person appears to be having difficulty understanding some particular word or phrase, repeat it only once or twice. Then try a less complex way of saying the same thing.
5. Establish a basic vocabulary of words and phrases and signs that works for the person.
6. Develop a predictable routine to conversations.
7. Talk about subjects, people, and events that the person has liked to talk about in the past and appears to continue to remember and value.
8. Assume greater responsibility for keeping conversations going.
9. Use every available clue, words, gestures, and expressions to understand what the person is saying.
10. Always assume that the person hears what you are saying.
11. Always assume that every attempt by the person to communicate is meaningful and deserves your attention.
12. Always say hello, and always say good-bye, and never talk about the person in her/his presence as if she/he is not there.

individually labeled in the same manner as on the list. For persons with intellectual disabilities, reading skills may not have been well developed. Pictures, signs, and symbols with which they have always been familiar may substitute for words.

Other memory aids are more focused on maintaining communication and socialization. For example, a *personal memory album* is a small photo album, usually a 4×6 index card size. This is large enough that images are clear but small enough to be carried around. Albums with cellophane covers on each page are particularly good. The album should reflect people and events who are important in the person's life, now and in the past, things that the person usually likes to talk about, and some information that the person often forgets that makes communication difficult. For example, one mother talked about how when she visited her son at the group home they never seemed to get past his complaints that he had not eaten lunch. Yet she always visited right after lunch. Indeed, a couple of times she had watched him eat lunch and he still complained of not eating. In his memory album she decided to include a picture of him eating lunch, and when he would begin to complain, she would have him open to this picture and ask him about it. He would explain that it was a picture of him eating lunch, and they would continue with a discussion of his favorite foods. The album contained some pictures of those foods. The mother said that he still began by complaining every time she visited, but now she knew what to do, and it made the visit more pleasant for both of them.

Items to consider including in a personal memory album include photographs of family, friends, and professional carers with whom the person with an intellectual disability has had a close relationship; postcards of favorite places; pictures from magazines; pictures of previous homes, gardens, program sites, cars, and buses that took the person to programs; pictures of favorite famous people; small items such as religious articles; and drawings to which the person has been particularly attached. Tabs can also be added to make it easier to turn the pages. It is important to remember that the picture or other image chosen should be important to and recognized by the person with an intellectual disability. Too often, family members and staff, with the best of intentions, choose what they believe is important, rather than respecting the person's choice, and the album is not effective.

Personal memory albums should support the expression of previously learned information, should be used all the time, not only when communication is frustrated, and should be used by everyone communicating with the person with an intellectual disability. In addition, the person should be encouraged to point to the appropriate page of the memory album when discussing the person, event, or topic to which it relates, even when the family member or professional caregiver understands the person's words. Alzheimer's dementia is progressive; working in the early stages of the dementia to build comfort and familiarity in using the personal memory album is likely to prolong its usefulness in later stages of the disease. Information on the effectiveness of memory aids, including memory albums, can be found in Bourgeois (1994), and specific directions on the development of albums can be found in McCallion and Toseland (1996) and Toseland and McCallion (1998).

Some persons with intellectual disabilities find it difficult to carry and utilize a personal memory album. This is particularly true in the later stages of Alzheimer's dementia. Selected items can instead be displayed on a *memory chart* which can be placed on the person's bedroom wall. The same poster may also be displayed in other rooms. Again, pictures can be used to support communication.

The use of memory charts may pose some concerns for staff who work in congregate settings. The display of personal information about individuals conflicts with rules about confidentiality. Also, the "homelikeness" of posting such charts is often questioned. This is a good example of where programming models and standards developed for other age groups and needs must be reexamined. Important points to consider are that the charts are created for the benefit of the person with an intellectual disability, not for staff convenience, and that they are a tool for maintaining independence and the person's current living situation. Their use should be clearly specified in any written plans for programming for the individual with an intellectual disability. Also information chosen to be displayed on the charts is intended to be read by everyone to encourage all carers and visitors to the home to continue to engage the person in conversation. This is not information that needs to be protected.

Other persons with intellectual disabilities may be visually impaired or may not respond to the prompts and supports offered by pictures. In these situations, a *memory audiotape* can be used. Again the focus is on identifying people, events, and topics likely to represent important memories and to be useful in maintaining conversation and communication. Individuals whose voices the person with an intellectual disability is likely to recognize are asked to tape short segments about the person, event, or topic. The segments may be supplemented with favorite music or sounds the person will recognize. People speaking on the tape should always identify themselves and speak conversationally. Persons playing the tape should then engage the person with an intellectual disability in a conversation about what was on the tape (see Woods & Ashley, 1995; McCallion & Toseland, 1996; and Toseland & McCallion, 1998, for further discussion of these memory aids).

☐   Caring for the Carer

Watching someone with an intellectual disability you care for steadily deteriorate because of progressive Alzheimer's dementia can be emotionally and physically draining. This is particularly true for families and other carers when the adult has an intellectual disability (as presented by Davis, this volume). Families have watched progressive growth and development throughout a lifetime and now with the onset of a devastating disease such as Alzheimer's all of those gains are compromised and eventually lost. Coping with such losses can be very difficult. Yet, even here, the strategies outlined in this chapter have application and have been found to help families and other caregivers cope.

It is helpful for family members and other caregivers to be able to get as much information as possible on Alzheimer's dementia and its progression, be able to obtain supports for themselves, and know when to take a break from caregiving. These three factors can often mean the difference between being able to cope with the changes due to dementia and continuing to provide for a high quality of life at home or becoming overcome by the caring role and the new demands of caring at home at a late age.

Information.   Help in the form of information and supports can usually be obtained from generic sources that aid families in distress because of Alzheimer's disease. Information can always be obtained by contacting a local chapter of the Alzheimer's Association or similar organizations in the United States (see Kendall, Rinck, & Wright, this volume, for addresses and contact numbers). There are similar groups in other countries. Another source of specialized help is the Arc of the United States, an advocacy and service organization for people with intellectual disabilities and their families (there are similar organizations in other countries). These organizations often can provide a variety of booklets, pamphlets, and videos on how to cope with dementia related to Alzheimer's disease or with other dementias.

A visit to the local office of one of these organizations will also provide an opportunity to see or borrow videotapes on the subject or to attend informational sessions. The organizations can also provide information on which physicians and clinics in the area are most knowledgeable and sensitive to the needs of persons with intellectual disabilities and dementia. Organizations such as the Alzheimer's Association work with families and wish to be responsive to their needs. Carers might be advised to join a chapter in their area, and after they become a member ask the chapter to get more information, or to organize a workshop that specifically addresses intellectual disabilities and dementia resulting from Alzheimer's disease.

Information is often also sought on issues that will become significant challenges if not attended to early. Although one such issue, guardianship, affects all families with a member with dementia, it is something that many confront with the increasing age of the person affected (Weiler, Helms, & Buckwalter, 1993). Other concerns that are among information requests include living wills and advance directives, as well as advice on sources of support for in-home care and alternatives in long-term care systems.

For staff in agencies providing residential supports, chapters of the Alzheimer's Association and of the Arc in the United States (and their equivalents in other countries) are also important sources of information. Agencies' staff development departments will also be helpful in getting additional materials and in organizing training workshops.

Support.   One service that many Alzheimer's dementia assistance groups, intellectual disability organizations, and churches provide is individual and group support. Often there is a staff person who families can turn to for information or just someone to listen. Families can be advised to find out who that person is, and get their number and the hours they are available to talk. Sometimes there is a support group that families can join. It is often helpful to be able to sit and hear from other families who are experiencing the same thing as the family (McCallion, Diehl, & Toseland, 1994). Families should ask chapters of the different support organizations or churches in their area to consider setting up such groups if none currently exist. As one mother reported,

> It can be so lonely. Sometimes it feels like you're the only person experiencing all of this. It helps me on the really rough days knowing that on Thursdays for two hours there are six other people who just know that this week all I want is someone to listen, whereas next week, I may need some ideas on how to get though it all.

For staff, it is often very difficult to watch a person with an intellectual disability's skills deteriorate when all their training has been on how to increase skills and independence. They too can benefit from having someone to talk to or from participating in a support group. Often such support groups can help carers sort out questions and other issues that may be of significant concern. For example, advice on technical help with care management, advance directives, and assistance with outside supports are often sought by staff attending such sessions. Such services, available through Alzheimer's dementia assistance groups, intellectual disability organizations, and churches, can be helpful. There have also been instances where agencies or the staff themselves have developed their own support groups (since as Service, Lavoie, & Herlihy, this volume, have noted, members of community support groups are not always receptive to having staff members join them).

Taking a Break.　Caring at home for a family member with an intellectual disability is often a full-time commitment for the person who is the primary carer. As the caregiving needs increase with the deterioration associated with Alzheimer's dementia, caring can become all-consuming, to the detriment of the carer's own health. It is important to suggest that they continue to accept help from other family members, neighbors, and friends and even to consider occasional paid in-home help, so that they get a break. In particular, the carer should ensure that he or she takes time to follow up on his or her own health needs, get adequate sleep and rest, and maintain a proper diet.

Even when assistance from others is limited, the carer should look for opportunities within the home to do things for himself or herself; for example, watch that favorite TV program, occasionally make a favorite meal, or take the opportunity at the end of the day to relax for 10 to 15 minutes. A carer in one of our support groups reported that she contacted her local senior center and they arranged for a volunteer to go to the local library for her each week to pick up favorite novels. She remarked that she was surprised that she could make time, often a half hour or so before she went to sleep, to read and how much she came to enjoy it and to look forward to it each day.

In residential care programs, staff get to go home at the end of their shift, but many report that they often carry home with them the concerns they have for the people with intellectual disabilities they care for who are experiencing Alzheimer's dementia. Sometimes this is coupled with care demands from their own family members who are affected by some condition (or even dementia). It is thus important that staff assigned to residential care homes where the residents have dementia have a chance to "decompress" from the job-related stresses as well as from stresses emanating from their own homes. Overstressed or distressed employees will pose particular problems for care management, as they may be preoccupied, neglectful of certain responsibilities, or even abusive to residents with acting-out or aggressive dementia. Thus, they too should identify activities that they like to do for themselves and make them part of their routine. Agency management must ensure that such considerations are accommodated in training and supervision of staff of homes where dementia may be the focus of care.

☐ Commentary

The goals in programming for persons with intellectual disabilities experiencing Alzheimer's dementia are to maintain independence, maintain living situations, and to prepare for increased deterioration. Independence and living situations can be maintained for a considerable period if steps are taken early in the disease to modify programs and to plan for the progression of the dementia and to ensure the well-being of family and other caregivers. Placing restrictions on the person with an intellectual disability and contemplating the disrupting of long-standing living situations usually indicates that emphasis is being placed on the deficits associated with Alzheimer's dementia. The deficits exist and will progress. However, quality of life for persons with intellectual disabilities experiencing Alzheimer's dementia is more likely to be maintained, even enhanced, when we emphasize the strengths that remain and explore environmental modification, proactive communication, and use of memory aids that capitalize on those remaining strengths and take care of the carer.

Strengths approaches similar to MCI have been shown to be effective for other populations with Alzheimer's dementia (Bourgeois, 1994; McCallion, Toseland, & Freeman, in press; Ripich, 1994). For persons with intellectual disabilities there are likely to be greater difficulties in the execution of communication strategies. There will be different levels of predementia attainment of communication skills, earlier onset of age-related changes, and a greater likelihood that dementia will be well advanced before a diagnosis occurs. However, the strength approach begins with an individual assessment of memory and communication strengths on which intervention may be based. All individuals with Alzheimer's dementia, including persons with intellectual disabilities, have remaining strengths to be built on. The key is the willingness of families and other carers to systematically identify those strengths and then to modify environments and communication practices to maximize them.

☐ References

Antonangeli, J. M. (1995). *Of two minds: A guide to the care of people with the dual diagnosis of Alzheimer's disease and mental retardation.* Malden, MA: Fidelity Press.

Aylward, E. H., Burt, D. B., Thorpe, L. U., Lai, F., & Dalton, A. J. (1997). Diagnosis of dementia in individuals with intellectual disability, *Journal of Intellectual Disability Research, 41,* 152–164.

Bourgeois, M. S. (1991). Communication treatment for adults with dementia. *Journal of Speech and Hearing, 34,* 831–844.

Bourgeois, M. S. (1994). Teaching caregivers to use memory aids with patients with dementia. *Seminars in Speech and Language, 15,* 291–305.

Burt, D., Loveland, K., & Lewis, K. (1992). Depression and the onset of dementia in adults with mental retardation. *American Journal on Mental Retardation, 96,* 502–511.

Calkins, M. P. (1988). *Design for dementia.* Washington, DC: National Health Publishing.

Christenson, M. A. (1990). *Aging in the designed environment.* New York: The Haworth Press.

Cohen, U., & Weisman, G. D. (1991). *Holding on to home.* Baltimore: The John Hopkins University Press.

Dalton, A. J., & Wisniewski, H. M. (1990). Down's syndrome and the dementia of Alzheimer disease. *International Review of Psychiatry, 2,* 43–52.

Frank, E. M. (1994). Effect of Alzheimer's disease on communication function. *Journal of the South Carolina Medical Association, 90,* 417–423.

Fujiki, M., & Brinton, B. (1993). Growing old with retardation: The language of survivors. *Topics in Language Disorders, 13*(3), 77–89.

Hart, B. D., & Wells, D. L. (1997). The effects of language used by caregivers on agitation in residents with dementia. *Clinical Nurse Specialist, 11,* 20–23.

Janicki, M. P., & Dalton, A. J. (1993). Alzheimer disease in a select population of older adults with mental retardation. *The Irish Journal of Psychology, 14,* 38–47.

Janicki, M. P., Heller, T., Seltzer, G., & Hogg, J. (1995). *Practice guidelines for the clinical assessment and care management of Alzheimer and other dementias among adults with mental retardation.* Washington, DC: American Association on Mental Retardation.

McCallion, P., Diehl, M., & Toseland, R. W. (1994). Support group interventions for family caregivers of Alzheimer's disease patients. *Seminars in Speech and Language, 15,* 657–670.

McCallion, P., & Toseland, R. W. (1996). The Family Visit Education Program. Albany, NY: School of Social Welfare, University at Albany.

McCallion, P., Toseland, R. W., and Freeman, K. (in press). Evaluation of a Family Visit Education Program. *Journal of the American Geriatrics Society.*

Ripich, D. N. (1994). *Functional communication with AD patients: A caregiver training program. Alzheimer Disease and Associated Disorders, 8,* 95–109.

Santo Pietro, M. J. (1994). Assessing the communicative styles of caregivers of patients with Alzheimer's disease. *Seminars in Speech and Language, 15,* 236–254.

Seltzer, M. M., & Krauss, M. W. (1987). *Aging and mental retardation: Extending the continuum.* Washington, DC: American Association on Mental Retardation.

Tomoeda, C., & Bayles, K. (1990). The efficacy of speech-language intervention: Dementia. *Seminars in Speech and Language, 11,* 311–320.

Toseland, R. W., & McCallion, P. (1998). *Maintaining communication with persons with dementia.* New York: Springer.

Weiler, K., Helms, L. B., & Buckwalter, K. C. (1993). A comparative study: Guardianship petitions for adults and elder adults. *Journal of Gerontological Nursing, 19,* 15–25.

Woods, P., & Ashley, J. (1995). Simulated presence therapy: Using selected memories to manage problem behaviors in Alzheimer's disease patients. *Geriatric Nursing, 16,* 9–14.

Brian Chicoine
Dennis McGuire
Stephen S. Rubin

Specialty Clinic Perspectives

In response to a request by the local parent group, a clinic was developed to provide for the medical and psychosocial needs of adults with Down syndrome. One of the concerns of the parents was that their sons and daughters were not receiving an adequate evaluation when they had a decline in function and were being given a diagnosis of Alzheimer's disease based on a presumption that all persons with Down syndrome develop Alzheimer's disease. The thorough evaluation that each patient receives at the clinic is described. The majority of the adults seen showed no decline in function. Of those that showed a decline in function, a small percentage were diagnosed with Alzheimer's disease, but most of those with a decline had a potentially reversible problem and, with treatment, most returned to their premorbid level of function.

The occurrence of Alzheimer's disease among persons with Down syndrome has caused a great deal of concern for families and care providers of adults with Down syndrome. As discussed by Holland (this volume), Dalton and Janicki (this volume), and others, research has found that all adults with Down's syndrome over the age of 40 develop plaques and tangles in their brains similar to those seen in persons with Alzheimer's disease. Based on this information, many parents and professionals often

Address correspondence to: Brian Chicoine, M.D., Adult Down Syndrome Center of Lutheran General Hospital, 1255 Milwaukee Ave., Glenview, IL 60025.

conclude that all persons with Down syndrome will eventually develop Alzheimer's disease. However, this conclusion is primarily based on autopsy data without a similar evaluation of premorbid clinical information. Many parent organizations are concerned that such conclusions may have deleterious effects if it is believed that all adults with Down syndrome eventually will be affected by Alzheimer's disease.

This was the case in the metropolitan Chicago, Illinois, area. Parents were concerned that, based on such conclusions, adults with Down syndrome were being given the clinical diagnosis of Alzheimer's disease whenever they had a decline in function and that these diagnoses were being made often without any substantive clinical evaluation. Their concern was strong enough to seek assistance in developing a center with sufficient expertise to offer periodic health and neurological reviews and to be able to conduct differential diagnoses when presented with the symptoms of dementia. Thus, at the request of the National Association for Down Syndrome (NADS, a parent group serving the Chicago metropolitan area), the Adult Down Syndrome Center of Lutheran General Hospital was developed.

This chapter discusses the concerns of the parents, describes the development of a multidisciplinary clinic to address their concerns, and offers information on how clinic staff evaluates persons with Down's syndrome who are declining in function and potentially developing Alzheimer's disease. Recommendations for the prescriptive care of persons who have been diagnosed with Alzheimer's disease are also discussed.

☐ The Down Syndrome Clinic Model

In the metropolitan Chicago area, the NADS has been providing advocacy services for persons with Down syndrome since 1961. This voluntary association was started by parents of young children and, therefore, for a number of years their focus was on children and adolescents with Down syndrome. However, as their sons and daughters grew beyond childhood, new concerns became evident. Parents felt that their children had received good care from their pediatricians and family physicians, but that as their children reached adulthood, they recognized that the dearth of practitioners experienced with adult development and intellectual disabilities could impede good health care. To address these concerns, NADS initially provided funds to help pay a social worker to meet with persons with Down syndrome, their families, and carers and provide counseling services, advocate for services, and support the parents when their sons or daughters were having problems.

During the early 1990s, NADS also surveyed its members regarding the psychosocial and medical concerns they had and confirmed the need to address the medical and psychosocial issues associated with aging of their sons and daughters with Down syndrome (Chicoine, McGuire, Hebein, & Gilly, 1994). A major concern expressed was a decline in function experienced by some persons with Down syndrome and whether the decline could be secondary to Alzheimer's disease. Parents expressed particular concern for how their sons and daughters were being evaluated when they presented with a decline in function. Numerous stories were shared of persons with Down syndrome presenting with a decline in function and being given a diagnosis of Alzheimer's disease after a brief history and physical exam, little or no diagnostic studies, and no discussion as to the differential diagnosis of Alzheimer's disease and the need to exclude other diseases that present similarly but are reversible. The parents sensed that many physicians had little training with regard to adults with an intellectual disability and were making a diagnosis without an adequate evaluation. They expressed interest in the development of a clinic that would specifically address the needs of adults with Down syndrome and their families and care providers.

These concerns led to a collaborative effort being undertaken by the NADS, the Lutheran General Hospital, and the University of Illinois at Chicago to develop a multidisciplinary clinic to serve the needs and concerns of persons with Down syndrome and their families and care providers. Using a community-oriented primary care model as a foundation, a new clinic was designed based on discussions with the NADS staff and other parents (Chicoine, McGuire, Hebein, & Gilly, 1995). Since so many of the concerns involved both medical and psychosocial issues, it was felt that a team approach would be the best strategy. Thus, the initial staff included a physician and a social worker working in a tandem. As the clinic began seeing adults, several other team members were added. One, a specialist on hearing assessment, was added because it was felt that hearing impairment was a common problem in persons with Down syndrome (Evenhuis, van Zanten, Brocaar, & Roerdinkholder, 1992). Audiology screening services were now included to help determine whether hearing was a cause in notable behavioral decline. In addition, a nutritionist was added because obesity was also common in persons with Down syndrome (Cronk, Chumlea, & Roche, 1985). Parents expressed significant concern about obesity and a need for sound nutrition.

As part of the development process, core staff also visited other local clinics and reviewed what services were being offered. Soon additional disciplines and services, such as medical consultants, physical therapists, and occupational therapists, as well as vision screening were included as part of the clinic's offerings. However, due to cost and inconsistent need, these were provided as referral services and not provided on-site. For example, it was observed that most adults had their own optometrist or ophthalmologist and, thus, providing these services would duplicate what the family was already accessing.

As now constructed, the Down syndrome clinic model used at the Adult Down Syndrome Center calls for each adult to be seen by a family practice physician, a social worker, an audiologist, and a nutritionist. Several assessments are carried out as part of normal data gathering. For example, a health maintenance checklist (based on the Down Syndrome Medical Checklist, Ohio/Western PA Down Syndrome Network, 1992) is completed. This checklist outlines appropriate health screening guidelines and is used to guide the health care provided. Questionnaires are used that focus on health problems that are seen more commonly in persons with Down syndrome. A social services review is carried out using the Checklist for Psycho-Social Concerns, which is administered in a structured interview with a family member or care provider or both and the adult. This interview screen is an adaptation of the diagnostic criteria for depression and other potential problem areas taken from the Diagnostic and Statistical Manual of Mental Disorders (DSM-IV; American Psychiatric Association [APA], 1994). An adaption of a standardized behavioral assessment instrument, the Developmental Disabilities Profile (Brown, Hanley, Nemeth, Epple, Bird, & Bontempo, 1986), is also used to assess adaptive and living skills. In addition to the annual evaluation by the physician, social worker, nutritionist, and audiologist, thyroid blood tests are ordered annually. Neck X rays are used to evaluate atlanto-axial instability and are administered on all new patients seen as needed. Hepatitis B screening and hepatitis immunizations are performed if indicated, and eye exams are carried out once every one to two years. Other routine preventive medical services are performed on a schedule indicated for the general population.

Personal well-being and an emphasis on health and wellness are foundations of the clinic's activities. Since hypothyroidism, atlanto-axial instability, chronic hepatitis, and other health problems are common in people with Down syndrome and can lead to physical or mental deterioration or both if left untreated, reviews for these conditions are included as part of the health status reviews. We have observed that the majority of the adults seen at the clinic are living healthy lives. In addition to benefiting from the availability of medical and psychosocial services, we have found that social opportunities afforded adults with Down's syndrome are correlated with being healthy (Fujiura, Fitzsimons, Marks, & Chicoine, 1997).

The clinic opened in 1992 with at least two adults being seen each of two mornings a month. The demand for the services has grown steadily,

and the clinic staff now sees referees five days a week. The clinic is operated by Advocate Health Care, a not-for-profit health system, with additional funding from Advocate Medical Group, a large multispecialty
medical group, and the Advocate Foundation. In addition to providing
the services of the physicians, the office staff, the audiologist, and the
nutritionist, Advocate Health Care provides for the office space and other
office expenses. NADS provides funding for a parent who serves as an
advocate who advises the adults, families, and care providers and helps
them obtain services. NADS also provides partial funding for the services
of the social worker. The University of Illinois at Chicago, another partner
in the clinic, provides additional funds for the services of the social
worker, a consulting psychiatrist, and a postdoctoral research fellow.

All of the collaborating organizations work together to provide several
other services, including an exercise program, patient and family group
sessions, a resource center, and educational programs for parents, care
providers and professionals. The exercise programs have been beneficial
in helping adults lose weight and improve cardiopulmonary fitness and
providing an opportunity to socialize. The group sessions, during which
the families meet in one room and the adults with Down syndrome meet
in another, each led by a social work student, have been very helpful for
both groups to discuss common concerns, support each other, and learn
more about solving problems that they have encountered. The staff of
the clinic has seen more than 400 adults with Down syndrome and have
become familiar with the similarities and differences of persons with
Down's syndrome to persons in the general population with regard to
general health care and, specifically, decline in function and Alzheimer's disease.

The clinic was developed and continues to function through a cooperative effort of a variety of organizations. The input of the parents is extremely important to the approach used to provide care as well as to the
success of the clinic. The majority of the referrals have come through
NADS. The staff and parents of NADS continue to advise on the functioning of the clinic and in developing additional programs to meet the needs
expressed by adults, families, and carers, and clinic personnel.

☐ Rationale for Thorough Screening and Evaluation

When a patient declines in function, a thorough evaluation is necessary
to look for reversible causes or, if no reversible cause is found, to confirm
that the decline is consistent with Alzheimer's disease. Alzheimer's disease is a diagnosis of exclusion in persons with Down syndrome, just as

it is in the general population. Traditional neuropsychological testing, used for persons in the general population who are suspected of having Alzheimer's disease, is less helpful for assessing persons with an intellectual disability (Janicki, 1994) and, therefore, often is not helpful in making the diagnosis. Therefore, careful clinical evaluation is necessary to avoid missing potentially reversible causes of the decline. The medical history and physical exam provide insight into the decline, evaluate for associated symptoms, and initiate the evaluation for etiology. Vision and hearing evaluations are important because loss of a sense can be very problematic for a person with an intellectual disability who has limited reserve (i.e., limited cognitive function) with which to compensate. Blood work should include thyroid function, vitamin B12, folic acid, CBC, and chemistry profile. A computerized tomography scan or magnetic resonance image scan can evaluate for intracranial lesions or atrophy. A lateral neck X ray in neutral, flexion, and extension is indicated to evaluate for atlanto-axial instability.

In addition, careful screening for psychological or social problems is a critical part of the evaluation. Mental health disorders often present differently in persons with Down syndrome and other disabilities because of cognitive and expressive language limitations in this population (McGuire & Chicoine, 1996; Sovner, 1986; Vitello, Spreat, & Behar, 1989; Wetzler & Katz, 1989; Zajecka & Ross, 1995). As a result, mental health disorders may be difficult to distinguish clinically from Alzheimer's dementia. For example, the following symptoms are common to both depression and Alzheimer's dementia in this population: loss of adaptive skills, disruption of sleep cycle and appetite changes, apathy, moodiness, irritation, aggressiveness, psychomotor agitation or retardation, memory loss, and the presence of psychotic features (such as extreme withdrawal, delusions, and an increase in hallucinatorylike self-talk) (McGuire & Chicoine, 1996; Pary, 1992). Alzheimer's dementia is particularly difficult to rule out because there is no definitive test for this disorder (Burt & Aylward, this volume; Dalton, Seltzer, Adlin, & Wisniewski, 1994). To further complicate matters, depression may coexist with Alzheimer's dementia (Burt, Loveland, & Lewis, 1992; also see Burt, this volume). In this case, prompt treatment of depression will preserve functioning for some time, even though a downhill course may be inevitable (Evenhuis, 1990; Storm, 1990; Warren, Holroyd, & Folstein, 1989).

Despite these difficulties, depression and other mental health disorders have been diagnosed in previous case studies (Collacott, Cooper, & McGrother, 1992; Harris, 1988; McGuire & Chicoine, 1996; Myers & Pueschel, 1991; Szymanski & Biederman, 1984; Warren et al., 1989). These reports demonstrate that diagnosis of mental health disorders is enhanced when behaviors, rather than subjective feelings, are emphasized as criteria and when care is taken to rule out all other sensory deficits and medical conditions such as Alzheimer's dementia or hypothyroidism. Additionally, results from previous case studies suggest that the differential diagnosis of depression and Alzheimer's dementia is enhanced if close attention is paid to the symptom course. Depression tends to show an up-and-down pattern of decline, which will show improvement and an eventual return to premorbid levels of functioning with time and treatment. Symptoms of Alzheimer's dementia tend to fluctuate up and down in the early stages, but over time will show a progressive and nonreversible pattern of decline (Evenhuis, 1990; Pary, 1992; Warren et al., 1989).

☐   A Review of the Cases Seen at the Clinic

A review of diagnosed disorders from the current clinical sample of the Adult Down Syndrome Center supports previous case reports showing reversible disorders, such as depression, to be a predominant cause of loss of functioning in this population (see McGuire & Chicoine, 1996, for a discussion of this sample). Of the 443 adults with Down's syndrome seen at the Adult Down Syndrome Center, 148 (33%) have presented with a decline in function. Of the 148 with a decline in function, only 11 individuals (2.5% of the 443 seen) have shown a progressive and nonreversible decline and deterioration over time which would merit the diagnosis Alzheimer's dementia. Several of these 11 initially showed a reduction in depressive symptoms in response to treatment, but the decline in function continued and all were later diagnosed with Alzheimer's dementia. For the remaining 137 of the 148 who also presented with a decline in function, all have shown significant improvement, or a return to premorbid state of functioning in response to treatments, which would not suggest Alzheimer's dementia.

Many of the 148 individuals with a decline in function had more than one health problem that caused or contributed or both to the decline. A mood disorder was the most commonly diagnosed problem. Seventy-six individuals, representing 51% of the 148 with a decline in function, were diagnosed with mood disorder alone or mood disorder in combination with a second disorder, which was most often anxiety or obsessive compulsive disorder. Including those with a mood disorder, 82 people (55%) had loss of function from a mental health disorder alone. Of the rest of the 148 who presented with a decline in function, 42 (28.5%) had a

TABLE 15.1.   Diagnosed disorders for 148 adults who presented with a decline in function.

Disorder	Frequency	Percent of Diagnosed Disorders (%)
Mood	76	31
Anxiety	31	13
Obsessive compulsive	29	12
Behavior	23	9
Hypothyroid	22	9
Adjustment	12	5
Alzheimer's	11	4
B12 deficiency	7	3
Menopause	7	3
Attention deficit hyperactive	6	2
Gastrointestinal or urinary	6	2
Sensory impairment	6	2
Psychotic	4	2
Other medical conditions*	4	2
Cardiac conditions	3	1
	247	100

*Includes parkinsonism, hyperthyroidism, and seizure disorder.

mental health disorder and a medical disorder, 13 (9%) had only a medical disorder (other than Alzheimer's disease), and 11 (7.5%) had Alzheimer's disease. The 148 adults received a total of 247 diagnoses (see Table 15.1). Treatment of multiple problems was necessary in some individuals to achieve improvement or a return to their premorbid state.

There are a number of additional findings from the Adult Down Syndrome Center sample that have a bearing on the issue of Alzheimer's dementia in Down syndrome. As shown in Table 15.2, the Adult Down Syndrome Center sample shows a large number of individuals who are

TABLE 15.2.   Age distribution of all adults seen at clinic (N=443).

Age	Total for Age	Percent of N
<20	21	4.8
21 to 30	115	26.5
31 to 40	136	31.4
41 to 50	115	26.5
51 to 60	38	8.8
61 to 70	15	3.5
71+	3	0.7

TABLE 15.3. Etiology of loss of function in all ages and in those over 40.

Etiology	All Ages (N=148)		Age 40+ (N= 53)	
Mental health disorder alone	82	(55%)	24	(45%)
Mental health and medical disorder	42	(28.5%)	13	(25%)
Medical disorder alone	13	(9%)	5	(9%)
Alzheimer's dementia	11	(7.5%)	11	(21%)

TABLE 15.4. Individuals by age: Total, those with loss of function and those with Alzheimer's dementia (AD) (N=443).

Age	Total for Age	Number with Loss of Function	Number with AD	Percent of AD by Age
<31	136	50	0	—
31 to 40	136	35	0	—
41 to 50	115	34	7	6
51 to 60	38	16	2	5
61 to 70	15	3	2	13
≥71	3	0	0	0

over the age of 30, who many professionals and carers believe to be at greater risk for Alzheimer's dementia. Of these, 307 (69%) adults were over the age of 30, while 171 (39%) were over the age of 40. Table 15.3 shows the diagnosis category of all the adults and for those over age 40 who presented with a loss of function. In our sample, the incidence of Alzheimer's dementia ranged from seven (6%) for individuals in their 40s, to two (13%) for individuals over the age of 60 (see Table 15.4). In the general population, the incidence of Alzheimer's disease ranges from 10% for persons in their mid 60s to up to 40% for persons over the age of 80 years (Evans et al., 1990). Our sample may not be representative of all persons with Down syndrome; therefore, we cannot make a broad statement about comparing the prevalence of Alzheimer's dementia in persons with Down syndrome with persons in the general population. However, in comparing our population with the general population, it is interesting to note that our population has a similar rate of Alzheimer's dementia, with an increase with age, except that it seems to occur 20 twenty years earlier. Our observations also suggest that some people with Down syndrome seem to age more rapidly as they reach their middle 30s. In many of our adults who are in their middle 30s, we have observed graying hair, physical slowness, and other changes associated with aging.

In addition, the estimated life expectancy of persons with Down syndrome is approximately 20 years less than the life expectancy for the general population (Baird & Sadovnick, 1988; Chicoine & McGuire, 1997; Janicki, Dalton, Henderson, & Davidson, in press). Therefore, the physical age of individuals with Down syndrome who are 40 or 50 years of age may be equivalent to individuals in the general population who are chronologically 60 to 70 years of age. Comparing the prevalence of Alzheimer's dementia by age of our sample with the prevalence in the general population suggests that the rates may be similar except that the higher rates with age in our sample occur approximately 20 years earlier. If the prevalence of our sample is comparable with the prevalence in all persons with Down syndrome, the higher rates in Down syndrome at any given age may be explainable by accelerated aging with an earlier onset of Alzheimer's disease. Therefore, the rate of Alzheimer's dementia in persons with Down's syndrome should be compared with the rate for the cohort 20 years older in the general population.

What may be a more compelling finding from the Adult Down Syndrome Center sample is the incidence of decline for older adults with Down syndrome that is not attributable to Alzheimer's dementia but to other reversible disorders. For example, for individuals more than 40 years of age in the sample, 53 out of 171 (30.9%) presented with a decline in function (see Table 15.4). Of this group, only 11 individuals out of 53 (21%) showed a pattern of continued decline and deterioration in functioning suggestive of Alzheimer's disease. The remaining 42 individuals (79%) with a decline in function were found to have reversible disorders that were responsive to treatment. In our sample, if the diagnosis of Alzheimer's disease was given based on an assumption that all persons with Down syndrome develop Alzheimer's disease rather than on a thorough evaluation, then more than three-quarters of those that presented with a decline in function would have received an inappropriate diagnosis of Alzheimer's dementia. As Szymanski (1988) warned, the result of this misdiagnosis of an "untreatable disease" may be to offer no treatment at all or to offer ineffective medications (such as an antipsychotic medication). In either case, this strategy could result in an increasing loss of functioning, which is then viewed by the practitioner as further evidence of Alzheimer's disease.

Some case studies are presented to highlight the importance of the complete evaluation. For example, a 35-year-old man was seen at his house because he would not leave his home and rarely left his bed. He would eat only beans and had a dramatic decline in function. His thyroid stimulating hormone (TSH) level was high, and he was diagnosed with hypothyroidism with depression. He was started on levothyroxine, and an occupational therapist was consulted to help him become ambulatory again. Over the next year he responded to the treatment, became ambulatory again, and started going outside.

Another example is a 38-year-old woman who was seen for a decline in function. The history revealed that she was very independent and came home from work each day on public transportation. She admitted (and the staff was able to confirm) that she disembarked from the bus one stop early each day and went into the local pub for multiple alcoholic drinks. She was diagnosed with depression probably secondary to her alcohol consumption. With the consent of her family, the staff was able to change her transportation and she stopped drinking. Interestingly, she later forgot or denied that she had ever drank alcohol, and she is doing well without any evidence of craving alcohol.

In yet another example, we encountered a 43-year-old man who presented with withdrawal, frequent crying, decline in function, and loss of memory. Within two to three months his depressive symptoms responded to antidepressant medications. However, his memory and decline in function continued on a downhill course and he developed seizures, gait apraxia, and incontinence and he was eventually given the diagnosis of probable Alzheimer's disease.

In this last example, a 52-year-old woman was brought by the staff of her residential facility for evaluation of a decline in function and a concern that she had Alzheimer's disease. She was losing money, bills that she previously paid without problem, and other items. The work-up revealed no clear etiology; however, she did not clearly fit the criteria for Alzheimer's disease. No diagnosis was given to her, and over the next 18 months there was no further significant decline. During this time, the carpeting in her room was changed and in the process the furniture was moved. Staff discovered the missing money, bills, and other objects neatly placed in small plastic bags and hidden in many places in her room. She was given the diagnosis of obsessive compulsive disorder and started on fluvoxamine (Luvox). Within a few weeks the staff stated that she was much better at attending to her finances and overall seemed much improved in her daily functions.

The criteria we use to determine a probable diagnosis of Alzheimer's disease include progressive decline in function, progressive memory loss, gait apraxia, incontinence of urine or stool or both, and seizures. While psychological symptoms often accompany Alzheimer's disease, we avoid making the diagnosis on the basis of these alone because of the difficulty differentiating between their etiology and the diagnosis of psychological and behavioral problems.

☐ Care Management

When an adult with Down syndrome is diagnosed with Alzheimer's disease, we focus on "the four S's": safety, stability (of the environment), social (emotional) issues, and symptoms. As the adult with Down syndrome experiences greater decline, family or carers will often have difficulty maintaining a safe environment. Falling because of gait apraxia, wandering from home, and touching or using objects in the home that can be harmful if used inappropriately (e.g., the stove) can all be problems that the family or carer cannot prevent. In addition, when the adults become bed-bound, frequent turning or changing the position to prevent bed sores is necessary and may be more than the family can provide. Safety is frequently the concern that requires a change in living arrangement and, if no specialty care programs are available, may require admission to a nursing facility.

As the person declines, stability of the environment helps reduce confusion. Persons with Down syndrome often have difficulty with change in environment including changes in carer and location. This is no less true for persons with Down syndrome who develop Alzheimer's dementia. Negotiating a new environment is more difficult and increases confusion and limits the remaining skills. This frequently presents a dilemma because the present environment may no longer be safe, but a new environment may increase confusion. We recommend maintaining the individual in the present environment as long as it is safely possible, making only minor changes as necessary and using canes, walkers, handrails, or other devices to prolong the length of time that the adult remains ambulatory and is able to remain in his or her present environment.

Emotional supports are also important. These include supporting the family and carers who are dealing with their own grieving issues of loss of the individual with Down syndrome. The rate of decline for a person with Down syndrome who develops Alzheimer's disease may be more rapid than in the general population, and family or carers may require a great deal of emotional support to deal with the change.

Another important social issue involves keeping the individual with Down syndrome as much involved in activities as possible. Keeping the adult involved in activities reflects the goal of maximizing function by stimulating the person at a level that is challenging but not overwhelming. Regular assessment is needed to determine the level of stimulation of activities to meet the ever-changing level of skill. Regular small changes seem to be beneficial so as not to confuse the patient but at the same time meeting the changing needs.

Incontinence is a problem and is even seen in some adults with Down syndrome who have no other decline in function. Therefore, evaluation for other causes can help reduce or delay this problem. Obstruction from benign prostatic hypertrophy or other causes, detrusor dysfunction, infections, and urinary dysfunction secondary to atlanto-axial subluxation should also be considered. For those whom no reversible cause is found, toileting regimens may be helpful.

Seizures will generally respond to standard medications. Tonic-clonic seizures are frequently seen but adults also may have petit mal seizures as well as less pronounced "jerking" type movements. These abnormal movements have also tended to respond to antiseizure medications. One woman had jerking or twitching movements of her arms and her body that actually caused her to fall or flip out of bed. These momentary abnormal movements responded nicely to phenytoin and helped prevent further injuries.

Many adults will also have psychological symptoms such as depression, psychotic features, and anxiety. Sleep disturbance and changes in eating are common. An evaluation for other causes will sometimes find a problem in addition to the Alzheimer's disease. Medical problems such as hypothyroidism, infections, peptic ulcers, and others may alter sleep, appetite, or behavior. Environmental issues may also contribute to these symptoms. Again, a careful evaluation of the environment is necessary to maximize function without overwhelming the individual's declining abilities. Antidepressants or antipsychotic medications are sometimes necessary to improve the function or reduce the symptoms. Using the adverse-effect profile of each to guide the selection of medication reduces the symptoms while minimizing additional problems. For example, for adults who develop depression and have problems with sleep, use of amitriptyline or other sedating antidepressants at night may benefit the sleep disturbance directly as well as treat the depression. However, another factor in the selection of the drug is that adults with Down syndrome do seem to be particularly sensitive to the anticholinergic side effects of medications, and many of the antidepressants and antipsychotics have adverse effects that could further reduce skills.

☐ Commentary

Careful evaluation of a person with Down syndrome who has a decline in function has broader public health implications. Many of the adults we have seen for a decline in function have either previously been given the diagnosis of Alzheimer's disease or there was a strong suspicion by the family or carers that the person had Alzheimer's disease. In discussing the concern with the family of carer, it is clear that many people believe that all persons with Down syndrome will develop Alzheimer's disease. Our experience and the research of others would suggest that not all persons with Down syndrome will develop clinical dementia stemming from Alzheimer's disease. The exact prevalence of Alzheimer's disease in persons with Down syndrome is still being investigated.

Unfortunately, the belief that all persons with Down syndrome get Alzheimer's disease appears to guide the evaluation of some people with Down syndrome who are declining in function. The misdiagnosis of Alzheimer's disease tends to increase the misperception that all people with Down syndrome will develop Alzheimer's disease. The use of this cyclical logic leads to more diagnoses of Alzheimer's disease. We have heard repeated stories of persons with Down syndrome who were declining in function, were given a brief evaluation, and were then given a diagnosis of Alzheimer's disease. The potentially reversible causes were not ruled out. Much of the decline in function that we have seen experienced by persons with Down syndrome is reversible, and the quality of the person's life can often be improved. Even if some of these people later develop Alzheimer's disease, they often receive benefit in the interim from treatment of reversible disease processes. The diagnosis of Alzheimer's disease is still a diagnosis of exclusion, and a thorough evaluation for potentially reversible causes for a decline in function is indicated.

A close working relationship with the families and carers of the adults with Down syndrome has provided insight into their needs and leads us to argue for a multidisciplinary approach to diagnosis and care management. We have found that such a multidisciplinary approach can be instrumental in providing for the diagnosis of adults with Down syndrome who present with a decline in function. In our sample, there were a variety of medical and psychosocial problems causing the decline, and the team approach helped provide insight into these problems. Both a thorough medical and psychosocial evaluation are important to avoid missing reversible causes and overdiagnosing Alzheimer's dementia. Further evaluation of this and other approaches will aid in developing improved services to adults with Down syndrome.

☐ References

American Psychiatric Association. (1994). *Diagnostic and statistical manual of mental disorders* (4th ed.). Washington, DC: Author.

Baird, P. A., & Sadovnick, A. D. (1988). Life expectancy in Down syndrome adults. *Lancet II*, 1354–1356.

Brown, M. C., Hanley, A. T., Nemeth, C., Epple, W., Bird, W., & Bontempo, A. (1986). *The Developmental Disabilities Profile, final report: The design, development, and testing of the core instrument.* New York: New York State Office of Mental Retardation and Developmental Disabilities.

Burt, D. B., Loveland, K. A., & Lewis, K. R. (1992). Depression and the onset of dementia in adults with mental retardation. *American Journal of Mental Retardation, 96,* 502–511.

Chicoine, B., & McGuire, D. (1997). Longevity of a woman with Down syndrome: A case study. *Mental Retardation, 35,* 477–479.

Chicoine, B., McGuire, D., Hebein, S., & Gilly, D. (1994). Development of a clinic for adults with Down syndrome. *Mental Retardation, 32,* 100–106.

Chicoine, B., McGuire, D., Hebein, S., & Gilly, D. (1995). Use of the community-oriented primary care model for a special-needs population: A clinic for adults with Down syndrome. *American Journal of Public Health, 85,* 869–870.

Collacott, R. A., Cooper, S. A., & McGrother, C. (1992). Differential rates of psychiatric disorders in adults with Down syndrome compared with other mentally handicapped adults. *British Journal of Psychiatry, 61,* 671–674.

Cronk, C. E., Chumlea, W. C., & Roche, A. F. (1985). Assessment of overweight children with trisomy 21. *American Journal of Mental Deficiency, 17,* 117–122.

Dalton, A. J., Seltzer, G. B., Adlin, M. S., & Wisniewski, H. M. (1994). Association between Alzheimer disease and Down syndrome: Clinical observations. In J. M. Berg, A. J. Holland, & J. Karlinsky (Eds.), *Alzheimer disease and Down syndrome* (pp. 1–24). London: Oxford University.

Evans, D. A., Scherr, P. A., Cook, N. R., Albert, M. S., Funkenstein, H. H., Smith, L. A., Hebert, L. E., Wetle, T. T., Branch, L. G., Chown, M., Hennekens, C. H., & Taylor, J. O. (1990). Estimated prevalence of Alzheimer's disease in the United States. *The Milbank Quarterly, 68,* 267–289.

Evenhuis, H. M. (1990). The natural history of dementia in Down's syndrome. *Archives of Neurology, 47,* 263–267.

Evenhuis, H. M., van Zanten, G. A., Brocaar, M. P., & Roerdinkholder, W. H. M. (1992). Hearing loss in middle-age persons with Down syndrome. *American Journal on Mental Retardation, 97,* 47–56.

Fujiura, G. T., Fitzsimons, N., Marks, B., & Chicoine, B. (1997). Predictors of BMI among adults with Down syndrome: The social context of health promotion. *Research in Developmental Disabilities, 18,* 261–274.

Harris, J. C. (1988). Psychological adaptation and psychiatric disorders in adolescence and adults with Down syndrome. In S. M. Pueschel (Ed.), *The young person with Down syndrome: Transition from adolescence to adulthood.* (pp. 35–52) Baltimore: Brookes Publishing.

Janicki, M. P. (1994). *Alzheimer disease among persons with mental retardation: Report from an international colloquium.* Albany: New York State Office of Mental Retardation and Developmental Disabilities.

McGuire, D., & Chicoine, B. (1996). Depressive disorders in adults with Down syndrome. *Habilitative Mental Healthcare Newsletter, 12,* 26–27.

Myers, B. A., & Pueschel, S. M. (1991). Psychiatric disorder in persons with Down syndrome. *Journal of Nervous and Mental Disorders, 179,* 609–613.

Ohio/Western PA Down Syndrome Network. (1992). Down syndrome preventive medical check list. *Down Syndrome Papers and Abstracts for Professionals, 15*(3), 1–10.

Pary, R. (1992). Differential diagnosis of functional decline in Down's syndrome. *Habilitative Mental Healthcare Newsletter, 11,* 26–27.

Pary, R. (1992). Down syndrome and aging. *Habilitative Mental Healthcare Newsletter, 12,* 26–27.

Sovner, R. S. (1986). Limiting factors in the use of DSM-III criteria with mentally ill/mentally retarded persons. *Psychopharmacological Bulletin, 22,* 1055–1059.

Storm, W. (1990). Differential diagnosis and treatment of depressive features in Down's syndrome. *Research in Developmental Disabilities, 11,* 131–137.

Szymanski, L. S. (1988). Integrative approach to diagnosis of mental disorders in retarded persons. In J. A. Stark, F. J. Menolascino, M. H. Albarelli, V. C. Grey (Eds.), *Mental retardation and mental health: Classification, diagnosis, treatment services* (pp. 124–139). New York: Springer-Verlag.

Szymanski, L. S., & Biederman, J. (1984). Depression and anorexia nervosa of persons with Down syndrome. *American Journal of Mental Deficiency, 89,* 246–251.

Vitello, B., Spreat, S., & Behar, D. (1989). Obsessive-compulsive disorder in mentally retarded adults. *Journal of Nervous and Mental Disorders, 177,* 232–234.

Warren, A. C., Holroyd, S., & Folstein, M. F. (1989). Major depression in Down's syndrome. *British Journal of Psychiatry, 155,* 202–205.

Wetzler, S., & Katz, M. M. (1989). Problems in the differentiation of anxiety and depression. *Journal of Psychiatric Research, 23,* 1–12.

Zajecka, J. M., & Ross, J. S., (1995). Management of comorbid anxiety and depression. *Journal of Clinical Psychiatry, 2* (Suppl.), 1–13.

Lawrence T. Force
Marie O'Malley

Adult Day Services

The number of older individuals in our society with lifelong disabilities is ever expanding. As a result of this increase in lifespan, there will be an accompanying increase in individuals with Alzheimer's disease and the need for community-based programs to address their needs. One such program is adult day services. This chapter argues that existing generic adult day services programs can meet the needs of individuals, with lifelong disabilities or without, who are presenting a diagnosis of Alzheimer's disease. Case studies are provided giving funding options and schedules of programs and activities supporting the integrative function of adult day services.

As people with intellectual disabilities live longer and grow older in greater numbers, programs and supports are needed to address community care issues related to age-associated problems, such as progressive dementia and other impairments. One group of such programs and supports is what is generally known as adult day services (this program was previously referred to by the aging network as "adult day care"). Adult

Address correspondence to: Larry T. Force, Ph.D., 38 Traver Road, Pleasant Valley, NY 12569.

day services programs are one of several community care alternatives to institutionalization (Sanborn, 1988; National Council on the Aging [NCOA], 1990; Tataru, 1997). Today, families and discharge planners view adult day services programs as both a respite option for carers and an alternative to nursing facility admission for elderly persons (Henry & Capitman, 1995; Wimo, Mattsson, Adolfsson, Eriksson, & Nelvig, 1993).

Adult day services, as a program concept, have a variety of specific service designs and provide one of several accommodations to the services often asked for by families and other carers (Adams, 1988; Conrad, Hughes, Hanrahan, & Wang, 1993; Force, 1993; Mace & Rabins, 1984; Montgomery & Kosloski, 1990; Sherman, Newman, & Frenkel, 1980; Tobin, 1975; Weiler & Rathbone-McCuan, 1978; Weissert, 1976; Weissert, Bolda, Zelman, Kalsbeek, & Rice, 1989). Adult day services often provide that last bulwark to institutionalization for an adult with an age-associated impairment. As Frenkel, Sherman, Newman, and Derico (1984) have noted, "no continuum of long-term care services is complete without day care programming." This program model has taken on more import with the steady rise in the incidence of dementia in the general population and among adults with intellectual disabilities.

This chapter examines adult day services models as well as other specialty programs for adults with intellectual disabilities and considers strategies for increasing the use of these programmatic approaches for individuals with intellectual disability who are affected by Alzheimer's disease and related dementias. Part of the chapter will provide an overview of the history of adult day services programs, identify existing models of adult day services programs, and examine the parallels of day programs for adults who are aging and those with lifelong disabilities. Another part will provide suggestions for the applications on starting an integrated program, as well as securing funding and accessing training resources within the aging and developmental disabilities networks. Knowledge of these issues can affect treatment outcomes and, ultimately, the success and quality of service provision during later life. In addition to these applications, some practical approaches are considered for daily schedules of activities and programs that can be incorporated into the adult day services program.

☐ Background

The roots of adult day services can be traced to several starting points. In the United States, adult day services were first provided by the Menniger Clinic in 1947 and the Yale Psychiatric Clinic in 1949 (Gelfand & Olsen,

1980). The original purpose was to serve adults with chronic mental illness who did not need to be placed in a fully controlled environment (Padula, 1985). Another beginning was in the partial hospitalization concept, when someone recovering from illness, surgery, or other medical treatment could attend a day treatment center under a physician's prescription and participate in a range of therapeutic activities designed to provide for aftercare services. This model is still in use within psychiatry as an alternative to full hospitalization of adults who need monitoring and rehabilitative care but not inpatient services. Still other models based on a social interaction therapeutic approach used day service environments for older adults who were in need of supervision, health oversight, and a place for social interaction and activities (Lurie, Kalish, Wexler, & Ansak, 1976). Another version, with application to adults with intellectual disabilities, is the variation of adult activity or habilitation day centers found in most communities. Today, the function of adult day services is broader (it now extends to the care of not only persons with short-term stay needs but also to long-term care groups, such as elderly and chronically impaired populations), and this program model has become a recognized part of the community long-term care continuum (Frenkel et al., 1984; Sanborn, 1988).

The operating styles of adult day services programs are quite varied. Beyond common operational denominators such as per diem cost, staffing, and activities, variability is reflected in the orientation, the setting, and the population being served (i.e., adults with Alzheimer's dementia, individuals with intellectual disabilities, persons with AIDS-related dementia, and impaired elderly persons in need of supervision). As has been noted, adult day services can take many different forms with regard to the persons served and the specific services provided. Yet, even with a lack of clarity surrounding definitional and function issues, there is agreement that this program model serves the primary purpose of providing a diversion to institutional admission (Australian Institute of Health and Welfare, 1995; Long Term Care Policy Coordinating Council, 1987).

☐ Program Classification

A variety of orientations and definitions of adult day services have been noted (Adams, 1988; Conrad et al., 1993; Chappell & Blandford, 1987; Frenkel, Newman, & Sherman, 1983; Frenkel et al., 1984; Gelfand, 1984; Mace & Rabins, 1984; Montgomery & Kosloski, 1990; Rathbone-McCuan, 1990; Sherman, Newman & Frenkel, 1980; Strain, Chappell, & Blandford,

1987; Tobin, 1975; Weiler & Rathbone-McCuan, 1978; Weissert, 1976; Weissert et al., 1989; Zimmerman, 1986). Different models of adult day services exist, often delineated by their structure, process, and client population. Conrad et al. (1993) surveyed approximately 800 such settings in the United States and identified six classes: Alzheimer's family care, rehabilitation, high intensity clinical/social, moderate intensity clinical/social, general purpose, and low scoring. However, most day services settings are classified by functional means. One such classification schema is that of Weissert (1976; Weissert et al., 1989), who classified adult day services programs according to particular orientations using two models of adult day services. Model I corresponds to a health/medical model of adult day services (operated under the auspices of a nursing home or hospital or both). Model II represents a social or nonmedical model of adult day services (this format of care can be free-standing and need not be associated with a medical facility). In 1989, Weissert expanded the parameters of his models to include a third type, special purpose. Weissert noted that special purpose programs serve a single type of clientele.

Thus, in practice, three general applications are found within these models: social model adult day services programs, adult day health services programs, and specialty day services, such as partial hospitalization, day psychiatric or community club programs within the psychiatric or head injury community, or day habilitation, day activities, or day treatment programs within the developmental disabilities community. In fact, national surveys have revealed that among the specialty day programs those serving adults with intellectual disabilities are well represented (Mace & Rabins, 1984; Von Behren, 1989; Weissert et al., 1989; Weissert 1990). This model also has gained prominence in the aging network and is used to complement the social centers, represented by senior centers, autumn clubs, and the like. Thus, in most localities, adult day services may be provided for older people who are frail or fragile, may have a significant impairment or dementia, live at home or by themselves, and who need some assistance in order to remain independent and active in their communities (Abraham, Onega, Chalifoux, & Maes, 1994). Adult day services may be built around the socialization (social model) or medical (adult day health model) needs of older adults. Adult day services offer supportive services in a group setting. Programming and services generally include a hot meal, socialization, recreation, individual and family counseling, and training in skills needed to remain independent despite one or more impairments. Adult day services can be defined as a program that provides services to adults with functional impairments in a structured, supervised setting.

These models are also subject to differing means of financing. For example, social model programs generally are covered by fees, donations, and allocations from local or state government. Health model programs are generally funded by the same funds as are hospitals and other medical facilities (Medicaid, Medicare, third party payments). In specialty adult day services programs, the funding often comes from particular state government agencies, for example, the mental health department for psychiatric day care, the intellectual disability/developmental disabilities' agency for day programs for adults with an intellectual disability, and the Department of Veterans Affairs for older veterans programs. Although specialty models of adult day services have been developed to serve particular populations, any variation of adult day services can be applicable to older adults with an intellectual disability who have been identified as also having dementia.

The emerging use of adult day services programs can in part be explained by the changes in the profile and circumstances of the aging population and their families in this country. Significant changes have occurred in the longevity of the American populace, so that when age-associated problems occur, they may occur in persons with significant years of life still to live. For example, in 1900 the life expectancy was in the mid-40s; currently it is in the late 70s (Schick, 1986). Further, it is estimated that the aging population of the United States will increase by 77% between 1985 and 2025 and expectations are that many persons will live into progressively older "old age" with acute, chronic, and debilitating diseases and conditions (Kosburg, 1992). Thus, the demand for adult day services programs has been generated by both an increased longevity and an increase of survivor mass in the older population. The impact of these longevity and survivor trends is being felt in all the institutions of society, including the service systems serving older and disabled individuals. These increases have also moved the long-term care system to see adult day services programs as a significant alternative care option.

☐ Program Components of the Adult Day Services Model

Adult day services programs are one piece of the patchwork of available programs that will by necessity grow in number and evolve as demands increase. As Von Behren (1989) has noted, adult day services is a community-based group program designed to meet the needs of functionally impaired adults through an individual plan of care, at a central location and through the provision of a set of core services, including nutrition, socialization, and some form of supervision and monitoring. Such services often serve two masters. The first are families, as these programs provide respite to families who are carrying the burden of full-time care for a relative who is impaired (Janicki, Krauss, Cotten, & Seltzer, 1986; Rathbone-McCuan, 1990). The second are older or chronically impaired adults, as these are individuals who need and can benefit from a setting that offers structure, engaging activities, and a place for socialization (NCOA, 1990; Williams & Roberts, 1995; Wimo et al., 1993).

Program Philosophies and Structures.   The individual and specific designs of an adult day services program are variations on a theme. The structure is built on an underlying foundation that includes set guidelines. These include, first, a mission statement or statement of purpose or both that defines the level of service to be provided and the values embodied by the program design. In most cases, these are specific and list individual program components and target population. Second, programs adhere to principles that note that all program participants using the program must be accorded nondiscriminatory equal access, confidentiality, privacy, consideration, and dignity. A formal, written "bill of rights" which provides a guarantee of self-determination and client participation in planning and operation may be appropriate (Bell & Troxel, 1996). Statements of such kind should recognize and communicate an essential approach of compassion and respect and acknowledge that participants of adult day services have the potential of growth, life enhancement, and reaching the highest level of their individual functioning. Last, the program states its obligation for providing activities and methods of operation that support each individual participant's sense of well-being, value, and individuality. Specific codes, standards, and guidelines for adult day services program generally are prescribed by state or other certifying or regulating agencies (NCOA, 1990, 1994).

With an accent on serving individuals with dementia (Cefalu & Heuser, 1993), it has been shown that the foremost guiding principle for all activities is prevention, that is, preventing further decline, providing a "good" day versus a "rough" day (Hasselkus, 1992), and helping participants maintain their sense of autonomy (Tataru, 1997). Thus, in using adult day services programs, participants must be guaranteed an environment that is safe, secure, clean, and visually inviting. To this end, adult day services programs generally use a variety of facilities to house their programs and participants and to provide these basic requirements. Since a building built specifically for the program may not be necessary (or is impractical in most instances), many localities have set up such services within second-use buildings or spaces, such as decommissioned schools, store fronts, church basements or social halls, or other appropriate space. Generally, within certifying agency guidelines, any variety of freestanding or attached structures can be used. What generally governs the nature of the space is cost, availability, local fire codes or operational regulations, and the nature of the population to be served.

Most programs are run in a flexible manner, so that as the participant's needs change, so must the activities and services. Thus, adult day services program facilities and program designs should be flexible and adaptable to those changes and must acknowledge that they will serve a spectrum of functional needs and levels. Most programs should be sited in buildings that can be modified. A safe, protective, and appealing environment with adequate space and well-maintained recreation, eating, and administration areas are required, as is a sufficient budget (or contract/lease agreement) to replace, repair, and maintain the physical plant, supplies, and equipment.

Entry into Adult Day Services.
Irrespective of the population served or the nature of the primary services offered, most adult day services programs follow a similar course for admission and assessment of new participants. A comprehensive evaluation serves as a starting point before a potential participant can be deemed to have the characteristic of a program's target population and condition of preparedness. Evaluations, consistent with an established written policy defining enrollment criteria, are performed prior to entry and reflect the broadest spectrum of guidelines allowed for participation. An adult day services agency that incorporates complete medical, psychosocial, and family histories into the assessment instrument may better serve participants and program goals. During interviews with carers and the potential participant for possible inclusion in adult day services, information is gathered on work life, leisure activities, personality, and particular likes and dislikes. Current diagnosis and treatment, mental and cognitive status, and conditions of financial and support resources of clients are integral ingredients and determinants of successful involvement. Full disclosure by carers and conscientious professional appraisal ensure that an adult day services model can integrate and benefit a participant.

Building and Spaces.
Local building codes and program regulations generally require that toileting areas are well ventilated and of sufficient size to permit a participant and aide(s) to move freely within the space. They require that they be positioned to guarantee privacy. Bathroom number, size, and plumbing appointments must meet the demands of the participants and health codes. Many programs have shower or bathing facilities to accommodate those participants who are incontinent or who may have an occasional accident. Many have on hand an extra supply of clothes when such accidents do occur. Targeting a population without any history of incontinence is not a guarantee that the circumstance will not occur.

Program standards for adult day services generally ask that sites be well-lit and safe and provide accessibility to wheelchairs, foot traffic, and vehicles (NCOA, 1990). The entrance is the program's invitation to the community, participants, and family. The adult day services is a part of the community and should be recognized as such by visibility and labeling. Community support is an important ingredient to the successful outcomes of an adult day services program.

Lighting within a structure (both natural and artificial), interior layout, furnishings, and flooring facilitate any activity and should provide ease of mobility. Overbright and glaring light is inappropriate and considered nontherapeutic. As some participants may be sensitive to loud, unexpected noise, programs should avoid overhead speakers and other sources of extraneous noise. Adult day services programs are usually required to provide training to staff so that all staff (including clerical, maintenance, drivers, etc.) can recognize and accommodate physical limitations and sensitivities.

Adult day services programs are generally required, under advisement of regulatory agencies, to secure storage and preparation of toxic substances, foodstuffs, medicines, and equipment. A requisite for medication dispensed during adult day services attendance is that it be in its original, labeled, prescription containers. Fire safety, universal precautions, infection control, and first aid need to be built into the daily adult day services operation and designed and monitored with regulatory agency supervision. A written, formal, and tested emergency plan should be posted in all areas of the program and agency-sponsored transportation vehicles; this posting should be used to notify staff, visitors, and participants of appropriate procedures and exit plans. In-service training and drills should be incorporated into emergency policies. All necessary emergency equipment (such as first aid kits and fire extinguishers) should be in working order and readily accessible.

Records.   Documentation and record keeping are necessary for adult day services management. Thus, programs should have formal procedural policies governing records and their use, storage, access, and contents. Regularly scheduled audits by regulatory agencies serve to ensure that participant and agency records are valid and comprehensive. Participants and personnel have a legal right to privacy and confidentiality; therefore, such programs should exercise discretion and caution in the storage and handling of records and the information contained in the records. Usually, by practice, such programs store records for a minimum of five years after a participant is discharged or the program is closed.

Specific participant problems (such as behavior or health issues) should be noted, monitored, and documented regularly and made part of a recommended daily log of participation, treatments, and therapies. A participant record or chart containing medical, psychosocial, and family histories should be maintained and updated as needed. A detailed physical description and current photograph of the participant can be kept in the record. These may be important, specifically within programs that have participants who may unexpectedly wander off-site. Many adult day services programs in operation today file standard release forms for participant photographs, off-site trips, and special or unusual activities (such as companion pet therapy). The participant's initial and ongoing assessments, progress notes, and care plans and reviews should be included in his or her permanent file. Usual requirements are that all notes be signed and complete with the writer's name and title.

If a participant is medically limited in activity participation or diet, program administrators should request a physician's written order to cover such limitation, otherwise modifications are made in the duration and nature of activities. Advance directives such as living wills, do not resuscitate orders, organ donorship, and health care proxies should follow the proper format for the jurisdiction and be kept in the participant's main record. A written, participant/carer signed notification should be kept on file in the event that an agency cannot honor an advance directive. Programs should also have on file information emergency contact, physicians to contact, power of attorney's, and next-of-kin telephone numbers.

The following should be considered essential documents for inclusion in a participant file: fee determination schedules, service contracts, correspondence, transportation plans, attendance logs, and consent for release of information forms. Which specific ones are often prescribed by regulatory and control or funding agency guidelines. It is the obligation of adult day services to provide knowledgeable assistance and referral to carers or participants or both in completing the documents held on file. This function may fall into the realm of either the social services unit or the program administrator. During its daily operation, but particularly in the event of an emergency or crisis (be it health, behavioral, injury, or family), an adult day services program should assume the role of temporary guardianship. Thus, there are often requirements for properly documenting and securing information that lends assurance that the adult day services program has fulfilled its responsibility in the role of participant stewardship.

Program Activities and Services. Adult day services programs generally operate within flexible hours. Service time may run from half-time days, Monday through Friday only, up to a comprehensive full-time seven-days-a-week schedule. Some programs provide coverage for additional early morning or post dinner hours for working carers. The individual participant's needs, wants, physical and emotional capabilities, and financial circumstances, are the factors that determine his or her length and frequency of participation.

Regardless of the length of day, all adult day services programs should have meals and snacks based on nutrition plans considering dietary restrictions, modifications, and state and federal guidelines for adult minimal daily nutritional requirements. Usually there are several options for sound nutrition. If a program does not have the approval or facility to cook meals on site, it can resort to commercial food preparation and delivery. If the program is attached to a senior center, nursing home, or hospital, food is often prepared and served from the kitchen facilities of the host program. Free-standing programs can have a congregate meal program on site or access one in an adjacent senior center. Other sources of hot or cold meals can include such entities as Meals-On-Wheels, community outreach, Veterans of Foreign Wars (V.F.W.) post, or church service groups. "Brown bag" lunches from the participant's home can also be a source. Although hot, freshly prepared food should be the accepted standard, cold lunches and snacks can be used if they are varied, nutritious, and appetizing. Ethnic tastes and religious mandates should be accommodated.

Large sites can have a formal nutritional program that is implemented by a professional dietitian, nurse, physician, administrator, or program director. The initial assessment care plan for a participant can be developed by a registered dietitian, dietetic technician, or a knowledgeable health care professional. However, a dietary assessment and nutritional plan is not complete without a home visit (to address problems there), a dietary, medical, and drug history, and written instructions to staff and family/carer.

Adult day services programs vary in their offerings, but generally any activities offered should address the participants' dysfunctions and cognitive levels. Often it is the training, creativity, and intuition of the program director that determines how varied and successful these activities are in meeting the needs of the program participants. A limited financial budget, while often restricting available activities, should not prevent enriching experiences and a well-planned and implemented program. Dementia-specific programs have some defining characteristics. As noted by Rosewarne, Bruce, and McKenna (1997) with application to dementia-specific hostel programs, dementia-capable programs were effective in a number of ways. While such programs do not appear to modify the capacities of participants by slowing rates of decline, they do provide specialist (non personal care) staff who focus on the individual participant's social and emotional needs. Such staff provide appropriate, targeted activities for participants with dementia, have a clearly defined role directed exclusively to these participants, and assume direct responsibility for them. Rosewarne, Bruce, and McKenna (1997) felt that dementia programs produced a system effect in that they increased the capacity of the programs to care for participants with dementia for longer periods and provided a longer period of community stay prior to admission to a nursing facility. Generally the principal reasons necessitating admission to a nursing facility are advancing dementia and the addition of a physical impairment (Lefroy, Hobbs, & Hyndman, 1992).

Transportation. Adult day service programs are usually responsible to arrange or provide for all transportation to and from the center and all off-site activities, and the success or failure of an adult day services program can hinge on its transportation arrangements. However, participant transportation is expensive, can become a drain on program resources, and is difficult to accommodate. Thus some programs encourage private transportation or, for fairly independent and capable participants, the use of a community transit system. Private carriers that specialize in transporting medically compromised passengers have vans equipped with wheelchair lifts. Agencies should consider providing transportation through (a) a contractual agreement with a private, commercial provider; (b) the use of a volunteer service conveyance; or (c) its own vehicles and drivers. However, whichever method is used, it must conform to regulatory standards (NCOA, 1990). For example, all drivers are required to be licensed and the licenses should be valid and free of restrictions. Drivers and aides should be trained in client assistance, transfer, and emergency response and must be familiar with and trained to respond appropriately to their passenger's limitations and disabilities.

Community Use. Adult day service programs are part of the community and thus should incorporate the amenities available in their proximity. Effective program managers can make use of the greater community as part of the participants' experiences. Participants can visit the community, and the general population can be welcomed to the center. When a participant may exhibit troublesome behavior (particular with loss of self-control or when the behavior may be seriously inappropriate or dangerous), then special considerations can be taken to manage and anticipate the behavior. Community use can be effective when done one-on-one or in small, select groups. Community activities can include outings to such places as zoos, museums, restaurants, schools, and libraries. Often for on-site entertainment, a speaker's bureau, travel or handiwork club, 4-H, or amateur choral group can be tapped. Crafts and "cooking class," a foster grandparent or senior companion participant, use of pets, modified dancing and aerobics, reminiscence hour, current events, an afternoon at the movies, music therapy, and the Internet are all entities or activities that can be integrated in the program day. Who and when are often choices that can be left to the individual or determined by the individual's level of functioning. Activities that stimulate the mind, provide enjoyment, and reaffirm individuality and competence can be used to retard deterioration and promote higher functioning.

☐ Speciality Adult Day Service Programs

As noted by Lepore and Janicki (1997), social model adult day service programs are similar in many respects to the day training or day habilitation programs operated for adults by agencies serving persons with intellectual and other developmental disabilities. These types of programs are prevalent in the United States and generally provide a program site for habilitative or vocational activities. They admit adults with intellectual disabilities of all ages and generally provide a full day of training and other experiences for adults who live at home or in group homes or other community care settings. Depending on the needs and level of cognitive functioning of the participants, such programs provide either a long-term day care setting or a stepping stone to other less supervised and habilitatively oriented programs or services in the community. As adults with intellectual disabilities age, the program focus often moves more toward that of a more traditional adult day services setting, with an increased emphasis on socialization and age-related experiences.

With regard to dementia care, many such programs are beginning to adapt their practices to accommodate aging adults whose behaviors are changing and who will be challenged by a loss of current skills. Whether there will be any large-scale new development or modification of day activity programs operated by intellectual disabilities agencies due to growing numbers of adults in community care with dementia remains to be seen. Experience (as exemplified by the vignettes that follow in this chapter) has shown that alternatively, local program managers are relying more on referral and admission to generic adult day services programs that already have experience with aiding and caring for adults with dementia.

One significant consideration in providing continued care within an existing intellectual disabilities day program is the need to reorient staff to a more focused "dementia capable" approach. By this, staff will have to consider the impact of progressive dementia on the functioning of the participant and how to both restructure activities and the environment as the dementia affects functioning. In most instances, adults affected by dementia will not do well in settings that provide for stimulation and the necessity of make choices. They also show progressive decline that becomes more pervasive with time. In fact, often the type of dementia (multi-infarct versus Alzheimer's type) will determine the rate and nature of that decline (Cohen-Mansfield, Gruber-Baldini, Culpepper, & Werner, 1996; Wells & Jorm, 1987). To compensate, most dementia capable programs adopt a more structured and directive approach to care and activities and limit choices within the program to one or two, so as to not provide for confusion and affect orientation, but yet provide supportive care. Because dementia causes loss of memory and affects perception and judgment, the participant benefits from the comfort provided by a stable and structured setting. This type of approach will generally be at odds with a development orientation that promotes choice and new experiences. Thus, staff will have to be trained in dementia care management and become familiar with activities and routines that offer stability and comfort to someone affected by Alzheimer's disease.

☐ Links to Caring at Home

The links from adult day services settings to families is crucial, since many older adults with intellectual disabilities and dementia are cared for at home by family. However, the effect on carers may be quite hard, as many have accepted the incremental gains made in self-direction and other skills over a lifetime and are now faced with decline that may wipe out all of these gains. At the same time, older carers may be facing their own aging, and the presence of dementia may be posing additional strains on physical, emotional, and financial resources (Graham, 1989). Thus, the goals of care at home are to minimize the burdens on the carer and at the same time maximize the quality of life of the adult with dementia.

Behavioral problems are common with dementia and can lead to significant stress on the family and primary carer. Most prevalent are behaviors related to memory disturbances, restlessness and agitation, catastrophic reactions, day/night disturbances, delusions, wandering, and aggression (Alessi, 1991). Stressors at home or in other environments may cause behavioral problems and may stem from fatigue, a change of routine, excessive demands, overwhelming stimuli, and acute illness or pain (Gallagher-Thompson, Brooks, Bliwise, Leader, & Yesavage, 1992). In addition, care difficulties may be evidenced by one particular effect of Alzheimer's disease—what has become known as "sundowning" or increased restlessness, agitation, and confusion in the late afternoon (Burney-Pucket, 1996; Little, Satlin, Sunderland, & Volicer, 1995). It has been proposed that such "sundowning" may be linked to sleep apnea, deprivation of REM (rapid eye movement) sleep, or other factors linked to fatigue or deterioration of the suprachiasmatic nucleus of the hypothalamus (Vitiello, Bliwise, & Prinz, 1992; Burney-Pucket, 1996).

Adult day services settings need to attend to these effects and help carers identify these stressors in order to prevent or alleviate troublesome behaviors (Flint, 1995; Keyes & Szpak, 1983; Wells & Jorm, 1987). Aiding with management of dementia at home can improve the quality of life for the adult with dementia and their carers. Avenues of approach can include support groups for carers, counseling, education and training classes or programs, or help with information and referral (LaBarge & Trtanj, 1995). For example, one adult day services program offered help to families by providing education, offered help with practical problem solving, and sought to provide a reduction in burden by providing respite via an adult day services program. The burden of care may be reduced by some of these techniques, but studies of interventions with families facing such care burdens show mixed results (Graham, 1989; Flint, 1995; Keyes & Szpak, 1983). It may be that the manner of presentation, the resilience and capabilities for coping of carers, and the nature of the behaviors presented by the adult with intellectual disability and dementia may be key to the success or failure of the applicability of such techniques.

☐ Financing Adult Day Services

While specialty adult day services programs may have dedicated funding, in the United States there is no uniform method used to finance generic adult day services (Cox & Reifler, 1994). Thus, most site funding is contingent on how each state manages or supports this program model. In many instances, funding is cobbled together by the host agency. Agencies use a variety of methods to calculate payment amounts and often create different rates for adult day services. Usually, the type of model dictates the source and amount of the reimbursement process. In some adult day services program, individuals may be eligible for reimbursement through public funds. When entitlement funding is used, a long-term care financing program such as Medicaid can help underwrite the participant's admission and use of medically prescribed adult day services program.

The use of Medicare is not a means for reimbursing most adult day services. Medicare covers only acute or rehabilitative adult day health services when provided by nursing facilities or hospitals, and the services that can be provided are limited to strict Medicare rules for acute care. If a person does not fall into an eligible class and cannot afford the full cost of purchasing adult day services, generally there is no source of public assistance (Long Term Care Policy Coordinating Council, 1987). Thus, most costs of social model adult day services are covered by fees for services, contract or per diem (daily cost) from aging or social services agencies or by speciality funds from intellectual disabilities state agencies.

The combined effort of the public and private sector to meet the cost factors of the ever spiraling health field is on the increase. The current program development climate is to reduce what was once considered to be a territorial issue. The result has evolved into a working partnership. Private sector corporations coupled with public agencies are launching successful campaigns to address the cost factors associated with health care. No place is this strategy more evident than in the adult day services arena (Cox & Reifler, 1994). It is common to find not-for-profit agencies operating adult day services with a combination of fee-for-service, Medicaid reimbursement, and private donations as their funding source (Reifler et al., 1997). When it comes to financing admission and use of adult day services by individuals with an intellectual disability, often agencies may cobble together funding or use dedicated funds available from the state developmental disabilities' agency. The costs for adults with an intellectual disability generally can be covered by the state's intellectual or developmental disabilities agency.

☐ Applications to Adults with Intellectual Disabilities

Increasingly, the adult day services model is being used for adults with dementia as well as for those adults with intellectual disabilities and dementia or other decline features. Given the similarities in functional levels and the need to have an environment that is dementia capable, the use of this program model is well suited for supervised day services provision for adults with both Alzheimer's disease and intellectual disabilities. Since most localities may have adult day services programs, admission to them by adults with intellectual disabilities can be handled the same way as admission is for anyone. The individual's functional needs and capabilities will be assessed, and if participation in daytime activities in a supervised setting is indicated, the individual will be admitted. Generally, such individuals are very compatible with adult day services environments, since the activities and daily routines are geared for individuals with varying capabilities. Thus, referral for admission can follow generally accepted practice in the community. Admission requirements for social adult day services may vary from program to program. Usually a person must be elderly or be "chronically impaired" and have an impairment that requires some assistance or guidance with activities of daily living.

The primary model used, social adult day services, generally is found in programs that provide a structured environment for seniors who are frail or require supervision or both. The programs offer participants socialization and usually have daily programming built around recreation and other structured activities. Assistance with personal care is usually provided, as is transportation. Since most of these programs have a nutrition component, typically a hot lunchtime meal, they can provide for a full daily set of activities. Such social model adult day services programs generally are similar to the day habilitation programs operated for adults by agencies serving persons with intellectual disabilities. Because of these similarities, many older adults with intellectual disabilities can readily adapt to the demands of such settings and their activities.

Lepore and Janicki (1997) have noted the use of such programs by persons with intellectual disabilities may be a two-edged sword. The advantages include the notion that programming is oriented on the basis of individual need, staff generally have experience with persons who have various disabilities and impairments, and other participants share similarities in functional abilities with older persons with an intellectual disability. However, there are also disadvantages, such as the staff ratios at day service sites tend to be lower than those found in the intellectual disabilities network day programs, and in some states, social adult day services programs generally do not operate under a fixed set of standards, so program offerings and quality may vary from site to site.

Where such adult day services resources do not exist, then intellectual disability providers often set up an appropriate day services program for adults with intellectual disabilities and functional decline, including decline associated with dementia. Such endeavors generally prove most useful when the program site is open to other adults with dementia from the community. Having staff specifically trained to work with adults with intellectual disabilities is an asset and the skill can be transferable to other adults with both physical and cognitive disfunctions. Special training in dementia care or having staff cross-trained from both population groups is necessary when serving individuals whose disfunctions are linked to Alzheimer's disease. Information on training information and curricula can be obtained from a number of organizations, including the National Council on Aging, the Alzheimer's Association, and the American Association on Mental Retardation (see also Kendall, Rinck, and Wright, this volume).

Case One—RT

RT is a very friendly 75-year-old woman with mild intellectual disability. She lives in a foster family care home. She has severe hearing loss, congestive heart failure, and is experiencing some losses indicative of early stage Alzheimer's disease. She had been attending an occupational center, but because of her age, concerns regarding her physical health, and the fact that she enjoys socializing so much, it was suggested that she visit a local adult day services program. Her first visit was successful. RT enjoyed the arts and crafts, especially the needlework, but she did not want to give up the paycheck she was receiving from the occupational center. She decided to continue working three days a week and attend the adult day service program for two days a week. In addition, staff put into effect some special changes due to her declining health and functional status.

Case Two—BK

BK is a 77-year-old woman with moderate intellectual disability. She currently lives in small group home. BK has been living in this particular house for six years. Prior to this, she lived in an institution for 56 years. She has worked her entire life; at present she is attending a day program located at an occupational center. She has been employed at this setting for the last 18 years. The residential and day program staff are quite concerned that BK, who had a heart attack eight months ago, has not regained her stamina. There is also evidence of dementia-like behavior. However, although she could use the environment of an adult day service site, none is available in the locality in which she resides.

The above vignettes are representative of the types of situations that are occurring with greater frequency as more individuals with lifelong disabilities and Alzheimer's disease are referred to existing adult day services programs. When faced with dementia, agencies often are presented with difficult choices as to what resources to tap that can help provide for respite or an appropriate day service. In the examples noted above, the individuals demonstrated a need for a day services type program, but its availability was questionable. In situations where such programs may not be available, agencies may opt to develop a specialty day program that has the capability to provide for participants with dementia and related functional decline. To gain support for the development of an adult day services program one can begin by developing a network of connections and resources. This can be done by contacting the local, regional, or state unit on aging, the county, region, or state intellectual agency, or the local Alzheimer's self-help organization. Also, it is helpful to investigate whether there is a local carers group or parents support group for individuals with lifelong disabilities. The use of traditional and nontraditional sources of information (e.g., the local library, United Way, newspapers, or community groups) can be helpful. In addition, linkage with existing sources of referral is vital. Upon review of specific systems and models (e.g., Alzheimer's and aging programs) certain successful strategies can be duplicated. Information can be obtained from the NCOA and in particular the National Adult Day Services Association at NCOA, as well as some of the following national organizations: National Institute on Aging (NIA), national and local alzheimer's associations, the Arc of the United States, and the American Association on Mental Retardation (AAMR)—see Kendall, Rinck, and Wright (this volume) for addresses of these organizations. These organizations should also be considered as resources for information that can be used in providing staff training.

Case Three—MW

MW is an 85-year-old man who is receiving services from a local intellectual disabilities agency. As a teenager, MW was referred by his older sister for admission to a state school because of behavior problems. He remained at the school for the next 38 years. After he was discharged, he lived in supported housing and attended an occupational center. As MW aged and his health declined concomitant with the onset of Alzheimer's disease, he moved to a foster family care home. Once there, he started using a walker and began attending the local adult day services program. MW seems to fit in perfectly and reports that he enjoys the diversity of activities offered (cooking, music, and art activities).

Case Four—DL

DL, a 51-year-old woman with a very friendly disposition, lives with her parents. Prior to returning to her family home, she lived in a developmental center. DL suffers from depression, shows signs of Alzheimer's disease, and takes an antidepression medication. She is independent in her activities of daily living (ADLs), but she does require some supervision in oral hygiene and selecting weather-appropriate clothing. After moving back with her parents, DL began to attend a local adult day services program. Initially, she had difficulty with feeling as part of the group and often felt that she was alone. It was not uncommon to find DL lying on the couch in the staff office, feeling nervous, and reporting that she was upset about her mental condition. However, after about six weeks, she made what seemed to be a successful adjustment to the adult day services program. She is only rarely found in the staff office these days. In fact, she has made friends with several of the other participants and is now joining in with many of the daily activities. She particularly loves playing Bingo and enjoys winning prizes. Staff note that she is quite the "fashion bug," loving jewelry and compliments about her appearance.

At times, staff may be apprehensive of the unknown. In judging the appropriateness of integrating older adults with lifelong disabilities into adult day services, staff training efforts should encourage strategies that minimize the use of stereotypes. Staff should be encouraged to look beyond the diagnosis of the individual and find the real person. A concerted effort should be made to provide program staff cross-training sessions with information targeting intellectual disabilities, aging, and Alzheimer's disease. As training continues and concerns surrounding background, history, and early experiences of the individual become less important, the focus should be on the strengths and interests of the adult. Most adult day services programs provide a programmatic format that includes, but is not limited to, the following activities: music and art activities, cooking, exercise/range of motion activities, outings, board games/table activities, reminiscence groups, and socialization. Indeed, research has shown that socialization and maintaining friendships, to the degree possible, has proven to be highly therapeutic (Williams & Roberts, 1995). Thus, program activities should be developed that exude a sense of purpose and enhance the dignity of the participants. When programs are implemented correctly, one is hard pressed to differentiate individuals with lifelong disabilities who now have Alzheimer's disease from those with Alzheimer's disease but not a lifelong disability. This message should be continually presented and reinforced to staff.

☐ Commentary

The adult day services model is providing a useful place in the community long-term care continuum. Findings from a Robert Wood Johnson Foundation demonstration program indicated that such community-based day centers can effectively care for people with dementia, a demand for these services does exist, and families consider these services of sufficient value that they are willing to pay for them out of pocket (Cox & Reifler, 1994). Further, as individuals with lifelong disabilities continue to enjoy an extended lifespan, community-based programmatic responses will be needed in greater mass to meet their needs. Adults with intellectual disabilities, if viewed by functional ability rather than diagnosis, can participate in the full complement of services offered to their normative age-mates. It is necessary to recognize that the deficits exhibited by an individual with lifelong disabilities experiencing Alzheimer's disease find common ground in the impairments and losses experienced by those in the general populace who are affected by Alzheimer's disease. The recognition, study, and teaching of the parallels in aging, be it with lifelong disabilities or not, can be constructed into "teachable entities." Thus, encouraging cooperation across agency networks and interagency staff cross training (between aging and developmental disabilities systems) will optimize the person's success rate in the new setting and strengthen the worker's knowledge base, therefore minimizing stereotypical assumptions. Concentrating on the universals of the people using the program and not on the differences will lead to the outcome noted by one adult day services manager, "they are really one group of people dealing with aging issues. . . . They are not two separate groups of people" (B. Engwiller, personal communication, June 25, 1996).

☐ References

Abraham, I. L., Onega, L. L., Chalifoux, Z. L., & Maes, M. J. (1994). Care environments for patients with Alzheimer's disease. *Nursing Clinics of North America, 29*(1), 157–172.

Adams, R. (1988). Attitudes of decision makers toward adult day care. *Journal of Applied Gerontology, 7,* 37–48.

Alessi, C. A. (1991). Managing the behavioral problems of dementia in the home. *Clinics in Geriatric Medicine, 7,* 787–801.

Australian Institute of Health and Welfare. (1995). *Aged and respite care in Australia.* Canberra: Author.

Bell, V. M., & Troxel, D. (1996, November). *An Alzheimer's disease bill of rights.* Paper presented at the annual meeting of the Gerontological Society of America, Washington, DC.

Burney-Pucket, M. (1996). Sundown effect: Etiology and management. *Journal of Psychosocial Nursing and Mental Health Services, 34*(5), 40–43.

Cefalu, C.A., & Heuser, M. (1993). Adult day care for the demented elderly. *American Family Physician, 47,* 723–724.

Chappell, N., & Blandford, A. (1987). Adult day care and medical and hospital claims. *The Gerontologist, 27,* 773–779.

Cohen-Mansfield, J., Gruber-Baldini, A. L., Culpepper, W. J., & Werner, P. (1996). Longitudinal changes in cognitive functioning in adult day care participants. *Journal of Geriatric Psychiatry and Neurology, 9*(1), 30–38.

Conrad, K. J., Hughes, S. L., Hanrahan, P., & Wang, S. (1993). Classification of adult day care: A cluster analysis of services and activities. *Journal of Gerontology, 48,* S112–S122.

Cox, N. J., & Reifler, B. V. (1994). Dementia care and respite services program. *Alzheimer Disease and Associated Disorders, 8*(Suppl. 3), 113–121.

Flint, A. J. (1995). Effects of respite care on patients with dementia and their caregivers. *International Psychogeriatrics, 7,* 505–517.

Force, L. T. (1993). *Spouses and children in accessing adult day care: Differences in attitudes and behaviors among daughters, husbands and wives.* Unpublished doctoral dissertation, University at Albany, NY

Frenkel, E., Newman, E., & Sherman, S. (1983). Classification decisions within psychogeriatric day care. *Community Mental Health Journal, 19,* 279–289.

Frenkel, E., Sherman, S., Newman, E., & Derico, A. (1984). The continuum of care within psychogeriatric day programming: A study of program evolution. *Journal of Gerontological Social Work, 7,* 17–27.

Gelfand, D. (1984). *The aging network: Program and services.* New York: Springer Publishing.

Gelfand, D., & Olsen, J. (1980). *Adult day care: The aging network.* New York: Springer Publishing.

Graham, R. W. (1989). Adult day care: How families of the dementia patient respond. *Journal of Gerontological Nursing, 15*(3), 27–31.

Hasselkus, B. R., (1992). The meaning of activity: Day care for persons with Alzheimer disease. *American Journal of Occupational Therapy, 46,* 199–206.

Henry, M. E., & Capitman, J. A. (1995). Finding satisfaction in adult day care: Analysis of a national demonstration model of dementia care and respite services. *Journal of Applied Gerontology, 14,* 302–320.

Janicki, M. P., Krauss, M. W., Cotten, P. C., & Seltzer, M. M. (1986). Respite services and older adults with developmental disabilities. In C. L. Salisbury & J. Intagliata (Eds.), *Respite care: Support for persons with developmental disabilities and their families* (pp. 51–67). Baltimore: Paul Brooke.

Keyes, B., & Szpak, G. (1983). Day care for Alzheimer's disease. Profile of one program. *Postgraduate Medicine, 73,* 245–250.

Kosburg, J . (1992). *Family care of the elderly: Social and cultural changes.* Newbury Park, CA: Sage Publications.

LaBarge, E., & Trtanj, F. (1995). A support group for people in the early stages of dementia of the Alzheimer type. *Journal of Applied Gerontology, 14,* 289–302.

Lefroy, R. B., Hobbs, M. S., & Hyndman, J. (1992). A five-year study of residents of a special hostel for people with dementia. *Australian Journal of Public Health, 15,* 98–102.

Lepore, P., & Janicki, M. P. (1997). *Wit to win—How to integrate older persons with developmental disabilities into community aging programs* (3rd ed.). Albany: New York State Office for the Aging.

Little, J. T., Satlin, A., Sunderland, T., & Volicer, L. (1995). Sundown syndrome in severely demented patients with probable Alzheimer's disease. *Journal of Geriatric Psychiatry and Neurology, 8,* 103–106.

Long Term Care Policy Coordinating Council. (1987). *The role of ADC in New York state's long-term care service continuum.* Albany, NY: Author.

Lurie, E., Kalish, R. A., Wexler, R., & Ansak, M. L. (1976). Symposium—the city: A viable environment for the elderly? Phase III: Planning and delivery of health services. On Lok Day Health Center; a case study. *Gerontologist, 16,* 39–46

Mace, N., & Rabins, P. (1984). *A survey of day care for the demented adult in the U.S.* Washington, DC: National Council on Aging.

Montgomery, R., & Kosloski, K. (1990). Secondary analysis of effects of intervention on family caregivers: Correlates of nursing home placement. *Final Report: Health Care Financing Administration (#HCFA-90-0435).* Washington, DC: Health Care Financing Administration.

National Council on the Aging (NCOA). (1990). *Standards and guidelines for adult day care.* Washington, DC: National Council on the Aging, Inc.

National Council on the Aging (NCOA). (1994). *Summary report—Questionnaire response from state adult day care associations regarding adult day care services in the U.S.* Washington, DC: National Council on the Aging, Inc. (National Institute on Adult Daycare).

Padula, H. (1985). *Developing adult day care—An approach to maintaining independence for unpaired older persons.* Washington, DC: National Council on the Aging, Inc.

Rathbone-McCuan, E. (1990). Respite and adult day care. In A. Monk (Ed.), *Handbook of gerontological services* (pp. 546–567). New York: Columbia University.

Reifler, B. V., Henry, R. S., Rushing, J., Yates, M. K., Cox, N. J., Bradham, D. D., & McFarlane, M. (1997). Financial performance among adult day centers: results of a national demonstration program. *Journal of the American Geriatrics Society, 45,* 146–153.

Rosewarne, R., Bruce, A., & McKenna, M. (1997). Dementia programme effectiveness in long-term care. *International Journal of Geriatric Psychiatry, 12,* 173–182.

Sanborn, B. (1988). Dementia day care: A prototype for autonomy in long term care. *American Journal of Alzheimer's Care and Related Disorders and Research,* July/August, 23–33.

Schick, F. L. (1986). *Statistical handbook on aging Americans.* Phoenix: Oryx Press.

Sherman, S., Newman, E., & Frenkel, E. (1980). Evaluation of continuum of care: Psychogeriatric day care. *AARP Report,* 1–34

Strain, L., Chappell, N., & Blandford, A. (1987). Changes in life satisfaction among participants of adult day care and their informal caregivers. *Journal of Gerontological Social Work, 11,* 115– 129.

Tataru, N. (1997). Project for the development of an ambulatory and semi-ambulatory community center for the third age. *Dementia and Geriatric Cognitive Disorders, 8,* 128–131.

Tobin, S. (1975). Social and health services for the future aged, Part II. *The Gerontologist, 15,* 32–37.

Vitiello, M. V., Bliwise, D. L., & Prinz, P. N. (1992). Sleep in Alzheimer's disease and the sundown syndrome. *Neurology, 42*(Suppl. 6), 83–93.

Von Behren, R. (1989). Adult day care: A decade of growth. *Perspectives on Aging,* July/August, 14–21.

Weiler, P., & Rathbone-McCuan, E. (1978). *Adult day care: Community work with the elderly,* New York: Springer Publishing.

Weissert, W. (1976). Two models of geriatric day care: Findings from a comparative study. *The Gerontologist, 16,* 420–427.

Weissert, W., Bolda, E., Zelman, W., Kalsbeek, W., & Rice, T. (1989). Models of adult day care: Findings from a national survey. *The Gerontologist, 29,* 640–649.

Weissert, W., Elston, J., Bolda, E., Zelman, W., Mutran, E., & Mangum, A. (1990). *Adult day care: Findings from a national survey.* Baltimore: Johns Hopkins University Press.

Wells, Y., & Jorm, A. F. (1987). Evaluation of a special nursing home unit for dementia sufferers: A randomized controlled comparison with community care. *Australian and New Zealand Journal of Psychiatry, 21,* 524–531.

Williams, B., & Roberts, P. (1995). Friends in passing: Social interaction at an adult day care center. *International Journal of Aging and Human Development, 41,* 63–78.

Wimo, A., Mattsson, B., Adolfsson, R., Eriksson, T., & Nelvig, A. (1993). Dementia day care and its effects on symptoms and institutionalization—a controlled Swedish study. *Scandinavian Journal of Primary Health Care, 11,* 117–123.

Zimmerman, S. (1986). Adult day care: Correlates of its coping effects for families of an elderly disabled member. *Family Relations, 35,* 305–311.

17

CHAPTER   *Leslie Udell*

Supports in Small Group Home Settings

This chapter covers what organizations that provide residential supports to adults with an intellectual disability need to consider in terms of planning and implementing program changes. Covered are areas that examine the nature of dementia and its possible impact on service provision. Its particular focus is on how agencies that decide to support people with dementia in small group home settings can accommodate their organizational and operational structure and offers insight on the perspectives and questions that agencies need to consider. Suggestions are offered on how to address some of the difficulties that organizations will encounter.

Supporting people with both an intellectual disability and dementia is a major challenge facing many organizations today. Due to vast improvements in health care provision, people with Down's syndrome are living well beyond earlier expectations. Unfortunately, this increased lifespan, as for those adults in the general population, has brought with it the threat of Alzheimer's disease. Based on the experiences that one agency has faced, this chapter contains information about how an organization can meet such a challenge in a proactive manner.

Organizations across the world provide a variety of supports to a range of persons with intellectual disabilities. Many of these people live in group

Address correspondence to: Leslie Udell, Winnserv, Inc., 101–960 Portage Avenue, Winnipeg, Manitoba R3G 0R4, Canada.

homes or supported apartments. As an example, Winnserv, a residential agency in the Winnipeg, Manitoba, area, supports some 100 adults ranging in age from their 20s to the their 70s. Of these adults, 25 have Down's syndrome and 10 of those 25 adults are older than age 40. In the past four years Winnserv has provided supports to three adults with Alzheimer's disease. To date no adult with Down's syndrome served by our agency has reached his or her 60th birthday without showing signs of dementia.

Agencies facing the challenge of coping with an aging service population often go through several phases before they come to terms with how to provide services. The initial phases include identification of the issue and coming to a consensus on how to approach it, and the latter phases involve trying program alternatives and changing organizational structures to accommodate new program practices. What follows is a description of considerations related to these phases.

☐ Identification Phase

People with Down's syndrome can show the early signs of Alzheimer's disease as young as 30 years old. Functional assessments should begin at this point in their life and should continue annually. This will assist in identifying the first signs of the disease and in monitoring its progression. If an organization is unable to complete the necessary assessments, then planning should be based on statistical information about the number and ages of people with Down's syndrome. For example, at Winnserv we estimate that of the people who are 40 years or older, 40% will show the signs of Alzheimer's disease within the next 10 years. We know that researchers have not accurately determined the percentage of people with Down's syndrome who will show signs of Alzheimer's disease, but estimates indicate that one in five older adults will most likely be affected. This lack of data means that when gathering information it is more useful to overestimate the figures than to underestimate. Consideration must also be given to those adults with a family history of Alzheimer's disease but who do not have Down's syndrome. Our planning takes into account that there is evidence that such a connection can be a risk factor and that Alzheimer's disease may be evident at some point in their lives.

☐ Organizational Commitment Phase

Many organizations are unaware of the impact that dementia will have on their service over time. A total commitment from every level of the organization will be necessary, and that begins with education. The first step in the education process is to provide an agency's board and management with detailed information about Down's syndrome and dementia. Included with this information will be the organization's statistics on how many people have Down's syndrome and their age ranges. The next step is to estimate how many of those people will be affected by dementia and the possible time lines. It is important to emphasize how service provision will need to change in the future. Special attention must be paid to the explanation of the true meaning of palliative care and supporting someone until death. It is a mistake to assume people will intuitively understand these implications.

Once the board of directors has a full understanding of the impact of Alzheimer's disease, the organization's mission statement needs reviewing. Does it lend itself to the changes necessary in supporting people with Alzheimer's disease? If not, the organization must decide whether it will make the adjustment to its mission statement and therefore its service provision. This decision-making process will probably involve philosophical discussions around placing someone in a personal care home versus assisting someone to age in place. Some people feel it is a natural progression of aging to move into a personal care home. However, it can be argued that group homes already accommodate people requiring assistance and that a move from a highly personalized setting to a larger institutional setting would cause rapid deterioration.

In Winnserv's case, a series of board of directors meetings were held to discuss accommodating the needs of people with Alzheimer's disease. Board members held very different perspectives and felt strongly about their positions. Several members were concerned about Winnserv's ability to be all things to all people and the expenses involved in providing such a service. Others took the position that a personal care home was the most appropriate place for residents who had Alzheimer's disease. When the final vote was taken, the motion to make the necessary changes was passed by a close margin.

Education of the board of directors and management does not stop once there is adoption of a suitable mission statement. Current and new members of the board of directors need to clearly understand how the mission statement translates to the day-to-day operation of the organization. A lack of understanding of the organization's philosophical commitment can lead to a questioning of the direction of service provision.

At this point, a program committee composed of board members and management staff needs to be established. This committee should provide direction to board and management through the development of a long-range plan. The program committee must be committed to developing a comprehensive plan and following through on each of the recommended changes. External environmental changes are so rapid that often it is impossible to predict anything beyond five years. Once the plan is in place, it should be reviewed annually and new goals set as appropriate.

A program plan should cover a number of areas, including accessible housing, assistive devices, staffing levels, and funding/financing implications. These are covered in more detail below.

Accessible Housing. Providing care to people with an intellectual disability and Alzheimer's disease will require accessible housing. It is unlikely that an organization will have wheelchair accessible homes unless it currently supports people with physical disabilities. Therefore, it is necessary to make a decision to renovate a current home or to find an alternative home. An evaluation of current homes will establish how easy it will be to meet specifications for wheelchair accessibility. Those specifications can be obtained from the appropriate government agency or an agency that supports people with a physical disability. There are also environmental needs specific to Alzheimer's disease that should be included in any alterations (Olsen, Ehrenkrantz, & Hutchings, 1993). The local Alzheimer's association will have this type of information (see Kendall, Rinck, & Wright, this volume).

An organization may want to investigate other alternatives while current housing is being evaluated. These alternatives include renting, buying, or building a wheelchair accessible home(s). Buying or renting an established home may be difficult, as wheelchair accessible housing is often not readily available. However, renovations can be costly, so this may not always be a viable option. Renovations also disrupt the lives of those people living in the home.

The planning around accessible housing should include factors above and beyond changes to physical structure. What if the home to be renovated is not where the individual with Alzheimer's disease lives? Do you make one person, or the whole group of people, move out of their home to accommodate the needs of other residents? Do you move the person with Alzheimer's disease out of a known environment and away from familiar staff and housemates? Is it better to move someone when they are in the earlier stages or the later stages of dementia? Answers to these questions are difficult. Winnserv has struggled with them and still has no magic answers. Some of the solutions came from the fact that only one of the 12 Winnserv houses could be made easily accessible. The house where people with Alzheimer's disease have been living was made accessible at a high cost to the organization. It became obvious early on that the only option was to set up specialized housing rather than supporting people within their current homes. Winnserv also concluded, after a lengthy review of options, that it was not acceptable to move others to accommodate the person or people with Alzheimer's disease. Such moves would have created much stress for many people including family members. The plan was and continues to be one that causes minimal disturbance.

What of those individuals who live independently and receive support from an organization? A move is disruptive for anyone. People who are living independently can find moving into a group home very traumatic. It may be feasible to provide additional supports for a short time but not once the person becomes a danger to themselves (i.e., when he or she wanders or forgets to turn off the stove after using it). At this point, moving the individual to a group home setting may be necessary. The cost of providing 24-hour supervision on a one-to-one basis is usually too prohibitive.

Assistive Devices. The provision of supports for people with deteriorating physical skills includes assistive devices such as bed rails, grab bars, and Hoyar lifts. Assessments by a physiotherapist and an occupational therapist are invaluable for identifying what equipment will best meet the needs of the individuals. In Canada, a recommendation from a therapist is often required for government funding of the necessary items. However, an organization may consider buying the equipment so that it is available for other individuals in the future.

Whether provided through government funding or bought by the organization, this equipment must be in place before the individual needs it. Obtaining assessments and equipment can take months and it is extremely difficult for staff and residents without the proper equipment to cope with deteriorating physical abilities.

Staffing Levels. The determination of appropriate staffing levels will depend on the number of people with Alzheimer's disease living in one home. Considering the care requirements and the financial constraints under which most organizations work, it is recommended that no more than four persons live in one home. Further, not more than two of those four should be persons who may be affected by the later stages of Alzheimer's disease.

An awake overnight staff position is needed to assist people experiencing night wakefulness. In the later stages of the disease, the job description will grow, by necessity, to include repositioning and toileting (or changing) the person. Sufficient numbers of daytime staff are necessary to allow each individual some one-on-one time each day. In both the evenings and daytime double staffing is required when there are more than two people at home. The staffing ratios may seem high, but it is essential that people living in the home receive quality supports and that staff always has adequate help. Staffing levels can be supplemented whenever possible with volunteers, practicum students, and people on work experience.

Another very important factor for sufficient staffing levels is a pool of trained casual staff who are willing to work with people who have Alzheimer's disease. If sufficient staff is not in place, small crises arise each time a regular staff person is ill or wants to take holidays. These small staffing crises can have a serious impact on the organization's ability to cope.

Funding/Financial Implications.   The funding or financial implications of supporting people with Alzheimer's disease until their death are clear from the information provided in this chapter. An organization's program plan must identify potential funding sources for accessible housing, assistive devices, increased staffing, and additional staff training. Realistic planning and creative problem solving will overcome this seemingly insurmountable obstacle.

Part of the solution is to seek funding from a variety of sources. Are additional resources available from the usual funding sources such as government departments? Once the organization knows what increases it can expect from its current funding base it can move on to identifying additional funding required from other sources. Such other sources may include foundations, grants, and fundraising initiatives. Organizations can also approach government departments that traditionally do not provide funds for people with an intellectual disability, such as the departments of health and housing. Another possibility is to ask the individual and their family to contribute more than is customary.

☐   Program Preparation Phase

Staff Training.   The information and training residential staff need to do their job can be quite different when they move from working with people who only have an intellectual disability to working with people who also have dementia. There will be new areas to be explored such as provision of information on Alzheimer's disease and Down's syndrome, palliative/hospice care, grieving and loss, personal care practices, and body mechanics training.

To be effective and proactive, staff need to know everything about Alzheimer's disease and more specifically how the disease impacts on people who have Down's syndrome. One source of this information is the local Alzheimer's association, which should be able to furnish such information. In addition, information about Down's syndrome and dementia can be found in the various AAMR-IASSID working group publications (Janicki, Heller, Seltzer, & Hogg, 1995, 1996; Aylward, Burt,

Thorpe, Lai, & Dalton, 1995, 1997) and is also often available from national organizations concerned with Down syndrome and intellectual disabilities (Marler & Cunningham, 1994; The Arc, 1995).

With the deterioration of skills associated with Alzheimer's disease, staff will soon recognize that their job will eventually entail care usually provided to those with a severe physical disability. They will need to learn proper body mechanics for lifts and repositioning so they can ensure the safety of themselves and the residents. They will also have to learn how to do range-of-motion exercises with the residents so that some degree of flexibility can be maintained. This type of training can be obtained through local physiotherapists, occupational therapists, nurses, and organizations that support people with a physical disability.

Staff is hired with the knowledge that they will be supporting people until death. However, they will need to further explore the issues around palliative/hospice care and grieving and loss. Many think they have a good grasp of these ideas until they look at them in greater detail. Only then do they realize what a truly difficult task lies ahead of them and what personal preparation they will need to accomplish. This personal preparation can be aided by seminars provided by people currently involved in palliative/hospice care and by people trained in grieving and loss. Staff may find it easier to talk to an outside person who has an objective perspective. The organization may want to consider several options in accomplishing staff training. It may want to hire consultants, contract out to another agency, employ the skills of some current staff, train current staff to provide a portion of the training, or make use of government-funded training sessions that may be offered free of cost.

Another point that does not relate directly to staff training, but does pertain to palliative care and grieving and loss, is the hiring process. The process must include very clear job descriptions and a way of ensuring that staff has a philosophical commitment to the type of support the agency is providing. Staff must know and accept that in all likelihood people will die in the home in which they work, that this death may happen without intrusive medical interventions, and that they will be administering pain control medications. A person should not be hired if he or she is not in agreement with these principles.

Philosophical Considerations. It is very important that all staff have the proper training, philosophy, and values base. The number one concern in the provision of care is what is best for the resident. Another important consideration is what residents would have chosen for themselves if they could still clearly communicate their needs and wishes. Convenience should not be a deciding factor. The focus should always be on respect and dignity for the resident and seeing the person rather than the illness.

Decisions based on what that person would have chosen for himself or herself are made using a thorough personal history of that individual. The history includes the person's habits, values, and interests and details such as which hand the person prefers to use. Obtaining this kind of information will require the involvement of family, significant others, current and past staff, housemates, and coworkers. The use of personal history, team consensus, and compromise will resolve most conflicts about the provision of care. Regular meetings are helpful in addressing issues promptly. Some conflicts around care provision will need to be resolved by involving family and/or significant others.

It is easy to make decisions for people who don't communicate clearly. It is a little more difficult to figure out what someone would choose if he or she still had decision-making skills. The effort to do this, however, gives meaning to the words "dignity" and "respect." People with Alzheimer's disease have a right to maintain their individuality in the face of such a devastating disease.

Physical Deterioration and Health Concerns.   Maintaining skills and health while providing quality care is an ongoing challenge for the staff supporting people with dementia. Each stage brings with it a new set of health concerns, but there are ways to cope with each of them. Risk factors, such as pressure sores, constipation, and dehydration, are preventable through the maintenance of good care practices. Other factors, such as incontinence, stiff joints, and weight loss, are manageable with changes in routine. Seizures, pneumonia, weakening of muscles, and choking are all aspects of the disease that continue to deteriorate with time. Proactive measures can slow down the pace of that deterioration.

Therapists, the medical profession, and books about Alzheimer's disease are all sources of good information about treatments for physical deterioration and health concerns. There are also excellent suggestions contained in the AAMR/IASSID practice guidelines (Janicki et al., 1995, 1996). However, there is one issue that has gone undocumented but is important to managing late onset seizure disorders. Staff at Winnserv have observed that the medication Dilantin has quite debilitating effects on people who have impaired cognitive functioning. It can be particularly harmful to someone who has both Down's syndrome and Alzheimer's disease. This medication can cause rapid and serious deterioration of physical skills, such as mobility and the ability to sit upright, and can lead to extreme agitation. We have observed that individuals return to their original functioning level within 24 hours of being removed from this medication.

Emotional/Behavioral Issues.   The individual with dementia experiences much anger and frustration over their loss of skills and ability to recall information. They also have to deal with the confusion and delusions that are a part of the disease. Much support, patience, and creativity are required when addressing these issues. It is just as frustrating to have something done for you as it is to try a familiar task and to fail. Tasks need to be set up in ways that encourage participation as well as success. Present information clearly, concisely, and step by step. If an activity becomes too confusing, it is time to either move on or begin the process again.

Delusions that are a part of the Alzheimer's disease process can be very difficult for staff to understand and handle. The most successful approach is to accept that person's version of reality and work within that context. Reality orientation at this point will only cause more emotional upheaval. Staff must provide reassurance and help the person move onto another topic or activity.

Day Time Supports and Activities.   The difficulties a person will experience when he or she has dementia are often first identified at the individual's work or day program. The person's ability to do his or her job or function adequately at a day program is seriously impaired by disorientation and confusion. This inevitably leads to the need for that person to retire. It is much easier for that person to adapt to such a change if it can be done gradually, going from full-time to part-time and then eventually to remaining at home every day.

Changes to daytime supports include a plan for how such persons are going to fill their day once they are at home all of the time. Interaction, involvement, and meaningful activities are key to maximizing skills and ensuring quality of life. Meaningful activities must have relevance to the individual, be voluntary, and offer him or her a reasonable chance for success. It must in some way address the person's personal psychosocial needs, and its purpose must be obvious to the him or her (Zgola, 1987). We have found it is useful to encourage contributions from the individual but also at the same time to rely on his or her history of work activities and recreation/leisure likes and dislikes. Always take into consideration the person's skills and abilities and build on these while ensuring that activities are age appropriate. Participation in seniors' programs, adult day programs for people with dementia, and generic community activities are all part of scheduled activities. Time at home can be spent involving the person in areas of personal care, home maintenance routines, and recreation/leisure activities. Ongoing inclusion is extremely important because its absence can quickly lead to more rapid deterioration. Community activities may be restricted to the afternoon at the point where the assistance needed to bathe, dress, and eat takes up all of the morning hours.

Providing Palliative Care. Despite all attempts to provide quality care and the use of preventive techniques, it is inevitable that over time care will move from active to palliative. The disease itself and its debilitating side effects, such as repeated bouts of pneumonia, take its toll and eventually leads to death. Seizures will increase and will require greater dosages of antiseizure medication, which will in turn lead to greater sedation. The person will become increasingly reluctant to eat or will be unable to eat. The person's health reaches the point where he or she is confined to home or bed. The primary responsibility of the program then becomes the alleviation of pain and discomfort and the provision of basic human touch, love, and caring.

Decisions about guardianship, advanced directives, and the provision of palliative care must be in place so that they are not being made in a time of crisis (see King, 1996). If the intention is to provide care at home until death, then repeated hospitalizations can cause untold stress and trauma for the person with Alzheimer's disease as well as staff, family, and significant others. In Winnserv's experience the decision to have the person die at home and to stop all intrusive medical measures is generally made by family, in conjunction with the individual's physician and agency staff. This is illustrated by the situation of one older man, MC, who recently died in our care.

> The decision was made after MC had been hospitalized twice for pneumonia. Everyone involved in MC's life believed that it was not in his best interest to continue to intervene when there was little or no quality left to his life. Once it was agreed that further care would be provided at home, MC's physician prescribed morphine in both oral and rectal forms. The medication was kept in the house and therefore accessible if necessary. In order to protect staff the physician suggested that he be the one to authorize the initiation of morphine. The physician also prescribed Dilantin to be injected if MC's seizure activity increased and he was no longer able to swallow. Oversedation was no longer a concern, so Dilantin became the drug of choice. Arrangements were made for a nurse to be on call to give the injections of Dilantin.
>
> One month after returning home from the final hospitalization for pneumonia, fever and congestion reoccurred. The initial response was to treat the fever with aspirin and cold compresses and alleviate breathing difficulties by raising the bed. Once the aspirin no longer produced any positive results and MC began experiencing a great deal of restlessness, agitation, and labored breathing, the decision was made to begin morphine. The morphine eased his breathing and he experienced a peaceful death.
>
> As soon as staff became aware of the onset of the pneumonia, they knew that death was near. In the final 24 hours everyone was made aware that

MC was dying, and someone was always there to hold and comfort him. Housemates took turns spending time in his room providing whatever support they could. MC was able to die in his own room surrounded and supported by people who cared deeply for him. Following MC's death, staff made the necessary arrangements for family, roommates, and staff to come and say their good-byes.

□ Coping with the Impact

Alzheimer's disease is not only devastating for the person who has it but also for that individual's family/significant others, housemates, and staff. The organization must have a plan in place for helping everyone cope with the stress. On the basis of Winnserv's experience, the following recommendations for staff, housemates, and family/significant others should prove helpful.

Staff. The job emphasis for residential staff is growth, learning, and achieving goals. Dementia is about trying to maintain skills for as long as possible. It is also about an individual losing those skills and becoming increasingly dependent. That can be hard for staff to witness. It also can be very difficult for staff to deal with the decision to no longer medically intervene. They may feel like "we're giving up, taking the easy way out, or putting our values on someone's life." In addition, they may not have come to terms with their own issues about death. Even when there is a commitment to the decision to cease intrusive medical measures, death suddenly becomes inevitable and ever present. The possibility exists for staff to walk into that person's room one day and find him or her dead. This too is a fear that needs addressing. For staff, the grieving really begins at this point.

As mentioned, part of the hiring process should include a very careful explanation of what the job entails so that the mental preparation can begin immediately. Regular staff meetings are a valuable tool for helping staff address their fears and concerns and for supporting one another. Management must emphasize to staff that they are providing quality care, dignity in death and are adding to that person's life through a secure, respectful, and loving environment. The organization must put together a team of objective people willing to provide staff with practical and emotional support during the dying process. Staff should be encouraged to participate in the funeral and, if necessary, provided with the opportunity to receive individual counseling at the organization's expense.

Housemates. To date, Winnserv has supported people who have dementia in a house with four other housemates who do not have the disease. The home was renovated to accommodate physical changes and to prevent people from being moved. In that home, two people have died of complications associated with Alzheimer's disease, and a new housemate with Alzheimer's disease has just moved in. The organization's plan was to always have one space at that house designated for someone with Alzheimer's disease. After the death of the second person, however, we realized how tremendously difficult it was for people to watch dearly loved housemates die. They had shown amazing strength and resilience, but clearly it was unfair to ask them to go through such trauma every two to three years. It was concluded that setting aside a house specifically for people who have dementia would eliminate the problem. Winnserv is struggling with how to resolve the problem of the people currently living with yet another housemate who is going to die of complications associated with Alzheimer's disease.

However, there will be organizations that cannot have everyone with Alzheimer's disease living in the same house. Staff will then need to deal with the concerns and questions of housemates. They will be addressing questions such as why the person with Alzheimer's disease can no longer do certain tasks, and why he or she no longer works. It's important to answer questions honestly and provide as much information about dementia as possible. Individual learning styles will determine how that information is presented. Housemates need encouragement to interact with the person who has dementia and to help whenever possible. It is also important to make sure there is sufficient staffing to accommodate everyone's needs so no one feels neglected.

The process of death and dying is a major issue for housemates (see Service, Lavoie, & Herlihy, this volume). Staff needs to encourage discussion about the issue and allow for grieving. Once death has occurred, people will need to say their farewells in their own way and be allowed to actively participate in the funeral.

Family/Significant Others.   It is important that family and significant others receive all available information about dementia and about the organization's plans to accommodate people who have the disease. Family and friends of those residents not currently affected by Alzheimer's disease can be educated through group sessions. Individual meetings are necessary for the family and friends of those people demonstrating the signs of dementia or living with someone who has the disease. Group sessions should cover the facts on dementia and Down's syndrome. Family and significant others also need to know about the organization's plans to accommodate changing needs. Information about the organization should include plans for accessible housing, changes to staffing patterns, and plans for provision of care. There should be an emphasis on the lifelong commitment to everyone within the organization.

Individual sessions should include all the above information but should take on a more personal meaning. The family and significant others of those with the disease need to be prepared for the deterioration that will occur. They also need to tackle the painful questions of guardianship and advanced directives. Staff must be particularly sensitive and supportive at this point. An important element of supporting family and friends is keeping them up to date on new developments and including them in decision making. The families and friends of housemates need reassurance that increased needs will not lead to neglect.

☐ Commentary

The information in this chapter came from Winnserv's experiences in supporting people with Alzheimer's disease. The organization learned as it went, and much of the learning was by trial and error. Although the struggles were more than worthwhile, it would have been best to have been able to avoid them wherever possible. Yet other agencies can benefit from our experience, as the challenge of coping with the aging in place of adults with dementia is something that all agencies will confront eventually. Thus, drawn from our experiences, the following recommendations are offered for agencies considering supporting people with Alzheimer's disease in some small group home settings.

- Preplanning is essential because Alzheimer's disease progresses quickly in people who have Down's syndrome. Unless supports are in place, caregivers will always be two steps behind, to the detriment of staff and residents.
- There should be a house/hospice in place exclusively for those individuals with Alzheimer's disease. This addresses the concern about healthy housemates having to watch people they care about die every two or three years.
- There must be a good support system in place for staff to assist them with the dying and death of residents. It is an emotionally draining process that must be handled appropriately.
- The key to a successful program is to ensure that everyone involved receives the information necessary to understand the process.

We have found that there are infinite rewards that come from supporting people with Alzheimer's disease in small group home settings. It is a gift to be able to maintain someone in a homelike setting and provide them with dignity and respect even in the most difficult times. The provision of this type of care has a lasting, positive impact on the organization and everyone associated with it.

☐ References

Aylward, E. H., Burt, D. B., Thorpe, L. U., Lai, F., & Dalton, A. J. (1995). *Diagnosis of dementia in individuals with intellectual disability.* Washington, DC: American Association on Mental Retardation.

Alyward, E., Burt, D., Thorpe, L., Lai, F., & Dalton, A. J. (1997). Diagnosis of dementia in individuals with intellectual disability: Report of the task force for development of criteria for diagnosis of dementia in individuals with mental retardation. *Journal of Intellectual Disability Research, 41,* 152–164.

Janicki, M. P., Heller, T., Seltzer, G., & Hogg, J. (1995). *Practice guidelines for the clinical assessment and care management of Alzheimer and other dementias among adults with mental retardation.* Washington, DC: American Association on Mental Retardation.

Janicki, M. P., Heller, T., Seltzer, G. B., & Hogg, J. (1996). Practice guidelines for the clinical assessment and care management of Alzheimer's disease among adults with intellectual disability. *Journal of Intellectual Disability Research, 40,* 374–382.

King, N. M. P. (1996). *Making sense of advance directives* (revised ed.). Washington: Georgetown University Press.

Marler, R., & Cunningham, C. (1994). *Down's syndrome and Alzheimer's disease.* London: Down's Syndrome Association.

Olsen, R. V., Ehrenkrantz, E., & Hutchings, B. (1993). *Homes that help: Advice from caregivers for creating a supportive home.* Newark: The Center for Architecture and Building Science Research, N.J. Institute of Technology.

The Arc. (1995). *Developmental disabilities and Alzheimer's disease: What you should know.* Arlington, TX: Author.

Zgola, J. M. (1987). *Doing things.* Baltimore: The John Hopkins University Press.

Kathryn Pekala Service
Diane Lavoie
Janice E. Herlihy

Coping with Losses, Death, and Grieving

As the number of older adults with mental retardation, dementia, and other fourth-age diseases grows, so does the need to develop functional responses to losses, dying, and death. A composite case is used to demonstrate strategies to address the issues related to losses and death for people with mental retardation and the diagnosis of dementia and for their families and staff. Dealing with the diagnosis and the changes are explained in the framework of the stages of death and dying as developed by Kubler-Ross. The responses to the losses of dementia that are manifested by affected individuals and members of their personal networks are reflective of a number of factors. The dilemma related to personal value systems, professional roles, and philosophies of care is explored in the context of ethical concerns. The impact of program considerations such as rules, regulations, policies, and economics is examined. Bereavement work for peers and housemates

Address correspondence to: Kathryn Pekala Service, M.S., R.N.C/N.P., C.D.D.N., Nurse Practitioner, Massachusetts Department of Mental Retardation, Franklin-Hampshire Area Office, One Roundhouse Plaza, Northampton, MA 01060.

The opinions and assertions contained herein are the private views of the authors and are not to be construed as official or as reflecting the views of the Massachusetts Department of Mental Retardation.

We would like to gratefully acknowledge the astute and kind assistance of Betsy Johnson, Health Care Ethicist, for her review of this chapter.

can be further developed for carers, family, and staff. Recommendations for research and interventions for public policy are given.

I would like to add a few thoughts. Until Teresa became ill, she was a joy to all of us. Bright, cooperative, we took her everywhere. Before her illness, there were a number of years that her disabilities did not interfere with her coming home and enjoying the time out. However, she is of course older—and so are we. So the problems seem, and definitely are, more. And too, I no longer have a car—and depend on family to drive me. I will visit her at the home as I can—and if—at some time she improves—will be taking her out—if possible. I trust and thank you for keeping us informed of her condition. Sincerely, Mrs. B——

P.S. She'll always be precious to me— her mother—and I care that she is happy and comfortable.

A letter from a parent.

Teresa B was a 52-year-old woman with Down's syndrome who moved from her family home into a large institution at the age of 22. At age 32, she moved from the institution to a community group home where she continues to reside. When she was 35 years old, she suffered a stroke with a residual left-sided weakness. Her gait was affected, but this did not impact greatly upon her lifestyle. She continued to attend a sheltered workshop during the day and enjoyed the resources and activities of her neighborhood and visits with her family. Always sociable, engaging in personality, pleasant to be around, Teresa B enjoyed a comfortable life with her two housemates whom she had known for years. These three women were a "threesome"—a family.

For the past several years, Teresa B had shown a progressive decline in cognitive, functional, and physical skills. More rapid deterioration occurred in the past six months. Neurological evaluations confirmed progressive multi-infarct dementia as well as probable dementia of the Alzheimer type. Toward the end of her life, Teresa was no longer able to walk and was incontinent. She required total care for all her activities of daily living (ADLs), except she would still try to feed herself. Yet, through all of this, her receptive and expressive language skills remained somewhat intact. However, these varied greatly from day to day. Often she screamed loudly for extended periods of time and could not be comforted. This was immensely disruptive to her housemates. She could no longer attend any type of day activity program. She no longer left her home and when asked to go outside, she refused vigorously by screaming and shouting "no." Most of her days were spent watching television and napping. Living at home had become more difficult, because the home was not handicap accessible, and environmental modifications had not been made because they were considered too costly. It took at least two persons to move her into her bed or a chair. Before she died, her carers and family had begun to discuss admission to a nursing facility.

Teresa B's situation illustrates the challenges that are confronting a greater number of agencies and families as the elderly population of persons with intellectual disability grows larger. With progress in medical technology and improvements in personal care procedures, people with intellectual disability are living to an older age. With advancing age there also occurs an increase in the occurrence of Alzheimer's and other dementias. As discussed in other chapters, adults with intellectual disability, particularly those individuals with Down's syndrome, appear to be at a greater risk for the development of dementia than individuals without this condition. We will use our experience with Teresa B to illustrate some of the issues and challenges related to dealing with dying and death among people with intellectual disability and the effects such deaths have on staff and families.

Teresa had been affected by dementia of the Alzheimer type. Such dementia is characterized by eventual profound losses in memory and judgment, ADL skills, and physical dignity, as well as challenges to remaining in one's residence or home. The time when this condition is first suspected marks the starting point for an anticipatory grieving process, since the condition results eventually in death. Several issues related to this grieving process have been studied including issues related to loss and grief among family caregivers of relatives with dementia (Collins, Liken, King, & Kokinakis, 1993). Loss associated with deterioration can be ambiguous. Grieving ambiguous loss is difficult because individuals must let go while finding ways to remain connected (Cutillo-Schmitter, 1996).

As applied to end-stage care of persons with dementia, Weddington (1994) noted that grieving processes can be more clearly appreciated using the five-stage model of grief developed by Kubler-Ross (1969). This model also provides a useful framework for examining the issues involved in dying and grieving among persons with intellectual disability. These five stages, *denial, anger, bargaining, depression,* and *acceptance,* can both overlap and flow together. Although these stages may not always be sequential and some stages may not occur, most people will experience at least one during the grieving process. Not all people will go through these stages the same way, and each individual generally finds his or her own way to become reconciled to the reality of death (Gruetzner, 1988). The feelings evoked are, of course, dependent on the intensity of the relationship between or among the persons involved.

In large part, materials produced for the general population have used these stages to provide useful information. In the general population, such materials have been adapted to help families cope with the terminal care and death of relatives with Alzheimer's disease. Several such reference sources are available (e.g., Oliver & Bock, 1978). In *The 36-Hour Day: A Family Guide to Caring for Persons with Alzheimer's Disease and Related Dementing Illnesses and Memory Loss in Late Life,* Mace and Rabins (1991) address issues of grieving by carers in the general population. Further, a number of sources have available informative educational materials, including books, videotapes, and brochures, as well as supportive advice and helpful activities for support groups for carers and their families (Alzheimer's Disease Education & Referral Center, 1993). Because of the changing nature and attitudes toward persons with intellectual disability, more attention is also now being given to the recognition that people with intellectual disability display similar grief responses. Materials are now beginning to emerge that address grieving among persons with intellectual disability, among them texts by Barbera, Pitch, and Howell (1989) and Oswin (1991).

In addition to these resource materials, studies and reports of grief and bereavement among people with intellectual disability are now being reported and these are beginning to provide insight into how to best approach the grieving process (Bihm & Elliot, 1982; Carder, 1987; Deutsch, 1985; Elliot, 1995; Emerson, 1977; French & Kuczaj, 1992; Harper & Wadsworth, 1993; Kauffman, 1994; Kennedy, 1989; Kloeppel & Hollins, 1989; McDaniel, 1989; McEvoy, 1989; McLoughlin, 1986; Moddia & Chung, 1995; Wadsworth & Harper, 1991; Yanok & Beifus, 1993). There is general agreement that some responses to death are universal, irrespective of the individual's age or degree of intellectual disability, as most everyone understands death as a loss. This loss is generally accompanied by some emotion, usually sadness or anger and sometimes by a sense of wonder. Other responses that may be evident are more likely a reflection of the individual's level of cognitive and emotional development.

With some exceptions (e.g., Antonangeli, 1995b; McLoughlin & Bhate, 1987), little information exists that addresses losses, death, and grieving in relation to persons with intellectual disability and their carers specifically in the area of psychopathology or dementia. A closer analysis of death and grief processes among this group reveals the presence of a sequence of responses which reflect a recognizable and somewhat predictable five-stage process. Thus, in this chapter, we address these issues as well as the process of grieving as it applies to persons with intellectual disability. Although these stages will be highlighted sequentially in this chapter, it must be remembered that these responses may occur at any point throughout the process, are very individual, and reflect the emotional dilemma that is presented by two types of death—the physical death and "the death of self," which may precede the physical death by many years (Cohen & Eisdorfer, 1986).

☐ Dealing with the Diagnosis

Denial

There are many issues related to denial, especially early in the emergence of dementia, that apply to people with and without intellectual disability. Initially, most persons "deny" the diagnosis as they look to rule out other treatable causes. Paradoxically, situations have been encountered in which many care providers, including physicians, hastily affix the diagnosis of Alzheimer's disease to behavioral changes because the individual has Down's syndrome. Because one of the major barriers to an early diagnosis is denial (Weddington, 1994), there needs to be a careful and thoughtful and balanced approach to the assessment, which includes sharing of information and comprehensive data collection.

Denial may also manifest itself in another unique manner. Caregivers and other service providers may be reluctant to combine both the diagnoses of dementia and intellectual disability because, as a stigma, it presents another opportunity for persons with intellectual disability to obtain another label that is devaluing. This has even evolved to a hesitancy to seek diagnostic help, as exemplified by the comment, "What difference does it make? It's just another label."

People with intellectual disability may receive services from specialist or generalist services, as well as from private or public agencies. Within the various levels of assistance or care, there exist many different types of carers from both the generic and specialized systems, from foster and natural families to direct care staff, and from among professionals, including clinicians. In many instances, teams of staff will either formally or informally be working with people with intellectual disability, and among these team members there exist many and diverse levels of capabilities, responsibilities, ethics, and personal values.

This diversity among the service team members may contribute to another issue related to denial when someone is facing death. This is the comparison of the team's goals with those of the family's. Team members, generally paid staff, need to examine the goals they set for the individual and ensure that they not try to have the family accept what they, the team, believes in the face of concerns or opposition from the family. It is important to let family members work through the process of acceptance of death on their own conditions and time frames. The following illustrates this point:

> The team had accepted the diagnosis of Alzheimer's disease for Teresa B and was aware of all of its implications. The members felt that Teresa's mother was not accepting her daughter's diagnosis because the mother avoided the use of the word and discussion of the possibility of Alzheimer's as a reason for the changes in her daughter. She also kept pressing the team to investigate other reasons for the changes in her daughter's behavior. In the past, Teresa had a blood clot in her brain, and her mother wondered if this could explain the changes in her daughter. Following a period of two years and extensive evaluations, Teresa's mother came to accept the diagnosis. One day, she turned to the service coordinator and said, "Tell me about Alzheimer's disease."

Anecdotal observations indicate that many care providers incorrectly interpret deterioration in behaviors as a sign of aggression or annoyance by the affected person rather than a function of the disease process. With Teresa, staff and her housemates would complain that "Teresa knew exactly what she was doing; she was just doing that to get back at me." An early diagnosis can help everyone understand the significance of deterioration in affected persons and in some ways alleviate fears that the individual affected is rejecting his or her friends or family. The Alzheimer's Association (Staff, 1994a) suggests that an early diagnosis reduces feelings of uncertainty resulting in stress reduction and that this, in turn, leads to better care, management, and planning for the future.

The difficulty with accepting a diagnosis of Alzheimer's disease may occur for a number of reasons. First, as noted in other chapters, it is difficult to provide a definite diagnosis of dementia until someone has died and, thus, the possibility of other causes may be clung to by family members and other carers. Further, to obtain a diagnosis of probable dementia among persons with an intellectual disability, comprehensive evaluations are necessary. Adults with an intellectual disability may present limitations to this process, because they may not be able to understand the need and level of participation or cooperation needed for certain diagnostic exams, such as a CAT scan. In addition, because of the slow, subtle changes in function that are generally the hallmarks of Alzheimer dementia, it may take several years before enough functional data are collected to document a pattern of decline. This, too, may provide for the hope that the changes may be attributed to other factors. Last, because of the lack of treatment for Alzheimer dementia, a pessimistic prognosis and a hopelessness of such a diagnosis may be present. Thus, many family members or carers may think, "No matter what you do, you cannot change the course of the disease."

For many families, this represents the culmination of a lifelong struggle that impacts on their attitudes and level of acceptance. Teresa's mother had noted that "we just didn't expect Teresa to live this long." This is the feeling of many parents. Davis (1987) notes that people with disabilities and their families experience chronic sorrow, which can be accompanied by ambivalence, dependence, and feelings of guilt. In addition, this sorrow may be complicated by social expectations of mourning. Personal values, beliefs, social resources, and experiences all affect how families cope with the long-term uncertainty related to a child with disabilities and impact on the family's capacity to adapt (Ramey, Krauss, & Simeonsson, 1989). Coping and adaptation may be further complicated when the affected person with intellectual disability no longer lives in the family home. The role that the family plays is changed now that strangers are caring for the family member. Consequently, there may be competition and conflict with regard to power and control among staff, family, and the affected individual with intellectual disability. Thus, in terms of the process, the focus needs to be directed onto the person with intellectual disability.

☐ Dealing with Changes

Denial

Affected individuals must be prepared and helped to understand the changes that occur as a result of dementia. Early during the course of the disease, Teresa would become frustrated when tasks that were previously easy required more and more effort and even became impossible to do. The team met with Teresa's mother and discussed Teresa's right to know what was going on. Together, the decision was made to try to explain Teresa's condition to her in concrete terms, so that she would understand that what was happening to her was not "her fault." Using a method suggested by Antonangeli (1995a), a nurse consultant, invited to come by the team, brought in a toy train set with dimmer switches that made the lights go off and on. She explained to Teresa that the train was like her mind and that like the train's lights, the lights in her mind were also going off. She told her,

> It's just like when it's hard for you to see to do things as it gets darker and darker when you are outside. It's hard for this train to see where its going and it gets lost [as the nurse put out a light, she moved the train off the track]. The lights are going off in your mind, so you get off track, too. It's hard because we can't put the lights back on, but just like we can help the train to get back on track, we'll be helping you to get back on track.

The explanation helped the other team members deal with Teresa's condition. The nurse consultant also provided other technical information for the staff and explained what changes they would see in Teresa over the months and years to come. The information she provided and her involvement with the team were very supported and helped the team members deal with their own emotions related to Teresa's illness and decline.

During the phase when changes or losses are becoming more evident, staff must also comprehend their changing role and accept that they will need to provide much more physical care as the disease progresses. They need to examine their values, feelings, and own abilities and decide for themselves on adjustments to these changes as the affected person loses skills. Some of the staff who had been working with Teresa felt that they were hired to work on more "recreational" activities since Teresa had been so independent in her ADLs. With the progressive course of the disease, they needed to make a considerable adjustment that included providing a greater amount of personal care.

The emotional attachment between carers and people with intellectual disability who are affected with dementia will vary. Many staff become members of extended families and may, in fact, be the only "family" that many persons with intellectual disability know. Thus, caregiving should be viewed both as a family role and as a professional role. As noted by Aroskar (1991) professionals are forced to struggle with finding and maintaining their own role boundaries while providing care and supports. Stress and confusion may result from the efforts of carers to identify and maintain these boundaries.

Anger/Guilt

In addition to denial, anger is a common response of many carers (Mace & Rabins, 1991; Weddington, 1994). Carers may take reactions personally and become upset with day-to-day inconsistent and unpredictable behavior. Although there frequently exists the opportunity for detachment when staff is not at work, many carers can still experience strong emotions, such as anger, when someone in their care is dying. For families in the general population, support groups offer an excellent opportunity for acknowledging anger and working through feelings. However, in most agency systems, such opportunities are very limited. Agency staff members often do not find that community support groups are able to meet their needs, so that talking at team meetings may be the only outlet for staff feelings.

From our experiences, we found that outside support groups involved additional time and that staff complained that, "We can't get coverage or the agency won't pay overtime for other staff to relieve us so that we can go to support group meetings." Further, we found that the nature of caring and how people with dementia are treated may be seen differently in outside support groups. Staff noted that the members of the local support group who they were starting to attend just "couldn't understand that we couldn't lock the doors when Teresa started to wander." Staff had to explain that if they locked the doors, then Teresa's housemates couldn't come and go as they please and that there would be concerns raised by the human rights committee. Because outside support groups generally are not helpful, team meetings should be used to help staff understand that their anger may be the result of their sense of helplessness. In our situation, we told staff, "When you get frustrated with Teresa, ask for help, call a time-out, get someone to cover for you, and go outside, and take a deep breath. . . . You cannot control your feelings, but you can control your behaviors." What is important is not to eliminate or suppress the anger but to understand and control it.

Guilt develops out of anger (anger turned inward) and frequently "what if's" may be hastened when carers reflect on the situation. It is a normal reaction to Alzheimer's disease and can arise from unresolved conflicts, especially with families (Gruetzner, 1988). Teresa's mother expressed guilt that she was responsible for having her daughter admitted into an institution when she was younger. She told us, "I wasn't strong enough to keep Teresa with me. It was what God gave to me and I just couldn't do it. I feel as if I failed as a good mother." We worked with Teresa's mother to help her understand that when she was a young parent, she did not receive the supports that were required to be able to meet her daughter's needs. In addition, we helped her accept many of the positive things that she had done for her daughter over the years.

Staff may also demonstrate feelings of guilt because of their own perceived omissions or angry acts during the provision of care. The provision of information by clinicians during staff meetings and at other appropriate occasions may help to alleviate some of these feelings (Kauffman, 1994). Carers can also be empowered to solve their own problems when they are given enough information to positively impact outcomes. Some have proposed holding workshops or clinics to help staff come to terms with their feelings (Kauffman, 1994; French & Kuczaj, 1992).

Carers may also demonstrate guilt over therapeutic lying (Volicer, Fabiszewski, Rheaume, & Lasch, 1988) or "fiblets" (J. M. Antonangeli, personal communication, 1994). This form of communication has been thought to work to the affected person's interest by protecting him or her from unnecessary emotional confrontations. Thus, at the team meetings, staff can be encouraged to express their feelings and review situations during which they felt that they were being "deceptive." In our situation, staff were told,

When you told Teresa that her father is not here right now and she must miss him when he's gone, you avoided a catastrophic reaction. She doesn't realize that her father died many years ago and if she heard that he is dead, she could get unnecessarily upset and act as if she's hearing that terrible news for the first time. By focusing on her feelings, you still showed respect for her.

It has been noted that it is not uncommon for members of the family to wish that their loved one would die and then feel guilty about that wish (Cohen & Eisdorfer, 1986; Gruetzner 1988). Staff, too, experience this emotional turmoil and a wish for death either because of the perceived suffering or because of the amount of resources, which are often limited, that are being "given" to the person. At team meetings, staff need to be encouraged to express their frustrations, counseled as to the validity of their feelings, and helped to explore ways in which limited resources could be modified. In our experience, one staff member told us,

> When I think of how much staff time goes into our care of Teresa, for what? It's not fair, because Helen and Kay are missing out on so much! Sometimes, I just think that it would be better if Teresa went sooner than later. It would be better for all of us if she wouldn't have to be suffering so much.

☐ Dealing with Housemates and Peers

Anger

Recognizing and addressing the issues that housemates confront can be challenging to carers. They are trying to cope with the losses and demonstrate grief in many ways. Sometimes they display behaviors that do not reflect their own stage of coping but those of the people around them (Barbera et al., 1989). We observed that Teresa's housemates faced these losses differently. One, Kay, at first tried to rationalize Teresa's challenging behaviors: "She's just being silly, that Teresa," she would say. However, as more disturbing behaviors appeared, Kay became frustrated, "How come we can't go out tonight? Not enough staff to stay home with Teresa?" Anger was also displayed by Kay's attempts to hit Teresa when she screamed because she could not hear the television. Some of Kay's old self-abusive behaviors also returned. As the situation worsened, staff tried several approaches. They would try to explain what was happening with Teresa and include both Kay and Helen (Teresa's housemates) in discussions. They would try to spend "one-on-one" time with each housemate. They would make a special effort to make Teresa's housemates feel valued when they helped in the care of Teresa (such as getting her a sweater or by singing to her). Yet even these approaches eventually proved difficult, for having staff diverted to these supportive functions meant they were not doing other things. In addition, the added cost to the agency of having to pay overtime or bringing in other staff proved difficult.

Bargaining

Another dynamic observed in the adjustment process was bargaining. Such bargaining is universal and some forms, like prayers, can be comforting (Weddington, 1994). Teresa's other housemate, Helen, first tried to reason with the situation as she went through the bargaining stage: "I'll go to Church and pray hard every Sunday, so that God will let Teresa get better." As Teresa's condition worsened, Helen became despondent and constantly retreated to her room. To help Helen cope, staff worked with her and taught her how to pray for more realistic requests, such as warmer weather so Teresa could be taken outside.

Depression

A chronic dementing illness takes a toll on everyone's emotions (Mace & Rabins, 1991). Because some components of depression form a normal and natural part of the grieving process, in our situation, staff members worked to acknowledge that it was "OK" for Helen to be sad about her friend and they gave her comforting hugs, recognizing the effectiveness of physical contact. They also tried to engage Helen in physical activities, such as taking walks in the neighborhood, since lack of exercise and poor nutrition can contribute to depression (Weddington, 1994). Yet Helen experienced a dramatic decrease in appetite and a resulting weight loss. Because of this, in the end staff sought individual therapy for her.

A social worker consultant visited the two housemates and worked with them on the development of collages which contained "cut-out pictures" from magazines of each woman's favorite things and old photographs of the housemates. During these periods they all reminisced about their "good times." Reminiscence can be a comforting (and relatively "cost-effective") activity, both for people with and without intellectual disability (Kauffman, 1994).

On a regular basis, the housemates joined part of the team support group and were encouraged to express their losses and grief in their own words. Eye contact and touch, which are powerful but gentle devices

(Barbera et al., 1989), were shared by all the members of the group. The inability to express feelings related to the losses can be a powerful predictor of future problematic problems, such as serious depression. If depression goes beyond or is different from the understandable feelings of discouragement caused by the illness (Mace & Rabins, 1991) or if, after several months after the death, life still seems empty and devoid of meaning and there continues to be no enjoyment of any activity, then professional attention should be sought (Cohen & Eisdorfer, 1986).

Acceptance

Barbera et al. (1989) note that given adequate time and support to work through these stages, a point is reached when all business is completed, the person is ready to die in peace, and the struggle is over. This is the time during which the carers need more help, understanding, and support than the individual. Communications become more nonverbal than verbal. The presence of supporting people confirms that those in grief will not be alone (Kubler-Ross, 1969).

An important guideline proposed by Barbera et al. (1989) centers on hope. They note that hope is an element that persists throughout all the stages. Hope allows persons to cope with the most difficult of times. Cutillo-Schmitter (1996) noted that staff can provide hope that the disease can be managed by making the unfamiliar familiar, thereby helping to build resiliency into the lives of the carers. Hope should always be respected and nurtured.

☐ Program Considerations

Regulations, Rules, and Policies

Overlaying any efforts at helping staff and families cope with the dying or death are problems that are caused by administrative practices or fiscal constraints. A complicating issue with formal care systems is the regulations, requirements, and other mandates under which the system must function and which may be blind to the realities of someone who is dying. These are rooted in the conventional wisdom that reflects policies of the funding agencies, such as the state, region, or facility/agency. Surveyors, licensors, quality assurance, and human rights personnel have differing interpretations of the regulations that generate conflicting messages for carers. These effects can be made even more complicated by restrictions on the amount of money for services that the person with intellectual disability receives and the limits for spending from governmental budgets. Thus, normal process, such as coping with dying and death, can be complicated by the formal structure that encompasses both the person who is dying and the staff who provide care.

One such area of complications is how services are funded. In the United States, there are both federal and state regulations concerning payment for services. This can be very complicated and confounding to the layperson. This is also confusing because each state may have its own "individual" rules and regulations. Thus, although assignment of services may be well-intended, how they are paid for may pose complications. For example, consideration needs to be given to avoid the "double-billing" trap. In our situation, Teresa received occupational therapy services at home. Because her housemates needed "special attention," the team considered having Teresa regularly attend a day habilitation program so they would have time to spend with them. This particular day program included occupational therapy services as a part of its contract for services. If Teresa were to go to that program, she could not continue to receive occupational therapy services at home, because the rules for the use of the federal funds that were used to pay for the day program prohibited double payment for the same service. Thus, if the day habilitation program was already receiving funds for Teresa to receive occupational therapy, the agency could not also bill for this service in the group home. Because the team valued the benefit of the education and reassurance provided by the occupational therapy in the group home, it was decided to maintain the status quo. Should there have been the opportunity for Teresa to attend the day program and receive the occupational therapy in the home, the team would have gladly approved Teresa's attendance. This funding peculiarity led to many of the team members raising concerns about being forced to make this perceived "choice" between Teresa and her housemates.

Another situation involving funding concerns environmental modifications. As people experience decline and need special accommodations with the progression of dementia, often such accommodations can be made by modifying their home. In our situation, Teresa's decline posed a special problem. Even though Teresa could no longer easily use the home's bathroom and needed special accommodations so we could bathe her, it was deemed too expensive to modify. This situation obviously raised questions as to the dignity of bed baths for the rest of Teresa's life. In fact, this situation was noted as a "deficiency" during a site survey and was questioned by the agency's human rights officer. The problem was further complicated by the fact that even though Teresa was incontinent and did not have a need for the toilet, she refused to go near the bathroom to be washed. It was felt that if the bathroom was modified to be accessible, we could work to alleviate her fears of going into it. There were many discussions regarding the possible alternatives, yet it was this situation that almost lead to Teresa to be admitted to a nursing facility. However, the consensus of the team was to keep Teresa in her home and to postpone a referral to a nursing facility for as long as they could safely provide for her in the home.

Another problem concerns funding for hospice care. Typically in the United States, hospice programs for the terminally ill are time-limited (generally to six months), although the concepts apply as well to terminally ill people whose prognoses are measured in years. In order to qualify for hospice care benefits through Medicare, Medicaid, and even some private insurance providers, the physician must indicate that the person has entered the "terminal" phase of the disease (Staff, 1994b). This service can be used in group homes but is limited by the time of "six months" determination for terminal care. A greater period of time is often necessary, since the time of death associated with dementia is often unpredictable.

These types of funding complications continue to pose problems. In the United States, Medicaid—the primary federal financing mechanism for funding services for people with intellectual disabilities—funding rules restrict community-based care. Because many of the rules governing the use of Medicaid do not adequately reflect the need for intensive care in community care settings, especially in the later stages of Alzheimer's disease, it puts many agencies in a quandary about how to best proceed with providing adequate and appropriate care. Ironically, under Medicaid regulations, even though more expensive to the state and inappropriate for the individual, admission to and care in nursing facilities may be the only feasible option for many community-dwelling individuals when care systems become overwhelmed or recommended services cannot be provided in the home due to funding restrictions (Governor's Conference on Alzheimer's Disease, 1995).

Philosophies of Care

The working philosophy in providing care for persons with intellectual disability typically rests on the notion of the development of new skills and productivity. This notion translates to "behavior modification" (as opposed to "behavior management") when providing care for persons affected with dementia. This distinction may be difficult for some paid staff, as they have to change their perspective and be able to reflect this change in mandated documentation, such as in the individual service plan.

The principle of "habilitation" as described by Raia (1992) is based on the notion of the maintenance of skills and the enhancement of well-being through a facilitation of personal worth, basic trust, and security in the environment and others. In our situation, Teresa's carers were able to develop service plan objectives that satisfied the official regulatory requirements, while simultaneously maintaining respect for Teresa. Activities under these objectives included sensory stimulation (such as massage, touching items, using flavored lip gloss and scented hand lotions, and windchimes), sensory motor movement (such as holding items), gross motor activities (such as reaching for items), and efforts at communication (such as making a choice between two items with one preferential item). Staff also grew to realize that "just sitting" with Teresa, even when she seemed to be unresponsive, was valuable and comforting for both Teresa and themselves. As noted by Post (1995), "the first task of dementia ethics is to secure the underpinnings of care, that is, the appreciation and respect for compassion. In a culture that is hypersensitive in its values and emphasizes productivity, it is easy to think that people with dementia lack any moral significance" (p. 314).

Another concept related to dementia and people with intellectual disability is the idea of the "then self" (Post, 1995), which is the person prior to the losses or prior to the dementia. This can affect care in two ways. First, many in the population-at-large have doubts about the value of people with an intellectual disability and may have mixed thoughts and feelings about their need for a quality of life (even before the complications brought on by the onset of dementia—or as the "then self"). These doubts are evident in the provision of generic services and may even increase as funding becomes more limited. One physician who had been covering for Teresa's primary care doctor had noted that if Teresa was his patient, he "would never give her a G-tube, even if she was having problems with eating because she was mentally retarded and now that she has Alzheimer's, what kind of a quality of life could she have?"

Second, the need to determine the nature and extent of life-sustaining treatments and other end-of-life decisions becomes inescapable as the disease progresses to the terminal phase. There are many affected people who lack the capacity to make informed decisions and may or may not be under guardianship. There are also many people with intellectual disability who have never been given the opportunity to participate in the treatment decision-making process. In some programs, there is frequent turnover of staff, so there may be few, if any, people who know the person and are familiar with his or her lifestyle preferences prior to the dementia. In our situation, Teresa's mother and other people who "knew" Teresa were able to make appropriate recommendations as to what they felt that Teresa would want.

As Teresa's abilities became more and more limited, it was hard for some staff to modify their former beliefs, which were based upon a strong commitment to independent choices and opportunities. As Teresa became more debilitated, she was more unable to participate in any processes that determined what would happen to her. This was disconcerting to staff who were accustomed to involving her in the decision-making process. Additionally, many staff members were personally connected with the management of dementia in their own families. Because of the drain on their emotional and personal resources, these experiences influenced their attitudes and behaviors. Many wrestled with why we continued to provide care for Teresa in her home. As an example, one told us: "We had to put my mother-in-law in a nursing home when she screamed like that. It was the best thing we could do for all of us."

Statements like the one made by the covering physician emphasize the need for carers to again reflect on their own values and attitudes and work together with the individual and their families or guardians or both in advocating and planning for treatment and end-of-life decisions. A proactive and empowering approach is to work with individuals before they become incapacitated by dementia. This can include such activities as development of health care proxies and advance directives, durable powers of attorney, or other plans that are appropriate and according to the laws of the specific state in which one resides. Although the concept of quality of life is complex and beyond the scope of this chapter (see Post & Whitehouse, 1995, for a discussion relating to quality of life and dementia), it can still be suggested that this be an area for self-examination and discussion and for the creation of a supportive environment to enhance the well-being of the person who has both intellectual disability and dementia.

☐ Helping with Bereavement

Part of "dying a good death" is that everyone (staff, family, and other members of affected individuals' personal network) acts together to do what they can do as long as possible and that they help one another. Despite the years of grieving and adjustment to the losses during the course of dementia, the moment of death is still painful. During the period after the death, carers will be adapting their patterns of living and will continue to feel great sadness (Cohen & Eisdorfer, 1986). The interventions that have been previously noted and those that follow are applicable throughout the process.

Working with Peers and Housemates

The process of grief management can involve a number of techniques (Kauffman, 1994; Fox, 1988; Moddia & Chung, 1995; Yanok & Beifus, 1993). One model, outlined by Fox (1988), has its origins in developmental theory and is composed of four tasks. Its applications can be extended to working with staff and families, as well as to persons with intellectual disabilities. These tasks are as follows.

Understanding.   Information needs to be given according to the individual's intellectual level with consideration toward the meaning and implications of the information. This should be given in extremely concrete terms. When consideration was given to the time of Teresa's physical death, staff discussed the use of the analogy of marigolds that died in the autumn and that the members of the household replanted in the following spring to explain Teresa's death to her housemates, Kay and Helen. These flowers were meaningful for Teresa for she loved the brightness and even the smell of her "maregoads." Staff would even be able to show how the marigolds eventually would die whether in the yard or being picked and kept and saved in a vase.

Expression of Feelings.   As noted earlier, staff (who learned that it is intrinsically OK to feel any feeling) worked diligently with the housemates to express their feelings appropriately and how to explore their feelings safely.

Commemoration.   There is a tremendous value in acknowledging that every life is special and "sacred." This uniqueness can be translated into some concrete activities. In our situation, formal portraits were taken of each housemate and displayed in the living room. Informal photos of Teresa with her housemates, staff, and family were given to individuals. They were used later to help illustrate stories and a memory book or collage of activities during bereavement.

Continuation of Life.   At times, Helen felt that she couldn't smile, that "it wasn't right." Kay noted to staff that when her grandmother died, she had laughed at the funeral and was punished. She "didn't mean to, but her cousin said something funny." While some may feel that a certain style of expression is not appropriate, the housemates were reassured that it was OK not only to have very sad or angry feelings, but feelings of happiness could also be expressed at this sad time. Plans were made to include funny stories, such as Teresa's affinity for beads, at the memorial service and to play the music of the singer, Elvis Presley, who was Teresa's favorite ("the more lively, the better" according to the people who knew Teresa the best).

Helping Carers, Family, and Staff

Many of the suggestions for the housemates can be further developed for carers. Most individuals wanted to have their picture taken with Teresa so they could have something to remember her by. People also discussed possibilities for other tangible remembrances, including such personal items as Teresa's "signature" beads. Teresa's mother shared family photos, including baby pictures of Teresa, and planned to include them in a photo collage for the memorial service. In comparison with her mother's knowledge of her daughter, which spanned a lifetime, the staff and her housemates knew Teresa for only a few short years. However, the combined knowledge of all of Teresa's personal network of friends and relatives was able to be woven into a meaningful fabric of comfort.

Religion and rituals often assume a role of comfort during the bereavement process. In our situation, there was some concern as to the formal role of religion. Teresa's mother was a practicing Roman Catholic and Teresa had been baptized in the church. She had made plans to bury Teresa in the family's plot at the Catholic cemetery. After Teresa moved in with Kay and Helen, she started attending services at a Protestant church for a number of reasons. Besides wanting to attend the same church as her housemates, she found very attractive the activities and social component that this church provided for its members with disabilities. After she was diagnosed with dementia, fellow parishioners and the minister of the church continued to visit Teresa and assisted and comforted her housemates and even some of the staff in their grief. Thus, the ties to this particular church were strong.

Although Teresa's mother was aware of and supported these connections while Teresa was alive, she still had very strong feelings and beliefs with regard to her religion and how Teresa's death would be handled. She requested that Teresa receive the sacraments of the sick and wanted Teresa to have a funeral mass at her home parish. She confided in the social worker that her desire was based on family custom and also reflected the wishes of other members of her and her late husband's families. Thus, both the wishes of Teresa's mother and those of her housemates had to be discussed and dealt with by staff and housemates. It was here that a conflict arose. There was a strong feeling that the other family members had "no right to dictate what should be done for Teresa, because they didn't know her and hardly ever visited her, if at all." Much discussion ensued; eventually staff were helped to understand the deep meaning of religious and ethnic rituals and customs for this family. Their reactions also illustrated the unresolved anger over Teresa's condition and death that was still present. With the assistance of the minister and priest, the team was able to work together to develop a plan that would satisfy everyone. In the end, it was agreed that there would be a Catholic funeral mass and burial at the time of her death, and at a later point there would be a special memorial service at the Protestant church. This memorial service, which would include the sharing of stories and listening to Teresa's favorite music, would be followed by a reception at the house.

Administrative practice is another concern that appears at the time of death. Often spaces in residential programs, such as Teresa's, are highly desirable and sought after. There is usually administrative pressure to move someone in and "fill the bed" as quickly as possible. Such pressures can meet an administrative need but can also pose difficulties for people still working through the death of someone for whom they cared. To see someone new quickly fill Teresa's room would have been disconcerting to her housemates and staff. The team worked closely with the agency administrators to help them understand that due respect for Teresa called for her room to remain as is for a brief time after her death. A colleague commented on a similar situation that occurred in another residence.

> We were able to keep Claudia's room just as it had been for two weeks after her funeral. People were able to go in and think about Claudia; in fact, you could still smell her rose perfume. One of her housemates who had very limited sight and hearing would often "trail" into that room and "move her hands and feel about the empty bed." I think it helped her understand that Claudia was gone.

☐ Commentary

Dealing with the dying and death of adults with dementia and intellectual disability in care settings is still relatively novel. Although we have outlined some stratagems for understanding the grieving process, there is a need for more research and demonstration projects in this area. Studies should be undertaken that examine the development of decision-making skills for people with intellectual disability as they pertain to life-sustaining treatment. In addition, there should be research centered on creative means by which to maintain a person in his or her own home for as long as possible.

There is a need to know the individual's subjective experience with a disease such as dementia because it adds an important dimension to care management. In addition, it adds to a better understanding of health promotion and prevention of complications of a preexisting disease (Cohen, 1991). Because there is scant information relating to the topics of loss and grief related to people with intellectual disability and the subjective experience of dementia for persons with intellectual disability, qualitative research should be undertaken to expand the knowledge in this area. This is particularly important because, as Gerhardt (1990) has noted, the purpose of clinical practice is to improve the condition of individuals, and it is on the basis of case-related evidence that clinical judgments can become more effective.

Models of care and technologies are not routinely shared among the intellectual disability, Alzheimer's disease, and aging networks (Antonangeli, 1995b). There is a need for cross-agency transfer of information and skills (Governor's Conference on Alzheimer's Disease, 1995). Such interagency-collaborative activities, like joint educational endeavors, have been found to be beneficial and an ideal time during which to network. There needs to be more training and other opportunities for reflecting on attitudes and values toward death and bereavement (French & Kuczaj, 1992), as more staff face this personal challenge with the impending growth of aging in place and community dementia care.

Public policy needs to address the expansion of the definition of "terminal" to include dementia so that hospice services could be accessed for people with dementia. There should be flexibility within federal Medicaid regulations in the United States so that funds could be allocated for a particular individual for long-term care or adult health services to be used for community residential care. Additionally, funding of day and residential care services needs to more adequately reflect the intensified care requirements for this population (Governor's Conference on Alzheimer's Disease, 1995, p. 40).

Until a cure is found, the eventualities of Alzheimer's disease are inescapable. Yet although the care that is provided does make a difference, many behaviors associated with this disease cannot be controlled by either the caregiver or the person afflicted. We need to grieve for the losses that we experience but also enjoy our good memories and live for each day (Staff, 1994b). Remembrance is important, for as Teresa's mother noted in her letter, "She'll always be precious to me."

☐ References

Alzheimer's Disease Education & Referral Center. (1993). *Alzheimer's disease: A guide to federal programs.* Silver Spring, MD: Author.

Antonangeli, J. M. (1995a, April). *Developing case management specialty services for the person with Alzheimer's disease and mental retardation.* Paper presented at the Annual Educational Conference of the Developmental Disabilities Nurses Association, Tempe, Arizona.

Antonangeli, J. M. (1995b). *Of two minds: A guide to the care of people with the dual diagnosis of Alzheimer's disease and mental retardation.* Malden, MA: Fidelity Press.

Aroskar, M. A. (1991). Caring—Another side. *Journal of Professional Nursing, 7,* 3.

Barbera, T. C., Pitch, R. J., & Howell, M. C. (1989). *Death and dying: A guide for staff serving adults with mental retardation.* Boston: Exceptional Parent Press.

Bihm, E., & Elliot, L. (1982). Concept of death in mentally retarded people. *Journal of Psychology, 3,* 205–210.

Carder, M. (1987). Journey into understanding mentally retarded people's experiences around death. *Journal of Pastoral Care, 41*(1), 18–31.

Cohen, D. (1991). The subjective experience of Alzheimer's disease: The anatomy of an illness as perceived by patients and families. *The American Journal of Alzheimer's Care and Related Disorders and Research, 6*(3), 6–11.

Cohen, D., & Eisdorfer, C. (1986). *The loss of self.* New York: W.W. Norton.

Collins, C., Liken, M., King, S., & Kokinakis, C. (1993). Loss and grief among family caregivers of relatives with dementia. *Qualitative Health Care Research, 3,* 236–253.

Cutillo-Schmitter, T. A. (1996). Managing ambiguous loss in dementia and terminal illness. *Journal of Gerontological Nursing, 22,* 32–39.

Davis, B. H. (1987). Disability and grief. *Social Casework, 68,* 352–357.

Deutsch, H. (1985). Grief counseling with the mentally retarded clients. *Psychiatric Aspects of Mental Retardation Reviews, 4,* 17–20.

Elliot, D. (1995). Helping people with learning difficulties to handle grief. *Nursing Times, 91,* 27–29.

Emerson, P. (1977). Covert grief reaction in mentally retarded adults. *Mental Retardation, 15*(6), 44–45.

Fox, S. (1988). *Good grief: Helping groups of children when a friend dies.* Boston: New England Association for the Education of Young Children.

French, J., & Kuczaj, E. (1992). Working through loss and change with people with learning disabilities. *Mental Handicap, 20,* 108–111.

Gerhardt, V. (1990). Qualitative research on chronic illness: The issue and the story. *Social Science and Medicine, 30,* 1149–1159.

Governor's Conference on Alzheimer's Disease. (1995). *Final Report.* Boston: Massachusetts Executive Office of Elder Affairs, Massachusetts Department of Public Health, and Alzheimer's Associations of Massachusetts.

Gruetzner, H. (1988). *Alzheimer's: A caregiver's guide and sourcebook.* New York: Wiley.

Harper, D. C., & Wadsworth, J. S. (1993). Grief in adults with mental retardation: Preliminary findings. *Research in Developmental Disabilities, 14,* 313–330.

Kauffman, J. (1994). Mourning and mental retardation. *Death Studies, 18,* 257–271.

Kennedy, J. (1989). Bereavement and the person with mental handicap. *Nursing Standard, 4*(6), 36–38.

Kloeppel, D. A., & Hollins, S. (1989). Double handicap: Mental retardation and death in the family. *Death Studies, 13*(1), 31–38.

Kubler-Ross, E. (1969). *On death and dying.* New York: Macmillan.

Mace, N. L., & Rabins, P. V. (1991). *The 36-hour day: A family guide to caring for persons with Alzheimer's disease and related dementing illnesses and memory loss in late life* (revised ed.). Baltimore: The Johns Hopkins University Press.

McDaniel, B. (1989). A group work experience with mentally retarded adults on the issue of death and dying. *Journal of Gerontological Social Work, 13,* 187–191.

McEvoy, J. (1989). Investigating the concept of death in adults who are mentally handicapped. *British Journal of Mental Subnormality, 35*, 115–121.

McLoughlin, I. J. (1986). Bereavement in mentally handicapped. *British Journal of Hospital Medicine, 36*, 256–260.

McLoughlin, I. J., & Bhate, M. S. (1987). A case of affective psychosis following bereavement in mentally retarded handicapped woman. *British Journal of Psychiatry, 151*, 552–554.

Moddia, B., & Chung, M. C. (1995). Grief reactions and learning disabilities. *Nursing Standard, 9*, 38–39.

Oliver, R., & Bock, F. A. (1978). *Coping with Alzheimer's*. New York: Dodd, Mead, & Company.

Oswin, M. (1991). *Am I allowed to cry? A study of bereavement amongst people who have learning disabilities*. London: Souvenir Press, Ltd.

Post, S. G. (1995). Alzheimer's disease and the "then" self. *Kennedy Institute of Ethics Journal, 5*, 307–321.

Post, S. G., & Whitehouse, P. J. (1995). Fairhill guidelines on ethics of the care of people with Alzheimer's Disease: A clinical summary. *Journal of the American Geriatrics Society, 43*, 1423–1429.

Raia, P. A. (1992). What are we trying to restore? A case for habilitation. *Generations, 16*, 37–39.

Ramey, S. L., Krauss, M. W., & Simeonsson, R. J. (1989). Research on families: Current assessment and future opportunities. *American Journal on Mental Retardation, 94*, ii–vi.

Staff. (1994a). Alzheimer's and stress: Caregivers at risk. *Alzheimer's Association National Newsletter, 13*(3), 1, 9.

Staff. (1994b). Families find comfort in hospice care. *Alzheimer's Association National Newsletter, 16*(1), 1, 7.

Volicer, L., Fabiszewski, K. J., Rheaume, Y. L., & Lasch, K. E. (1988). *Clinical management of Alzheimer's disease*. Rockville, MD: Aspen Publishers.

Wadsworth, J. S., & Harper, D. C. (1991). Grief and bereavement in mental retardation: A need for a new understanding. *Death Studies, 15*, 281–292.

Weddington, D. (1994). *Early-stage Alzheimer's care*. New York: Springer Publishing Company.

Yanok, J., & Beifus, J. A. (1993). Communicating about loss and mourning: Death education for individuals with mental retardation. *Mental Retardation, 31*, 144–147.

6

EDUCATION AND POLICY CONSIDERATIONS

In this last section we provide both an overview of the resources available to help agencies cope with dementia and functional decline, as well as explore some of the policy and education issues still remaining unresolved within the field. We also offer a final view of the main issues of this handbook from the eyes of the editors and a fellow colleague. Kendall, Rinck, and Wright, in their chapter on dementia assistance resources, reveal that the programs serving persons with intellectual disabilities and dementia are based on duplication or modification of the programs that have been designed for persons with dementia from the community at large. They indicate that families seeking services typically are confronted with an enormously complex situation and often struggle to obtain accurate information. They define succinctly the most frequent needs families are trying to grapple with, such as the lack of programs, inadequate diagnostic services, absence of clinics, supports and education, respite, adult day programs, and residential services. They illustrate the potential value of the work of the self-help organizations such as the Alzheimer's Association for individuals with dementia and intellectual disabilities. Specific attention is devoted to dementia support groups, case management, and information and referral services. Throughout, it is apparent that cooperation and sharing of resources between the professionals in the field of aging and in the field of intellectual disabilities is gradually reshaping services for persons affected with dementia. This development is particularly evident in the description of educational efforts and the content and format of dementia and intellectual disabilities training, which is both theory-backed and practical.

The authors then outline some of the major coalition building activities currently in progress in the United States and touch on the development of international networks through the Alzheimer's Disease International organizations. They conclude that duplication of effort and competition for limited resources should be avoided between organizations that serve individuals with intellectual disabilities and those that serve persons with Alzheimer's disease from the population in general. Their overview takes us through what can be useful to workers in either of these two care systems as they attempt to help older adults with intellectual disabilities, and their families and other carers, who are experiencing dementia. The appendices and resource listings at the end of the chapter should prove to be an invaluable resource.

As the editors of this text, our differing perspectives have helped us reflect on the best work of our colleagues and then bring harmony to the varying viewpoints offered. In the next chapter, we examine some of the underlying issues related to dementia care and explore the various approaches that care system agencies are beginning to take. We approach this task from both an analytical and historical perspective, recognizing that public policy, by its very nature, will always be grounded within the political and administrative climate of care systems. Thus, we realize that no one method or response will work universally and have provided information on the issues, rather than prescriptions. Since much depends on how health and social services are funded, their philosophical underpinnings, and what agenda drive review of care practices, such considerations are best left open, and the role of a chapter like ours on policy can only anticipate and point out areas that warrant discussion, decision, and action. In this chapter, we define the policy and related concerns that are being forced on all of us by a dramatic shift in the age composition of the population in general, and the population with intellectual disabilities, in particular. The higher prevalence of dementia of the Alzheimer type among persons with Down's syndrome and the longer lifespan of persons with other etiologies of intellectual disabilities are singled out for particular attention.

The reader is invited to consider whether or not agencies should obtain services for their clientele from the general care system (the aging or health care systems, for example) or through the development of specialist services within agencies that serve persons with intellectual disabilities. Should nursing home facilities be utilized for persons with dementia and intellectual disabilities when there is still disagreement about their effectiveness in caring for persons with Alzheimer's disease? A similar dilemma arises in considering utilization of specialized units for the care of affected individuals with intellectual disabilities because the literature suggests that there are no substantial differences in the needs of affected individuals with or without intellectual disabilities. The progressive nature of dementia leading to the need for complete care has confronted care providers with the unresolved policy question of how best to handle the changes in function from relatively independent, capable self-direction to complete functional incapacity and immobilization. These changes can occur in as short a time as 16 months and may last for as long as 20 years. Solutions are hard to find and the authors suggest that the prospects for the future are dim unless wide-ranging discussions and exchanges of ideas are conducted with the aims of developing comprehensive care and management practices. Advances will also require an examination of how the whole care and support system is distributed and managed. This activity may involve fundamental redistribution of staff, financial, and other resources. At the present time, strategic planning and resource allocation are yet undetermined, and little progress will be made without a better knowledge base about the changing demographics and detailed knowledge about the characteristics of affected individuals and their families, the patterns of service agency development and growth, service distribution, and service utilization patterns.

In Chapter 21, we—along with Henryk Wisniewski—provide a synthesis of the key points made by our contributors and where their thinking has taken the issues that drove this handbook in the first place. We have also taken the liberty to explore the future and make some suppositions about the next steps that need to be undertaken. Thus, in this last word, we offer a synthesis of what is known and projection into the future for what still remains to be uncovered. We trust that the final chapter of this book does justice to this end and will serve to stimulate new research inquiries and dialogues in the area of services and care policy.

Liz Kennedy Kendall
Christine Rinck
Linda Wright

Dementia Assistance Resources

Families and providers struggle with a complex service environment whose access becomes more confusing and remote when a dual diagnosis of dementia and intellectual disability occurs. This chapter describes relevant aspects of the aging, Alzheimer, and developmental disability networks that serve these populations. These networks operate on parallel courses which interface formally and informally through the coexisting responsibilities of professionals who work in their respective networks. Educational and support needs and their accessibility for persons with dementia and intellectual disability are described. The histories and capabilities of these networks to meet such needs are reviewed. Dementia-specific programs designed and currently operating are discussed with regard to their potential to be replicated or modified to serve persons with intellectual disability and dementia.

Families and providers typically find the service environment complex and often struggle to obtain accurate information about services and

Address correspondence to: Liz Kendall, Caregiving Program Specialist, Center on Aging Studies, University of Missouri-Kansas City, 5100 Rockhill Road, Kansas City, MO 64110-2499.

359

funding for the services they need (Advisory Panel on Alzheimer's Disease, 1993; U.S. Congress, 1990). When the combined diagnosis of dementia and intellectual disability is present, it is likely that access to services will be even more difficult and confusing than is experienced within either the intellectual disability or dementia care system. The aging, intellectual disability, and Alzheimer networks operate on parallel courses, but they often overlap in formal or informal ways through the multiple responsibilities of professionals involved within these networks. However, even though some confluence occurs, those dealing with both dementia and intellectual disabilities still run into numerous barriers in trying to access these networks. This is in part due to differing histories, funding streams, target populations, professional paths, and bureaucracies. To help better understand how to access resources related to Alzheimer disease and intellectual disabilities, this chapter describes some aspects of these networks. We give particular attention to dementia and later life issues and activities, enumerate some of the existing barriers to network access, and suggest approaches to resource access and cooperation. Further, we discuss education and support programs that have the potential to serve older persons with intellectual disability and dementia.

☐ Dementia, Alzheimer's Disease, and Aging in Intellectual Disability

Dementing illness is characterized by intellectual decline, behavioral symptoms, and personality change (Tariot, 1994; Grafstrom & Winblad, 1995). The most common cause of dementia is Alzheimer's disease, a progressive brain disease with no certain etiology or cure (Tariot, 1994). The prevalence of Alzheimer's disease increases with age, and it has been estimated that approximately 40% of those persons age 85 and older may have Alzheimer's disease (Evans et al., 1989; Evans et al., 1990). Researchers debate whether age at onset might describe subtypes of Alzheimer's disease, but this question remains to be answered (Brooks, 1995). Still, the relationship that exists between aging and increased risk for dementia, combined with the rapid increase in the older population in the United States, will have a profound impact on care systems.

Given the relationship between aging and the increased prevalence of Alzheimer's disease, it is also useful to note that the number of older adults with intellectual disabilities is growing (Altman, 1995). This trend and its implication for increased risk for dementia has been well recognized in the general population as well (U.S. Congress, 1990). Although chronological definitions may not accurately define aging in adults with intellectual disabilities, these individuals are likely subject to the same age-related changes as the overall population, including increased risk for dementing illnesses such as Alzheimer's disease (Evenhuis, this volume). Specifically, the coincidence of Alzheimer's disease and Down's syndrome has been recognized and studied (Dalton & Wisniewski, 1990; Lott, 1988). Yet, with all of this, it appears as if states and service providers are not prepared to meet the needs that these trends of longevity and their consequences will demand (Heller & Factor, 1995; Janicki, 1995).

Dementia Needs.   Reports prepared for the U.S. Congress by the U.S. Office of Technology Assistance detail the needs of persons with dementia and link the care needs of these individuals with a range of services (e.g., diagnosis, adult day service, hospice care) needed throughout the course of the illness (U.S. Congress, 1987; 1990). Further, this range of services is needed by persons with dementia regardless of the setting in which they live. Ideally the services should be available to people in both home and residential settings, including board and care assisted living, foster homes, and sheltered housing, as well as nursing homes (U.S. Congress, 1990). Unfortunately, this ideal service delivery system does not exist in most communities. Persons with dementia and their families must deal with a system that is fragmented, lacking in services, underfunded, or nonreimbursed by private and public payers (Petty, 1990).

Because of the fragmentation and gaps in service confronted by those who care for persons with dementia, including Alzheimer's disease, a 1990 congressional report called for a national uniform linking system (U.S. Congress, 1990). The report described various national organizations and agencies that provide information, education, and services for persons with dementia that might associate to create a national linking system. One of these organizations was the Alzheimer's Association (U.S. Congress, 1990).

The Alzheimer's Association.   This association is the largest national organization focused on dementia and the needs of carers (U.S. Congress, 1990). Established in 1981, the Alzheimer's Association developed as a nonprofit, self-help, voluntary organization for persons with Alzheimer's disease and their families. Community-based chapters, formed by family carers and caring professionals, work in concert with the national office staff to carry out the mission of the association. The Alzheimer's Association supports research, provides information, education, support and advocacy programs, as well as services for individuals with the disease. These programs and services are provided at local, state, and national levels. Both the Alzheimer's Association and its chapters target services and programs to family and professional carers, medical professionals, persons from public and private sector organizations, and other individuals who share the same concerns. Similar organizations exist in many other countries.

Lack of Programs.   Although the Alzheimer's Association does recognize other brain diseases that cause irreversible forms of dementia, few programs are specifically targeted at either national or chapter levels by the Alzheimer's Association to address dementias other than those associated with Alzheimer's disease. Further, the availability of informational materials, specific education or training programs, and services relevant to other dementias is not consistent throughout the Alzheimer's Association in the United States. In some cases, individual chapters may have developed non-Alzheimer's dementia-targeted programs, but these are not the norm. Further, information on intellectual disabilities and dementia is quite limited across the Alzheimer's Association network, and specific programs and services that target adults with these two conditions are almost nonexistent.

Given that considerable obstacles exist to creating links across dementia, aging, and intellectual disability organizations, the imperative still remains to attempt to build community services within existing programs. The 1990 congressional report contends that four components are needed in an effective linking system for people with Alzheimer's disease and other dementias; these include public education, information and referral, outreach, and case management (U.S. Congress, 1990). As conceptualized, this service structure would operationally assist the person and his family throughout the progression of the illness. Specific information and referral resources could relate to public awareness, diagnostic resources, family education and training, service identification and access, and professional education and training. If adapted further, such efforts would also address the diagnosis and care of persons with intellectual disability and dementia as well.

Diagnostic Process.   The need for a comprehensive assessment of older adults with an intellectual disability experiencing symptoms of dementia is comparable, within certain limits, to the needs experienced by other adults with similar presenting symptoms. Adults with intellectual disability, particularly those with Down's syndrome, may experience concomitant chronic conditions, such as early degeneration of the spine (Diamond, 1992), thyroid disease (Friedman, Kastner, Pond, & O'Brien, 1989; McCoy, 1992) and obstructive sleep apnea (Pueschel, 1992; Strome & Strome, 1992). Some of these conditions may present similarly to symptoms of dementia (Thorpe, this volume; Wherrett, this volume). Thus, differential diagnosis between dementia and depression can be problematic (Wisniewski, Hill, & Wisniewski, 1992; Burt, this volume). Given this, both diagnosis and care of persons with intellectual disabilities and dementia must encompass not only attention to dementia but also to the health-related problems of older persons with intellectual disabilities. In this framework, both the aging network and the Alzheimer's Association can serve as primary resources for information about the components of a comprehensive diagnostic work-up and often can provide resource lists of diagnostic centers, specialty clinics, and physicians capable of doing such work-ups.

Understanding the dynamics involved in cognitive testing and differential diagnosis of an individual with intellectual disability may call for additional education of the medical dementia-diagnostic community. The need for training for health care professionals concerning aging and resource access for persons with intellectual disability has been cited repeatedly (Jaskulski, Metzler, & Zierman, 1990; Crocker, 1989, 1992). Training and education in the diagnosis and care of dementia in persons with intellectual disability is recommended by the AAMR-IASSID Working Group on Intellectual Disability and Dementia (Janicki, Heller, Seltzer, & Hogg, 1995; 1996; see also Appendix, this chapter). To accomplish these ends, the aging, intellectual disability, and dementia-relevant networks should serve as resources to each other and work cooperatively with one another.

Diagnostic Clinics.   The number of clinics that focus on assessing adults with intellectual disabilities (including Down's syndrome) is beginning to grow. Some of these clinics are now also developing expertise in diagnosing Alzheimer's disease, other dementias, and associated aging conditions. Most are sponsored by universities or medical training facilities; others are run by local voluntary associations or agencies. Examples of such clinics and their operations are presented by Chicoine, McGuire, and Rubin (this volume) and Henderson, Ladrigen, Davidson, Bishop, Janicki, Miles, and Houser (1988). While the number of individuals with Down's syndrome and other intellectual disabilities in any geographic area may limit the viability of such clinics, specialized clinical services organized on a regional basis are necessary and should be made available.

Families Approach Support and Education.   When an individual is diagnosed with dementia, carers are confronted with the need for education about the illness and often seek long-range planning information and systems of support for the person and for themselves. For persons with intellectual disability the carer is often not a family member, but a provider, which differs from that of the typical aging population. While staff may be familiar with the intellectual disability network, their knowledge of aging resources is usually quite limited (Seltzer, 1994). And while there may be more similarities than differences, some characteristics of persons with intellectual disability and their families may influence their approach to education and support services (Seltzer & Krauss, 1995). For example, carers of persons with intellectual disability are often older parents unattached to services and so may be less aware of and less likely to seek education and support (Seltzer & Krauss, 1995). As a possible consequence, families caring for adults with intellectual disability may not recognize dementia symptoms and, regardless of resources available, may delay diagnostic or support services.

Sources of Information and Education. Basic information about dementia, especially Alzheimer's disease, is generally available from both national and local sources (see Table 19.1 and 19.2). The national office of the Alzheimer's Association, its chapters and the Benjamin Greenfield Library; Alzheimer's Disease Education and Referral Center (ADEAR); state, county, and local aging government agencies; libraries; private aging-related organizations; county extension programs; public health departments; and local universities and colleges are among the many potential resources for basic information about dementia. (Indeed, AD-EAR, 1993, quite concisely catalogues many of these resources.) However, much of the information received from these organizations is not targeted toward dementia in adults with intellectual disabilities. This type of information is now beginning to emerge from the national intellectual disabilities organizations (see, in particular, Marler & Cunningham, 1994; The Arc, 1995a, 1995b). Likewise, many of the educational programs made available to both families and professionals as an introduction to dementia do not have content on intellectual disability and dementia. There is an ongoing need for more dissemination of the resources of both the intellectual disability and dementia networks, especially those designed specifically for carers dealing with dual diagnoses.

☐ Programs with Cooperative Potential

Numerous dementia and aging agencies have developed support and educational programs for dementia. These offer potential adaptation, replication, or cooperation opportunities for the intellectual disability network.

Residential. Numerous residential options have been explored and developed over the past two decades to help persons with dementia in the general population. These options include adult day service, board, and care facilities; assisted living; shared living in private homes and institutions; and nursing homes, which may segregate dementia residents in

TABLE 19.1.   Aging Alzheimer network

Service	Agency
1. Adult Day Services Programs	Alzheimer's Association Chapters Brookdale Foundation Respite Program Health Care Organizations Public/Private Agencies or Programs Robert Wood Johnson Respite Program
2. Advocacy	Alzheimer's Association Chapters Alzheimer's Association National American Association of Retired Persons Chronic Care Consortium Families USA National Coalition on Aging National Council on Aging
3. Case Management Case/Care Coordination	Alzheimer's Association Chapters Area Agencies on Aging Mental Health Agencies Private Agencies-Social Service State Units on Aging
4. Differential Diagnosis of Dementia	Acute Care/Hospital Dementia Screening Clinic Alzheimer's Disease Research Centers Neurologists and Psychiatrists Private Practice Internists: General Practitioners, Neurologists, and Psychiatrists
5a. Education and Training: Family Caregivers Public Workshops, Forums	Alzheimer's Association Chapters Alzheimer's Association National Alzheimer's Disease Research Centers Area Agencies on Aging Public and Private Nursing Homes Universities and Colleges
5b. Education and Training: Materials: Brochures, Guides, Manuals, Videos	Administration on Aging Alzheimer's Association Chapters Alzheimer's Association National Alzheimer's Disease Education and Referral Center (ADEAR) American Association of Retired Persons Area Agencies on Aging Greenfield Library-National Alzheimer's Association National Institute on Aging
5c. Education and Training: (Conferences) Professionals, Practitioners, Providers	Alzheimer's Association Chapters Alzheimer's Association National Alzheimer's Disease Research Centers American Public Health Association American Society on Aging Association of Gerontology in Higher Education National Association of Area Agencies on Aging Public and Private Nursing Homes Universities and Colleges University Extension

TABLE 19.1. (continued)

Service	Agency
6. Helplines	Alzheimer's Association Chapters
	Alzheimer's Association National 800 Line
	Area Agencies on Aging
	State Units on Aging
7. Home Care	Area Agencies on Aging
	Churches
	Companion Programs
	Home Health Agencies
8. Home Chores/Delivered Meals	Area Agencies on Aging-Senior Centers
	Private Organizatins (Churches, Shepherd Centers)
9. Information and Referral	Alzheimer's Association Chapters
	Alzheimer's Association National
	Alzheimer's Disease Research Centers
	Area Agencies on Aging
	Private Agencies/Organizations (e.g., Pharmaceutical Companies)
	State Units on Aging
10. Legal and Financial Materials Education	Alzheimer's Association Chapters
	Alzheimer's Association National
	American Association of Retired Persons
	Area Agencies on Aging
	Legal Aid Societies
	Private Financial Consultants
	Private/Public Attorneys
	Social Service Agencies
	State Units on Aging
11. Research	Alzheimer's Association National
	Alzheimer's Disease Research Centers
	American Health Assistance Foundation
	National Institute on Aging
	State Alzheimer's Initiatives, Public and Private
12. Skilled Nursing	Public and Private Nursing Homes
13. Support Groups	Alzheimer's Association Chapters
	Alzheimer's Association National
	Private Long-Term Care Agencies
	Social Service Agencies

special care units or integrate them into the existing population (Heller, 1993; Kane & Wilson, 1993). The American Association of Retired Persons (AARP) published a study of board and care residences and found few regulations and very inconsistent programming and safety in such settings (Hawes, Wildfire, & Lux, 1993). Appropriate environments for dementia care have been avidly studied and will continue to be an important subject of research (U.S. Congress, 1990). For example, Calkins (1988) describes ways in which visual and textured stimuli serve as critical cues for daily activities. The national Alzheimer's Association Patient

TABLE 19.2.   Intellectual and developmental disabilities network.

Service	Agency/Organization
Advocacy	American Association on Mental Retardation
	The Arc
	National Down Syndrome Congress
	Protection and Advocacy
	Regional Centers
	University Affiliated Programs
Case Management	County Boards
	Occupational Centers/Vocational Rehabilitation
	Private/Public Agencies
	Regional Centers
	State Councils
Day Programs	Occupational Centers
	Private Agencies
Regional Centers	Occupational Centers
Education and Training: Families Public	Regional Centers
(Workshops, Forums)	University Affiliated Programs
Materials: Brochures, Guides, Manuals	Arcs-Local and National
	National Down Syndrome Congress
	University Affiliated Programs
Practitioners, Professionals, Providers	American Association on Mental Retardation
Conferences	The Arc
	National Down Syndrome Society/Congress
	University Affiliated Programs
Information and Referral	The Arc
	National Down Syndrome Congress
	Fanny Baker Center
	Regional Centers
	State Developmental Disabilities Councils
	University Affiliated Programs

and Family Services (1992a) has distributed a book describing ideal criteria for the institutional care of persons with dementia. Further, two Association publications *(Guidelines for Quality Alzheimer Care* and more recently, *Key Elements of Dementia Care)* expand this focus to include the entire continuum of residential care from retirement communities to skilled nursing. In the early 1990s, the National Institute on Aging (NIA) funded a series of studies of special care for dementia. Each of these studies focused on different aspects of care, such as environment, activities, and behaviors. The results of these studies have contributed to the continuing controversy about the definition and content of special care (U.S. Congress, 1992).

Respite.   Respite care evolved to fill gaps in the continuum of care and to provide relief to family carers providing primary care. Respite is a formal name for the types of assistance families, neighbors, and others provide when they help a family or person in need who is trying to live in the community or at home. In general, respite services are those intended to provide temporary relief for the primary carer; however, there is still active debate among government funded programs over eligibility, duration, and service elements. Anecdotal information from the Alzheimer's network and preliminary research on respite indicate positive outcomes including reduced carer stress, prolongation of care at home, and increased time for personal and family activities (Petty, 1990).

Respite programs may, in fact, benefit persons with intellectual disability and dementia. Senior centers that currently informally incorporate persons with intellectual disability and persons with dementia into center and community activities can formalize these by cooperative arrangements with neighboring occupational centers. Memorandums of agreement, regular combined staff meetings, shared training that crosses agencies and disciplines, and concerted marketing may also foster such cooperation. However, while the health and aging needs of older persons with intellectual disability and those of the general population are more similar than not, the heterogeneity of the populations pose administrative and programmatic demands that act as barriers to sharing such resources (Janicki, 1995). There may be no one method to support older persons and adults with intellectual disability, especially in light of their dependence on state and local policies for program development and sustenance (Lepore & Janicki, 1997). Occupational centers and other congregate work models that have begun to recognize this need and now offer leisure programs and community activities can augment and establish these in formal ways. Increased numbers of older persons with intellectual disability who can no longer sustain their jobs will need programs or other retirement age activities to provide meaningful leisure activities (Janicki et al., 1995). Meaningful activities are equally important to persons with dementia. Persons with dementia may be incorporated into occupational centers to assist in tasks or support older persons with intellectual disability or both who are needing additional supervision and help. Group home personnel and family involvement will enhance the planning and implementation of these possibilities.

Research on respite has included examinations of utilization, programming, training, and staffing. Several recent studies have demonstrated the effectiveness of respite care in the intellectual disability field where respite care is more often provided for young children than for older persons (Rinck & Eddy, 1988). However, an Illinois home-based support program found that when respite was available to them, carers of older persons with intellectual disability also experienced a decreased feeling of burden and need for out-of-home placement (Heller, Smith, Kopnick, & Braddock, 1992). A national evaluation of the Family Friends program identified many variables (e.g., stress, burden of care) that decreased when either a visitor or respite care program was implemented (Rinck, Naragon, & St. Clair, 1995). However, many families who provide care at home are still disengaged from formal systems and have not made use of available respite services. With the onset of dementia in someone with an intellectual disability in their care, this may eventually prove to be a significant problem (Smith, Fullmer, & Tobin, 1995).

Adult Day Services.   These services (previously referred to as adult day care) are a type of respite for families who are caring for family members who cannot care for themselves. An adult day services program can be defined as a community-based program designed to meet the needs of adults with impairment through an individual plan of care. It is structured, comprehensive, nonresidential, and provides a variety of health, social, and related support services in a protective setting. It reflects the assessed needs of participants and the program's ability to meet those needs. Participating individuals attend on a planned basis. By supporting families and other carers, adult day services programs enable participants to live in the community (National Council on the Aging, 1977). Adult day services are less restrictive than institutional care for individuals and can provide peer group support and social interaction not connected to other care settings, such as home care (Conrad, Hanrahan, & Hughes, 1990; see also Force & O'Malley, this volume). Although adult day programs initially served the needs of physically impaired, cognitively intact individuals, programs have now been established to specifically serve individuals with a dementing disorder. Many adult day programs now have a mix of dementia and nondementia participants (Conrad & Guttman, 1991). Although adult day services represent opportunities to serve persons with intellectual disability, by and large this is not currently done on a consistent basis. With regard to the Alzheimer's Association, chapters often train staff, refer families, and support adult day programs and a few operate companion in-home and adult day programs. Further, to identify best practice models, the Alzheimer's Association and Robert Wood Johnson Foundation jointly sponsored the National Respite Care Demonstration Project and Partners in Dementia, which was dedicated to the development of exemplary dementia-specific respite models (Alzheimer's Association Patient and Family Services, 1992b).

Adult Day Services for Persons with Intellectual Disability.   The nation's community-based senior services (including senior centers, nutrition sites, and community recreation programs) are generally designed for the well-elderly who are ambulatory and function with a high degree of autonomy. In many communities, adult day services for more dependent adults (including those with dementia) are either nonexistent or oversubscribed. When specialized Alzheimer's programs do exist, family members as well as administrators and staff of both adult day services and residential programs are often reluctant to include persons with intellectual disabilities. Partly due to the limited number of individuals with intellectual disability and Alzheimer's disease in each community, few specialty programs have been developed for this group. Further, limited staff experience with intellectual disabilities and subtle (or overt) discrimination are often factors discouraging inclusion of older adults with intellectual disability into local senior center activities. This leaves few viable formal options for an older person with an intellectual disability and dementia.

The social and medical models of adult day services that have been successful in serving adults with dementia and their family may need to be modified, enhanced, or replicated to address the needs of a person with dementia and intellectual disability (see Force & O'Malley, this volume). An initial step would be to identify such programs through relevant aging, Alzheimer's, and intellectual disability networks. Once staff from both networks recognize the need and potential for the integration of persons with intellectual disability into adult day settings, training and education that address the medical, social, and behavioral issues unique to persons with intellectual disabilities and dementia must follow. Inclusion must be ongoing with communication and mutual trust between staff and family. Support groups may be an additional source of comfort for families and providers. Well-trained activity directors and appropriate programming enhance adult day services.

Support Groups.   Such groups provide the foundation for many grassroots, self-help organizations. Self-help groups evolved as a means to address the lack of information and resources available to family carers. Support groups offer participants information, sharing of common problems, and emotional supports (Janicki, Heller, Seltzer, & Hogg, 1996b). Participants often benefit from the experiences of others dealing with similar illnesses and issues (Zarit, Orr, & Zarit, 1985). Support groups offer unique benefits to carers but may be most valuable as a part of an overall program. Support groups, however, may not help all individuals; some people may receive more benefit from one-on-one counseling (Zarit et al., 1985).

Dementia Support Groups.   Support groups have been the mainstays of local chapters of the Alzheimer's Association. Collectively, the Alzheimer's Association chapters sponsor thousands of support groups throughout the United States for family members and significant others. These groups are often cofacilitated by family carers with assistance from professional carers such as a social worker or nurse. Many have specialized foci, such as adolescents or newly diagnosed persons. Several association chapters sponsor support groups online. Those affiliated with the association meet basic standards, but often the expertise of the facilitator or format and evaluation of the process may not be consistent across the network.

Support Groups for the Intellectual Disability Network. Support groups for the parents of young children with intellectual disability are common. However, as the child becomes an adult, participation by families often declines. There are few, if any, support groups for families or carers for older persons with dementia and intellectual disability. The expertise, experience, and effectiveness of Alzheimer's Association support groups clearly have the potential to be shared or replicated or both throughout the network serving persons with intellectual disability and dementia. The more than 3,000 support groups and tens of thousands of participants within the Alzheimer network provide opportunities into which families and carers of persons with intellectual disability could be integrated. However, the interface between the two networks and the specific needs of carers for persons with intellectual disability would first need to be addressed.

Information and Referral. Many agencies and institutions offer resources for information on dementia (National Association of Area Agencies on Aging, 1996). The information and referral practices for persons with dementia from Alzheimer's Association chapters, area agencies on aging, private consultants, discharge planners, and other social service agencies offer multiple sources of information depending on the path carers or clients choose. Increasingly, many of these organizations extend comprehensive information online through the World Wide Web (for example, at //www.alz.org). The consistency of information provided is quite diverse. Some systems are linked by computers, such as the online interfaced capacities of all Alzheimer's Association chapters and their national office. Assistance given often depends on the training and information available to agency personnel and volunteers. Because of the nature of parallel networks, case managers need to stay abreast of the resources that are available. When it comes to advocating for individuals with an intellectual disability who have dementia, advocates relaying information or making referrals must be aware of resources that serve multiple populations, update these, and maintain regular communication among networks and agencies.

Case Management. The dynamic nature of dementia and the diverse needs of the populations complicate the management of care. In 1990, the Office of Technology Assessment reported great frustration over the many unmet needs that it found with regard to case management for persons with dementia (U.S. Congress, 1990). Further, one longitudinal study found that case management providing information on residential programs, financial plans, guardianship, family counseling, and respite was the highest unmet service need for adults with intellectual disability (Heller & Factor, 1993). Repeatedly, case management has been identified as a critical linchpin for both persons with dementia and adults with intellectual disability (U.S. Congress, 1990; Heller, Smith, Kopnick, & Braddock, 1992).

The changes in the way health care is and will be delivered in the United States will have an affect on case management. Now many organizations, such as long-term care insurance companies, managed care organizations, and private consultants are developing their own case coordination capacities. While the competition for clients may bring more attention and conscientiousness by sheer quantity, one might argue that numbers alone do not ensure quality or that needs will be met. More fragmentation may result in more confusion for the families and consumers. How this will all fall out is still uncertain.

Case Management and Intellectual Disability.   Case management has been a hallmark of care in the intellectual disability field. Almost all individuals served by state agencies receive some form of case management. Such case managers, however, are often not cognizant of dementias in an older population, nor of their diagnosis or care needs. Case managers within the aging network, Alzheimer's Association chapters, and other social service agencies and departments that serve persons with dementia are likely to be aware of dementia-specific support services; however, they are not consistently aware of resources for persons with intellectual disability. Family advocates may be the catalysts to insist on communication, referrals, and information exchange among case managers from different networks. Public policy at state and federal levels needs to address regulatory, reimbursement, and eligibility issues that intersect across these distinct populations.

The intellectual disabilities network has recently embraced person-centered planning as a vehicle for assuring individualized services (Heller, Factor, Sterns, & Sutton, 1996). Using this approach, anyone concerned with permanency planning for an older person with an intellectual disability, together with the person and all others involved, examines all related residential, financial, and legal implications (Heller & Factor, 1995). These topics are particularly relevant for adults with intellectual disabilities, even if they are currently living in a setting outside of their family's home. Planning for guardianship and residential changes needs to be conducted in an interdisciplinary milieu with the individual's desires taken into account. These services may be integrated into dementia case management programs or, at the least, be part of a coordinated referral component.

☐ Education and Training.

The Congressional Office of Technology Assessment reported that there is a great need for information and education for carers of dementia (U.S. Congress, 1990). The study of dementia caregiving has confirmed its high level of burden (George & Gwyther, 1986; Perlin, Mullan, Semple, & Skaff, 1990; Zarit, 1994). The positive outcomes and benefits of education, skill training, information, resource identity, and access for carers has been generally accepted (Schmall, 1994). There is recognition that older adult needs are most effectively addressed when providers have aging-specific knowledge and skill (Wendt & Peterson, 1992). The need to proffer education to professionals and families who plan and care for older persons with intellectual disability has also been established (Heller & Factor, 1995). Yet it has also been found that providers in the aging network are often unaware of issues in the intellectual disabilities field (Kultgen & Rominger, 1993). Many carers for persons with intellectual disabilities often report a need for information on a wide range of aging topics (Rominger, Mash, & Kultgen, 1990), including the intellectual disabilities system, how to access resources, introduction to the diverse range of disabilities, and help with better understanding behavior and communication strategies. The American Association of University Affiliated Programs' Task Force on Aging, as well as the AAMR/IASSID Working Group on Intellectual Disability and Dementia have recommended a focus on information, training, and education for professional and family carers of persons with dementia and intellectual disability (Davidson et al., 1987; Janicki, Heller, Seltzer, & Hogg, 1995, 1996).

Training for Intellectual Disability and Dementia. The symptoms of Alzheimer's disease, diagnostic process, implications for care, community resources, and effective coping strategies are topics for training sessions that could prove useful for the public and professional and family carers (Antonangeli, 1995; see the training package developed by the University of Stirling—McLennan, Murdoch, & McIntosh, 1993). The families of young and adult family members with intellectual disability should also receive education and support relating to Alzheimer's disease. Educational efforts should begin early, at minimum when their family member reaches their mid-30s, the age at which Alzheimer neuropathology may first appear in persons with Down's syndrome (see Evenhuis, this volume). However, information may not be available in all locales; persons may not identify themselves with the training subject or understand terminology; and the changes in policies may create difficulties in keeping resource identification and education current.

Existing Educational Efforts.   The national Alzheimer's Association and local chapters, Alzheimer's Disease International and the Alzheimer's Disease Research Centers, all drawing on the foremost experts in the field, have offered workshops, training manuals, conferences, and seminars on most aspects of dementia. Some conference presentations have included an overview of dementia and intellectual disability. However, these have been few in number. Intellectual disabilities agencies, regional centers, state councils, Alzheimer's Association chapters, and agencies on aging have begun to turn to one another for more information on intellectual disability and dementia. Those training programs that have emerged, have come predominately from the intellectual disability network and focus on aging changes and related programs and target professionals and paraprofessionals who serve persons with developmental disabilities.

Content and Format of Dementia and Intellectual Disability Training.   Interest from all networks is growing with the potential need for multidisciplinary education on aging, dementia, and intellectual disability. The content of such education should be both theory-based and practical. Content should include the following: backgrounds of aging, dementia, and intellectual disability networks; the aging process; and its impact on and implication for persons with intellectual disability. Content should also encompass the incidence, description, symptom/signs, risk factors, research foci, and community support and educational resources (local and national) for both Alzheimer's disease and Down's syndrome. Both common and differentiating issues of both populations should be articulated. Finally, content could reflect the caregiving, abuse, and ethical implications affecting the family, carer, and person with dementia or intellectual disability or both.

Content of training could be enhanced by attention to adult learning principles (e.g., appropriate audiovisual support, role playing, practical application, and appeal to the experiences of the audience). Inclusion of a variety of aging, Alzheimer's, and intellectual disability professionals and practitioners presents opportunities for on-site exchanges of interest, solutions, and referrals. Further, providing content regarding coalition-building can serve as a catalyst to its development. Training should be consistently offered several times per year and should be a cooperative venture among Alzheimer's, aging, and intellectual disability agencies.

☐ Coalitions

The aging and disability coalitions that have been most successful are those that are based on committed and sustained participation of diverse public and private community agencies and professionals. A foundation of common interests and needs for advocacy and services, mission, goals, and objectives and business plan and time line helps to fosters success. Involvement of participants in activities suited to their expertise and sustained interest may have more positive outcomes. Coalition leadership should include key community players and the responsibilities allotted should be equitably distributed and staffed. The inclusion of projects that focus on specific areas of interest, such as transportation or legislative interests that cross diverse populations, bode well for the continuation of a coalition. Training should be provided in the context of a coalition that crosses multiple networks. Educational components with topics of common interest could be used as an integral part of a meeting format or an occasional event. Coalescing around legislation that serves common interests may also be the focus. Although one agency initially assumes the leadership, responsibility should be passed equally among the network's participating agencies. Format for coalition meetings can vary; it may be an informal brown bag lunch gathering or formal structured meeting. However, the critical outcome is how the group works together and what it eventually accomplishes.

Existing Cooperative Initiatives.   One effort that united organizations concerned with aging, intellectual disability, and dementia was the Long-Term Care Coalition lead by the Alzheimer's Association in the late 1980s. This initiative brought together diverse networks, agencies, and disciplines and used the meetings to inform and advocate on behalf of long-term care. This model was first used in Washington, DC and was then replicated throughout the nation. Another, still ongoing, is the Annual Public Policy Forum that is sponsored by the Public Policy Division of the Alzheimer's Association (located in Washington, DC). This coalition provides ongoing training and strategies in state and local advocacy efforts on behalf of dementia and acts as a clearinghouse for public policy information and promotes coalition building. Such a national model could serve as a basis for future cooperation efforts that links these efforts to those concerned with the area intellectual disabilities. Another example of a broad range coalition is The Safe Return Program. This advocacy project, funded by the U.S. Department of Justice, was implemented through the Alzheimer's Association. The Safe Return Program is an example of a national coalition on a grand scale, for it has enrolled more than 27,000 persons and offers the potential to incorporate persons with intellectual disability and their families, agencies, and professionals who serve them (Alzheimer's Association, personal communication, 1997).

Development of Coalitions for Intellectual Disability and Dementia.   The Alzheimer's Association does not provide for all of the needs of individuals with Alzheimer's disease and their carers; however, the organization serves as a valuable resource for professional and family carers and those individuals with Alzheimer's disease. The Alzheimer's Association might likewise prove to be a helpful resource for those individuals with intellectual disability who, as they grow older, develop a dementing illness. The ability of the Alzheimer's Association to serve adults with both an intellectual disability and dementia will be enhanced if a successful partnership can be created between the Alzheimer's disease and the intellectual disability networks. Despite the fact that both the Alzheimer's disease and the intellectual disability networks are composed of committed families, volunteers, and professionals, their energies have been channeled into the rather specific interests of either persons with intellectual disability or of persons with dementia.

In order to find ways to work together, it may be necessary to rethink organizational programs and services, to find common areas of interest, to learn new concepts about the needs of individuals with dementia and intellectual disability, and to discover how partnership might strengthen rather than dilute the efforts of the two networks. This process will take thoughtful deliberation, cooperation, and program analysis in order to be successful.

Other Dementia-Specific Organizations.   There are organizations and networks beyond the Alzheimer's Association that theoretically could serve those with intellectual disability and dementia (see the Appendix, this chapter). Aging organizations and other groups and associations that serve individuals with dementia should be regarded as potential partners in the formation of coalitions for service. Although aging-related networks and organizations are found at local, state, and national levels, a philosophy that includes all older adults may not convert into services that are comprehensive enough to benefit the older adult with an intellectual disability and dementia. For example, May and Marozas (1994) studied the involvement of older adults with an intellectual disability in senior centers. They found that the needs of this population were not being adequately met by available community services, and that staff training was needed to provide for the varied needs of these older adults. Thus, even when services are being received, it is possible that many needs are not being met and that it will be necessary to adapt programs and services in order to address the needs of older adults with an intellectual disability (Coelho & Dillion, 1990).

International Interests. The more than 50 Alzheimer's disease organizations across the world have coalasced into an international network through Alzheimer's Disease International (see the Appendix, this chapter, for a listing). Its yearly conference brings together international scientists and practitioners who share their information on the research and programs currently in operation. There is also international cooperation in research and programming in the area of intellectual disability through the AAMR/IASSID Working Group on Intellectual Disability and Dementia. In addition, internationally, dementia-specific materials and videos have been developed and disseminated, but overall they appear to be less prevalent in other countries than in the United States.

Federal Aging and Dementia Research. Research on aging and dementia includes biomedical, clinical, and social science approaches. In the United States, the NIA has historically provided federal oversight and funding for research in the areas of aging and age-related diseases. While NIA has produced some educational materials focused on aging, such as "The Age Pages" (National Institute on Aging, n.d.), and invested considerable monies into dementia research, the NIA funding does not usually extend to service delivery, carer training, or support. This is the purview of the United States Administration on Aging which funds program evaluation and applied scientific endeavors.

NIA has funded more than 30 Alzheimer's Disease Research Centers (ADRCs), located in a variety of university settings throughout the country (Alzheimer's Disease Education and Referral Center, 1996). They offer clinical diagnostic and pathology services and some family and professional carer education, often sponsored with local Alzheimer's Association chapters. However, the main focus of the ADRCs is the instigation and support of Alzheimer's disease research projects. A few do have relationships with their local university-affiliated programs in developmental disabilities and offer limited research and educational opportunities for persons with intellectual disability and dementia (but this is not consistent across the country).

Alzheimer's Association Research. Advocacy efforts through the public policy arm of the Alzheimer's Association have lead to increased funding for Alzheimer's research; it is currently at $315 million nationally. Additionally, the national Alzheimer's Association's Medical and Scientific Advisory Board has granted more than $50 million to Alzheimer research since 1982. Brain chemistry, genetics, proteins, structural changes, nerve cells, behaviors, assessment, family dynamics, language, adult day care, and nursing home management are but a few subjects of study that have been funded over the last two decades (Alzheimer's Association, 1996). Although much emphasis has been given to finding a cause and productive treatment for Alzheimer's disease, this has not happened without some criticism. Some have complained that this effort has redirected funds that could have been made available for pure aging research (Adelman, 1995).

With regard to intellectual disabilities, the National Institute on Disability and Rehabilitation Research (NIDRR) funds research and demonstration projects, some of which focus on aging and disabilities. The Administration on Developmental Disabilities' university affiliated program network centers its research, programming, and education efforts generally in the area of developmental disabilities; however, little or none of this effort is directed toward pathological aging. Even with these efforts, research in the area of aging within the disability community and programmatic studies of care management and dementia are particularly lacking.

☐ Commentary

Rather than duplicate efforts and compete for limited resources, organizations that serve individuals with intellectual disability, as well as those that serve older adults and those that serve persons with Alzheimer's disease, should combine their efforts to benefit persons with dementia and intellectual disability. This could be done by tapping into the resources and bases of knowledge held by one another. However, to accomplish this, it will require a multilevel effort by the organizations, including building a base of knowledge and gaining an understanding of the philosophy, mission, and services offered by each group. In some instances, it may require adaptation of existing services to meet the needs of this special population, and in others, it will require the development of new services where currently none exist.

Unfortunately, the ideal of cooperation, coalition-building, and linking may be conceptualized more easily than operationalized. Studies of organizational behavior in a fragmented service environment indicate that the impetus of organizations operating in this type of system is toward maintaining the status quo and retaining prestige and power as opposed to developing cooperative interorganizational arrangements (Bolland & Wilson, 1994). Further, other variables may act to impede interorganizational cooperation, including the fear of loss of control and decision-making capacity. At the community level, the apparently successful growth of dedicated agencies to address specific problems (like Alzheimer's disease, aging, or intellectual disability) can serve as a disincentive to cooperative arrangements as each of the agencies competes for the same service dollars (Bolland & Wilson, 1994).

Despite such impediments, there are compelling reasons to cooperate. Inevitably diminishing public and private support for educational and support programs and materials will have to draw agencies into cooperative initiatives (Roybal, 1988). Common neuropathology, similar client behavioral issues, and unique professional competencies argue for the need for training across networks and disciplines (Seltzer &Luchterhand, 1994). Coalitions and cooperative projects may provide access to education and support resources for families and providers. These will happen if policy makers, scientists, providers, and families respond to individual needs on functional status rather than on chronological age; providers, and scientists from the Alzheimer's, intellectual disability, and aging networks acknowledge the benefits of joint research, shared programs, reciprocal referrals, and training across networks; and family carers and providers abandon stereotypes, misconceptions, and conceptions of turf, while remaining secure about their identities and affiliations within a given network.

☐ References

Adelman, R. C. (1995). The Alzheimerization of aging. *Gerontologist, 35,* 526–532.

Advisory Panel on Alzheimer's Disease. (1993). *Fourth report of the advisory panel on Alzheimer's disease* (NIH Publication No. 93-3520). Washington, DC: U.S. Government Printing Office.

Altman, B. M. (1995). *Elderly persons with developmental disabilities in long-term care facilities* (Monograph No. 95-0084). Agency for Health Care Policy and Research, Center for General Health Services Intramural Research, Washington, DC: U.S. Government Printing Office.

Alzheimer's Association. (1996). *Research in progress: Annual report on research grants.* Chicago: Alzheimer's Disease and Related Disorders Association (Medical and Scientific Department).

Alzheimer's Association Patient and Family Services. (1992a). *Guidelines for dignity: Goals of specialized Alzheimer/dementia care in residential settings.* Chicago: Alzheimer's Disease and Related Disorders Association.

Alzheimer's Association Patient and Family Services. (1992b). *Taking care: Alzheimer/dementia respite care experiences and advice.* Chicago: Alzheimer's Disease and Related Disorders Association.

Alzheimer's Disease Education & Referral Center. (1993). *Alzheimer's disease: A guide to federal programs.* Silver Spring, MD: Author.

Alzheimer's Disease Education & Referral Center. (1996). *Alzheimer's disease centers program directory.* Silver Spring, MD: Author.

Antonangeli, J. M. (1995). *Of two minds: A guide to the care of people with the dual diagnosis of Alzheimer's disease and mental retardation.* Malden, MA: Fidelity Press.

Bolland, J. M., & Wilson, J. (1994). Three faces of integrative coordination: A model of interorganizational relations in community-based health and human services. *Health Services Research, 29,* 341–366.

Brooks, J. O., III. (1995). A comment on age at onset as a subtype of Alzheimer's disease. *Alzheimer's Disease and Associated Disorders, 9*(1), S28–S29.

Calkins, M. P. (1988). *Design for dementia.* Owings Mills, MD: National Health Publishing.

Coelho, R. J., & Dillion, N. F. (1990). Older adults with developmental disabilities: An interdisciplinary approach to grouping for service provision. *Western Reserve Geriatric Education Center Interdisciplinary Monograph Series.* Cleveland, OH: Western Reserve Geriatic Education Center, Case Western Reserve University School of Medicine.

Conrad, K. J., & Guttman, R. (1991). Characteristics of Alzheimer's versus non-Alzheimer's adult day care centers. *Research on Aging, 13*(1), 96–116.

Conrad, K. J., Hanrahan, P., & Hughes, S. L. (1990). Survey of adult day care in the United States. *Research on Aging, 12*(1), 36–56.

Crocker, A. C. (1989). The spectrum of medical care for developmental disabilities. In I. L. Rubin & A. C. Crocker (Eds.), *Developmental disabilities: Delivery of medical care for children and adults* (pp. 10–22). Philadelphia: Lea & Febiger.

Crocker, A. C. (1992). Expansion of the health-care delivery system. In L. Rowitz (Ed.), *Mental retardation in the year 2000* (pp. 163–183). New York: Springer.

Dalton, A. J., & Wisniewski, H. M. (1990). Down syndrome and the dementia of Alzheimer's disease. *International Review of Psychiatry, 2,* 43–52.

Davidson, P. W., Calkins, C. F., Griggs, P. A., Sulkes, S., Burns, C., Chandler, C., & Bennett, F. (1987). The implementation of postgraduate training programs through state and local resources. *Research in Developmental Disabilities, 8,* 487–498.

Diamond, L. S. (1992). Orthopedic disorders in Down syndrome. In I. T. Lott & E. E. McCoy (Eds.), *Down syndrome: Advances in medical care* (pp. 111–126). New York: Wiley-Liss.

Evans, D. A., Funkenstein, H. H., Albert, M. S., Scherr, P. A., Cook, N. R., Chown, M. J., Hebert, L. E., Hennekens, C. H., & Taylor, J.O. (1989). Prevalence of Alzheimer's disease in a community population of older persons. *JAMA—Journal of the American Medical Association, 262,* 2551–2556.

Evans, D. A., Scherr, P. A., Cook, N. R., Albert, M. S., Funkenstein, H. H., Smith, L. A., Hebert, L. E., Wetle, T. T., Branch, L. G., Chown, M., Hennekens, C. H., & Taylor, J. O. (1990). Estimated prevalence of Alzheimer's disease in the United States. *The Milbank Quarterly, 68,* 267–289.

Friedman, D. L., Kastner, T., Pond, W. S., & O'Brien, D. R. (1989). Thyroid function in individuals with Down syndrome. *Archives of Internal Medicine, 149,* 1990–1993.

George, L., & Gwyther, L. (1986). Caregiver well-being. A multidimensional examination of family caregivers of demented adults. *Gerontologist, 26,* 253–259.

Graftstrom, M., & Winblad, B. (1995). Family burden in the care of the demented and nondemented elderly—a longitudinal study. *Alzheimer's Disease and Associated Disorders. 9*(2), 78–86.

Hawes, C. Wildfire, J. B., & Lux, L. J. (1993). *The regulation of board and care homes—Results of a survey in the 50 states and the District of Columbia: National summary.* Washington, DC: American Association of Retired Persons.

Heller, T. (1993). Community living options. In E. Sutton, A. Factor, B. Hawkins, T. Heller, & G. B. Seltzer (Eds.), *Older adults with developmental disabilities: Optimizing choice and change* (p. 185). Baltimore, MD: Paul Brookes.

Heller, T., & Factor, A. (1993). Aging family caregivers: Support resources and changes in burden and placement desire. *American Journal on Mental Retardation, 98,* 417–426.

Heller, T., & Factor, A. (1995). Facilitating future planning and transitions out of the home. In M. M. Seltzer, M. W. Krauss, & M. P. Janicki (Eds.), *Life course perspectives on adulthood and old age* (pp. 39–50). Washington, DC: American Association on Mental Retardation.

Heller, T., Factor, A., Sterns, H., & Sutton, E. (1996). Impact of person-centered later life planning training program for older adults with mental retardation. *Journal of Rehabilitation, 62*(1), 77–83.

Heller, T., Smith, B., Kopnick, N., & Braddock, D. (1992). *The Illinois home-based support service program evaluation report.* Chicago: University of Illinois at Chicago, Illinois University Affiliated Program in Developmental Disabilities.

Henderson, C. M., Ladrigan, P. M., Davidson, P. W., Bishop, K. M., Janicki, M. P., Miles, R., & Houser, K. (1998). *Comprehensive geriatric assessment for the evaluation of functional decline in adults and elders with intellectual disability.* Unpublished manuscript, Strong Center for Developmental Disabilities, University of Rochester School of Medicine and Dentistry, Rochester, New York.

Janicki, M. P. (1995). Policies and supports for older persons with mental retardation. In M. M. Seltzer, M. W. Krauss, & M. P. Janicki (Eds.), *Life course perspectives on adulthood and old age* (pp. 143–165). Washington, DC: American Association on Mental Retardation.

Janicki, M. P., Heller, T., Seltzer, G., & Hogg, J. (1995). *Practice guidelines for the clinical assessment and care management of Alzheimer and other dementias among adults with mental retardation.* Washington, DC: American Association on Mental Retardation.

Janicki, M. P., Heller, T., Seltzer, G. B., & Hogg, J. (1996). Practice guidelines for the clinical assessment and care management of Alzheimer's disease among adults with intellectual disability. *Journal of Intellectual Disability Research, 40,* 374–382.

Janicki, M. P., (1996). *Help for caring for older people caring for an adult with a developmental disability.* Albany: New York State Developmental Disabilities Planning Council.

Jaskulski, T., Metzler, C., & Zierman, S. A. (1990). *Forging a new era: The 1990 report on people with developmental disabilities.* Washington, DC: National Association of Developmental Disabilities Councils.

Kane, R., & Wilson, K. B. (1993). *Assisted living in the United States: A new paradigm for residential care for frail older persons?* Washington, DC: American Association of Retired Persons.

Kultgen, P., & Rominger, R. (1993). Cross-training within the aging and developmental disabilities services system. In E. Sutton, A. Factor, B. Hawkins, T. Heller, & G. B. Seltzer (Eds.), *Older adults with developmental disabilities: Optimizing choice and change* (pp. 239–256). Baltimore: Paul Brookes.

Lepore, P., & Janicki, M. P. (1997). *Wit to win: How to integrate older persons with developmental disabilities into community aging programs* (3rd rev.). Albany: New York State Office for the Aging.

Lott, I. T. (1988). Down's syndrome, aging and Alzheimer's disease: A clinical review. *Annals of the New York Academy of Science, 396,* 15–26.

Marler, R., & Cunningham, C. (1994). *Down's syndrome and Alzheimer's disease.* London: Down's Syndrome Association.

May, D. C., & Marozas, D. S. (1994). Are elderly people with mental retardation being included in community senior centers? *Education and Training in Mental Retardation, 29,* 229–235.

McCoy, E. E. (1992). Endocrine function in Down syndrome. In I. T. Lott & E. E. McCoy (Eds.), *Down syndrome advances in medical care* (pp. 71–82). New York: Wiley-Liss.

McLennan, J. M., Murdoch, P. S., & McIntosh, I. B. (1993). Dementia touches everyone: A guide for trainers and trainees in general practice. Stirling, Scotland: Dementia Services Development Centre, University of Stirling.

National Association of Area Agencies on Aging. (1996). *National directory of eldercare information and referral—1996–1997 directory of state and area agencies on aging.* Washington, DC: Author.

National Council on the Aging. (1977). *Standards and guidelines for adult day services.* Washington, DC: Author (National Adult Day Services Association).

National Institute on the Aging. (n.d.). *Bound for good health: A collection age pages.* Washington, DC: Author.

Perlin, L. L. I., Mullan, J. T., Semple, S. J., & Skaff, M. M. (1990). Caregiving and the stress process: An overview of concepts and their measures. *Gerontologist, 30,* 583–594.

Petty, D. M., (1990). Respite care: A flexible response to service fragmentation. In N. L. Mace (Ed.), *Dementia care: Patient, family and community* (pp. 243–269). Baltimore: The Johns Hopkins University Press.

Pueschel, S. M. (1992). The person with Down syndrome: Medical concerns and educational strategies. In I. T. Lott & E. E. McCoy (Eds.), *Down syndrome: Advances in medical care* (pp. 53–60). New York: Wiley-Liss.

Rinck, C., & Eddy, B. (1988). *Analysis of the purchase of service system of the Missouri Division of MR/DD.* Kansas City, MO: University of Missouri, Kansas City, Institute for Human Development, A University Affiliated Program.

Rinck, C., Naragon, P., & St. Clair, B. (1995). *Family friends: A national evaluation of six Administration on Aging sites.* Kansas City, MO: University of Missouri, Kansas City, Institute for Human Development, A University Affiliated Program.

Rominger, R., Mash, C., & Kultgen, P. (1990). *Planning for the 1990s: A survey of training needs regarding older adults with developmental disabilities.* Bloomington, IN: University Institute for the Study of Developmental Disabilities, A University Affiliated Program.

Roybal, E. R. (1988). Mental health and aging: The need for an expanded federal response. *American Psychologist, 43,* 189–194.

Schmall, V. L. (1994). A training and education perspective on family caregiving. In M. H. Cantor (Ed.), *Family caregiving agenda for the future* (pp.49–65). San Francisco, CA: American Society on Aging.

Seltzer, G. B., & Luchterhand, C. (1994). Health and well-being of older persons with developmental disabilities: A clinical review. In M. M. Seltzer, M. W. Krauss, & M. P. Janicki (Eds.), *Life course perspectives on adulthood and old age* (pp. 109–142). Washington, DC: American Association on Mental Retardation.

Seltzer, M. M. (1994). Education in gerontology: An avolutionary analogy. *Gerontologist, 14,* 308–311.

Seltzer, M., & Krauss, M. W. (1995). Aging parents with coresident adult children: The impact of lifelong caregiving. In M. M. Seltzer, M. W. Krauss, & M. P. Janicki (Eds.), *Life course perspectives on adulthood and old age* (pp. 3–18). Washington, DC: American Association on Mental Retardation.

Smith, G., Fullmer, E., & Tobin, S. (1995). Living outside the system: An exploration of older families who do not use day programs. In M. M. Seltzer, M. W. Krauss, & M. P. Janicki (Eds.), *Life course perspectives on adulthood and old age* (pp. 19–37). Washington, DC: American Association on Mental Retardation.

Strome, M., & Strome, S. (1992). Recurrent otitis and sleep obstruction in Down syndrome. In I. T. Lott & E. E. McCoy (Eds.), *Down syndrome advances in medical care.* (pp. 127–133). New York: Wiley-Liss.

Tariot, P. N. (1994). Alzheimer's disease: An overview. *Alzheimer's Disease and Associated Disorders, 9,* S4–S11.

The Arc. (1995a). *Developmental disabilities and Alzheimer's disease . . . What you should know.* Arlington, TX: Author.

The Arc. (1995b). *Q & A: Alzheimer's disease and people with mental retardation.* Arlington, TX: Author.

U..S. Congress, Office of Technology Assessment. (1990). *Confused minds burdened families: Finding help for people with Alzheimer's and other dementias* (OTA-BA-403). Washington, DC: U. S. Government Printing Office.

U.S. Congress, Office of Technology Assessment. (1987). *Losing a million minds: Confronting the tragedy of Alzheimer's disease and other dementias* (OTA-BA-323). Washington, DC: U.S. Government Printing Office.

U.S. Congress, Office of Technology Assessment. (1992). *Special care units for people with Alzheimer's and other dementias: consumer education, research, regulatory, and reimbursement issues* (OTA-H-543). Washington, DC: U.S. Government Printing Office.

Wendt, P. F., & Peterson, D. A. (1992). Transition in use of human resources in the field of aging. *Journal of Aging and Social Policy, 4*, 107–123.

Wisniewski, K. E., Hill, A. L., & Wisniewski, H. M. (1992). Aging and Alzheimer's disease in people with Down syndrome. In I. T. Lott & E. E. McCoy (Eds.), *Down syndrome: Advances in medical care* (pp. 167–183). New York: Wiley-Liss.

Zarit, S. (1994). Research perspectives on family caregiving. In M. H. Cantor (Ed.), *Family caregiving agenda for the future* (pp. 9–24). San Francisco, CA: American Society on Aging.

Zarit, S. H., Orr, N. K., & Zarit, J. M. (1985). *The hidden victims of Alzheimer's disease: Families under stress.* New York: New York University Press.

Appendix

☐ Listing of Resources

AAMR/IASSID Working Group on Intellectual Disability and Dementia
% American Association on
Mental Retardation
444 North Capitol Street, N.W.
Suite 846
Washington, DC 20001-1512
(202) 387-1968
1-800-424-3688
Webstie: www.thirdageinc/sirgaid

Administration on Aging
Department of Health and Human
Services
330 Independence Avenue, S.W.
Washington, DC 20201
(202) 245-0556
Website: www.aoa.dhhs.gov

Administration on Developmental Disabilities
Department of Health and Human
Services
Room 338-D, HHH Building
200 Independence Avenue, S.W.
Washington, DC 20201
(202) 690-6590
Website: www.acf.dhhs.gov/
programs/add

Alzheimer's Association
919 North Michigan Avenue
Suite 1000
Chicago, IL 60611-1676
(312) 335-8700 / (800) 272-3900
Website: www.alz.org

The Alzheimer's Association Public Policy Division
1334 G Street, N.W., Suite 500
Washington, DC 20005
(202) 393-7737

Alzheimer's Disease Eduation and Referral Center
NIAC P.O. Box 8250
Silver Spring, MD 20907-8250
(800) 438-4380

Alzheimer's Disease International
% Secretary General
45/46 Lower Marsh
London SE1 7RG
United Kingdom
(44) 171 620 3011
Website: www.alz.co.uk

American Society on Aging
833 Market Street, Suite 511
San Francisco, CA 94103-1824
(800) 537-9728, (415) 974-9600

384

**American Association on
Mental Retardation**
444 North Capitol Street, N.W.
Suite 846
Washington, DC 20001-1512
(202) 387-1968
Website: www.aamr.org

**American Asociation of
Retired Persons**
Disability Initiative
601 E. St., N.W.
Washington, DC 20049
(202) 434-2000
Website: www.aarp.org

American Society on Aging
833 Market Street,
Suite 511
San Francisco, CA 94103-1824
(415) 974-9600/(800) 537-9728
Website: www.asaging.org

**American Association of
University Affiliated
Programs (AAUAP)**
8630 Fenton St., Suite 410
Silver Spring, MD 20810
(301) 588-8252

**American Health Assistance
Foundation**
15825 Shady Grove Road
Suite 140
Rockville, MD 20850
(800) 437-AHAF, (301) 948-3244

The Arc of the United States
National Headquarters
500 East Border Street
Suite 300
Arlington, TX 76010
(817) 261-6003,
Website: www.arc.org

**The Baker International
Resource Center on Down
Syndrome**
10900 Euclid Avenue
Cleveland, OH 44106-4921
(800) 288-8804, (216) 368-8806

**Assisted Living Facilities
Association of America**
9411 Lee Highway, Suite J
Fairfax, VA 22031
(703) 691-8100

**CSAVR (Vocational
Rehabilitation)**
P.O. Box 3776
Washington, DC 20007
(202) 638-4634

**Gerontological Society of
America**
1030 15th St, NW
Suite 250
Washington, DC 20005-1503
(202) 842-1275

**Institute for Human
Development
University of Missouri—Kansas
City UAP**
2220 Holmes
Kansas City, MO 64108
(816) 235-1770

**National Adult Day Services
Association**
The National Council on the
Aging, Inc.
409 Third Street, S.W.
Suite 200
Washington, DC 20024
(202) 479-1200
Webstie: www.ncoa.org

National Aging Information Center (NAIC)
500 E. Street, N.W.
Suite 910
Washington, DC 20024-2710
(202) 554-9800
Website: www.aoa.dhhs.gov/naic

National Association of Developmental Disabilities Councils
1234 Massachusetts Ave., N.W.
Suite 103
Washington, DC 20005
(202) 347-1234
Website: www.igc.apc.org/NADDC

National Association of Protection and Advocacy Systems, Inc.
220 Eye St., N.E.
Suite 150
Washington, DC 20002
(202) 546-8202
Webstie:
www.protectionandadvocacy.com

National Association of State Directors of Developmental Disabilities Services, Inc.
113 Oronoco Street
Alexandria, VA 22314
(703) 683-4202
Website: None listed

National Association of State Units on Aging
20033 Eye Street, N.W.
Suite 304
Washington, DC 20006
(202) 785-0707
Website: None

National Council on the Aging
409 Third Street S.W.
Suite 200
Washington, DC 20024
(202) 479-1200
Website: www.ncoa.org

National Down Syndrome Congress
1605 Chantilly Drive
Suite 250
Atlanta, GA 30324
(404) 633-1555/(800) 232-NDSC
Website: www.members.carol.net/-ndsc

National Down Syndrome Society
666 Broadway
New York, NY 10012-2317
(212) 460-9330/(800) 221-4620
Website: www.ndss.org

National Institute on Aging
National Institutes of Health
Information Center
P.O. Box 8057
Gaithersburg, MD 20898-8057
(800) 222-2225
Website: www.nih.gov/nia

National Institute on Mental Health
Parklawn Building
5600 Fishers Lane
Rockville, MD 20857
(301) 443-4513
Website: www.nimh.nih.gov

Rehabilitation, Researach and Training Center on Aging with Mental Retardation
University of Illinois-Chicago
1640 Roosevelt Road
Chicago, IL 60608
(312) 413-1510
Website: www.uic.edu/orgs/
rrtcamr/index/html

U.S. Department of Health and Human Services
Public Health Service
Agency for Health Care Policy and Research
2101 East Jefferson Street
Suite 501
Rockville, MD 20852
(800) 358-9295

Matthew P. Janicki
Arthur J. Dalton

Dementia and Public Policy Considerations

The focus of this chapter is on the major public policy considerations related to the aging of adults with intellectual disabilities who evidence change due to dementia. Specifically addressed is the changing structure of at-risk adult populations with intellectual disabilities in service systems; the programmatic and policy issues raised by providers attempting to cope with these changes; needs for further training, education, and dissemination of information on aging; and, last, the challenges and policy imperatives to be confronted with the new millennium.

A dramatic shift in the age composition of the population of most developed nations will occur over the next 20 years. Where currently, from between 12 and 20% of these nations' populations is elderly, we will see the percentage climb in some nations to more than 30% (Kinsella & Taeuber, 1993; U.S. Department of Commerce, 1991). With increasing risk of age-associated dementia as populations age, these demographics portend a significant public health policy challenge (Evans et al., 1990). Until recently, the related focus of concern in the field of intellectual

Address correspondence to: Matthew P. Janicki, Ph.D., 31 Nottingham Way South, Clifton Park, NY 12065-1713. E-mail: janickimp@aol.com

Special appreciation to Debra Lamp of Oregon State University for sharing her experience with setting up a dementia-capable group home in Corvallis, Oregon.

disabilities singled out aging persons with Down's syndrome because they are uniquely at risk for developing Alzheimer's disease (Bauer & Shea, 1986; Eisner, 1985; Ellis, McCulloch, & Corley, 1974; Haberland, 1969; Heston, 1984; Jenkins, Hildreth, & Hildreth, 1993; Owens, Dawson, & Losin, 1971). This focus has now broadened to include all adults with an intellectual disability because as greater numbers of people with intellectual disabilities live to an old age, are in community settings, and with increasing age are at demonstrative risk of a compounding disability resulting from Alzheimer's disease and other dementias, the presentation of dementia as a diagnostic and care issue has gained momentum (Antonangeli, 1995b; Deb & Janicki, 1995; Janicki, 1994; Koenig, 1995a, 1995b, 1995c; The Arc, 1995).

Thus, the focus of this chapter will be on the major public policy considerations related to the aging of adults with intellectual disabilities who evidence change due to dementia. Specifically, we will address the changing structure of at-risk adult populations with intellectual disabilities in service systems; the programmatic and policy issues raised by providers attempting to cope with these changes; needs for further training, education, and dissemination of information on aging; and last, the challenges and policy imperatives facing us with the new millennium.

☐ Emergence of an At-Risk Population

Emergence of onset of dementia at a relatively earlier age (when most adults are still working or involved in other gainful activities) is one reason why care systems are concerned with the rate of dementia among adults with Down's syndrome (Visser, Aldenkamp, van Huffelen, Kuilman, Overweg, & van Wijk, 1997; Wisniewski & Merz, 1985; Zigman, Silverman, & Wisniewski, 1996). Certainly, it is alarming when a significant portion of the adult population of persons with an intellectual disability is experiencing diminished abilities and premature death at a time of their lives when others are still learning and gaining from life experiences. The potential implications for staffing and financing services are enormous. Yet, even with precocious aging and early signs of Alzheimer's disease among adults with Down's syndrome, they are not the only group at risk of dementia. Adults, with etiologies other than Down's syndrome, are progressively evidencing higher rates of survival (Strauss & Eyman, 1996; Janicki, Dalton, Henderson, & Davidson, 1996, in press) and thus are living to the point where heightened risk for Alzheimer's disease or other dementias is also a concern. As increased age poses a greater risk for the onset of dementia and with successive generations of adults with intellectual disabilities living longer, expectations are that the rate of Alzheimer's disease and other dementias may approach or equal that of the general population.

Further, even among the dementias, differential patterns are a rising concern. For example, the type of dementia primarily seen among adults with Down's syndrome is mostly attributable to Alzheimer's disease, and because adults with Down's syndrome are younger when affected, the onset and course patterns are atypical (Visser et al., 1997). Only when we look at the overall population of individuals with intellectual disability do we begin to see patterns of a more normative distribution of dementia and onset and course at ages more consistent with those of the general population. For example, in one systematic statewide survey of the prevalence of dementia among some 27,000 adults with intellectual disabilities, Janicki and Dalton (1997a, 1997b, 1998) found that of adults age 40 and older, 60 and older, and 80 and older, some 3%, 6%, and 12%, respectively, were identified as having either diagnosed or suspected dementia. Of those identified as having dementia, about one-third were adults with Down's syndrome. Overall, dementia in adults with Down's syndrome was present in about 20% of the adults over age 40 and in about 60% of adults over age 60. The authors noted that with increasing age, the proportional prevalence of dementia among adults with other intellectual disabilities increased similarly to that of the general population. The implication of these data is that when compared with the general population, with increasing age, adults with Down's syndrome show a higher than expected rate of occurrence of dementia, but that adults with etiologies for intellectual disability other than Down's syndrome show a more typical rate of occurrence.

Janicki and Dalton (1998) also revealed a clear dichotomy of diagnosed (48%) and suspected (52%) dementia, suggesting that physician-diagnosed dementia was present in only about half of the group. Among the diagnosed group, adults with Down's syndrome were more apt to have dementia of the Alzheimer type (DAT—77%), while the adults without Down's syndrome had a variety of dementias (e.g., 26% had DAT; 34% had nonspecified dementia). The duration of dementia also varied. Some 85% of the Down's syndrome group had been diagnosed within the past three years, while only 55% of the non-Down syndrome group had been. Janicki and Dalton (1994) also noted that most referrals for diagnosis originally come about as a result of staff suspicions and that staff indicated a high need for training in raising the "index of suspicion." Others, too, have reported that with increasing frequency, agencies are finding more individuals in their care who are evidencing dementia and that staff need training for coping with the demands of dementia care (Koenig, 1995a;

Hammond & Benedetti, this volume; Udell, this volume; Visser et al., 1997). These reports, albeit preliminary, are indicative of a growing trend.

Increased longevity is adding to the issue. Recent reports are documenting lifespan increases for adults with intellectual disabilities (Janicki et al., 1996; Janicki, Dalton, Henderson, & Davidson, in press). The mean age at death was 66 years for a group of 2,750 adults with intellectual disabilities (Janicki et al., 1996; 1998). This compared with the mean age of death of 56 for adults with Down's syndrome in the same group, a finding which was consistent with a contemporary report based on the study of individuals in the Netherlands (Visser et al., 1997). These data reflect a lengthening of average lifespan over reports published in the 1970s and 1980s (e.g., Carter & Jancar, 1983). Thus, expectations are that with increased survival rates of older adults with intellectual disabilities, coupled with greater numbers of survivors among the current "baby boomers," there will be an increased probability that dementia and other old age associated decline will be a significant challenge to care systems. Additionally, with dementia rates approaching 40% by the time adults in the general population are in their late 80s (Evans et al., 1989; Evans et al., 1990), this increase in the numbers of old age survivors with intellectual disabilities and the potential for higher rates of dementia among these adults should be worrisome for care systems.

Dementia is becoming more prevalent and is being recognized as a challenging problem among intellectual disabilities providers because many agencies are ill-prepared to accommodate the diagnostic and care needs of individuals who are at risk of or evidence onset of dementia. This is reinforced by a recent survey of state intellectual disabilities agencies in which it was found that few state intellectual disabilities agencies had policies related to dementia assessment or care (Janicki, 1996). What, then, are some of the consequences of this lack of preparedness? At the level of the individual providers, it may mean that few will have information on where to turn to in the intellectual disabilities system for guidance on the provision of appropriate services. The alternative source for such information may be the aging or health care systems. Yet these generic services have financing, administrative, and implementation structures that are quite different from those found in the disabilities field. Further, they may not see adults with intellectual disabilities as their source of clientele and expect the intellectual disabilities agencies to provide for this population. Given this, the issue is unresolved as to whether intellectual disabilities providers should look to such generalist providers or develop their own organizations that offer such specialized services to individuals with intellectual disabilities.

☐ Programmatic and Policy Issues

Generalist vs. Specialist Care

With regard to providing supports for older adults with intellectual disabilities, a prominent policy issue is where to seek services. Should providers seek services within the generalist system (whether the aging network or health care system) or develop specialist services within the intellectual disabilities system? When considering supports for aging problems, or dementia care, this issue becomes particularly acute. With the expected growth of the older population there will be a significant demand for services related to supports for old age and dementia care. Yet, currently in the United States, there is no stable source of funding that underwrites in-home supports or respite for family carers who need aid with dementia care, nor is there funding for dementia care in small group community care settings. The predominant models, support groups for carers and adult day services for respite care, when available, are not always within the financial means of most older families. In most states, adult social day services are poorly underwritten and depend mostly on local resources and user fees. Adult day health model programs, providing services on a physician's prescription, exist and are funded by Medicaid or day hospitalization financing schemes. Yet even these services are not prevalent, and many are being cut back following diminished support or decreased reimbursement rates because of the restructuring of the U.S. health care system. At the same time, managed care organizations, which are becoming more prominent, have yet to assume responsibility for provision of adult day services or reimbursement for its use by subscribers. Even though there is some availability, the poor state of adult day services in the United States means that the generalist structure will not be able to absorb the growing number of adults with intellectual disability who manifest dementia and need supervised care during the day (Administration on Aging, n.d.). At the same time, many state mental retardation agencies are dismantling their infrastructure of day services in favor of buying care in generalist services or programs under the home- and community-based waiver program (Government Accounting Office, 1996). However, when it comes to dementia care, there is often no place from which to purchase these services. This decrease in day program availability will mean that when greater numbers of adults are emerging who need dementia-related supervised day services, the specialist system which is decreasing its base for specialty services will not have the program capacity, nor, unless greatly increased efforts at expansion are undertaken, will the generalist system.

The obvious impact will be on residential care providers and families with whom these individuals are living. With diminished community care resources, residence providers will have to absorb the cost of day care since they have primary responsibility (alternatively, the long-term health care system may become the primary carer). Yet in most states, housing reimbursement rates do not take into account the increased need for 24-hour staffing for persons aging in place or who have retired, nor for the augmented individualized programming which may be required for house residents with dementia. The same applies for supports given to family carers. The tragedy for families will be acutely felt as aging families are confronted with new care demands at a time when they are expecting their sons or daughters to be able to help them in their old age, as they experience their own frailty, diminishing capacities for coping, and reduced personal and financial resources (Freedman, Krauss, & Seltzer, 1997). Many will be forced to seek admission to nursing facilities for their son or daughter because the alternatives are unavailable. Thus, while some generalist services are available, it is not expected that without a marked increase in capacity, they will be able to absorb the growing number of older adults with dementia needing this type of care. Also, if these capacities are made available, they will only apply to adults with early- to midstage dementia. This still does not address care demands for late-stage dementia.

The use of nursing facilities poses another dilemma. For the most part, these settings have become the repository of older adults with dementia from the general population. Some have recognized the need for specialized care and have begun to develop Alzheimer's special care units or group living programs (Mor, Banaszak-Holl, & Zinn, 1995; Annerstedt, 1993; 1997). These units depend on specially trained personnel and specialized environmental modifications that enhance the autonomy and quality of life of residents while at the same time reducing health and safety risks that arise from wandering, physical abuse, stealing and hoarding, and other problems associated with mid- to late-stage dementia. Yet even though these specialized units may offer a more directed focus for management of dementia patients, the gerontological literature is not in agreement on their feasibility or effectiveness (Sloan, Lindeman, Philipps, Moritz, & Koch, 1995). Further, the use of nursing facilities may be problematic as many such facilities are ill-equipped to deal with seriously challenging behaviors which are prevalent among adults with dementia of the Alzheimer type (Jakubiak & Callahan, 1995; Annerstedt,

1993). Many do not offer specialized care and offer only custodial and related support services to persons with intellectual disabilities (who often need specialized services). Thus, many families are left with few service options when they most need settings that can handle dementia care in a humane and supportive manner. This problem becomes even more acute when admission is sought on behalf of an older person with an intellectual disability. Admittedly, while many such facilities can provide basic care in a manner that is of acceptable quality and do so against remarkable odds (in spite of low budgets, staff changes, lack of training in intellectual disabilities), others lack staff or training capacities to accommodate the special needs of adults with intellectual disabilities and dementia (Department of Health and Social Services, 1995). Thus, in some sectors, these facilities offer a poor resource or none at all.

Developing specialist programs offers a different set of challenges. If specialist program availability is present or support programs are in place, how should dementia care management be practiced in such settings? Generally, little or no mention is made in the generic care literature of care for adults with intellectual disabilities, yet the interest in this area is growing rapidly (Antonangeli, 1995a, 1995b; Janicki, 1995; Janicki, et al., 1996; The Arc, 1995; Noelker & Somple, 1993; Marler & Cunningham, 1994). Is there a substantial difference in care management practices as applied to adults with intellectual disabilities? From an examination of the intellectual disabilities literature, the answer is "no." If this is the case, why place a distinct focus on specific dementia services for those with intellectual disabilities? The most practical reason is that because the intellectual disabilities system is a dedicated system, changes in care practice of individuals' aging in place takes on more import. In the general population, care prescriptions are either for continued care by families (and this applies to adults with intellectual disabilities as well) or for admission to long-term care settings. Thus, the transfer from being under one's own direction to a care setting addresses the issue of specialization. In the intellectual disabilities field the care is linear and transfers only in fashion and not intersetting. What is clearly evident is that because the intellectual disabilities system generally provides both financial and programmatic supports for adults, concerns over changes in capabilities and continued independence are raised by the onset of dementia.

As dementia related to a disease process progresses, significant changes in supports have to be put in place. These responses to aging in place have generally been unplanned or unexpected, for the intellectual disabilities system expects either static or continued development and ever-growing independence following interventions, supports, or programs and does not easily accommodate to functional decline. Diminishing abilities create a demand for more staff time and supervision, a change in the level of intensity of programs or supports, and potentially a change in residence (and potentially greater costs for care). One of the unresolved policy areas is how to constructively handle diminishing abilities among persons who had been relatively independent and capable of extensive self-direction. Philosophical and pragmatic considerations become mired in a need for personal care which becomes more intense and necessary each year following the onset of progressive dementia. As dramatically revealed by Davis (this volume), Hammond and Benedetti (this volume), Udell (this volume), and others (e.g., Visser et al., 1997), adults with Down's syndrome can experience an early and precipitous decline and, because of this immediacy, care management practices can take their toll on family and staff resources (Service, Lavoie, & Herlihy, this volume). Others, with different etiologies, will have a later onset and longer duration of decline, taxing intellectual disabilities agency resources in a different manner (such as prolonged care with progressively diminished capacities). Thus, how to anticipate and manage care in these situations is an issue.

Care Practices

The foregoing considerations suggest that the prospects for the future are dim unless wide-ranging discussions and exchanges of ideas are conducted with the aims of developing comprehensive care and management practices. A major step in this direction was taken with the convening of an international colloquium in 1994 on the subject of Alzheimer's disease and intellectual disabilities (Deb & Janicki, 1995; Janicki, 1994). It was quickly recognized that there was no solid base of knowledge on the criteria for diagnosis, nor a consensus on methods for the care and management of dementia, nor agreement on the prevalence, incidence, and risk factors for dementia among persons with intellectual disabilities. Given the absence of any formal practice guidelines in the area of intellectual disabilities, clinicians and carers have had little guidance that proffered specific suggestions for assessment prior to, and service provision following, the diagnosis of Alzheimer's dementia among adults with mild or moderate intellectual disabilities. As a result, services often were a patchwork of methods based on anecdotal evidence and trial and error, and many adults with intellectual disabilities and Alzheimer's dementia were being referred unnecessarily to long-term care settings. Further, because such settings lacked familiarity with intellectual disabilities, admissions were often inappropriate, care was overly restrictive, and both factors contributed to a hastening of functional decline.

Together with available information with regard to care, management, and diagnostics (e.g., Harper, 1993; Holland, Karlinsky, & Berg, 1993;

Kultgen & Holtz, 1992; Newroth & Newroth, 1981; Noelker & Somple, 1993), it was acknowledged that one solution to this was the application of modifications of those practices that guide diagnostics and treatment of individuals with dementia from the community at large. Colloquium participants noted that with the continued emphasis on providing personalized supports to adults with intellectual disability in their communities and the increasing lifespan of people with intellectual disability, the occurrence of Alzheimer's dementia would continue to have a profound impact on many social agencies and families. Given the lack of direction in the social, mental health, and intellectual disability service systems, it was recommended that a set of practice guidelines be developed that would suggest methods for diagnosis and for the provision of care to persons with intellectual disability and dementia. The availability of such guidelines would prevent scarce resources from being misdirected or wasted because agencies were unfamiliar with how to best access or provide supports to adults with intellectual disability and Alzheimer's disease.

The AAMR/IASSID practice guidelines (see Appendix 1) that resulted from this colloquium (Janicki, 1995; Janicki, Heller, Seltzer, & Hogg, 1996) recommend an initial and periodic dementia screening, advise when to obtain a more thorough diagnostic assessment, and then provide suggestions regarding the provision of dementia-specific services. The guidelines suggest a three-step process to follow: recognize changes, conduct assessments and evaluations, and institute medical and care management. In large part, the AAMR/IASSID guidelines draw from the care model adopted by the Alzheimer's Association in the United States (Alzheimer's Association, 1994), which considers attitudes and assumptions about aging in place, safety versus risk, expectations for individualization of services, and appropriateness of family roles. To emphasize consistency with prevailing practice in the field of intellectual disabilities, the guidelines used the following assumptions: each person's needs must determine how care is provided; age-associated changes are a normal part of life; persons with Down's syndrome are at greater risk for Alzheimer's disease; some behavioral changes may look like Alzheimer's dementia but may be due to other causes and be reversible; and the individual's own abilities and levels of function should be the basis for evaluating subsequent changes (Janicki, 1995; Janicki et al., 1996). The guidelines were complemented by three additional reports produced by the AAMR/IASSID workgroup, including one on diagnostics (Aylward, Burt, Thorpe, Lai, & Dalton, 1995, 1997; see also Burt & Aylward, this volume), one of instrumentation (Burt & Alyward, 1998), and one on epidemiological considerations (Zigman, Schupf, Haveman, & Silverman, 1995, 1997). Given their comprehensiveness, these guidelines (and other guidance materials currently in distribution, e.g., The Arc, 1995; Koenig, 1995a,

1995b, 1995c; Marler & Cunningham, 1994) can provide the foundation on which many care systems can base planning, program development, and everyday care practices. The question remains as to what specific settings or care may be most useful for addressing dementia in persons with intellectual disabilities and in which these practice guidelines may apply.

Specialty Service Capability Issues

Care systems wrestle with the challenge of having to provide care for dementia, particularly since the prevailing form of dementia, linked to Alzheimer's disease, is slow and progressive and results in severe loss of skills and capabilities and then death. Although early-stage care practices may be less taxing, late-stage care practices call into question how agencies can adopt new care practices and restructure their staff and services, and whether they will need to seek services elsewhere. Several alternative strategies of prolonged care are worth exploring with regard to adults with intellectual disabilities. In the general population, dementia care practices are accommodated in a range of settings, including informal in-home care, formal in-home care supports, respite and adult day services programs, and formal specialized group living programs and institutional long-term care settings (e.g., nursing facilities).

The services provided in support of informal caregiving for dementia generally are the same as those for other dependent care needs of adults with an intellectual disability (i.e., respite, in-home supports, transportation). With regard to formal settings, the issue is more of the appropriateness. For example, with regard to adults in the general population, one may ask, why do these adults end up in long-term care settings? Outside of major postoperative or specialized nursing care, most older adults do so because they can no longer care for themselves and their informal support structure has broken down (Mittelman, Ferris, Shulman, Steinberg, & Levin, 1996). The example of the surviving spouse, with diminishing stamina and spirit, who can no longer cook or provide for self-care and who has no proximate family is typical. In such a situation, the nursing facility serves as a board and care option, with medication and health management as add-ons. The threshold for admission to such facilities is generally set in state regulations or policies and involves the use of a screening instrument. Such instruments look for loss of abilities in activities of daily living (ADLs) and instrumental activities of daily living (IADL) and note the need for basic personal care assistance and the absence of direct support from family members. In most states, adults with an intellectual disability easily pass through these nursing facility screens, as their ADLs and IADLs and personal care levels are generally already below or at the threshold for admission (Governor's Commission on Mental Retardation, 1996). However, most adults with an intellectual disability, unless living alone or with their family, have some degree of formal or informal supports available and generally do not need admission. These support structures, exemplified generally by small group homes and structured supports for independent living, are often the envy of senior services advocates, for they include safe and decent housing, meals, activities, and, in group homes, a staff ratio that can provide for around-the-clock care and supervision. Thus, with these support aspects in place, what drives requests for admission to nursing facilities in the intellectual disabilities system?

The notion of "threshold" is a probable answer. In the general population, families who find they can no longer cope with providing primary care for a relative with mid- to late-stage dementia request help with admission to a long-term care facility (Mittelman et al., 1996). At what point do staff of a residence for adults with intellectual disabilities come to the same conclusion? When this type of question is raised, then the answer most likely is that the core element of the threshold for long-term care setting referral cannot be the *nature of care* but the *tolerance* and *capability* of staff. For the nature of care can always be adjusted, just like it is for anyone who lives at home and who is sick. But sickness is temporary and the wear and tear on staff who offer personal care in times of illness may not be comparable with that when the duration is the balance of one's life. Residence program administrators note that the nature of care will often vary from residence to residence, even when the program structure of the residence and the character of the residents are reasonably equivalent. These same administrators note that the threshold for referral to a nursing facility has been shifting upward—often unquantifiably—but shifting upward, so that overall staff tolerance for increased care has been noticed. The threshold issue comes down to what degree is each agency willing to accept lifetime care management and adapt care practices accordingly when adults age, potentially experience a decline in skills, and develop new care demands. Generally, such a commitment is present when planning care for children. However, care of adults with dementia is a good example of equivocation on this lifelong care commitment.

If a commitment for lifetime care of persons with dementia is made, then administrative and staff practices need to be redefined. This may involve a fundamental redistribution of staff and other resources. It may also involve a reexamination of how the whole care and support system is distributed and managed. Many agencies have expressed concerns over assignments of staff and training needs for both direct care staff and managers in dementia care. Staff who were originally hired for one function may find their jobs redefined as they take responsibility for more adults with dementia. Physical changes also pose new demands. For example, many agencies note that they have observed losses in physical movement or mobility and that they are in a quandary over how to redesign the housing to make it more barrier-free. The solution to this problem is usually driven by money (i.e., limited renovation budgets) and is affected by limitations in physical plant (i.e., problems due to stairs, room layouts, etc.). This problem is often made worse in areas where multistory buildings constitute housing for most, if not all, of the residents.

Programs for older adults can help. Activities can be directed toward adapting and extending models currently in use and providing enhanced services. For example, most localities have small group homes where full or limited supervision is available. With the onset of dementia and an understanding of its duration and course, agencies could plan and project supportive care using "aging in place" models, drawing up the same innovative supports that are offered by the aging network for the community care of others with Alzheimer's disease. Under these models, older adults could remain in their homes, and staff as well as technological and environmental enhancements could be added. This would mean training staff to make them "dementia capable," making physical changes to the dwellings to make them more usable when losses due to dementia take place (for example, in room design and color choices, door controls, and name signs; see Olsen, Ehrenkrantz, & Hutchings, 1996), and enhancing supports to the homes so that staff can cope with the changing demands of dementia care. This approach can also apply to families; parents and other carers can be afforded supports for as long as they are capable of providing extended care.

In communities where small speciality group homes are not readily available, agencies might consider developing new or adapting existing *assisted living* residences. Like the housing in the intellectual disability system, the assisted living model provides for or coordinates flexible personal care services, and offers 24-hour supervision and assistance, activities, and health-related services in a small group living environment (Alzheimer's Association, 1996; Wilson, 1996). Such settings are generally designed to provide a safe environment and supports for aging in place, with consumer autonomy and preferences, as well as community governance, as principal features. As many assisted living residence programs also offer dementia care, physical space and staffing adaptations would permit using this model for early- to middle-stage dementia care. For late-stage care, extended care programs generally have been the norm. However, as applied to adults with intellectual disabilities already in supported housing, small dedicated group homes with special care staff could be used (see the vignette for an illustration of one such effort.)

If consideration is to be given to a specialty care setting for adults with intellectual disability, it is important to consider the two unique facets of a dementia care model; one, that dementia (particularly that resulting from Alzheimer's disease) is a condition that is progressive and ever-diminishing abilities are an expectation, and two, that cognitive function is severely compromised even though the person remains ambulatory. The focus, thus, is on compensation for cognitive loss and disorientation and primary care practices should support safety, mobility, and serve to protect against disease. A question, however, remains as to how to handle community care for early stage dementia when aging in place is the norm. Do agencies enhance supports to the home or setting in which an affected adult resides or do they ask the individual to move to a setting better equipped to handle such care? Udell (this volume) considered this dilemma. She also recognized that, with increasing numbers, whether adults with dementia care need die in their own dwellings or after being relocated to homes with dementia care capability, the toll of recurring deaths on house mates and staff has to be considered. How the intellectual disability system will cope with this new phenomenon on a large scale is unknown.

☐   Vignette: An Oregon Experience

The project started a couple of years ago when I met two housing managers working for an intellectual disabilities organization in western Oregon. During our discussion it came up that they were unsure of how to deal with an adult with Down's syndrome who had been diagnosed with Alzheimer's disease. I volunteered to help train their staff in strategies that could be used to provide care for him. During the course of these trainings and meetings I suggested some environmental modifications that could be used to help this man make better use of his home. As time went on, staff and his housemates were becoming very frustrated with the demands of his new behaviors. Staff found it difficult to continually switch back and forth from dealing with the man with dementia and the others residents in the home. His housemates were wondering why he was getting treated differently than they were and did not seem to be able to grasp the idea that he had a disease that was causing his behavior to change.

I also found a similar level of frustration at several other corporations in another Oregon community in which I was doing carer trainings for dementia. The managers and I started a task force to study the feasibility of creating a dementia-specific home to be operated by the local intellectual disabilities organization. I recommended that they try it. The executive director agreed and began looking for a home to transform within their organization. In the meantime, the man with dementia had died and several others (all adults with Down's syndrome) had been diagnosed with dementia as well. Two houses were chosen and remodeling was begun on both. Although the remodeling is not complete, several adults with dementia are now living in one of the houses. The first house was designated a dementia-capable residence and started operating as such. I was hired to train and oversee the transition of this house and staff to a dementia care home. The first house provides for six residents (currently only five live there), and the second house provides for eight. Currently, the financing is by the private corporation, but an application has been submitted for grant funding. Residents are admitted after receiving a formal diagnosis of dementia from Oregon Health Sciences University. To help prepare the staff, staffing meetings have been increased to weekly, and we have modified the shift rotation to include more people per shift and are using shorter shifts to try to reduce burnout of staff. We continue to use weekly staffing meetings. I attend these at least once a month and am on call all other times in case of questions or emergencies.

Debra Lamp
Oregon Health Sciences Center

With regard to the care system, this redefinition may also include a redistribution of day services funding resources when general intellectual disability day programs are no longer appropriate. It may mean using program models that make better use of what is rather than developing models that need new resources. It may involve working out new cooperative agreements with the aging network regarding the use of social program and in-home elder care supports. It may involve new outreach efforts to long-term care and health agencies to help provide in-home supports, training for staff, and other supports for community living (Department of Health and Social Services, 1995). Some reports of such approaches are beginning to emerge that illustrate how states are making the effort to prepare for aging in place and make their providers dementia-capable. These variations involve intellectual disabilities funding of aging network supports and services (Janicki & Bradbury, 1993; Janicki, McCallion, Force, Bishop, & Lepore, 1998), specialty assistance teams drawn from area specialists on dementia care (Antonangeli, 1995b), assessment and prescription clinics (Carlsen, Galluzzi, Forman, & Cavalieri, 1994; Chicoine, McGuire, Hebein, & Gilly, 1994; Gambert, et al., 1988; Henderson, Davidson, Overeynder, Bishop, & Ladrigan, 1996; Henderson, Ladrigan, Davidson, Bishop, Janicki, Miles, & Houser, 1998; McCreary, Fotheringham, Holden, Ouellette-Kuntz, & Robertson, 1993), and supports for families (Janicki et al., 1998b; Meltzer, 1996; Magrill, Handley, Gleeson, & Charles, 1997).

One approach is to extend the funding of intellectual disabilities services to the aging network, while also supporting intellectual disabilities providers to develop specialty aging-related services (Davis & Berkobein 1994; Janicki et al., 1998b). Using this approach, state intellectual disabilities funds can be used to underwrite specialty services or purchase services from generalist adult day services programs. This helps broaden the base of available services, makes use of existing services with expertise in providing physical aging-related or dementia care during the day, and has financing originate within the intellectual disabilities system (thus ensuring some control over quality of care). Such approaches can also tap volunteer programs, such as the federal Senior Companion program or locally sponsored senior friends, to provide one-on-one assistance during the early stages of dementia.

In the second approach, specialty clinics and assessment teams can be developed to accommodate the needs for dementia assessment referrals. In a number of areas, generic intellectual disabilities clinics are already beginning to see patients who may manifest dementia or where suspicions have been heightened by onset of behavioral changes (Carlsen et al., 1994; Chicoine et al., 1994; Chicoine, McGuire, & Rubin; this volume; Henderson et al., 1996, 1998; McCreary et al., 1993). Such regional clinic models can help serve as assessment centers for agencies that have someone in their care who is suspected of having dementia. Such suspicions need to be acted on, because the behavioral changes may be attributed to other causes than Alzheimer's disease. If this is the case, the changes may prove to be reversible and treatable, if identified early. Such assessment clinics can also help guide staff and family activities during the course of the decline and be used to help with medical management.

Another approach can involve using specialty services to help families cope with long-term care of adults and to provide in-home assistance upon request. Such models have proved successful in a series of projects reported by Janicki et al. (1998b), in which the area agencies on aging were given intellectual disabilities agency funds to help support outreach and assistance efforts, and by Meltzer (1996) and Magrill et al. (1997) in which local voluntary associations did the outreach. Any of these innovations can help agencies develop the capability to help their staff, other personnel, or families cope with dementia care. The growth of the number of adults with dementia over the next 20 years will force us to examine even more innovative alternatives to help cope with the changing demands of this aging population. Without seeking alternatives within these and other innovations, the intellectual disabilities field will be forced into reliance on congregate-institutional models (Governor's Commission on Mental Retardation, 1996) that will only force the field to regress from the overall gains in community care it has achieved over the past 20 years (Heller, Factor, & Hahn, 1995).

Planning and Development

There is no doubt about the growing size of the aging population, but how this will figure in strategic planning and resource allocation is yet undetermined. Local services and care agencies need to consider the immediate and eventual impact of dementia and care management on their clientele. As noted by Udell (this volume), having a good understanding of the demographics of the local service population helps in planning for anticipated changes of the population, as well as determining physical housing and staffing levels in the future. One starting point is collecting data on age, sex, place of residence, and needs of the service population. Another point is obtaining diagnostic data to provide the basis for projections of future need. Identifying current supports levels, as well as determining the variations of future support and care levels, is essential. Zigman and colleagues (1995, 1997) defined the characteristics of a "minimum data set" for epidemiological dementia research. Elements of this data set can also be used for planning purposes (see Figure 20.1). Collection of such demographic and diagnostic data can provide the basis for considering the needs and impact of future cohorts of aging persons with intellectual disabilities.

A precursor to planning should also involve a system analysis and administrative review. Here the focus is on what the agency can do today with the resources it has and what it will have to do in the future when the population changes. Such a review should also focus on short- and long-term needs and changes. Short-term needs and change reviews should include exploring training and resource allocations. Long-term needs and change reviews should include exploring how to derive more resources, achieve modification of environments and programs, and staff up for changing demands. These short- and long-term reviews should also involve an assessment of costs, financing, personnel capabilities and levels, and physical space and other program requirements.

Planning also involves knowing the detailed characteristics of the population at risk and the changes its members will experience due to aging. Not only is "aging in place" a consideration, but dementia care planning is important. It is helpful to know that premature aging is common among adults with Down's syndrome after 40 years of age, that one in five will probably show clinical dementia associated with Alzheimer's disease, and that most will be affected by dementia if they survive past the age of 70 (Dalton, 1995; Dalton, Seltzer, Adlin, & Wisniewski, 1994; Dalton &

A. Demographic Information
- age (full date of birth)
- sex
- level of intellectual disability
- other disabilities
- ethnicity
- residential situation
- occupational or occupational activity
- etiological and categorical diagnosis
- height and weight
- sensory status
- general physical condition
- major life events over past 10 years

B. Diagnostic Criteria
- operational criteria for significant regression in adaptive/functional skills
- core symptoms of Alzheimer disease (measured by standardized scales)
- operational criteria for case definition
- suspected stage of Alzheimer's disease
- diagnostic certainty (probable, possible, uncertain)

C. Medical Information
- risk factor of family history of Alzheimer's disease
- indication of whether blood was banked for future tests
- blood samples for current tests
- any current or historical neuroimaging data that is available

Adapted from Zigman, Schupf, Haveman, & Silverman (1995)

FIGURE 20.1   Components of Minimum Data Set for Dementia Research Projects

Wisniewski, 1990; Visser et al., 1997). It is also useful to understand that the disease course following the onset of Alzheimer's disease among adults with Down's syndrome is comparatively short, with a duration of between five and seven years. However, when considering adults with other intellectual disabilities, the course of Alzheimer's dementia has a different consequence. Onset will occur at an age which is more consistent with what has been observed in the aging general population, most often after the age of 60 years, and it may have a longer duration of approximately 20 years. Further, if the dementia is not due to Alzheimer's disease, it may have an acute and unpredictable course, posing different care demands. Planning for early- to midstage associated services, such as housing, day services, and clinical supports, and for late-stage services, such as (in addition to the others already noted) nursing care and hospice services, needs to consider all of these factors.

Existing clinical services that offer diagnostic and consultative information for children and young adults must begin to assume more responsibilities for geriatric assessment and supports. This may mean a greater initial investment in staff training or recruitment of personnel trained in gerontology, geriatrics, and related disciplines to add to staff numbers or to replace existing personnel. Over the long term, it will provide lasting results as subsequent generations of aging adults will benefit from a structure that understands aging and is prepared to address the problems inherent with the onset of dementia and other old age associated conditions. Last, it is crucial to link agency planning and development to what is being done generally in the locality by organizations concerned with Alzheimer's disease or dementia care (such as the Alzheimer Association, public health offices or departments, and aging agencies). Planning outside of these existing community structures will introduce unnecessary barriers to obtaining support services for dementia care for adults with intellectual disabilities.

☐ Education and Training Issues

The advent of the new millennium invites us to look back critically and to look forward creatively in our preparations to provide appropriately trained personnel. Retrospectively, the National Institute on Aging (NIA—U.S. Department of Health and Human Services [DHHS], 1987), in an extensive examination of the needs for health care personnel in the new millennium, noted that through 2020, the demand for health care services will double for the elderly, and the pressure to provide practitioners trained to work with elderly persons will show a corresponding increase. Yet, the NIA recognized that the nation was unprepared for this growth and there was an insufficient number of health care professionals trained to work with this age group and, without a special effort, the nation will be largely unprepared when the new millennium arrives. This concern has been echoed by others (Arie, 1985; Kovar & Feinleib, 1991). To date, most of the public health effort has been directed toward postponing mortality. This has resulted in increased lifespan, and the fact that much of that increased lifespan may not be disability-free (Kovar & Feinleib, 1991) poses new challenges for the intellectual disability system. Yet, even with this advance in basic knowledge, the nation is unprepared for the dramatic increase in its older population. Resources and training to accommodate an older population have not been made available. In the public health field, it has been recognized that without an increase in the number of health care professionals, special efforts to prevent and minimize disability in old age will fail. This same concern applies to the area of intellectual disabilities.

The NIA (U.S. DHHS, 1987) and others (Davidson, Janicki, Seltzer, & Rose, 1988) have noted that the intellectual disabilities field would also have to considerably increase the number of new personnel focusing on aging to be able to fully accommodate the growing number of elderly persons. Given the notion that age-associated disability must be prevented or minimized, coming to old age with a preexisting condition provides an added dimension to this concern. The call is not only for the generic needs of aging but also to cope with the special problems inherent in pathological aging and the effects of lifelong disability and aging. The U.S. Administration on Developmental Disabilities began, in the late 1980s, to provide substantial financial support for training programs within the nation's university-affiliated programs (UAPs) in developmental disabilities and to expand the training of professionals interested in aging. Although this support produced a surge of new training and research efforts through the mid-1990s, it has been greatly reduced in recent years, partly as a result of congressional budget cuts for federal programs. However, another factor has been the competition for scarce federal dollars within the UAPs, which are still dominated by interests in pediatrics and not by those who are willing to accommodate their activities to the needs of the emerging at-risk aging population. Political forces within the intellectual disabilities public policy community of the United States, such as the Joseph P. Kennedy, Jr. Foundation and The Arc of the United States (The Arc, 1997), have attempted to keep supports for aging alive at the national level and are continuing to aggressively push this agenda.

Because educating new professionals in the field of aging people with intellectual disabilities has received diminished emphasis by the university community, most training is now being done by the community care system and its focus is on existing personnel. The leadership role in training is now being taken over by the groups most intimately affected, that is, the service provider sector. Many have set up strong "train-the-trainers programs" with staff from both the aging and intellectual disabilities networks. Others have tried to directly influence administrators and public policy makers. Over the past years, training in aging has promoted age-specific program models that stress integration and use of the aging network (Lepore & Janicki, 1991, 1997; May & Morazas, 1994; Turner, 1994). However, the health care needs of old age have not been the crux of many training programs. As noted in numerous reports, there is still a need to train many more health care professionals who will work with older persons with disabilities and a need to link research to examining expanded levels of care that reflect changing needs of aging persons. There is agreement that clinicians, workers, family carers, and others should receive training in normal aging processes and indicators of change signaling a dementing process (Janicki, 1995). Training staff in care management techniques is also critical. Staff need new information to strengthen their current competencies in working with adults with dementia. An increased understanding of the process of coping with the complexities of functional impairments, deterioration, and death will greatly enhance their effectiveness. Social and psychological supports should also be made available for staff to deal with the experiences of loss and grief.

Numerous workers have noted the need to promote early recognition and referrals of persons with suspected dementia (Janicki & Dalton, 1993a, 1993b, 1994, in press; Antonangeli, 1995b; Burt & Aylward, this volume). Recently, family-oriented materials have been developed and made available to assist carers with information and assistance (Antonangeli, 1995a; Kerr, 1997; Marler & Cunningham, 1994; Rinck, Kendall, & Cohen, 1992; The Arc, 1995). The Alzheimer Association in the United States has made available to its chapters the AAMR/IASSID practice guidelines (see Appendix 1) and other family-oriented materials. These distribution schemes are directed toward family carers to enable them to more effectively maintain their relative's functioning and to know how to search for and find needed services. In many localities, as noted by Kendall (this volume), some information about program supports, such as day services, respite, and in-home services, is being made available. Materials on intellectual disabilities and Alzheimer's disease are being distributed in many countries and information about the AAMR/IASSID workgroup reports has been made available in variety of languages (e.g., Japanese—Takahashi, 1996a, 1996b; Italian—Janicki, 1995). Regional and local intellectual disabilities and aging network providers are linking families to support organizations for Alzheimer's disease or for intellectual or developmental disabilities and others providing opportunities for support. With the expansion of interest in using the World Wide Web, more resources are rapidly becoming available, 24 hours per day, at no cost, on the Internet. Many Alzheimer's disease organizations and university centers on aging throughout the world are offering information and resources on the World Wide Web which will continue to expand and make these materials instantly available all over the world.

The medical community is now receiving more targeted diagnostic and practice information (e.g., McLennan, Murdoch, & McIntosh, 1993). However, to adequately address the needs of the older population with intellectual disabilities, physicians and other workers at acute, managed, and long-term care facilities should become more familiar with how the dementing process is manifested in adults with intellectual disability and how to carry out effective evaluations. This knowledge is important to both preservice and continuing education. Workshops and training courses are another new development. These need to be developed specifically for service providers, health practitioners, and family carers. These should all provide information on Alzheimer's disease, diagnostic and treatment practices, and their relevance to intellectual disability. Workshops and courses should at minimum contain a basic core of information on normal aging, Alzheimer's disease, recognition of the early signs of dementia, the characteristics and value of regular, periodic assessments or evaluations, general care management, available services, supporting carers, and effective practices for early-, mid-, and late-stage interventions (Janicki & Dalton, 1994).

☐ Public Policy Issues and Implications

Three main areas have significant public policy implications: services planning and financing, human rights, and research. The need for expanded program capacity in the area of dementia care for adults with intellectual disabilities has already been explored. The first major public policy challenge is how to produce widespread recognition that this is a public health problem and how states can respond to the allocation, on the short term, of sufficient resources to bolster existing programs that are coping with aging in place. Second, states must invest financial and other resources in training and education of personnel as well as in moderate-term planning and funding and begin to finance alternative care models for adults with intellectual disabilities and Alzheimer's disease that maintain them in community settings. Long-term efforts are crucial to ensure that the current middle-aged segment of the at-risk population and those who are old enough to be in the "third age" (60 years and older) have prevention programs in place. Increased investments in the planning and modification of program practices will save enormous expenditures on the long term (CARF, 1996). With demographic projections of a restricted work force interested or available to work in long-term care services (Government Accounting Office [GAO], 1991), planning now to create constructive environments will go far to protect these resources and promote a better lifestyle for adults under the care of intellectual disabilities agencies.

In the future, human rights will receive much more attention from professionals in the intellectual disabilities field, as well as from the general public (Janicki, in press). With contemporary research directed toward identifying the cause and finding treatments for Alzheimer's disease, there is an inherent danger that with new discoveries of genetic or other screening technologies, people at risk or with a predisposition for Alzheimer's disease will be marked, and deleterious consequences will be the result (Post et al., 1997). Although such information can be beneficial for treatment, it can also form the basis of discrimination. Thus, public policies must recognize the implications of research on genetic testing and the fact that it may provide reliable advance warning of susceptibility to or risk for Alzheimer's disease. These same public policies must, however, as does national legislation in the United States (i.e., the Americans with Disabilities Act [ADA]) and in other nations, ensure that discrimination on the basis of such tests be prohibited. Such policies must also go further. They must reflect a commitment to aggressive care of persons with Alzheimer's disease and intellectual disability and avoidance of institutionalization solely on the basis of a diagnosis of dementia. Training on alternative approaches of care should be emphasized so that practices are consistent with these policies (Department of Health and Social Services, 1995). Under no circumstances should a commitment to community care and interventions be minimized or denied solely because the individual has Alzheimer's disease or dementia of any other type.

Support of research, both basic and applied, is the third area. With the emergence of an ever-larger at-risk population, we see a rapidly escalating need for investment in research aimed at making discoveries of improved and more effective models of care, staff training, and how the aging and intellectual disabilities resources can best be deployed to achieve shared results. Demonstrations of community support programs, shared housing models, geriatric assessment clinics and teams, and other ways of delivering services in an efficient and effective manner need to be supported and carried out. Only when we test what works best for us and under what conditions will we have a rational basis for making the necessary choices to provide a dignified quality of life for persons as they grow older.

☐ References

Administration on Aging. (n.d.). *Infrastructure of home and community based services for the functionally impaired elderly: State source book.* Washington, DC: U.S. Department of Health and Human Services.

Alzheimer's Association. (1994). *Residential settings: An examination of Alzheimer issues.* Chicago: Author.

Alzheimer's Association. (1996). *Assisted living quality initiative: Building a structure that promotes quality*. Chicago: Author.

Annerstedt, L. (1993). Development and consequences of group living in Sweden. A new mode of care for the demented elderly. *Social Science and Medicine, 37*, 1529-1538.

Annerstedt, L. (1997). Group living care: An alternative for the demented elderly. *Dementia and Geriatric Cognitive Disorders, 8*, 136–142.

Antonangeli, J. M. (1995a). *Of two minds—A guide to the care of people with dual diagnosis of Alzheimer's disease and mental retardation*. Malden, MA: Cooperative for Human Services.

Antonangeli. J. M. (1995b). The Alzheimer project: Formulating a model of care for persons with Alzheimer's disease and mental retardation. *The American Journal of Alzheimer's Disease, 10*(4), 13–16.

Arie, T. H. D. (1985). Education in the care of the elderly. *Bulletin of the New York Academy of Medicine, 61*, 492–500.

Aylward, E., Burt, D., Thorpe, L., Lai, F., & Dalton, A. J. (1995). *Diagnosis of dementia in individuals with mental retardation: Report of the task force for development of criteria for diagnosis of dementia in individuals with mental retardation*. Washington, DC: American Association on Mental Retardation.

Aylward, E., Burt, D., Thorpe, L., Lai. F., & Dalton, A. J. (1997). Diagnosis of dementia in individuals with intellectual disability: Report of the task force for development of criteria for diagnosis of dementia in individuals with mental retardation. *Journal of Intellectual Disability Research, 41*, 152–164.

Bauer, A. M., & Shea, T. M. (1986). Alzheimer's disease and Down syndrome: A review and implications for adult services. *Education and Training of the Mentally Retarded, 21*, 144–150.

Burt, D., & Aylward, E. (1998). Test battery for the diagnosis of dementia in individuals with intellectual disability. Washington, DC: American Association on Mental Retardation.

CARF. (1996). *CARF strategic plan, 1997–1999*. Tucson, AZ: CARF (Rehabilitation Accreditation Commission).

Carlsen, W. R., Galluzzi, K. E., Forman, L. F., & Cavalieri, T. A. (1994). Comprehensive geriatric assessment: Applications for community-residing elderly people with intellectual disability/ developmental disabilities. *Mental Retardation, 32*, 334–340.

Carter, G., & Jancar, J. (1983). Mortality in the mentally handicapped: A 50 year survey at the Stoke Park group of hospitals (1930–1980). *Journal of Mental Deficiency Research, 27*, 143–156.

Chicoine, B., McGuire, D., Hebein, S., & Gilly, D. (1994). Development of a clinic for adults with Down syndrome. *Mental Retardation, 32*, 100–106.

Dalton, A. J. (1995). Alzheimer disease: A health risk of growing older with Down syndrome. In L. Nadel & D. Rosenthal (Eds.), *Down syndrome: Living and learning in the community* (pp. 58–64). New York: Wiley-Liss.

Dalton, A. J., Seltzer, G. B., Adlin, M. S., & Wisniewski, H. M. (1994). Association between Alzheimer disease and Down syndrome: Clinical observations. In J. M. Berg, A. J. Holland, & J. Karlinsky (Eds.), *Alzheimer disease and Down syndrome* (pp. 1–24). London: Oxford University.

Dalton, A. J., & Wisniewski, H. M. (1990). Down's syndrome and the dementia of Alzheimer's disease. *International Reviews of Psychiatry, 2*, 43–52.

Davidson, P. W., Janicki, M. P., Seltzer, M. M., & Rose, T. (March, 1988). *Proceedings of "Aging and developmental disabilities: Windows to the aging network"* (Symposium presented at the ADD Commissioner's Annual Forum, New Orleans, LA). Rochester, NY: University of Rochester University Affiliated Program in Developmental Disabilities.

Davis, S., & Berkobein, R. (1994). *Meeting the needs and challenges of at-risk, two-generation, elderly families*. Arlington, TX: The Arc.

Deb, S., & Janicki, M. (1995). Conference report: International colloquium on intellectual disability and Alzheimer's disease. *Journal of Intellectual Disability Research, 39,* 149–150.

Department of Health and Social Services. (1995). *Review of policy for people with a learning disability.* Belfast, Northern Ireland: Author.

Eisner, D. A. (1985). Down's syndrome and aging: Is senile dementia inevitable? *Psychological Reports, 52,* 119–124.

Ellis, W. G., McCulloch, J. R., & Corley, C. L. (1974). Presenile dementia in Down's syndrome. *Neurology, 24,* 101–106.

Evans, D. A., Funkenstein, H. H., Albert, M. S., Scherr, P. A., Cook, N. R., Chown, M. J., Hebert, L. E., Hennekens, C. H., & Taylor, J. O. (1989). Prevalence of Alzheimer's disease in a community population of older persons. *JAMA—Journal of the American Medical Association, 262,* 2551–2556.

Evans, D. A., Sherr, P. A., Albert, M. S., Funkenstein, H. H., Hebert, L. E., Wetle, T. T., Branch, L. G., Chown, M., Hennekens, C. H., & Taylor, J. O. (1990). Estimated prevalence of Alzheimer's disease in the United States. *Milbank Quarterly, 68*(2), 267–289.

Freedman, R. I., Krauss, M. W., & Seltzer, M. M. (1997). Aging parents' residential plans for adult children with mental retardation. *Mental Retardation, 35,* 114–123.

Gambert, S. R., Crimmins, D., Cameron, D. J., Heghinian, M., Bacon-Prue, A., Gupta, K. L., & Escher, J. E. (1988). Geriatric assessment of the mentally retarded elderly. *The New York Medical Quarterly, 8,* 144–147.

Government Accounting Office. (1991). *Long-term care: Projected needs of the aging baby boom generation* (GAO/HRD-91-86). Washington, DC: Author.

Government Accounting Office. (1996). *Waiver program for developmentally disabled is promising but poses some risks* (GAO/HEHDS-96-120). Washington, DC: Author

Governor's Commission on Mental Retardation. (1996). *Nursing homes as residential placements for persons with mental retardation.* Boston: Author.

Haberland, C. (1969). Alzheimer's disease in Down's syndrome. *Acta Neurologica Belgica, 69,* 369–380.

Harper, D. C. (1993). A primer on dementia in persons with intellectual disability: Conclusions and current findings. In R. J. Fletcher & A. Dosen (Eds.), *Mental health aspects of intellectual disability: Progress in assessment and treatment* (pp. 169–200). New York: Lexington Books.

Heller, T., Factor, A., & Hahn, J. E. (1995). Nursing home reform: The impact of moving out of nursing homes on people with developmental disabilities. *Policy Research Brief* (University of Minnesota—Center on Residential Services and Community Living), 7(1), 1–8.

Henderson, C. M., Davidson, P. W., Overeynder, J., Bishop, K., & Ladrigan, P. (1996, April). *Functional decline and aging in older adults with intellectual disability: Origins, diagnosis and prognosis.* Paper presented at conference on aging and intellectual disability, Ospedale Bambini Gesu, Rome, Italy.

Henderson, C. M., Ladrigan, P. M., Davidson, P. W., Bishop, K. M., Janicki, M. P., Miles, R., & Houser, K. (1998). *Comprehensive geriatric assessment for the evaluation of functional decline in adults and elders with intellectual disability.* Unpublished manuscript, Strong Center for Developmental Disabilities, University of Rochester School of Medicine and Dentistry, Rochester, New York.

Heston, L. L. (1984). Down's syndrome and Alzheimer's dementia: Defining an association. *Psychiatric Developments, 4,* 287–294.

Holland, A. J., Karlinsky, H.. & Berg, J. M. (1993). Alzheimer's disease in persons with Down syndrome: Diagnostic and management considerations. In J. M. Berg, H. Karlinsky, A. J. Holland (Eds.), *Alzheimer's disease, Down syndrome, and their relationship* (pp. 96–114). Oxford: Oxford University Press.

Jakubiak, C. H., & Callahan, J. J. (1995). Treatment of mental disorders among nursing home residents: Will the market provide? *Generations, 19*(4), 39–42.

Janicki, M. P. (1994). *Alzheimer disease among persons with mental retardation: Report from an international colloquium*. Albany: New York State Office of Mental Retardation and Developmental Disabilities.

Janicki, M. (1995). La malattia di Alzheimer tra le persone con ritardo mentale (translation in Italian). *Phoenix, 2*(1), 11–24.

Janicki, M. P. (1996). *State mental retardation agency polices related to Alzheimer dementia*. Albany, NY: Office of Mental Retardation and Developmental Disabilities.

Janicki, M. P. (in press). Public policy and service design for older adults with intellectual disability. In S. Herr & G. Weber (Eds.), *Aging, rights, and quality of life for older persons with developmental disabilities*. Baltimore: Paul Brookes.

Janicki, M. P. & Bradbury, S. (1993). *Creating choices: New York's third age programs*. Albany, NY: Office of Mental Retardation and Developmental Disabilities.

Janicki, M. P., & Dalton, A. J. (1993a). Alzheimer disease in a select population of older adults with mental retardation. *Irish Journal of Psychology, 14*, 37–46.

Janicki, M. P. & Dalton, A. J. (1993b, August). *Clinical/training implications of Alzheimer disease among older adults with mental retardation*. Paper presented at the 101st annual meeting of the American Psychological Association, Toronto, Ontario, Canada.

Janicki, M. P., & Dalton, A. J. (1994, March). *Alzheimer disease among older adults with mental retardation: Findings of two surveys in New York State*. Paper presented at the 40th annual meeting of the American Society on Aging, San Francisco, California.

Janicki, M. P., & Dalton, A. J. (1997a). *Pending impact of dementia related care on intellectual disability providers*. Proceedings of the International Congress III on the Dually Diagnosed-Mental Health Aspects of Mental Retardation (Montréal, P.Q., Canada), 188–190.

Janicki, M. P., & Dalton, A. J. (1997b, August). *Occurrence of dementia in a population of adults with intellectual disability*. Paper presented at the 16th World Congress on the International Association of Gerontology (Adelaide, S.A., Australia).

Janicki, M. P., & Dalton, A. J. (1998). *Prevalence of dementia and impact on intellectual disability services*. Manuscript submitted for publication.

Janicki, M. P., & Dalton, A. J. (in press). Current practice in the assessment and care of persons with intellectual disabilities. In N. Bouras (Ed.), *Psychiatric and behavioral disorders in mental retardation*. Cambridge: Cambridge University Press.

Janicki, M. P., Dalton, A. J., Henderson, M., & Davidson, P. W. (1996, July). *Deaths among adults with mental retardation: Demographic and policy considerations*. Paper presented at the 10th Congress of the International Association for the Scientific Study of Intellectual Disabilities, Helsinki, Finland.

Janicki, M. P., Dalton, A. J., Henderson, M., & Davidson, P. W. (in press). Mortality and morbidity among older adults with intellectual disabilities: Health services considerations. *Disability and Rehabilitation*.

Janicki, M. P., Heller, T., Seltzer, G. B., & Hogg, J. (1996). Practice guidelines for the clinical assessment and care management of Alzheimer's disease among adults with intellectual disability. *Journal of Intellectual Disability Research, 40*, 374–382.

Janicki, M. P., McCallion, P., Force, L., Bishop, K., & Lepore, P. (1998). Area agency on aging outreach and assistance for households with older carers of an adult with a developmental disability. *Journal of Aging and Social Policy, 10*, 13–36.

Jenkins, E. L., Hildreth, B. L., & Hildreth, G. (1993). Elderly persons with mental retardation: An exceptional population with special needs. *International Journal of Aging and Human Development, 37*, 69–80.

Kerr, D. (1997). *Down's syndrome and dementia*. Birmingham, UK: Venture Press.

Kinsella, K., & Taeuber, C. M. (1993). *An Aging World 11.* Washington, DC: U.S. Department of Commerce (Bureau of the Census).

Koenig, B. R. (1995a). *Aged and dementia care issues of people with intellectual disability: Literature review and survey of carers.* Brighton, S.A.: MINDA, Inc.

Koenig, B. R. (1995b). *Aged and dementia care issues of people with intellectual disability: Best practices,* Brighton, S.A.: MINDA, Inc.

Koenig, B. R. (1995c). *Aged and dementia care issues of people with intellectual disability: Assessing change.* Brighton, S.A.: MINDA, Inc.

Kovar, G. M., & Feinleib, M. (1991). Older Americans present a double challenge: Preventing disability and providing care. *American Journal of Public Health, 81,* 287–288.

Kultgen, P., & Holtz, P. (1992). *Age change and what to do about it.* Indianapolis: Indiana University Institute for the Study of Developmental Disabilities.

Lepore, P., & Janicki, M. P. (1991). *The wit to win: How to integrate older persons with developmental disabilities into community aging programs.* Albany, NY: State Office for the Aging.

Lepore, P., & Janicki, M. P. (1997). *The wit to win: How to integrate older persons with developmental disabilities into community aging programs* (3rd rev.). Albany, NY: State Office for the Aging.

Magrill, D., Handley, P., Gleeson, S., & Charles, D. (1997). *Crisis approaching! The situation facing Sheffield's elderly carers of people with learning disabilities.* Sheffield, England: Sheffield Mencap (Norfolk Lodge, Park Grange Road, Sheffield, UK S2 3QF).

Marler, R., & Cunningham, C. (1994). *Down's syndrome and Alzheimer's disease.* London: Down's Syndrome Association.

May, D. C., & Morazas, D. S. (1994). Are elderly people with mental retardation being included in community senior citizen centers? *Education and Training in Mental Retardation, 29,* 229–233.

McCreary, B. D., Fotheringham, J. B., Holden, J. J. A., Ouellette-Kuntz, H., & Robertson, D. M. (1993). Experiences in an Alzheimer clinic for persons with Down syndrome. In J. M. Berg, H. Karlinsky, & A. J. Holland (Eds.), *Alzheimer's disease, Down syndrome, and their relationship* (pp. 115–131). Oxford: Oxford University Press.

McLennan, J. M., Murdoch, P. S., & McIntosh, I. B. (1993). *Dementia touches everyone: A guide for trainers and trainees in general practice.* Stirling, Scotland: Dementia Services Development Centre, University of Stirling.

Meltzer, N. (1996). *Washington statewide senior family initiative—A project to assist regions plan for the needs of aging family caregivers of individuals with developmental disabilities.* Seattle, WA: The Arc of King County.

Mittelman, M. S., Ferris, S. H., Shulman, E., Steinberg, G., & Levin, B. (1996). A family intervention to delay nursing home placement of patients with Alzheimer disease: A randomized controlled trial. *Journal of the American Medical Association, 278,* 1725–1731.

Mor, V., Banaszak-Holl, J., & Zinn, J. (1995). The trend toward specialization in nursing care facilities. *Generations, 19*(4), 24–29.

Newroth, S., & Newroth, A. (1981). *Coping with Alzheimer disease: A growing concern.* Downsview, Ontario, Canada: National Institute on Mental Retardation.

Noelker, E. A. & Somple, L. C. (1993). Adults with Down syndrome and Alzheimer's. In K. A. Roberto (Ed.), *The elderly caregiver: Caring for adults with developmental disabilities* (pp. 81–92). Newbury Park, CA: Sage Publications.

Olsen, R. V., Ehrenkrantz, E., & Hutchings, B. (1993). *Homes that help: Advice from caregivers for creating a supportive home.* Newark: The Center for Architecture and Building Science Research, NJ Institute of Technology.

Owens, D., Dawson, J. C., & Losin, S. (1971). Alzheimer's disease in Down's syndrome. *American Journal of Mental Deficiency, 75,* 606–612.

Post, S. G., Whitehouse, P. J., Binstock, R. H., Bird, T. D., Eckert, S. K., Farrer, L.A., Fleck, L. M., Gaines, A. D., Juengst, E. T., Karlinsky, H., Miles, S., Murray, T. H., Quaid, K. A., Relkin, N. R., Roses, A. D., St. George-Hyslop, P. H., Sachs, G. A., Steinbock, B., Truschke, E. F., & Zinn, A. B. (1997). The clinical introduction of genetic testing for Alzheimer disease. An ethical perspective. *JAMA—Journal of the American Medical Association, 277*, 832–836.

Rinck, C., Kendall, E., & Cohen, G. (1992). *Alzheimer's disease and Down syndrome. Fast Facts on Aging #1.* Kansas City, MO: University of Missouri, Kansas City, Institute for Human Development.

Sloan, P. D., Lindeman, D. A., Phillips, C., Moritz, D. J., & Koch, G. (1995). Evaluating Alzheimer's special care units: Reviewing the evidence and identifying potential sources of study bias. *Gerontologist, 35*, 103–111

Strauss, D., & Eyman, R. K. (1996). Mortality of people with mental retardation in California with and without Down syndrome, 1986–1991. *American Journal on Mental Retardation, 100*, 643–653.

Takahashi, R. (1996a). Practice guidelines for the clinical assessment and care management of Alzheimer's disease and other dementias among adults with intellectual disability (Japanese translation). *Social Welfare Research Series (Japan), 19*, 9–29.

Takahashi, R. (1996b). Diagnosis of dementia in individuals with intellectual disability: Report of the task force for development of criteria for diagnosis of dementia in individuals with mental retardation (Japanese translation). *Social Welfare Research Series (Japan), 20*, 11–31.

The Arc. (1997). *Policy statement on aging.* Arlington, TX: Author.

The Arc. (1995). *Developmental disabilities and Alzheimer's disease: What you should know.* Arlington, TX: Author.

Turner, K. W. (1994). Modeling community inclusion for older adults with developmental disabilities. *Southwest Journal on Aging, 10*(1/2), 13–18.

U.S. Department of Commerce. (1991). Global aging: Comparative indicators and future trends. Washington, DC: Bureau of the Census.

U.S. Department of Health and Human Services. (1987). *Personnel for health needs of the elderly through the year 2020.* Bethesda, MD: National Institute on Aging.

Visser, F. E., Aldenkamp, A. P., van Huffelen, A. C., Kuilman, M., Overweg, J., & van Wijk, J. (1997). Prospective study of the prevalence of Alzheimer-type dementia in institutionalized individuals with Down syndrome. *American Journal on Mental Retardation, 101*, 400–412.

Wilson, K. B. (1996). *Assisted living: Reconceptualizing regulations to meet consumers' needs and preferences.* Washington, DC: American Association of Retired Persons.

Wisniewski, H. M., & Merz, G. (1985). Aging, Alzheimer's disease and developmental disabilities. In M. P. Janicki & H. M. Wisniewski (Eds.), *Aging and developmental disabilities: Issues and approaches.* Baltimore: Paul H. Brookes.

Zigman, W., Schupf, N., Haveman, M., & Silverman, W. (1995). *Epidemiology of Alzheimer disease in mental retardation: Results and recommendations from an international conference.* Washington, DC: American Association on Mental Retardation.

Zigman, W., Schupf, N., Haveman, M., & Silverman, W. (1997). Epidemiology of Alzheimer disease in mental retardation: Results and recommendations from an international conference. *Journal of Intellectual Disability Research, 41*, 76–80.

Zigman, W., Silverman, W., & Wisniewski, H. M. (1996). Aging and Alzheimer's disease in Down syndrome: Clinical and pathological changes. *Mental Retardation and Developmental Disabilities Research Reviews, 2*, 73–79.

Arthur J. Dalton
Henryk M. Wisniewski
Matthew P. Janicki

Future Prospects

This chapter provides a brief overview of the matter covered in this text, explores areas of new findings, and proposes directions for further research in the years to come. In it, we note that we expect a continued increase in interest in refinements in diagnosis and assessment. Particularly promising will be the rapid advance in the development of highly specific and powerful drugs with fewer sedative, anticholinergic, extrapyramidal, and hypotensive side effects and that pharmacological interventions will be more useful and pose less danger than in the past, substantially improving quality of life and preserving functions for much longer periods. Promising also will be the emergence of new and more reliable measures that will more definitively define dementia marked behavior and provide indicators for physiological changes associated with dementia. Notwithstanding these areas of promise, we also note the lack of forward-looking health policy and care management research focusing on older adults with dementia and intellectual disabilities and note the need for a greater emphasis in work in this area. Last, we explore the new avenues of information exchange, in particular the World Wide Web, and predict that their contributions to furthering new research and practices will become invaluable to the world-wide network of families, researchers, and workers affected by and interested in this condition.

Address correspondence to: Arthur J. Dalton, Ph.D., New York State Institute for Basic Research in Developmental Disabilities, 1050 Forest Hill Road, Staten Island, NY 10314. email: daltonaj@aol.com.

The contents of this handbook reflect the current status of knowledge on the practical, applied, and clinical aspects of dementia as it affects individuals with intellectual disabilities. It is quite evident that more is known about the condition as it affects persons with Down's syndrome than those with intellectual disabilities of other etiologies. This is not surprising because the causes of intellectual disabilities in persons other than those with Down's syndrome are numerous and diverse and are completely unknown in more than 50% of cases. Consequently, it is generally not possible to examine relationships between Alzheimer's disease and these other conditions for lack of sufficient numbers of adults affected with similar etiologies.

The current status of biological and biomedical knowledge is examined in the second section. The more recent research efforts on the assessment and diagnosis of dementia among individuals with intellectual disabilities have yielded new information which is reflected in the chapters of the third section. Similarly, the increasing pressure in recent years to provide adequate clinical services for a growing number of individuals suspected of suffering from dementia has yielded impressive contributions which reveal frequently overlooked psychiatric disorders and other reversible conditions, including depression, which accompany dementia and which are treatable. These advances are presented in some detail in the fourth section. It is expected that in the near future a continued increase in interest will attract many more psychiatrists and other professionals leading to better characterization of these conditions as well as important refinements in diagnosis and assessment. Particularly promising for the future is the rapid advance in the development of highly specific and powerful drugs with fewer sedative, anticholinergic, extrapyramidal, and hypotensive side effects. Pharmacological interventions will be more useful and less dangerous than in the past, substantially improving quality of life and preserving functions for much longer periods.

Today's knowledge base about the behavioral, social, habilitative, management, and care of persons with intellectual disabilities and dementia is comparatively small. Progress in behavioral and nonmedical interventions will continue to be slow because psychologists and related professionals have been insufficiently stimulated to develop interest in the problems of aging persons with intellectual disabilities. Yet in this volume we have included some noteworthy examples of activities that can address care issues, including a program for enhancing communication skills in persons affected with dementia (see McCallion Chapter 14) and methods for addressing death in care settings (see Service, Lavoie, & Herlihy

Chapter 18). Many of the chapters in this text that focus on care management issues are based on real-life experiences dealing with care management and how clinicians or agencies have coped with the day-to-day demands of decline associated with dementia. Similarly, the handbook titled *Coping with Alzheimer's Disease: A Growing Concern* (Newroth & Newroth, 1981) was developed from the trial-and-error experience of a single agency. The staff of this agency decided to undertake the demanding responsibility for caring for several individuals with Down's syndrome on a 24-hour basis from the onset of Alzheimer's disease until their death. Portions of the handbook are included as a supplement in this text. In this vein, the chapter by Udell on supports in small group living settings is another outstanding example of how practical experience has provided information on how to address troublesome facets of caring for people with this condition. It flows from these works that a systematic body of knowledge in the care and management of affected individuals will not be created by the academic community but rather will rely almost entirely on the courage and initiative of individuals and care agencies.

In the immediate future, research into the underlying nature of Alzheimer's disease as it affects individuals with intellectual disability will continue to advance. Of particular interest in this regard is the notion of "brain reserve," which is considered to be limited in persons with intellectual disability and which may partly explain hypothesized premature aging and the known susceptibility of adults with Down's syndrome to Alzheimer's disease (Zigman, Silverman, & Wisniewski, 1996). Three decades of vigorous laboratory research have led to the conclusion that Alzheimer's disease is polyetiological with multiple genes involving several chromosomes, and there has been no significant progress in establishing any causative role for potential environmental agents such as trace metals. Consequently, the likelihood that a single discovery will be made that adequately explains Alzheimer's disease is unlikely.

On the other hand, progress in the development of pharmacological agents has been substantial in the past 10 years. The number and variety of drugs being developed to prevent or slow the progression of the disease are increasing dramatically, and this trend is likely to accelerate as better agents are found and hypotheses about the pathogenesis of the disease are verified. It seems very unlikely, however, that a single "magic bullet" will be found for the treatment of Alzheimer's disease. Currently approved treatments (such as tacrine and donepezil) provide, at best, only symptomatic and temporary relief from further declines in cognitive functions. In the future an increasing number of treatments will be aimed at modifying or interfering with one or more of the underlying mechanisms of pathogenesis.

There are several particularly active and promising directions aimed at reducing free radical damage, immune system abnormalities, and cholinergic deficits. One source of promising results are the multicenter studies of vitamin E, prednisone (a steroidal antiinflammatory agent), and estrogen that are currently underway. For example, one international consortium has developed a multicenter, three-year, double-blind, placebo-controlled trial of vitamin E with persons with Down's syndrome over the age of 50 years. The driving force behind this project is the successful multicenter trial of vitamin E in the treatment of patients with moderately severe Alzheimer's disease (Sano et al., 1997). Individuals with intellectual disabilities, particularly those with Down's syndrome, who are affected by Alzheimer's disease will ultimately also reap the benefits of these efforts.

Progress in the clinical management of dementia will also continue to rely heavily on individual initiatives and the courage of agencies to adopt trial and error methods since there is no established body of knowledge to serve as a guide. This situation was illustrated in the chapter by Chicoine, McGuire, and Rubin who established a community-based clinic specifically designed to meet the concerns of families who are trying to cope with the onset and progression of functional decline and deterioration in their older relatives with Down's syndrome. It is also reinforced by the efforts of national and international associations, such as the American Association on Mental Retardation (AAMR) and the International Association for the Scientific Study of Intellectual Disability (IASSID), to establish and place into general distribution practice guidelines that will aid in the care management of individuals affected by dementia (see Janicki, Heller, Seltzer, & Hogg, 1996 and Appendix 1) and will serve to stimulate public policy as well as new research endeavors on care practices.

Kendall, Rinck, and Wright (Chapter 19), and in their exploration of dementia assistance resources, revealed that the programs serving persons with intellectual disabilities and dementia are based on duplication or modification of the programs that have been designed for persons with dementia from the community at large. This absence of specialized resources will continue as long as the care and management of dementia in persons with intellectual disability is deemed to be adequate within the framework of the model of care employed for those persons from the community at large. Present day knowledge is scanty and fragmentary concerning the needs of those with intellectual disabilities and dementia from those of affected people without intellectual disabilities. Only recently has the research required to delineate these differences gotten underway.

Policy and organizational issues have received the shortest attention in this handbook, reflecting the absence of basic knowledge on the impact of dementia in persons with intellectual disabilities on the larger social environment. In particular, the paucity of adequate epidemiological studies and the preponderance of small sample studies mean that there are no reliable figures on prevalence and incidence rates to guide public health and social policy. Organizational issues are currently addressed by individual agencies. There has been little pressure to develop regional or national policies in the absence of compelling data which would define realistically the magnitude of the problem of dementia, its distribution in different groups at risk, and its impact on the community defined at regional or national levels. Epidemiologists are particularly hindered in doing research in this area because there is no litmus test for detecting dementia of the Alzheimer's type, and existing methods of diagnosis are costly, time consuming, and subject to substantial errors (Erkinjuntti, Ostbye, Steenbuis, & Hachinski, 1997).

The prospects of advances in diagnostic accuracy will, for some time to come, hinge mainly on the advances in the biological and physiological sciences which are making rapid strides in identifying possible "biomarkers" and other heretofore unbeknownst physiological process indicators of dementia. The emerging work on visual process deficiencies associated with neuropathological changes in the brain when dementia is present has potential for applications with populations with limited verbal skills, such as people with intellectual disabilities. Until these "breakthroughs" occur, work on behavioral measures will have to continue, albeit this means can be limiting because the development of new behavioral tests for diagnosis of cognitive and related functions is a long, arduous, and equally costly undertaking. In the meantime, modifications of existing behavioral and other tests as well as questionnaires, ratings scales, and informant-based instruments will continue to be a relatively haphazard process with little coordination between investigators in the foreseeable future. The development of a set of guidelines for the diagnosis of dementia and recommendations for using a particular battery of neuropsychological tests (as reported by Burt & Aylward, this volume, and by Burt & Aylward, 1998) represents a significant advance. However, the benefits of this advance will come only with changes and improvements, which can only emerge after there is widespread adoption of the guidelines and test recommendations.

Such advances may require 5 to 10 years before we will see any substantial results. We also know that policy issues are affected by factors such as funding levels; rapid changes in funding mechanisms; local, regional, and national political considerations; as well as prevailing attitudes toward the provision of health care services in general. The necessity to avoid duplication of effort and competition for limited resources, particularly in the United States, are important considerations for providers of services for those with intellectual disabilities as well as for those responsible for the care of persons with Alzheimer's disease from the population in general. The prospects for the future and the ultimate outcome are unclear at this time.

The need for more effective education and training in assessment, diagnosis, management, and care of dementia is directly or indirectly acknowledged by nearly every contributor to this handbook. What this means is that everyone recognizes the existence of an important problem. While the advent of the new millennium invites us to look back critically and to look forward creatively in our preparations to provide appropriately trained personnel, there is no obvious solution in sight. The United States, for example, will see a doubling in the demand for health care services for the elderly through the year 2020 and the nation is largely unprepared, according to the National Institute on Aging. Even though a knowledge base has grown rapidly in recent years, the transfer and assimilation of this knowledge into effective education and training programs has been largely on a fragmentary basis, resting mostly in optimistic aspirations, vaguely defined goals, and only rarely in postgraduate training (and then only in a few universities). Paradoxically, even though we know more about the impending needs for elder care and about the changing demographics of the older population, education in aging and geriatrics of new professionals in the field of intellectual disabilities has received diminished interest in the university community. To its credit, most training now is being done by the community care system with its focus on existing personnel. Adequate educational and training programs appear to be only a dim prospect for the future.

In the meantime, however, some of the demand for knowledge will be met by the growing World Wide Web and the new communication resources available on the Internet. These new resources will no doubt provide an important source of information, knowledge, and opinion to a vast new and growing audience of families, students, professionals, agencies, and other interested individuals and organizations. The web offers a new dimension previously inconceivable, namely, quick access to specialized "listserves," where one can interact with others all over the globe at relatively low cost and exchange knowledge and opinions. Not only will the research community benefit, but such resources will help expand our thinking about treatment and care management. There will be wide distribution of knowledge about the quality of service providers and those services and agencies that fall short in the quality of their services will be highly visible to consumers of these services who will organize into informal "listserves," a current practice which will no doubt grow by leaps and bounds. The web will provide opportunities for the exchange of a range of information to be put on the Internet in electronic form, making it available almost instantaneously to anyone in the world who has access to a computer and a modem.

These cumulative exchanges of quickly available information will eventually lead to the definition of the causes and effective treatments of Alzheimer's disease and related dementias in the population at large, and the specialized exchanges of information will help us better relate these greater findings to older people with intellectual disabilities. Such information will also help families and other carers cope with the significant changes in behavior and function exhibited by individuals with intellectual disabilities affected by dementia.

☐ References

Burt, D. B., & Aylward, E. H. (1998). *Test battery for the diagnosis of dementia in individuals with intellectual disability* (Report of the working group for the establishment of criteria for the diagnosis of dementia in individuals with intellectual disabilities). Washington, DC: American Association on Mental Retardation.

Erkinjuntti, T., Ostbye, T., Steenbuis, R., & Hachinski, V. (1997). The effect of different diagnostic criteria on the prevalence of dementia. *New England Journal of Medicine, 337*, 1667–1674.

Janicki, M. P., Heller, T., Seltzer, G. B., & Hogg, J. (1996). Practice guidelines for the clinical assessment and care management of Alzheimer's disease among adults with intellectual disability. *Journal of Intellectual Disability Research, 40*, 374–382.

Newroth, S., & Newroth, A. (1981). *Coping with Alzheimer disease: A growing concern.* Downsview, Ontario, Canada: National Institute on Mental Retardation.

Sano, M., Ernesto, C., Thomas, R. G., Klauber, M. R., Schafer, L., Grundman, M., Woodbury, P., Growdon, J., Cotman, D. W., Pfeiffer, E., Schneider, L. S., & Thal, L. S. (1997). A controlled trial of selegiline, alpha-tocopherol, or both as treatment for Alzheimer disease. *New England Journal of Medicine, 336*, 1216–1222.

Zigman, W., Silverman, W., & Wisniewski, H. M. (1996). Aging and Alzheimer's disease in Down syndrome: Clinical and pathological changes. *Mental Retardation and Developmental Disabilities Research Reviews, 2*, 73–79.

APPENDIX **1**

AAMR/IASSID Practice Guidelines for Diagnosis and Care Management of Adults with Intellectual Disability and Dementia

☐ **Step 1. Understanding Changes in Normal Aging, Being Aware of Risk Factors, and Recognizing Changes Indicating Onset of Dementia**

Normative aging results in certain sensory, physical, psychological, and behavioral changes. To understand pathological changes it is important to know the differences between these normative changes and changes that result from disease or other pathological processes. Further, although the staging of dementia symptoms does not appear to differ among persons with intellectual disability in general, the timing and manner that symptoms may be expressed can vary widely from individual to individual. These symptoms may also appear differently among adults with

[Adapted from Janicki, Heller, Seltzer, & Hogg (1996). Practice guidelines for the clinical assessment and care management of Alzheimer's disease and other dementias among adults with intellectual disability. *Journal of Intellectual Disability Research, 40,* 374–382.]

Down's syndrome than among adults with other etiologies of intellectual disability.

Adults with intellectual disability who are at risk for Alzheimer's disease include those over age 50, those with Down's syndrome over the age of 40, or those who are from families with a history of Alzheimer's disease. The presence of any of these factors does not necessarily mean that Alzheimer's dementia (or another form of dementia) will occur. However, the presence of one or more of these risk factors may indicate an increased risk of an adult with intellectual disability manifesting dementia.

When these risk factors are present, periodic screenings are particularly helpful for identifying potential changes in behavior that may suggest pathological aging. Changes that may be early indicators include unexpected changes in routine behaviors; a decrement in functional abilities, such as cooking, dressing, or washing; memory losses or difficulty in learning new activities; changes in affect or attitude or demeanor; a loss of job or social skills; withdrawal from pleasurable activities; nighttime awakenings and other altered time difficulties; increases or decreases in rigid behavioral patterns; and onset of seizures. Because observable changes in behavior may be due to causes other than dementia (e.g., depression, sensory impairments, hypo/hyperthyroidism) and may be treatable and reversible, referral for a diagnostic work-up should be made as soon as possible after observing any of the signs noted above.

A periodically applied screening instrument should be used to establish both a behavioral baseline and to obtain longitudinal measures that indicate change. A baseline screening should be undertaken that includes cognitive, health, and functional assessments beginning with age 40 in individuals at increased risk for premature aging, such as persons with Down's syndrome, and beginning with age 50 in others. The individual should also receive periodic cognitive, health, and functional assessments. These on-going assessments could reveal significant changes in function. Where periodic screenings are not practical or possible, an alternative means of assessing change should be used. One means is to ask the adult to keep a "life-history" diary in which are noted significant events, abilities, and documentation of capabilities. Such baseline measures or life histories can help others understand the adult's normative behavior and thus any changes that suggest pathological aging will be highlighted.

☐ Step 2. Conducting Assessments and Evaluations

When there is suspicion of dementia, referral for a thorough evaluation should be done to assure a proper differential diagnosis. Thus, the second step includes (1) gathering information on behavior to further confirm noticed changes, preferably from multiple informants such as staff or carers; (2) continuing to monitor behavior/functioning for presentation to clinicians; and (3) making a referral for a diagnostic work-up for a differential diagnosis. To make a distinction between *possible* and *probable* diagnosis of Alzheimer's disease, it is necessary to observe a well-documented progression of symptoms substantiated by appropriate clinical test results. Because periodic observation of behavior is a critical feature of the diagnostic evaluation among adults with intellectual disability, obtaining a confident diagnosis requires repeated evaluations.

Resources for general diagnostic evaluations may include geriatric assessment clinics, memory assessment and memory disorder clinics, Alzheimer's disease assistance centers, Alzheimer's disease centers, specialist or geriatric health care teams, general practitioners, neuropsychologists, neurologists, geriatric psychiatrists, and other physicians. Other, more specialized resources may include special clinics of local intellectual disability, mental health or psychiatric, aging or senior services agencies, and university programs in intellectual or developmental disabilities.

☐ Step 3. Instituting Medical and Care Management

The third step involves two interwoven paths: *medical management* and *care management.* Contact between these two paths should be routine and ongoing, depending on the individual's needs.

The *medical management* path calls for systematic treatment of all treatable medical conditions, such as hearing disabilities, seizure disorders, or cataracts. Treatment of these conditions should be as thorough as it is in the general population. Comorbid mental disorders (such as depression) should be treated aggressively. In particular, the treatment must be tailored to a clearly established diagnosis, rather than to vague behavioral symptoms, such as aggression. The use of psychoactive medications for behavioral control should be limited to acute situations and should be replaced, when possible, by appropriate behavioral, cognitive, and environmental interventions. Frequent review of all medications is necessary, with the goal of using the fewest number and lowest possible doses of effective medications. Continued monitoring of medical, psychiatric, and cognitive changes must occur, as conditions tend not to be static but evolve with time. Pharmacological therapies must consider carefully the increased vulnerability of the central nervous system to further cognitive impairments. Particularly likely to cause impairment is the use of multiple medications (polypharmacy). With progression of the disease, medical management takes on a more intensive course, often inverse to the time spent in care management. When there is an overwhelming loss of personal care skills and mobility during the last stage, the person may no longer be able to walk, sit up, chew and swallow food, or control bowel or bladder. Added to these losses of function and general unresponsiveness, the person may experience the onset of seizures and is at greater risk of infection. Given the total loss of body functions, practitioners must put more emphasis on primary nursing care and medical management to deter infections and defer death for as long as possible.

The *care management* path calls for documenting and carrying out a treatment strategy appropriate to each stage of the disease. General principles of care management include (1) helping the person preserve and maximize function; (2) using interventions and supports that are appropriate to the stage of the disease; and (3) conducting care planning that is multidisciplinary and involves information from multiple sources. Care management involves structural activities such as making referrals for appropriate services, making environmental modifications, changing the general plan of care according to identified sustainable abilities of the individual, and determining whether to use aging or Alzheimer's disease related services in addition to or instead of intellectual disability services. Care management also involves individualized applications of clinical strategies to address problem management and carer concerns. Written documentation is crucial in this step, as it helps identify changes and personal care needs.

Once the suspicion of Alzheimer's disease has been clinically confirmed, the person's family or other carers need to be made aware that what may have been comfortable and familiar for the individual in the past may become unrecognizable and result in unpredictable behavior. Changes may need to be made in daily routine and environment so that the adult can feel safe and secure in his or her environment. Carers should be encouraged to promote this feeling of safety, because although the adult may be mobile, his or her judgment may be decreasing and he or she may be at risk of falling or other injuries. Under these circumstances, some of the person's responsibilities may need to be modified or curtailed.

Family, friends, and companions (including providers and staff) are integral to care management. They should be used as genuine supports and encouraged to gain a better understanding of the nature and course of the disease. A balance should be maintained between providing supports that compensate for the loss of skills and encouraging the individual to perform activities that may preserve function. As the disease progresses, treatment practices need to be modified to meet the changing needs of the individual with probable Alzheimer's disease. These modifications need to accommodate diminishing self-care, communication, and orientation skills.

Attention should be paid to addressing eating, balance and mobility difficulties, and problems with continence and wandering. Simplifying the environment, establishing a regular routine, and applying common-sense oversight and direction will help address these changes. It may be necessary to reduce the number of alternatives in the person's daily life, because making choices can be confusing and frustrating for someone with dementia. While reducing the extent of individual alternatives to minimize confusion, the carer should simultaneously offer a variety of broad experiences drawn from programs and amenities available within the community. The person should not be isolated but should be encouraged to continue membership for as long as possible in his or her community. Supports, services, and care management strategies should be designed to accommodate differing needs at the various stages of the disease, including early, mid, and late.

Early-Stage Practices

As the onset of symptoms often appears very gradually, changes in supports and services may be minimal at first. There may be some small memory loss, particularly of recent events. Adults may have trouble in finding the right words to use during casual conversations. Work performance may begin to deteriorate and changes in behavior may start to become obvious. Adults may also experience some altered time concepts, loss of familiarity with routine activities, or loss of interest in favored hobbies, events, or activities. There may be periods of lessened alertness and slowing of movement. Early signs and symptoms of Alzheimer's dementia do not mean that a change of familiar program or residence is necessary or even desirable. Maintaining routine and familiarity with the environment can help compensate for any changes or disorientation in the adult's behavior. To the extent possible, the adult should be allowed to "age in place" with dignity and respect. The adult's program or home environment should be adapted for safety, ease of access, and ultimately to maintain or slow down loss of function. Supervision or personal assistance levels should be modified to accommodate changing abilities. Early-stage care practices often include providing supports that buttress the person's ability to enjoy normal activities, by adapting or simplifying the activities to the person's changing cognitive abilities; providing structure and supports for performing daily routines; using explicit, short directions or instructions, cues, and verbal prompts; maintaining favorite activities;

implementing approaches that match the changing abilities of the individual; and engaging the individual in activities involving other members of the household or program. Adults who experience changes related to dementia should be involved in activities and exercises that can support their positive sense of involvement, accomplishment, and well-being and specifically aid in the preservation of muscle tone and strength. The practice goal is to optimize the person's sense of success in everyday activities, encourage positive self-esteem, and maintain autonomy and good physical and emotional health for as long as possible.

Middle-Stage Practices

During this stage, the behavioral changes noted during the early stage become more obvious. Distinct losses of language abilities are frequently the most obvious sign that the individual is progressing to this stage. For example, adults affected may have difficulty naming objects or with maintaining a logical conversation. They may also have difficulty understanding directions or instructions. They often become disoriented as to time, place, and person. Memory losses and confusion often lead to frustration. Thus, carers need to acknowledge with enthusiasm what the individual is saying and doing and to do so using the adult's perceptual field as the point of reference. There may also be the beginning of a loss of self-care skills and continence. Significant changes in personality and social behavior begin to appear. These changes are often associated with paranoia and delusions. Late onset seizures may become evident for the first time. Thus, additional supports such as respite, personal care assistance, physical alterations to the home, and more frequent health monitoring at this stage may help continue to maintain the individual in his or her residence and moderate some of the behavioral changes. Questions may also arise regarding self-determination, advanced directives, and guardianships. Where legally permissible, a health care proxy should be executed authorizing a named individual to make health care decisions after the adult becomes too incapacitated to make his or her own decisions. The proxy should cover artificial hydration, nutrition, extraordinary medical procedures, and resuscitation. When a guardian has not been appointed, the adult or carers may want to start guardianship, using whatever legal processes exist in the jurisdiction. Overall, the following practices are useful in midstage of the disease: preservation of function, maintenance of physical and dental health, adequate nutrition, protection and maintenance of safety, aid with self-care, participation in stimulating activities, strategies to reduce agitation, and a periodic review of physical function and health for ongoing planning of appropriate interventions.

With increasing disorientation, forgetfulness, and sometimes personal agitation, greater care should be given to the design of the person's routine, activities, and safety. Since wandering, disorientation, and agitation, together with a loss of orientation to visual cues, may occur, the person's negotiation of his or her environment is enhanced by using special markings, colors, and textures. Continence can be maintained by monitoring of fluid intake, timing of voiding, and ensuring that toileting facilities are carefully marked. Carers should ensure that adult is maintained on a balanced diet and receives adequate nutrition by using techniques that encourage safe eating, including using appropriate food consistency and portions, allowing adequate time for eating, and taking advantage of times when the person is not fatigued. Maintaining flexibility in nutrition management, such as simplifying meal routines, avoiding excess stimuli during meal time, providing finger foods and more frequent smaller meals, and supplementing dietary needs by vitamins or healthy snacks can help maintain good nutrition and safe eating as the disease progresses. Some families or other carers may benefit from respite and information on care management techniques. Persons helping carers cope should be aware of carer stresses or problems associated with lack of relief for caring, coping with their own health difficulties, and caring for others in the household. Carers in these situations may also benefit from counseling and future planning, particularly as the adult continues to lose function.

Late-Stage Practices

Late- or end-stage needs require special attention and sensitivity. During this stage, adults experience substantial dysfunction. Basic skills such as eating or drinking are lost. Because of eating problems, activity level, and changes in metabolism, many adults may experience a substantial loss of body weight. They may eventually lose their ability to maintain balance and walk. Their long- and short-term memories are typically lost, as is their ability to recognize other persons and their environment. At the very late stage, persons affected require 24-hour care and supervision. They often become bedridden and inactive. Because they are bedridden, they are at increased risk for any infection, specially pneumonia, and consequently are far more likely to die. Special care must be exercised to prevent dehydration, choking, or aspiration pneumonia, and skin pressure sores. Preventive care may curb these conditions and thus support the maintenance of comfort. In this stage, adults also lose their ability to care for themselves, and bowel and bladder incontinence becomes a problem. Previously simple activities like eating, washing, and grooming will require extensive personal care attention. Adults will require constant direction and supervision and will generally not be able to be left alone. When adults are still able to walk, wandering presents a significant risk to safety and health. If excessive wandering cannot be prevented, environmental modifications, such as special pathways, or targeted supervision needs to be designed into the program. With advancing decline, adults may be lacking any affect and have a complete lack of unawareness of their surroundings. Although most verbal abilities may be lost, some use of words or phrases may be retained. When this occurs, carers should consider methods for retaining these abilities. Late-stage interventions should also attend to the problems of carers burdened by the strain of caregiving. At this stage more effort should be given to supporting the family or other carers directly involved in caring for the individual. Special consideration should be given to helping staff and carers handle bereavement and deal with the stresses inherent in providing terminal care. Use can be made of clergy or other spiritual supports, and also hospice.

Guidelines for Coping with Alzheimer's Disease in Persons with Down's Syndrome

Can the three-stage model of dementia described in Dalton & Janicki (this volume) serve as a useful and practical guide for the management and care of individuals with intellectual disabilities from the onset of Alzheimer's disease until their death in the terminal stage? One answer to this question has been provided by the staff and residents of a residential community called Daybreak. Daybreak is important because it represents a pioneering effort at meeting the challenges of dementia while at the same time dealing successfully with the consequences of adopting an "aging-in-place" philosophy.

Daybreak is the name of a residential community north of Toronto, Canada, of about 50 men and women who live and work together with the specific purpose of providing a home, as well as training and work for about 30 of its members with an intellectual disability. The philosophy

The editors are grateful to the National Institute on Mental Retardation publishers, who kindly gave permission to reproduce the charts from *Coping with Alzheimer Disease: A Growing Concern*, by Ann and Stephen Newroth, ISBN 0-919648-26-6, 1980. They have been reproduced with minor modifications. Copies of the manual including the charts are available from L'Institut Roeher Institute, Kinsmen Building, York University, 4700 Keele Street, North York, Ontario, Canada, M3J 1P3. Phone (416) 661-9611.

of Daybreak maintains that people with intellectual disabilities are like other people, with unique personalities, with rights to individualized education, vocational training, and job opportunities. It also maintains that they have a right to a home that gives them a sense of belonging and a right to respect and dignity in all relationships. When two of the residents succumbed to Alzheimer's disease, one alternative was placing the residents in a nursing home. After agonizing over the alternatives, Daybreak chose to accept the responsibility of caring for its failing members for as long as possible, up to and including their death. Being fully aware of the extraordinary amount of additional care that would be required by these persons affected with dementia, the staff of Daybreak felt that the necessary human and technical resources were available and could be utilized in the residential setting. The introduction of more intensive and specialized care for two frail and aging person with Down's syndrome represented a major programmatic addition to the operation of Daybreak. It had serious implications for daily routines, staffing patterns, staff education and training, qualifications of staff, type of care, activities, emotional climate, general expectations for certain residents, and for the cost of operation. This resulted in a definite change in the type of care provided by the staff, from residential counseling to an increased amount of specialized personal health care.

After much discussion, the staff of Daybreak felt that the intense changes that would be required in order for them to properly care for persons with Alzheimer's disease would not pose insurmountable problems, and so the decision to care for these people at Daybreak rather than to place them in a nursing home was made. The decision made by Daybreak was a difficult one, although probably not as difficult as it would be for a family faced with the same problem concerning a family member. Daybreak, with its paid, experienced staff, was able to provide professional care for its failing members after some reorganization of its residential facilities. The purchase of such requirements as wheelchairs, lift apparatus for baths, and other equipment may not be possible for a single family, and thus eventual care in a nursing home may be the only possible solution for some families.

At the time that Daybreak had to provide care for several individuals showing signs of dementia, there was no information available in plain language to help human service workers and families understand the nature of this process, its signs and symptoms, and more significantly for a care-provider agency, the implications of the signs for care. The directors of Daybreak, therefore, put together a 27-page manual based on their observations and experiences over a five-year period of providing care for person with intellectual disabilities affected by Alzheimer's disease. This work was published by Ann and Stephen Newroth of Daybreak

(1980), directors of the residential community. The manual contains a set of charts which provide a helpful set of guidelines for recognizing the changes associated with dementia and for providing practical solutions to each problem as it developed. The charts are divided into three sections corresponding to the conceptual division of Alzheimer's dementia into stage one (early), stage two (middle), and stage three (late or terminal). These charts describe ways and means by which persons having symptoms of Alzheimer's disease can be helped in the community. The charts utilize plain language to help families and human service workers understand the nature of the process of dementia.

The guidelines clearly demonstrated the value and need for a team approach in order to maintain organized and consistent care for persons with Alzheimer's disease. As this disease will eventually leave the individual virtually helpless, the onus falls on the carers to provide for all of the person's basic needs. This job is one that cannot be done by just one or two people without great physical and emotional sacrifice on their part. Caring for a person with Alzheimer's disease is a demanding task that involves a primacy of human presence, sensitivity, and stability over technology and organization. It is not easy for staff people to consistently maintain devotion to these necessary human qualities over long periods of care. Therefore, the charts must be used while active support and encouragement is given to the staff in order to help the quality of care to remain high. The kinds of problems encountered are best met by an interlocking support system of counseling, training, and supportive management. The authors also recognize that government fiscal planners need documentation on the more intensive kind of care required by people with Alzheimer's disease in order to allow for adequate budget increases. These issues are discussed by Janicki and Dalton in Chapter 20 in the context of more recent developments and relevance to many other service providers.

Adaptations of the charts for the three stages of dementia are provided below. The charts consists of four columns. The first column presents a series of physical and psychological signs; the second, a list of observed behaviors that appear to be related to the signs; and the third, a list of implications of each of those behaviors for the individual and for those who render care (be they staff, family, or friends). The fourth, and most important column, provides a list of practical suggestions on how to respond to the consequences of the signs to meet the needs of those involved. The suggestions are based on extensive experience in caring for a number of middle-aged men with Down's syndrome on a 24-hour-per-day basis for more than five years. Postmortem examination of brain tissue specimens for the men revealed the characteristic lesions and a neuropathological diagnosis of Alzheimer's disease.

STAGE ONE

SIGNS	BEHAVIOR EXAMPLES	IMPLICATIONS	SUGGESTIONS
1. Impairment of memory including: • diminished ability in decision making and judgment • time disorientation • confusion and general intellectual disorientation	Person cannot remember names of acquaintances and names of common objects.	Social life becomes limited. Person is not satisfying social needs of acquaintances. Therefore, people may begin to by-pass the person.	Staff should not take behavior personally. The person may show recognition through other behaviors. People need to expect less interaction, but to stimulate with maximum opportunities for socialization, e.g., meals with others, attend parties, etc.
	Forgets words and sentences.	Unable to explain personal needs or condition adequately (doctor's visit, banking, etc.). Experiences frustration and irritability results.	Provide advocate or "interpreter."
	Cannot remember what he/she did with familiar articles (gloves, cigarettes, etc.).		Needs help to find personal possessions. Familiar articles should be placed within easy access in sight.
	Loss of interest in personal hygiene and appearance. Dresses inappropriately for social functions.	May appear unkempt, dirty and smelly and, therefore, less socially acceptable. May draw unfavorable attention to self.	Provide supervision to choose appropriate clothing, leaving room for personal preference. Eliminate clothing that is difficult to manage (ties, shoelaces, flies that button, etc.). Give reminders to wash, brush teeth, etc., and offer encouragement and direction to maintain appearance and hygiene routines. Supervision should be sensitive and made available only when necessary.

STAGE ONE (continued)

SIGNS	BEHAVIOR EXAMPLES	IMPLICATIONS	SUGGESTIONS
	Forgets what time of day it is.	Is frequently late for meals, appointments, etc., and upsets routines.	*Requires frequent reminders.*
Apparent loss of sensory feedback re: 1. sleep, 2. appetite 3. climate.	1. Wakes in the middle of the night and dresses. 2. Doesn't know what meal he/she has just eaten, or what meal to expect next (breakfast, lunch, or supper—may expect a meal just after finishing one). 3. Dresses inappropriately for climate.	Wakes others, risks injury, loses sleep, and further confuses self. Annoys others with inappropriate expectations or questions. Risk of catching cold.	*Provide someone to supervise at night.*
	Starts to undress at bedtime and forgets what he/she is doing and begins to dress again.	Exasperates care providers	*Exercise patience and share responsibility for gentle reminders about routines, meal times, time of day, etc.*

STAGE ONE (continued)			
SIGNS	BEHAVIOR EXAMPLES	IMPLICATIONS	SUGGESTIONS
2. Spatial disorientation including • loss of sense of direction.	Can't find his/her bedroom or bathroom even in familiar home setting. Gets lost easily in familiar neighborhood. Tries to enter bus from wrong side.	Gets lost easily as daily activities change (especially in strange environment and routine). Often late, risks personal injury. Therefore, others worry and get impatient, which may cause overreaction in the form of undue restrictions.	*Be prepared to provide increased supervision and direction within the house and to provide escorts on neighborhood outings. Outings alone should be limited to daytime and fair weather.* *Avoid radical changes in physical setting (redecorating, moving furniture) and daily routine.*
	Difficulty in focusing and successfully grasping, holding fixed object and bringing to desired spot (finding fork, placing food on fork, putting fork in mouth).	Drops food, spills things; mealtimes may become burdensome to others.	*Person should be adequately supplied with serviette, apron, etc. Simplify tableware (spoon instead of knife and fork, mug instead of cup and saucer).* *"Cheerful cleaner-upper." It is important for morale that staff and others do not blame the person for the inconveniences caused by the deteriorating condition.*
	Sits on half of chair. Difficulty in orienting self to place setting at table.	May fall or annoy others at table.	
Unable to place body in correct reference to activity.			

STAGE ONE (continued)

SIGNS	BEHAVIOR EXAMPLES	IMPLICATIONS	SUGGESTIONS
3. Lack of spontaneity • dimished spontaneous movement	Does not initiate activities for self and interest in outside activities diminishes.	Not included in mainstream of activity. Tendency to become withdrawn, left out. Experiences loneliness. Not stimulated by surroundings.	*Encourage increased external motivation from peers or supervisor. Make the person central to group activities and offer help to participate and feel "part of."*
	Generally decreased body movement. Remains sedentary for long periods.		*Don't leave the person alone for long periods of time.*
	General decreased alertness and eye contact.	People tend to ignore the value of eye contact and no longer encourage it. May offend others.	*Encourage, seek out, and maintain eye contact. Use bright objects to capture attention.*
• diminished spontaneous reaction to people	Manifestations of greeting, reception, interest in, and a awareness of people's physical presence and emotional states are reduced.	May not be greeted by others.	*Increase effort to affirm person's presence. Help others to appreciate that this decline is not a personal rejection. Try to maintain continuity of relationships.*
	Inability to respond to simple questions without repetition. Misses cues for social interactions.	May be avoided by others. Friendship and social contacts "fall off" because colleagues may find the relationship unsatisfactory.	*Encourage social interaction with others, especially with old friends. Friends may require assistance (counseling) to understand why the relationship has changed.*

STAGE ONE (continued)

SIGNS	BEHAVIOR EXAMPLES	IMPLICATIONS	SUGGESTIONS
4. Physical dysfunction • increasing drowsiness • tires easily • general slowing of movements • loses balance	Falls asleep at work or home, tires easily. Walks, responds, works slowly.	Cannot be counted on to produce and, therefore, loses status and employment opportunities as a worker. Frustrates coworkers and staff. May need workday rescheduled. May need transportation and escort at other than usual times. Needs close work supervision. Will receive less pay for work. May lose or have to change job and may lose employability. Cannot work indefinitely.	*Should be employed in sheltered work or attend a "flexible" program determined by individual's potential.* *Should be provided with opportunity to rest during the day at work or home.* *Physical condition needs respect and to be accepted in work environment by staff and coworkers. Staff and coworkers should be counseled on the special needs of this person.* *Determine flexibility in work schedule in consultation with those in home life (e.g., may work half-days). This alteration in work situation is one of the first major decisions which may be made, and a team approach will be essential.* *Arrange to have personnel available for supervision, escort, and travel needs.* Discuss pay and job changes, as deemed appropriate, offer consolation and support. Provide alternative program and maintenance of stimulating routines.

STAGE ONE (continued)

SIGNS	BEHAVIOR EXAMPLES	IMPLICATIONS	SUGGESTIONS
Diminished fine motor control and coordination	Unable to strike a match, fasten buttons, cut meat, dress himself, feed himself, manage stairs, etc. Stumbles frequently. Body may list to one side or the other. May not sit or stand up straight. Apparent loss of body awareness.	Risks injury. Reduced ability for independent ambulation. May easily slip out of a sitting position.	*Give help and reassurance to move around especially on stairs and uneven ground. Provide security in a chair or prop him up with pillows.*
		May get frustrated and leave things undone. This may give rise to "nagging." May not be able to be held responsible for safety of himself and others (e.g., cannot smoke without supervision).	*Exercise patients and provide help with fine motor tasks, "hand-over-hands." Provide easy access to a responsible person.*
Restricted blood circulation	Results in cold, dry hands and feet and discoloration of limbs.	Will suffer discomfort. May need massages and/or medical advice. May need extra warmth.	*Make the person more comfortable. Provide for medical attention, massages, etc. Turn up the heat. Use extra blankets. Put on socks to wear in bed. Keep out of drafts. Use of portable electric heater may be helpful for certain rooms in the house. Provide support to move around. Develop a program of physical stimulation to maintain limb functions*

STAGE ONE (continued)

SIGNS	BEHAVIOR EXAMPLES	IMPLICATIONS	SUGGESTIONS
Changes in physical functioning.	Loss of bladder control.	Person gets wet and uncomfortable. May smell and be embarrassed and resent invasion of privacy. Bedding, carpets, and chairs are vulnerable.	*Provide discreet reminders of toileting. Give good-natured help to clean up. Use rubber protective coverings on mattresses, etc. Provide easy access to laundry facilities. Use easy-care clothing. Make extra changes of clothing available. Ensure adequate privacy.*
	Becomes constipated.	Person will be uncomfortable and may need laxative, suppositories, and/or medical attention.	*Note dates and times of bowel movements. Monitor diet more closely.*
	Sporadic sucking of thumbs or fingers.	May draw negative attention.	
	Diminished use of communication skills -dimished use of speech -apparent hearing impairment (which may be explained otherwise as a result of decreased awareness of the significance of verbal communication) -loss of reading and writing skills.	Loses touch with friends. Becomes frustrated. May lose desire for social interactions and may become more passive and unresponsive to stimulation. May resent care.	*Increased efforts should be made to exercise the remaining communication skills of the person. Provide assistance in dialing telephone numbers. Write letters on his/her behalf. Read to the person in quiet surroundings. Reassure friends that this is not a personal rejection but the result of a deteriorating medical condition.*
	May experience visual impairments and/or deterioration (e.g., double vision).	Risks of accidents greatly increase (e.g., falling, knocking things over, especially at tables).	

STAGE TWO

SIGNS	BEHAVIOR EXAMPLES	IMPLICATIONS	SUGGESTIONS
By this stage, pathology in the brain is readily evident by CT scan or MRI imaging techniques. Specific neurological and behavioral consequences of deterioration are evident as follows:			
1. Perceptual failure in which the person loses the ability to recognize the significance of what he/she sees, hears, tastes, smells, or feels with the skin senses.	Person does not recognize the names or faces of close friends. Little response to voices. Does not appear to understand verbal communication attempts. Person does not remembers what he/she has in his/her hand. Without setting an object down, person may attempt to pick up three or four more objects in the hand.	Interaction with others is seriously impaired. The person now seems despondent. Likes, dislikes, and emotions seem to be flattened.	*Continue conversations and social occasions as long as the individual responds positively.* *Continue conversations and include attempts to cheer him/her up.* *Preferences, likes, and dislikes should be documented and shared with all those taking care of the person.*
2. Speech and language difficulties	Very seldom speaks spontaneously. When person speaks, speech is slowed down and now hard to understand. Person mumbles.	Person may be ignored and physically isolated. People will fear him and find him upsetting.	*Others should be made aware that this is part of the condition.* *Person may need a private room.* *Repeat questions. Offer yes/no options as answers.*

STAGE TWO (continued)

SIGNS	BEHAVIOR EXAMPLES	IMPLICATIONS	SUGGESTIONS
3. Movement disorders & dyspraxia). Failure to make voluntary or purposeful movements although muscles and reflexes are otherwise normal.	Spontaneous activity and movements are largely reduced. Person may now largely be confined to bed and a wheelchair. Person is unable to feed himself. Increased sleeping during the day. All movements are very slow and awkward. May have "myoclonic jerks." (See below.)	Person may need to be lifted from bed to chairs, etc. May need specialized equipment. May need to have bed baths and to be spoon-fed. Needs to vary location and sitting/lying positions. Needs to be taken to the toilet. Needs to be taken to meals. When this is absolutely impossible, have meals taken to him/her.	*Provide attending team. Carers require basic training and support in caregiving. For example, all actions should be preceded by explanations (i.e., removing false teeth from the mouth, changing bed position, moving the person from one place to another). Carers need to learn how to lift, turn, bathe, and provide all personal hygiene and grooming routines.* *Person needs to be fed (carers should be aware of person's preferences). Move person frequently and provide extra pillows or props. Arrange for a wheelchair, hospital bed, rubber sheets, incontinence pads, bedpan, invalid tray, when necessary. Installation of a "grab bag" in the bathroom may be necessary.* *Finances must allow for specialized equipment and additional personnel as needed.*

STAGE TWO (continued)

SIGNS	BEHAVIOR EXAMPLES	IMPLICATIONS	SUGGESTIONS
4. Other physical dysfunction. Beginning of epileptic seizure activity, lost of sphincter control, increased vulnerability to infections (especially pneumonia), marked weight loss may occur, and fluid retention. Progressive deterioration in both motor abilities and general interests in the environment.	Involuntary muscle action (myoclonic jerks) including jumping movements of arms, legs, twitching of the face and/or shoulders. Trembling of the chin and other abnormal facial reflexes. Increased muscle tone.	Premature expectations of death on the part of the patient, staff, and others. Needs medical attention by physician willing to make house calls. If ill, person may need some nursing care at home. Needs monitoring of diet and weight. Those immediately involved may become overtired and emotionally drained. If person becomes seriously ill, he/she may need temporary acute care hospitalization. Person now needs physical comforting and reassurance.	*Team should increasingly shift to a "medical model" of care. Participation of a nurse or doctor on the team is useful. Death should be freely discussed. Honest answers must be available. Have physician make regular house calls, review, and change medications. Keep physician informed of any significant change in the patient. Physician or nurse should make diet recommendations. Good nutrition is imperative to avoid infections. Extra time off and/or relief personnel should be made available to those intimately involved in care. Also provide a forum for discussions of staff emotional reactions, sources of stress, etc. Hospitalize if necessary. Handle person lovingly, massage often, rub body with pleasant-smelling body lotion. Offer physical displays of affection, touches, kisses, holding hands and face. Spend time with the person even if there is only silence in response. Conduct passive exercise and offer changes in scenery.*

STAGE TWO (continued)

SIGNS	BEHAVIOR EXAMPLES	IMPLICATIONS	SUGGESTIONS
5. Psychological distress may frequently be associated with this stage.	Crying, screaming, moaning, manifestations of fear, anxiety.	Severe distress to others who may feel upset, worried, and even agitated.	*Provide increase support for caregivers, including more frequent time off. This may require administrative resolve.*

STAGE THREE

SIGNS	BEHAVIOR EXAMPLES	IMPLICATIONS	SUGGESTIONS
Complete dementia. Often accompanied by cerebral seizures.	Severely reduced spontaneous movements and reactions to people and other stimuli. Completely bedridden. Person is very prone to pneumonia and bed sores. Incoherent muttering. Limited facial expressions.	Person needs constant supervision and physical and social attention. Person needs continuous comfort, reassurance, and understanding.	*Person will need to be turned in bed every 3 to 4 hours to prevent pneumonia and lower risks of decubitus ulcers. Patience. Person needs to be kept dry, clean, and comfortable. Needs to be watched for bed sores and other secondary types of infection. Provide companionship and visitors. Extra efforts should be made to interpret minor facial expressions. Make life as pleasant and normal as possible for all concerned. Prepare those close at hand for the person's impending death and recognize a human consciousness.*

Instruments and Tests

AAMR Adaptive Behavior Scale
Aberrant Behavior Checklist
Balthazar Scales of Adaptive Behavior
Basic Life Skills Scale
Buschke Selective Reminding Test
Cain–Levine Social Competency Scale
CAMCOG-Cambridge Cognitive Examination
Cambridge Assessment for Mental Disorders in the Elderly (CAMDEX)
CERAD (Consortion to Establish a Registry for Alzheimer's Disease)
Checklist for Psycho-Social Concerns
Client Development Evaluation Report
Dalton/Murrary Visual Memory Test
Dementia Questionnaire for Mentally Retarded Persons
Dementia Scale for Down Syndrome (DSDS)
Developmental Disabilities Information System (DDIS)
Developmental Disabilities Profile (DDP)
Diagnostic Assessment for the Severely Handicapped
Disability Assessment Schedule
Down Syndrome Medical Checklist
Down Syndrome Mental Status Examination
Dyspraxia Scale for Adults with Down Syndrome
Emotional Problems Scales
Hachinski Ischemic Score
Hampshire Assessment for Living with Others

Leiter International Performance Scale
Mental Status Exam
Mini-Mental Status Examination (MMSE)
Minnesota Developmental Programming System Behavior Scales (MDPS)
Mood Assessment Scale for Demented Adults
One Word Picture Vocabulary Test
Otacoustic Emissions
Psychiatric Assessment Schedule for Adults with a Developmental
  Disability (PAS-ADD)
Peabody Picture Vocabulary Test
Progress Assessment Chart of Social and Personal Development
Psychopathology Inventory for Mentally Retarded Adults
Pyramid Scales
Reiss Screen for Maladaptive Behavior
Rivermead Behavioural Memory Test
Scales of Independent Behavior
Stanford–Binet
System of Multicultural Pluralistic Assessment
Test of Severe Impairment
Vineland Adaptive Behavior Scales
Vineland Social Maturity Scale
Wechsler Adult Intelligence Scale
Wechsler Memory Scale

GLOSSARY

This glossary contains some common terms and descriptors associated with Alzheimer's disease, other dementias, medications, and psychopathologies related to aging, dementia, intellectual disabilities, and care management practices.

acetylcholine—a neurotransmitter released at autonomic synapses and neuromuscular junctions, active in the transmission of nerve impulse, and formed enzymatically in the tissues from choline. It appears to be involved in learning and memory. Acetylcholine is severely diminished in the brains of patients with Alzheimer's disease.

activities of daily living (ADLs)—basic activities that are important to self-care, such as bathing, dressing, using the toilet, and eating.

adaptive behavior—skills and capabilities that permit productive and independent daily functioning (also adaptive functioning).

adult day services—a program that provides services to adults with functional impairments in a structured, supervised setting for fewer than 24 hours a day.

advance directive—a written statement that is intended to govern health care decision making for its author, should he or she lose decisional capacity in the future; generally applies to end-of-life issues (includes both "living wills" and "health care proxies").

agitation—a state of anxiety accompanied by motor restlessness.

agnosia—loss or diminution of the ability to recognize familiar objects or stimuli usually as a result of brain damage and distinguished as visual, auditory, olfactory, gustatory, and tactile agnosia.

agoraphobia—irrational fear of being helpless in a situation from which escape may be difficult or embarrassing; characterized initially often by anticipatory anxiety, panic attacks, and finally by avoidance of open or public places.

akathisia—a condition of motor restlessness, ranging from a feeling of inner disquiet to inability to sit or lie quietly, or to sleep.

alogia—inability to speak due to central nervous system lesion.

alprazolam—a drug of the benziodiazepine group indicated for the management of generalized anxiety disorder or for the short-term relief of the symptoms of anxiety.

Alzheimer's disease—a progressive, neurodegenerative disease characterized by loss of function and death of nerve cells in several areas of the brain leading to loss of cognitive function such as memory and language. The cause of nerve cell death is unknown. Alzheimer's disease is the most common cause of dementia.

Alzheimer's disease, familial (FAD)—an early-onset form of Alzheimer's disease that appears to be inherited. In FAD several members of the same generation in a family are often affected.

Alzheimer's disease, sporadic—same as FAD, except that there is no obvious family history of the disease. Nevertheless, twin studies suggest that there are genetic factors for most cases of Alzheimer's disease. (See Percy, this volume.)

amantadine—a drug indicated in the treatment of idiopathic parkinsonism (paralysis agitans; shaking palsy), postencephalitic parkinsonism, symptomatic parkinsonism, drug-induced extrapyramidal reactions, and parkinsonism associated with cerebral arteriosclerosis in the elderly.

amnesia—loss of memory sometimes including the memory of personal identity due to brain injury, shock, fatigue, repression, or illness or sometimes induced by anesthesia.

amphetamines—a group of drugs, namely amphetamine, dextroamphetamine, and methamphetamine, used for attention-deficit hyperactivity disorder (ADHD) as part of a total treatment program which typically includes other remedial measures for a stabilizing effect in children and adults. Also indicated for well-established and proven narcolepsy.

amyloid angiopathy—the accumulation in blood vessels of amyloid, an abnormal complex material, most probably a glycoprotein. The material is frequently found in the blood vessels of brain specimens from individuals with Down's syndrome who have died in later life with Alzheimer's disease.

amyloid beta protein—a breakdown product of a large protein encoded by a single gene located on chromosome 21, called the amyloid precursor protein (APP). It is thought that there is a problem with APP metabolism in all persons who develop Alzheimer's disease. (See Percy, this volume.)

amyloid precursor protein (APP)—the larger protein from which beta amyloid is formed.

amitriptyline—a tricyclic antidepressant drug indicated for the relief of symptoms of major depressive episodes, the depressed type of bipolar disorder, dysthymia, and atypical depressions.

anti-inflammatory agent—a group of medications that counteract or suppress inflammation. They include steroidal and nonsteroidal agents.

antioxidants—a substance that deactivates oxygen free radicals which can cause damage to cell membranes in the nervous system and elsewhere. Antioxidants, particularly vitamin E, are currently being investigated as possible therapeutic agents for arresting Alzheimer's disease.

anxiolytic—a drug which relieves anxiety.

apathy —indifference, lethargy, or general lack of emotion or feeling.

aphasia—refers to loss or impairment of the power to use or comprehend words, usually resulting from brain damage. There are many forms—**anomic aphasia:** the loss of the power of naming objects or of recognizing or recalling their names; **motor aphasia:** the inability to speak or to organize the muscular movements of speech (also called Broca's aphasia); and **sensory aphasia:** the inability to understand spoken, written, or tactile speech symbols due to a brain lesion.

apoE4 (apolipoprotein E4)—one form of the apoE gene, which produces the protein apolipoprotein E4; this form of the gene occurs more often in people with Alzheimer's disease than in the general population. However, more than 90% of people who have the apoE4 allele do not have Alzheimer's disease. In addition, apoE4 is not specific for Alzheimer's disease because its presence is also a risk factor for heart disease, multi-infarct dementia, and Parkinson's disease. The most frequent form of the gene is apoE3. ApoE2, like apoE4, is less common than apoE3. Most people have two apoE3 genes. (See Percy, this volume, for details.)

apoE gene—a genetic blueprint made of DNA that has three slightly different (allele) forms and in which particular combinations might confer greater or lesser risk of the development of Alzheimer's disease. This gene is the subject of intense research at the present time as a possible marker for Alzheimer's disease.

apraxia—loss or impairment of the ability to execute familiar purposeful movements in the absence of paralysis or other motor or sensory impairment.

arthritis—inflammation of joints due to infectious, metabolic, or constitutional causes.

aspartate—a neurotransmitter mainly present in the brain's cortex causing excitatory responses; aspartate can be an excitotoxin that is a poison in certain brain cells.

asphyxia—a lack of oxygen or excess of carbon dioxide in the body that is usually caused by interruption of breathing.

atherosclerosis—an arteriosclerosis characterized by atheromatous deposits within the inner layer of the arteries.

audiology—the science of hearing.

audiometry—the testing and measurement of hearing acuity for variations in sound intensity and pitch and for tonal purity; can include speech and pure tone assessments for each ear separately.

auditory brain stem response—method for recording and amplifying small electrical signals emitted by the brain stem when auditory stimuli are presented to either ear or both. It is a nonverbal method for detecting hearing impairments but is insensitive to determination of hearing for speech.

avolition—a psychiatric term referring to the loss of the will.

axon—a usually long and single nerve-cell process that conducts impulses away from the cell body. It is the "arm" of a nerve cell that normally transmits outgoing signals. Each nerve cell has one axon, which can be over a foot long. A nerve cell communicates with another nerve cell by transmitting signals from the branches at the end of its axon.

Barrett's metaplasia—a particular variation in a condition in which there is a change in the type of adult cells in a tissue to a form that is not normal for that tissue.

behavioral symptoms—changes in typical behavior that are markers or indicators for a disease or psychiatric pathology. Behavioral symptoms typically indicative of onset of Alzheimer's disease will include memory loss, disorientation, personality changes, and difficulties performing higher level tasks (previously easily mastered and performed). Behavioral symptoms of latter-stage Alzheimer's disease, which are particularly troublesome for families and professional carers, include wandering, pacing, agitation, screaming, depression, anxiety, aggressive reactions, and sleep disturbances.

benztropine—an antidyskinetic drug indicated for the treatment of mild cases of parkinsonism (idiopathic, postencephalitic, arteriosclerotic), and as an adjunct with more potent medicines to maximize improvement of symptoms of parkinsonism. Also used in the control of extrapyramidal disorders secondary to neuroleptic drug therapy (e.g., phenothiazines).

beta amyloid—a protein found in dense deposits forming the core of neuritic plaques.

Binswanger disease—a presenile (occurring before age of 65 years or so) dementia marked by loss of memory and mental lethargy.

biperiden—an antidyskinetic drug indicated for the treatment of mild cases of parkinsonism and as an adjunct with more potent medicines to maximize improvement of symptoms of parkinsonism. Also used in the control of extrapyramidal disorders secondary to neuroleptic drug therapy.

blood-brain barrier—a group of mechanisms that keep most substances in the bloodstream from entering cells in the brain.

bradykinesia—abnormal slowness of movements; sluggishness of physical and mental responses.

brain—one of the two components of the central nervous system, the brain is the center of thought and emotion. It is responsible for the coordination and control of bodily activities and the interpretation of information from the senses (sight, hearing, smell, etc.). (See also **spinal cord**.)

bronchopneumonia—a name given to an inflammation of the lungs which usually begins in the terminal bronchioles. These become clogged with a mucopurulent exudate forming consolidated patches in adjacent lobules. The disease is essentially secondary in character, following infections of the upper respiratory tract, specific infectious fevers, and debilitating diseases.

buproprion—a drug used for the treatment of major depression. It may cause generalized seizures in a small fraction of persons, especially with higher doses.

buspirone—a drug used for the management of anxiety disorders and the short-term relief of symptoms of anxiety.

cachexia—a profound and marked state of constitutional disorder characterized by general ill health and wasting away in terminal stage of Alzheimer's disease.

calcium—an element taken in through the diet that is essential for a variety of bodily functions, such as neurotransmission, muscle contraction, and proper heart function. Imbalances of calcium can lead to many health problems, and excess calcium in nerve cells can cause their death.

calcium channel blocker—a drug that inhibits or blocks the entry of calcium into heart cells, thereby dilating coronary arteries and peripheral arteries and arterioles. Calcium channel blockers are indicated in the treatment of certain heart conditions, stroke, hypertension, and vascular headaches, and are being studied as potential treatment for Alzheimer's disease.

cancer—malignant abnormal cellular growths (lay term for **carcinoma**).

capillary—any of the smallest blood vessels connecting the arterioles and venules and forming networks throughout the body. Capillary walls act as semipermeable membranes for the exchange of substances between the blood and tissue fluid.

carcinoma—a malignant new growth made up of epithelial cells tending to infiltrate the surrounding tissues and gives rise to metastases. (See also **cancer.**)

cardiovascular—pertaining to the heart and blood vessels.

carer—anyone who provides care to a physically or cognitively impaired person, including both family and other carers at home and professional carers in health care settings.

case management—a component of community care system that involves assessing an individual's functional level and impairments, developing a plan of care, identifying and arranging for coordinated delivery of services, monitoring changes, and periodically reassessing needs. (See **casework** and **service coordination.)**

casework—(See **care management** and **service coordination**.)

cataract—an opacity of the crystalline eye lens or of its capsule, impairing vision or causing blindness.

cell—the smallest unit of a living organism that is capable of functioning independently.

cell body—the central portion in nerve cells, which contains the cell nucleus, from which axons and dendrites sprout. The cell body is primarily concerned with carrying out the life-sustaining functions of a cell.

cell membrane—the outer boundary of the cell; the cell membrane helps control what substances enter and leave the cell.

central nervous system (CNS)—the **brain** and **spinal cord**.

cerebral cortex—the outer part or "mantle" of the brain most involved in the higher order functions, including learning, language, reasoning, perception, and voluntary movements. The cerebral cortex is the part of the brain in which thought processes take place. In Alzheimer's disease, nerve cells in the cerebral cortex die in large numbers over an extended period of time.

cerebrospinal fluid (CSF)—a clear, colorless liquid containing small quantities of glucose and protein that is secreted from the blood into the lateral ventricles of the brain. It fills the ventricles of the brain and the central canal of the spinal cord and maintains uniform pressure within both.

cerebral vascular disease—disease of the blood vessels of the brain, particularly the cerebrum.

cerebrovascular—pertaining to the blood vessels of the brain, particularly the cerebrum.

ceroid-lipofuscinosis—a lethal, developmental disorder marked by intellectual disability and characteristic insoluble pigments in various tissues.

chelation—the chemical process of binding and removing metal ions from the body. Chelation is used to treat metal poisoning, such as copper poisoning in Wilson's disease, and to reduce aluminum levels in blood of persons affected by Alzheimer's disease.

chloral hydrate—a drug indicated preoperatively as an anesthesia adjunct to relieve anxiety and produce sedation or sleep or both. Chloral hydrate has been used as a routine sedative, but it generally has been replaced by safer and more effective agents.

choline—a natural substance required by the body that is obtained from various foods, such as eggs; one essential component of acetylcholine.

choline acetyltransferase (CAT)—an enzyme that controls the production of acetylcholine; appears to be depleted in the brains of persons affected by Alzheimer's disease.

cholinergic—stimulated, activated, or transmitted by choline (acetylcholine); a term applied to those neurons that liberate acetylcholine at the synapse as a nerve impulse passes. Nerve cells in the cholinergic system are damaged in the brains of persons with Alzheimer's disease, particularly in the nucleus basalis.

cholinergic system—the system of nerve cells that uses acetylcholine as its neurotransmitter; nerve cells in the cholinergic system are damaged in the brains of persons with Alzheimer's disease, particularly in the brain structure called the *nucleus basalis*.

cholinesterase—an enzyme that breaks down acetylcholine to stop its action.

cholinesterase inhibitors—chemicals that slow down or stop the action of cholinesterase.

chromatin—the more readily stainable portion of the cell nucleus, forming a network of nuclear fibrils within the achromatin of a cell. It is a deoxyribonucleic acid (DNA) attached to a protein structure base and is the carrier of the genes in inheritance.

chromosome—a structure in the nucleus of a cell containing a thread of DNA, which transmits genetic information. Humans have 23 pairs of chromosomes, one set from the mother, one from the father. These can only be visible on staining at the time cells divide (metaphase). At other times, the genetic material in the chromosomes is scattered throughout the nucleus as chromatin.

chromosome 21—the twenty-first chromosome; associated with Down's syndrome and some forms of Alzheimer's disease. Persons with Down's syndrome have an extra copy of chromosome 21 in their cells. A site on chromosome 21 has been identified as the location for a gene associated with Alzheimer's disease. Specifically, it is the locus for the beta peptide, which has been implicated in the accumulation, deposition, and formation of neuritic plaques. Chromosome 21 is also the locus for superoxide dismutase, an essential enzyme that continuously removes free radicals. It is elevated in Down's syndrome, and it is hypothesized that free-radical damage may account for the development of dementia of the Alzheimer type in persons with Down's syndrome.

clinical drug trial—a study designed to test whether an intervention, such as a drug, is safe and effective in human beings. There are several kinds, including an *open drug trial* in which participants are all given the active treatment with their knowledge (a weak method, scientifically); *single-blind* trial, in which the principal investigator knows which participants are receiving the active treatment and which participants are receiving a ''placebo,'' but where no one else knows, including the participants who are enrolled (it is a strong method, scientifically, but not the best); *double-blind, randomized assignment,* where no one knows which participants are getting the active treatment and which ones are are receiving the placebo. Assignment of participants to either treatment or placebo is controlled by using a table of random numbers, so that every candidate for the study has an equal probability of being assigned to either condition.

cognitive disintegration—loss of cognitive skills.

cognitive functions—an expression from psychology that refers to all aspects of thinking, perceiving, and some types of memory.

cognitive impairment—a weakening or deterioration of the mental processes of perception, memory, judgment, and reasoning.

cognitive symptoms—an expression from psychology that refers to all aspects of thinking, perceiving, and some types of memory.

cohort effect—influence of the characteristics of a group (e.g., age, generation, sex, ethnic group, skill level) on an outcome.

comorbidity—one or more conditions or diseases that occur at the same time in the individual. For example, persons with symptoms of Alzheimer's disease may also have diabetes or symptoms of Parkinson's disease.

computerized tomography scan (CT or CAT scan)—a diagnostic test that uses computer and X rays to obtain a highly detailed picture of the brain.

congenital abnormality—a condition that is present at birth, regardless of cause(s).

copharmacy—use of a combination of different classes of psychotropic drugs to treat a person with one or more psychiatric disorders. (See also **polypharmacy**.)

coronary heart disease—a disease process that involves a sufficiently large build-up of plaques within the vessel walls of the coronary blood vessels of the heart to interfere with the flow of blood to the heart muscle.

cross-sectional design—a research design that examines the comparative nature and characteristics of a sample of a population at one point in time; a method of testing hypotheses about aging, for example, in which experimental groups are composed of people of different age subgroups. (See also **longitudinal design**.)

delirium—a mental disturbance marked by illusions, hallucinations, short unsystematized delusions, cerebral excitement, physical restlessness, and incoherence, and having a comparatively short course. It may occur in the course of a more prolonged mental disorder or as a result of fever, disease, or injury.

delusion—a false belief that cannot be corrected by reason. It is logically founded and cannot be corrected by argument or persuasion or even by the evidence of the person's own senses.

dementia—cognitive decline from any cause (e.g., head injury, stroke, anoxia) that occurs at any stage of life beyond the acquisition of ADLs. The term is applied to patients in whom cognitive decline is sufficient to impair personal, social, or occupational adaptation, is persistent and progressive, and is associated with a chronic diffuse or multifocal brain disorder. The pathological processes producing dementia may involve brain structures that subserve functions other than cognition, such as motor function. Signs and symptoms of the involvement of these structures are often specified in the research criteria for the diagnosis of individual dementing disorders. Most research criteria also specify neuropathological criteria (disease or damage of the brain itself). Although these criteria are commonly regarded as the "gold standard," it should be appreciated that all of them, including those for Alzheimer's disease, are to some extent controversial and neither universally nor uniformly applied.

dementia, Alzheimer's type (DAT)—cognitive decline characterized by loss of higher-order brain functions, including cognitive, noncognitive, and other functions and attributed to Alzheimer's disease.

dementia, cortical—cognitive decline that includes higher cortical functions such as memory, language, integrated motor control, and integrated perception (amnesia, aphasia, apraxia, agnosia). Ultimately will involve subcortical functions. (See also **dementia, subcortical**.)

dementia, frontotemporal—cognitive decline characterized by prominent behavioral features with frontal executive, but minimal memory, impairment as a result of frontal lobe and temporal lobe nerve cell losses, ballooned neurons, proteinaceous cell inclusions called Pick bodies, and subcortical gliosis. There is a high familial incidence.

Occurrences in adults with intellectual disability have not been reported.

dementia, multi-infarct (MID)—cognitive decline characterized by loss of higher-order brain functions, including cognitive, noncognitive, and other functions caused by multiple blockages of brain blood vessels. The blockages interrupt the blood supplies of those parts of the brain where the blockage occurs. The onset of symptoms are usually abrupt and can be mild to fatal. Many persons with dementia of the Alzheimer type also show evidence of multi-infarct dementia. CT scans of the brain can be particularly helpful in diagnosis as well as use of a number of rating scores, such as the Hachinski Ischemia Score.

dementia, subcortical—cognitive decline characterized by impaired retrieval of memory in the face of preserved storage, impaired "executive" function, and disordered mood. Motor disturbances also occur early. Includes the dementias occurring in Huntington's and Parkinson's diseases, progressive supranuclear palsy, communicating hydrocephalus, and vascular dementias such as Binswanger disease. (See also **dementia, cortical,** and **Lewy body dementia.**)

dementia, vascular(VaD)—cognitive decline characterized by strokes that can occur anywhere in the brain and with highly variable damage and effect on cognitive functions. Diagnosis is made complicated by the observation that vascular function may be impaired in Alzheimer's disease. These strokes can cause specific symptoms, depending on their severity and location, and can cause general symptoms of dementia. This type of dementia cannot be treated; once the nerve cells die, they cannot be replaced. However, the underlying condition leading to strokes (e.g., high blood pressure, diabetes) can be treated, which may help prevent further damage.

dementia capable—staff and environment being capable of accommodating the special needs of persons affected by dementia.

dendrites—the branchlike extensions of neurons that receive messages from other neurons through synaptic connections. Each nerve cell usually has many dendrites.

deoxyribonucleic acid—(See **DNA.**)

depression—a disorder of mood that is characterized by sadness, inactivity, difficulty with thinking and concentration, a significant increase or decrease in appetite and time spent sleeping, feelings of dejection and hopelessness, and sometimes suicidal thoughts or an attempt to commit suicide. When first episode occurs later in life, it is more likely to be associated with cognitive impairment, cerebral atrophy, deep white matter changes, recurrences, medical comorbidity, and mortality.

developmental disability—any of the cognitive, sensory, or physical conditions present at birth or occurring before the 22nd birthday that compromise full vocational, social, economic, and personal functional independence over a lifetime and that can be aided by special compensatory, remedial, or assistive services. (See also **intellectual disability**.)

diagnostic overshadowing—instance when a significant impairment or condition tends to obviate further examination for other less prominent impairments or conditions (often found in examinations of people with intellectual disability, when the intellectual disability diagnosis is given and thus other conditions are overlooked).

differential diagnosis—clinical evaluation of possible causes of dementia to rule out all other factors before settling on Alzheimer's disease.

diphenhydramine—an antihistamine used as a sedative–hypnotic to treat insomnia.

divalproex—an anticonvulsant medication indicated for the treatment of various forms of epilepsy, and also approved for the treatment and prevention of manic episodes in bipolar disorder.

DNA (deoxyribonucleic acid)—a nucleic acid that constitutes the genetic material of all cellular organisms. DNA is a large double-stranded molecule containing nucleotides and sugar moieties joined by phosphate linkages. Most of the DNA is located in the cell nucleus as chromatin. When cells prepare to divide, the DNA coils into a highly compact structure, called a chromosome, which is readily visible under the light microscope. Certain sequences of DNA make up genes.

dopamine—a neurotransmitter that is essential for normal movement, such as walking. The brains of persons with Parkinson's disease are deficient in dopamine.

dopaminergic system—the system of nerve cells that uses dopamine as its neurotransmitter.

Down's syndrome—a condition brought about by a chromosomal abnormality consisting of an extra chromosome 21 in each cell of the body. The condition produces an amplified disturbance in homeostatic mechanisms associated with disturbed development. It is characterized by a small antero-posteriorly flattened skull, short, flat-bridged nose, epicanthus, short phalanges, and widened space between the first and second digits of hands and feet, with a wide range of intellectual functions from mild (rare), moderate to severe (about one-half to two-thirds), to profound (about 10%–15%). (See also **chromosome**.)

dual diagnosis—situation when coexistent conditions are present, as in intellectual disability and a psychiatric impairment.

dyskinesia—difficulty of moving characterized by impairment in making voluntary movements, resulting in fragmentary or incomplete movements.

dyspepsia—an impairment of the function of digestion.

dyspnea—difficult or labored breathing.

dyspraxia—a partial loss of the ability to perform purposeful or skilled motor acts in the absence of paralysis, sensory loss, abnormal posture or tone, abnormal involuntary movements, incoordination, poor comprehension, or inattention.

dysthymia—mental depression present for more than two years but without symptoms severe enough to meet the requirements for major depression.

dystonia—a disorder of tonicity of the muscles.

encephalitis—inflammation of the brain.

enuresis—involuntary discharge of urine, often specifically with involuntary discharge during sleep at night (termed *nocturnal enuresis).*

epilepsy—any of the various disorders marked by disturbed electrical rhythms of the central nervous system and typically manifested by convulsive attacks, usually with clouding of consciousness. It can be characterized by one or more of the following symptoms: paroxysmally recurring impairment or loss of consciousness, involuntary excess or cessation of muscle movements, psychic or sensory disturbances, and perturbations of the autonomic nervous system. The symptoms are based on a substrate of paroxysmal disturbance of the electrical activity of the brain. (See also **seizure.**)

excitotoxin—a chemical substance that can damage and kill nerve cells by overstimulating them.

extrapyramidal—comprises all neural structures other than the cortex sending impulses to the spinal cord from the brain. It is a complex "servo-mechanism" of the brain for the control of the final common motor pathway. Six nuclear masses belong to the extrapyramidal system: globus pallidus, subthalamic nucleus of Luys, substantia nigra, nucleus ruber, nucleus dentatus, and the inferior olive. Only these brain nuclei give a "positive" reaction for iron ions.

floor effect—condition present in a testing procedure when the individual is unable to score above the base items on a test.

free radicals—(See **oxygen free radicals.**)

functional impairment—limitation of an individual's functional abilities, the inability to perform personal and instrumental activities of daily living and associated tasks, or the inability to live independently.

ganglioside storage disease—a disease of the brain involving accumulation of galactose cerebrosides.

Gaucher's disease—a familial disorder of lipid metabolism characterized clinically by splenomegaly, skin pigmentation, scleral pingueculae, and the presence of distinctive kerasin-containing cells in the liver, spleen, lymph nodes, alveolar capillaries, and bone marrow. The three clinical forms are Type I or adult, Type II or infantile, and Type III or juvenile.

gene—the biologic unit of heredity. Each gene is located at a definite position on a particular chromosome and is made up of a string of chemicals, called bases, arranged in a certain sequence along the DNA molecule.

gene, mutant (mutation)—a gene in which the loss, gain, or exchange of material has resulted in a permanent transmissible change in functioning. Genetic "blueprints" can be abnormal from a wide variety of causes with the result that they have abnormalities that translate into the building of defective products. Some of these can be lethal, others produce subtle changes, and still others may show no effects until later life.

geriatrician—a medical specialist in geriatrics. (See also **psychogeriatrician**.)

glaucoma—a condition of the eye associated with increased intraocular pressure which impairs the blood supply to parts of the retina that may cause impaired vision, ranging from slight loss to absolute blindness. The cause(s) are not known. Effective treatment using certain medications in the eye can halt or slow the progression of glaucoma. Other forms of treatment include laser surgery to open the canals of Schlemm to facilitate the movement of the intraocular fluids, and the use of some systemic medications, depending on the form of glaucoma.

gliosis—a disease condition associated with the presence of gliomas or with the development of tumors made up of neuroglial tissue.

glucose metabolism—the process by which cells turn food into energy.

glutamate—a neurotransmitter that is normally involved in learning and memory. Under certain circumstances it can be an excitotoxin, and it appears to cause the death of nerve cells in a variety of neurodegenerative disorders. Early research has shown that glutamate may cause nerve cell death in Alzheimer's disease.

gold standard—a point of reference against which other things are compared.

grasp reflex—a reflex consisting of a grasping motion of the fingers or of the toes in response to stimulation. It is one of the reflexes that reappear in the later stages of Alzheimer's disease.

group living program—a care situation in which a small cluster of individuals affected by dementia are housed; specialized staff provide security, integrity-promoting therapies, and activation specifically designed to aid in coping with dementia. (See also **special care unit**.)

hallucination—a sense perception not founded upon objective reality; it can affect any of the senses.

health care proxy—durable power of attorney with a named proxy decision maker or agent for health related decision making.

hemianopia—defective vision or blindness in half of the visual field.

hemiparesis—muscular weakness affecting one side of the body.

hippocampus—a structure deep in the brain involved in memory storage.

hospice—a facility or program designed to provide a caring environment for supplying the physical and emotional needs of persons who are terminally ill.

Hoyar lift—a portable hydraulic lift with a sling seat that is used to transfer or lift an individual from bed to chair or chair to bed in a safe, comfortable manner, for both the person and the carer.

Huntington's disease (chorea)—a chronic hereditary condition involving the ceaseless occurrence of a wide variety of rapid, jerky, but well-coordinated movements performed involuntarily, and progressive intellectual deterioration.

hydrocephalus—a condition characterized by abnormal accumulation of fluid in the cranial vault, accompanied by enlargement of the head, prominence of the forehead, atrophy of the brain, mental weakness, and convulsions.

hyperammonemia (hyperammoniemia)—the presence of an excess of ammonia in the blood.

hypertension—abnormally elevated blood pressure.

hyponatremia—deficiency of sodium in the blood.

hypothermia—subnormal temperature of the body.

hypothyroidism—deficiency of thyroid activity or the condition resulting therefrom. It is more frequent among persons with Down's syndrome than in the general population and may be a comorbid condition associated with onset of dementia of the Alzheimer type in persons with Down's syndrome.

imipramine—a tricyclic antidepressant drug administered in the form of its hydrochloride.

information and referral—a function that provides assistance on locating and being referred to a service that is desired.

informed consent—the agreement of a person (or his or her legally authorized representative) to serve as a research subject, in full knowledge of all anticipated risks and benefits of the experiment.

instrumental activities of daily living (IADLs)—functions or tasks of living independently, including housekeeping, shopping, meal preparation and cleanup, laundry, taking medications, money management, transportation, correspondence, telephoning, and related tasks.

intellectual disability—a condition of intellectual ability that is characterized by cognitive development of from two or more standard deviations below the norm, is present from birth or infancy, and is often associated with lifetime learning difficulties and needs for social and vocational supports.

interactions, drug—the effects (positive or negative) caused by the administration of two or more medications taken at the same time. (See also **side effects**.)

keratoconus—a conical protrusion of the cornea.

lethargy—a condition of drowsiness or stupor.

leukemia—a disease of the blood-forming organs, characterized by a marked increase in the number of leukocytes and their precursors in the blood, together with enlargement and proliferation of the lymphoid tissue of the spleen, lymphatic glands, and bone marrow. The disease is attended with progressive anemia, internal hemorrhage, and increasing exhaustion.

leukodystrophy—disturbance of the white substance of the brain. Metachromatic and globoid leukodystrophies are inheritable enzyme deficiencies characterized by progressive paralysis, dementia, and retardation.

leukodystrophy (metachromatic)—a hereditary neurological disorder or lipid metabolism characterized by the accumulation of cerebroside sulfates, loss of myelin in the central nervous system, and progressive deterioration of mental and motor activity.

Lewy bodies—a proteinaceous cellular inclusion restricted to the midbrain, occurring in the cerebral cortex in persons with both dementia and parkinsonism but without pathological findings of Alzheimer's disease.

Lewy body dementia—an irreversible brain disease associated with protein deposits called Lewy bodies, which appear in deteriorating nerve cells and are often found in damaged regions deep within the brains of persons with Parkinson's disease. Lewy body dementia is a less common form of dementia and can easily be misdiagnosed as Alzheimer's disease, because symptoms are similar.

lithium—the primary agent used to treat acute manic episodes in bipolar disorder and for maintenance therapy to help diminish the intensity and frequency of subsequent manic episodes in persons with a history of mania.

living will—document in which the signer requests to be allowed to die rather than be kept alive by artificial means in the event of becoming disabled beyond a reasonable expectation of recovery.

longitudinal design—a research design that examines the nature and characteristics of a sample of a population over a period of time; a method of testing hypotheses in experiments in which each person is examined more than once and thereby serves as his or her own control. (See also **cross-sectional design**.)

long-term memory—memory that involves the storage and recall of information or events over a long period of time (as days, weeks, or years). (See **short-term memory**.)

loxapine—a drug used in the management of the symptoms of psychotic disorders; can be associated with the development of tardive dyskinesia and parkinsonian extrapyramidal effects.

maprotiline—a medication indicated for the treatment of depression in patients with major depressive disorder, dysthymia, and the depressed type of bipolar disorder. Also effective in the relief of anxiety associated with depression. Seizures have been associated with the use of this drug, usually with higher doses.

memory—process of reproducing or recalling what has been learned and retained. (See **long-term memory** and **short-term memory**.)

meningitis—an inflammation of the meninges, the three membranes (the dura mater, pia mater, and arachnoid) that envelop the brain and spinal cord.

meprobamate—a drug indicated for the management of anxiety disorders or for the short-term relief of the symptoms of anxiety.

mesoridazine—a drug of the phenothiazine group used in the treatment of psychotic conditions, especially schizophrenia, by essentially reducing the severity of emotional withdrawal, conceptual disorganization, anxiety, tension, hallucinatory behavior, suspiciousness, and blunted affect. It is also used in the management of hyperactivity in children and adults and uncooperativeness associated with intellectual disability and chronic brain syndrome.

metabolism—the normal process of turning food into energy; the complex chemical and physical processes of living organisms that promote growth, sustain life, and enable all other bodily functions to take place.

micturition—the passage of urine.

mitochondria—structures inside cells where glucose metabolism and the generation of energy takes place.

monoamine oxidase (MAO)—an enzyme that breaks down certain neurotransmitters, including dopamine, serotonin, and noradrenaline.

monoamine oxidase inhibitor (MAOI)—a drug that interferes with the action of monoamine oxidase, slowing the breakdown of certain neurotransmitters in the treatment of major depression.

multi-infarct dementia (MID)—also known as vascular dementia. (See **dementia, multi- infarct**, and **dementia, vascular**.)

multiple sclerosis (MS)—an autoimmune disease of the central nervous system that damages myelin, the insulating sheath surrounding the axons of some nerve cells, and slows the conduction of nerve impulses along the axons. Persons with MS show a variety of symptoms (weakness, incoordination, speech difficulties, dizziness, cognitive disabilities, pain, spasticity, and visual complaints), depending on where in the central nervous system lesions occur.

myoclonus—shocklike contractions of a portion of a muscle, an entire muscle, or a group of muscles, restricted to one area of the body or appearing synchronously or asynchronously in several areas.

nadolol—a drug indicated in the treatment of angina pectoris and hypertension. It may be used alone or in combination with other antihypertensive agents, especially thiazide diuretics.

naltrexone—an agent that binds to opioid receptors in the central nervous system and competitively inhibits the action of opioid (narcotic) drugs. Naltrexone is indicated as an adjunct to other measures, psychological and social, in the treatment of detoxified, formerly opioid-dependent persons.

neoplastic disorder—a condition involving any new and abnormal growth, such as a tumor.

nerve growth factor (NGF)—a protein that promotes nerve cell growth and may protect some types of nerve cells from damage, including nerve cells in the cholinergic system.

neuritic plaques—deposits of amyloid mixed with fragments of dead and dying neurons. Abnormal cluster of dead and dying nerve cells, other brain cells, and protein. Neuritic plaques are one of the characteristic structural abnormalities found in the brains of persons with Alzheimer's disease. Upon autopsy, the presence of neuritic plaques and neurofibrillary tangles is used to positively diagnose Alzheimer's disease.

neurodegenerative disorder—a type of neurological disease marked by the loss of nerve cells. (See **Alzheimer's disease, Parkinson's disease**.)

neurofibrillary tangles (NFTs)—collections of twisted nerve cell fibers or paired helical filaments found in the cell bodies of neurons in Alzheimer's disease. Neurofibrillary tangles are one of the characteristic structural abnormalities found in the brains of persons with Alzheimer's disease. Upon autopsy, the presence of neuritic plaques and neurofibrillary tangles is used to positively diagnose Alzheimer's disease.

neuroleptic—a drug or agent indicated for the treatment of psychosis; a term referring to the effects of antipsychotic drugs.

neurological disorder—disturbance in structure or function of the central nervous system resulting from developmental abnormality, disease, injury, or toxin.

neurologist—a physician who diagnoses and treats disorders of the nervous system.

neuron—any of the conducting cells of the nervous system. A neuron consists of a cell body, dendrites, and axon.

neuron thread protein (NTP)—a family of immunologically related molecules expressed in brain and primitive neuroectodermal tumor cell lines.

neuropathology—pathology of the nervous system.

neuropeptide Y—a substance that sometimes functions as a neurotransmitter. Some research shows that neuropeptide Y may be involved in Alzheimer's disease.

neuroscientist—a scientist who studies the brain, its development, molecular basis, function, and relationships to behavior.

neurotransmission—passage of signals from one nerve cell to another via chemical substances or electrical signals.

neurotransmitter—a chemical messenger between neurons; a chemical released by the axon of a neuron that excites or inhibits activity in a neighboring neuron. Acetylcholine, dopamine, norepinephrine, and serotonin are examples of neurotransmitters produced and secreted on excitation of a presynaptic neuron of the central or peripheral nervous systems. Neurotransmitters play different roles throughout the body, many of which are not yet fully understood.

neurotransmitter system—a group of nerve cells that use the same neurotransmitter to communicate.

neurotrophic factors—a family of substances that promote growth and regeneration of neurons.

Niemann–Pick disease—a familial disorder of lipid metabolism in which sphingomyelin accumulates in the reticuloendothelial cells because of a deficiency of the enzyme sphingomyelinase. Characterized by massive hepatosplenomegaly, brownish discoloration of the skin, nervous system involvement, and presence of foamy reticular cells or histiocytes in the liver, spleen, lungs, lymph nodes, and bone marrow, which store phospholipids, chiefly lecithin and sphingomyelin. Called also *lipid histiocytosis* and *sphingomyelin lipidosis*.

noradrenaline (norepinephrine)—a neurotransmitter that plays a role in mood, pain, and possibly learning and memory. Noradrenaline may be involved in Alzheimer's disease.

noradrenergic system—the system of nerve cells that uses noradrenaline (norepinephrine) as its neurotransmitter.

norepinephrine—a hormone secreted by the adrenal medulla in response to splanchnic stimulation and stored in the chromaffin granules, being released predominantly in response to hypotension; a sympathomimetic drug administered intravenously as a pressor agent to increase blood pressure in the treatment of shock.

normal aging—a characterization of aging that normally follows an expected pattern and is differentiated as either usual or successful aging. (See **usual aging** and **successful aging**.)

nystagmus—an involuntary, rapid movement of the eyeball, which may be horizontal, vertical, rotatory, or mixed.

osteoarthrosis—chronic arthritis of noninflammatory character.

oxazepam—a drug indicated for the management of anxiety disorders or for the short-term relief of the symptoms of anxiety. Anxiety associated with depression may respond to treatment with this agent.

oxygen free radicals—an oxygen molecule with an unpaired electron that is highly reactive, combining readily with other molecules and sometimes causing damage to cells. (See also **antioxidants**.)

Parkinson's disease (paralysis agitars)—a progressive, neurodegenerative disease characterized by the death of nerve cells containing the neurotransmitter dopamine in a specific area of the brain; the cause of nerve cell death is unknown. Persons affected by Parkinson's disease have such symptoms as tremors, speech impediments, movement difficulties, and often dementia. Secondary parkinsonism is often caused by treatment with neuroleptic drugs.

parkinsonism—a group of neurological disorders characterized by hypokinesia, tremor, and muscular rigidity.

pathological aging—aging affected by diseases or age-related impairments or disabilities.

peripheral nervous system (PNS)—one of the two major divisions of the nervous system. Nerves in the PNS connect the central nervous system (CNS) with sensory organs, other organs, muscles, blood vessels, and glands.

perphenazine—a neuroleptic drug of the phenothiazine group used in treatment of persons with psychotic conditions. Tardive dyskinesia may be developed in persons treated with antipsychotic agents (neuroleptics).

personal care—care provided that assists an individual with his or her activities of daily living.

PET scan—(See **position emission tomography**.)

pharmacodynamics—physiological and biochemical effects produced by a given drug.

pharmacokinetics—action of drugs on the body over a period of time.

phospholipids—the major form of lipids or fats in all cell membranes.

Pick's disease—a type of dementia in which the prominent behavioral features are changes in executive functions, minimal memory impairment, with brain atrophy most conspicuous in the frontal regions in combination with cortical cell loss, ballooned neurons, proteinaceous cell inclusions called Pick bodies, and subcortical gliosis. Pick's disease is a rare, progressive, degenerative disease similar in clinical course and manifestations to Alzheimer's disease.

placebo—a dummy treatment, often a sugar pill having no specific pharmacological activity against the person's illness and given solely for psychophysiological effects; also, a dummy treatment or sometimes an active drug used for comparison in controlled clinical trials of medications. (See **clinical drug trial**.)

plaques—(See **neuritic plaques**.)

polypharmacy—the use of more than one drug of the same category to treat a person (e.g., two neuroleptics).

positron emission tomography (PET)—an imaging technique that allows researchers to observe and measure brain activity by monitoring blood flow and concentrations of substances such as oxygen and glucose in brain tissues.

prodromal syndrome—premonitory symptoms of disease.

prospective assessment strategy—an assessment strategy that involves collecting baseline data and then conducting follow-up assessments of individuals to measure changes in a particular behavior or condition over time. (See also **retrospective assessment strategy**.)

protease—an enzyme that catalyzes the splitting of a protein into smaller sections.

protective factor—some factor that is associated with lower prevalence of Alzheimer's disease; examples include estrogen for postmenopausal women undergoing treatment for osteoporosis and ibuprofen (a nonsteroidal antiinflammatory agent) as a treatment for arthritis in aging individuals.

protein—a molecule made up of amino acids arranged in a specific order which is determined by a gene. Proteins include neurotransmitters, enzymes, hormones, and hundreds of other substances.

pseudodementia—a condition of extreme apathy that outwardly resembles dementia but is not the result of actual mental deterioration.

psychiatrist—a physician who specializes in the branch of medicine that deals with the study, treatment, and prevention of behavioral abnormalities and mental disorders.

psychogeriatrician—a medical specialist in psychiatry and geriatrics.

psychomotor retardation—slowing of movements, diminution of activity, particularly noteworthy as one of the symptoms of depression and dementia of the Alzheimer type.

receptor—a protein in a cell membrane that recognizes and binds to chemical messengers, such as neurotransmitters. In the nervous system, a site on a nerve cell that receives a specific neurotransmitter.

receptor agonist—a substance that mimics a specific neurotransmitter, is able to attach to that neurotransmitter's receptor, and thereby produces the same action that the neurotransmitter usually produces. Drugs are often designed as receptor agonists to treat a variety of diseases and disorders when the original chemical substance is missing or depleted.

respite care—temporary relief from the burden of caregiving provided in the home or elsewhere in the community.

retrospective assessment strategy—an assessment strategy that involves review and analysis of data from past assessments of individuals which have been employed to measure changes in a particular behavior or condition over time. (See also **prospective assessment strategy**.)

risk factor—something that increases risk or susceptibility.

seizure—a sudden attack, a convulsion. (See **epilepsy**.)

selective serotonin reuptake inhibitors (SSRIs)—A group of antidepressant medications that increase the level of the neurotransmitter, serotonin, in the spaces between the nerve cells in the brain, thereby reducing depression.

self-talk—talking to oneself (not "hearing voices" or verbalizations symptomatic of severe cognitive problems) where conceptualization, problem solving, or emotional conflict resolution has not been internalized; thinking out loud among persons with limited cognitive abilities and generally performed in private.

senile dementia—an outdated term, previously used for dementia developing after the onset of the "senium," that is, after the age of 65 years or so. It was distinguished from presenile dementia for many years because the symptoms were less severe, slower in progression, and duration of the illness was longer than in the dementia conditions observed at younger ages. Several decades of careful neuropathological investigations have revealed that the underlying neuropathology is similar, regardless of age of onset or severity of symptoms. Consequently, the term senile dementia has gradually been abandoned with preference now given to distinctions based on neuropathological criteria. (See **dementia**.)

senile (neuritic) plaques (SPs)—one of the characteristic neuropathological lesions of Alzheimer's disease. They are extracellular deposits or accumulations of a mixture of fibrillar proteins and incomplete necrosis of the aging cerebral cortex. They have been the subject of intensive research for more than three decades on the pathogenesis of Alzheimer's disease.

serotonergic system—the system of nerve cells that uses serotonin as their neurotransmitter.

serotonin—a neurotransmitter that plays a role in mood, sleep, and pain.

service coordination—assistance provided to a family or person that includes information and referral, benefits counseling, linkages to services, advocacy, and other assistance; also known as case management or casework.

Shapiro syndrome—neurological condition that includes an absence of the corpus callosum.

short-term memory—memory that involves recall of information of events occurring in the immediate past. (See **long-term memory**.)

side effect—an undesired effect of drug treatment that may range in severity from barely noticeable, to uncomfortable, to dangerous. Side effects are usually predictable. (See also **interactions, drug**.)

single photon emission computerized tomography (SPECT)—an imaging technique that allows researchers to monitor blood flow to different parts of the brain; used for visualizing the interior of the brain as part of diagnostic evaluations for a number of neurological conditions.

somatostatin—a substance that sometimes functions as a neurotransmitter. Some research indicates that somatostatin may be involved in Alzheimer's disease.

special care unit—a long-term care facility with environmental features or programs or both designed for people with dementia. (See also **group living program**.)

SPECT—(See **single photon emission computerized tomography**.)

spinal cord—one of the two components of the central nervous system. The spinal cord is the main relay for signals between the brain and the rest of the body. (See also **brain**.)

strabismus—deviation of the eye that the person cannot overcome. The visual axes assume a position relative to each other different from that required by the physiological conditions.

stroke—damage to a group of nerve cells in the brain as a result of interrupted blood flow, usually caused by a blood clot or blood vessel bursting. Depending on the area of the brain that is damaged, a stroke can cause coma, paralysis, speech problems, or dementia or all of these.

subdural hematoma—a blood clot situated under the membrane (dura) that covers the brain.

successful aging —aging when there is a low risk for pathology and strong evidence of high function.

sucking reflex—normally, a totally inhibited reflex that reappears to stimulation of the region around the mouth and lips when there is widespread parenchymal damage to the brain, as in Alzheimer's disease.

sundowning—the tendency for the behavioral symptoms of Alzheimer's disease, such as confusion or agitation, to grow worse in the afternoon and evening.

survivor effect—recognition in an experimental design that certain study cohorts may live longer for whatever reason, independent of the study variables, and thus influence the study outcomes.

synapse—the minute gap between nerve cells across which a nerve impulse passes; the junction or site at which a signal is transmitted from the axon of one neuron to the dendrites of another, usually by electrical or chemical (neurotransmitter) means.

synaptic vesicles—small sacs located in the interior and in the area of nerve cell axons that contain neurotransmitters. During activity, the vesicles release their contents at the synapse, and the neurotransmitter stimulates receptors on other cells.

tachycardia—excessively rapid heart rate.

tacrine—a drug indicated for the symptomatic treatment of mild to moderate dementia of the Alzheimer type. Benefits are minor and restricted to the earliest phase of dementia. Hepatotoxicity or damage to the liver is a frequent side effect. Donezepil is a similar medication with fewer side effects. Tacrine and donezepil are thought to increase the levels of acetylcholine by blocking its breakdown in the central nervous system.

tangles—(See **neurofibrillary tangles**.)

tardive dyskinesia—a syndrome consisting of potentially irreversible, involuntary, dyskinetic movements of the lips, cheeks, tongue, and the arms and legs that may develop during treatment with neuroleptic (antipsychotic) drugs. The prevalence appears to be highest among the elderly, women, and persons with brain damage. Tardive dyskinesia may become irreversible as the duration of treatment and the total cumulative dose of administered drug are increased. However, tardive dyskinesia can develop at low doses and after relatively brief treatment periods.

tau—a protein that is a principal component of paired helical filaments in neurofibrillary tangles. Abnormal phosphorylation of this protein is hypothesized to be one of the important mechanisms in the pathogenesis of Alzheimer's disease.

thalassemia—a hereditary, genetically determined hemolytic anemia with familial and racial incidence, divided into a number of categories based on clinical severity and the type(s) of hemoglobin contained in the erythrocytes.

toxin—a substance that can cause illness, injury, or death.

tremor—an involuntary trembling or quivering.

usual aging—nonpathologic (that is, free of disease) aging where there is a recognition that there may be a risk or potential of aging becoming pathologic.

valproic acid—anticonvulsive drug indicated for the various forms of epilepsy. Valproic acid may also be useful in the prevention and treatment of manic–depressive illness refractory to lithium or other agents.

vascular dementia—(See **dementia, vascular.**)

vitamin E—one of a group of antioxidants indicated for prevention and treatment of documented vitamin E deficiency. Vitamin E supplementation in large doses has been hypothesized to diminish the rate of decline in Alzheimer's disease.

withdrawal—psychiatric symptom associated with reduced social interaction.

INDEX

Cell body, definition of, 452
Cell membrane, definition of, 452
Central nervous system (CNS), definition of, 452
Cerebral cortex
    atrophy in, 24
    definition of, 452
Cerebral vascular disease
    definition of, 452
    secondary dementia from, 98*t*
Cerebrospinal fluid (CSF)
    antemortem tests of, for Alzheimer's disease, 56, 58, 59*t*, 68–69, 70*t*, 71–74, 73*t*, 81
    definition of, 452
Cerebrovascular, definition of, 452
Ceroid–lipofuscinosis
    continuation into adulthood, 97
    definition of, 452
Chelation therapy
    definition of, 453
    dementia treated with, 64–65
Childhood disorders, with cognitive impairment, continuing into adulthood, 97–98
Chloral hydrate, 239
    definition of, 453
Chlordiazepoxide, 238*t*, 239
Chlorpromazine, 237, 238*t*
Choline acetyltransferase (CAT), definition of, 453
Choline, definition of, 453
Cholinergic, definition of, 453
Cholinergic system, definition of, 453
Cholinesterase, definition of, 453
Cholinesterase inhibitors, 248
    definition of, 453
Choroid plexus, acute phase response in, 69, 70*t*
Chromatin, definition of, 453
Chromosome(s). *See also* Genetic risk factors
    definition of, 453
Chromosome 21
    beta–amyloid deposits associated with, 8–9, 60, 185
    definition of, 453–454
    partial trisomy of, 76–77, 78*f*
Chronic granulomatous lesions, 65
Chronic obstructive pulmonary disease, 22, 109

Cingulate region, neuritic plaques/NFTs in, 24
Clinical criteria. *See* Diagnosis
Clinical drug trial, definition of, 454
Clinical perspective, of Alzheimer's disease, case history of, 16–25, 23*t*
Clomipramine, 237, 238*t*
Clonazepam, 238*t*, 239, 245–246
Clorazepate, 238*t*, 239
Clozapine, 238*t*, 242
Coalitions, on aging/disabilities, 375–378
Coffin–Lowry syndrome, 97
Cognitive disintegration, definition of, 454
Cognitive functions, definition of, 454
Cognitive impairment. *See also* Case histories
    from antipsychotic medications, 237
    assessment of, 19–20, 124–127, 146–148
    definition of, 454
Cognitive symptoms, definition of, 454
Cohort effect, 126
    definition of, 454
Communication
    deficits in, 264–265. *See also* Audiology; Speech impairment
    effective, suggestions for, 268–269, 270*f*
Community use, of adult day services, 304–305
Comorbidity
    definition of, 236–237, 454
    with Down's syndrome/Alzheimer's disease, 14–16
Complement proteins, associated with neuritic plaques, 9–11
Computerized tomography (CT) scan
    of Alzheimer's disease brain, 19
    definition of, 454
    used in differential diagnosis, 150
Congenital abnormality, definition of, 454
Congenital cataracts, with Down's syndrome, 106–107
Congenital rubella syndrome, secondary dementia from, 98
Constipation, with intellectual disability, in aging population, 110
Cooperative initiatives, on aging/disabilities, 375–376
Copharmacy, definition of, 237, 454
Copper, role of, in Alzheimer's disease, 62